CW01022458

Cisco Network Admission Control, Volume II:

NAC Network Deployment and Troubleshooting

Jazib Frahim, CCIE No. 5459, Omar Santos, David White, Jr., CCIE No. 12021

Cisco Press

Cisco Press
201 West 103rd Street
Indianapolis, IN 46290 USA

Cisco Network Admission Control, Volume II
NAC Framework Deployment and Troubleshooting

Jazib Frahim, CCIE No. 5459, Omar Santos, David White, Jr., CCIE No. 12021

Copyright © 2007 Cisco

Published by:
Cisco Press
800 East 96th Street
Indianapolis, IN 46240 USA

All rights reserved. No part of this book may be reproduced or transmitted in any form or by any means, electronic or mechanical, including photocopying, recording, or by any information storage and retrieval system, without written permission from the publisher, except for the inclusion of brief quotations in a review.

Library of Congress Catalog Card Number: 2004114756

Printed in the United States of America 1 2 3 4 5 6 7 8 9 0

First Printing November 2006

ISBN: 1-58705-225-3

Warning and Disclaimer

This book is designed to provide information about the Cisco NAC Framework. Every effort has been made to make this book as complete and as accurate as possible, but no warranty or fitness is implied.

The information is provided on an "as is" basis. The authors, Cisco Press, and Cisco shall have neither liability nor responsibility to any person or entity with respect to any loss or damages arising from the information contained in this book or from the use of the discs or programs that may accompany it.

The opinions expressed in this book belong to the author and are not necessarily those of Cisco.

Trademark Acknowledgments

All terms mentioned in this book that are known to be trademarks or service marks have been appropriately capitalized. Cisco Press or Cisco cannot attest to the accuracy of this information. Use of a term in this book should not be regarded as affecting the validity of any trademark or service mark.

Feedback Information

At Cisco Press, our goal is to create in-depth technical books of the highest quality and value. Each book is crafted with care and precision, undergoing rigorous development that involves the unique expertise of members from the professional technical community.

Readers' feedback is a natural continuation of this process. If you have any comments regarding how we could improve the quality of this book or otherwise alter it to better suit your needs, you can contact us through e-mail at feedback@ciscopress.com. Please make sure to include the book title and ISBN in your message.

We greatly appreciate your assistance.

Corporate and Government Sales

Cisco Press offers excellent discounts on this book when ordered in quantity for bulk purchases or special sales.

For more information please contact: U.S. Corporate and Government Sales 1-800-382-3419

corpsales@pearsontechgroup.com

For sales otuside the U.S. please contact: International Sales international@pearsoned.com

Publisher	Paul Boger
Cisco Representative	Anthony Wolfenden
Cisco Press Program Manager	Jeff Brady
Executive Editor	Brett Bartow
Production Manager	Patrick Kanouse
Development Editor	Andrew Cupp
Project Editor	Tonya Simpson
Copy Editor	Krista Hansing Editorial Services, Inc.
Technical Editors	Darin Miller
	John Stuppi
Publishing Coordinator	Vanessa Evans
Book Designer	Louisa Adair
Cover Designer	Louisa Adair
Composition	Carlisle Publishing Services
Proofreader	Chrissy White
Indexer	Julie Bess

Americas Headquarters
Cisco Systems, Inc.
170 West Tasman Drive
San Jose, CA 95134-1706
USA
www.cisco.com
Tel: 408 526-4000
800 553-NETS (6387)
Fax: 408 527-0883

Asia Pacific Headquarters
Cisco Systems, Inc.
168 Robinson Road
#28-01 Capital Tower
Singapore 068912
www.cisco.com
Tel: +65 6317 7777
Fax: +65 6317 7799

Europe Headquarters
Cisco Systems International BV
Haarlerbergpark
Haarlerbergweg 13-19
1101 CH Amsterdam
The Netherlands
www-europe.cisco.com
Tel: +31 0 800 020 0791
Fax: +31 0 20 357 1100

Cisco has more than 200 offices worldwide. Addresses, phone numbers, and fax numbers are listed on the Cisco Website at **www.cisco.com/go/offices.**

©2006 Cisco Systems, Inc. All rights reserved. CCVP, the Cisco logo, and the Cisco Square Bridge logo are trademarks of Cisco Systems, Inc.; Changing the Way We Work, Live, Play, and Learn is a service mark of Cisco Systems, Inc.; and Access Registrar, Aironet, BPX, Catalyst, CCDA, CCDP, CCIE, CCIP, CCNA, CCNP, CCSP, Cisco, the Cisco Certified Internetwork Expert logo, Cisco IOS, Cisco Press, Cisco Systems, Cisco Systems Capital, the Cisco Systems logo, Cisco Unity, Enterprise/Solver, EtherChannel, EtherFast, EtherSwitch, Fast Step, Follow Me Browsing, FormShare, GigaDrive, GigaStack, HomeLink, Internet Quotient, IOS, IP/TV, iQ Expertise, the iQ logo, iQ Net Readiness Scorecard, iQuick Study, LightStream, Linksys, MeetingPlace, MGX, Networking Academy, Network Registrar, Packet, PIX, ProConnect, RateMUX, ScriptShare, SlideCast, SMARTnet, StackWise, The Fastest Way to Increase Your Internet Quotient, and TransPath are registered trademarks of Cisco Systems, Inc. and/or its affiliates in the United States and certain other countries.

All other trademarks mentioned in this document or Website are the property of their respective owners. The use of the word partner does not imply a partnership relationship between Cisco and any other company. (0609R)

About the Authors

Jazib Frahim, CCIE No. 5459, has been with Cisco Systems for more than seven years. With a Bachelor's degree in computer engineering from Illinois Institute of Technology, he started out as a TAC engineer with the LAN Switching team. He then moved to the TAC Security team, where he acted as a technical leader for the security products. He led a team of 20 engineers as a team leader in resolving complicated security and VPN technologies. Jazib is currently working as a Senior Network Security Engineer in the Worldwide Security Services Practice of Cisco's Advanced Services for Network Security. He is responsible for guiding customers in the design and implementation of their networks, with a focus in network security. He holds two CCIEs, one in Routing and Switching and the other in Security. He also authored the Cisco Press book *Cisco ASA: All-in-one Firewall, IPS, and VPN Adaptive Security Appliance* (ISBN: 1-58705-209-1). Additionally, Jazib has written numerous Cisco online technical documents and has been an active member on Cisco's online forum, NetPro. He has presented at Networkers on multiple occasions and has taught many onsite and online courses to Cisco customers, partners, and employees.

Jazib is currently pursuing a Master of Business Administration (MBA) degree from North Carolina State University.

Omar Santos is a Senior Network Security Consulting Engineer in the Worldwide Security Services Practice of Cisco's Advanced Services for Network Security. He has more than 12 years of experience in secure data communications. Omar has designed, implemented, and supported numerous secure networks for Fortune 500 companies and the U.S. government, including the United States Marine Corps (USMC) and Department of Defense (DoD). He is also the author of the Cisco Press book *Cisco ASA: All-in-one Firewall, IPS, and VPN Adaptive Security Appliance* (ISBN: 1-58705-209-1) and many Cisco online technical documents and configuration guidelines. Prior to his current role, he was a technical leader of Cisco's Technical Assistance Center (TAC), where he taught, led, and mentored many engineers within the organization. He is an active member of the InfraGard organization, a cooperative undertaking between the Federal Bureau of Investigation and an association of businesses, academic institutions, state and local law-enforcement agencies, and other participants that are dedicated to increasing the security of the critical infrastructures of the United States of America. Omar has also delivered numerous technical presentations to Cisco customers, partners, and other organizations.

David White, Jr., CCIE No. 12021, has more than ten years of networking experience with a focus on network security. He is currently an Escalation Engineer in the Cisco TAC, where he has been for more than six years. In his role at Cisco, he is involved in new product design and implementation and is an active participant in Cisco documentation, both online and in print. David holds a CCIE in Security and is also NSA IAM certified. Before joining Cisco, David worked for the U.S. government, where he helped secure its worldwide communications network. He was born and raised in St. Petersburg, Florida, and received his Bachelor's degree in computer engineering from the Georgia Institute of Technology.

About the Technical Reviewers

Darrin Miller is an engineer in Cisco's security technology group. Darrin is responsible for system-level security architecture. He has worked primarily on policy-based admission and incident response programs within Cisco. Previous to that Darrin conducted security research in the areas of IPv6, SCADA, incident response, and trust models. This work has included protocol security analysis and security architectures for next-generation networks. Darrin has authored and contributed to several books and whitepapers on the subject of network security. He has also spoken around the world at leading network security conferences on a variety of topics. Before his eight years at Cisco, Darrin held various positions in the network security community.

John Stuppi, CCIE No. 11154, is a Network Consulting Engineer for Cisco Systems. John is responsible for creating, testing, and communicating effective techniques using Cisco product capabilities to provide protection and mitigation options to Cisco customers facing current or expected security threats. John also advises Cisco customers on incident readiness and response methodologies and assists them in DoS and worm mitigation and preparedness. John is a CCIE and a CISSP, and he holds an Information Systems Security (INFOSEC) professional certification. In addition, John has a BSEE from Lehigh University and a Master of Business Administration degree from Rutgers University. John lives in Ocean Township, New Jersey, with his wife, Diane, and his two wonderful children, Thomas and Allison.

Dedications

I would like to dedicate this book to my parents, Frahim and Perveen, who support and encourage me in all of my endeavors. I would also like to dedicate it to my siblings, including my brother, Shazib; my sisters, Erum and Sana; my sister-in-law, Asiya; and my cute nephew, Shayan; and my newborn niece, Shiza, for their patience and understanding during the development of this book.

—Jazib

I would like to dedicate this book to my lovely wife, Jeannette, and my two beautiful children, Hannah and Derek, who have inspired and supported me throughout the development of this book. I would also like to dedicate this book to my parents, Jose and Generosa. Without their knowledge, wisdom, and guidance, I would not have achieved many of my goals.

—Omar

I would like to dedicate this book to my wife, Holly, who has patiently put up with me (or the lack of me) during this writing process. And to our newborn son, Blake, who reminds us every day how much joy can be found in small things.

I would also like to dedicate this to my loving parents, David and Connie, who have always supported me and pushed me to strive for perfection and to be the best I can be. And to my sister, Patricia, who is a true genius and someone I have always looked up to.

Finally, I would not be the person I am without the strong influence that Jimmy Collins, Art and Shirley Cheek, and Brenda Markland have had on my life. To each, I am eternally grateful.

—David

Acknowledgments

We would like to thank the technical editors, John Stuppi and Darrin Miller, for their time and technical expertise. They verified our work and provided recommendations on how to improve the quality of this manuscript. Special thanks go to Jay Biersbach for reviewing this book before final editing.

We would like to thank the Cisco Press team, especially Brett Bartow and Andrew Cupp, for their patience, guidance, and consideration. Their efforts are greatly appreciated.

Additionally, special thanks go to the NAC product and development teams, especially to Russell Rice, Jason Halpern, David Anderson, Thomas Gary Howard, and Darrin Miller for their unlimited support.

Many thanks to our managers, William Beach, Ken Cavanagh, Mike Stallings, and Joe Dallatore, for their continuous support throughout this project.

Finally, we would like to acknowledge the Cisco TAC. Some of the best and brightest minds in the networking industry work there, supporting our customers often under very stressful conditions and working miracles daily. They are truly unsung heroes, and we are all honored to have had the privilege of working side by side with them in the trenches of the TAC.

This Book Is Safari Enabled

The Safari® Enabled icon on the cover of your favorite technology book means the book is available through Safari Bookshelf. When you buy this book, you get free access to the online edition for 45 days.

Safari Bookshelf is an electronic reference library that lets you easily search thousands of technical books, find code samples, download chapters, and access technical information whenever and wherever you need it.

To gain 45-day Safari Enabled access to this book:

• Go to http://www.ciscopress.com/safarienabled

• Complete the brief registration form

• Enter the coupon code KICN-3ZJD-SDBH-RUD6-TDNM

If you have difficulty registering on Safari Bookshelf or accessing the online edition, please e-mail customer-service@safaribooksonline.com.

Contents at a Glance

Contents

Command Syntax Conventions

The conventions used to present command syntax in this book are the same conventions used in the IOS Command Reference:

- **Boldface** indicates commands and keywords that are entered literally as shown. In actual configuration examples and output (not general command syntax), boldface indicates commands that are manually input by the user (such as a **show** command).

- *Italics* indicate arguments for which you supply actual values.

- Vertical bars (|) separate alternative, mutually exclusive elements.

- Square brackets [ ] indicate optional elements.

- Braces { } indicate a required choice.

- Braces within brackets [{ }] indicate a required choice within an optional element.

Foreword

Cisco pioneered Network Admission Control (NAC) in 2003. Until then, client and network security were two disjointed worlds and islands, with little linkage between them. NAC has been an industry-wide effort to overcome this gap and create explicit trust boundaries and policies that did not exist before. Today, NAC is more than technology or product only. It is a system, requiring important architectural and design guidelines as well as collaboration between industry partners. Cisco's NAC alliance has grown from three to more than 75 partners in the past three years.

Successfully deploying and troubleshooting the Cisco NAC solution requires thoughtful builds and design of NAC in branch, campus, and enterprise topologies, of any size network. It requires a practical and methodical view toward building layered security and management with troubleshooting, auditing, and monitoring capabilities. NAC has unified wired with wireless, networks with devices, and transcends traditional boundaries for security decisions.

The authors of *Cisco Network Admission Control, Volume II: Deployment and Troubleshooting*, Omar Santos, David White Jr., and Jazib Frahim, are industry veterans in network security, switching, and customer deployments, with cumulative expertise of more than 20 years. I hope you enjoy their comprehensive, informative, and thoughtful review of NAC highlighting real-world recommendations.

Jayshree V. Ullal

Cisco Systems, Inc.

Senior Vice President, Datacenter, Switching, and Security Technology Group

August 22, 2006

Introduction

This book is the second volume of *Cisco Network Admission Control* from Cisco Press. The first volume, *NAC Architecture and Design,* examines the protocols used in NAC and covers each individual component's function in detail. Design guidance is provided to assist the reader in implementing NAC in an existing network infrastructure. This includes examining existing hardware and software to determine whether it is NAC capable, providing suggestions for logical enforcement points, and offering guidance on defining an admissions policy.

This book focuses on the key components that make up NAC and how one can successfully deploy and troubleshoot each component as well as the overall solution. Emphasis is placed on real-world deployment scenarios, and the reader is walked step by step through the individual component configurations. Along the way, best practices are called out along with mistakes to avoid. Component-level and solution-level troubleshooting techniques are also presented.

Three common deployment scenarios are covered in Part III, "Deployment Scenarios." They include a small business, a medium-size enterprise, and a large enterprise. Each topology builds on the previous one and adds additional components of NAC to the solution. The small business becomes the branch (or remote) office in the enterprise topologies, while the medium-size enterprise becomes a separate geographically located part of the large enterprise design. This approach also demonstrates how one can phase in NAC in any size network.

Who Should Read This Book?

This book serves as a guide for any network professional who wants to implement the Cisco NAC Framework solution in a network to identify, prevent, and adapt to threats. It systematically walks the reader through installing, configuring, deploying, troubleshooting, and maintaining the NAC solution. Any network professional should be able to use this book as a guide to successfully deploy NAC in a network. The requirements of the reader include a basic knowledge of TCP/IP and networking, familiarity with Cisco routers/switches and their CLI, and a general understanding of the overall NAC Framework solution.

How This Book Is Organized

Part I includes Chapter 1, which provides an overview of the NAC Framework solution and the technology and components used to implement it. The remainder of the book is divided into three parts. Part II encompasses Chapters 2 through 12 and covers the installation, configuration, deployment, and troubleshooting of the individual components that make up the NAC solution. The chapters should be read in order, but if you are not using one of the components of the NAC solution in your network, you will want to skip the corresponding chapter.

Part III encompasses Chapters 13 through 15, which cover how to deploy and troubleshoot the overall NAC solution in your network. Each deployment chapter builds off the previous; therefore, they should be read in order. However, if you are deploying NAC in only a small business, you will want to skip the chapters devoted to deploying NAC in an enterprise.

Part IV encompasses Chapters 16 and 17, which explain how to manage and monitor the NAC solution. Some readers might find it useful to read Chapter 16 after Chapter 1. This will get your mind thinking about the overall tasks and processes in your business that need to be lined up before deploying NAC.

The core chapters, Chapters 2 through 17, cover the following topics:

Part II, "Configuration Guidelines," includes the following chapters:

- **Chapter 2, "Cisco Trust Agent"**—This chapter covers the installation, configuration, deployment, and troubleshooting of the Cisco Trust Agent (CTA). CTA is a small application, installed on end hosts in the NAC solution that provides posture information about the end host to ACS.

- **Chapter 3, "Cisco Secure Services Client"**—This chapter covers the installation, configuration, deployment, and troubleshooting of the Cisco Secure Services Client. The Cisco Secure Services Client is a full-featured wired and wireless 802.1X supplicant that natively supports NAC Framework by passing posture credentials through an EAP-FAST tunnel within the Layer 2 802.1X session.

- **Chapter 4, "Configuring Layer 2 NAC on Network-Access Devices"**—This chapter covers the configuration, operation, and troubleshooting of both Layer 2 IP and Layer 2 802.1X NAC on network-access devices.

- **Chapter 5, "Configuring Layer 3 NAC on Network-Access Devices"**—This chapter discusses the packet flow in an IOS NAD when NAC is enabled and then provides detailed steps to configure Layer 3 NAC on the NAD. This chapter also covers how to monitor and troubleshoot the NAC sessions by examining various log and debug messages.

- **Chapter 6, "Configuring NAC on Cisco VPN 3000 Series Concentrators"**—This chapter starts by covering the packet flow in a concentrator when NAC is enabled. Next, detailed configuration steps to enable NAC on the concentrator are provided, followed by a section on monitoring the remote-access VPN tunnels. For troubleshooting purposes, this chapter closes by covering various debug and log messages to help you isolate the issues related to remote-access tunnels and NAC.

- **Chapter 7, "Configuring NAC on Cisco ASA and PIX Security Appliances"**—This chapter covers the configuration required to enable NAC on the ASA or PIX security appliance for remote-access tunnels. In addition, for troubleshooting purposes, various debug and log messages are explained to help you isolate the issues related to remote-access tunnels and NAC.

- **Chapter 8, "Cisco Secure Access Control Server"**—At the core of NAC is the Cisco Secure Access Control Server. It is often considered the "brains" of NAC because ACS interprets the posture credentials returned from the end hosts and assigns a posture token and policy to them. This chapter covers an overview of ACS and walks the reader step by step through the installation and configuration of ACS for NAC. ACS logging is covered along with a troubleshooting section, which focuses on troubleshooting NAC issues on ACS.

- **Chapter 9, "Cisco Security Agent"**—This chapter starts with an overview of the Cisco Security Agent and then walks the reader step by step through the installation of the management center and creation of agent kits. The remainder of the chapter focuses on NAC-specific features in CSA, such as the capability to dynamically activate or deactivate rules based on system posture token returned.

- **Chapter 10, "Antivirus Software Integration"**—This chapter looks at the antivirus software vendors that interoperate with the NAC Framework. Installation of the antivirus posture plug-in on CTA is covered along with the HCAP protocol (the protocol used to communicate between ACS and antivirus servers). Finally, the reader is walked systematically through the configuration steps necessary to add an antivirus policy server to ACS.

- **Chapter 11, "Audit Servers"**—This chapter looks at the integration of the QualysGuard Scanner appliance into the NAC Framework solution. This chapter provides step-by-step configuration for both the Cisco devices and the QualysGuard Scanner appliance.

- **Chapter 12, "Remediation"**—Remediation servers provide a way of automatically patching end hosts to bring them into compliance with network policies. This chapter examines the software provided by two of the remediation server vendors, Altiris and PatchLink.

Part III, "Deployment Scenarios," includes the following chapters:

- **Chapter 13, "Deploying and Troubleshooting NAC in Small Businesses"**—This is the first of three chapters in the deployment section of the book. It focuses on the small business and what requirements a typical small business would have when deploying NAC in the network. After the requirements are defined, an example small business network is provided and the topology is reviewed. Next, the reader is walked through detailed steps on configuring ACS and the network devices to enable NAC-L2-IP and enforce the requirements drawn up earlier in the chapter. Finally, techniques for troubleshooting the NAC solution are covered.

- **Chapter 14, "Deploying and Troubleshooting NAC in Medium-Size Enterprises"**—This chapter focuses on the requirements of a medium-size enterprise to protect its network from both internal and external unknown threats. Based on the requirements, a solution is presented to the company. This chapter shows step-by-step configurations of all the devices involved. We discuss NAC-L2-IP on a Catalyst switch and NAC-L3-IP on a VPN3000 concentrator. The configurations of an Altiris server for remediation and a QualysGuard server for agentless hosts auditing are also covered. We walk through the steps required to configure ACS and define all the policies.

- **Chapter 15, "Deploying and Troubleshooting NAC in Large Enterprises"**—This chapter builds off the previous two deployment chapters and focuses on the large enterprise (greater than 5,000 users and multiple geographic locations). The requirements of the branch, regional, and headquarters sites are covered. Within the headquarters site, different policies are created for each of the following: executive floor, call center, human resources, finance, sales, engineering, conference center, and data center. Topics such as high availability and scalability are also covered.

Part IV, "Managing and Monitoring NAC," includes the following chapters:

- **Chapter 16, "NAC Deployment and Management Best Practices"**—Some readers may find it useful to read this chapter first. The first half of the chapter is focused on the process of successfully deploying NAC in your network. Topics such as completing a readiness assessment, talking with stakeholders, deploying NAC in a lab, and creating test plans are covered. The second half of the chapter covers the following topics: provisioning user/client software (CTA and third-party software), handling CSA management, maintaining NAC policies, providing technical support, and performing education and awareness of end users as well as the support staff.

- **Chapter 17, "Monitoring the NAC Solution Using the Cisco Security Monitoring, Analysis, and Response System"**—This chapter discusses how to monitor the NAC solution using the Cisco Security Monitoring, Analysis, and Response System (CS-MARS). Detailed instructions on how to configure the individual components of NAC to report to CS-MARS are covered, along with the reporting capabilities of CS-MARS. Troubleshooting the CS-MARS appliance is also covered.

NAC Overview

This chapter covers the following topics:

- Introduction to Network Admission Control
- Review of NAC Phase I and Phase II architecture
- Overview of the components that make up the NAC Framework solution, including:
  - Cisco Trust Agent
  - Cisco Security Agent
  - Network-access devices
  - Cisco Secure Access Control Server
  - Event monitoring, correlation, and reporting

## CHAPTER 1

NAC Solution and Technology Overview

One of the biggest challenges corporations face today is securing the internal network. When the words *network security* are mentioned, most people immediately associate this phrase with protecting their network from external threats. Few people think of the internal threats that already exist. Unpatched end-host systems, out-of-date antivirus signatures, and disabled or nonexistent personal firewalls all weaken the internal security of corporate networks and make them vulnerable to data theft and attacks. Preventing or limiting these hosts' access to the corporate network has been difficult to do until now.

Cisco Systems has launched the Self-Defending Network Initiative (SDNI) to dramatically improve the network's capability to identify, prevent, and adapt to threats. A key part of this initiative is Network Admission Control (NAC). NAC is a multipart solution that validates the security posture of the endpoint before admitting it on the network. If admitted, NAC can also be used to define what resources the endpoint has access to, based on the endpoint's overall security posture.

This chapter is meant to provide you with an overall review of the NAC Framework solution. We start by covering what NAC is and why companies would want to deploy it. Then we cover an architectural overview of the initial NAC solution (NAC Phase I), followed by an architectural overview of the current NAC solution (NAC Phase II). In the remainder of the chapter, we provide an overview of the individual components that make up NAC. Each component has a dedicated chapter in this book where we cover the installation, configuration, and steps to troubleshoot that component in the NAC solution. After reading this chapter, you should be familiar with the concepts and components that make up the NAC Framework and should be ready to start installing and configuring NAC in your network.

If you are unfamiliar with NAC or are interested in learning more about the architecture of the NAC solution, we invite you to read *Cisco Network Admission Control, Volume I: NAC Architecture and Design* (ISBN 1587052415), published by Cisco Press.

Network Admission Control

Reports of data and identity theft have become hot topics in the news recently. Unfortunately, they have also become fairly common, often resulting in millions of dollars' worth of damage to the companies affected. Traditionally, network security professionals have focused much of their time securing the front door to their networked companies—their Internet presence. Stateful firewalls often sit at the gateways, and, in most cases, these are supplemented with inline intrusion-prevention devices (IPS), antivirus scanners, and denial-of-service (DoS) mitigation devices. Behind this virtual fortress of protection sit hardened servers, which serve up the corporate web presence. Many companies are proud of their investment in this type of security and advertise this fact. Now, don't get me wrong—this type of security is important. However, sometimes in the zeal to make the web presence secure, we forget that a huge threat exists from within.

It is becoming mandatory these days for employees to have access to the Internet; often it is a critical component of their jobs. However, have you thought about devices that your employees are using to access the Internet? How secure are they? If they are corporate assets, they should have the corporate antivirus software installed and possibly a personal firewall. But how do you know the employee has not disabled one or more of these and thereby reduced the security of not only the device, but also your internal network, and opened it up to threats?

While you are pondering that thought, let me give you another. How many noncorporate assets connect to your network? How many employees bring in their personal laptop, their personal digital assistant (PDA), or even their cell phone and connect it to the corporate network? What about partners and outside vendors? How much control do you have over these devices? Imagine what could happen if a rootkit or some other Trojan back door was installed on one of these devices and now has access to your internal network. How many confidential documents or corporate secrets could be stolen by attackers within?

It is often easier to consider the mistakes or ignorance of others, but how many times have you been guilty of letting the security of your own PC lapse? How many times have you been notified of a new critical security patch for your laptop or desktop and clicked the Not Now button, choosing instead to install it later? I am sure all of us are guilty of this; I know I am.

Installing security patches, especially to the operating system, usually results in the mandatory reboot. This usually comes at the worst time of the day, when shutting down your applications and rebooting is not an option. So we make a mental note to install the patches when we leave for the day, but how many times do we actually follow through? More often than not, weeks or months could go by before we find the time to install the patches. During this time, the PC remains susceptible to the targeted attack.

Although I have highlighted only a few of the common threats to the internal security of your corporate network, I am sure you can think of many more. Home users connecting via a VPN tunnel, remote sales forces connecting from the local hotspot or hotel, partners with direct site-to-site tunnels to your company—the list goes on. These are the types of threats NAC was designed to protect you against and eliminate.

NAC is a Cisco-led, multivendor initiative focused on eliminating threats to the corporate network caused by insecure endpoints attaching to the network. In its simplest form, NAC defines a set of policies that are used to evaluate the security posture of an endpoint that wants to join the network. The endpoint can be a PC, a PDA, a server, an IP phone, a printer, and so on. Based on the security posture of the endpoint, it can be given unrestricted access to the network—if it meets all the security requirements. Devices that fail to fully satisfy the security requirements can be quarantined where autoremediation ensues. (Remediation servers can automatically push out patches and updates to software running on the endpoints to improve their security posture.) Alternatively, devices can be denied access to the network altogether, or they can be placed in their own VLAN and given limited access to the network. All of these actions are fully configurable, along with the security policy to be enforced.

NAC: Phase I

Cisco rolled out NAC in a series of phases. Phase I was launched in the summer of 2004. It includes using Cisco routers as the enforcement point, running Cisco IOS Release 12.3(8)T or later. When NAC is deployed on Cisco IOS routers, it is called NAC-L3-IP because the router operates at Layer 3 (the IP layer) and contains noncompliant endpoints using Layer 3 Access Control Lists (ACLs). As endpoints attempt to access devices through the router, they are queried to determine their security posture. Based on the endpoint's security posture, a security policy for the endpoint is pushed down to the router that permits or restricts access. Figure 1-1 shows a NAC-L3-IP architecture overview.

Figure 1-1   *NAC-L3-IP Architecture Overview*

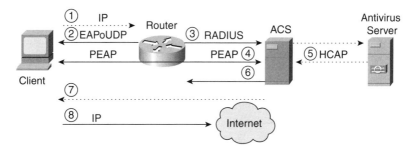

Follow along in Figure 1-1 as we walk through each step of this process:

1. The endpoint sends a packet, which passes through the router, on to its destination. The packet matches the *Intercept ACL* applied to the router's interface, which triggers the NAC-L3-IP posture-validation process.

2. The router initiates an EAP over UDP (EAPoUDP) tunnel to the Cisco Trust Agent (CTA) on the endpoint. This is the first part in setting up a secure tunnel between the endpoint and the Cisco Secure Access Control Server (ACS).

3. Next, the router initiates a RADIUS tunnel to the Cisco Secure ACS server. This is the second part in establishing a secure tunnel between the endpoint and Cisco Secure ACS.

4. With the EAPoUDP and RADIUS tunnels established, the Cisco Secure ACS server establishes a Protected Extensible Authentication Protocol (PEAP) tunnel with the endpoint and queries it for posture credentials. The posture credentials are sent to Cisco Secure ACS using EAP type-length-values (EAP-TLVs). The EAP-TLVs allow for any number of posture credentials to be returned from the end device.

5. (Optional) Cisco Secure ACS proxies some of the posture credentials to additional validation servers (in this case, an antivirus server) using the Host Credentials Authorization Protocol (HCAP).

6. Cisco Secure ACS analyzes the end host's security posture by passing the posture credentials through rules, defined by the administrator in Cisco Secure ACS, or by sending them to external posture-validation servers. The host is then assigned an overall security posture, based on those results. The overall security posture is then forwarded to the router, along with the associated access list, which restricts the host's access to the network, based on its security posture.

7. (Optional) Cisco Secure ACS can also send a message to the endpoint, which, in turn, is displayed to the user to provide notification about the security posture of the host. Cisco Secure ACS can also redirect the user's browser to a remediation server, where patches and updates can be applied.

8. If the host is deemed "healthy" (its security posture meets the requirements of the company), it is permitted to access the network unrestricted.

The protocols used in Figure 1-1 are discussed in more detail in later chapters. For now, it is important to know only that the posture credentials and security policy are carried over authenticated and encrypted tunnels for added security. Figure 1-2 illustrates the relationship among these protocols in a graphical way. The PEAP-encrypted tunnel is carried over both the RADIUS and EAPoUDP tunnels. It contains the EAP-TLVs used to determine the host's posture.

Figure 1-2 *Graphical Representation of Protocols Used in Phase I NAC*

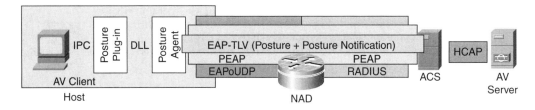

NAC: Phase II

Cisco launched NAC Phase II in the summer of 2005. Phase II expands on Phase I by placing NAC capabilities into several more product lines, including the Catalyst line of switches, the VPN 3000 series concentrators, the ASA 5500 series and PIX 500 series security appliances, the Aironet wireless access points, and the Wireless LAN Service Module. With these new additions, the enforcement point has moved to the network edge, providing enforcement and containment at a port (or host) level instead of at the gateway. These additions also created some new terminology:

- **NAC-L2-IP**—The term *NAC-L2-IP* is used when NAC is applied to a Catalyst switch, on a per-port basis. You can think of NAC-L2-IP as being identical to NAC-L3-IP, but the enforcement policy is an IP-based ACL applied to a switch port instead of a routed port. Likewise, the protocol flow as defined in Figure 1-1 is the same for NAC-L2-IP.

  One other difference between NAC-L2-IP and NAC-L3-IP is that, in NAC-L2-IP, the posture assessment is triggered when the switch port receives a Dynamic Host Configuration Protocol (DHCP) packet or an Address Resolution Protocol (ARP) packet from the endpoint attempting to connect to the network. Then the switch establishes the EAPoUDP tunnel to the endpoint to start the posture-validation process.

- **NAC-L2-802.1X**—The term *NAC-L2-802.1X* is used when NAC is applied to a switch port along with 802.1X authentication. 802.1X provides for both user- and machine-based authentication of the endpoint before the switchport forwards any traffic to the network. NAC-L2-802.1X adds security posturing to 802.1X by way of the Extensible Authentication Protocol–Flexible Authentication via Secure Tunneling (EAP-FAST) protocol. Thus, the posture credentials are carried through EAP-FAST over a Transport Layer Security (TLS) tunnel from the endpoint directly to Cisco Secure ACS. Consequently, an 802.1X supplicant that supports EAP-FAST is needed for NAC-L2-802.1X.

  When NAC-L2-802.1X is enabled and a PC is connected to a switch port, 802.1X authentication and posture validation occur within the same EAP transaction. The posture credentials are included within the EAP-FAST messages that are transmitted on top of the 802.1X protocol. However, unlike NAC-L3-IP and NAC-L2-IP, posture enforcement is done not through ACLs but instead solely through VLAN assignment.

Figure 1-3 illustrates NAC-L2-802.1X on a switch that uses 802.1X authentication as the Layer 2 protocol.

Figure 1-3 *NAC-L2-802.1X Architecture Overview*

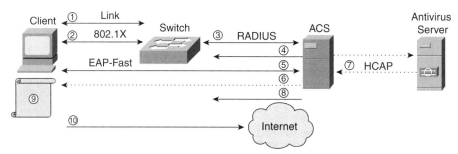

Follow along in Figure 1-3 as we walk through the process of what happens when an endpoint connects to a switch with NAC-L2-802.1X enabled on the port:

1. The end device is attached to a switch port.

2. As the link comes up, the client's 802.1X supplicant initiates an authentication request with the switch via 802.1X.

3. The user's (or machine's) credentials are sent from the switch to the Cisco Secure ACS server via RADIUS.

4. The Cisco Secure ACS server authenticates the user (or machine).

5. CTA and Cisco Secure ACS now establish an EAP-FAST tunnel over the existing 802.1*x* and RADIUS sessions.

6. The Cisco Secure ACS server queries CTA for posture credentials using the EAP tunnel.

7. (Optional) Cisco Secure ACS optionally proxies some of the posture credentials to additional validation servers (in this case, an antivirus server) using HCAP. These validation servers can notify the agents on the endpoint and trigger their own updates.

8. Cisco Secure ACS applies the security policy to the retrieved posture credentials, and the host is assigned an overall posture. This security posture is forwarded to the switch along with the associated VLAN to be applied to the port the host is connected to.

9. (Optional) Based on the posture credentials, Cisco Secure ACS can send a message to the end host to be displayed to the user or can redirect the browser to a remediation server. The remediation server can automatically push out patches and updates to the endpoint to bring it in compliance with the corporate security policy.

10. The host is now permitted (or denied) access to the network, based on its posture and the VLAN it is assigned to.

Periodic Revalidation

Periodic revalidations are built into the NAC-L3-IP and NAC-L2-IP solution. The network-access device (NAD) initiates the process by periodically polling validated endpoints to determine whether a change has been made in their posture. CTA alerts the NAD of any changes on the end host, and the NAD then issues a full revalidation and posture assessment.

This security measure prevents users from validating their host and then lowering their security posture after they have been granted access to the network.

Additionally, a separate revalidation timer requires all active hosts to be fully revalidated every 30 minutes, by default. This enables the network administrator to change the security policy on the fly. All already-validated end hosts must meet this new policy when their revalidation timer expires. The following example further illustrates this point:

Bob, the network administrator of example.com, receives a new alert about a critical security vulnerability in Microsoft Windows. Realizing the security impact that this vulnerability might have on his network, Bob immediately modifies his NAC security policy to require the hotfix that addresses this vulnerability to be applied on all end hosts on his network. Because it is during the day, most users validated their machines on the network when they arrived in the morning. Without periodic revalidation, Bob would have to wait until each user disconnects and reconnects to the network before the endpoint is revalidated. However, the revalidation timer solves this by requiring all active, validated hosts to be fully revalidated every 30 minutes (by default).

NAC Agentless Hosts

A NAC agentless host (NAH) (or a clientless endpoint) is a device that does not have CTA installed. Therefore, it cannot respond to the EAPoUDP or EAP-FAST request from the NAD. A printer, a webcam, an IP phone, and a guest PC are all examples of NAHs.

Individual policies can be defined on the NAD for NAHs. The policy can be designed to exclude a specific MAC or IP address or a range of addresses. Alternatively, a global policy can be defined on Cisco Secure ACS for NAHs. After the EAPoUDP or EAP-FAST session times out, the NAD can notify Cisco Secure ACS of the NAH, and Cisco Secure ACS can apply the appropriate authorization rights. We look at NAHs in more detail in Chapters 4, "Configuring Layer 2 NAC on Network-Access Devices," through 8, "Cisco Secure Access Control Server."

Another option for NAHs (which is part of NAC Phase II) is to use an audit server to scan the host for the services running on it and potential vulnerabilities. Cisco Secure ACS instructs the audit server on which hosts to scan by using the Generic Authorization Message Exchange (GAME) protocol. When the scan is complete, the audit server returns the results to Cisco Secure ACS through the GAME protocol, and Cisco Secure ACS uses these results to apply a security posture and overall policy to the end host.

NAC Program Participants

Cisco Systems leads the NAC program, but is open to any vendor that wants to participate. To ensure interoperability, Cisco requires all vendors shipping NAC-enabled code to have it tested either by an independent third-party testing center or by Cisco Systems. At the time of publication, more than 75 vendors were enrolled in the NAC program. A current list of program participants is maintained by Cisco at http://www.cisco.com/web/partners/pr46/ nac/partners.html.

Components That Make Up the NAC Framework Solution

The following sections examine the individual components that make up the NAC Framework solution. Although only an overview is provided here, each component is covered in detail in its associated chapter in this book.

Cisco Trust Agent

Cisco Trust Agent (CTA) is a small software application (approximately 3MB) that is installed locally on a PC and that allows Cisco Secure ACS to communicate directly with the PC to query it for posture credentials. Some common posture credentials are the OS name, the service pack installed, and specific hotfixes applied. Table 1-1 lists the posture credentials that CTA supports or for which CTA is a broker.

CTA is a core component of NAC and is the only communications interface between the NAD and the applications that reside on the PC. It receives posture credential queries from Cisco Secure ACS, brokers them to the correct application, and then forwards the application responses to Cisco Secure ACS. CTA has three key responsibilities (see Figure 1-4):

- **Communication**—Provides a communications link with the NAD using EAPoUDP or EAP-FAST.

- **Security**—Authenticates the device requesting posture credentials and ensures that all information is sent out encrypted on the wire.

- **Broker**—Provides an application programming interface (API) to query other applications running on the system and notifies them of the current system posture so they can react to posture changes.

Table 1-1   *Posture Credentials Supported by CTA*

Application	Posture Credentials
CTA (version 2)	CTA version
	Operating system name
	Operating system version
	Installed service packs
	Installed hotfixes
	Custom credentials returned through the optional scripting interface
Cisco Security Agent (CSA)*	CSA version
	CSA status (enabled/disabled)
	Fully qualified domain name (FQDN) of Cisco Security Agent Management Center (CSA-MC)
	Last poll of CSA
Antivirus*	Antivirus software name or identifier
	Software version
	Scan engine version
	DAT/pattern file version
	DAT/pattern file release date
	Antivirus enabled/disabled
	On-access scan enabled
Other software*	Varies by vendor

*CTA must be installed and acts as a broker agent to forward the posture credentials to Cisco Secure ACS.

Figure 1-4   *Responsibilities of CTA*

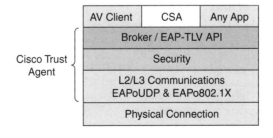

NOTE   CTA is involved only in the posture query and response process; it does not take part in any enforcement action on its own. Thus, if a user disables (or removes) CTA, the host becomes clientless (a NAC agentless host). However, it still cannot bypass the NAC validation process and be granted unrestricted access to the network. Instead, the NAC agentless host policy takes effect, which can greatly restrict or even deny access to the network. This is unlike common personal firewall software or antivirus software, in which disabling the application lessens the protection provided.

Software Availability and Operating System Support

CTA is available free of charge to all registered Cisco.com users at http://cisco.com/cgi-bin/tablebuild.pl/cta. CTA supports the Windows NT, Windows 2000, Windows XP, Windows 2003, Red Hat Linux, and MAC OS 10.3 host operating systems. Internationalization support for CTA includes English, Japanese, Korean, French, Spanish, Arabic, Hebrew, and Russian.

CTA also includes an 802.1X supplicant bundled with it that supports EAP-FAST when running NAC. The 802.1X supplicant is needed to implement NAC-L2-802.1X. However, the 802.1X supplicant is limited to wired interfaces only—no wireless interfaces.

Chapter 2, "Cisco Trust Agent," fully covers the installation, configuration, operation, and troubleshooting of CTA.

Cisco Security Agent

Cisco Security Agent (CSA) is the Cisco award-winning host-based intrusion-prevention system (HIPS) installed on a desktop or server PC that protects it from known and unknown threats. CSA adds a shim into the network layer and into the kernel layer (to watch both network traffic and API calls to kernel). This allows CSA to not only be a personal firewall, but also to protect against buffer-overflow attacks and spyware/adware. In addition, it provides file protection, malicious application protection, and operating-system integrity protection. CSA is one of the few HIPS products that provide true protection against "Day Zero" attacks.

Starting with version 4.5, CSA integrates seamlessly with NAC through CTA. CTA queries CSA to establish the presence of the agent and determine whether it is in protect mode. This information is part of the posture credentials returned to Cisco Secure ACS and is used to determine the end host's overall security posture. Based on this posture, Cisco Secure ACS can apply a policy that alters the state of CSA. CSA's state change dynamically activates additional rules within CSA, thereby providing another level of protection to the host.

Cisco Security Agent Management Center (CSA MC) provides a powerful, scalable application used to manage all agents. When an agent is installed on a host, it first registers with CSA MC and downloads any updates to its rule set. Thereafter, the agent periodically polls CSA MC to check for any new software or rule updates. Besides the configuration and software update function, CSA MC receives real-time security events from the agents and immediately displays them in the Event Monitor for the network administrator to see. In addition, CSA MC correlates the events, received from all agents in the network, to detect suspicious activity across several hosts. If similar threats are detected across several agents, CSA MC creates and deploys dynamic rules to all the agents to provide an additional layer of protection against this newly spreading threat.

Chapter 9, "Cisco Security Agent," covers the installation, configuration, and operation of CSA.

Software Availability and Operating System Support

CSA MC versions 4.5 and 5.0 are a separately licensed product under the CiscoWorks VMS umbrella. They are supported on Windows 2000 Server and Windows 2000 Advanced Server. CSA MC Version 5.1 and higher are standalone products (no longer part of VMS) and are supported on Windows 2003 R2 Standard and Enterprise editions. CSA MC is capable of managing up to 100,000 agents in distributed mode.

CSA agents are supported on the following operating systems: Windows 2003, Windows XP, Windows 2000, Windows NT, Solaris, and Red Hat Linux. Internationalization is supported on Windows 2000 and later and includes all languages except Arabic and Hebrew. Localization is included for English, French, German, Italian, Japanese, Korean, Simplified Chinese, and Spanish language desktops. The agent UI, events, and help system all appear in the language of the end user's desktop. Additional information can be found online at http://www.cisco.com/go/csa/.

Licensed users of CSA MC can obtain software updates at http://www.cisco.com/cgi-bin/tablebuild.pl/csa.

See Chapter 9 for installation and configuration information about CSA and CSA MC.

Network-Access Devices

NADs query the CTA installed on the endpoint. In NAC Phase I, the NAD could be only an IOS router. In Phase II, any of the following devices can be a NAD:

- Cisco IOS router
- Cisco Catalyst Switch running Cisco IOS or CAT OS
- Cisco VPN 3000 series concentrator

- Cisco ASA 5500 series adaptive security appliances and PIX 500 series security appliances
- Cisco wireless access device

NOTE   Future phases of NAC will continue to expand the list of supported network devices.

Cisco IOS Router

Cisco IOS routers first supported NAC in Cisco IOS Release 12.3(8)T, in the Advanced Security, Advanced IP Services, or Advanced Enterprise Services feature sets. Table 1-2 lists Cisco IOS routers by platform and current NAC capability.

NOTE   For the most up-to-date list of NAC-enabled routers, check online at http://www.cisco.com/go/nac/.

Table 1-2   *NAC Support in IOS Routers*

Cisco Router Platform	NAC Support
7500 series	Yes
7300 series	Yes
7200 series	Yes
7100 series	No
4500 series	No
3800 series	Yes
3700 series	Yes
3640, 3640A, 3660-ENT series	Yes
3620, 3660-CO series	No
2800 series	Yes
2600XM series, 2691	Yes
2600 series (non-XM Models)	No
1800 series	Yes
1701, 1711, 1712, 1721, 1751, 1751-V, 1760	Yes
1710, 1720, 1750	No
830 series	Yes
AS5850, AS5400, AS5400HPX, AS5350	No

When NAC is implemented on a router, this is called NAC-L3-IP. That is, the security enforcement point becomes the Layer 3 gateway instead of the physical port into which the end host is plugged.

Posture validation is triggered by defining an *intercept* ACL on the router's interface. Any traffic arriving on the interface from a nonpostured source that matches the *intercept* ACL triggers the posture-validation process, as illustrated in Figure 1-1. When the overall security posture of the host is determined, Cisco Secure ACS sends a host-based downloadable ACL to the router to restrict, prohibit, or permit that client's access to the network. Thus, policy enforcement takes place at Layer 3 with an ACL on the router's interface.

Online Resource: Cisco Routers

For more information about the line of IOS routers available from Cisco Systems, visit http://www.cisco.com/go/routers/.

See Chapter 5, "Configuring Layer 3 NAC on Network-Access Devices," for more information on configuring and troubleshooting NAC on a Cisco IOS router.

Cisco Catalyst Switch Running Cisco IOS or CAT OS

Catalyst switches first supported NAC in the summer of 2005 across various platforms and release trains. One benefit of adding NAC on the switch is enhanced posture-enforcement capabilities through containment. On Cisco IOS routers, policy enforcement was applied with a downloadable ACL on the router's interface. This enabled the administrator to restrict (or even deny) the endpoint's access through the router. However, the endpoint could not be restricted from sending packets to Layer 2–adjacent devices (because those packets did not traverse the router and, therefore, would not be subject to the downloadable ACL). However, on access switches, the endpoints are typically directly connected to a physical port on the switch. This allows for policy enforcement (through VLAN or ACL) as well as containment (because the endpoint is typically the only device connected to that port).

Catalyst switches can implement NAC on a per-port basis at Layer 2 or Layer 3. As mentioned previously in this chapter, when NAC is implemented at Layer 2, it is known as NAC-L2-802.1X because 802.1X is used as the underlying Layer 2 transport protocol. When NAC is implemented on a switch at Layer 3, it is known as NAC-L2-IP.

NAC-L2-802.1X and NAC-L2-IP have several administrative and operational differences that you should fully consider before selecting which one to deploy.

The following are attributes of NAC-L2-802.1X:

- 802.1X authentication must be implemented on the switch.
- The client's 802.1X supplicant triggers authentication and posture validation.
- The client's 802.1X supplicant must be CTA aware.
- Posture enforcement is provided by VLAN assignment only.
- EAP-FAST authenticates CTA to Cisco Secure ACS; therefore, no client-side certificate is needed.
- Endpoints must be directly connected, or be connected through an IP phone.

The following are attributes of NAC-L2-IP:

- Posture validation is triggered when the switch receives Address Resolution Protocol (ARP) packets from the endpoint. Optionally, Dynamic Host Configuration Protocol (DHCP) snooping can be enabled on the port to trigger posture validation when the switch receives the first DHCP packet.
- Posture enforcement is provided by downloadable ACLs.
- VLAN assignment is not supported.
- EAPoUDP is used to communicate between CTA and the NAD. PEAP is used between CTA and Cisco Secure ACS.
- URL redirection of the endpoint's web browser to a remediation server is supported.
- Endpoints can be directly connected, connected through an IP phone, or connected through a shared-media device (hub, non-NAC-capable switch, and so on.)

No "right" or "wrong" choice exists between the two. But there is a best choice for your network. If you don't know what that choice is, read *Cisco Network Admission Control, Volume I: NAC Architecture and Design,* which walks through several design scenarios, discusses the options available, and provides the rationale for the choices made.

An additional consideration (and probably the most important one) is which one will run on your existing switch hardware. Table 1-3 should come in handy in making that determination; it lists the various models of Catalyst switches and their NAC capabilities based on the OS.

NOTE   For the most up-to-date list of NAC-enabled switches, check online at http://www.cisco.com/go/nac/.

Table 1-3   *NAC Support in Catalyst Switches*

Platform, Supervisor	OS	NAC-L2-802.1*x*	NAC-L2-IP	NAC-L3-IP	NAC Agentless Host
6500 - Sup32, Sup720	Native IOS	Planned	Yes, 12.2(18)SXF2	Planned	Yes, NAC-L2-IP
6500 – Sup2	Native IOS	No	No	No	No
6500 – Sup32, Sup720, Sup2	Hybrid	Yes, 8.5	Yes, 8.5	No	Yes, NAC-L2-IP
6500 – Sup32, Sup720, Sup2	Cat OS	Yes, 8.5	Yes, 8.5	No	Yes, NAC-L2-IP
6500 – Sup1A	All	No	No	No	No
5000 Series	All	No	No	No	No
4900 Series	IOS	Yes, 12.2(25)SG	Yes, 12.2(25)SG	Planned	Yes, NAC-L2-IP
4000/4500 Series – SupII+, II+TS, II+10GE, IV, V, V-10GE	Cisco IOS	Yes, 12.2(25)SG	Yes, 12.2(25)SG	Planned	Yes, NAC-L2-IP
4000 – SupI, II, and III	All	No	No	No	No
3750, 3560	Cisco IOS; advanced IP services, IP services, IP base	Yes, 12.2(25)SED	Yes, 12.2(25)SED	No	Yes, NAC-L2-IP
3550	Cisco IOS; IP services and IP base	Yes, 12.2(25)SED	Yes, 12.2(25)SED	No	Yes, NAC-L2-IP
3500XL, 2900XL	All	No	No	No	No
2970	Cisco IOS; LAN base	Yes, 12.2(25)SED	No	No	No
2960	Cisco IOS; LAN base	Yes, 12.2(25)SED	No	No	No
2950	Cisco IOS; EI, SI	Yes, 12.1(22)EA6	No	No	No
2955, 2940	Cisco IOS	Yes, 12.1(22)EA6	No	NO	No

continues

Table 1-3 *NAC Support in Catalyst Switches (Continued)*

Platform, Supervisor	OS	NAC-L2-802.1*x*	NAC-L2-IP	NAC-L3-IP	NAC Agentless Host
2948G-GE-TX	Cat OS	No	No	No	No
1900	All	No	No	No	No
Express 500	Cisco IOS	No	No	No	No

Catalyst switches are an integral part of the NAC solution, providing protection and containment of hosts that do not meet corporate security policies at the access layer. As such, Cisco is committed to providing NAC support on all new switch hardware.

Online Resource: Cisco Catalyst Switches

You can find more information about the Cisco Catalyst line of high-performance LAN switches at http://www.cisco.com/go/catalyst/.

See Chapter 4 for more information on configuring and troubleshooting NAC on a Catalyst switch.

Cisco VPN 3000 Series Concentrator

NAC support for the VPN 3000 series concentrators was first added in Release 4.7. The concentrator is a Layer 3 NAD and postures remote-access IPSec (or Layer 2 Tunneling Protocol [L2TP] over IPSec) clients. The posturing process is almost identical to that of NAC-L3-IP, described previously in the section "NAC: Phase I" (refer to Figure 1-1). The only difference is that the router is replaced with a VPN 3000 concentrator, and an IPSec tunnel is first established to the concentrator before the EAPoUDP session starts.

When the EAPoUDP session starts, a PEAP session is established between the client and the Cisco Secure ACS so posture validation can take place. Cisco Secure ACS then notifies the concentrator (through RADIUS) of the client's posture and passes down a filter list to be applied to the client. The filter list is the 3000's equivalent to a downloadable ACL.

One unique option that the concentrator provides is that clients can be excluded from posture validation based solely on OS type. This is because the Cisco VPN client sends its OS information during IPSec tunnel establishment, which occurs before NAC posture validation. Host exemption, along with all other NAC configuration, is specified under the group policy settings on the 3000. NAC configuration on the VPN 3000 concentrator is covered in detail in Chapter 6, "Configuring NAC on Cisco VPN 3000 Series Concentrators."

Online Resource: Cisco 3000 Series VPN Concentrators

For more information about the Cisco VPN 3000 series concentrators, see http://www.cisco.com/go/vpn3000/.

Cisco ASA 5500 Series Adaptive Security Appliance and PIX 500 Series Security Appliance

The NAC implementation on the Cisco 5500 series Adaptive Security Appliances (ASA) and PIX 500 series security appliances is identical to the implementation on the VPN 3000 concentrators. NAC-L3-IP is supported starting with Version 7.2(1) on all IPSec and L2TP over IPSec remote-access tunnels. Posture enforcement is provided by way of a downloadable ACL from Cisco Secure ACS. Additionally, just as with the VPN 3000, remote-access clients can be exempted from NAC posture validation based on OS type.

The ASA and PIX also support clientless authentication. Those hosts connecting through a remote-access tunnel that do not have CTA installed are marked as clientless. Cisco Secure ACS can then apply the clientless policy to those hosts, to limit (or remove entirely) their access to the network. Chapter 7, "Configuring NAC on Cisco ASA and PIX Security Appliances," contains the complete configuration of NAC on the ASA 5500 series appliances and PIX 500 series security appliances.

Online Resource: Cisco Adaptive Security Appliances

For more information about the Cisco ASA 5500 series adaptive security appliances, see http://www.cisco.com/go/asa/.

Cisco Wireless Devices

NAC Framework support for wireless devices is available on autonomous Access Points (AP), lightweight access points running the Lightweight Access Point Protocol (LWAPP), and the Wireless LAN Services Module (WLSM) for the Catalyst 6500. Table 1-4 lists the wireless devices and minimum supported software.

Table 1-4   *NAC Support in Wireless Devices*

Wireless Device	Minimum Supported Software
Autonomous APs running IOS: Aironet 1100, 1130AG, 1200, 1230AG, 1240AG, 1300 IOS-based access points	Cisco IOS Release 12.3(7)JA or later
Lightweight APs running LWAPP: Aironet 1000, 1130AG, 1200, 1230AG, 1240AG, 1500 + WLAN Controller 2000, 4100, or 4400	Cisco Unified Wireless Network Software Release 3.1 or later
Catalyst 6500 series WLSM	Cisco IOS Release 1.4.1 or later

Wireless devices are Layer 2 termination devices and, as such, support NAC-L2-802.1*x* as the posturing method. The process that a wireless client connecting to a wireless device goes through for posture validation is the same as for a wired client. Figure 1-3 depicts this posture. Note that wireless devices provide posture enforcement through VLAN only. This means that, to support NAC, the wireless devices must be configured for multiple VLANs per service set identifier (SSID).

Configuration and troubleshooting of NAC on Cisco wireless access points is covered along with other Layer 2 network-access devices in Chapter 4.

Online Resource: Cisco Wireless Access Points

For more information about the wireless line of products available from Cisco Systems, see http://www.cisco.com/go/wireless/.

Cisco Secure Access Control Server

The Cisco Secure Access Control Server (ACS) for Windows is another core required component of NAC. Cisco Secure ACS first supported NAC in Version 3.3, which was launched concurrently with Phase I in the summer of 2004. Cisco Secure ACS 4.0, released in the fall of 2005, added support for NAC Phase II, including all the NADs listed in the previous section.

Cisco Secure ACS is the central controller for all NAC policy decisions. It receives posture credentials from all agents and either processes them locally or forwards them on to partner validation servers for processing. If the posture credentials are forwarded on, Cisco Secure ACS waits to receive the application posture token (APT) back from the external validation server. It then combines this APT with the local APTs it created based on the defined policy; the result is an overall system posture token (SPT).

The SPT has one of the following values: Healthy, Checkup, Quarantine, Infected, or Unknown, which are mapped to a network access policy. The network-access policy and SPT are then transmitted to the NAD as part of policy enforcement. Optionally, Cisco Secure ACS can send a user-notification message that CTA displays on the end host. This message usually indicates the posture of the system along with some instructions (for the un-Healthy hosts). Cisco Secure ACS can also send a URL redirect to the end host via the NAD if either NAC-L3-IP or NAC-L2-IP is being used.

Chapter 8 covers installation, configuration, and troubleshooting of Cisco Secure ACS.

Online Resource: Cisco Access Control Server

For more information about the Cisco Secure Access Control Server, see http://www.cisco.com/go/acs/.

Event Monitoring, Analysis, and Reporting

Protecting the network from threats is the first step toward securing it. However, event monitoring, analysis, and reporting are also vital pieces in understanding the *network's* security posture:

- **Event monitoring**—The process of receiving events (or alerts) from the network and presenting them to the user in real time and in a meaningful way. This is usually provided with some sort of "dashboard" where new events are displayed as they come in.

- **Analysis**—The process of taking the events received and normalizing and correlating them to produce the most relevant set of data. The correlation process takes multiple streams of events from various device types and finds similarities in their data that can be linked to provide a detailed composite picture. The normalization process then removes the redundant data and improves data consistency.

- **Reporting**—The process of querying historical data for specific events and presenting those events in a useful way to the user.

Monitoring, analysis, and reporting are powerful tools that show the network administrator the state of the network at any given point in time. These tools are very important in networks where NAC is enabled because the volume of events that each network device generates for each postured host is huge. Monitoring the network devices individually for problems or anomalies is neither practical nor efficient. This is why Cisco has enhanced its Cisco Security Monitoring, Analysis, and Reporting System (CS-MARS) to support NAC.

The CS-MARS appliance is a topologically aware, high-performance event-correlation system. Syslogs, NetFlow data, Simple Network Management Protocol (SNMP) traps, and other network logging information can be sent to it from a variety of network sources. This includes routers, switches, firewalls, intrusion-prevention devices, Cisco Secure ACS, and even end hosts. All this information is then correlated within CS-MARS to detect network attacks and other types of security threats. When an attack is detected, an incident is fired and the attacker, victim, and path from attacker to victim are displayed in the CS-MARS interface. Additionally, based on the attack vector, CS-MARS can inform the user of the best way to mitigate the attack.

In support of NAC, CS-MARS parses, normalizes, correlates, and reports on posture-validation events for NAC-L3-IP, NAC-L2-IP, and NAC-L2-802.1X. Predefined reports enable network administrators to view the number of hosts in Healthy, Quarantined, Clientless, or other states throughout the entire network. Administrators can further drill down to determine the posture status on a per-device basis. They may also choose to receive daily reports (via e-mail) of the number and location of nonhealthy hosts in their network.

Help-desk support teams can use CS-MARS to identify problems reported from end users. CS-MARS can display IP addresses, machine/usernames, and the logical switch port number the user is connected to, along with the posture information or authentication information of end hosts. This information can be displayed in real time and allows the help-desk teams to quickly and easily identify problems end users are having.

Chapter 17, "Monitoring the NAC Solution Using the Cisco Security Monitoring, Analysis, and Response System," covers the configuration and operation of CS-MARS in a NAC Framework solution.

Online Resource: Cisco Security Monitoring, Analysis, and Reporting System

For more information about the Cisco Security Monitoring, Analysis, and Reporting System, see http://www.cisco.com/go/mars/.

Summary

This chapter answered the question, "What is network access control?" by providing a solution overview as well as taking a look at the individual components that make up NAC. The different implementations of NAC were also explained, including NAC-L3-IP, NAC-L2-IP, and NAC-L2-802.1X. Network-access devices supporting NAC were presented, along with the version of software required.

Looking ahead, subsequent chapters focus on the installation, configuration, and operation of each individual NAC component. Once complete, the individual components are combined to illustrate real-world deployment scenarios in Part III, "Deployment Scenarios." Finally, Part IV, "Managing and Monitoring NAC," focuses on the overall management and monitoring of the NAC solution.

Review Questions

You can find the answers to the review questions in Appendix A, "Answers to Review Questions."

1. Which of the following is a required component of NAC?

    a. Remediation server

    b. Antivirus server

    c. Cisco Security Agent

    d. Cisco Secure Access Control Server

2. What is the posture-enforcement method for NAC-L3-IP?

3. What is the posture-enforcement method for NAC-L2-802.1X?

4. NAC-L3-IP and NAC-L2-IP use which of the following protocols to secure the communication between the endpoint and Cisco Secure ACS?

   a. EAP over UDP

   b. EAP-FAST

   c. 77RADIUS

   d. PEAP

5. The network-access device uses what protocol to send NAC-related messages to Cisco Secure ACS?

   a. EAP over UDP

   b. EAP-FAST

   c. RADIUS

   d. PEAP

6. The VPN 3000 concentrator and the ASA and PIX security appliances support NAC on which of the following:

   a. Remote-access IPSec and L2TP over IPSec connections

   b. Remote-access and LAN-to-LAN IPSec connections

   c. Remote-access PPTP and L2TP over IPSec connections

   d. Remote-access IPSec connections only

Configuration Guidelines

This chapter covers the following topics:

- Preparing for deployment of CTA
- Deploying CTA in a lab environment
- Understanding user notifications
- Understanding how to customize CTA by editing *.ini files
- Understanding CTA's Scripting Interface
- Understanding CTA's logging service
- Deploying CTA in a production network
- Troubleshooting CTA

CHAPTER 2

Cisco Trust Agent

Cisco Trust Agent (CTA) is a required, integral component of NAC deployments. CTA is a small software application (about 3MB) installed on end-host machines that performs the following functions:

- Provides a secure communications channel between the host and the ACS server through which posture information is transmitted

- Provides OS and patch information from the host, along with the machine running state, through its included posture plug-in

- Provides state, version, and status information about other NAC partner applications installed on the host through the partner's posture plug-in

- Reports any arbitrary posture information back to ACS through an optional Scripting Interface (SI)

Currently, two versions of CTA are available: CTA Version 1 (released with NAC Phase I) and CTA Version 2 (released with NAC Phase II). CTA Version 1 was limited in the posture credentials it could report by itself. It required the installation of Cisco Security Agent (CSA) to retrieve the hotfixes installed on a Windows client machine. CTA Version 2 improves upon Version 1 by adding these new features:

- Included plug-in module for reporting the host OS and hotfix information, along with running state

- Support for Macintosh OS X operating system

- Support for Linux operating systems

- Silent installation options to ease large CTA deployments

- Included 802.1X supplicant (wired interfaces only), with support for the optional Cisco Secure Services Client, which supports wired and wireless interfaces

- Capability to change the security level of CSA, based on the posture of the host

- Customizable end-user notifications, through a pop-up window

- Scripting interface to provide arbitrary posture information for third-party applications from the host to ACS

CTA Version 2 is backward-compatible with Version 1 and allows for automated silent upgrades (from Version 1 to Version 2) without user intervention.

NOTE	Because of a format change, the CTA 2.0 wired supplicant .xml configuration files are not compatible with those of CTA 2.1. After the CTA upgrade, new configuration profiles must be pushed to the clients.

TIP	Before attempting to deploy CTA in a production environment, it is highly recommended that you read this chapter in its entirety. As a network administrator, you have several available options in the deployment of CTA. Understanding these options and correctly configuring them before pushing CTA out to your users could save you a lot of time and headaches.

Preparing for Deployment of CTA

As a network administrator, you must make a few key decisions before starting the deployment of CTA. The first and most important is whether your NAC deployment will include IEEE 802.1X port-based authentication. 802.1X authentication is an optional component of NAC that provides end-user authentication. When deployed, it is typically done company-wide as part of an overall security architecture. Therefore, you first need to determine whether your security policy requires that all devices authenticate before being granted access to the network. If so, you will want to deploy IEEE 802.1X authentication along with NAC.

NOTE	To learn more about IEEE 802.1X authentication and the benefits it can provide, see *Cisco Network Admission Control, Volume I: NAC Architecture and Design*.

The second decision that needs to be made is whether you will deploy the optional Scripting Interface for CTA. The Scripting Interface provides a way to gather posture information from non-NAC-compliant applications that reside on the end host. You can use it to pass back any arbitrary information that you want to use in the posture policy on ACS to determine the machine's posture state. Typically, the Scripting Interface is used only when the existing posture plug-ins do not provide the posture credentials necessary for you to determine the overall policy of the endpoint.

The next decision that must be made is whether your ACS server will use a self-signed certificate or a certificate obtained from a public Certificate Authority (CA, such as Verisign), or whether you plan to use your own CA server. The root CA certificate must reside on the CTA client machine to validate the identity certificate that ACS presents to

CTA during the negotiation of the PEAP (for NAC-L3-IP and NAC-L2-IP) or EAP-FAST (for NAC-L2-802.1X) tunnels. This certificate can be bundled in the CTA software distribution to aid in deployment.

The final decision that needs to be made is how to distribute the CTA client to end hosts. For small offices or lab setups, it might be possible to manually install the software or have it installed through a startup script on the host. However, for large enterprise deployments a software-distribution tool such as Microsoft's SMS or Altiris is the recommended way to push CTA out to end hosts. Additionally, if you are using the Cisco Security Agent (CSA) in your environment, CTA can also be deployed with an agent kit from CSA. See Chapter 9, "Cisco Security Agent," for more information about deploying CTA with CSA.

Supported Operating Systems

CTA Version 2.1 improves on CTA 1.0 by adding support for non-Windows platforms with the addition of Red Hat Linux and Mac OS X. Table 2-1 lists the supported operating systems for CTA.

Table 2-1   *CTA-Supported Operating Systems*

Operating System	CTA Version 1.0	CTA Version 2.1
Windows 2003 Standard Server	✓	✓
Windows XP Professional and Home*	✓	✓
Windows 2000 (Professional and Server)	✓	✓
Windows NT 4.0**	✓	
Mac OS X***		✓
Red Hat Enterprise Linux Versions 3 and 4***		✓

* Windows XP Home does not support the CTA Wired 802.1X supplicant. However, it does support CTA without the supplicant.

** Beginning with CTA Version 2.1, Windows NT is no longer a supported operating system.

*** Cisco currently does not have a wired 802.1X supplicant version of CTA for Mac OS X and Linux.

NOTE   If you are using the CTA 802.1X supplicant, be aware that user and machine profiles created with CTA 2.0.0 are not compatible with CTA 2.1. On upgrade, the profiles are deleted and new profiles must be created and pushed out to clients. Profiles created with CTA 2.0.1 are compatible with CTA 2.1 and are not deleted during the upgrade.

NOTE   CTA also supports localized versions of the operating systems listed in Table 2-1.

Cisco plans to continue to expand on the supported base of operating systems. Support for Solaris is on the roadmap.

Minimum System Requirements

The CTA client software is a small software package that requires very few hardware resources. Table 2-2 lists the minimum system requirements for Windows, Mac, and Linux operating systems. In short, the machine needs to meet just the minimum OS requirements.

Table 2-2 *Windows, Mac, and Linux Minimum System Requirements*

Component	Requirement
Processor	Windows: Pentium II class or higher
	Mac: G3 processor or better
	Linux: Pentium class or higher
RAM	256MB: Windows XP, 2003, Mac
	128MB: Windows 2000, NT, Linux
Hard Drive Space	20MB
Network Connectivity	UDP port 21862 (default)
Software Installer	Windows: MSI Version 2.0 or later
	Linux: Red Hat Package Management (RPM) v4.2 or greater

TIP   To determine the version of MSI installed, run **msiexec** from a DOS command prompt or from **Start > Run**. A GUI window appears displaying the current version of MSI. Windows NT (supported only on CTA 2.0 and earlier) and some Windows 2000 clients might need to upgrade their MSI before installing CTA.

Installation Packages and Files

Cisco has created several installation packages for CTA, based on the host's operating system. All the Admin packages include a bundled CTA executable that can be installed interactively or silently on end-user machines. The silent option is useful if you plan to push CTA out to users using a software-distribution tool. This method also allows the distribution of CTA with customized configuration files and certificates. The interactive installation options perform noisy installs. With noisy installs, the user is prompted to accept the End User License Agreement (EULA) and for information on where to install CTA. With either installation method, you have the option of choosing to install the optional 802.1X wired supplicant and Scripting Interface.

NOTE	The 802.1X wired supplicant is currently supported only on Windows installations of CTA. Cisco also offers a full-featured supplicant, the Cisco Secure Services Client, which supports both wired and wireless network interfaces. This supplicant used to be the Meetinghouse AEGIS SecureConnect client, before Cisco acquired Meetinghouse in the summer of 2006. We cover the installation and configuration of the Cisco Secure Services Client in Chapter 3, "Cisco Secure Services Client."

See Table 2-3 for a complete list of the available installation packages.

Table 2-3   *CTA Installation Packages**

Windows Installation Packages	
Filename	**Description**
CtaAdminEx-win-*version*.exe	Admin install package contains ctasetup-win-*version*.msi. No 802.1X supplicant.
CtaAdminEx-supplicant-win-*version*.exe	Admin install package contains ctasetup-supplicant-win-*version*.msi. 802.1X wired supplicant.
ctasetup-win-*version*.msi	Client MSI installation file. No 802.1X supplicant.
ctasetup-supplicant-win-*version*.msi	Client MSI installation file. 802.1X wired supplicant.
Mac Installation Packages	
Filename	**Description**
ctaadminex-darwin-*version*.tar.gz	Admin installation package contains cta-darwin-*version*.dmg. No 802.1X supplicant.
cta-darwin-*version*.dmg	Installation disk image.
Linux Installation Packages	
Filename	**Description**
ctaadminex-linux-*version*.tar.gz	Admin installation package contains cta-linux-*version*.i386.rpm. No 802.1X supplicant.
cta-linux-*version*.i386.rpm	Installation RPM. No 802.1X supplicant.

*The [*version*] string is a representation of the current version of CTA. It is represented in 4-tuple dotted-decimal format. Example: 2.1.0.11.

NOTE	You must have Administrator privileges to install CTA. One exception is on Windows. If the group policy allows the MSI to have elevated privileges, users with Standard or Restricted accounts can install CTA.

The latest versions of CTA are available to users with a Cisco Connection Online (CCO) account. You can find them on the Cisco website at http://www.cisco.com/cgi-bin/tablebuild.pl/cta.

Deploying CTA in a Lab Environment

It is highly recommended that you deploy NAC in a lab environment before deploying it in a production network. Deploying it in a lab gives you invaluable hands-on experience and time to learn and understand all the configuration options available to you, under minimal pressure. Heed this warning: Do not attempt to deploy NAC in a production environment without any lab testing ahead of time. NAC is a complex solution with many components. Each one needs to be tested and fully understood before a production rollout. With that in mind, the next several sections walk you through the installation of CTA—with and without the 802.1X supplicant—in a lab environment.

CTA Windows Installation

Installing CTA for windows is simple and very straightforward. For initial testing of CTA in a lab, download the CtaAdminEx-win-*version*.exe file and execute it on your test machine. The installer presents the End User License Agreement (EULA). You must read and accept the EULA before proceeding. After you accept the EULA, the .msi installation file is extracted to the same directory as the CTA Admin executable. Double-click the .msi file to start the CTA installation using the interactive wizard.

When the wizard window appears, select **Next**. You are prompted one more time to accept the EULA before being allowed to continue. On the following screen, you are prompted to choose the location where you want CTA installed (the default is C:\Program Files\Cisco Systems\). The next screen presents you with three installation types: Typical, Complete, and Custom. The only difference among the three is whether the Scripting Interface (SI) is installed. Refer to Table 2-4, which summarizes the installation options.

Table 2-4 *CTA Installation Options*

Installation Type	What Is Installed
Typical	CTA only.
Complete	CTA with Scripting Interface.
Custom	CTA with the option to install the Scripting Interface. *Note:* The Scripting Interface is not selected by default.

After choosing the installation type, choose **Next** to begin the installation. The installer copies the files and inserts the associated Registry entries, and then notifies you that installation is complete. At this point, you might be prompted to reboot. Go ahead and reboot if needed.

With CTA installed, the final step is to install the CA certificate (or ACS's self-signed certificate) into the host's trusted certificate store. See the section "Installing the CA Certificate," later in this chapter, for instructions on how to complete this step.

CTA Windows Installation with the 802.1X Wired Supplicant

Installation of CTA on Windows with the wired supplicant follows the same steps covered in the last section. The only difference is that you download and run the CtaAdminEx-supplicant-win-*version*.exe file to begin the install.

Installing the CTA Admin 802.1X Wired Client

As mentioned previously, download and run the CtaAdminEx-supplicant-win-version.exe file to begin the installation of the CTA Admin 802.1X wired client. The installer presents the EULA. You must read and accept the EULA before proceeding. After you accept the EULA, the .msi installation file (which contains the wired supplicant) is extracted to the same directory as the CTA Admin executable. Double-click the .msi file to start the CTA installation wizard for the administrative version of the wired client.

When the installation wizard completes, you are prompted to reboot your computer. A reboot is required because of the installation of the 802.1X supplicant. After reboot, the Cisco Trust Agent 802.1X wired client icon appears in the system tray. The icon is color-coded to represent the authentication status of the 802.1X client. Additionally, a status balloon pops up indicating your current authentication status. See Table 2-5 for a list of icon colors and their meanings.

Table 2-5   *CTA 802.1X Wired Client Icon Color Codes*

Icon Color	Status
Green	The device is authenticated and connected to the network. This is the normal state.
Yellow	802.1X authentication is in progress.
Red	802.1X authentication failed; the device is not connected to the network.
Blue	The device is connected to the network, but no authentication was required. This is normal when connecting to non-802.1X-enabled switches.
No Color	The connection is idle.

A PC with the 802.1X supplicant installed can still connect to networks that do not have 802.1X authentication enabled. The supplicant displays "No Authentication Required" when connected to non-802.1X networks. However, the converse is not always true. If a PC without a supplicant connects to an 802.1X-enabled switch, it might not be capable of accessing the network. Access to 802.1X-enabled networks by non-802.1X-enabled clients is based on the policy set forth by the network administrator.

The administrative version of the 802.1X wired client is preconfigured with the following policies and profiles:

- It does not validate ACS's certificate.

- It performs both machine and user authentication.

- It requests and stores user credentials and passwords.

- It does not allow certificate-based authentication.

- It uses anonymous as the identity in the outer (unprotected) tunnel during Phase 1 of the EAP-FAST negotiation.

Therefore, after the administrative version of the 802.1X wired client is installed on a machine and connected to an 802.1X-enabled switch port, you should be prompted for user credentials. If you enter valid user credentials, you are authenticated to the network. However, these preconfigured policies might not be what you want deployed to end users in your network. Next, we look at customizing the policies in preparation for client deployments.

Creating a Customized Deployment Package

Before deploying the CTA 802.1X wired client to your network, you will most likely want to customize the client's policies. The option to edit the client's default policies is available only through the creation of a custom deployment package. However, before a custom deployment package can be created, you must decide which of the following authentication methods the client should support:

- **User authentication only**—The network connection is established only after the user logs on to the machine and successfully authenticates.

- **Machine authentication only**—The network connection is established only after the machine's credentials have been authenticated. You can configure the client to provide the machine's credentials at boot-up or after the user successfully logs into the machine.

- **User and machine authentication**—The network connection is established only after both the user and the machine credentials have been authenticated.

Depending on which devices you plan to deploy the CTA 802.1X wired client to, you might want to create more than one deployment package to allow different devices to have different authentication methods.

Follow these steps to launch the deployment wizard, which walks you through creating a deployment package.

Step 1   Right-click the CTA admin 802.1X wired client icon in the system tray and choose **Open**.

Step 2   Select the **Administration** pull-down menu and choose **Create Deployment Package.**

Step 3   A new window appears, titled Create Deployment Package. Click the **Start** button to begin the deployment wizard. You should see the client's Station Policy configuration screen, shown in Figure 2-1.

Figure 2-1   *CTA 802.1X Wired Client Custom Deployment Configuration—Station Policy*

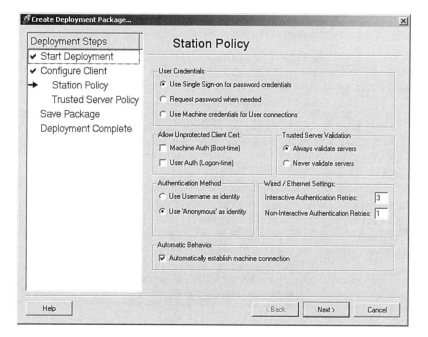

Step 4   In the User Credentials section, select one of the following options:

— **Use Single Sign-On for Password Credentials**—This option uses the user's Windows login credentials. Therefore, the user is not prompted for 802.1X authentication. (This is the default and most common selection.)

— **Request Password When Needed**—This option prompts the user for credentials when needed.

— **Use Machine Credentials for User Connections**—This option replaces the user credentials with the machine's credentials. This option should be selected only when performing machine authentication.

Step 5   The Allow Unprotected Client Certification section defines whether a certificate should be used during Phase 1 of the EAP-FAST PAC provisioning. By default, neither option is selected. (This is the most common case.)

— **Machine Auth (Boot-time)**—This method authenticates the client to ACS using the Microsoft Active Directory–provided machine certificate.

— **User Auth (Logon-time)**—This method authenticates the client using a predeployed client certificate.

NOTE   Selecting these options has no effect on the use of a certificate during the protected portion of the EAP-FAST PAC provisioning. If ACS is configured to request a client certificate within the secure tunnel, the CTA wired client will always attempt to send one. If a certificate is not available, the connection attempt will fail.

Step 6   The Trusted Server Validation section enables you to choose whether the client should validate the identity certificate presented by ACS. It is highly recommended that you select the **Always Validate Servers** option. Choosing the **Never Validate Servers** option allows the client to accept the credentials from any ACS server.

WARNING   The **Never Validate Servers** option is not recommended because it greatly reduces the level of security and could allow the client to communicate to a rogue authentication server.

Step 7   The Authentication Method section enables you to choose whether the real username should be sent in the clear during the Phase 1 PAC provisioning, or whether the username anonymous should be sent. If you are unsure of what to select here, choose **Use Anonymous as Identity.**

NOTE   This option does not affect the username sent during the actual user or machine authentication. If user credentials are required for authentication, the client will send username@domain, regardless of the option selected here.

NOTE   ACS 3.3 supports only the **Use Anonymous as Identity** option. For all other versions of ACS, the selection chosen here must match what is configured on ACS.

Step 8   The Wired/Ethernet Settings section controls the number of retries the client should attempt before failing authentication. The default is three retries for Interactive authentications (the client is prompted for credentials) and one retry for noninteractive authentications when the client is authenticated via a certificate and the user is not prempted for credentials. It is recommended that you keep the default options unless you have a specific reason to change them and have thoroughly tested the impact of the change before general deployment. Increasing **Interactive Authentication Retries** results in additional user dialog prompts. Increasing **Noninteractive Authentication Retries** adds delays to the machine or user logon to Windows when network connectivity fails.

NOTE   If you are using the auth fail vlan feature on your switch, the values for these fields must be one greater than the max-attempts value on the switch. If the switch is set for two max-attempts, both retry values should be 3.

Step 9   In the Automatic Behavior section, you have the option of automatically establishing the machine connection. Select this option only if you want to perform machine-only authentication or machine and user authentication.

Step 10   When you are finished making the selections on this page, click the Next button.

Step 11 The Trusted Server Policy window appears. If on the previous page you selected **Never Validate Servers,** you can skip to Step 16; however, for security reasons, this is greatly discouraged.

Step 12 Click the **Add Server Rule** button.

Step 13 The Trusted Server configuration window opens. In the **Rule Name** text box, fill in a user-friendly name for this rule. It can be any name that represents your ACS server (because it is not used in the validation), but I suggest using the *ACS* keyword somewhere in the rule so that it is easily recognizable.

Step 14 In the Validation Method drop-down box, select **Certificate**. (The **PAC** method is not supported at this time.)

Step 15 Under the Match ANY Certification Validation Rule section, deselect **Subject Alternative Name** and select **Subject/Common Name**. Choose **Exactly Matches** and fill in the Common Name (CN) listed in ACS certificate; then click **OK.** (Alternatively, you could choose to match on the subject alternative name, which is typically the DNS name of the ACS server, but this must be included in the certificate). When ACS presents its certificate to the client, one of these rules must match or the client will reject the certificate. See Figure 2-2 for a screen shot of a configured trusted server rule.

Figure 2-2 *CTA 802.1X Wired Client Custom Deployment Configuration—Trusted Server Policy*

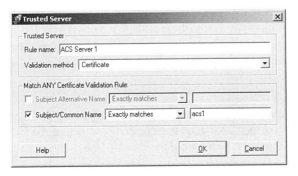

NOTE You can easily determine the Subject/Common name (CN) by opening ACS's identity certificate and selecting the Details tab. See the sidebar "Obtaining the CN from ACS's Identity Certificate" for more information.

NOTE   If you are using multiple ACS servers in your network, you can configure additional trusted server rules or create one rule that will match all servers.

Step 16 Click the **Next** button to advance to the Save Package screen. By default, the deployment package configuration files are saved in the C:\Program Files\Cisco Systems\Cisco Trust Agent 802_1X Wired Client\ directory. Click the **Browse** button if you want to save them in a different location.

Step 17 In the **Deployment Package Filename** field, specify a prefix to be appended to the .xml configuration files that the wizard creates. In this chapter, we use 802_1x-auth to easily distinguish the files.

Step 18 When finished, click the **Save** button. The Deployment Complete screen appears, showing the three configuration files created: 802_1x-auth-policy.xml, 802_1x-auth-networks.xml, and 802_1x-auth-credentials.xml.

Step 19 Click the **Close** button to complete the deployment package wizard.

Obtaining the CN from ACS's Identity Certificate

You can determine the CN for your ACS identity certificate by opening the Microsoft Management Console (MMC) on the ACS box. Choose **Start > Run > mmc**. If Certificates (Local Computer) is not listed under the Console Root, you need to add the snap-in by selecting **File > Add/Remove Snap-In**. In the window that appears, choose **Add**. Select **Certificates** from the list and then **Add**. You are prompted for the certificates you want to manage. Choose **Computer Account** and then **Next**. In the final window, use the default **Local Computer** and click **Finish**. Finally, click **OK** and you should be back to the MMC.

Expand Certificates (Local Computer) and also ACSCertStore. Select the **Certificates** folder; on the right pane, you should see the identity certificate issued to ACS. Double-click it and choose the **Details** tab. Select the **Subject** field; the CN is listed.

Installing the Customized CTA 802.1X Wired Windows Client

It is recommended that you load the customized 802.X wired client on an alternate machine (aside from the one the admin client was installed on). This enables you to test the customized deployable client and make any necessary changes by rerunning the deployment wizard on the admin client machine.

Follow these steps to install the customized client:

Step 1   Run the ctasetup-supplicant-win-*version*.msi file on the client machine. However, do *not* reboot the machine when requested by the installer.

Step 2   Copy the 802_1x-auth-policy.xml configuration file to the machine and place it in the following directory: C:\Program Files\Cisco Systems\ Cisco Trust Agent 802_1x Wired Client\profiles\policies\.

Step 3   Copy the 802_1x-auth-networks.xml configuration file to the machine and place it in the following directory: C:\Program Files\Cisco Systems Cisco Trust Agent 802_1x Wired Client\profiles\networks\.

NOTE   The 802_1x-auth-credentials.xml file is not used on the Cisco CTA 802.1X wired client.

Step 4   Reboot the machine for the configuration to take affect.

The final step is to install the CA certificate (or ACS's self-signed certificate) into the host's trusted certificate store. See the section "Installing the CA Certificate," later in this chapter, to complete this task. When the certificate is installed, you are ready to begin testing.

NOTE   You can also install the CA certificate during the installation of the client by creating a certs\ directory in the directory the .msi client executable resides. Copy the CA certificate into the certs\ directory; during the client installation, it will install any certificate in that directory to the trusted root store.

CTA Mac Installation

The Cisco Trust Agent first supported Macintosh operating systems starting with Version 2.1 of CTA and Version 10.3.9 (or higher) of OS X. Installation of CTA on the Mac can be accomplished one of the following ways:

- Installation with the installation wizard
- Custom installation from the command line

In this section, we cover the installation of CTA using the installation wizard. Later, in the "Deploying CTA in a Production Network" section, we cover the installation of CTA using the command line.

Before installing CTA, you must have administrative privileges on the machine, and you must extract the installation disk image.

Extracting the Installation Disk Image

Before you can begin the installation of CTA using the wizard or the command line, you must extract the installation disk image and accept the EULA. Follow these steps to accomplish this task:

Step 1 Download the ctaadminex-darwin-*version*.tar.gz administrative archive file to the machine you want to install CTA on.

Step 2 Open a terminal window and change to the directory where you saved the ctaadminex-darwin-*version*.tar.gz archive file.

Step 3 Expand the compressed archive by typing the following command: **tar zxvf ctaadminex-darwin-***version***.tar.gz**

Step 4 The contents of the archive are extracted in the same directory. Next, execute the command **./ctaadminex.sh**.

Step 5 You are presented with the EULA. After you have read the EULA, type **y** if you agree to the terms. The cta-darwin-*version*.dmg file is then extracted.

Step 6 Finally, execute the command **open cta-darwin-***version***.dmg** to open the CTA disk image. This places the CiscoTrustAgent volume icon on the desktop and in Finder.

With the disk image opened, you are ready to begin the installation process.

Installing CTA on Mac OS X Using the Installation Wizard

With the CiscoTrustAgent disk image opened, follow these steps to install CTA using the installation wizard:

Step 1 Open Finder and select the **CiscoTrustAgent** volume.

Step 2 Double-click the **CiscoTrustAgent.mpkg** icon.

Step 3 The installation wizard opens, displaying the window shown in Figure 2-3. Choose **Continue**.

Figure 2-3   *CTA Mac Installation Wizard*

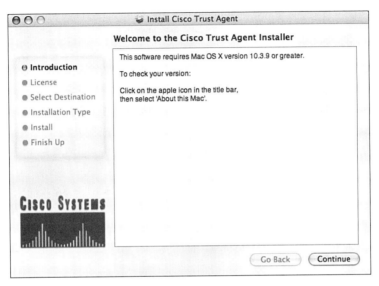

Step 4   The End User License Agreement is displayed. Read it and click the **Continue** button. You are then prompted to agree to the terms of the license agreement. Click **Agree** to accept the terms and continue.

Step 5   The Select a Destination window appears. Select the drive where you want CTA installed, and then click **Continue**.

Step 6   The Easy Install window appears. Click the **Customize** button if you want to install the CTA Scripting Interface (see the section titled "CTA Scripting Interface" for more information about the Scripting Interface); otherwise, skip to step 8.

Step 7   The Custom Install window appears. Select the **Scripting Interface for Cisco Trust Agent** package from the list.

Step 8   Next, choose **Install** to start the installation process. The installer prompts you to authenticate with a user account that has administrative rights. Enter a username and password, and then click **OK**.

Step 9   The installer begins to copy the files to the machine. When the process is complete, you will see the message "The software was successfully installed." Choose **Close** to exit the installation wizard.

The final step is to install the CA certificate (or ACS's self-signed certificate) into the host's trusted certificate store. See the section "Installing the CA Certificate," later in this chapter, to complete this task. When the certificate is installed, you are ready to begin testing.

CTA Linux Installation

Installation of CTA on Linux requires superuser privileges. In addition, the RPM Package Manager (RPM) must be installed. To begin the installation of CTA on a Linux machine, follow these steps:

Step 1   Download the ctaadminex-linux-*version*.tar.gz administrative archive file to the machine on which you want to install CTA.

Step 2   Open a terminal window and change to the directory where you saved the ctaadminex-linux-*version*.tar.gz archive file.

Step 3   Expand the compressed archive by typing the following command: **tar zxvf ctaadminex-linux-*version*.tar.gz**.

Step 4   The contents of the archive are extracted in the same directory. Next, execute this command: **./ctaadminex-linux-*version*.sh**.

Step 5   You are presented with the EULA. After you have read the EULA, type **y** if you agree to the terms. The script creates a directory named CTA-*version* and extracts the cta-linux-*version*.i386.rpm file.

Step 6   Change to the CTA-*version* directory (**cd CTA-*version***) and begin the installation by typing this command: **rpm –ivh cta-linux-*version*.i386.rpm**.

Example:

```
[root@linux CTA-2.1.0-11]# rpm -ivh cta-linux-2.1.0-11.i386.rpm
Preparing...       ################################# [100%]
    1:cta-linux    ################################# [100%]
```

NOTE   To upgrade from a previous version of CTA, use this command: **rpm –Uvh cta-linux-*version*.i386.rpm**.

NOTE   The CTA Scripting Interface is installed by default on Linux installations.

When you finish installing CTA, the CA certificate needs to be installed. Follow the instructions in the next section to complete this final step.

Installing the CA Certificate

When the CTA installation is complete, you must install the CA certificate (or ACS's self-signed certificate) into the client's trusted certificate store. This allows the client to accept the certificate that ACS provides during the negotiation of the PEAP or EAP-FAST tunnel. Without the certificate, CTA will not form the protected tunnel with ACS to transmit posture credentials. On Windows machines, CTA accepts a PEM (Privacy Enhanced Mail) (Base64) or DER (Distinguished Encoding Rules) encoded binary X.509 certificate. On Mac and Linux, only PEM (Base64) encoded certificates are supported.

NOTE   If you do not have a CA and do not want to purchase a certificate for ACS from a public CA, you can have ACS generate a self-signed certificate. This self-signed certificate must be installed into the trusted certificate store on the CTA host instead of the CA certificate. However, for scalability reasons, it is strongly suggested that you do not use a self-signed certificate. ACS's self-signed certificate is valid for only one year. After that, you must regenerate it. If you do not currently have a CA server, Microsoft provides one free of charge with its Windows Server operating systems. Just install it from **Add/Remove Programs** -> **Add/Remove Windows Components**. For more information on getting a CA certificate or on retrieving ACS's self-signed certificate, see the documentation that came with those products.

Follow these steps to install the CA certificate (or ACS self-signed certificate) into the trusted certificate store on the CTA client.

Installing a CA Certificate (or ACS Self-Signed Certificate) on Windows

Follow these steps to install a CA certificate (or ACS self-signed certificate) on Windows:

Step 1   Copy the certificate to the client.

Step 2   Open a command prompt and change to the root directory where CTA is installed:

Example: C:\Program Files\Cisco Systems\CiscoTrustAgent\

Step 3   Install the certificate by entering the following command: **ctaCert.exe / ui** *x* **/add** "*path_to_cert*" **/store "Root"**, where *x* represents the level of user interaction (2 or 3 is no interaction, 4 or 5 is full interaction) and *path_to_cert* is the full path and filename to the certificate.

Example:

```
c:\Program Files\Cisco Systems\CiscoTrustAgent> ctaCert.exe /ui 4 /add
"C:\root_ca.cer" /store "Root"
```

A pop-up appears indicating that the certificate was successfully imported.

Installing a CA Certificate (or ACS Self-Signed Certificate) on Mac OS X

Follow these steps to install a CA certificate (or ACS self-signed certificate) on Mac OS X:

Step 1   Copy the certificate to the client.

Step 2   Open a terminal window and change to the following directory: **/opt/ CiscoTrustAgent/bin/**.

Step 3   Install the certificate by entering the following command: **sudo ./ctacert –add** */path/cert_file*.**cer**, where */path/cert_file*.**cer** is the full path and filename to the certificate.

Example:

```
mac:/opt/CiscoTrustAgent/bin Admin$ sudo ./ctacert -add /Users/admin/
root_ca.cer
```

You are prompted to enter the admin password.

Step 4   When the certificate is successfully installed, you will see the message "Certificate successfully added to store with Hashed Name *hash*."

Installing a CA Certificate (or ACS Self-Signed Certificate) on Linux

Follow these steps to install a CA certificate (or ACS self-signed certificate) on Linux:

Step 1   Copy the certificate to the client.

Step 2   Open a terminal session.

Step 3   At any prompt, install the certificate by entering the following command: **ctacert --add** */path/cert_file*.**cer**, where */path/cert_file*.**cer** is the full path and filename to the certificate.

Example:

```
[root@linux cta]# ctacert --add root_ca.cer
Certificate successfully added to store with Hashed Name 0c23cfaa.0
```

Post-Certificate Installation Tasks

After you install the CA certificate, CTA is ready to go. You can begin testing in your lab network. But before you do, you might want to continue reading. The rest of the chapter is devoted to customizing optional CTA components, deploying CTA in a production environment, and troubleshooting CTA.

User Notifications

The CTA client includes a GUI-based user-notification system. With the exception of the 802.1X supplicant, this is the only user-visible part of CTA. Notifications are defined in ACS and sent to users for various reasons. Notifications can include a message along with a clickable URL. The notification system can also autolaunch a web browser to direct the user to a website specified by the ACS policy. Figure 2-4 shows an example of a Healthy user-notification message displayed on a client with CTA installed.

Figure 2-4   *CTA Healthy User-Notification Message*

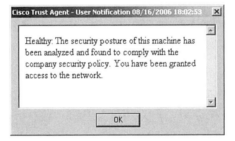

A few configurable options exist for user notifications, such as the capability to display the notification message before or after user logon, the length of time to display the message before it automatically closes, and whether the user must acknowledge the notification message before being able to continue working. All these options and more are defined in the [UserNotifies] section of the ctad.ini file. If an option is not specified (or a ctad.ini file does not exist), the default value is used. See the next section for a complete list of configurable options.

Customizing CTA with the Optional ctad.ini File

The ctad.ini file is an optional file that contains CTA daemon configuration information. This file is not installed with a default installation of CTA, but it can be included in a customized package deployment. The presence of the ctad.ini file allows the Administrator to customize various components of CTA. In the absence of the file, CTA takes the default values.

The ctad.ini file is a standard configuration file and can be created in any text editor. Each configuration setting is in *attribute=value* format. The default CTA installation comes with a ctad.ini.*operating_system* template file, which you can rename to ctad.ini and edit to make modifications as necessary. You can also use the sample file shown in Example 2-1 at the end of this section for reference. The ctad.ini template files are located in the same directory where the ctad.ini file must be saved:

> **Windows:** C:\Program Files\Cisco Systems\CiscoTrustAgent\
> **Mac:** /etc/opt/CiscoTrustAgent/
> **Linux:** /etc/opt/CiscoTrustAgent/

The file is divided into the following sections:

- [main]
- [EAPoUDP]
- [UserNotifies]
- [ServerCertDNVerification]
- [Scripting_Interface]

[main] Section

The [main] section is optional and contains global configuration options for CTA. If you are using optional posture plug-ins, you might consider altering some of these options from their default. Specifically, if your antivirus posture plug-in returns very large messages, you might consider increasing the PPMsgSize attribute to from 1 K to 4 K. Likewise, you might want to change how frequently CTA polls the plug-ins to detect a change in their status. This option is configurable by changing the SQTimer attribute. See Table 2-6 for the complete list of available options.

Table 2-6   *[main] Configuration Options*

Attribute	Description	Operating System(s)
EnableVFT	Notifies CTA of whether the Cisco IOS running on the NAD supports the Validation-Flag TVL. 0 = Cisco IOS does not support Validation-Flag TVL 1 = Cisco IOS does support Validation-Flag TVL Default value: 0 Range of values: 0, 1	Windows, Mac, Linux

continues

Table 2-6 *[main] Configuration Options (Continued)*

Attribute	Description	Operating System(s)
PPInterfaceType	Defines how CTA gathers posture plug-in information. Block: CTA requests posture information serially, from one plug-in at a time. It waits for a response before requesting information from the next plug-in. NonBlockConcurrent: CTA requests posture information from all plug-ins simultaneously. The request completes when CTA receives a response from each plug-in or when the PPWaitTimeout expires, whichever is sooner. NonBlockSerial: CTA requests posture information from one plug-in at a time. It waits for a response from the plug-in or for the PPWaitTimeout to expire before requesting information from the next plug-in. Default value: Block Range of values: Block, NonBlockConcurrent, NonBlockSerial	Windows, Mac, Linux
PPWaitTimeout	This attribute is valid only if PPInterfaceType is set to NonBlockConcurrent or NonBlockSerial. It defines the maximum time allowed (in seconds) for CTA to receive the response from the posture plug-in query. Default value: 5 seconds Range of values: 1–4294967295 seconds	Windows, Mac, Linux
PPMsgSize	Specifies the maximum size of the posture plug-in message. Default value: 1024 bytes Range of values: 1024–4096 bytes	Windows, Mac, Linux
SQTimer	The status query (SQ) timer defines how often CTA queries the posture plug-ins to detect a change in their status. This is applicable only for NAC-L2-802.1X. Default value: 300 seconds Range of values: 5–4294967295 seconds	Windows, Mac, Linux
UserActionDelayTimeout	Defines the length of delay before a web browser window is launched upon receiving a redirect URL. Increasing this value gives the client more time to obtain an IP address (if using NAC-L2-802.1X) before the web browser attempts to access the URL. Default value: 15 seconds Range of values: 0–4294967295 seconds	Windows, Mac, Linux

[EAPoUDP] Section

The [EAPoUDP] section contains the configurable communication settings for the EAP over UDP connection. The only option that you might consider changing in this section is the LocalPort. However, changing the LocalPort also requires making this change on all the NADs. See Table 2-7 for the complete list of available options.

Table 2-7   *[EAPoUDP] Configuration Options*

Attribute	Description	Operating System(s)
LocalPort	UDP port that CTA will listen on. Default value: 21862 Range of values: 1–65535	Windows, Mac, Linux
MaxSession	Number of simultaneous EAP over UDP sessions allowed. *Note:* CTA supports multiple sessions, but only one from a given NAD at a time. Default value: 8 Range of values: 1–256	Windows, Mac, Linux
SessionIdleTimeout	Number of seconds after which idle EAP over UDP sessions times out. Default value: 3600 Range of values: 60–172800	Windows, Mac, Linux
BootTimeUDPExemptions	This attribute alters the Windows XP SP2 firewall policy to allow CTA to receive EAPoUDP packets during boot. 0 = Exemptions are disabled. 1 = Exemptions are enabled. Default value: 1 Range of values: 0, 1	Windows

[UserNotifies] Section

The [UserNotifies] section contains the configurable options for the user-notification messaging system. You might want to disable SysModal or tweak some of the timeout values. See Table 2-8 for a complete list of the available options in this section.

Table 2-8 *[UserNotifies] Configuration Options*

Attribute	Description	Operating System(s)
SysModal	If enabled, the user must acknowledge the CTA notification message before being allowed to access any other windows. In addition, if multiple notifications are received, only the newest one is viewable. 0 = Disabled 1 = Enabled Default value: 1 Range of Windows values: 0, 1 Range of Mac values: 1	Windows, Mac, Linux
EnableNotifies	Enables or disables user notifications. 0 = Disabled 1 = Enabled Default value: 1 Range of values: 0, 1	Windows, Mac
MsgTimeout	Amount of time, in seconds, the notification message appears. A value of 0 indicates no timeout. Default value: 30 seconds Range of values: 0, 30–4294967	Windows, Mac, Linux
EnableLogonNotifies	Specifies whether user notification messages are displayed on the login screen. 0 = Disabled 1 = Enabled—For Windows, messages are displayed on the logon screen. For Mac and Linux, messages are saved and presented to user after successful login. Default value: 0 Range of values: 0, 1	Windows, Mac, Linux
LogonMsgTimeout	Number of seconds a user notification message is displayed (Windows) or saved (Mac and Linux) when EnableLogonNotifies is set to 1. A value of 0 disables this timeout. Default value: 0 (Windows), 300 (Mac and Linux) Range of values: 0, 30–4294967	Windows, Mac, Linux

Table 2-8   *[UserNotifies] Configuration Options (Continued)*

Attribute	Description	Operating System(s)
ClearOldNotification	Clears or saves notification messages. 0 = Notification messages are saved. 1 = CTA clears old notification messages before displaying new ones. Default value: 1 Range of values: 0, 1	Mac, Linux
TermFont	Specifies the font used to display messages. The TermFont for Asian languages will be implemented in a future release. Default value: -misc-fixed-medium-r-semicondensed--13-120-75-75-c-60-iso10636-1 For Asian languages, set this attribute equal to: -misc-zysong18030-medium-r-normal—0-0-0-0-c-0-iso10646-1	Linux
Display Type	Specifies whether user-notification messages sent from ACS to CTA are displayed in a GUI interface or in a terminal window. In Linux, if term is specified, messages are written to /var/opt/ CiscoTrustAgent/msg directory. Default value: gui Range of values: term, gui (Linux); gui (Mac)	Mac, Linux
BrowserPath	Specifies the full path to the user's web browser. This value is used to open a web browser during URL redirection. For Red Hat Enterprise v3 use: /usr/bin/mozilla For Red Hat Enterprise v4 use: /usr/bin/firefox	Linux

[ServerCertDNVerification] Distinguished Name-Matching Section

Distinguished name matching provides additional security for CTA by requiring additional validation checks for the certificate presented by the ACS server. These checks are similar to, but in addition to, the Trusted Server Policy used with the CTA wired client; they apply to all CTA installations.

The additional checks are created by adding distinguished name matching rules in the [ServerCertDNVerification] section of the ctad.ini file. If this section does not exist, CTA accepts any certificate with a validated certificate chain. If rules do exist, the certificate must match one of the rules for the certificate to be accepted. See Table 2-9 for a complete list of options for this section.

Table 2-9   *[ServerCertDNVerification] Configuration Options*

Attribute	Description	Operating System(s)
TotalRules	Defines the number of DN matching rules that will follow. If the number of rules is greater than 1, the rules are connected by an OR statement. A value of 0 disables DN matching Default value: (none) Range of values: 0–64	Windows, Mac, Linux
RuleX	The RuleX parameters are DN matching rules, where X is the index of the rule. Example: Rule1=CN="acs01", OU="Cisco"	Windows, Mac, Linux

Each DN matching rule is an OR of the next rule. Therefore, the first rule that matches will cause the certificate to be accepted. Each rule can contain one or more subrules, separated by a comma. If any subrule fails, the entire rule fails. Rules are limited to 255 characters total and must be in this format:

RuleX=subrule_a, subrule_b, subrule_c, ...

Here, each subrule is comprised of a DN attribute, an operator, and a value:

DN_attribute<operator>"value"

Table 2-10 lists the valid DN attributes that CTA will accept. There are two possible operators:

= **(equals)**—The certificate must exactly match the value.
* **(contains)**—The certificate presented must contain the value.

If the ACS server's certificate had a Common Name of acs01, an Organization Unit of Cisco, a State of NC, and a Country of US, a validation rule would be written as follows:

Rule1=CN="acs01", OU="Cisco", ST="NC", C="US"

Table 2-10   *Valid DN Attributes*

Attribute	Definition	Attribute	Definition
CN	Common Name	L	Locality
SN	Surname	SP	Province
GN	Given Name	ST	State
N	Unstructured Name	O	Organization
I	Initials	OU	Organization Unit
GENQ	Generation Qualifier	T	Title
C	Country	EA	E-mail address

In addition to the server certificate, you can validate the issuer attributes (the CA that issued the certificate to ACS). To do so, you must prefix the attribute with the string ISSUER-. For example:

> Rule1=ISSUER-CN="ca-server1"

TIP	If you are using distinguished name matching rules, you will most likely want to have one rule for each ACS server that the client might need to posture with. The alternative option, if you have multiple ACS servers, is to choose attributes that will be common across each certificate assigned to the ACS servers. This way, only one rule is needed.

[Scripting_Interface] Section

The [Scripting_Interface] section currently contains only one option that is used to determine when to expire old posture data retrieved through the Scripting Interface, from the posture database. This attribute is defined in Table 2-11. For more information on the Scripting Interface, see the section titled "CTA Scripting Interface."

Table 2-11 *[Scripting_Interface] Configuration Options*

Attribute	Description	Operating System(s)
delta_stale	Defines the amount of time, in minutes, before the posture database record is deemed outdated. Default value: 43200 minutes Range of values: 0–5256000 minutes; a value of 0 means never age out the records	Windows, Mac, Linux

Example ctad.ini

This section closes with a sample ctad.ini file. Example 2-1 shows a sample ctad.ini file that can be used as a template for Windows, Mac, or Linux systems. All attributes listed are shown at their default values, with the exception of the distinguished name matching section. Lines proceeded by a semicolon are commented out.

Example 2-1 *Sample ctad.ini File*

```
; You can comment out a line
; by preceding it with a semi-colon
[main]
EnableVFT=0
PPInterfaceType=Block
PPWaitTimeout=5
PPMsgSize=1024
SQTimer=300
UserActionDelayTimeout=15

[EAPoUDP]
LocalPort=21862
BootTimeUDPExemptions=1
MaxSession=8
SessionIdleTimeout=3600

[UserNotifies]
; The following apply to Windows and MAC only
SysModal=1
EnableNotifies=1
; The following apply to Windows, MAC and Linux
MsgTimeout=30
FnableLogonNotifies=0
LogonMsgTimeout=0
; The following apply to MAC and Linux only
;ClearOldNotification=1
;DisplayType=gui
; The following apply to Linux only
;TermFont=-misc-fixed-medium-r-semicondensed--13-120-75-75-c-60-iso10636-1
 (default)
;BrowserPath=/usr/bin/firefox

; There are no defaults for Distinguished
; Name matching in the certificates, so all
; the below lines are commented out.
;[ServerCertDNVerification]
;TotalRules=2
;Rule1=CN="acs01", OU="cisco", ST="NC", ISSUER-CN*"ca-server1"
;Rule2=CN="acs02", OU="cisco", ST="NC", ISSUER-CN*"ca-server1"

[Scripting_Interface]
delta_stale=43200
```

CTA Scripting Interface

CTA provides an optional Scripting Interface as a way for non-NAC-aware applications to provide CTA with posture information about that application. Cisco Secure ACS can then combine this additional posture information with the posture information received from NAC-aware applications and use it in determining the overall posture of the host. Although this is not a commonly used feature, it might be useful for companies that have a requirement to validate a specific attribute before making a posture decision.

You have the option of installing the Scripting Interface during the installation by selecting either a **Complete** or **Custom** installation type. (Linux installations have the Scripting Interface installed by default.) If you choose a **Custom** Windows or Mac install, you must also manually select the Scripting Interface option and choose to install it on the local hard drive. By default, the Scripting Interface is not installed during a custom installation. See Figure 2-5, which illustrates this step on Windows.

Figure 2-5   *Scripting Interface Option Selected during Custom Windows Install*

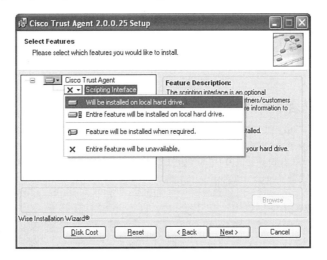

NOTE	If you are distributing CTA out to your users and silently installing it on their Windows machines, you must use the **ADDLOCAL** option to install the Scripting Interface. For example:

```
C:\temp>Msiexec.exe /I "C:\temp\ctasetup-win-2.1.0.11.msi"
ADDLOCAL=Scripting_Interface
```

Requirements for Using the Scripting Interface

After installing the Scripting Interface executable and posture plug-in module, you must perform the following steps before you can use your user-defined posture credentials in a posture policy on ACS:

Step 1 Create an executable script (in any programming language) on the client. The script should run periodically and output a posture data file with current posture information in attribute-value pair format.

Step 2 Create an .inf file to register the script with the ctascriptPP posture plug-in.

Step 3 Add the new user-defined attributes (created by the script) to the ACS dictionary.

Before you can begin with Step 1, you need to determine what information you want to retrieve from the host that will help you make a policy decision about the posture of the host. Some common examples are whether a particular non-NAC compatible application is installed (personal firewall, antivirus application, and so on), whether it is enabled, and what its current version is. When you have determined the information that you would like to get from the host, you are ready to proceed. The next few subsections walk you through each step.

Step 1: Create a Posture Data File

You can use any programming or scripting language you want to create a script that will generate a posture data file. The only requirement is that the posture data file must contain only ASCII text and that it must comply with the format shown in Example 2-2.

Example 2-2 *Sample Posture Data File Excerpt*

```
[attr#0]
vendor-id=9
vendor-name=Cisco
application-id=61440
application-name=Script-001
attribute-id=32768
attribute-name=Script-Name
attribute-profile=in
attribute-type=string
attribute-value=Script "posture_file_01"

[attr#1]
vendor-id=9
vendor-name=Cisco
application-id=61440
application-name=Script-001
attribute-id=32769
```

Example 2-2 *Sample Posture Data File Excerpt (Continued)*

```
attribute-name=Unsigned-Integer
attribute-profile=in
attribute-type=unsigned integer
attribute-value=31

...
```

Each posture data file contains one or more posture-validation attribute definitions. Each attribute definition begins with an attribute identifier, followed by a series of attribute value pairs. Table 2-12 lists the valid attributes and their possible values.

Table 2-12 *Valid Attributes in the Posture Data File*

Attribute	Description	Value	Required
[attr#n]	Attribute identifier. Each file must start with [attr#0].	The string "attr#", enclosed in brackets [], and followed by an integer. The integer should start with zero and increment by one.	Yes
vendor-id	Globally unique vendor ID (used by Radius) assigned by the IANA.	Cisco Systems is assigned ID 9.	No
vendor-name	Vendor name that corresponds to the vendor-id.	Cisco	No
Application-id	Globally unique value that must match the AppType in the .inf file. The application-id must be the same throughout a posture data file.	Must be in the range of 61440–65535.	Yes
Application-name	The name of the script that created the posture data file.	String—no spaces allowed. Only characters, numbers, underscore, or hyphen.	No
attribute-id	Globally unique value assigned to each attribute definition.	Must be in the range of 32768–65535.	Yes
attribute-name	Describes the attribute.	String—no spaces allowed. Only characters, numbers, underscore, or hyphen.	No
attribute-profile	Always ignored. It is included to be consistent with the attribute definition file for ACS.	in, out	No
attribute-type	Format of the attribute-value.	String, integer, unsigned integer, ipaddr, date, version, octet-array	Yes
attribute-value	The posture information passed back to ASC and used in making a policy decision.	See Table 2-13 for a list of the possible values.	Yes

Table 2-13 lists the possible formats for the attribute-values used in the posture data file. Remember that the entire point of your script is to create a file of attribute-values. CTA passes these custom attribute-values to ACS, which compares them against the posture policy to help determine the host's overall posture.

Table 2-13 *Possible Formats for the attribute-value Data*

Data Type	Description	Example
octet-array	A stream of hexadecimal octets, separated by spaces	0x23 0x11 0x0B
integer	A 32-bit signed integer value Valid range: –2147483647–2147483646	–12
unsigned integer	32-bit unsigned integer	430
string	Free text string	CustomApp_01
ipaddr	Standard 4-tuple dotted-decimal representation of an IP address	192.168.1.1
date	32-bit unsigned value representing the number of seconds elapsed since midnight January 1, 1970, Coordinated Universal Time (UTC)	1134439111
version	String representation of version, in dotted-decimal format. major.minor.revision.rebuild	5.0.1.214

The posture data file can be saved anywhere on a Windows system, but it is recommended that it be saved under the \Program Files\Cisco Systems\CiscoTrustAgent directory. On Linux systems, the posture data file must be saved in the directory /var/tmp/CiscoTrustAgent/pdata.

Step 2: Create an .inf File

An .inf file is required for each script. It must be saved in the \PostureAgent\Plugins\install directory on the host machine. (For Windows, the directory is C:\Program Files\Common Files\PostureAgent\Plug-Ins\Install; for Mac and Linux, it is /opt/PostureAgent/Plug-Ins/Install). CTA uses the .inf file to register the CTA script posture plug-in, and as a means of locating your custom posture attributes in the local posture database. For this reason, the AppType value must match the application-id value used in the posture data file generated by your script.

Example 2-3 shows a sample .inf file that can be used as the basis for all your scripts. You should modify only the last three lines. The AppList is a string (without spaces) that should uniquely describe your script. Also change the corresponding section heading, and ensure that the AppType is in the range 61440–65535 and matches the application-id used in the posture data file created in Step 1. That is all there is to creating and registering the .inf file.

Example 2-3 *Sample .inf File*

```
[main]
PluginName=ctascriptPP.dll
; For MAC and Linux hosts use the following line instead
; PluginName=ctascriptpp.so
VendorID=9
Styles=SupportAsync
AppList=script_1

[script_1]
AppType=61440
```

Step 3: Add Attributes to ACS Dictionary

The final step is to add the attribute definitions to the ACS dictionary so that ACS is aware of their existence and they can be used in the posture policy definition. To begin, take the posture data file created by your script and copy it to a new file. It is a good idea to maintain the same name on the file but change the suffix to .ini. Next, edit the file and remove the attribute-value line from each of the attribute definition sections. *Note that this will be the last line of each section.* Finally, move the file to the ACS server and import it into the ACS dictionary using the CSUtil.exe utility.

Example:

```
CSUtil.exe -addAVP script1_data_file.ini
```

NOTE   The CSUtil.exe is located in the following directory starting with ACS Version 4.0:

C:\Program Files\CiscoSecure ACS v*X.X*\bin

where *X.X* is the version of your Cisco Secure ACS software.

NOTE   After adding the attributes to the ACS dictionary, you must stop and restart the CSAuth, CSAdmin, and CSLog services. All services can be restarted from the ACS GUI interface by selecting System Configuration, Service Control, Restart.

With the new custom attributes added to the ACS dictionary, you are now ready to use them in your posture policy.

Executing the Scripting Interface

When all these steps are complete, the only remaining task is to have your script run the ctasi executable file to import the policy data file into the policy database. On a Windows box, the ctasi.exe file is located in the following directory:

C:\Program Files\Common Files\PostureAgent\

On Mac and Linux, it is located here:

/opt/PostureAgent/

ctasi will accept two variables passed in. The first is required. It must be the full path to the posture data file. The second is optional and represents whether the script has detected a posture change since the last time it was run. A value of 1 indicates that the script detected a change in posture and CTA should be alerted to this, regardless of the contents of the data file. A value of 2 indicates that the script did not detect a change in posture, and CTA should accept this, regardless of the contents of the data file. If no value is specified, CTA will determine whether a status change occurred by comparing the most recent posture reported with the previous one for the same application-id.

In the following example, the posture data file is named script1_data_file.txt and is located in the C:\PostureDataFiles\ directory. The CTA Scripting Interface executable is run, passing in the full path to the file, along with the optional variable 1, to alert CTA that a change has taken place since the previous time the script ran.

```
ctasi.exe C:\PostureDataFiles\script1_data_file.txt 1
```

An external process (scheduled task, startup script, and so on) should execute your script on a periodic basis so that the data saved to the policy database does not become stale. However, CTA also ages out data added to the posture database by the Scripting Interface if it exceeds a *delta_stale* value. The default *delta_stale* value is 43200 minutes (approximately one month). This value can be changed by specifying a new *delta_stale* value in the ctad.ini file. Example 2-4 shows part of a sample ctad.ini file with the *delta_stale* value set to 720 minutes.

Example 2-4 *Sample ctad.ini File Specifying a delta_stale Value*

```
Example:
; Sample ctad.ini file

[Scripting_Interface]
delta_stale=720
```

Remember that this value applies to all posture data added to the database through the Scripting Interface. If more granular control is required, ACS can be configured to age out data on a per-AppType (or per-script) basis. To use this method, you must first add the **WriteTimeStamp** attribute to the ACS dictionary using CSUtil.exe. Example 2-5 shows a sample WriteTimeStamp.ini file.

Example 2-5 *Sample WriteTimeStamp.ini file*

```
[attr#0]
vendor-id=9
vendor-name=Cisco
application-id=61440
application-name=Script-001
attribute-id=15
attribute-name=WriteTimeStamp
attribute-profile=in
attribute-type=date
```

The **WriteTimeStamp** attribute applies only to the specified application-id. If additional application-ids are used, modify the *application-id* and *application-name* attributes in the WriteTimeStamp.ini file and add it to the ACS dictionary again. When the WriteTimeStamp is added to ACS, you can use it in your policy definition to provide more granular control over when to age out stale data.

NOTE   The local *delta_stale* attribute on the host overrides any aging policy set on the ACS. For this reason, the *delta_stale* value should be larger than any value used in a posture policy on ACS.

CTA Logging Service

CTA includes its own logging service, ctalogd, for recording events and troubleshooting issues with CTA and posture plug-ins. Because CTA is designed to be a silent application on the end host, logging is disabled by default. However, logging can be enabled through one of two methods:

- Creating a ctalogd.ini file
- Using the clogcli utility

With logging enabled, CTA saves the log files in the following directories by default:

   Windows: C:\Program Files\Cisco Systems\CiscoTrustAgent\Logging\Logs\
   Mac and Linux: /var/log/CiscoTrustAgent/

You can change the default log directory by specifying a different directory in the LogDir attribute in the ctalogd.ini file. With logging enabled, CTA will write all logs to a single file in the log directory. A new file is created every time the log service restarts (when the system reboots) or after the file has reached a specified size (4MB, by default). Each log file has a unique name and follows the following naming convention:

CTALOG-*YYYY-MM-DD*T*HH-MM-SS_N*.txt

Where file values are

- *YYYY*—Four-digit year
- *MM*—Month
- *DD*—Day
- *T*—Literal character separator between date and time
- *HH*—Hour
- *MM*—Minute
- *SS*—Second
- *N*—Integer indicating the *N*th log file created since the service was started

Creating a ctalogd.ini File

The ctalogd.ini file defines the configuration of the logging service. It includes parameters for enabling/disabling logging, log retention policies, and the logging levels for each CTA component. A sample ctalogd.ini file (named ctalogd.tmp) is created when CTA is installed and can be found in the /Logging directory. Edit this file to meet your logging needs, and then save it as ctalogd.ini in the same directory. Example 2-6 shows a sample ctalogd.ini file with all options listed and all logging components set to level 3 (High).

Example 2-6 *Sample ctalogd.ini File*

```
[main]
EnableLog=1
LogDir=C:\Program Files\Cisco Systems\CiscoTrustAgent\Logging\Logs
MaxFileSize=1
MaxDiskSize=50
FileDeleteAge=30

[LogLevel]
PADaemon=3
NetTrans=3
PAPlugin=3
CTAMsg=3
CTAD=3
PEAP=3
EAPTLV=3
EAPSQ=3
PPMgr=3
```

Example 2-6 *Sample ctalogd.ini File (Continued)*

```
PSDaemon=3
HostPP=3
CTASI=3
ScriptPlugin=3
CTASC=3
CTAVSTLV=3
CTASTATE=3
```

Table 2-14 lists the configurable options in the ctalogd.ini file. If any attribute is not listed in the ctalogd.ini file, then the default value is used.

Table 2-14 *ctalogd.ini Configurable Options*

Attribute	Description	Value
[main]	Main section header—required.	[main]
EnableLog	Specifies whether logging is enabled.	0 = Disabled (default)
		1 = Enabled
		2 = Enabled temporarily (until reboot)
LogDir	Full path where log files are stored.	Any full, valid path
MaxFileSize	Maximum size of a single log file in megabytes. If this size is reached, a new log file is created.	0 = no limit
		4 = (default)
		50 = Max
MaxDiskSize	Maximum allowable disk space for log files in megabytes.	0 = no limit
		50 = Min, 100 = Max
		50 = (default)
FileDeleteAge	Max age of files before they are deleted.	0 = never delete
		30 = (default)
[LogLevel]	Section header for specifying individual component logging levels.	[LogLevel]
PADaemon	CTA Posture Agent daemon logging component	0 = Disabled (default)
		1 = Low (critical)
		2 = Medium (warnings)
		3 = High (informational)
		15 = Debug (Packet Dump)

continues

Table 2-14 *ctalogd.ini Configurable Options (Continued)*

Attribute	Description	Value
NetTrans	Network Transport logging component	0 = Disabled (default)
		1 = Low (Critical)
		2 = Medium (warnings)
		3 = High (informational)
		15 = Debug (Packet Dump)
PAPlugin	Posture Plug-In logging component	0 = Disabled (default)
		1 = Low (Critical)
		2 = Medium (Warnings)
		3 = High (Informational)
		15 = Debug (Packet Dump)
CTAMsg	CTA's User Notify logging component	0 = Disabled (default)
		1 = Low (Critical)
		2 = Medium (Warnings)
		3 = High (Informational)
		15 = Debug (Packet Dump)
CTAD	CTA daemon service logging component	0 = Disabled (Default)
		1 = Low (Critical)
		2 = Medium (Warnings)
		3 = High (Informational)
		15 = Debug (Packet Dump)
PEAP	PEAP logging component	0 = Disabled (default)
		1 = Low (Critical)
		2 = Medium (Warnings)
		3 = High (Informational)
		15 = Debug (packet dump)
EAPTVL	EAP TVL logging component	0 = Disabled (default)
		1 = Low (Critical)
		2 = Medium (Warnings)
		3 = High (Informational)
		15 = Debug (packet dump)

Table 2-14   *ctalogd.ini Configurable Options (Continued)*

Attribute	Description	Value
EAPSQ	EAP Status Query logging component	0 = Disabled (default)
		1 = Low (Critical)
		2 = Medium (Warnings)
		3 = High (Informational)
		15 = Debug (packet dump)
PPMgr	Third-party posture plug-in logging component. If enabled, this specifies the logging level for all third-party plug-ins.	0 = Disabled (default)
		1 = Low (Critical)
		2 = Medium (Warnings)
		3 = High (Informational)
		15 = Debug (Packet Dump)
PSDaemon	CTA Policy Server daemon logging component	0 = Disabled (default)
		1 = Low (Critical)
		2 = Medium (Warnings)
		3 = High (Informational)
		15 = Debug (Packet Dump)
HostPP	CTA's built-in host posture plug-in logging component. The HostPP is used to retrieve posture information from the host OS.	0 = Disabled (default)
		1 = Low (Critical)
		2 = Medium (Warnings)
		3 = High (Informational)
		15 = Debug (Packet Dump)
CTASI	CTA Scripting Interface logging component	0 = Disabled (default)
		1 = Low (Critical)
		2 = Medium (Warnings)
		3 = High (Informational)
		15 = Debug (Packet Dump)
ScriptPlugin	CTA Scripting Interface posture plug-in logging component	0 = Disabled (default)
		1 = Low (Critical)
		2 = Medium (Warnings)
		3 = High (Informational)
		15 = Debug (Packet Dump)

continues

Table 2-14 *ctalogd.ini Configurable Options (Continued)*

Attribute	Description	Value
CTASC	CTA Status Change Logging component	0 = Disabled (default) 1 = Low (Critical) 2 = Medium (Warnings) 3 = High (Informational) 15 = Debug (Packet Dump)
CTAVSTLV	CTA Vendor Specific TLV logging component	0 = Disabled (default) 1 = Low (Critical) 2 = Medium (Warnings) 3 = High (Informational) 15 = Debug (Packet Dump)
CTASTATE	CTA State logging component	0 = Disabled (default) 1 = Low (Critical) 2 = Medium (Warnings) 3 = High (Informational) 15 = Debug (packet dump)

If your company policy is to record critical events on the host machines, you can set the logging level to 1 (Low). Levels 2 and 3 are generally reserved for troubleshooting. There is no harm in setting these higher logging levels because the logs will be limited in the amount of disk space they can consume, and they will have negligible impact on the CPU. By default, the logging service will keep 50MB of files and up to 30 days' worth of files. Logging level 15 should be used at the direction of the Cisco TAC, to troubleshoot a problem with you.

Using the clogcli Utility

CTA provides a command-line utility, clogcli, that enables and disables logging on the fly to assist in troubleshooting CTA issues. This utility does not require the presence of the ctalogd.ini file, and thus is simple yet quick and easy to use. All logging configuration parameters are passed to the utility at execution time and take affect immediately. The clogcli utility is located in the following directories:

Windows: C:\Program Files\Cisco Systems\CiscoTrustAgent\
Mac and Linux: /opt/CiscoTrustAgent/sbin/

Table 2-15 provides a description of the command-line options for the clogcli utility. The command syntax is as follows:

```
clogcli {enable [-t] | disable | clear | loglevel [1-3, 15] | maxfile [0-50]
| maxdisk [0, 50-100] | fileage [0 - ...n] | logdir [any valid local dir | default]
| zipit}
```

Table 2-15   *clogcli Utility Options*

Option	Description
clear	Clears the current log file. If logging is enabled, a new log file is created.
disable	Disables logging.
enable	Enables logging.
enable –t	Enables logging temporarily until the host is rebooted.
fileage	Specifies the maximum age that a log file will be kept, in days [0–[el]]. The default is 30 days. A value of 0 keeps the files forever.
logdir	Specifies a valid full path where the log file should be written. If this option is not specified, the log will be written to the default directory.
loglevel	Sets the logging level for all CTA components at once and to the same level. 1 = Low (Critical) 2 = Medium (Warnings) 3 = High (Informational) 15 = Debug (Packet Dump)
maxdisk	Specifies the maximum amount of disk space that can by used by logging (in megabytes). When this limit is reached, the oldest log files are deleted until the space used falls below this limit. The default is 50MB.
maxfile	Specifies the maximum size a single log file can grow to, in megabytes (MB). If this option is not specified, the default of 4MB is used.
zipit	Captures the log files and zips them into a compressed archive.

When executing the clogcli command, you can pass only one option at a time. Therefore, if you wanted to temporarily enable logging and set the level to High, you would issue the following two commands:

```
clogcli enable -t
clogcli loglevel 3
```

In the background, the clogcli executable checks whether a ctalogd.ini file exists. If not, it creates one. If one does exist, it modifies the file by inserting or adjusting the appropriate option.

NOTE   If you use comments in the ctalogd.ini file, note that the executing clogcli will cause all comments to be removed from the ctalogd.ini file.

Deploying CTA in a Production Network

When you have thoroughly tested CTA in conjunction with the other components of NAC Framework in a lab environment and have decided on the configuration options for CTA, you can proceed with preparations for a production rollout.

NOTE   Before continuing, it is assumed that you have already read most of the remaining chapters in this book and have made a detailed, phased plan for a production rollout of CTA. You should have identified the ACS boxes you will be using for NAC and obtained the respective CA certificates. You should also know whether you will be using any third-party posture plug-ins that you can deploy with the CTA custom installation.

The first step in the production deployment is to download the appropriate CTA Admin package to an administrative workstation. Refer to Table 2-3 for a list of the available Admin packages. Execute the admin package to extract the client installation file. In addition, the process prompts you to accept the EULA. Because you will be pushing the application out to your users silently, they will not be prompted to accept the EULA. Therefore, your acceptance of the EULA here is on behalf of your end users.

The next step is to gather all the files needed for the customized deployment and place them in a temporary directory. These files might include the following:

- CTA client executable (with or without the wired supplicant)
- ctad.ini file with communication settings, user-notification options, and certificate-matching rules specified
- ctalogd.ini file, specifying logging settings and logging levels
- CA certificate to authenticate ACS's server certificate
- Microsoft Windows Installer (MSI)
- Third-party posture plug-ins
- Customized .inf files for the Scripting Interface

Finally, prepare to create the distributable archive by copying the configuration files, certificates, and plug-ins to the appropriate directories for CTA to access during the install. Create all directories under the directory where the CTA silent package is located. Table 2-16 lists the files and directories that can be included.

Table 2-16   *CTA Custom Installation Files*

File or Directory	Description
ctasetup-win-*version*.exe ctasetup-supplicant-win-*version*.exe CiscoTrustAgent.mpkg cta-linux-*version*.i386.rpm	CTA client installation file. Select the appropriate one for your custom installation package.
ctad.ini	Configuration file that specifies communication settings, user notifications, and certificate validation.
ctalogd.ini	Configuration file that specifies the logging settings.
certs\	Create this directory and place the CA certificates for the ACS servers in it. These certificates are required. During CTA installation, any certificate located in this directory is added to the system root certificate store.
plugins\	Create this directory and place any third-party posture plug-in files in it, to be provisioned at install time. If using the optional Scripting Interface, place any custom .inf files in this directory as well.
802_1x\policies\	(Optional) This directory should contain the custom .xml policy file for the 802.1X wired supplicant that you saved at the end of the supplicant configuration wizard.
802_1x\networks\	(Optional) This directory should contain the custom .xml network file for the 802.1X wired supplicant that you saved at the end of the supplicant configuration wizard.
*.inf	(Optional) INF files for custom scripts. Place these files in the plugins\ directory.
instmsiw.exe	(Optional) Microsoft Windows installer application. This is needed only for clients that do not have MSI 2.0 already installed (older Windows NT clients).

Create the custom installation package by including the extracted silent installation file, along with any custom configuration files, certificates, and plug-ins in a distributable file set. One example is to include the files in a compressed zip archive, as shown in Figure 2-6, and push the zip file out to the individual clients. However, there is no restriction on how the files are deployed to the clients.

NOTE   If you deploy the CTA executable file without any custom configuration files, then CTA installs with all the defaults. However, you must still install the CA certificate before CTA could be operational.

Figure 2-6 *CTA Distribution Package Example*

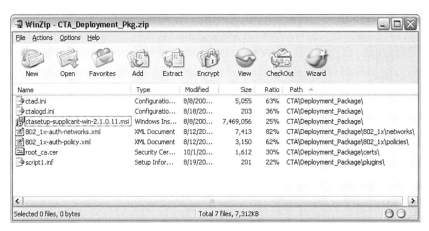

With the distribution package deployed to the clients, complete the installation instructions in the corresponding section for your operating system.

Deploying CTA on Windows

With the deployment package pushed out to the end clients, extract the files to a temporary directory to prepare for installation. CTA uses the standard MSI installer; options are included on the command line to determine the level of user interaction and what features to install. Table 2-17 lists the common MSI installation options

Table 2-17 *MSI Common Installation Options*

Option	Description
/I *"path_to_file"*	Installs the MSI program located at *path_to_file* using an interactive installation wizard. Example: `msiexec.exe /I "C:\temp\ctasetup-win-2.1.0.11.msi"`
/x *ProductCode*	Uninstalls the program with the *ProductCode* specified. CTA's ProductCode can be found by using the Windows Registry editor and navigating to HKEY_LOCAL_MACHINE\Software\Cisco Systems\Cisco Trust Agent.

ADDLOCAL=*option*	Enables you to specify which features you want to install. The only two valid features for CTA are: **8021x_Wired_Client** and **Scripting_Interface**. Both can be installed by using the ALL option or by separating them with a comma. Examples:
	
	`msiexec.exe /I "C:\temp\ctasetup-supplicant-win-2.1.0.11.msi"`
	`ADDLOCAL=8021x_Wired_Client,Scripting_Interface`
	
	`msiexec.exe /I "C:\temp\ctasetup-supplicant-win-2.1.0.11.msi"`
	`ADDLOCAL=ALL`

Table 2-17   *MSI Common Installation Options (Continued)*

Option	Description
REBOOT=*option*	By default, the MSI installer will detect when a reboot is needed and automatically prompt the user. This action can be overridden by specifying the **REBOOT** option on the command line. The **Force** option automatically reboots the system when the installation completes, without prompting the user. The **ReallySuppress** option suppresses all reboots (both during and after the installation), and the user is never prompted. Example: ```msiexec.exe /I "C:\temp\ctasetup-supplicant-win-2.1.0.11.msi" ADDLOCAL=8021x_Wired_Client REBOOT=Force```
/L*V *"path_to_file"*	The **/L** option instructs the installer to create a log file during the installation. ***V** indicates to use verbose logging. The *path_to_file* is the full path and filename of the log file to be created. The path must already exist. Example: ```msiexec.exe /I "C:\temp\ctasetup-win-2.1.0.11.msi" /L*V "C:\temp\cta_install.log"```
/q, /qf, /qr, /qn+, /qb, /qb+	These options specify how much user interaction occurs during the CTA installation. **/q**—Quiet, no interaction. Silent install. **/qf**—Full user interaction. Users must walk through the installation wizard. **/qr**—Users see some of the installation wizard windows and a progress bar, but they are not prompted for any action. **/qn+**—Users receive a pop-up message at the end of the installation, indicating success or failure. **/qb**—Users see messages alerting them that CTA is being installed and configured, but they are not prompted to take any action. **/qb+**—Same as **/qb**, plus at the end, they receive a pop-up message indicating success or failure. Example: ```msiexec.exe /I "C:\temp\ctasetup-win-2.1.0.11.msi" /q```

To solidify this section, we cover three of the very common CLI options to install the client on end machines, and we show the files and directory structure needed for the installation. In all cases, a customized ctad.ini and ctalogd.ini file were included in the deployment package.

The most common deployment is to install CTA completely silently, without any other features. This command is needed to execute this installation:

```
C:\> msiexec.exe /I "C:\temp\ctasetup-win-2.1.0.11.msi" /q
```

The CTA installation file, along with the corresponding custom configuration files and the root CA certificate, was deployed as part of a deployment package. The directory structure and files needed are shown in Example 2-7.

Example 2-7 *Directory Structure and Files Needed for Standard Installation*

```
C:\temp>dir /S /B /A-D
C:\temp\ctasetup-win-2.1.0.11.msi
C:\temp\ctad.ini
C:\temp\ctalogd.ini
C:\temp\certs\root_ca.cer
```

Likewise, for the CTA wired client, with a completely silent install and no reboot at the end (which is required before the 802.1X supplicant will operate) the command would be

```
C:\> msiexec.exe /I "C:\temp\ctasetup-supplicant-win-2.1.0.11.msi"
ADDLOCAL=8021x_Wired_Client REBOOT=ReallySuppress /q
```

Example 2.8 shows the directory structure and files needed for this installation.

Example 2-8 *Directory Structure and Files Needed for Supplicant Installation*

```
C:\temp>dir /S /B /A-D
C:\temp\ctasetup-supplicant-win-2.1.0.11.msi
C:\temp\ctad.ini
C:\temp\ctalogd.ini
C:\temp\certs\root_ca.cer
C:\temp\802_1x\policies\802_1x-auth-policy.xml
C:\temp\802_1x\networks\802_1x-auth-networks.xml
```

Finally, to install the CTA wired client, along with the Scripting Interface and a custom script .inf file, allow the user to see the installation occur and let Windows determine whether a reboot is needed, use the following command:

```
C:\> msiexec.exe /I "C:\temp\ctasetup-supplicant-win-2.1.0.11.msi"
ADDLOCAL=8021x_Wired_Client,Scripting_Interface /qr
```

The directory structure and files needed for this installation are shown in Example 2-9.

Example 2-9 *Directory Structure and Files Needed for Supplicant and Scripting Interface Installation*

```
C:\temp>dir /S /B /A-D
C:\temp\ctasetup-supplicant-win-2.1.0.11.msi
C:\temp\ctad.ini
C:\temp\ctalogd.ini
C:\temp\certs\root_ca.cer
C:\temp\plugins\script1.inf
C:\temp\802_1x\policies\802_1x-auth-policy.xml
C:\temp\802_1x\networks\802_1x-auth-networks.xml
```

NOTE   For a complete list of MSI command-line options, see the Microsoft Windows Installer SDK:

http://msdn.microsoft.com/library/default.asp?url=/library/en-us/msi/setup/about_windows_installer.asp

NOTE   CTA will not create a program group once installed, or an icon on the desktop or in the system tray. It is essentially hidden from the end user. If the 802.1X wired supplicant is installed, an icon appears in the system tray to alert the user about the connection status.

The procedure for installing CTA on Mac and Linux is similar and is covered in the next two sections.

Deploying CTA on Mac OS X

Earlier in this chapter, we extracted the cta-darwin-*version*.dmg disk image from the CTA admin installation file. The disk image includes the CiscoTrustAgent.mpkg package, which is used to install CTA. The disk image can also be customized by adding configuration .ini files, as well as the root CA certificate. Follow these steps to customize the disk image and install CTA on end clients:

Step 1   Locate the cta-darwin-*version*.dmg disk image file in Finder and rename it to indicate that is has been customized. In this example, you will name it cta-custom-darwin-*version*.dmg.

Step 2   Double-click the custom disk image to open its contents.

Step 3   Copy the root CA certificate for your ACS server (or ACS's self-signed certificate, if not using a CA) to the Certs directory.

Step 4   (Optional) Copy any third-party plug-ins for the plug-ins directory.

Step 5   (Optional) Create a ctad.ini file to customize CTA and copy it to the CiscoTrustAgent disk image (at the same level as the CiscoTrustAgent.mpkg file).

Step 6   (Optional) Create a ctalogd.ini file to customize CTA's logging and copy it to the CiscTrustAgent disk image (at the same level as the CiscoTrustAgent.mpkg file).

Step 7   (Optional) Copy any custom .inf files that you created to use with the Scripting Interface to the plug-ins directory.

Step 8   Eject the customized disk image.

Step 9 Deploy the custom disk image file to your Macintosh machines.

Step 10 On the remote client machine, change to the directory where the custom disk image was deployed and execute the command **open cta-custom-darwin-***version***.dmg**.

Step 11 Change to the directory /Volumes/CiscoTrustAgent.

Step 12 Install CTA by executing the following command (all on one line):

```
sudo installer -verbose -pkg /Volumes/CiscoTrustAgent/
CiscoTrustAgent.mpkg/ -target /Volumes/Macintosh\ /HD
```

If you want to install the optional Scripting Interface, use the following command instead:

```
sudo installer -verbose -pkg /Volumes/CiscoTrustAgent/
CiscoTrustAgent.mpkg/CiscoTrustAgentSI.pkg/ -target /Volumes/
Macintosh\ /HD
```

Step 13 When prompted, enter the Administrator's password. CTA will now be installed. When finished, you will see the message "The install was successful."

Step 14 Exit the /Volumes/CiscoTrustAgent directory by typing **cd ..**

Step 15 Complete the installation by detaching the CiscoTrustAgent volume. To do this, execute the command **hdiutil detach /Volumes/ CiscoTrustAgent**.

Step 16 A message appears, indicating that the volume was unmounted and ejected. This completes the installation of a custom deployment package of CTA on a Mac.

Deploying CTA on Linux

As indicated earlier in this section, you need to create a custom distribution package that contains the cta-linux-*version*.i386.rpm file, along with the root CA certificate (located in the /certs subdirectory) and, optionally, ctad.ini and ctalogd.ini, plus any third-party plug-ins (in the /plugins subdirectory) you plan to use. With the custom distribution package created, follow the steps below to install CTA on Linux client machines.

Step 1 Deploy the custom distribution package to your end clients and extract the contents to a temporary directory. In this example, we use /tmp/CTA. Example 2-10 shows files and directories our distribution package created.

Example 2-10 *Directory Structure and Files Needed for Supplicant and Scripting*

```
[root@linux CTA]# ls -bR1
.:
certs
ctad.ini
cta-linux-2.1.0-11.i386.rpm
ctalogd.ini
plugins

./certs:
root_ca.cer

./plugins:
script1.inf
```

Step 2   Install CTA by executing the command **rpm –ivh cta-linux-**
version.**i386.rpm.** You will receive messages indicating that CTA was
installed.

Example:

```
[root@linux CTA]# rpm -ivh cta-linux-2.1.0-11.i386.rpm
Preparing...     ################################# [100%]
     1:cta-linux   ################################# [100%]
```

Step 3   This completes the installation of a custom deployment package of CTA
on Linux.

Troubleshooting CTA

This section includes some common problems you might run into during the deployment
of CTA, along with examples. We begin with installation issues.

Installation Issues

If you have successfully installed CTA but are not being postured, or are seeing any
indication that CTA is operational, first verify that the services are running. For Windows,
you should see the following services running:

- Cisco Posture Server Daemon
- Cisco Systems, Inc., CTA Posture State Daemon
- Cisco Trust Agent EOU Daemon
- Cisco Trust Agent Logger Daemon

If the 802.1X lite supplicant is installed, you will also see the following services:

- Cisco Trust Agent 802.1X wired client

For Mac and Linux installations, verify that the following daemons are running:

- ctad
- ctalogd
- ctapsd
- ctaeoud

This can be verified by executing the command:

```
ps -A | grep cta
```

If one or more of the services are not running, reboot the machine to see if that resolves the issue. If not, enable logging in the ctalogd.ini file and examine the logs to see if they give a reason why a service failed to start. If necessary uninstall, reboot, and then reinstall CTA.

Communication Issues

CTA communicates on UDP port 21862 with the NAD. If you are experiencing communication issues, ensure that this port is not blocked by a host-based firewall or an ACL on a device between your client and the NAD. Take a sniffer trace on the client and verify that you are seeing two-way communications.

You can also use the ctastat utility to view the current status of CTA. This executable is located in the default CTA installation directory. When run, the command returns the session type, the system posture token, and the last time posture information was sent or received. It also includes information about each of the posture plug-ins installed. See Examples 2-11 and 2-12 for the output of this command on EAPoUDP and 802.1X-enabled clients.

Example 2-11   *ctastat Output for an EAPoUDP Session*

```
C:\Program Files\Cisco Systems\CiscoTrustAgent>ctastat

CTA Statistics Reporting Tool

Cisco Trust Agent Statistics
Current Time: Sat Aug 19 16:11:50 2006


Session Information
    Session Number (Hex): 01000000
        Session Type: EOU
            IP Address: 172.18.173.99:21862
```

Example 2-11 *ctastat Output for an EAPoUDP Session (Continued)*

```
                System Posture Token Value: Healthy
                    Received on: Sat Aug 19 14:47:58 2006
                    Total Postures Received: 38
                Last SQ Response was "No Status Change"
                    Last "Status Change": Sat Aug 19 14:47:57 2006
                Plugin Vendor/Application: 9/1
                    Application Posture Token Value: Healthy
                        Received: Sat Aug 19 14:47:58 2006
                    Posture Request last received: Sat Aug 19 14:47:58 2006
                        Length of last response to Posture Req: 42
                        Sent: Sat Aug 19 14:47:58 2006


Plug-ins:
    Vendor: Cisco Systems
        Application ID: 1
            Status: Operational
        Application ID: 2
            Status: Operational
```

Example 2-12 *ctastat Output for an 802.1X Session*

```
C:\Program Files\Cisco Systems\CiscoTrustAgent>ctastat

CTA Statistics Reporting Tool

Cisco Trust Agent Statistics
Current Time: Sun Aug 13 18:25:37 2006


Session Information
    Session Number (Hex): 02000000
        Session Type: 802.1X
            Local MAC Address: 00D0B74C46EC
            Remote MAC Address: 0014A9386882
        System Posture Token Value: Healthy
            Received on: Sun Aug 13 17:24:51 2006
            Total Postures Received: 2
        Plugin Vendor/Application: 9/1
            Application Posture Token Value: Healthy
                Received: Sun Aug 13 17:24:51 2006
            Posture Request last received: Sun Aug 13 17:24:51 2006
                Length of last response to Posture Req: 42
                Sent: Sun Aug 13 17:24:51 2006

Plug-ins:
    Vendor: Cisco Systems
        Application ID: 1
            Status: Operational
        Application ID: 2
            Status: Operational
```

System Logs

Enabling logging is also a great way to troubleshoot any problem on CTA after installation. Logging can be enabled quickly and easily just by executing the following two commands:

```
clogcli enable -t
clogcli loglevel 3
```

This set of commands enables logging temporarily (using the **-t** variable), until the next reboot, at an Informational level (using the **loglevel 3** variable). Some example log messages follow.

The following error indicates that CTA was unable to retrieve a key from the Windows Registry:

```
2    15:55:56.186  10/02/2005   Sev=Critical/1   PSDaemon/0xE3C0001C    Failed
to Open Registry Key, error code 13
```

Table 2-18 lists the Registry entries created by CTA. If you encounter this problem, verify that these entries exist. If any are missing, attempt a reinstall after rebooting the machine.

Table 2-18 *Windows Registry Entries Created by CTA*

Description	Registry
Cisco Trust Agent Service	\HKEY_LOCAL_MACHINE\SYSTEM\CurrentControlSet\Services\ctad
Cisco Trust Agent Logging Service	\HKEY_LOCAL_MACHINE\SYSTEM\CurrentControlSet\Services\ctalogd
Cisco Trust Agent MSI Product Code	\HKEY_LOCAL_MACHINE\SOFTWARE\CiscoSystems\Cisco Trust Agent\ProductCode\
Cisco Trust Agent Install Paths	\HKEY_LOCAL_MACHINE\SOFTWARE\CiscoSystems\Cisco Trust Agent
MSI Install Information	\HKEY_LOCAL_MACHINE\SOFTWARE\Microsoft\Windows\CurrentVersion\Installer\UserData\S-1-5-18\Products\
MSI Uninstall Information	\HKEY_LOCAL_MACHINE\SOFTWARE\Microsoft\Windows\CurrentVersion\Uninstall*Product_code* *Product_code* refers to the code in the Cisco Trust Agent MSI Product Code key in the registry.

The following message indicates that ACS is requesting posture information through the NAD:

```
30    17:07:14.443  10/02/2005   Sev=Info/4   PSDaemon/0x63C0001B  Posture is
being requested on session 0x02FFFFFE
```

The following messages indicate that ACS evaluated the posture credentials returned from the client and assigned a Healthy posture token to both the application and the system:

```
60    17:15:55.763   10/02/2005    Sev=Info/4    PAPlugin/0x63200001    Application
Posture Result = Healthy

61    17:15:55.763   10/02/2005    Sev=Info/4    PAPlugin/0x63200002    System
Posture Result = Healthy
```

The following messages show a certificate that was successful in passing the DN certificate-validation rules:

```
21    14:17:40.683      10/04/2005      Sev=Info/5      PEAP/0x6340000D
Server certificate (/C=US/ST=NC/O=RTP/OU=cisco/CN=acs01) has been        validated
by local CA certificate (/DC=com/DC=cisco/CN=ca       server1).
22    14:17:40.733      10/04/2005      Sev=Info/5      PEAP/0x6340000F
Server certificate matches following DN checking rule: CN="acs01"
```

The following messages show a certificate that failed to match the DN certificate-validation rules.

```
266   14:07:51.671      10/04/2005      Sev=Info/5      PEAP/0x6340000D
Server certificate (/C=US/ST=NC/O=RTP/OU=cisco/CN=acs01) has been        validated
by local CA certificate (/DC=com/DC=cisco/CN=ca       server1).
267   14:07:51.671      10/04/2005      Sev=Warning/2      PEAP/0xA3400009
Server certificate failed DN verification (no matching rules),        connection is
rejected.
```

Many of the log messages are meaningful and can be interpreted literally. However, some require the assistance of the Cisco TAC to interpret.

CTA Client Fails to Receive a Posture Token

You can quickly validate the posture token a client receives by checking either the NAD (for NAC-L2-IP and NAC-L3-IP) or the Passed and Failed attempts logs on ACS. The following output from a Cisco IOS switch shows a client that failed to receive a posture token.

```
c3750#show eou all
---------------------------------------------------------------------------
Address           Interface           AuthType   Posture-Token Age(min)
---------------------------------------------------------------------------
172.18.173.69     GigabitEthernet1/0/4   EAP       -------        6
```

Next, if the NAD device does not have too many clients, we can enable **debug radius authentication** to watch the authentication debugs. Once enabled, we will force a re-posturing of the client by issuing the following command on the NAD **clear eou ip 172.18.173.69**. From the output of the RADIUS debugs, we see that the ACS server returned an Access-Reject packet.

```
6w2d: RADIUS: Received from id 1645/111 172.18.173.77:1645, Access-Reject, len 56
6w2d: RADIUS: authenticator DB 61 F7 FD 4F 2A 40 75 - C4 A5 2C E2 47 9F 24 10
6w2d: RADIUS: EAP-Message           [79] 6
6w2d: RADIUS:  04 1C 00 04                                    [????]
6w2d: RADIUS: Reply-Message         [18] 12
6w2d: RADIUS:  52 65 6A 65 63 74 65 64 0A 0D                  [Rejected??]
```

The next step is to check the Failed Attempts logs on the ACS server. We find the current log for our client and see that the Authen-Failure-Code is that EAP-TLS or PEAP authentication failed during SSL handshake. This indicates a certificate issue. If other clients are successfully getting postured, you know that the ACS certificate is fine. So the next step is to check the client.

On the client, execute **ctalogd enable**, followed by **ctalogd level 3**. This causes the client to start logging CTA events at level 3 (High). Next, we force a new revalidation by issuing the command **clear eou ip 172.18.173.69** on the NAD, and we check the CTA log file. In it, we see the following:

```
22    16:44:31.216   08/19/2006   Sev=Warning/2      PEAP/0xA340000A
PEAP certificate verification failure: self signed certificate in certificate chain.
Subject of current certificate: /DC=com/DC=cisco/CN=ca-server1.
```

This tells us that the client did not establish the PEAP session because the certificate verification failed. Also note that the client thinks the certificate provided is a self-signed certificate. However, we know it is not. The reason the client thinks this is because it does not have a valid root CA certificate installed in its trusted root store.

This problem is resolved by installing the root CA certificate on the client by issuing the command:

```
C:\Program Files\Cisco Systems\CiscoTrustAgent>ctaCert.exe /ui 4 /add
"C:\root_ca.cer" /store "Root"
```

We can verify that the client received a valid posture token by issuing the command **show eou all** on the NAD again.

```
c3750#show eou all
- - - - - - - - - - - - - - - - - - - - - - - - - - - - - - - - - - - - - - - -
Address         Interface            AuthType   Posture-Token Age(min)
- - - - - - - - - - - - - - - - - - - - - - - - - - - - - - - - - - - - - - - -
172.18.173.69   GigabitEthernet1/0/4 EAP        Healthy       0
```

CTA 802.1X Wired Client

The following sections apply only to the Cisco Trust Agent 802.1X wired client and cover troubleshooting wired client specific issues only. This does not apply to the CTA nonwired client.

CTA Wired Client System Report Utility

Troubleshooting issues with 802.1X authentication can be complicated. However, the CTA 802.1X wired client comes with a nice tool called System Report, found in the Cisco Trust

Agent 802.1X wired client program group. When executed, this tool gathers the following information from the client:

- *-networks.xml and *-policy.xml—Network- and policy-configuration files
- The contents of the profiles/ directory—Contains all the configuration files for the client
- log_current.txt—CTA 802.1X wired client's current log file
- CiscoLiteSysRepLog*date*.txt—This file contains information about the client PC, including processor information, memory usage, active process list, network adapter information, Cisco Secure Services Client network, and policy profiles, as well as a list of all client files with their corresponding versions.

The System Report utility zips up all these files into a file named CiscoLiteSysRep*date*stamp.zip. This .zip file is then placed on the user's desktop where it can be e-mailed to the support team. Additional files are included in the .zip archive, including older log files, the client's license file, and client debug logs, which can be sent to the Cisco TAC for additional troubleshooting, if necessary. Because some of these files contain sensitive information, the System Report utility allows you to encrypt the sensitive files with a password.

Follow these steps to generate the System Report archive:

Step 1   From the Windows Start menu, select **Programs > Cisco Trust Agent 802.1X Wired Client > Cisco Trust Agent 802.1X Wired Client System Report**. You should see the System Report utility screen shown in Figure 2-7.

Figure 2-7   *System Report Utility*

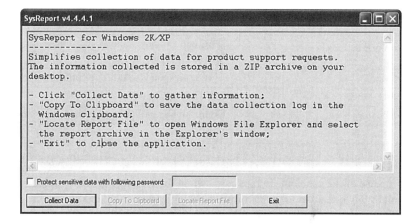

Step 2   (Optional) Select the **Protect Sensitive Data with the Following Password** check box to encrypt the configuration and licensing files. If selected, the .zip utility you use to extract the .zip archive must also support encrypted files. I have tested and used WinZip 9.0, and it works fine.

Step 3   Click the **Collect Data** button to generate the report.

Step 4   When complete, the archive file is placed on the user's desktop. Click the **Locate Report File** button to launch a Windows Explorer window showing the location of the file.

The most important file in the archive is the log_current.txt file, which contains the most recent messages generated by the client. Each message in the log file is encoded in the following format:

```
date time [process] msg_id severity context_ID string
```

The *Severity* field can be one of the following values:

- I: Informational message
- W: Warning message
- E: Error message

When troubleshooting a client issue, it is best to search for error messages first to quickly locate the problem. Once located, examine the logs leading up to the error, to gain additional contextual information. The *context_id* field provides further information about the interface and device the client is authenticating with. Table 2-19 lists the possible values for the *context_id* field.

Table 2-19   *Possible Values for context_id Field*

Code	Description
\<AD *MAC*>	*MAC* corresponds to the MAC address of the client interface adaptor.
\<AC *MAC*>	*MAC* corresponds to the MAC address of the access device.
\<MT Ethernet|WiFi>	Media Type identifier.
\<CN *integer*>	Connection identifier—an incrementing integer.
\<PR *name*>	Profile name, truncated to 16 characters.

Usually, the log_current.txt file provides enough information to assist you in determining the cause of the problem. In rare cases when the message is not completely clear, you can lookup the msg_id in the table of possible messages at the end of the Cisco Trust Agent 802.1X Wired Client's User Guide.

Viewing the Client Logs and Connection Status in Real Time

You can view the client logs and watch the connection status in real time by opening the CTA 802.1X wired client GUI and selecting the **Manage Networks** tab. Select the interface and network you are attempting to connect to from the list, and then select the **Details** button. A new Information window opens, displaying the real-time logs from the client. The current client status also appears at the top of the window. See Figure 2-8 for a screen shot of the Information window just after connecting to a NAC-L2-802.1x enabled wireless network.

Figure 2-8   *Client Information Window*

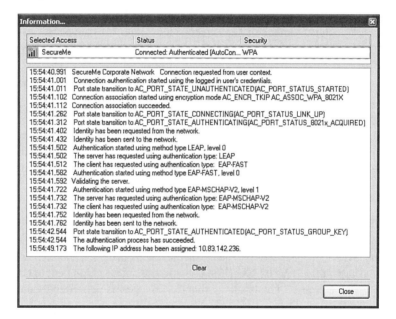

Client Icon Does Not Appear in System Tray

If you do not see the CTA 802.1X wired client icon in the system tray, open the client GUI and select the **Client** menu; deselect **Show System Tray** and then reselect it.

Client GUI Does Not Start

If you receive an error when you attempt to start the client GUI, run the System Report utility. In the .zip archive that it creates, open the clientDebug_current.txt file and scroll down to the bottom to read the most current events. Most errors are printed in plain English (not encoded hex strings) and are, therefore, straightforward to understand and diagnose.

Note that installation of the client over Remote Desktop (RDC) is not supported. If attempted, upon reboot and logon via RDC, the client GUI will fail to start, even though the services are running. If you reboot the PC again and log on via the console (or over a VNC session), you can successfully start the client GUI, but, again, this is unsupported.

Client Does Not Prompt for Password

One common reason the user is never presented with a password dialogue box is if the ACS server is not in the Trusted Server list or if none of the rules can validate ACS's certificate. When this happens, if the user clicks the **Connect** button in the client GUI, the connection fails and the icon changes to red. In addition, in the bottom of the client window reads the message "Connection failed: The server is not trusted." If you see this message, follow the instructions in the Defining Trusted Servers section in this chapter to add a trusted server rule for ACS.

You can also validate this issue remotely by having the end user run the System Report tool and sending in the .zip file it creates. To verify that this is the problem, open the .zip file and look in the /log directory for the log_current.txt file. Open the file and scroll to the bottom (where the most recent messages are) and look for the message "Trusted server list empty, server cannot be validated." If some trusted server rules are defined on the client, you should also see messages indicating why these rules failed to validate ACS's certificate.

Wireless Client Is Immediately Dissociated after 802.1X Authentication

If your wireless client is authenticating via 802.1X but then immediately dissociates from the access point, check the CPU usage on the client during the authentication process. If the CPU is high, the CTA 802.1X wired client might not be getting enough CPU time to complete the protocol handshake within the time period permitted by the access point.

If the CPU is high, check that you are running antivirus software that automatically scans files that are written to disk. Most current antivirus software does this automatically. Because the CTA 802.1X wired client software generates a lot of log messages during the authentication phase, the antivirus software is busy monitoring all these disk writes. This often prevents the client from getting enough CPU time to complete the handshake within the time period allowed. To resolve this issue, exclude the following directories from being monitored by the antivirus software:

C:\Program Files\Cisco Systems\Cisco Trust Agent 802_1x Wired Client\system\log
C:\Program Files\Cisco Systems\Cisco Trust Agent 802_1x Wired Client\log

Client Is Disconnected (Suspended)

If the status of the client shows up as Disconnected (Suspended), on the Manage Networks tab, you just need to press the **Connect** button to allow the client to reconnect to the network. However, sometimes the **Connect** button is grayed out. In these cases, right-click the Cisco Trust Agent 802.1X wired client tray icon and deselect **Enable Client**; then wait a second and re-enable it. This should cause the Connect button to no longer be grayed out.

Chapter Summary

This chapter opened with an introduction to CTA, followed by a list of decisions that must be made before deployment. The minimum system requirements were covered next, along with step-by-step instructions for installing CTA in a lab environment. Deploying CTA in a production environment came next. The remainder of the chapter described the various configuration files, along with the options available in each. Quite a bit of time was also spent describing the optional Scripting Interface and how to use it. Finally, we wrapped up by devoting a section to configuring logging and troubleshooting.

References

NAC2 Deployment Guide

Cisco Trust Agent Administrator Guide 2.1

Review Questions

You can find the answers to the review questions in Appendix A, "Answers to Review Questions."

1. What port does CTA use to communicate with the NAD?

   a. 12628

   b. 1812

   c. 1813

   d. 21862

2. What type of certificate is required to be installed on the CTA client?

   a. Identity certificate

   b. Root certificate

   c. Self-signed certificate

3. The 802.1X supplicant bundled with CTA supports what interface types?

    a. Wired interfaces only

    b. Wireless interfaces only

    c. Both wired and wireless interfaces

4. On default CTA installs, logging is

    a. Enabled at level High

    b. Enabled at level Medium

    c. Enabled at level Low

    d. Disabled

5. To temporarily enable CTA logging:

    a. Manually start the ctalogd service

    b. Execute the **clogcli** command

    c. Create a log.ini file

6. What command will allow you to view the current status of CTA?

    a. show status

    b. ctad -status

    c. ctastat

7. What file must be edited to disable user notifications?

    a. ctalogd.ini

    b. ctad.ini

    c. ctaconfig.ini

8. True or false: The CTA Scripting Interface is installed by default.

9. When using the Scripting Interface, which of the following is not true:

   a. The AppType value in the .inf file must match the application-id used in the posture data file.

   b. The application-id can be any positive integer.

   c. The ctasi executable is used to load the output of your custom script into the posture database on the client.

10. How do you add custom attributes to the ACS database?

   a. Use CSUtil.exe

   b. Import a csv file, attributes.def, into ACS

   c. Enter each one into the GUI under the Posture Validation section

This chapter covers the following topics:

- Installing and configuring the Cisco Secure Services Client
- Deploying the Cisco Secure Services Client in a production network
- Viewing the current status of the Cisco Secure Services Client
- Understanding interaction of the Cisco Secure Services Client with Windows Wireless Zero Configuration
- Troubleshooting the Cisco Secure Services Client

## CHAPTER 3

Cisco Secure Services Client

In Chapter 2, "Cisco Trust Agent," we covered CTA and its included 802.1X wired supplicant. In this chapter, we look at the Cisco Secure Services Client. This is a full-featured 802.1X supplicant for wired and wireless interfaces that integrates natively with NAC. This is important because the integration allows the posture validation to take place in the 802.1X exchange itself, within the authentication phase. Thus, posture information can be used along with authentication credentials for VLAN assignment.

NOTE   The Cisco Secure Services Client was previously the Meetinghouse AEGIS SecureConnect client. Cisco acquired Meetinghouse in August 2006.

Table 3-1 compares the CTA 2.1 wired 802.1X client with the Cisco Secure Services Client.

Table 3-1   *Comparison of CTA Wired Client and the Cisco Secure Services Client*

Features/OS Support	CTA 2.1	Cisco Secure Services Client 4.0
Wired connections	✓	✓
Wireless connections		✓
Windows 2003 Server (Enterprise, Standard, and Web)	✓	✓
Windows XP Professional	✓	✓
Windows 2000 (Professional and Server)	✓	✓
EAP support	FAST v.1a	FAST v.1a, EAP-LEAP, EAP-PEAP, EAP-TTLS, EAP-TLS
Network profiles	One	Multiple profiles allowed
Network adapter support	Wired only	Unlimited adapter support

NOTE   Note that the Microsoft 802.1X supplicant is not included in this chapter. This is because the current Microsoft supplicant does not natively support NAC. This means that posture validation cannot occur in the 802.1X authentication phase. You can still use the Microsoft supplicant for 802.1X authentication, and when authentication is complete, CTA can be used for posture validation using NAC-L2-IP or NAC-L3-IP. However, in this case, authentication and posture validation are completely independent of one another. Cisco and Microsoft have agreed to work together to allow interoperability between NAC and Microsoft's Network Access Protection (NAP). Both Windows Vista and the next release of Windows Server (code-named Longhorn) will natively support NAC without the need for CTA.

If you do not plan to install the Cisco Secure Services Client, it is safe to skip this chapter and continue on to Chapter 4, "Configuring Layer 2 NAC on Network Access Devices."

Installing and Configuring the Cisco Secure Services Client

The Cisco Secure Services Client is a full-featured 802.1X supplicant that supports multiple network profiles for both wired and wireless connections. CTA's 802.1x wired supplicant is actually a stripped-down version of the Cisco Secure Services Client. Therefore, the installation and operation of the two are very similar, but the Cisco Secure Services Client has much more configurable options and can be used in any 802.1X-enabled network.

In the next few sections, we cover how to install, configure, and deploy the Cisco Secure Services Client to hosts in your network. As always, before making any network deployment, we recommend that you fully test the client and deployment method in a lab or nonproduction environment. The time spent installing, configuring, and troubleshooting hands-on in a lab will make for a much smoother (and less stressful) production rollout.

Two versions of the Cisco Secure Services Client exist:

- Administrator version
- End-User version

Both versions are installed using the same executable file, but the Administrator version (default install) enables you to create a deployable End-User version. The End-User version is defined by the configuration files that you will create when stepping through the Deployment Package Wizard. The installation of the configuration files during the Cisco Secure Services Client installation causes the client to become an end-user client.

Minimum System Requirements

The Administrator version of the Cisco Secure Services Client requires a user with administrative privileges to install. Table 3-2 lists the minimum system requirements; as you can see, these are minimal.

Table 3-2   *Cisco Secure Services Administrative Client—Minimum System Requirements*

Component	Requirement
Operating system	Windows 2003
	Windows XP Professional (SP1, SP2)
	Windows 2000 (SP4)
	Windows 2000 Server (SP4)
RAM	256MB: Windows XP, 2003
	128MB: Windows 2000
Hard drive space	24MB
Software installer	Microsoft System Installer (MSI) Version 2.0 (Version 3.0 or higher recommended)

You should experience no problem installing the Administrative Client on any system that supports the minimum OS requirements.

Before installing the Cisco Secure Services Administrative Client, you need to install CTA on the host machine. See Chapter 2 for instructions on installing CTA. The Cisco Secure Services Client requires a CTA version of 2.0.0.30 or greater. (This was the first FCS build of CTA 2.0.) Also when installing CTA, make sure you choose the nonsupplicant version because you will be using the supplicant included with the Cisco Secure Services Client.

Installing the Cisco Secure Services Administrative Client

Installation of the Cisco Secure Services Administrative Client is very simple and straightforward. The Windows version comes packaged as an .msi executable. The format of the file name is as follows:

Cisco_SSC-*OS-version*.msi

For example, the XP/2000 version of the client has the filename Cisco_SSC-2KXP-4.0.5.4783.msi. Double-click the .msi file to start the InstallShield installation wizard. The installer presents the End User License Agreement (EULA). You must read and accept the EULA before proceeding. Next, you are prompted to choose the location where you want the Cisco Secure Services Client installed (the default is C:\Program Files\Cisco Systems\Cisco Secure Services Client\). The next screen presents you with two installation options: Complete (recommended) and Custom. The only difference is that, with the Custom option, you can choose not to install the documentation and a shortcut to the client GUI in the Program Group. After making your choice, click **Install** to start the installation.

When the installation completes, choose **Finish** to close the InstallShield wizard. Next, you see a pop-up window requesting that you restart your computer. You must restart the computer before using the Administrative Client.

NOTE   The Cisco Secure Services Administrative Client contains its own full-featured 802.1X supplicant. This enables you to test the client configuration settings before packaging them in a deployment bundle.

The client installs itself as a Windows service entitled Cisco Secure Services Client. The service starts automatically at bootup using the local system account. After the reboot, you will notice the gray and blue Cisco Secure Services Client icon, which now appears in the system tray. Right-clicking the icon brings up a menu that enables you to open the configuration utility, disable the client, or disable the WiFi radio.

Additionally, the installation creates the Cisco Secure Services Client Program Group, which contains the client configuration utility, the Release Notes and User's Guide, and the System Report utility, which we look at later. With the installation complete, the next step is to configure the client by creating a network profile and policy.

Configuring the Cisco Secure Services Administrative Client

With the Administrative Client installed, the next step is to configure it in your lab environment and test it. This step is crucial and should not be overlooked. Take time to thoroughly test the client in the lab before any production rollout. Lessons learned in the lab can prevent major issues from appearing during the production rollout. The first step in configuring the client is to create a network profile. The next section walks you through completing this task.

Creating a Network Profile

With the Administrative Client installed, follow these steps to create a network profile:

Step 1   Right-click the Cisco Secure Services Client tray icon and choose **Open** from the pop-up menu, as shown in Figure 3-1.

Figure 3-1   *Cisco Secure Services Client Tray Status Icon*

Step 2   You will see a screen similar to the one in Figure 3-2. However, you
might see more or fewer networks listed, depending on the number of
interfaces on your device and the number of wireless networks detected.

Figure 3-2   *Cisco Secure Services Client GUI*

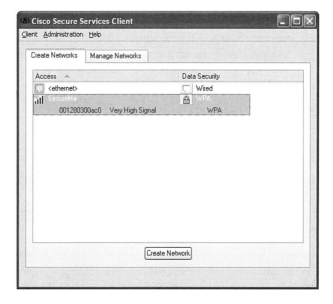

Step 3   Click the **Create Network** button at the bottom of the window to open
the Network Profile Configuration window.

Step 4   In the **Name** field, fill in a user-friendly name for the network profile. In
this example, we use **SecureMe Corporate Network**.

Step 5 To make this network profile available to all users of the machine, check the **Available to All Users (Public Profile)** check box. It is enabled by default, allowing all users to see this network in their main network display list.

Step 6 Determine how and when authentication should take place.

— Select **Automatically Establish Machine Connection** if you want to allow the machine to be authenticated on its own, without requiring a user to log in to it.

— Select **Automatically Establish User Connection** if you want this profile to be available in the automatic-selection process.

— Select **Before User Account** if this profile requires authenticating to a domain or Active Directory (this is the default and the most common configuration). This option allows the authentication to take place before the Windows Domain Login, thus allowing network connectivity for Microsoft GPOs. However, this method supports only password authentication and smart cards; it does not support client certificates that are stored in the Microsoft Certificate Store.

See Figure 3-3 for an example of this screen.

NOTE If you are performing both machine and user authentication, you must deselect the **Before User Account** option. This option is not needed because the machine authentication will establish the network connectivity.

Step 7 Configure the authentication method by clicking the **Modify** button. The default option is no authentication, which you would choose for open hotspots or home wireless access points. For enterprise networks, an authentication method is almost always selected.

After selecting **Modify** in Step 7, the Network Authentication window appears, as shown in Figure 3-4. On the left of the screen is the Authentication Methods selection. Select **Turn On** to enable authentication; then select **Use Anonymous as Identity** if authenticating to an ACS server. This prevents the username from appearing in the outer (unprotected) tunnel.

Step 8 Next, select one or more authentication protocols from the list provided. For NAC-L2-802.1X, you must select **FAST** from the list and then choose the **Configure** button to modify the EAP-FAST settings.

Figure 3-3   *Network Profile Screen*

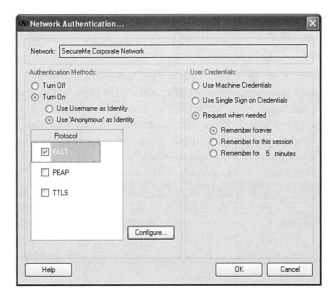

Figure 3-4   *Network Authentication Screen*

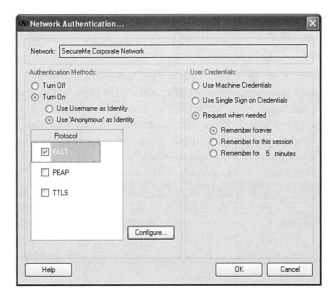

Step 9   A new window appears, enabling you to configure the EAP method. **Use Client Certificate**, if selected, is used only initially to provision the PAC (phase 1). This is deselected by default and is not required. Select this box only if you will be using client certificates to establish the initial EAP-FAST tunnel. (If you do not know, do not select it).

Step 10 Ensure that both **Validate Server Certificate** boxes are checked (default), to validate the certificate that ACS presents during the EAP-FAST and optional EAP-TLS authentication. Deselecting these options is not recommended because this can substantially weaken the security posture of the client.

NOTE   This option requires the CA certificate to be installed in the client's Trusted Root Store and for the server to be in the client's Trusted Servers list. Deselecting this option is not advised because it weakens the security posture.

Step 11 Select **Allow Fast Session Resumption** to allow cached credentials to be used for reauthentication.

Step 12 Under Tunneled Method, if you want to restrict the inner EAP method used, select it from the list. Otherwise, use the default of **Any Method**.

Step 13 Under the EAP-TLS Settings, the **Use Smart Card–based Client Certificates Only** option restricts the client to presenting only certificates contained on smart cards and not a locally stored certificate. This option is not selected by default.

Step 14 Select the **OK** button to close this window.

Step 15 You should be back at the Network Authentication screen, where you can configure the user credentials on the right pane. Select **Use Machine Credentials** only if you want all users of the machine to authenticate using the machine's certificate (not common). Otherwise, choose **Use Single Sign-On Credentials** to use the credentials provided during Windows login, or **Request When Needed** to have a pop-up box appear when authentication is required (default). This last option further enables you to configure whether you want the credentials cached forever (default), or for the life of the session (connection), or for a preset number of minutes. After making your selection, click the **OK** button to return to the Network Profile screen.

Step 16 At the bottom of the Network Profile screen, choose the **Add** button to add an access device (network connection) that you want to apply your configured policy to. This opens a new window with a list of available network devices shown in the upper half.

Step 17 For wired connections, select the **<ethernet>** access method and then choose the **Add Access** button. For wireless connections, choose the SSID from the list. This prepopulates the **Access (SSID)** field, along with the **Mode** (encryption type). If the SSID is not currently available, manually enter it in the **Access (SSID)** field and choose the encryption method from the **Mode** drop-down list. Finally, choose **Add Access**. Repeat this step to add additional network interfaces or SSIDs. The client can support up to ten network access devices. See Figure 3-5 for an example of this step.

Figure 3-5 *Add Access Device Screen*

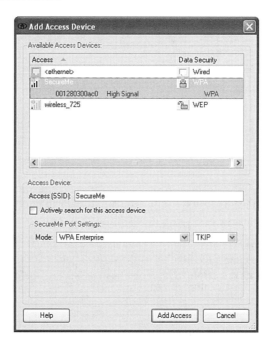

NOTE	Check the box **Actively Search for This Access Device** only if the wireless access point does not broadcast beacons or probes.

Step 18 You should now be back at the Network Profile screen, and it should look similar to what you see in Figure 3-6.

Figure 3-6 *Completed Network Profile Screen*

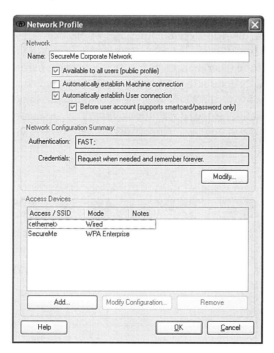

Step 19 Click the **OK** button to close the Network Profile screen and return to the Cisco Secure Services Client GUI.

Upon closing the screen in Step 17, you might be prompted to authenticate to the network. However, if you enabled validation of the server's certificate in Step 10, you must complete the steps in the next section, "Defining Trusted Servers," before you can authenticate.

NOTE It is assumed that you previously installed the CA certificate into the Trusted Root Store of the client machine, as described in Chapter 2. If not, refer to the section in that chapter entitled "Installing the CA Certificate" for step-by-step instructions before proceeding.

Defining Trusted Servers

If the client is configured to validate the server certificate in the EAP exchange (highly suggested, for security reasons), after configuring the network profile, you must define at least one trusted server in the client. Add ACS as a trusted server by completing these steps:

Step 1 Select the **Client** menu and choose **Trusted Servers** > **Manage Machine/All Users Trusted Servers**. Optionally, you can choose to add ACS as a trusted server for just that user account by selecting **Manage Current User Trusted Servers**, but this is not recommended.

Step 2 A new window opens displaying the current server rules. Select the **Add Server Rule** button to create a new rule.

Step 3 The Trusted Server configuration window opens. In the **Rule Name** text box, fill in a user-friendly name for this rule. I suggest using the **ACS** keyword somewhere in the rule so that it is easily recognizable.

Step 4 In the **Validation Method** drop-down box, select **Certificate**.

Step 5 Under the Match ANY Certification Validation Rule section, select the check box next to either (or both) of the options. The **Subject Alternative Name** in the certificate is typically the fully qualified domain name of the ACS machine. The **Subject/Common Name** is whatever string you specified when requesting the certificate. It can be easily determined by opening the certificate and selecting the **Details** tab. When ACS presents its certificate to the client, one of these rules must match or the client will reject the certificate. See Figure 3-7 for a screen shot of a configured trusted server rule.

Figure 3-7 *Create a Trusted Server Rule*

TIP   If you have multiple ACS servers and do not to define a unique rule for each server's certificate, then consider choosing to validate the ACS certificates against the subject alternative name with a match option of Ends With followed by the domain name.

Step 6   With the rule defined, click the **OK** button to return to the Manage Machine/All Users Trusted Servers window. Your new rule should be visible as shown in Figure 3-8. If you need to define additional rules for multiple ACS servers, do so now before continuing. When finished, select the **Close** button to return to the Cisco Secure Services Client GUI window.

Figure 3-8   *Rule Added to the Trusted Server List*

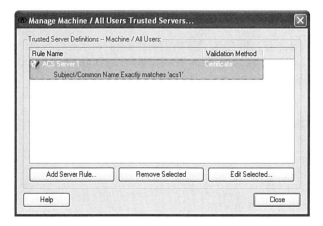

This completes the process of defining a rule to validate a trusted server's certificate.

If a user is never prompted to enter the password, it is possible that the ACS server's certificate did not match any of the trusted server rules. See the "Troubleshooting the Cisco Secure Services Client" section in this chapter for more information on how to troubleshoot this type of issue.

Deploying the Cisco Secure Services Client in a Production Network

After thoroughly testing the client in a lab environment, you are ready to deploy the client in your network. The following sections walk you through this process.

End-User Client Deployment Installation Prerequisite

Before deploying the Cisco Secure Services End-User Client, you need to install CTA on the client machines. See Chapter 2 for instructions on installing CTA. The Cisco Secure Services Client requires a CTA version of 2.0.0.30 or greater (this was the first FCS build of CTA 2.0). Also, when installing CTA, make sure you choose the nonsupplicant version because you will be using the supplicant included with the Cisco Secure Services Client.

Creating End-User Client-Configuration Files

When you are ready to create End-User Client configuration files, select the **Create Deployment Package** item from the **Administration** menu. This launches a wizard that walks you through the process. Along the way, you create client policies and network profiles, which you package into a distribution along with the End-User Client (supplicant). Follow these steps to create the client-configuration files:

Step 1   After selecting the **Administration > Create Deployment Package** option, the Enterprise Deployment Wizard window appears, as shown in Figure 3-9.

Figure 3-9   *Enterprise Client Deployment Wizard*

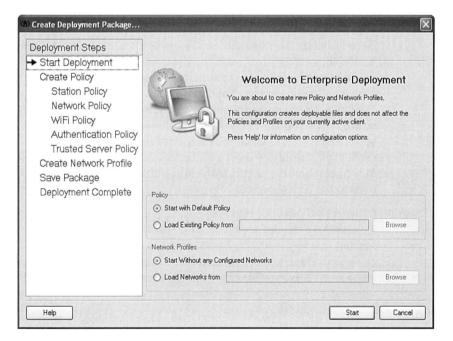

Step 2   Unless you are editing an existing deployment, choose **Start with Default Policy** and **Start Without Any Configured Networks**. Select the **Start** button to begin.

Step 3   The Station Policy screen appears. You must first select whether you want the end users to be able to create new networks using a configurable client (needed for sales or traveling users) or whether you want to provide them with a preset client. Users with a preset client will be able to access only the networks that you have defined; they will not have the ability to create new networks, and their user interface will show them only the status of the client.

Step 4   If you chose a configurable client in Step 3, under the General Settings section, you have the option **Allow Users to Create Public Profiles**, or profiles that are available to all users of the computer. This option must be selected if you want to allow the user to create machine-authentication connection profiles (uncommon). The default and most common deployment is to leave this option unchecked. Additionally, you might select the **Remove Activation menu option,** which removes the activation item from the Help menu (default). This option needs to be visible to end users only if you plan to have them manually install new licenses.

Step 5   Under the Trusted Server Validation section, if you chose a preset client, you can choose only **Always Validate Servers** (most secure option) or **Never Validate Servers** (least secure option). The configurable client has the additional option to allow the end user to select whether to validate the server on a per-network basis (most flexible option). Additionally, if the **Always Validate Servers** option is selected, then you can choose to **Allow user to add new servers**, or **Do not allow the user to add new servers.** Selecting **Do not allow the user to add new servers** removes the **Manage Trusted Servers** option from the **Client** menu. If you are unsure about what options to select, choose the defaults: a configurable client that always validates the server and does not allow users to add new servers.

Step 6   Under the WPA/WPA2 Handshake Validation section, you can disable the handshake-validation process if the client's end stations have wireless adapters that do not support RSN probe response/beacon IE verification performed within a four-way handshake. Disabling this option reduces the security. Also, you have an option to allow the client to choose by selecting the Advanced Settings from the Client menu.

Step 7   Finally, in the Simultaneous Connections pane, you can choose **Allow Only One Connection at a Time** or **Allow Multiple Simultaneous Connections.** Allowing multiple connections lets multihomed machines use all connections to the network at the same time. Finally, you can allow the user to choose the connection setting option.

Step 8   Figure 3-10 shows a configured Station Policy screen. When you are finished defining the station policy, click the **Next** button.

Figure 3-10   *Station Policy Screen*

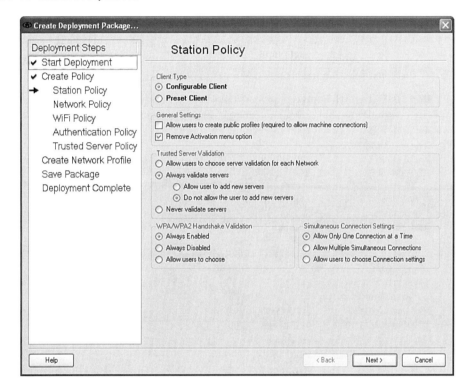

Step 9   The Network Policy screen now appears. The User Credentials section enables you to prohibit machine authentication by deselecting the **Allow Machine Credentials** check box (uncommon). It also has an option **Allow Single Sign-On and Request Credentials,** which must be selected to perform user authentication. You can also specify how long the client should retain the authentication credentials. The default, **For the User Session**, is the most common. **Forever** is the equivalent of static credentials (less secure). Specifying a time limit reprompts the user to reenter credentials when the specified time elapses.

Step 10   The Allow Media Types section enables you to restrict the client to a specified network interface type (wired or wireless). It is uncommon to deselect either of these.

Step 11 The Wired/Ethernet Settings control how many **Interactive Authentication Retries** and **Noninteractive Authentication Retries** are allowed before marking the connection as failed. You should not change the defaults here unless you have a strong reason to do so and have tested the configuration thoroughly before deploying in your network. Increasing the interactive retries causes more pop-up boxes for your users, and increasing the noninteractive retries could add delay to the machine boot/user logon. These same options are provided under the WiFi Settings section, along with the Association Retries.

Step 12 Figure 3-11 shows a configured Network Policy screen. When you are finished making your selections, select the **Next** button.

Figure 3-11 *Network Policy Screen*

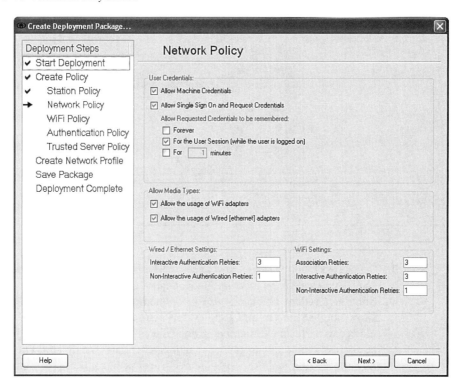

Step 13 The WiFi Policy screen now appears, listing all the wireless modes the client license supports. None of the modes is selected by default. If **Configurable Client** was selected in Step 3, I suggest selecting each

mode listed. If **Preset Client** was chosen, you can choose only the modes being used in your enterprise network. When you are finished, click the **Next** button.

Step 14 The Authentication Policy screen appears, listing the licensed authentication methods. Choose the outer tunnel authentication methods you want available to the end users. For NAC-L2-802.1X, you must select **FAST**. If you are using non-NAC-capable 802.1X switches or wireless access points in your network, select the authentication method used on those devices and then click **Next**.

Step 15 The Trusted Server Policy window appears. Click the **Add Server Rule** button to create a new rule.

Step 16 The Trusted Server configuration window opens. In the **Rule Name** text box, fill in a user-friendly name for this rule, I suggest using the **ACS** keyword somewhere in the rule so that it is easily recognizable.

Step 17 In the **Validation Method** drop-down box, select **Certificate**.

Step 18 Under the Match Any Certification Validation Rule section, select the check box next to either (or both) of the options. The **Subject Alternative Name** in the certificate is typically the fully qualified domain name of the ACS machine. The **Subject/Common Name** is whatever string you specified when requesting the certificate. When finished, click the **OK** button. If you have multiple ACS servers, you might need to define additional rules. When finished, click the **Next** button.

Step 19 The Create Network Profile screen appears. Click the **Create Network** button to open the Network Profile window.

Step 20 In the **Name** field, fill in a user-friendly name for the network profile.

Step 21 Determine how and when authentication should take place.

— Select **Automatically Establish Machine Connection** if you want to allow the machine to be authenticated on its own, without requiring a user to log in to it.

— Select **Automatically Establish User Connection** if you want this profile to be available in the automatic-selection process.

— Select **Before User Account** if this profile requires authenticating to a domain or Active Directory (this is the default and the most common configuration). This option allows the authentication to take place before the Windows Domain Login, thus allowing network connectivity for Microsoft GPOs. However, this method supports only password authentication and smart cards; it does not support client certificates that are stored in the Microsoft Certificate Store.

NOTE   If you are performing both machine and user authentication, you must deselect the **Before User Account** option. This option is not needed because the machine authentication will establish the network connectivity.

Step 22 Configure the authentication method by clicking the **Modify** button. The default option is No Authentication, which you would choose for open hotspots or home wireless access points. For enterprise networks, an authentication method is almost always selected.

Step 23 After selecting **Modify** in Step 22, the Network Authentication window appears, as shown in Figure 3-2. On the left of the screen is the Authentication Methods selection. Select **Turn On** to enable authentication; then select **Use Anonymous as Identity** if authenticating to an ACS server. This prevents the username from appearing in the outer (unprotected) tunnel. Next, select one or more authentication protocols from the list provided. For NAC-L2-802.1X, you must select **FAST** from the list and then click the **Configure** button to modify the EAP-FAST settings.

Step 24 A new window appears that enables you to configure the EAP method. **Use Client Certificate**, if selected, is used only initially to provision the PAC (phase 1). This is deselected by default.

Step 25 The **Validate Server Certificate** box is checked if you selected it back in Step 5. When checked, ACS's certificate is validated during the EAP-FAST and optional EAP-TLS authentication.

NOTE   Validating ACS identity certificate requires the CA certificate to be installed in the client's Trusted Root Store and for the server to be in the client's Trusted Servers list. Deselecting this option is not advised because it weakens the security posture.

Step 26 Select **Allow Fast Session Resumption** to allow cached credentials to be used for reauthentication.

Step 27 Finally, under Tunneled Method, if you want to restrict the inner EAP method used, select it from the list. Otherwise, use the default of **Any Method.**

Step 28 Under the EAP-TLS Settings, the **Use Smart Card–based Client Certificates Only** option restricts the client to presenting only certificates contained on smart cards and not a locally stored certificate. This option is not selected by default.

Step 29 Select the **OK** button to close this window.

Step 30 You should be back at the Network Authentication screen, where you can configure the user credentials in the right pane. Select **Use Machine Credentials** only if you want all users of the machine to authenticate using the machine's certificate (not common). Otherwise, choose **Use Single Sign-On Credentials** to use the credentials provided during Windows login, or choose **Request When Needed** to have a pop-up box appear when authentication is required (default). After making your selection, click the **OK** button to return to the Network Profile screen.

Step 31 In the bottom of the Network Profile screen, click the **Add** button to add an access device (network connection) that you want to apply your configured policy to. This opens a new window with a list of available network devices shown in the upper half.

Step 32 For wired connections, select the **<ethernet>** access method and then click the **Add Access** button. For wireless connections, choose the SSID from the list. This prepopulates the **Access (SSID)** field, along with the **Mode** (encryption type). If the SSID is not currently available, manually enter it in the **Access (SSID)** field and choose the encryption method from the **Mode** drop-down list. Finally, choose **Add Access.** Repeat this step to add network interfaces or SSIDs. The client can support up to ten network access devices.

NOTE Check the box **Actively Search for This Access Device** only if the wireless access point does not broadcast beacons or probes.

Step 33 You should now be back at the Network Profile screen, and it should look similar to what you see in Figure 3-4.

Step 34 Click the **OK** button to close the Network Profile screen and return to the Create Network Profile screen. Your network profile, along with the Network Configuration Summary, is displayed on the right side of the screen, as shown in Figure 3-12. Click the **Next** button to continue.

Figure 3-12 *Completed Network Profile Screen*

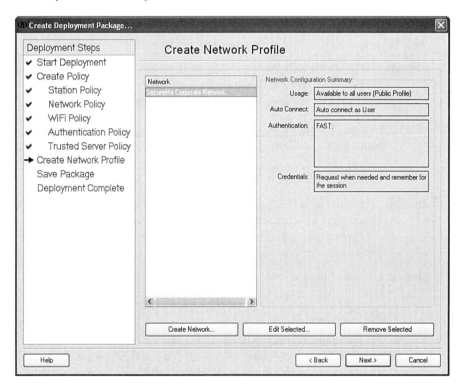

Step 35 The Save Package screen now appears. Click the **Browse** button to choose the directory where you want to save the deployment package. In the **Deployment Package Filename** field, specify a prefix to be appended to the .xml configuration files that the wizard creates. I used 802_1x-auth to easily distinguish the files.

Step 36 Finally, click the **Save** button. The Deployment Complete screen appears, as shown in Figure 3-13, providing a summary of the files created.

Figure 3-13 *Deployment Package Complete*

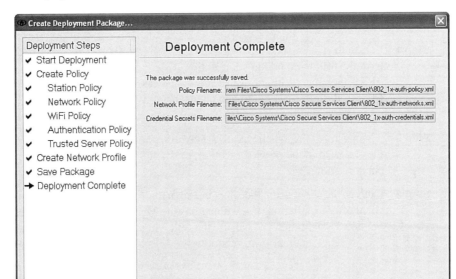

The deployment package that you just created is really just a set of three .xml configuration files. The files are saved in the directory you specified in the last step and have the following naming conventions:

- *prefix*-policy.xml
- *prefix*-networks.xml
- *prefix*-credentials.xml

Creating the License File

Before deploying the client to end users, you must create a license file. To do this, open a text editor and paste the license string (obtained from Cisco) into the file. If you have more then one license, paste in each one a separate line. When you are finished, save the file with the name licenseTransport.txt. This file will be moved to the installation directory during the deployment process.

Deploying the End-User Client

Now you have everything you need to deploy the End-User Client. Follow these steps to push the client out to machines in your network:

Step 1   Locate the Cisco Secure Services Client .msi installation file. It should have the following naming convention: Cisco_SSC-*OS-version*.msi (this is the same file that was used previously to install the Administrative Client). Push this file out to end clients using your company's standard software-publishing process (Microsoft SMS, Altiris, and so on).

Step 2   Also push out the *-policy.xml, *-networks.xml, and *-credentials.xml files, created in the previous section, to a temporary directory on the client machine.

Step 3   Execute the client using the silent install method, and try not to reboot the client after installation. If the client has the Microsoft System Installer Version 3.0 or higher, you can use the following to perform a silent install and prevent the client from rebooting:

```
msiexec /i Cisco_SSC-XP2K-4.0.5.4783.msi /quiet /norestart
```

Step 4   After the Cisco Secure Services Client has been installed, the *.xml configuration files need to be moved to the following locations:

— Policy .xml file:

$INSTALL_DIR\profiles\policies\

— Networks .xml file:

$INSTALL_DIR\profiles\networks\

— Credentials .xml file:

$INSTALL_DIR\profiles\users\settings\

Step 5   With the correct configuration files installed, delete the default policy-configuration file located in

$INSTALL_DIR\profiles\policies\default\.

Step 6   Move the license file to $INSTALL_DIR. Example:

```
C:\Program Files\Cisco Systems\Cisco Secure Services
Client\licenseTransport.txt
```

Step 7   With configuration now complete, restart the end user's machine. You can accomplish this using the tsshutdn /REBOOT command. On Windows XP and Windows 2000 machines with the Resource Kit installed, you can also use the shutdown –r command to reboot the machine.

Example 3-1 contains a sample .bat file that moves the .xml configuration files from C:\Temp to their proper locations. Then it removes the default policy and moves the license file to the correct location.

Example 3-1 *Sample Executable .bat File Used to Configure Clients*

```
REM  Move configuration files to correct locations
move C:\temp\802_1x-auth-policy.xml "C:\Program Files\Cisco Systems\Cisco Secure
  Services Client\profiles\policies\"
move C:\temp\802_1x-auth-networks.xml "C:\Program Files\Cisco Systems\Cisco Secure
  Services Client\profiles\networks\"
move C:\temp\802_1x-auth-credentials.xml "C:\Program Files\Cisco Systems\Cisco
  Secure Services Client\profiles\users\settings\"

REM  Delete the default policy
del "C:\Program Files\Cisco Systems\Cisco Secure Services
  Client\profiles\policies\default\*"

REM  Move the license file to the correct location
move C:\temp\licenseTransport.txt "C:\Program Files\Cisco Systems\Cisco Secure
  Services Client\"
```

It is highly recommended that before you push the client out on a large scale, you test the deployment process in the lab. This enables you to verify the process and ensure that everything works as expected before pushing it out to your end users.

NOTE   If you modify the client's configuration by pushing out a new network or policy .xml file with a different name, the Cisco Secure Services Client will use the file with the latest time stamp. However, it is still a good idea to remove the older configuration files to prevent confusion.

Viewing the Current Status of the Cisco Secure Services Client

The Cisco Secure Services Client installs an icon in the system tray, as shown in Figure 3-1. The icon changes colors to represent the current status of the client. Table 3-3 lists the possible colors for the Cisco Secure Services icon and what they mean.

Table 3-3 *Cisco Secure Services Client—System Tray Icon Colors*

Color	Meaning
Green	Connected (authenticated, or no authentication required)
Yellow	Connecting (authenticating)
Red	Failed authentication
Gray	Disconnected (idle/not connected)—default state when not in any of the previous states

Additional information about the connection status can be obtained by opening the client GUI (right-click the status icon and choose the **Open** menu item). Select the network from the list that you want to retrieve additional status from, and then click the **Status** button. A screen similar to the one shown in Figure 3-14 appears, providing additional connection details. For wireless connections, selecting the **WiFi Details** tab displays additional information about the wireless link.

Figure 3-14 *Additional Connection Status Details*

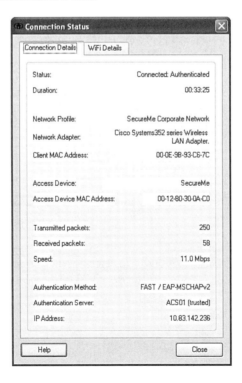

Windows Wireless Zero Configuration

The Cisco Secure Services Client disables the Windows Wireless Zero Configuration (WZC) utility automatically when it binds to the network interfaces. Disabling the Cisco Secure Services Client by right-clicking the system tray status icon and deselecting **Active** restores the WZC on the interfaces previously controlled by the Cisco Secure Services Client.

NOTE   You can define several network policies in the client to allow end users to connect to various open wireless networks. However, you must know the SSID of the network to add it to the list of managed networks.

If you are deploying a preset client, laptop users will most likely disable the Cisco Secure Services Client when roaming from the office. However, if a configurable client is deployed, the Cisco Secure Services Client will display all wireless networks it detects, and the user can select the network SSID to join the network (much like the WZC utility). Whichever deployment model you choose, make sure you educate the user community on how to connect to nonenterprise networks.

Troubleshooting the Cisco Secure Services Client

In this section, we cover troubleshooting tools and techniques to use when troubleshooting issues with the client. Common problems along with their solutions are also presented.

System Report Utility

Troubleshooting End-User Client issues or issues with 802.1X authentication can be complicated. However, the Cisco Secure Services Client comes with a very nice tool called System Report, which can be found in the Cisco Secure Services Client program group. When executed, this tool gathers the following information from the client:

- *-networks.xml and *-policy.xml, network- and policy-configuration files.
- The contents of the profiles/ directory, which contains all the configuration files for the client.
- log_current.txt, the Cisco Secure Services Client's current log file.
- Cisco_SSCSysRepLog*date*.txt contains information about the client PC, including processor information, memory usage, active process list, network adapter information, Cisco Secure Services Client network and policy profiles, and a list of all client files with their corresponding versions.

The System Report utility zips up all these files in a file named
Cisco_SSCSysRep*date*stamp.zip. This .zip file is then placed on the user's desktop, where
it can be e-mailed to the support team. Additional files are included in the .zip archive,
including older log files, the client's license file, and client debug logs, which can be sent to
the Cisco TAC for additional troubleshooting, if necessary. Because some of these files
contain sensitive information, the System Report utility enables you to encrypt the sensitive
files with a password.

Follow these steps to generate the System Report archive:

Step 1   From the Windows Start menu, select **Programs > Cisco Secure
Services Client > Cisco Secure Services Client System Report**. You
should see the System Report utility screen shown in Figure 3-15.

Figure 3-15   *System Report Utility*

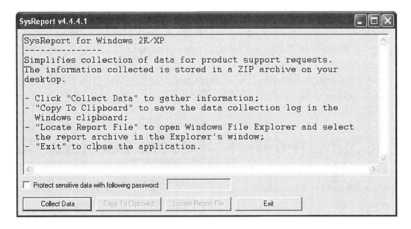

Step 2   (Optional) Select the **Protect Sensitive Data with the Following
Password** check box to encrypt the configuration and licensing files.
If selected, the .zip utility you use to extract the .zip archive must also
support encrypted files. I have tested and used WinZip 9.0, and it
works fine.

Step 3   Select the **Collect Data** button to generate the report.

Step 4   When complete, the archive file is placed on the user's desktop. Press the
Locate Report File button to launch a Windows Explorer window
showing the location of the file.

The most important file in the archive is the log_current.txt file, which contains the most recent messages generated by the client. Each message in the log file is encoded in the following format:

date time [process] msg_id severity context_id string

The *severity* field can be one of the following values:

- I: Informational message
- W: Warning message
- E: Error message

When troubleshooting a client issue, it is best to search for error messages first to quickly locate the problem. Then examine the logs leading up to the error, to gain additional contextual information. The *context_id* field provides further information about the interface and device the client is authenticating with. Table 3-4 lists the possible values for the *context_id* field.

Table 3-4   *Possible Values for context_id Field*

Code	Description
<AD *MAC*>	MAC corresponds to the MAC address of the client interface adaptor.
<AC *MAC*>	MAC corresponds to the MAC address of the access device.
<MT Ethernet|WiFi>	Media Type identifier.
<CN *integer*>	Connection identifier, an incrementing integer.
<PR *name*>	Profile name, truncated to 16 characters.

Usually, the log_current.txt file provides enough information to assist you in determining the cause of the problem. In the rare cases in which the message is not completely clear, you can look up the msg_id in the table of possible messages at the end of the Cisco Secure Services Client's User Guide.

Viewing the Client Logs and Connection Status in Real Time

You can view the client logs and watch the connection status in real time by opening the Cisco Secure Services Client GUI and selecting the **Manage Networks** tab. Select the interface and network you are attempting to connect to from the list, and then click the **Details** button. A new Information window opens, displaying the real-time logs from the client; the current client status appears at the top of the window. See Figure 3-16 for a screen shot of the Information window just after connecting to a NAC-L2-802.1X–enabled wireless network.

Figure 3-16 *Client Information Window*

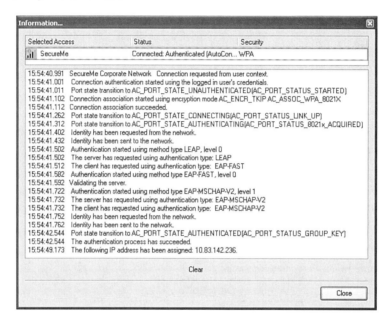

Client Icon Does Not Appear in System Tray

If you do not see the Cisco Secure Services Client icon in the system tray, open the client GUI and select the **Client** menu; deselect **Show System Tray,** then reselect it.

Client GUI Does Not Start

If you receive an error when attempting to start the client GUI, run the System Report utility. In the .zip archive that it creates, open the clientDebug_current.txt file and scroll down to the bottom to read the most current events. Most errors are printed in plain English (not encoded hex strings) and are therefore straightforward to understand and diagnose.

Note that installation of the client over Remote Desktop (RDC) is not supported. If attempted, upon reboot and logon via RDC, the client GUI will fail to start, even though the services are running. If you reboot the PC again and log on via the console (or over a VNC session), you can successfully start the client GUI, but, again, this is unsupported.

Client Does Not Prompt for Password

One common reason the user is never presented with a password dialogue box is that the ACS server is not in the Trusted Server list or if none of the rules can validate ACS's certificate. When this happens, if the user clicks the **Connect** button in the client GUI, the connection fails and the icon changes to red. In addition, in the bottom of the client window is the message "Connection failed: the server is not trusted." If you see this message, follow the instructions in the Defining Trusted Servers section in this chapter to add a trusted server rule for ACS.

You can also validate this issue remotely by having the end user run the System Report tool and sending in the .zip file it creates. To verify that this is the problem, open the .zip file and look in the /log directory for the log_current.txt file. Open the file and scroll to the bottom (where the most recent messages are) and look for the message, "Trusted server list empty, server cannot be validated." If some trusted server rules are defined on the client, you should also see messages indicating why these rules failed to validate ACS's certificate.

Wireless Client Is Immediately Dissociated after 802.1X Authentication

If your wireless client is authenticating via 802.1X but then immediately is dissociated from the access point, check the CPU usage on the client during the authentication process. If the CPU is high, the Cisco Secure Services Client might not be getting enough CPU time to complete the protocol handshake within the time period permitted by the access point.

If the CPU is high, check whether you are running antivirus software that automatically scans files that are written to disk. Most current antivirus software does this automatically. Because the Cisco Secure Services Client software generates a lot of log messages during the authentication phase, the antivirus software is busy monitoring all these disk writes. This often prevents the client from getting enough CPU time to complete the handshake within the time period allowed. To resolve this issue, exclude the following directories from being monitored by the antivirus software:

    C:\Program Files\Cisco Systems\Cisco Secure Services Client\system\log
    C:\Program Files\Cisco Systems\Cisco Secure Services Client\log

Client Is Disconnected (Suspended)

If the status of the client shows up as Disconnected(Suspended), on the Manage Networks tab, you just need to press the **Connect** button to allow the client to reconnect to the network. However, sometimes the **Connect** button is grayed out. In these cases, right-click the Cisco Secure Services Client tray icon and deselect **Enable Client**, then wait a second an re-enable it. This should cause the **Connect** button to no longer be grayed out.

Summary

This chapter covered the Cisco Secure Services Client, a full-featured 802.1X client for both wired and wireless networks, that natively integrates with NAC Framework. The minimum system requirements were covered, followed by step-by-step instructions on how to install, configure, and deploy the client to end users. We finished the chapter by covering troubleshooting steps and common problem seen by end users.

References

Cisco Secure Services Client's User Guide

Review Questions

You can find the answers to the review questions in Appendix A, "Answers to Review Questions."

1. What is the difference between the Administrator version and the End-User version of the Cisco Secure Services Client?

   a. The End-User Client version has a different .msi executable file than the Administrator version.

   b. The Administrator version is licensed separately.

   c. The clients are the same; the only difference is the configuration files.

2. The Cisco Secure Services End-Client configuration is defined by what three files?

   a. *-networks.xml, *-config.xml, *-profile.xml

   b. *-config.xml, *-profile.xml, *-policy.xml

   c. *-config.xml, *-networks.xml, *-policy.xml

   d. *-networks.xml, *-policy.xml, *-credentials.xml

3. True or false: The Cisco Secure Services Client must always validate ACS's identity certificate.

4. True or false: Cisco Secure Services Preset Clients cannot add new networks to their profiles.

5. The Cisco Secure Services Client must be configured for which Authentication method to support NAC-L2-802.1X?

   a. EAP-MD5

   b. EAP-TLS

   c. FAST

   d. PEAP

6. What utility is included with the Cisco Secure Services Client to assist you in troubleshooting client issues?

   a. Debugger

   b. System Report

   c. Cisco Secure Services Troubleshooter

   d. None of the above

This chapter covers the following topics:

- NAC-L2-IP architecture, configuration, and troubleshooting
- NAC-L2-802.1X architecture, configuration, and troubleshooting

## CHAPTER 4

Configuring Layer 2 NAC on Network Access Devices

The Cisco Catalyst switches are capable of enforcing device security policy compliance when local-area network (LAN) users attempt to access the network. Switches that support NAC Framework features are capable of denying access to noncompliant devices and placing them in a quarantined area and allowing restricted access to network resources for remediation purposes. This posture validation is done at the Layer 2 network edge using two different technologies:

- NAC Layer 2 IP (NAC-L2-IP)
- NAC Layer 2 802.1X (NAC-L2-802.1X)

This chapter guides you in configuring and troubleshooting these technologies on Cisco Catalyst switches.

NAC-L2-IP

This section covers the details about NAC-L2-IP, including the following:

- Architecture of NAC-L2-IP
- Configuration of NAC-L2-IP
- Troubleshooting tips for NAC-L2-IP

Architecture of NAC-L2-IP

NAC-L2-IP uses EAP over UDP (EoU) as the transport mechanism to complete the posture assessment of a device attempting to connect to the corporate network. This is similar to NAC Layer 3; however, the posture is done on a Layer 2 switch port. The posture assessment is triggered when the Cisco Catalyst switch receives a Dynamic Host Configuration Protocol (DHCP) or an Address Resolution Protocol (ARP) request from the device attempting to connect to the network. When the switch detects the DHCP or ARP request, it challenges the host by sending an EoU packet to start the posture validation.

Figure 4-1 illustrates how the posture validation is performed in NAC-L2-IP.

Figure 4-1 *NAC-L2-IP Posture Validation*

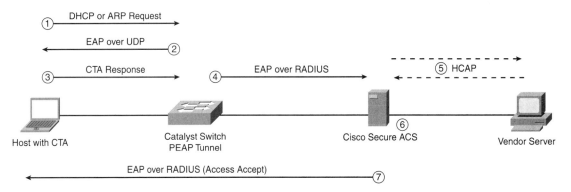

The following steps describe the process illustrated in Figure 4-1:

Step 1 A DHCP or ARP request triggers the Cisco Catalyst switch to start the posture-validation process.

Step 2 The Cisco Catalyst Switch sends an EAP over UDP message to the end host.

Step 3 The Cisco Trust Agent (CTA) application replies to the Cisco Catalyst with the host credentials (antivirus signature-definition information, operating system hotfixes, and service packs).

Step 4 The Cisco Catalyst switch sends the host's posture credentials to Cisco Secure Access Control Server (ACS) through EAP over RADIUS.

Step 5 Optionally, Cisco Secure ACS can send portions of the host credentials to a third-party vendor server (such as antivirus) for further policy enforcement through the Host Credential Authorization Protocol (HCAP).

Step 6 Cisco Secure ACS completes posture validation based on the configured policies and determines the authorization rights of the machine. For example, it determines whether the host complies with the configured policies and classifies it as Healthy, Infected, Quarantined, and so on.

Step 7 The Catalyst switch receives the response from the Cisco Secure ACS server and downloads appropriate Access Control Lists (ACLs) to allow or deny the end host from communicating with the rest of the network.

Table 4-1 lists the NAC feature compatibility matrix, including all the supported switch platforms.

Table 4-1   *Switch Support Matrix*

Platform/ Supervisor	Operating System	NAC L2 802.1X	NAC L2 IP	NAC L3 IP
6500 with Sup32 or Sup720	Native IOS	Future	Yes	Future
6500 with Sup2	Native IOS	No	No	No
6500 with Sup32 or Sup720	Hybrid	Yes	Yes	No
6500 with Sup2 or Sup32 or Sup720	CatOS	Yes	Yes	No
4500 Series with SupII+, II+TS, IV, V, V-10GE	IOS	Yes	Yes	Future
4900	IOS	Yes	Yes	Future
3550, 3560, 3750	IOS	Yes	Yes	No
2950, 2940, 2955, 2960, 2970	IOS	Yes	No	No
6500 with Sup1A	All	No	No	No
5000	All	No	No	No
4000—Sup I, II,	CatOS	No	No	No
4000-SUP III	IOS	No	No	No
3500XL, 2900XM, 1900	All	No	No	No

NOTE   All the switches that support NAC L2 IP also support NAC agentless hosts (NAH) with a third-party audit server.

Configuring NAC-L2-IP

This section guides you on how to configure NAC-L2-IP on Cisco Catalyst switches running Cisco IOS and CatOS. Figure 4-2 illustrates the topology used in the following examples.

Figure 4-2 *Configuring NAC-L2-IP Example Network*

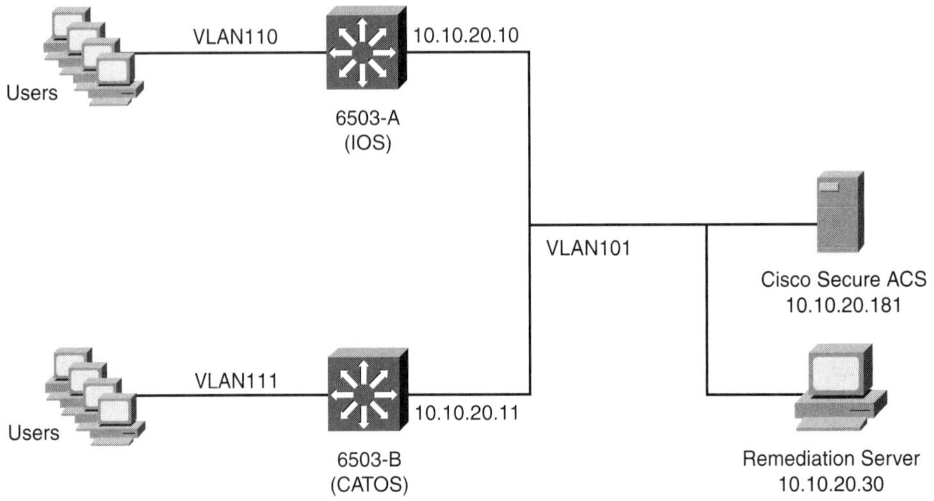

NAC-L2-IP Cisco IOS Configuration

The following steps are necessary to configure NAC-L2-IP on a Cisco Catalyst running Cisco IOS:

Step 1 Enable Authentication, Authorization, and Accounting (AAA) services:

```
6503-A(config)#aaa new-model
```

Step 2 Enable EAPoUDP RADIUS authentication:

```
6503-A(config)#aaa authentication eou default group radius
```

Step 3 Configure the switch to run authorization for all network-related service requests:

```
6503-A(config)#aaa authorization network default group radius
```

Step 4 Enable AAA RADIUS accounting:

```
6503-A(config)# aaa accounting network default start-stop group radius
```

Step 5 Next, you must specify the host name or IP address of the RADIUS server using the **radius-server host** command. The Cisco Secure ACS RADIUS server IP address is 10.10.20.181. The default RADIUS port number for authentication is 1645 and for accounting is 1646; however, you can optionally change the port. In this example, the default ports are used.

```
6503-A(config)#radius-server host 10.10.20.181
```

Step 6   Enter the RADIUS server encryption key:

```
6503-A(config)#radius-server key cisco123
```

NOTE   The RADIUS server key must match the key configured in the Cisco Secure ACS server. If they do not match, the switch and Cisco Secure ACS will not be capable of communicating with each other. In this example, cisco123 is the key configured. Chapter 8, "Cisco Secure Access Control Server," covers the configuration of the Cisco Secure ACS server.

Step 7   Configure the switch to send the Framed-IP-Address RADIUS attribute (attribute 8) in access-request or accounting-request packets:

```
6503-A(config)#radius-server attribute 8 include-in-access-req
```

Step 8   Configure the switch to recognize and use vendor-specific attributes from and to the Cisco Secure ACS server:

```
6503-A(config)#radius-server vsa send authentication
```

Step 9   Optionally, you can specify the interface from which all outgoing RADIUS packets will be sourced. This is an optional step; however, it is recommended when multiple paths might exist for the communication between the switch and the RADIUS server. In this example, all RADIUS packets will be sourced from the VLAN 101 virtual interface.

```
6503-A(config)#ip radius source-interface Vlan101
```

Step 10   Enable the IP Device Tracking feature on the switch. This feature is used for the switch to maintain a table that includes the IP and MAC addresses of the host attempting to access the network and information about what interface on the switch detected the host. IP Device Tracking enables the inspection of ARP packets to start the posture process.

```
6503-A(config)#ip device tracking
```

Step 11   In NAC-L2-IP, an ARP request from the host can trigger the security posture-validation process. Optionally, you can enable the DHCP Snooping feature in the switch to trigger NAC posture validation after a DHCP request is detected. To enable DHCP snooping on VLAN 110, use the following commands:

```
6503-A(config)#ip dhcp snooping
6503-A(config)#ip dhcp snooping vlan 110
```

Step 12   Create a default interface Access Control List (ACL) to be applied to the client ingress switch port. This ACL is used as the default security policy. After NAC posture validation, an ACL is downloaded from the Cisco Secure ACS server that allows or denies traffic to the user based on the security posture results.

```
6503-A(config)#ip access-list extended interface_acl
6503-A(config-ext-nacl)#remark Allow EAPoUDP
6503-A(config-ext-nacl)#permit udp any any eq 21862
6503-A(config-ext-nacl)#remark Allow DHCP
6503-A(config-ext-nacl)#permit udp any eq bootpc any eq bootps
6503-A(config-ext-nacl)#remark Allow HTTP access to remediation server
6503-A(config-ext-nacl)#permit tcp any host 10.10.20.30 eq www
```

NOTE   Unlike NAC Layer 3 IP, there is no concept of an intercept ACL for NAC-L2-IP.

In this example, the ACL is named interface_acl and allows EAPoUDP traffic from the end host (CTA), DHCP requests, and HTTP traffic to a web server where quarantined clients can be redirected to obtain more information on how to download OS patches, hotfixes, service packs, and any other software needed to be compliant.

Step 13   Create the IP admission rule to enable the EAPoUDP posture process. The rule name in this example is NAC-L2-IP.

```
6503-A(config)#ip admission name NAC-L2-IP eapoudp
```

Step 14   Apply the interface ACL and the IP admission rule to the switch interfaces where the clients reside. In this example, we apply it to the GigabitEthernet2/48 interface:

```
6503-A(config)#interface GigabitEthernet2/48
6503-A(config-if)# switchport
6503-A(config-if)# switchport mode access
6503-A(config-if)# switchport access vlan 110
6503-A(config-if)# ip access-group interface_acl in
6503-A(config-if)# ip admission NAC-L2-IP
```

NOTE   The **ip admission** command can be applied only to physical ports; it cannot be applied to VLAN interfaces. The switch will not accept the **ip admission** command if **switchport mode access** is not enabled on the interface.

Step 15 Configure the EAPoUDP hold-period timer to specify the time to wait (in seconds) after a client-credential validation fails (accept-reject from RADIUS) or an EAPoUDP association fails. The default is 180 seconds. In this example, the switch is configured to wait 160 seconds.

```
6503-A(config)#eou timeout hold-period 160
```

Step 16 After a client-credential validation and security posture session is successfully established, the switch sends a status-query to the client (CTA). If the switch does not receive a response from CTA, it waits 300 seconds, by default, before sending a new status-query message. To change the default value, use the **eou timeout status-query** command:

```
6503-A(config)#eou timeout status-query 360
```

Step 17 To verify whether any changes in the client admission policy have occurred, the switch sends a revalidation EAPoUDP message to CTA every 36,000 seconds (10 hours) by default. However, you can change the default revalidation period timer using the **eou timeout revalidation** command. In this example, the timer is configured to wait 18,000 seconds (five hours) before revalidating the security posture of the end-host machine.

```
6503-A(config)#eou timeout revalidation 18000
```

NOTE The status query and revalidation timeouts can also be configured in the Cisco Secure ACS server and sent to the switch during posture validation. The Cisco Secure ACS timers take precedence over the switch global EAPoUDP timers. This is the recommended method for controlling session timers, especially when interacting with a remediation server.

Step 18 To configure URL redirection, you can configure an ACL on the switch to allow HTTP traffic to the server that has additional information for the user after being quarantined. The ACL must match the ACL defined in the Cisco Secure ACS server. In this example, the name of the ACL is quarantine_url_redir_acl.

```
6503-A(config)# ip access-list extended quarantine_url_redir_acl
6503-A(config-ext-nacl)# deny tcp any host 10.10.20.30 eq www
```

Step 19 For URL redirection to work, you must enable the HTTP server service in the Catalyst switch.

```
6503-A(config)#ip http server
```

NOTE | To increase the security of your switch, it is recommended that you protect against any HTTP vulnerability by restricting access to the switch HTTP services with other devices within your infrastructure, such as firewalls, infrastructure ACLs, and so on.

NAC-L2-IP Cisco CatOS Configuration

This section covers the steps necessary to configure NAC-L2-IP on a Cisco Catalyst switch running CatOS. NAC-L2-IP is supported on Cisco Catalyst switches running CatOS version 8.5 or later.

The following steps are necessary to configure the switch for NAC-L2-IP:

Step 1 Configure the RADIUS server information on the switch. The RADIUS server in this example is 10.10.20.181, and it is set as the primary RADIUS server. The RADIUS shared secret key is cisco123.

```
Console> (enable)set radius server 10.10.20.181 primary
Console> (enable)set radius key cisco123
```

Step 2 Enable EAP over UDP on the switch:

```
Console> (enable)set eou enable
```

Step 3 Enable EAP over UDP for the switch port that will require posture validation:

```
Console> (enable)set port eou 2/48 auto
```

Step 4 Optionally, remove any previously configured Access Control Lists on the switch:

```
Console> (enable)clear security acl all
```

Step 5 Configure a policy-based ACL to allow the necessary services for NAC-L2-IP and to restrict access based on the posture of the end host.

Permit ARP:

```
Console> (enable)set security acl ip nac permit arp
Console> (enable)set security acl ip nac permit arp-inspection any any
```

Permit DHCP snooping:

```
Console> (enable)set security acl ip nac permit dhcp-snooping
```

Allow EAPoUDP communication:

```
Console> (enable)set security acl ip nac permit eapoudp
```

Allow DHCP communication:

```
Console> (enable)set security acl ip nac permit udp any eq 67 any
Console> (enable)set security acl ip nac permit udp any eq 68 any
```

Optionally, permit DNS services to resolve any internal hosts for remediation or used by URL redirect:

```
Console> (enable)set security acl ip nac permit udp any any eq 53
```

Create an Access Control List entry that defines the level of access Healthy hosts will have after security posture validation. This must match the Healthy policy group name defined in the Cisco Secure ACS server.

```
Console> (enable)set security acl ip nac permit ip group Healthy_hosts
    any
```

NOTE   In this example, the Healthy policy group name is Healthy_hosts. Refer to Chapter 8 to learn how to configure the Cisco Secure ACS server.

Allow limited access for quarantined hosts. In this example, the quarantine policy group name defined in the Cisco Secure ACS server is Quarantine_hosts. This is a policy-based ACL (PBACL).

```
Console> (enable)set security acl ip nac permit ip group
    Quarantine_hosts 10.10.20.30 0.0.0.0
Console> (enable)set security acl ip nac permit ip 10.10.20.30 0.0.0.0
    group Quarantine_hosts
```

NOTE   In this example, quarantined hosts are allowed to communicate to only an internal server (10.10.20.30) to obtain further instructions, patches, or any other software necessary for remediation.

PBACLs are Access Control Lists that are created dynamically with policy-based definitions in each Access Control Entry (ACE). These represent groups of network users. Enforcement on Catalyst 6500s is restricted to PBACLs. These PBACLs are commonly referred as intelligent VACLs. PBACLs are expanded in the Catalyst 6500 TCAM ACL implementation when the switch detects a new IP address on a specific port. The Catalyst 6500 looks at the group policy of the port and creates a specific ACE in the TCAM with the new IP address substituting for the group definition in the ACE.

These group definitions are either static definitions or dynamic definitions done through a RADIUS assignment. In NAC-L2-802.1X, the most common implementation is the dynamic assignment from Cisco Secure ACS. On the other hand, PBACLs are not restricted to NAC-L2-802.1X; PBACLs are also supported with NAC L2 IP as a way to dynamically implement access control policy.

Step 6 Commit the configured ACL:

```
Console> (enable)commit security acl all
```

Step 7 Map the ACL to the VLAN that will be used for NAC-L2-IP. In this case, VLAN 111 is used.

```
Console> (enable)set security acl map nac 111
```

NAC Nonresponsive Hosts

NAC nonresponsive hosts are often referred to as NAC agentless hosts (NAH). These are devices that do not or cannot run CTA. Consequently, NAH are incapable of performing NAC functions. Examples of these devices are printers, scanners, IP phones, and hosts with unsupported operating systems.

You can allow these hosts network access in several ways:

- Using static exceptions defined on the switch based on the MAC address or IP address of such device
- Configuring Network Access Profile (NAP) filtering on the Cisco Secure ACS server
- Using CDP, in the case of Cisco IP Phones
- Using a third-party audit server

This section teaches you how to configure static exceptions on the switch. Refer to Chapter 8 to learn how to configure NAP filtering and NARs on the Cisco Secure ACS server. Chapter 11, "Audit Servers," covers the integration of third-party audit servers.

In Figure 4-3, a printer with IP address 10.10.10.145 and an IP-enabled camera with MAC address 0099.1234.abcd need to be statically authorized. Additionally, all Cisco IP phones need to be excluded using CDP.

Take the following steps to accomplish this task:

Step 1 Configure an identity profile for EoU:

```
6503-A(config)#identity profile eapoudp
```

Step 2 Use the **device authorize ip-address** command to statically authorize the printer's IP address 10.10.10.145:

```
6503-A(config-identity-prof)#device authorize ip-address 10.10.10.145
```

Step 3   Use the **device authorize mac-address** command to statically authorize
the camera's MAC address:

```
6503-A(config-identity-prof)#device authorize mac-address
0099.1234.abcd
```

Step 4   Use the **device authorize type cisco ip phone** command to statically
authorize the IP using the CDP protocol:

```
6503-A(config-identity-prof)#device authorize type cisco ip phone
```

Figure 4-3   *NAH Exception Lists Example Network*

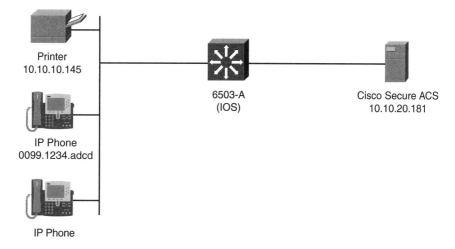

Printer
10.10.10.145

IP Phone
0099.1234.adcd

IP Phone

6503-A
(IOS)

Cisco Secure ACS
10.10.20.181

Troubleshooting NAC-L2-IP

This section provides several tips on how to troubleshoot NAC-L2-IP problems. It includes
the most useful **show** commands, debugs, and log messages that will help you troubleshoot
any unexpected problems and monitor the NAC solution.

Useful **show** Commands

You can use several **show** commands to monitor and report the state of NAC-L2-IP
connections. The **show eou all** command is one of the most commonly used because it
displays a table that summarizes all current NAC sessions. However, the **show eou**
command has several options that can help you get more specific information about a NAC
session. The following are all the options of the **show eou** command:

```
show eou {all | posture token | authentication | ip | mac}
```

Example 4-1 shows sample output of the **show eou all** command.

Example 4-1   *Output of the show eou all Command*

```
6503-A#show eou all
-------------------------------------------------------------------
Address           Interface        AuthType   Posture-Token Age(min)
-------------------------------------------------------------------
10.10.10.5        GigabitEthernet2/44    EAP        Infected       4
10.10.10.6        GigabitEthernet2/45    EAP        Quarantine     2
10.10.10.2        GigabitEthernet2/46    EAP        Healthy        3
10.10.10.133      GigabitEthernet2/48    EAP        Healthy        5
```

The switch has performed posture validation for four end hosts in Example 4-1. Two of the hosts are Healthy, one is Infected, and one is Quarantined.

Example 4-2 shows sample output of the **show eou ip** command. In this example, details about the end host with IP address 10.10.10.133 are shown.

Example 4-2   *Displaying EoU Session Details for a Specific IP Address*

```
6503-A# show eou ip 10.10.10.133
Address            : 10.10.10.133
MAC Address        : 0004.5aa8.2bde
Interface          : GigabitEthernet2/48
AuthType           : EAP
Audit Session ID   : 0000003843C75E400000002AC1FE192
PostureToken       : Healthy
Age(min)           : 15
URL Redirect       : NO URL REDIRECT
URL Redirect ACL   : NO URL REDIRECT ACL
ACL Name           : #ACSACL#-IP-healthy-42c46e7c
User Name          : PC123:User1
Revalidation Period : 3600 Seconds
Status Query Period : 300 Seconds
```

The output of the **show eou ip** command, as in Example 4-2, shows useful information such as the following:

- Interface on which the end host resides
- Posture token assigned to this session
- Age of the token
- URL redirect information
- Posture ACL name
- Username information
- Revalidation period
- Status query period

NAC-L2-IP EoU sessions can be reset on the switch on a per-interface, per-session basis or all at once. To clear all EoU sessions on the switch, use the **clear eou all** command. This command completely resets all existing NAC-L2-IP sessions. This command also clears all the information about existing sessions.

Several other options in the **clear eou** command enable you to reset specific EoU sessions, as shown in Example 4-3.

Example 4-3 *clear eou Command Options*

```
6503-A#clear eou ?
  all              All EAPoUDP clients
  authentication   Authentication Type
  interface        Interface information
  ip               IP Address
  mac              MAC Address
  posturetoken     Posture Token
```

The **clear eou** command enables you to reset specific EoU using the following keywords:

all—Clears all EoU sessions
authentication—Clears EoU sessions based on authentication type (for example, clientless, EAP, and static)
interface—Clears EoU sessions terminated on a specific interface/switch port
ip—Clears a specific EoU session using the end host's IP address
mac—Clears a specific EoU session using the end host's MAC address
posturetoken—Clears all EoU session for a specific posture token (Healthy, Quarantine, Infected, and so on)

In CatOS, you can verify the NAC-L2-IP functionality and posture with the **show policy group all** command. Example 4-4 shows sample output of this command.

Example 4-4 *Verifying NAC-L2-IP Posture in CatOS*

```
6503-B (enable) show policy group all
------------------------------------------------
Group Name            = Healthy
Group Id              = 1
No.of IP Addresses    = 1
Is Changed flag       = 0
Src Type              = ACL CLI
      List of Hosts in group.
      ----------------------
      Interface      = 2/48
      IpAddress      = 10.10.10.133
      Src type       = NAC
```

You can also use the **show eou config** command to display the current EoU configuration on the switch running CatOS, as shown in Example 4-5.

Example 4-5 *show eou config Command*

```
6503-B (enable) show eou config
Eou Protocol Version : 1
Eou Global Config
-----------------
Eou Global Enable        : Enabled
Eou Clientless           : Enabled
Eou IP-Station-Id        : Enabled
Eou Logging              : Enabled
Eou Radius Accounting    : Disabled
Eou MaxRetry             : 3
Eou AAA timeout          : 60
Eou Hold timeout         : 180
Eou Retransmit timeout   : 30
Eou Revalidation timeout : 3600
Eou Status Query timeout : 300
Eou Rate Limit           : 0
Eou Udp Port             : 21862
```

In CatOS, you can also use the **show eou all** command as demonstrated earlier for Cisco Catalyst switches running Cisco IOS. You also can use the **show eou ip** *ip-address* command to obtain EoU information about a particular host. For example, if you want to see EoU information for a host with the IP address 10.10.21.123, you can use the **show eou ip 10.10.21.123**.

You can also use the **show access-list** command to see the URL redirect access list and its hit count.

EoU Logging

You can obtain detailed information about NAC-L2-IP sessions by enabling EoU logging on the Cisco Catalyst switch that is acting as a NAC network access device. This information can then be sent to a syslog server or an event-correlation system, such as CS-MARS. To enable EoU logging, use the **eou logging** command, as shown in Example 4-6.

Example 4-6 *Enabling EoU Logging*

```
6503-A(config)# eou logging
```

Example 4-7 shows the log entries of a security posture session of a Healthy host (10.10.10.5).

Example 4-7   *Event Log Messages of a Healthy Host*

```
w0d: eou-ev:eou_send_eap_msg: Send EAP Msg host= 0.0.0.0 eou_port= 5566 (hex)
5w0d: eou-ev:Stopping All timers
5w0d: eou-ev:Starting AAA timer 60(10.10.10.5)
5w0d: eou-ev:Stopping Retransmit timer
5w0d: %EOU-6-POLICY: IP=10.10.10.5¦ ACLNAME=#ACSACL#-IP-healthy_acl-43c0799b
5w0d: %EOU-6-POLICY: IP=10.10.10.5¦ TOKEN=Healthy
5w0d: %EOU-6-POLICY: IP=10.10.10.5¦ HOSTNAME=PC-UY303MGWIN:user
5w0d: %EOU-6-POSTURE: IP=10.10.10.5¦ HOST=AUTHORIZED¦ Interface=GigabitEthernet2
/48
5w0d: eou-ev:Stopping AAA timer
```

The shaded lines show the access control list downloaded from Cisco Secure ACS, the Healthy token, the username and end-host machine name, and the interface from which the end host is attempting to connect to the network.

Useful Debugs

You can enable the following useful **debug** commands on the Cisco Catalyst switches when troubleshooting EoU or with authentication problems:

- **debug eou events**—Shows EoU basic event information
- **debug eou packets**—Displays detailed packet information on EoU transactions
- **debug eou all**—Enables both **debug eou events** and **debug eou packets**
- **debug radius authentication**—Displays RADIUS authentication transactions in detail
- **debug radius brief**—Displays a summary of RADIUS authentication transactions
- **debug aaa authentication**—Displays general AAA authentication messages

---

WARNING   Be careful when enabling any of these debugs on busy devices. It is recommended to first start by enabling **debug eou events** and/or **debug radius** to troubleshoot authentication and communication problems. However, they need to be carefully enabled in production switches.

Example 4-8 includes the output of **debug eou events** and **debug radius authentication**. In this example, the Cisco Secure ACS was offline.

Example 4-8 *Debugging RADIUS and EoU Communication Problems*

```
5w0d: eou-ev:69.171.218.244: msg = 33(eventEouCreateSession)
5w0d: AAA/BIND(00000021): Bind i/f
5w0d: %EOU-6-SESSION: IP=10.10.10.5 | HOST=DETECTED| Interface=GigabitEthernet2/48
5w0d: eou-ev:10.10.10.5: msg = 3(eventEouStartHello)
5w0d: eou-ev:Starting Retransmit timer 3(10.10.10.5)
5w0d: eou-ev:eou_send_hello_request: Send Hello Request host= 0.0.0.0 eou_port= 5566
 (hex)
5w0d: eou-ev:Stopping All timers
5w0d: %EOU-6-CTA: IP=10.10.10.5| CiscoTrustAgent=DETECTED
5w0d: eou-ev:10.10.10.5: msg = 21(eventEouEapStart)
5w0d: eou-ev:Starting Retransmit timer 3(10.10.10.5)
5w0d: eou-ev:eou_send_eap_msg: Send EAP Msg host= 0.0.0.0 eou_port= 5566 (hex)
5w0d: eou-ev:Stopping All timers
5w0d: eou-ev:Starting AAA timer 60(10.10.10.5)
5w0d: eou-ev:Stopping Retransmit timer
5w0d: AAA/AUTHEN/EOU (00000021): Pick method list 'default'
5w0d: RADIUS(00000021): Config NAS IP: 10.10.20.10
5w0d: RADIUS/ENCODE(00000021): acct_session_id: 48
5w0d: RADIUS(00000021): sending
5w0d: RADIUS(00000021): Send Access-Request to 10.10.20.181:1645 id 1645/152, len
 192
5w0d: RADIUS:   authenticator 63 F9 BF 20 E9 5E E7 E5 - 1D 37 10 10 0D 4F 70 BA
5w0d: RADIUS:   User-Name         [1]   2    ""
5w0d: RADIUS:   Called-Station-Id [30]  16   "0014.1c6b.864f"
5w0d: RADIUS:   Calling-Station-Id [31] 16   "0006.5b02.944c"
5w0d: RADIUS:   Framed-IP-Address [8]   6    10.10.10.5
5w0d: RADIUS:   Vendor, Cisco     [26]  32
5w0d: RADIUS:    Cisco AVpair     [1]   26   "aaa:service=ip_admission"
5w0d: RADIUS:   Vendor, Cisco     [26]  57
5w0d: RADIUS:    Cisco AVpair     [1]   51   "audit-session-
 id=00000000B84E5D4C000000110A0A0A05"
5w0d: RADIUS:   NAS-Port-Type     [61]  6    Virtual              [5]
5w0d: RADIUS:   Message-Authenticato[80] 18
5w0d: RADIUS:    80 F0 8D B5 7F C5 B5 57 29 08 9D B3 D6 8A 3A DF  [???????W)?????:?]
5w0d: RADIUS:   EAP-Message       [79]  7
5w0d: RADIUS:    02 01 00 05 01                                   [?????]
5w0d: RADIUS:   Service-Type      [6]   6    EAPoUDP              [25]
5w0d: RADIUS:   NAS-IP-Address    [4]   6    10.10.20.10
5w0d: RADIUS: no sg in radius-timers: ctx 0x53E6DFC0 sg 0x0000
5w0d: RADIUS: Retransmit to (10.10.20.181:1645,1646) for id 1645/152
5w0d: RADIUS: no sg in radius-timers: ctx 0x53E6DFC0 sg 0x0000
5w0d: RADIUS: Retransmit to (10.10.20.181:1645,1646) for id 1645/152
5w0d: RADIUS: no sg in radius-timers: ctx 0x53E6DFC0 sg 0x0000
5w0d: RADIUS: Retransmit to (10.10.20.181:1645,1646) for id 1645/152
5w0d: RADIUS: no sg in radius-timers: ctx 0x53E6DFC0 sg 0x0000
5w0d: RADIUS: No response from (10.10.20.181:1645,1646) for id 1645/152
5w0d: RADIUS/DECODE: parse response no app start; FAIL
5w0d: RADIUS/DECODE: parse response; FAIL
```

The shaded lines show the Cisco Catalyst switch starting the EoU negotiations with the end host and subsequently trying to send its information to the Cisco Secure ACS RADIUS server. After several retransmissions, the connection times out and the RADIUS session fails.

TIP   In the previous example, only one RADIUS server is configured on the switch. You can specify backup RADIUS servers (if available) for higher availability.

NAC-L2-802.1X

NAC-L2-802.1X leverages the Identity-Based Network Services (IBNS) solution to provide user- and machine-based authentication and adds security posture capabilities with the use of the Extensible Authentication Protocol–Flexible Authentication via Secure Tunneling (EAP-FAST). This section details the architecture of NAC-L2-802.1X and guides you on how to configure and troubleshoot NAC-L2-802.1X on Cisco Catalyst switches.

Architecture of NAC-L2-802.1X

The NAC-L2-802.1X feature enables you to perform a security posture assessment of a host using 802.1X proven technologies on a Layer 2 switch port. NAC-L2-802.1X uses EAP-FAST as the transport mechanism to carry identity and security posture information within a Transport Layer Security (TLS) tunnel. Consequently, an 802.1X supplicant that supports EAP-FAST is needed for NAC-L2-802.1X.

NOTE   The embedded supplicant included with CTA supports EAP-FAST. It also supports EAP-GTC, EAP-MSCHAPv2, and EAP-TLS for client-side authentication. CTA is covered in Chapter 2, "Cisco Trust Agent."

Cisco initially developed EAP-FAST to support customers who cannot enforce a strong password policy and want to deploy an 802.1X EAP type that does not require digital certificates, supports a variety of user and password database types, supports password expiration and change, and is flexible, easy to deploy, and easy to manage.

Two different sets of credentials can be sent from the client to the NAD and, subsequently, to ACS and back-end servers in a Microsoft Windows environment:

- Machine credentials (machine authentication)
- User credentials (user authentication)

Microsoft Windows allows a client machine (using machine authentication) to send its identity information before authenticating a user. This information is sent at boot time, establishing a secure channel to update and participate in the domain Group Policy Objects (GPO) model. This enables the end host to subsequently communicate with a Windows domain controller to obtain machine group policies.

The second method is user authentication. A user can log in to the local computer or to a Windows domain. The username and password can be used as the identity credentials for 802.1X authentication.

EAP-FAST uses a unique shared credential called the Protected Access Credential (PAC) to mutually authenticate the client and the RADIUS server. The PAC is linked to the client username and a server authority ID. A PAC supplements the use of digital certificates in a Public Key Infrastructure (PKI) environment. EAP-FAST has three basic phases:

> **Phase 0 (optional)**—This is a special case of Phase 1 and Phase 2 provisioning. This phase is used infrequently to enable the client to be dynamically provisioned with a PAC. During this phase, a per-user access credential is generated securely between the user and the network. This per-user credential, known as the PAC, is used in Phase 1 of EAP-FAST authentication.
>
> **Phase 1**—A secure tunnel is established using the provided PAC.
>
> **Phase 2**—The client is authenticated via the secure tunnel.

Two methods of provisioning the PAC are used:

- Out-of-band
- In-band

NOTE   The 802.1X supplicant bundled with CTA supports only in-band provisioning. Additionally, CTA's supplicant provisions a PAC to the client only if the Cisco Secure ACS server is configured to allow in-band provisioning and if there is a successful machine authentication using a digital certificate or a successful user authentication.

In NAC-L2-802.1X, security posture is performed in addition to the user and/or machine authentication. After a security posture token is assigned, the policy enforcement for NAC-L2-802.1X is done via dynamic VLAN assignment. Figure 4-4 illustrates the NAC-L2-802.1X authentication process.

The following steps describe the NAC-L2-802.1X authentication process illustrated in Figure 4-4:

Step 1   The 802.1X connection is set up between the switch and the end host (supplicant).

Step 2   The switch requests the credentials from the end host through EAP over 802.1X. This can include user and machine credentials and posture information (antivirus version and state, OS type, version, and so on).

Step 3   The end host (CTA using the NAC-compatible supplicant) sends the user/device credentials.

Step 4   The switch forwards the credentials to Cisco Secure ACS via EAP over RADIUS.

Step 5   Cisco Secure ACS can send user/device credentials to external authentication databases such as Microsoft Active Directory, Lightweight Directory Access Protocol (LDAP), and so on.

Step 6   Cisco Secure ACS can also send security posture information to a third-party vendor server through HCAP.

Step 7   Cisco Secure ACS validates credentials and determines authorization rights.

Step 8   Cisco Secure ACS sends the authorization policy, including VLAN assignment, to the switch.

NOTE   Optional notifications can also be sent to applications on end-host machines.

Figure 4-4   *NAC-L2-802.1X Authentication Process*

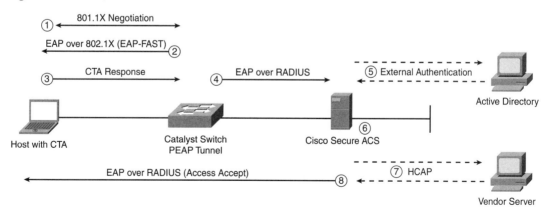

Configuring NAC-L2-802.1X

This section guides you on how to configure NAC-L2-802.1X on Cisco Catalyst switches.

NAC-L2-802.1X Cisco IOS Configuration

The following steps are necessary to configure NAC-L2-802.1X on a Cisco Catalyst switch running Cisco IOS.

Step 1   VLAN assignment is the method used in NAC-L2-802.1X for policy enforcement. In this example, the following VLANs are used:

— VLAN 10—Healthy Employees

— VLAN 20—Guests

— VLAN 30—Quarantine

— VLAN 40—Infected

— VLAN 50—Contractors

Configure the appropriate VLANs as follows:

```
6503-A#configure terminal
Enter configuration commands, one per line.  End with CNTL/Z.
6503-A(config)#vlan 10
6503-A(config-vlan)#name Healthy_Employees
6503-A(config-vlan)#exit
6503-A(config)#vlan 20
6503-A(config-vlan)#name Guests
6503-A(config-vlan)#exit
6503-A(config)#vlan 30
6503-A(config-vlan)#name Quarantine
6503-A(config-vlan)#exit
6503-A(config)#vlan 40
6503-A(config-vlan)#name Infected
6503-A(config-vlan)#exit
6503-A(config)#vlan 50
6503-A(config-vlan)#name Contractors
6503-A(config-vlan)#exit
```

Step 2   Enable the switch AAA services:

```
6503-A(config)#aaa new-model
```

Step 3   Configure the switch to use RADIUS for 802.1X authentication:

```
6503-A(config)#aaa authentication dot1x default group radius
```

Step 4   Enable authorization for all network-related service requests:

```
6503-A(config)#aaa authorization network default group radius
```

Step 5   Enable accounting with the following command:

```
6503-A(config)#aaa accounting network default start-stop radius
```

Step 6   Next you need to specify the host name or IP address of the RADIUS server using the **radius-server host** command. The Cisco Secure ACS RADIUS server IP address is 10.10.20.181. The default RADIUS port number for authentication is 1645 and for accounting is 1646; however, you can optionally change the port. In this example, the default ports are used.

```
6503-A(config)#radius-server host 10.10.20.181
```

Step 7   Enter the RADIUS server encryption key:

```
6503-A(config)#radius-server key cisco123
```

Step 8   Optionally, you can specify the switch interface from which all outgoing RADIUS packets will be originated (GigabitEthernet 2/12 is used in this example):

```
6503-A(config)#ip radius source-interface GigabitEthernet 2/12
```

Step 9   Enable 802.1X on the switch:

```
6503-A(config)#dot1x system-auth-control
```

Step 10   After enabling 802.1X globally, configure 802.1X parameters on all the switch interfaces where NAC-L2-802.1X end hosts reside. Configure 802.1X port control to auto. This enables 802.1X port-based authentication and allows the port to begin in the unauthorized state, allowing only EAPOL packets to be sent and received. The authentication process starts when an EAPOL-start frame is detected or when the link state of the port changes to up.

```
6503-A(config)#interface GigabitEthernet 2/38
6503-A(config-if)#dot1x port-control auto
```

NOTE   All end hosts attempting to access the network are uniquely identified by their MAC addresses.

Step 11   Configure the 802.1X reauthentication timer. In this case, the switch uses the timer configured in the Cisco Secure ACS server:

```
6503-A(config-if)#dot1x timeout reauth-period server
```

Step 12 Enable 802.1X reauthentication:

```
6503-A(config-if)#dot1x reauthentication
```

NAC-L2-802.1X Cisco CatOS Configuration

The following steps are necessary to configure NAC-L2-802.1X on a Cisco Catalyst switch running CatOS. NAC-L2-802.1X is supported on Cisco CatOS Version 8.5 and later.

Step 1 Configure the RADIUS server information on the switch. The RADIUS server in this example is 10.10.20.181, and it is set as the primary RADIUS server. The RADIUS shared secret key is cisco123.

```
Console> (enable) set radius server 10.10.20.181 primary
Console> (enable) set radius key cisco123
```

Step 2 Enable 802.1X authentication globally in the switch:

```
Console> (enable) set dot1x system-auth-control enable
```

Step 3 Enable 802.1X control on the switch ports that the end hosts are connected to. In this example, an NAC-L2-802.1X client is connected to port 2/38.

```
Console> (enable) set port dot1x 2/38 port-control auto
```

Step 4 Enable reauthentication on the port:

```
Console> (enable) set port dot1x 2/38 reauthentication
```

MAC Authentication Bypass

MAC authentication bypass or MAC Auth Bypass is an 802.1X feature to control policies for NAC agentless hosts. MAC authentication bypass is configured on a per-port basis and currently is supported only on the Catalyst 6500 running CatOS. When this feature is enabled, the switch makes a RADIUS request to the Cisco Secure ACS server with the MAC address of the client machine that is attempting to connect to the network. If Cisco Secure ACS finds the MAC address of the client machine in its internal database, it sends an access-accept to the switch, and the host is allowed onto the network. This MAC authentication happens after NAC-L2-802.1X. It bypasses the default NAC-L2-802.1X security policy of denying access for all devices that cannot complete an EAP authentication.

TIP   You can use the MAC address OUI to wildcard and allow devices with MAC addresses within the same OUI range to access the network. This avoids an administrator having to enter each individual MAC address for devices such as printers or terminals that don't have an 802.1X supplicant and need to be allowed access to the network.

The Cisco Catalyst 6500 configuration for MAC authentication bypass consists of only a few commands. It must be enabled globally and then applied to a port. To enable MAC authentication bypass globally, use the **set mac-auth-bypass enable** command:

```
Console> (enable) set mac-auth-bypass enable
```

Then apply it to an specific port, as follows:

```
Console> (enable) set port mac-auth-bypass 2/3 enable
```

This enables MAC authentication bypass on port 2/3.

TIP   Refer to Chapter 8 for the configuration of Cisco Secure ACS for MAC authentication bypass.

Troubleshooting NAC-L2-802.1X

This section lists several **show** and **debug** commands useful for troubleshooting NAC-L2-802.1X problems.

The **show dot1x all** command displays a detailed table of authentication and posture information. This table includes information such as the following:

- Authentication state
- Current posture token
- Reauthentication information
- Timer settings
- VLAN information
- Maximum attempts

Example 4-9 shows sample output of the **show dot1x all** command.

Example 4-9 *Output of **show dot1x all** Command*

```
6503-A#show dot1x all
Dot1x Info for interface GigabitEthernet2/38
--------------------------------------------------
Supplicant MAC 000f.4321.1234
    AuthSM State       = AUTHENTICATED
    BendSM State       = IDLE
    Posture            = Healthy
    ReAuthPeriod       = 3600 Seconds (From Authentication Server)
    ReAuthAction       = Reauthenticate
    TimeToNextReauth   = 3590 Seconds
PortStatus             = AUTHORIZED
MaxReq                 = 2
MaxAuthReq             = 2
HostMode               = Single
PortControl            = Auto
QuietPeriod            = 60 Seconds
Re-authentication      = Enabled
ReAuthPeriod           = From Authentication Server
ServerTimeout          = 30 Seconds
SuppTimeout            = 30 Seconds
TxPeriod               = 30 Seconds
Guest-Vlan             = 216
AuthFail-Vlan          = 0
AuthFail-Max-Attempts  = 3
```

TIP

You can also display this information on a per-interface basis with the **show dot1x interface** *interface* command. For example, to display information about the host connected on port GigabitEthernet 0/1, use the **show dot1x interface GigabitEthernet 0/1** command.

You can also use **show dot1x interface** *interface* **detail** to display detailed information on a specific interface. In addition, you can use the **show dot1x interface** *interface* **statistics** command to provide 802.1X interface statistics.

Example 4-10 includes a summarized view of the output of the **show vlan** command after the end host on port GigabitEthernet 2/38 was successfully authenticated and its security posture was Healthy. VLAN 10 (Healthy_Employees) was assigned to interface GigabitEthernet 2/38.

Example 4-10 *Output of **show vlan** Command after Authentication and Posture*

```
6503-A#show vlan
VLAN Name                             Status    Ports
-----------------------------------------------------
1    default                          active    Gi3/2
10   Healthy_Employees                active    Gi2/38
```

Unlike NAC-L2-IP, on NAC-L2-802.1X, no logging is available. However, the 802.1X accounting features provide useful information when troubleshooting 802.1X authentication issues. To enable 802.1X accounting, use the following command:

```
aaa accounting dot1x default group radius
```

The following are some useful debug commands when troubleshooting 802.1X issues:

```
debug dot1x errors
debug dot1x events
debug dot1x packets
debug dot1x state-machine
```

NOTE   The output of the **debug dot1x packets** command can be very lengthy and can impact performance on busy switches.

Similar to NAC-L2-IP, the **debug radius** command can help you troubleshoot RADIUS negotiation issues on NAC-L2-802.1X.

Configuring NAC-L2-802.1X on Cisco Wireless Access Points

Wireless networks are being deployed more every day. The increased deployment of these networks has also increased the need to secure them. Several different security methods, such as WEP keys, have classically been used by companies that deploy wireless networks. However, these methods have not been enough. NAC-L2-802.1X not only provides the secure mechanisms to perform authentication and identity, but it also provides advanced admission-control features. This section includes the steps necessary to configure NAC-L2-802.1X on Cisco wireless access points.

Cisco's authentication scheme is based on the Extensible Authentication Protocol (EAP). Cisco Wireless provides mutual authentication, in part to guard against man-in-the-middle authentication attacks from rogue access points. The client device authenticates the network via a RADIUS server. The RADIUS server authenticates the client. The two sides of this authentication scheme are decoupled on separate secure channels, with the access point in the middle. Figure 4-5 illustrates this.

The following steps are illustrated in Figure 4-5:

1. The client machine initiates the wireless association process with the Wireless Access Point.

2. The access point blocks client requests for LAN access and establishes a tunnel using EAP-FAST.

Figure 4-5 *Summary of Wireless NAC-L2-802.1X*

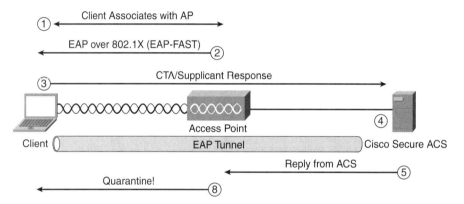

3. The user and machine credentials are sent from CTA and the wireless 802.1X supplicant.

4. Cisco Secure ACS processes the authentication request and also checks its NAC policies for admission control.

5. Cisco Secure ACS replies and sends RADIUS attributes to the wireless access point.

6. The wireless access point enforces security based on the security posture of the device. In this example, the client is quarantined because it didn't comply with the policies configured on Cisco Secure ACS.

The EAP protocol has a very detailed authentication process. Figure 4-6 illustrates the details of the EAP authentication sequence.

Now that you have learned the protocol details of EAP and NAC-L2-802.1X, it's time you learn how to configure the wireless access points. The configuration of NAC-L2-802.1X on Cisco wireless access points is basically the same as the traditional configuration for 802.1X. Follow these steps to configure NAC-L2-802.1X on the Cisco wireless access point:

1. Log in to the Cisco wireless access point via its web console.

2. Select **Security** from the navigation menu and click **Server Manager**. This section enables you to enter the authentication settings and to configure the RADIUS server information.

3. Configure the Cisco Secure ACS server information, identifying its IP address (10.10.20.181 in this example), as illustrated in Figure 4-7.

Figure 4-6   *Details of the EAP Authentication Sequence*

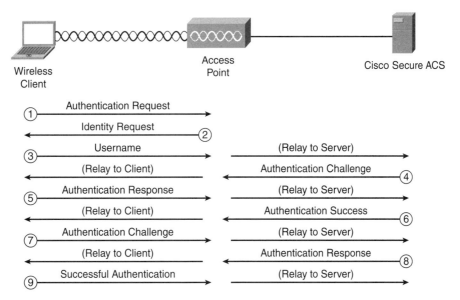

Figure 4-7 *Adding Cisco Secure ACS Information to the Cisco Wireless Access Point*

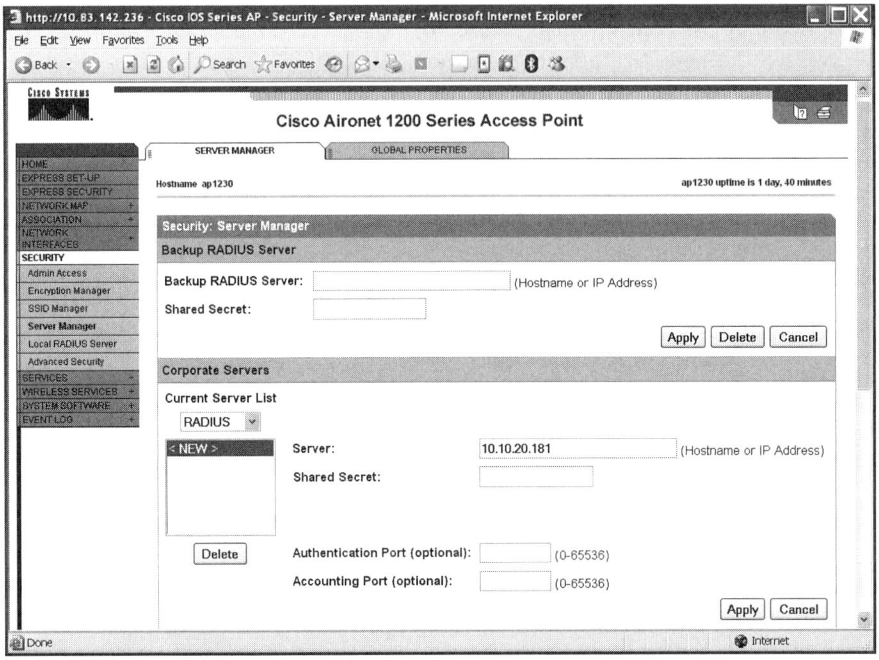

4. Enter a shared secret key between the Cisco wireless access point and the Cisco Secure ACS server.

   The shared secret on the Cisco wireless access point must match the shared secret on the Local/Backup server.

5. Click **Apply**.

6. Navigate to **Security > SSID Manager**.

7. Enter your SSID information and select **Network EAP**. SecureMe is entered as the SSID in this example in Figure 4-8.

   The SSID is the unique identifier that client devices use to associate with the wireless access point. The SSID can be any alphanumeric, case-sensitive entry from 2 to 32 characters.

8. Click **Apply**.

NOTE   Refer to Chapter 3, "Cisco Secure Services Client," for the configuration of the 802.1X supplicant, and Chapter 8 for the configuration of Cisco Secure ACS.

Figure 4-8 *Configuring the SSID Information on the Cisco Wireless Access Point*

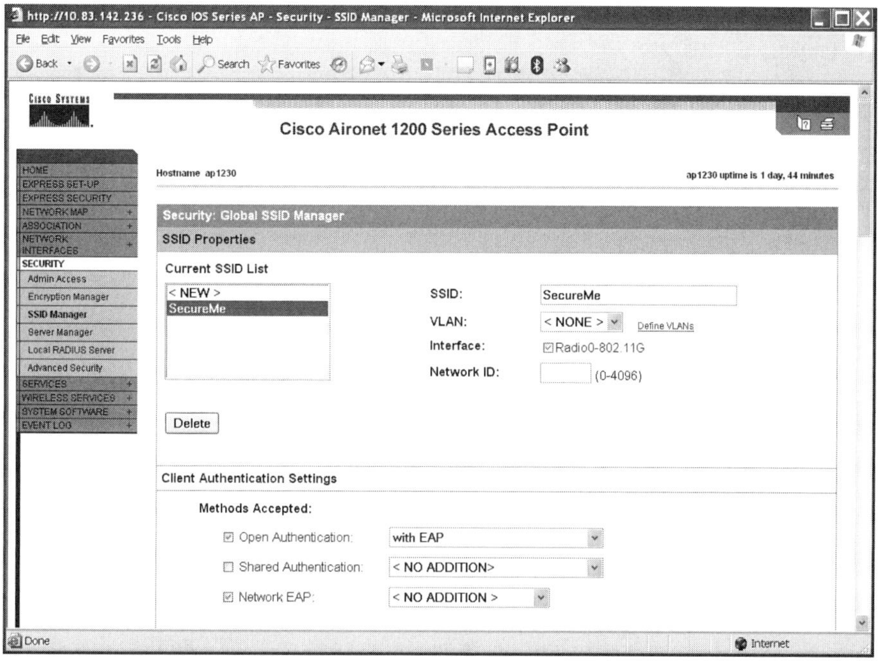

Summary

This chapter covered the configuration of NAC-L2-IP and NAC-L2-802.1X on the Cisco Catalyst switches. It provided a step-by-step guide on how to configure these NAC features on switches running Cisco IOS and Cisco CatOS. It also included useful **show** and **debug** commands, as well as several tips on how to troubleshoot NAC-L2-IP and NAC 802.1X problems on the Cisco Catalyst switches. This chapter described the methods used in wireless NAC-L2-802.1X. It also demonstrated how to configure NAC-L2-802.1X on Cisco wireless access points.

Review Questions

You can find the answers to the review questions in Appendix A, "Answers to Review Questions."

1. What command do you use to enable 802.1X globally on a switch running CatOS?

   a. **dot1x system-auth-control**

   b. **set dot1x system-auth-control**

   c. **dot1x enable**

   d. **set dot1x enable**

2. True or false: EAP-FAST Phase 0 is used very frequently to enable the client to be dynamically provisioned with a PAC. Phases 1 and 2 cannot complete without Phase 0.

3. True or false: VLAN assignment is the method used in NAC-L2-802.1X for policy enforcement.

4. True or false: The output of the **debug dot1x packets** command can be very lengthy and might impact performance on busy switches.

5. NAC nonresponsive hosts are often referred to as NAC agentless hosts (NAH). These are devices that do not or cannot run CTA. What command can you use to statically authorize a NAH though its IP address in a Catalyst switch running IOS?

   a. **set device authorize ip** *ip-address*

   b. **device authorize ip-address** *ip-address*

   c. **ip device authorize** *ip-address*

   d. **device ip authorize** *ip-address*

6. What command is used to enable EoU logging on a Catalyst switch running Cisco IOS?

   a. **eou logging enable**

   b. **set eou logging**

   c. **ip logging eou**

   d. **eou logging**

7. True or false: In NAC-L2-IP, the security posture process is triggered by an EAP-START.

8. True or false: You can configure only one RADIUS server on a Catalyst switch running CatOS.

9. True or false: The connection between CTA and a Catalyst switch running EoU is encrypted using IPSec.

10. True or false: By default, a Catalyst switch configured for NAC-L2-IP and running Cisco IOS will reauthenticate every 275 seconds.

This chapter covers the following topics:

- Architectural overview of NAC on Layer 3 devices
- Configuration steps of NAC on Layer 3 devices
- Monitoring and troubleshooting NAC on Layer 3 devices

## CHAPTER 5

Configuring Layer 3 NAC on Network Access Devices

The Layer 3 NAC solution ensures that posture validation is done before packets are allowed to pass through the Cisco IOS network-access devices (NADs). A number of Cisco IOS routers support this solution. This way, the NADs apply appropriate access restrictions when an end host tries to access network resources. These restrictions are based on the end hosts' state, such as the information about their antivirus software and their signature definitions. The Layer 3 NAC solution is useful in network deployments where

- You have Layer 2 devices but they do not support NAC.
- You want to implement NAC on a central routing device instead of enabling it on all the Layer 2 and wireless devices.
- You are using a site-to-site VPN tunnel to a partner and want to check the posture of your partner's machines before allowing access to your network.
- You have SSL- or IPSec-based remote-access VPN tunnels that NAC does not support.

This chapter discusses Layer 3 NAC implementation by providing an architectural overview of the solution and then step-by-step configuration examples.

NOTE   NAC Layer 3 support on Cisco IOS routers was introduced in the first phase of the NAC framework; NAC Layer 3 support on Cisco IOS—based Catalyst 6500 switches is currently planned.

Architectural Overview of NAC on Layer 3 Devices

The posture-validation process on a Layer 3 device starts when an end host requests access to the network. Figure 5-1 provides a complete flow of the posture-validation process on a Layer 3 NAD. A Cisco 3845 router is acting as the Layer 3 NAD to validate the end host's posture before allowing access to the corporate network. This assessment is checked against the policies defined on the Cisco Secure Access Control Server (Cisco Secure ACS).

Figure 5-1   *Layer 3 Posture-Validation Process for a Host*

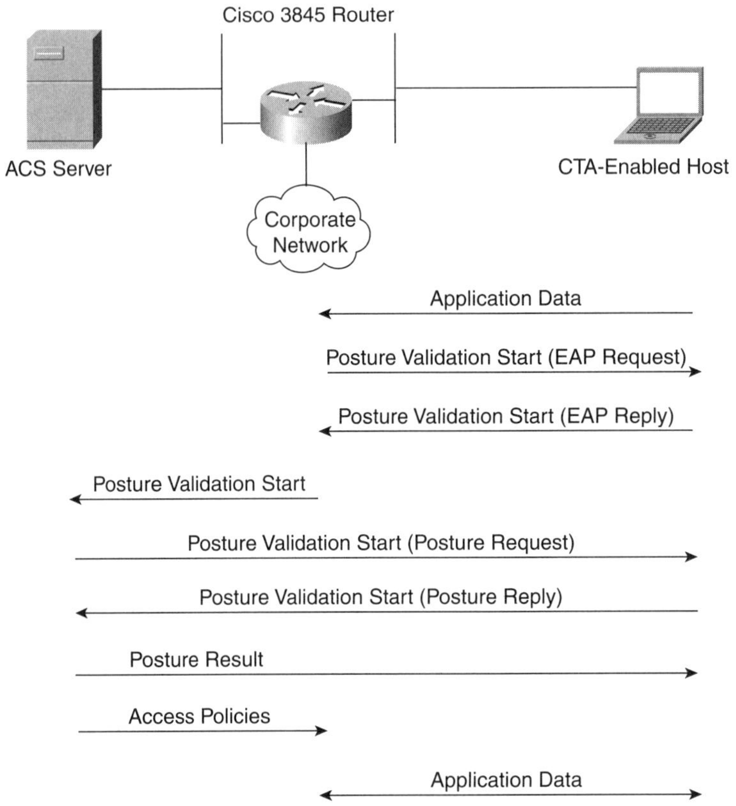

The end host, the Cisco IOS router, and the Cisco Secure ACS server go through the following process when a host tries to access the network:

1. The end host tries to access the network by sending traffic. The NAD identifies a new host when it sees a host's IP address that is not registered in its table.

2. The NAD checks its exception list to determine whether the device is exempt from the posture-validation process. If the reported device identity (IP address, MAC address, IP phone) is

   — In the exception list, the device is not subject to NAC verification. The NAD can optionally apply an access list (ACL) to restrict the traffic from these exempted hosts.

   — Not in the exception list, the host is subject to posture validation, and the NAC process continues.

3. The NAD creates an Extensible Authentication Protocol (EAP) session and applies a default access list until the host is fully validated. The NAD sends an Extensible Authentication Protocol over User Datagram Protocol (EAPoUDP) hello packet to the host. If an EAPoUDP hello response is

— Received, the NAD initiates the NAC posture validation process.

— Not received after a number of retries, the NAD assumes that it is an agentless or unresponsive host. The NAD skips to step 11 for further processing of the agentless hosts.

4. The NAD sends an EAP-identity request to the host. The host sends an EAP-identity response that is forwarded to the Cisco Secure ACS server as a part of the NAC access-request packet.

5. The Cisco Secure ACS server initiates a Protected Extensible Authentication Protocol (PEAP) session to establish a secure communication channel, to ensure integrity of the packets that follow.

6. The Cisco Secure ACS server requests posture information from the host. The NAD simply forwards this request to the host. The host responds with the requested posture information.

7. The Cisco Secure ACS server sends either an access-accept or accept-reject packet based on the assessment. If it is

— Access-accept, the Cisco Secure ACS server sends the NAC configuration and an ACL to be applied on the end machine.

— Access-reject, the Cisco Secure ACS server displays an error, and the NAD treats the host as an agentless host. The NAD skips to step 10 for further processing of the agentless hosts.

8. The Cisco Secure ACS server closes the PEAP session with the end host. The NAD starts the status query and revalidation timers.

9. The NAD sends a status query to the end host when it expires. If the response is

— Invalid or the host does not respond, the NAD initiates a full revalidation of the host machine by going back to step 4.

— Valid, and the validation flag is not set, the NAC processing enters into the idle state.

— Valid, and the validation flag is set, the NAD initiates a full revalidation of the host machine by going back to step 4.

10. The NAD discards the EAPoUDP association when the revalidation timer expires. In this case, it goes back to step 3.

11. The NAD starts a hold-off timer if the end host is agentless or if it does not respond to EAPoUDP communication. In this state, the NAD ceases the EAPoUDP and other NAC-related activities until the hold-off timer expires. When it expires, the NAD initiates a full revalidation and goes back to step 3.

12. If the end host does not respond to an EAPoUDP hello message, it is deemed to be agentless. The NAD requests agentless (clientless) policies from the Cisco Secure ACS server by forwarding the clientless user credentials.

NOTE For clientless hosts, you can use an audit server to determine the current state of the machine. Consult Chapter 11, "Audit Servers," for more information.

Configuration Steps of NAC on Layer 3 Devices

Figure 5-2 illustrates a network topology in which a Cisco IOS 3845 router is acting as a NAD. Two Cisco Secure ACS servers are connected to the GigabitEthernet0/0 interface. These servers are used for EAPoUDP sessions and posture validation. On the GigabitEthernet0/1 interface, two end machines are connected. One is running the Cisco Trust Agent (CTA); the other acts as an agentless machine.

Figure 5-2 *Network Topology for Layer 3 NAC*

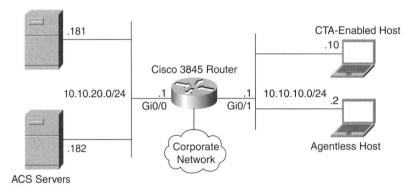

The implementation of NAC on a Layer 3 device can be divided into the following eight steps:

Step 1 Configure Authentication, Authorization, and Accounting (AAA) authentication.

Step 2 Define a Remote Authentication Dial-In User Service (RADIUS) server.

Step 3   Specify the interface Access Control List (ACL).

Step 4   Configure the NAC parameters.

Step 5   (Optional) Define the NAC intercept (ACL).

Step 6   (Optional) Set up the exception policies.

Step 7   (Optional) Configure the clientless host parameters.

Step 8   (Optional) Optimize the NAC parameters.

NOTE   You need Cisco IOS Release 12.3(8)T or higher to enable NAC on Cisco routers.

Step 1: Configuring AAA Authentication

The first step in configuring NAC on a Layer 3 Cisco IOS device is to enable AAA for posture validation. The NAC framework uses an external RADIUS server to validate the posture presented by the end hosts. Consequently, it is mandatory that the Cisco IOS NAD be set up to pass EAPoUDP sessions to the RADIUS server.

A Cisco IOS NAD device can be set up for AAA by using the **aaa new-model** command, if it is not already configured to do so. This command enables the AAA process globally on a Cisco IOS device. Use the **aaa authentication eou** command to enable EAPoUDP processing by the AAA process. This command ensures that the Cisco IOS NAD requests the appropriate posture information from the end hosts and forwards them to the RADIUS server for authentication and verification. In Example 5-1, a Cisco IOS router is set up for the AAA process. It is then configured to process the EAPoUDP packets with the **aaa authentication eou default group radius** command. The **default group radius** option instructs the Cisco IOS NAD to send all EAPoUDP queries to a RADIUS server, defined in the next step.

Example 5-1   *AAA Configuration for Cisco IOS NAD*

```
IOS-NAD# configure terminal
IOS-NAD(config)# aaa new-model
IOS-NAD(config)# aaa authentication eou default group radius
IOS-NAD(config)# aaa accounting network default start-stop group radius
```

You can optionally enable **aaa accounting network** if you want the Cisco IOS NAD to send an accounting record for each EAPoUDP session. In Example 5-1, the Cisco IOS NAD is set up to send an accounting record to the RADIUS server after it creates an EAPoUDP session and to send another accounting record when it tears down that session.

NOTE	If the **aaa new-model** command is not configured, you will not see any AAA commands in the Cisco IOS command syntax.

NOTE	Using NAC with authentication proxy (Auth-Proxy) is fully supported. In this case, the Cisco IOS NAD subjects the received traffic to the Auth-proxy process first, followed by the NAC process. The ACLs for auth-proxy get overwritten by the ACLs that NAC downloads after posture validation.

Step 2: Defining the RADIUS Server

After the IOS NAD is set up for the AAA process, the next step is to define a list of the RADIUS servers. The Cisco IOS NAD checks their availability on a round-robin basis. If the first server is not reachable, it tries the second server, and so on. It is highly recommended that you set up more than one RADIUS server, in case the first server is not reachable. A RADIUS server entry can be defined by using the **radius-server host** command followed by the IP address of the RADIUS server. You can optionally provide the following information for each of the RADIUS servers:

- **Authentication and authorization port**—If no default port is specified, the Cisco IOS NAD uses UDP port 1645 to send the authentication and authorization requests. The authentication port can be defined by using the auth-port keyword followed by the new port number.

- **Accounting port**—If no default port is specified, the Cisco IOS NAD uses UDP port 1646 to send the accounting records. The accounting port can be defined by using the acct-port keyword followed by the new port number.

- **Shared secret**—If all your RADIUS servers are configured to use the same shared secret, you can define a global key. You can use the **radius-server key** command followed by the actual shared secret. The Cisco IOS NAD authenticates itself to the RADIUS server by using a preconfigured shared secret. For security reasons, this shared secret is never sent over the network.

NOTE	User passwords are sent as encrypted messages from the Cisco IOS NAD to the RADIUS server. This is useful to protect this critical information from an intruder. The Cisco IOS NAD hashes the password using the shared secret that is defined on the NAD and the RADIUS server.

As shown in Example 5-2, a Cisco IOS NAD is configured for two RADIUS servers located at 10.10.20.181 and 10.10.20.182. Because both servers use the same shared secret, the administrator has defined a global key of cisco123. It is a best practice to encrypt the specified shared secret by using the **service password-encryption** command. This way, an intruder will not be able to get this key even if he gets access to the NAD's configuration.

Example 5-2 *Configuration of RADIUS Servers*

```
IOS-NAD# configure terminal
IOS-NAD(config)# service password-encryption
IOS-NAD(config)# radius-server host 10.10.20.181
IOS-NAD(config)# radius-server host 10.10.20.182
IOS-NAD(config)# radius-server key cisco123
IOS-NAD(config)# ip radius source-interface loopback0
```

If the Cisco IOS NAD can reach the RADIUS server through multiple interfaces, it is highly recommended that you use the **ip radius source-interface** command to send and receive the RADIUS traffic on a particular interface. In Example 5-2, a loopback0 interface is configured as the source interface for the RADIUS packets.

TIP   It is a best practice to use a loopback interface to source the RADIUS packets from the NAD to the RADIUS server. This is because a loopback interface is always up, and the source IP address in the RADIUS packets will be the same, regardless of the egress interface from the router.

Step 3: Specifying the Interface Access Control List

The next step is to define an ACL that limits the inside hosts' capability to send traffic until the RADIUS server validates their posture. In other words, this ACL defines exception rules for the traffic that needs to skip posture validation. This ACL is applied to the interface facing the end hosts. In Figure 5-2, the end hosts (client machines) reside on the inside interface of GigabitEthernet0/1. It is recommended that this ACL allows only EAPoUDP packets that are destined to the router on UDP port 21862. You can optionally allow other traffic such as Dynamic Host Configuration Protocol (DHCP) and Domain Name System (DNS) if those servers reside on different subnets. In Example 5-3, an ACL called intf-ACL is configured to allow UDP port 21862 to access the router's inside interface IP address of 10.10.10.1. The ACL is then applied on the interface facing the end-host network as an inbound list.

Example 5-3 *Configuration of Interface ACL*

```
IOS-NAD# configure terminal
IOS-NAD(config)# ip access-list extended intf-ACL
IOS-NAD(config-ext-nacl)# permit udp any host 10.10.10.1 eq 21862
IOS-NAD(config-ext-nacl)# exit
IOS-NAD(config)# interface GigabitEthernet0/1
IOS-NAD(config-if)# ip access-group intf-ACL in
```

NOTE	An implicit deny (as in **deny ip any any**) is at the end of every ACL on Cisco IOS NADs.

If you have agentless hosts or other network devices such as IP phones, printers, switches, and routers, you can configure their IP addresses in this list. However, it is recommended that you specify those networking devices in the exception list, discussed in step 6.

Step 4: Configuring the NAC Parameters

After specifying the interface ACL, the next step is to set up the NAC parameters. In this step, you configure a global rule that enables the EAPoUDP posture-validation process. This global policy is then applied to the interface facing the end hosts. Use the **ip admission name** command followed by a policy name to set up this policy. In Example 5-4, a NAC global policy called IOS-NAC is set up for the EAPoUDP posturing process. This policy is applied to the GigabitEthernet0/1 interface by using the **ip admission IOS-NAC** command under interface subconfiguration mode.

Example 5-4 *Configuration of NAC Parameters*

```
IOS-NAD# configure terminal
IOS-NAD(config)# ip admission name IOS-NAC eapoudp
IOS-NAD(config)# interface GigabitEthernet0/1
IOS-NAD(config-if)# ip admission IOS-NAC
```

NOTE	You can optionally define an ACL that lists the networks that are subject to the posture-assessment process. This is discussed in the next step.

NOTE	Use the **eou allow ip-station-id** command to use an end machine's IP address as the Calling-Station-Id. Otherwise, the IOS NAD uses the MAC address of the host machine. `IOS-NAD(config)# eou allow station-ip-address`

Step 5: Defining the NAC Intercept Access Control List (Optional)

If you would rather include a few networks (or hosts) to go through the posture-validation process, you can define those interesting entities in an ACL. You can then map the ACL to the **ip admission name** command. This way, the Cisco IOS NAD subjects to the posture process only the entities that are defined in the mapped ACL. Example 5-5 shows the

configuration of a Cisco IOS NAD that is validating hosts on 10.10.10.0. Other networks
behind the NAC-enabled interface are not checked for NAC.

Example 5-5 *Configuration of NAC Intercept ACL*

```
IOS-NAD# configure terminal
IOS-NAD(config)# ip access-list extended NAC-ACL
IOS-NAD(config-ext-nacl)# permit ip 10.10.10.0 0.0.0.255 any
IOS-NAD(config-ext-nacl)# exit
IOS-NAD(config)# ip admission name IOS-NAC eapoudp list NAC-ACL
```

Step 6: Setting Up the Exception Policies (Optional)

If you are not using an audit server in your environment, you must install the CTA
application in all your networking devices. However, in many instances installing CTA is
not possible on all devices. As discussed in Chapter 2, "Cisco Trust Agent," CTA is
currently available for the Windows, Linux, and Macintosh platforms. Therefore, if you
have other operating systems or network printers, you need to exempt them so that they are
not subject to the posture-validation process. You can except these devices based on the
following three attributes:

- IP address
- MAC address
- Type

If you assign static IP addresses to the non-CTA-enabled devices, you can define their IP
addresses in the exception rules. When the Cisco IOS NAD receives a packet from the IP
address specified in the exception rule, the Cisco IOS NAD does not challenge the host for
the posture-validation process. Using an IP address in the exception list can contradict your
security polices because an inside intruder can try to bypass the posture-validation process
by spoofing the address.

The other option is to define an exception list consisting of the MAC addresses of the
devices to be exempt from this process. This option is useful if you use a DHCP server to
allocate IP addresses in your organization. You can specify the MAC addresses of your non-
CTA-supported devices in this exception list even if they receive dynamic IP addresses.

The third option is to specify the type of device you are using in your network. Currently,
Cisco IP phones are the only valid device type.

The exempt devices are added in the list by using the **identity profile eapoudp** command.
Issuing this command places you into identity profile subconfiguration mode. All the
exempt devices can be specified by using the **device authorize** command followed by one

of the three options discussed previously. In Example 5-6, a device with a MAC address of 0011.2582.399d is allowed to exempt the posture process.

Example 5-6 *Configuration of Exemption List*

```
IOS-NAD# configure terminal
IOS-NAD(config)# identity profile eapoudp
IOS-NAD(config-identity-prof)# device authorize mac-address 0011.2582.399d
```

The Cisco IOS NAD also enables you to map a policy to the exempted devices to further define their network-access attributes. For example, you can limit the exempted devices to access only the allowed hosts on the network. You can create this policy by using the **identity policy** command followed by the policy name. You then are placed in identity-policy subconfiguration mode, where you can apply an ACL to limit network access. As shown in Example 5-7, an extended ACL called Policy-ACL is created that permits traffic from the 10.10.10.0 subnet to a host located at 10.10.20.50. This ACL is mapped to an identity policy called Exempt-Devices by using the **access-group Policy-ACL** command. Finally, this policy is linked to the exemption rules by using the **device authorize** command.

NOTE   In a large enterprise network, it is a best practice to use centralized exemptions using Cisco Secure ACS. Consult Chapter 8, "Cisco Secure Access Control Server," for more information about central device exemption.

Example 5-7 *Configuration of Exemption List*

```
IOS-NAD# configure terminal
IOS-NAD(config)# ip access-list extended Policy-ACL
IOS-NAD(config-ext-nacl)# permit ip 10.10.10.0 0.0.0.255 host 10.10.20.50
IOS-NAD(config)# identity policy Exempt-Devices
IOS-NAD(config-identity-policy)# access-group Policy-ACL
IOS-NAD(config)# identity profile eapoudp
IOS-NAD(config-identity-prof)# device authorize mac-address 0011.2582.399d policy
  Exempt-Devices
```

NOTE   The ACL mapped to the exempt devices must be a named ACL, not a numbered ACL.

The NAC feature of the Cisco IOS NAD also provides protection against infected devices that are exempted. You can set appropriate policies to redirect unallowed traffic to an internal web page. For example, if an infected machine tries to browse the Internet, you can redirect the connection so that the user on the infected machine is instructed to load the appropriate software before granting access to the requested hosts. In Example 5-8, a redirect URL of internal.securemeinc.com is specified under the identity policy called Exempt-Devices.

Example 5-8 *Configuration of Exemption List*

```
IOS-NAD(config)# identity policy Exempt-Devices
IOS-NAD(config-identity-policy)# access-group Policy-ACL
IOS-NAD(config-identity-policy)# redirect url http://internal.securemeinc.com
```

NOTE   Cisco Secure ACS can instruct the Cisco IOS NAD to apply a redirect ACL to the user sessions. The ACL defined on Cisco Secure ACS for URL redirect must have an identical name because it is case sensitive.

Cisco Secure ACS RADIUS attributes:

- url-redirect=http://IP-Address-Of-Remediation-Server

- url-redirect-acl=quarantine_url_redir_acl

Cisco IOS NAD configuration:

```
IOS-NAD(config)# ip access-list extended quarantine_url_redir_acl
IOS-NAD(config-ext-nacl)# permit tcp any 10.0.0.0 0.0.0.255 eq www
```

Step 7: Configuring the Clientless Host Parameters (Optional)

If you own a relatively large network, adding all non-CTA-enabled devices in the exception list can be a cumbersome task. Alternatively, you can enable the clientless authentication feature for the hosts that do not respond to the EAPoUDP packets. This way, the unresponsive hosts are treated as clientless, and the Cisco IOS NAD sends the preconfigured authentication credentials for the RADIUS server. If authenticated successfully, the RADIUS server returns appropriate attributes such as an ACL that will be enforced on those machines. It is recommended that clientless machines such as guests' and contractors' end hosts not be given access to the trusted network of the company. Therefore, the RADIUS server can send a downloadable ACL to be applied to the clientless machines. In Example 5-9, a clientless user named clientless is set up with a password of cisco123cisco. The **eou allow clientless** command initiates the clientless machine authentication for the unresponsive hosts. This command requires that you set up a user account on the Cisco Secure ACS server with the same username and the password, and specify the appropriate restrictions on it.

Example 5-9 *Configuration of Clientless Host Credentials*

```
IOS-NAD(config)# eou clientless username clientless
IOS-NAD(config)# eou clientless password cisco123cisco
IOS-NAD(config)# eou allow clientless
```

If the clientless authentication parameters do not match the configuration on Cisco Secure ACS, an authentication failure occurs. This causes the unresponsive hosts to be unsuccessful if they try to access the network.

NOTE   The Cisco IOS router running the 12.4(6)T or higher version of the code does not use clientless user authentication. The **eou clientless username** and **eou clientless password** commands have been deprecated. To have the clientless functionality on the IOS NAD devices running the 12.4(6)T or higher version of code, follow these steps:

1. Enable the **eou allow clientless** and **eou allow ip-station-id** commands in the Cisco IOS router.

2. Configure the Cisco Secure ACS server to use an external audit server for posture validation. Please consult Chapter 11, "Audit Servers,"for the configuration steps.

Step 8: Optimizing the NAC Parameters (Optional)

The Cisco IOS NAD supports five EAPoUDP timeouts when a machine goes through the posture-validation process:

- **Status query timeout**—This timeout ensures that the Cisco IOS NAD periodically checks the posture state of the CTA-enabled host, in case it has changed from the last time. The default status query timer is 300 seconds. In Example 5-10, the status query timer is changed to 600 seconds, which is recommended if the number of concurrent sessions is high. If this value is set too low, the Cisco IOS NAD will use a lot of system resources in sending status queries to the agents.

- **Revalidation timeout**—This timeout initiates a complete posture-validation process on the CTA-enabled host. The default timer is set to 36,000 seconds (10 hours). You can lower this timer to 5 hours, as shown in Example 5-10, if your organization requires you to revalidate the hosts more often. This is helpful when new antivirus patches are continuously updated on the servers and you want the end machines to update them as soon as they go through a new posture validation.

- **Hold period timeout**—This timeout instructs the Cisco IOS NAD to initiate the posture-validation process if the host fails the EAPoUDP association in the previous attempt or if the Cisco Secure ACS server fails the authentication. In Example 5-10, the hold period timeout is changed from its default value of 180 seconds to 300 seconds. The hold period timeout varies between 60 and 86,400 seconds.

- **Retransmission timeout**—The retransmission timeout indicates how long the Cisco IOS NAD waits if it fails to receive a reply from the end host. The default is 3 seconds, and it varies from 1 to 60 seconds. This timeout must be greater than the expected round-trip delays. If you have a slow network in which the round-trip delay might take more than 3 seconds, you should change it to a higher value, such as 10 seconds, as shown in Example 5-10.

- **AAA timeout**—The default is 60 seconds; it varies from 1 to 60 seconds.

Example 5-10 *Changing the NAC Timeouts on Cisco IOS NAD*

```
IOS-NAD(config)# eou timeout status-query 600
IOS-NAD(config)# eou timeout revalidation 18000
IOS-NAD(config)# eou timeout hold-period 300
IOS-NAD(config)# eou timeout retransmit 10
```

NOTE   If the Cisco Secure ACS server is also set up to specify the status query and revalidation timeouts, the Cisco IOS NAD prefers the received timeouts from the Cisco Secure ACS server over the statically configured global timeouts in Cisco IOS.

In addition to the previously discussed NAC timeouts, you can modify the following NAC EAPoUDP parameters:

- **EAPoUDP port**—If you have a requirement to use an EAPoUDP port different than 21862, you can achieve that by using the **eou port** command. It is recommended that you not change this port, if possible. In Example 5-11, the EAPoUDP port has been changed to port 21800.

- **EAPoUDP max-retry**—The Cisco IOS NAD sends a retransmission EAPoUDP packet if it does not receive a response from a host. By default, it retransmits the EAPoUDP packet three times before declaring the host as agentless. If you would rather have the Cisco IOS NAD retransmit only two times, you can use the **eou max-retry 2** command, as shown in Example 5-11.

- **EAPoUDP revalidation**—In Cisco IOS NAD, the revalidation process for the CTA-enabled hosts is enabled by default. If you do not want the existing EAPoUDP connections to go through the revalidation process, you can use the **no eou revalidate** command, as shown in Example 5-11.

- **EAPoUDP rate-limit**—You can set the Cisco IOS NAD to rate-limit the number of simultaneous posture validations for EAPoUDP. This way, if your Cisco IOS NAD gets overwhelmed with the number of simultaneous EAPoUDP requests, it will not run out of memory or CPU cycles. (This can occur if the entire building has a power outage and all clients boot and attempt to access the network at the exact same time.) Use the **eou rate-limit** command in global configuration mode to set the limit. In Example 5-11, the simultaneous number of EAPoUDP sessions has been limited to 100. If the 101st client tries to connect, the Cisco IOS NAD will not proceed with the posture-validation process until it is finished with one of the older sessions.

If you want to configure the Cisco IOS NAD to the default values of EAPoUDP, use the **eou default** command.

Example 5-11 *Changing the EOU Parameters on Cisco IOS NAD*

```
IOS-NAD(config)# eou port 21800
IOS-NAD(config)# eou max-retry 2
IOS-NAD(config)# no eou revalidate
IOS-NAD(config)# eou rate-limit 100
```

Monitoring and Troubleshooting NAC on Layer 3 Devices

This section provides several tips on how to troubleshoot NAC Layer 3 issues. It includes the most useful **show** commands, debugs, and log messages that will help you troubleshoot any unexpected problems and monitor the NAC solution.

Useful Monitoring Commands

Several **show** commands help monitor and report the state of NAC Layer 3 IP connections. The **show eou all** command is one of the most commonly used because it displays a table that summarizes all current NAC sessions. As shown in Example 5-12, the first entry indicates a clientless host that resides at 10.10.10.2. It was authenticated 3 minutes earlier, and the posture token is not known. The second entry indicates a static host that resides at 10.10.10.5 IP address. The last entry indicates a CTA-enabled host whose posture-assessment result is Healthy.

Example 5-12 *Output of show eou all*

```
IOS-NAD# show eou all
Address         Interface       AuthType    Posture-Token Age(min)
10.10.10.2      GigabitEthernet CLIENTLESS  -------       3
10.10.10.5      GigabitEthernet STATIC      -------       0
10.10.10.10     GigabitEthernet EAP         Healthy       15
```

If you would rather get detailed information about a particular EAPoUDP session, you can use the **show eou ip** command followed by the IP address of the host you are interested in. Example 5-13 shows the output of the **show eou ip** command to see detailed connection information about 10.10.10.10. The host resides out the GigabitEthernet0/1 interface of the router and has been given a Healthy posture token. Cisco Secure ACS is pushing a corresponding ACL called #ACSACL#-IP-healthy-42c46e7c to the Cisco IOS NAD that is applied to this host.

Example 5-13 *Displaying EOU Session Details for a Specific IP Address*

```
6503-A# show eou ip 10.10.10.10
Address               : 10.10.10.10
Interface             : GigabitEthernet0/1
AuthType              : EAP
PostureToken          : Healthy
Age(min)              : 15
URL Redirect          : NO URL REDIRECT
ACL Name              : #ACSACL#-IP-healthy-42c46e7c
User Name             : PCT00:User1
Revalidation Period : 18000 Seconds
Status Query Period : 600 Seconds
```

You can view the global EAPoUDP parameters on Cisco IOS by using the **show eou** command, as shown in Example 5-14. It displays the EAPoUDP port that the Cisco IOS NAD uses, along with all the EAPoUDP timers. It also shows the clientless authentication parameters, if configured.

Example 5-14 *Displaying Global EOU Parameters*

```
IOS-NAD# show eou
Global EAPoUDP Configuration
----------------------------
EAPoUDP Version      = 1
EAPoUDP Port         = 0x5566
Clientless Hosts     = Enabled
IP Station ID        = Enabled
Revalidation         = Disabled
Revalidation Period = 18000 Seconds
ReTransmit Period    = 10 Seconds
StatusQuery Period   = 600 Seconds
Hold Period          = 300 Seconds
AAA Timeout          = 60 Seconds
Max Retries          = 3
EAP Rate Limit       = 20
EAPoUDP Logging      = Enabled
Clientless Host Username = clientless
Clientless Host Password = cisco123

Interface Specific EAPoUDP Configurations
-----------------------------------------
Interface GigabitEthernet0/1
  No interface specific configuration
```

Troubleshooting NAC

If the inside hosts are not going through the posture-validation process or they are having difficulties accessing the network resources, make sure that you have the proper debugs and logging turned on. To troubleshoot a NAC issue, start by enabling EAPoUDP logging by using the **eou logging** command, as shown in Example 5-15. This command shows information about EAPoUDP for the new and existing sessions. In Example 5-15, a new host is detected on the GigabitEthernet0/1 interface with an IP address of 10.10.10.10. The Cisco IOS NAD initiates the EAPoUDP process and authorizes the host. The host has CTA installed, as detected by the Cisco IOS NAD.

Example 5-15   *Enabling EOU Logging*

```
IOS-NAD# configure terminal
IOS-NAD(config)# eou logging
*Feb  1 00:48:22.511: %EOU-6-SESSION: IP=10.10.10.10 | HOST=DETECTED |
 Interface=GigabitEthernet0/1
*Feb  1 00:48:22.515: %EOU-6-CTA: IP=10.10.10.10 | CiscoTrustAgent=DETECTED
*Feb  1 00:48:22.531: %EOU-6-POLICY: IP=10.10.10.10 | HOSTNAME=
*Feb  1 00:48:22.531: %EOU-6-POSTURE: IP=10.10.10.10 | HOST=AUTHORIZE D| Interface=
 GigabitEthernet0/1
*Feb  1 00:48:22.531: %EOU-6-AUTHTYPE: IP=10.10.10.10 | AuthType=EAP
```

By enabling the previous command, you can send the information to a syslog server or an event-correlation system, such as CS-MARS.

NOTE   Chapter 17, "Monitoring the NAC Solution Using the Cisco Security Monitoring, Analysis, and Response System," covers monitoring the NAC solution using CS-MARS.

If the EOU logging does not give you enough information about a NAC session, you can enable the EAPoUDP debugs using the **debug eou all** command, as shown in Example 5-16. When a host tries to access the network through the Cisco IOS NAD, the Cisco IOS NAD initiates the EAPoUDP process, as shaded in the first debug entry. It creates the EAPoUDP session and sends an EAPoUDP hello to the host. If the CTA service is active on the client, it responds to the hello packet. The Cisco IOS NAD contacts the Cisco Secure ACS server to determine the posture state of the client. In this example, the Cisco Secure ACS server returns a failed attribute to the Cisco IOS NAD. View the logs on the Cisco Secure ACS server to determine why it failed the session for this host.

Example 5-16   *Output of **debug eou all***

```
IOS-NAD# debug eou all
*Feb  1 01:02:51.983: eou-obj_create:EOU Init Validation for idb= GigabitEthernet0/
 1 src_mac= 0011.2582.399d src_ip= 10.10.10.10
*Feb  1 01:02:51.987: eou-ev:32.98.114.105: msg = 33(eventEouCreateSession)
```

Example 5-16   *Output of **debug eou all**   (Continued)*

```
*Feb  1 01:02:51.987: eou_auth 10.10.10.10: initial state eou_initialize has enter
*Feb  1 01:02:51.987: eou-obj_create:10.10.10.10: EAPoUDP Session Created
*Feb  1 01:02:51.987: eou-obj_link:10.10.10.10: EAPoUDP Session added to Hash table
*Feb  1 01:02:51.987: %EOU-6-SESSION: IP=10.10.10.10¦ HOST=DETECTED¦
 Interface=GigabitEthernet0/1
*Feb  1 01:02:51.987:     eou_auth 10.10.10.10: during state eou_initialize, got
 event 1(eouCheckProfile)
*Feb  1 01:02:51.987: @@@ eou_auth 10.10.10.10: eou_initialize -> eou_initialize
*Feb  1 01:02:51.987: eou-ev:10.10.10.10: msg = 3(eventEouStartHello)
*Feb  1 01:02:51.987:     eou_auth 10.10.10.10: during state eou_initialize, got
 event 3(eouStartHello)
*Feb  1 01:02:51.987: @@@ eou_auth 10.10.10.10: eou_initialize -> eou_hello
*Feb  1 01:02:51.987: eou-ev:Starting Retransmit timer 10(10.10.10.10)
*Feb  1 01:02:51.987: eou-ev:eou_send_hello_request: Send Hello Request host=
10.10.10.1 eou_port= 5566 (hex)
<output omitted>
*Feb  1 01:02:51.987:     eou_auth 10.10.10.10: during state eou_hello, got event
 5(eouHelloResponse)
*Feb  1 01:02:51.987: @@@ eou_auth 10.10.10.10: eou_hello -> eou_client
*Feb  1 01:02:51.987: %EOU-6-CTA: IP=10.10.10.10¦ CiscoTrustAgent=DETECTED
*Feb  1 01:02:51.987: eou-ev:10.10.10.10: msg = 21(eventEouEapStart)
*Feb  1 01:02:51.987:     eou_auth 10.10.10.10: during state eou_client, got even
t 12(eouEapStart)
<output omitted>
*Feb  1 01:02:52.019: @@@ eou_auth 10.10.10.10: eou_client -> eou_server
*Feb  1 01:02:52.019: eou-ev:Starting AAA timer 60(10.10.10.10)
*Feb  1 01:02:52.027: %EOU-6-POLICY: IP=10.10.10.10¦ HOSTNAME=
*Feb  1 01:02:52.027: %EOU-6-POSTURE: IP=10.10.10.10¦ HOST=AUTHORIZED | Interface=
 GigabitEthernet0/1
*Feb  1 01:02:52.027:     eou_auth 10.10.10.10: during state eou_server, got even
t 16(eouEapFail)
*Feb  1 01:02:52.027: @@@ eou_auth 10.10.10.10: eou_server -> eou_fail
IOS-NAD# undebug all
```

WARNING   Enabling **debug eou all** on a production router is not recommended because it can overwhelm your Cisco IOS NAD with the debug output. You can try to schedule a maintenance window if you need to enable this debug for detailed troubleshooting.

Summary

The NAC implementation on the Cisco IOS NAD provides a complete solution to check the posture state of an internal host. If the posture is not validated, the Cisco IOS NAD applies appropriate ACLs to filter traffic. This chapter discussed the packet flow in a Cisco IOS NAD when NAC is enabled and then provided detailed configuration steps. This chapter provided guidance on how to monitor the NAC sessions. For troubleshooting purposes, this chapter discussed various debug and log messages to help you isolate the issues related the NAC sessions.

Review Questions

You can find the answers to the review questions in Appendix A, "Answers to Review Questions."

1. You can exempt devices from the posture-validation process by using the following attributes: (Multiple answers)

   a. IP address

   b. MAC address

   c. Operating system

   d. Type

2. True or false: The Cisco IOS NAD does not allow you to use an audit server for determining the current state of clientless machines.

3. True or false: The **radius-server key cisco123** command encrypts the shared secret defined on Cisco IOS NAD.

4. The Cisco IOS NAD supports the following EAPoUDP timeouts when a machine goes through the posture-validation process: (Multiple answers)

   a. AAA timeout

   b. NAD timeout

   c. Retransmission timeout

   d. Max-retry timeout

5. True or false: In the hold-off state, the NAD ceases the EAPoUDP and other NAC-related activities until the hold-off timer expires.

6. The purpose of a NAC Intercept Access Control List is to

   a. Define the interesting hosts and networks that are bypassed from the posture-validation process.

   b. Define the interesting hosts and networks that are subject to the posture-validation process.

   c. Define the interesting hosts and networks that are considered clientless hosts and networks.

   d. Define the interesting hosts and networks that are allowed to pass traffic even if they are infected.

This chapter covers the following topics:

- Architectural overview of NAC on Cisco VPN 3000 concentrators
- Configuration steps of NAC on Cisco VPN 3000 concentrators
- Testing, monitoring, and troubleshooting NAC on Cisco VPN 3000 concentrators

## CHAPTER 6

Configuring NAC on Cisco VPN 3000 Series Concentrators

The Cisco VPN 3000 series concentrators provide a scalable, reliable, and flexible solution for the site-to-site as well as remote-access VPN tunnels. In the site-to-site IPSec tunnel, network professionals can reduce the high maintenance cost of point-to-point WAN links by connecting branch offices to the corporate network resources. The remote-access VPN tunnels provide a way to connect home and mobile users to the corporate network by leveraging dialup, wireless hotspots, digital subscriber line (DSL), and cable-modem connections.

This chapter focuses on Network Admission Control (NAC) implementation on the VPN 3000 concentrators by providing an architectural overview of the solution and step-by-step configuration examples.

Architectural Overview of NAC on Cisco VPN 3000 Concentrators

The current implementation of NAC provides posture validation (PV) to the remote-access VPN connections, including Cisco remote-access IPSec tunnels and Layer 2 Tunneling Protocol (L2TP) over IPSec tunnels. The PV ensures that VPN clients run the latest patches and antivirus signature files, the most recent personal firewall rules, and updated host-based intrusion-prevention system (HIPS) rules and software.

The Cisco VPN 3000 concentrator, as your remote-access solution, allows mobile and home users to establish a VPN tunnel by using any of the following clients:

- Cisco software clients
- Microsoft L2TP over IPSec clients
- Cisco Secure Sockets Layer (SSL) clients

NOTE   The VPN 3000 concentrator currently does not support SSL-based clients for posture assessment.

Cisco Software Clients

The Cisco VPN client uses aggressive mode if preshared keys are used and uses main mode when public key infrastructure (PKI) is used during Phase 1 of the tunnel negotiations. After bringing up the Internet Security Association and Key Management Protocol Security Association (ISAKMP SA) for secure communication, the Cisco VPN 3000 concentrator prompts the user to specify the user credentials. In this phase, also known as *X-Auth* or extended authentication, the VPN 3000 concentrator validates the user against the configured authentication database. If the user authentication is successful, the Cisco concentrator sends a successful authentication message back to the client. After X-Auth, the Cisco VPN client requests configuration parameters such as the assigned IP address, the Domain Name System (DNS) server's IP address, and the Windows Internet Naming Service (WINS) server's IP address. During this phase, known as *mode-config*, the VPN 3000 concentrator sends the configured parameters back to the client. The final step for a successful VPN tunnel is the negotiation of Phase 2 parameters, as illustrated in Figure 6-1.

Figure 6-1   *Tunnel Negotiations for Cisco VPN Client*

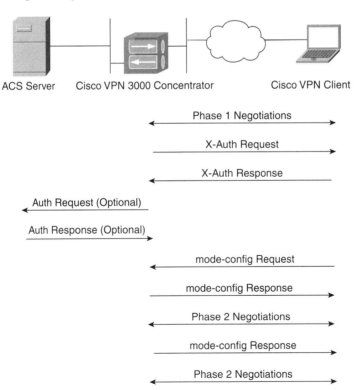

NOTE	It is a best practice to use main mode for Internet Key Exchange (IKE) authentication using RSA signatures because of the known vulnerabilities in aggressive mode. For more information, consult http://www.cisco.com/warp/public/707/cisco-sn-20030422-ike.html.

After completing the tunnel negotiations, the VPN client and the concentrator follow this process:

1. If NAC is enabled on the group the client connects to, a NAC session is created and NAC-related parameters are retrieved from the group configuration.

2. The exception list is checked against the reported operating system of the VPN client. If the reported OS is

   — In the exception list, the IPSec session is not subject to NAC verification. An exception access-control list (ACL), if configured, is applied to the IPSec sessions. In the VPN 3000 concentrators, an ACL is also referred as a filter.

   — Not in the exception list, the IPSec session is subject to posture validation, and the NAC process continues.

3. The concentrator creates an Extensible Authentication Protocol over User Datagram Protocol (EAPoUDP) session and applies a default ACL to the IPSec sessions. This default ACL is configured under the NAC section of user-group.

4. The EAPoUDP packet is sent to the IPSec client. If an EAPoUDP response is

   — Received, the concentrator initiates the NAC authentication process.

   — Not received after a number of retries, the concentrator assumes that it is an agentless host. The concentrator skips to step 13 for further processing of an agentless host.

5. The concentrator sends an EAP-identity request to the host. The host sends an EAP-identity response.

6. The concentrator forwards the EAP-identity response from the host to the ACS server as a part of a NAC access-request packet. At this point, a Protected Extensible Authentication Protocol (PEAP) session is established between the ACS server and the VPN client.

7. The ACS server requests posture information directly from the host. The concentrator simply forwards this request to the host. The host responds with the requested posture information.

8. The ACS server evaluates the response based on the configured policies. It sends either an access-accept or accept-reject packet. If it is

   — Access-accept, the ACS server sends NAC-specific configuration and an ACL to be applied on the VPN client.

   — Access-reject, the ACS server displays an error, and the VPN 3000 concentrator treats the host as an agentless host. The concentrator skips to step 13 for further processing of the agentless hosts.

9. The concentrator starts the status query and revalidation timers.

10. The concentrator sends a status query to the IPSec client when it expires. If the response is

    — Invalid or the host does not respond, the concentrator puts the IPSec client in the hold-off state. The concentrator skips to step 12 for further processing.

    — Valid, and the validation flag is not set, NAC processing enters into the idle state until the next status query timer expires.

    — Valid, and the validation flag is set, the concentrator initiates a full revalidation of the IPSec client. The concentrator goes back to step 4.

11. If the revalidation timer expires, the concentrator discards the EAPoUDP association and goes back to step 3.

12. The concentrator starts a hold-off timer if the IPSec client is agentless or if it does not respond to EAPoUDP communication. In this state, the concentrator ceases the EAPoUDP communications and other NAC-related activities until the hold-off timer expires. When it expires, the concentrator initiates a full revalidation and goes back to step 3.

13. If the IPSec client does not respond to an EAPoUDP hello message, it is deemed to be agentless. The concentrator requests agentless (clientless) policies from the ACS server by forwarding the clientless user credentials.

Figure 6-2 depicts this process of posture validation.

NOTE   If you are using downloadable ACLs for IPSec, those ACLs will be overwritten by the downloadable ACLs for NAC.

Figure 6-2   *Posture-Validation Process for Cisco VPN Client*

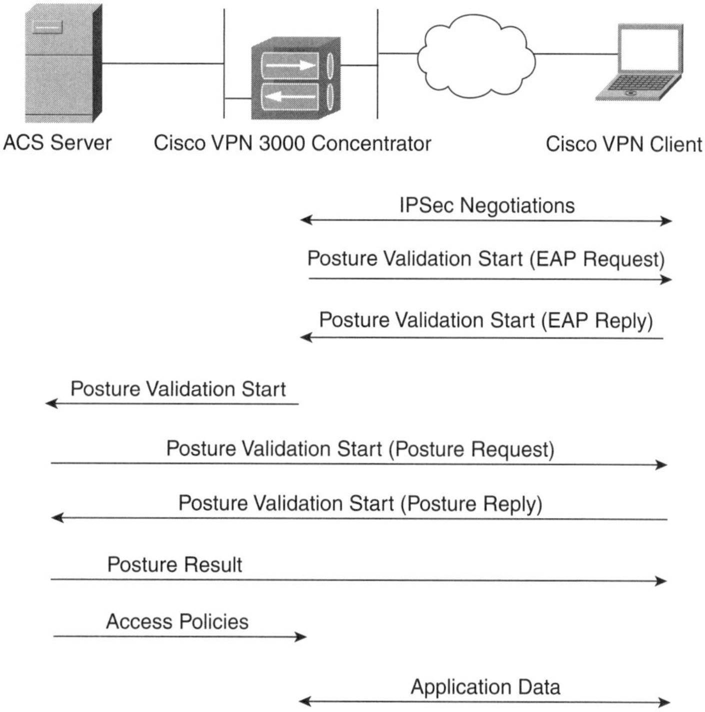

Microsoft L2TP over IPSec Clients

When a Microsoft L2TP over an IPSec client is used to establish the VPN tunnel, the VPN 3000 concentrator can start the PV process as soon as the VPN tunnel is established. In the L2TP over IPSec tunnel, an IPSec tunnel is negotiated first to provide data protection. When the IPSec SAs are established, the VPN devices negotiate the L2TP tunnel within the IPSec tunnel. When the L2TP over IPSec tunnel is successfully established, the VPN devices go through the posture-validation process, described earlier. Figure 6-3 illustrates the entire process of establishing an L2TP over IPSec session between a Windows-based operating system and the Cisco VPN 3000 concentrator.

Figure 6-3 *Tunnel Negotiation for L2TP over IPSec Client*

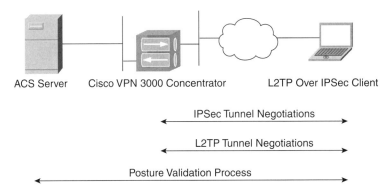

Table 6-1 lists major differences between the Cisco software clients and the L2TP over IPSec clients.

Table 6-1 *Contrasting Cisco IPSec and L2TP over IPSec Clients*

Feature	Cisco IPSec Client	L2TP over IPSec Client
Installation	This needs to be installed on the end workstations.	This is preinstalled on the Windows-based operating systems, such as Windomws XP, Windows 2000, and Windows 2003.
Authentication	Sessions are authenticated with X-Auth.	Sessions are authenticated using Point-to-Point Protocol (PPP)–based authentication methods.
Encapsulation	Data packets are encapsulated into IPSec.	Data packets are encapsulated first into L2TP and then into IPSec.
Compression	Data can be compressed using the Lempel-Ziv Stac (LZS) compression algorithm.	Data can be compressed using the Microsoft Point to Point Compression (MPPC) protocol.
Operating Systems	This works in Windows-, Solaris-, Linux-, and MAC based operating systems.	This works mostly in Windows-based operating systems.

Configuration Steps of NAC on Cisco VPN 3000 Concentrators

Figure 6-4 illustrates a network topology in which a Cisco VPN 3000 concentrator is terminating VPN sessions from Cisco VPN clients. The public IP address of the concentrator is 209.165.201.2, and the private IP address is 172.18.0.2. The concentrator leverages a Cisco Secure Access Control Server (CS-ACS) for user authentication. The CS-ACS also participates in the client's posture validation and applies appropriate policies. The concentrator is set up with a pool of addresses from the 172.18.200.0/24 subnet. During the mode-config phase of the VPN tunnel negotiations, the concentrator assigns an IP address from this pool to the VPN client.

Figure 6-4 *VPN 3000 Topology to Terminate IPSec Connections*

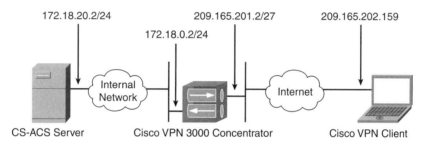

NOTE   You need to run Version 4.7 or later on the VPN 3000 concentrator to enable NAC.

The implementation of NAC on a VPN 3000 concentrator can be divided into three stages:

1. VPN configuration on the VPN 3000 concentrator
2. VPN configuration on the Cisco VPN client
3. NAC configuration on the VPN 3000 concentrator

NOTE   This chapter focuses on the configuration of the Cisco VPN 3000 concentrator and how it interacts with the Cisco VPN client because this is the most commonly deployed scenario. Consult the configuration guide of VPN 3000 concentrator for setting up L2TP over an IPSec tunnel.

VPN Configuration on the VPN 3000 Concentrator

This section discusses the configuration of remote-access IPSec tunnels on the VPN 3000 concentrator that can be used to accept connections from the Cisco VPN clients. The following are the four steps for setting up a basic remote-access IPSec tunnel:

Step 1   Group configuration

Step 2   User authentication

Step 3   Address assignment

Step 4   Mode-config assignment

NOTE   This chapter assumes that you have some familiarity with the VPN 3000 graphical user interface (GUI) and that you have administrative rights to set up different functions and features. For more information about the Cisco VPN 3000 concentrators, visit http://www.cisco.com/go/vpn3000.

Step 1: Group Configuration

The first step in configuring a remote-access IPSec VPN tunnel is to set up a group that the Cisco VPN client can connect to. A group, also known as user-group, can be created by navigating to **Configuration > User Management > Group** and clicking **Add**. The GUI shows the Identity tab, where a group name and a group password can be entered, as shown in Figure 6-5. The administrator has added NAC-Group as the group name and cisco123, shown as asterisks, as the group password. You can define the group as either an internal or an external group. In an internal group, all the policy and mode-config attributes are defined locally on the concentrator; in an external group, all the attributes are stored on an external server, such as Remote Authentication Dial-In User Service (RADIUS). In most implementations, these attributes are defined locally on the concentrator. In Figure 6-5, NAC-Group is set up as an internal group.

Click **Add** to create this VPN group in the local configuration file.

NOTE   If a group is set up as external, all tabs except for the Identity tab disappear.

Figure 6-5   *Creating a VPN Group*

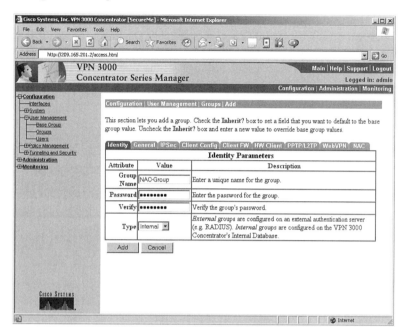

Step 2: User Authentication

Although the VPN 3000 concentrator supports a variety of authentication servers, such as RADIUS, Windows NT domain, Kerberos, Security Dynamics Incorporated (SDI), and the local database, the NAC implementation on the concentrator supports only RADIUS. The RADIUS server not only participates in authenticating the VPN user, but it also checks the current posture state of the VPN client. You can define the RADIUS server at the following two locations:

- Configuration > System > Servers > Authentication
- Configuration > User Management > Groups > Authentication Servers

If an authentication server is defined under **Configuration > System > Servers > Authentication**, it is referred to as a global authentication server. Any user-group that does not have an authentication server bound to it can use the global authentication server. When a VPN client needs to be authenticated and an authentication server is not found for that group, the user is authenticated against the global authentication server. If an authentication server is defined under **Configuration > User Management > Groups > Authentication Servers**, only that particular user group can use the authentication server. Defining an authentication server under each group is important if you will use a unique RADIUS server for each user group. If you have one RADIUS server that is responsible for authenticating users for all groups, you must define it as a global authentication server.

In Figure 6-6, a global RADIUS server is defined. The IP address of the RADIUS server is 172.18.20.2. Because this server acts as an authentication server for VPN users and then a posture-validation server to check the status of the VPN clients, the Used For option is set to User Auth and PV.

Figure 6-6   *Configuration of a RADIUS Server*

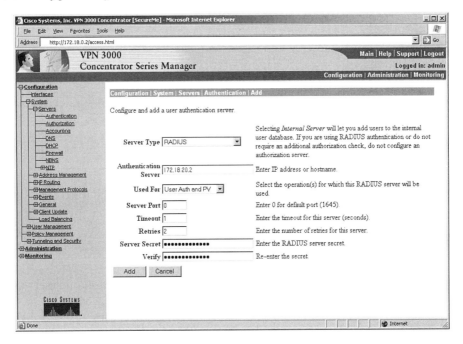

The other options under the User For drop-down menu include these:

- **User Authentication**—This option specifies that the RADIUS server should be used for authentication purposes only. The VPN 3000 concentrator does not contact this RADIUS server for posture validation.

- **Posture Validation**—This option specifies that the RADIUS server should be used only for validating the postures on the VPN clients. This is helpful if you want to use the RADIUS server for NAC purposes without user authentication.

The server port is set to 0, which means that the VPN 3000 concentrator uses the default UDP port of 1645 to communicate with the RADIUS server. If the RADIUS server is set up to use a different port, such as 1812, which RFC 2138 requires, you can specify that port here. In Figure 6-6, the RADIUS server port is 0 because CS-ACS uses 1645 for RADIUS authentication.

NOTE   Cisco Secure ACS listens on both UDP ports 1645 and 1812 for authentication purposes.

The Timeout value instructs a VPN 3000 concentrator to wait for a response after sending a request to the RADIUS server. The default timeout value is 4 seconds. If the connection between the VPN 3000 concentrator and the RADIUS server is slow or congested, you can increase the timeout value to a higher value, up to a maximum value of 30 seconds. In Figure 6-6, the timeout value is 2 seconds, so the VPN 3000 concentrator has to wait only 2 seconds before timing out the request, in case it does not get a response from the RADIUS server.

You can specify the number of times the VPN 3000 sends a RADIUS query if it does not get a response within the configured timeout interval. When the timeout interval expires, the VPN 3000 retransmits the query until the number of retries is reached. The default number of retries is 2, which is good enough if the connection between the concentrator and the RADIUS server is not congested. If the concentrator does not receive a response from the RADIUS server after the configured number of retries, it declares this server as unresponsive and tries to contact the next server, if any, in the list.

The Cisco VPN 3000 concentrator authenticates itself to the RADIUS server by using a preconfigured shared secret. For security reasons, this shared secret is never sent over the network. When the VPN 3000 concentrator sends a user password during the authentication phase, it hashes this critical information using the shared secret, to protect it from hackers. You can specify a secret key up to a maximum length of 64 characters. In Figure 6-6, a secret key of cisco123cisco is entered, which the concentrator masks using asterisks. The VPN 3000 concentrator requires you to retype the key to verify the key that is entered under the Server Secret field. When all the required fields have been configured, click **Add** to create this server in the authentication database of the concentrator.

After adding the RADIUS server in the database, the next step is to set up the user-group to consult the RADIUS server for user authentication. You can achieve this by modifying the user-group NAC-Group that was configured earlier. As shown in Figure 6-7, RADIUS is selected in the Authentication drop-down list of the Remote Access Parameters section.

Figure 6-7 *User-Group Configuration to Use RADIUS Server*

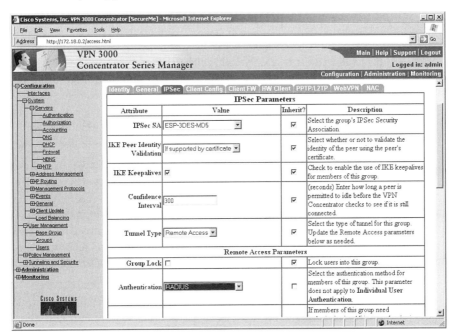

Step 3: Address Assignment

After a successful user authentication, the VPN client requests an IP address to be assigned to the VPN adapter on the workstation. The VPN client uses this address to source the clear-text traffic to be sent over the tunnel. For a Cisco VPN client, this address is assigned to the IPSec VPN adapter, while for the L2TP over IPSec client, this IP address is assigned to the L2TP VPN adapter. The Cisco VPN 3000 concentrator supports four different methods to assign an IP address to the client:

- **Use Client Address**—This option requires that an IP address be set up on the PPP-based VPN client such as L2TP over IPSec. This is not a recommended option for security reasons because you want to control address assignment from the concentrator.

- **Use Address from Authentication Server**—This option requires that an IP address be assigned from the RADIUS server. After a user is authenticated, the RADIUS server assigns an IP address in RADIUS attribute 8, Framed-IP-Address. This is a preferred method for large VPN deployments in which the pool of addresses is centrally managed on the authentication server.

- **Use DHCP**—For ease of management, the VPN 3000 concentrator can contact a DHCP server when allocating an IP address. After user authentication, the concentrator sends a request to the DHCP server and, when an address is allocated, assigns it to the VPN client.

- **Use Address Pools**—For small to midsize deployments, the preferred method for assigning an IP address is through the local database. When the client requests an IP address, the concentrator checks the local pool and assigns the next available IP address.

NOTE	The address-assignment process checks the selected methods in the sequential order of the preceding bullets until an address is found. If all methods are exhausted and an address cannot be allocated, the concentrator disconnects the VPN connection.

In Figure 6-8, the concentrator is being set up to assign an IP address from the RADIUS server and from a local pool of addresses. Address assignment is configured under **Configuration > System > Address Management > Address Assignment**. The concentrator checks the configured options in sequential order by trying to allocate an address from the RADIUS server. In this example, if the RADIUS server does not assign an address, the concentrator tries to allocate an address from the locally configured pool.

You need to define a pool of IP addresses in the concentrator if address assignment is using that option. To set up a pool of addresses, browse to **Configuration > System > Address Management > Address Pools** and click **Add**. The concentrator displays an option to enter the start and end of an IP range. As shown in Figure 6-9, the start IP address is 172.18.200.1 and the end IP address is 172.18.200.254. The subnet mask is set to 255.255.255.0, which means that the VPN client will be assigned an address from the 172.18.200.0 subnet. If no subnet mask is provided, the VPN 3000 concentrator assigns a default Class B mask of 255.255.0.0 because 172.18.200.0 is a Class B subnet.

Figure 6-8 *Address Assignment*

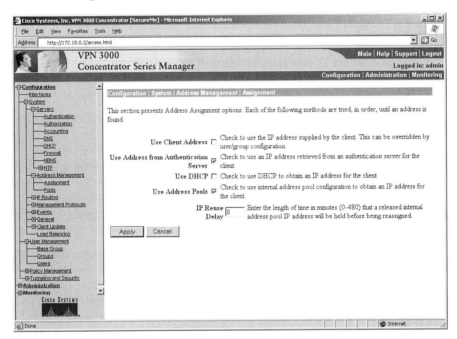

Figure 6-9 *Configuration of Address Pool*

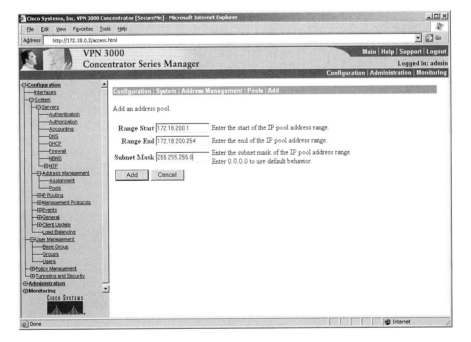

Step 4: Mode-config Assignment

As mentioned earlier, after user authentication, the VPN client requests mode-config attributes. The VPN 3000 concentrator replies with the configured values that the VPN client uses for proper operations. These attributes are configured under **Configuration > User Management > Groups** by modifying the group that was created earlier. All the attributes that are set up under the General, IPSec, Client Config, and Client FW tabs are considered mode-config attributes.

In Figure 6-10, the VPN 3000 concentrator is configured to assign 172.18.20.100 and 172.18.20.101 as the primary and secondary IP address of the DNS server. Additionally, the Idle Timeout value is changed from 30 minutes to 20 minutes. An idle timeout value helps save system resources by disconnecting the VPN clients that have been idle for 20 minutes. Consult the configuration guide of VPN 3000 concentration for a detailed explanation of all the other mode-config attributes.

Figure 6-10 *Mode-config Configuration*

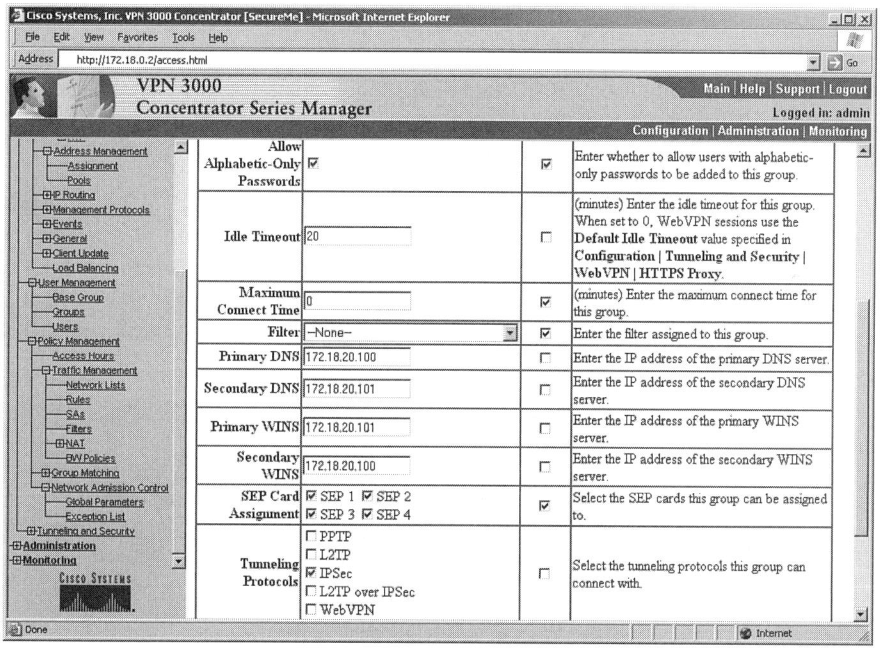

VPN Configuration on the Cisco VPN Client

The Cisco VPN Client, also known as the Cisco Easy VPN Client, initiates an IPSec tunnel to the VPN 3000 concentrator. If the configuration and user credentials are valid, the tunnel is established and traffic is processed over it. The Cisco VPN clients come in two different flavors:

- Software-based VPN clients
- Hardware-based VPN clients

However, the Cisco NAC implementation is currently supported only on the software-based VPN clients.

The software-based VPN client runs on a variety of operating systems, such as Windows, Solaris, Linux, and MAC OS X. Because the Cisco Trust Agent (CTA) is supported on Windows, Linux, and MAC OS X platforms, posture validation is performed only on those VPN clients. The VPN clients can be downloaded from Cisco.com free of charge as long as the Cisco VPN 3000 concentrator is under a valid service contract.

Before you configure the Cisco VPN Client, it must be installed on the host machine. Refer to http://www.cisco.com/go/vpnclient for the installation instructions. NAC is supported on VPN Client version 4.*x* or higher.

NOTE   The installation of Cisco VPN Client requires administrative privileges on the workstation.

In the Windows-based operating systems, if a VPN client is installed, it can be launched by running the VPN client executable found under **Start > Program files > Cisco Systems VPN Client.** The operating system runs the executable and displays the VPN Client utility, as depicted in Figure 6-11.

Figure 6-11 *Initial VPN Client Window*

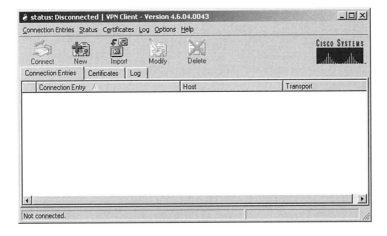

The configuration of a Windows-based VPN client requires five parameters:

- Name of the connection entry
- Public IP address of the VPN 3000 concentrator
- Group name that the VPN client will be connecting to
- Group preshared key
- Tunnel encapsulation

You can configure these parameters on the Cisco VPN client by clicking the **New** icon. The Cisco VPN client shows a different window in which you can enter the necessary information. In Figure 6-12, the user has specified the Connection Entry as Headend Concentrator. You can name this entry any name you like; it has only local significance and is not forwarded to the concentrator. You can optionally enter the description for this connection entry. In this example, the connection description is Connection to the Headend Concentrator. The VPN client requires you to input the IP or the host name of the concentrator. Because the public IP address of the concentrator is 209.165.201.2, the VPN client is set up to use this address. The group name that the VPN client is configured to use is NAC-Group, and the group password is cisco123, displayed as asterisks. The group password on the client is the preshared key configured on the concentrator.

Figure 6-12 *VPN Client Configuration*

You can specify what type of data encapsulation the Cisco VPN client should be using. This is set up under the Transport tab, as shown in Figure 6-13. If IPSec over UDP or NAT-T is the encapsulation mode, check the Enable Transparent Tunneling box with IPSec over UDP (NAT/PAT) as the selected option. If IPSec over TCP is the required encapsulation, select

IPSec over TCP and specify the appropriate port number. In this example, IPSec over UDP is the selected transport protocol.

NOTE NAC is fully supported on all the transparent tunneling protocols.

Figure 6-13 *Transparent Tunneling Configuration*

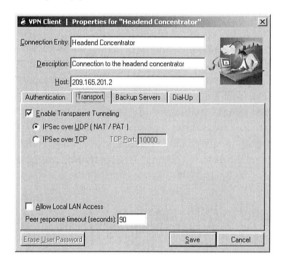

NOTE The concentrator needs to be set up for transparent tunneling as well with the appropriate encapsulation type. If you plan to use IPSec over TCP, it must be set up on the concentrator also.

NOTE If the Enable Transparent Tunneling box is disabled, the VPN client uses only the native IPSec encapsulation mode using encapsulating security payload (ESP).

After configuring the VPN client, the user can click the **Connect** icon to establish the connection to the VPN 3000 concentrator.

NAC Configuration on the VPN 3000 Concentrator

This section discusses the configuration of NAC-related parameters on the VPN 3000 concentrator. These parameters are applied after a VPN tunnel is established. The following three steps are required in configuring NAC on the VPN 3000 concentrator:

Step 1 Set up global NAC parameters.

Step 2 Configure the NAC exception list.

Step 3 Enable NAC on user-groups.

These configuration steps are discussed next.

Step 1: Setting Up NAC Global Parameters

The first step in setting up NAC on the concentrator is to ensure that the global NAC parameters are properly configured. You can modify the default values of these parameters by navigating to **Configuration > Policy Management > Network Admission Control > Global Parameters**. As shown in Figure 6-14, the Retransmission Timer is modified from 3 seconds to 5 seconds. When the concentrator sends an EAPoUDP packet to the VPN client, it waits for 5 seconds before resending another request. This way, the VPN clients that use dialup connections to connect to the Internet can reply to the concentrator within a reasonable time. If a response is not received, the concentrator sends another request and starts the retransmission timer. The concentrator sends the EAPoUDP packets three times before failing the communication and initiating the hold timer. The hold time of 180 seconds ensures that no EAPoUDP request is sent to the VPN client. As soon as this timer expires, the VPN 3000 concentrator initiates EAPoUDP communication with the VPN client and goes through the process discussed earlier. The active VPN clients are periodically challenged to determine whether posture validation can be done on the client machine based on the configured value of the hold timer.

The EAPoUDP communication is done on UDP port 21862. It is recommended that you not change this port unless there is a port conflict in your network.

For agentless hosts, you can enable the clientless authentication and specify a username and password. The user authentication credential is sent to the RADIUS server for proper action, such as applying appropriate ACLs or requesting an audit server to scan the host. In Figure 6-14, a clientless user named clientless is set up with a password of cisco123cisco. It is recommended that clientless machines such as guest hosts and contractors' computers not be given access to the trusted network of the company. Therefore, the RADIUS server can send a downloadable ACL to be applied to the VPN clients that do not have a CTA agent installed.

If clientless authentication is not enabled, the VPN 3000 concentrator applies a default ACL, discussed in Step 3 of this section. Traffic from the VPN client is subject to this ACL based on the permit and deny entries.

Figure 6-14 *NAC Global Parameter Configuration*

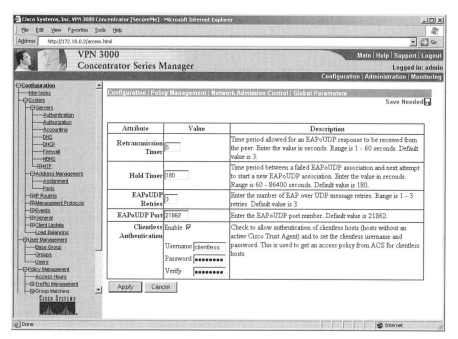

Step 2: Configuring the NAC Exception List

The Cisco VPN client is supported on a number of operating systems, including Solaris, MAC OS X, Windows, and Linux. However, Cisco CTA is currently supported only on Windows, Linux, and MAC OS X. During the tunnel negotiations, the VPN client reports its version information, such as Windows 2000, Windows XP, or MAC OS X, to name a few. You can specify an exception list based on the reported version from the VPN client. This list excludes the configured operating systems to go through the posture-validation process. After the IPSec tunnel is negotiated, the VPN clients that are in the exception list can be subject to an ACL to restrict their activities on the network. For example, if you want only Solaris-based VPN clients to access an internal mainframe system, the exception list ACL should allow only traffic destined to the mainframe server in the ACL and should deny all other traffic.

An ACL, also known as a filter, is a collection of rules. These rules can be added under **Configuration > Policy Management > Traffic Management > Rules > Add**. To allow bidirectional traffic between the Solaris VPN client and the mainframe server, you must configure two rules, one inbound and one outbound. The inbound rule inspects the traffic coming into the concentrator from the VPN client; the outbound rule inspects the traffic leaving the concentrator to the VPN client. In Figure 6-15, an inbound rule called Solaris-Inbound is being set up. This rule will be applied in the inbound direction of traffic with the action set to forward if

- Traffic is sourced from the VPN clients. Thus, the VPN client pool of 172.18.200.0 with a wildcard mask of 0.0.0.255 is specified as the source address.

- Traffic is destined to the Solaris server with an IP address of 172.18.50.100 and a wildcard of 0.0.0.0.

Figure 6-15 *Inbound Rule*

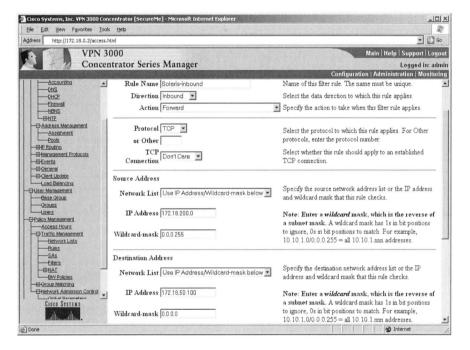

In Figure 6-16, an outbound rule called Solaris-Outbound is being set up. This rule will be applied in the outbound direction of traffic with the action set to forward if

- Traffic is sourced from the Solaris server with an IP address of 172.18.50.100 and a wildcard of 0.0.0.0.

- Traffic is destined to the VPN clients. Thus, the VPN client pool of 172.18.200.0 with a wildcard mask of 0.0.0.255 is specified as the destination address.

Figure 6-16 *Outbound Rule*

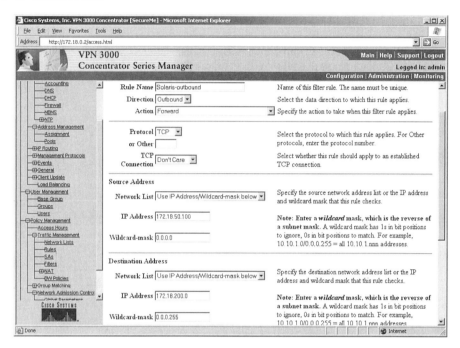

When both the inbound and outbound rules are configured, the next step is to set up a filter (an ACL) that consists of these rules. You can add a filter under **Configuration > Policy Management > Traffic Management > Filters > Add Filter**. In Figure 6-17, a new filter called Solaris is being added. Because you want to allow only the traffic that is permitted in the two rules we configured earlier, the default action is set to drop all other traffic. A description of Filter to restrict Solaris-based clients is added to describe the function of this filter. Click **Add** to create this filter.

The VPN 3000 concentrator shows all the current and available rules in the database. Move Solaris-inbound and Solaris-outbound from the available rules to the current rules, as shown in Figure 6-18. Click **Done** to complete this process.

Figure 6-17 *Configuration of a New Filter*

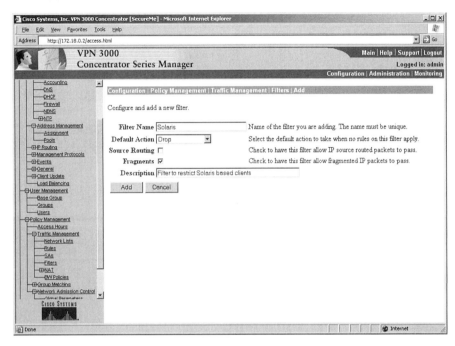

Figure 6-18 *Add Rules to Filter*

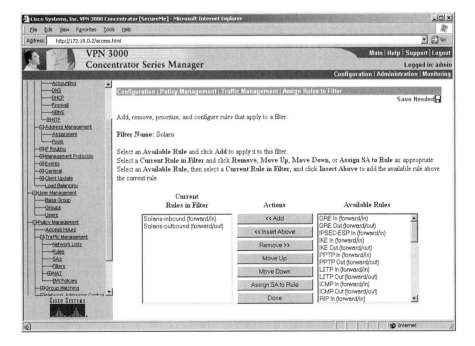

An exception list can be added under **Configuration > Policy Management > Network Admission Control > Exception List > Add**. As shown in Figure 6-19, an exception list is enabled for the Solaris version of the VPN client. An ACL named Solaris is applied to allow traffic from the VPN client to access the mainframe server.

Figure 6-19 *NAC Exception List*

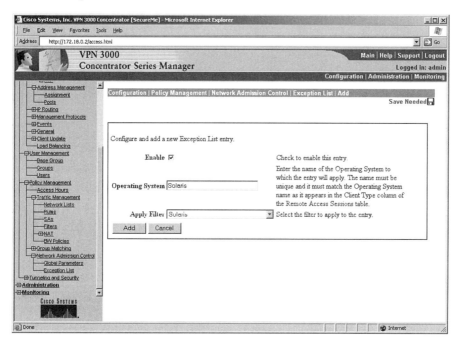

Step 3: Enabling NAC on User Groups

As mentioned earlier, after a VPN tunnel is established, the VPN 3000 concentrator initiates the posture-validation process. During this process, a default ACL is applied on the users to restrict traffic. The VPN 3000 concentrator also applies this default ACL if the EAPoUDP communication fails between the client and the Cisco Secure ACS server. The purpose of this default ACL is to ensure that remote users do not send unnecessary traffic until their posture is fully validated. You want this ACL to be as restrictive as possible. Therefore, it is a best practice to allow EAPoUDP communication between the VPN clients and the VPN concentrator and to deny all traffic passing through the VPN 3000 concentrator using the inbound and outbound rules. This is illustrated in Table 6-2.

Table 6-2   *Inbound and Outbound Rules in the Default ACL*

Parameters	Inbound Rule	Outbound Rule
Direction	Inbound	Outbound
Action	Forward	Forward
Protocol	UDP	UDP
Source address	172.18.200.0	172.18.0.2
Source wildcard mask	0.0.0.255	0.0.0.0
Source port	Range 21862 to 21862	Range 0 to 65535
Destination address	172.18.0.2	172.18.200.0
Destination wildcard mask	0.0.0.0	0.0.0.255
Destination port	Range 0 to 65535	Range 21862 to 21862

You can define a new filter and add both rules to it. The default action should be to drop all traffic. This filter is mapped to a user-group under **Configuration > User Management > Groups > Modify NAC-Group > NAC**. As shown in Figure 6-20, the default ACL name is Default-Filter.

Figure 6-20   *User-Group Configuration for NAC*

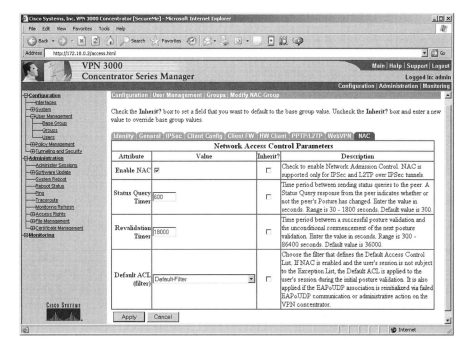

The VPN 3000 concentrator supports two timers after successfully completing posture validation for the VPN clients:

- **Status query timer**—This timer ensures that the concentrator periodically checks the posture state of the VPN client, in case it is changed from the last time. The default status query timer is 300 seconds. In Figure 6-20, the status query timer is changed to 600 seconds, which is recommended if the number of concurrent session is high. If this value is set too low, the concentrator will use a lot of system resources in sending status queries to the VPN clients.

- **Revalidation timer**—This timer initiates a complete posture-validation process on the VPN client. The default timer is set to 36,000 seconds (10 hours). You can lower this timer to 18,000 seconds (5 hours) if your organization requires you to revalidate the VPN clients more often. This is helpful when new antivirus patches are continuously updated on the servers and you want the VPN clients to update them as soon as they go through a new posture validation.

When all the parameters are set up, the last step is to enable NAC on the group.

Testing, Monitoring, and Troubleshooting NAC on Cisco VPN 3000 Concentrators

This section discusses the different test scenarios that are useful in implementing the NAC solution in the VPN 3000 concentrators. Each test scenario helps in gathering the statistical information about a connection. The scenarios also discuss the related debugs that are helpful in troubleshooting any IPSec or NAC deployments. The following test scenarios are discussed:

- Remote-access IPSec tunnel without NAC
- Remote-access IPSec tunnel from an agentless client
- Remote-access IPSec tunnel from a CTA client

Remote-Access IPSec Tunnel Without NAC

If you are setting up a new group on the concentrator that will validate the posture on the VPN clients, follow the first two configuration stages, as discussed earlier in the section "Configuration Steps of NAC on Cisco VPN 3000 Concentrators." The next step is to make a VPN tunnel from a test VPN client machine to ensure that you do not run into any misconfigurations. If you want to enable logging on the concentrator, navigate to **Configuration > System > Events > Classes** and add the classes and their recommended severities, as shown in Table 6-3.

Table 6-3   *Recommended Event Logging*

Class	Recommended Severity (Events to Log)
AUTH	1 to 9
IKE	1 to 9
IKEDBG	1 to 9
EAP	1 to 9
EAPoUDP	1 to 9
NAC	1 to 9

If NAC is disabled on the user-group, you will not see EAP, EAPoUDP and NAC debugs. Browse to **Monitoring > Filterable Event Log** to view these system logs. The tunnel negotiations begin by exchanging the ISAKMP proposals. The VPN 3000 concentrator shows the tunnel group—NAC-Group, in this case—that the VPN client is trying to connect to. If the proposal is acceptable, the VPN 3000 concentrator displays a message indicating that the IKE SA proposal is acceptable, as shown in Example 6-1. It also displays the chosen IKE SA proposal, CiscoVPNClient-3DES-MD5, and the public IP address of the VPN client, which is 209.165.202.159.

Example 6-1   *Log Output to Display IKE SA Proposal Is Acceptable*

```
377 10/18/2005 12:03:50.520 SEV=7 IKEDBG/28 RPT=15 209.165.202.159
Group [NAC-Group]
IKE SA Proposal # 1, Transform # 10 acceptable
Matches global IKE entry # 1 Proposal (CiscoVPNClient-3DES-MD5)
```

If the IKE proposal negotiation is successful, the Cisco VPN 3000 concentrator authenticates the user-group that the VPN client is trying to connect to. The concentrator displays an "Authentication successful" message if the client-specified group credential is accurate. In Example 6-2, the VPN client is connecting to the NAC-Group user-group, and the authentication succeeds.

Example 6-2 *Log Output to Display a Successful Group Authentication*

```
524 10/18/2005 12:04:02.550 SEV=6 AUTH/41 RPT=46 209.165.202.159
Authentication successful: handle = 56, server = Internal, group = NAC-Group
```

The Cisco VPN 3000 concentrator prompts the user to specify user credentials after group authentication. Upon successful user authentication, the VPN 3000 concentrator displays a message indicating that the user (testuser, in this example) is authenticated, as shown in Example 6-3.

Example 6-3 *Log Output to Display User Authentication*

```
594 10/18/2005 12:04:02.750 SEV=4 IKE/52 RPT=11 209.165.202.159
Group [NAC-Group] User [testuser]
User (testuser) authenticated.
```

The client requests mode-config attributes by sending a list of client-supported attributes, as shown in Example 6-4. The Cisco VPN 3000 concentrator replies with all its supported attributes and the appropriate information.

Example 6-4 *Log Output to Display Mode-Config Requests*

```
610 10/18/2005 12:04:02.810 SEV=9 IKEDBG/1 RPT=220
Processing cfg Request attributes

611 10/18/2005 12:04:02.810 SEV=9 IKEDBG/53 RPT=161
MODE_CFG: Received request for IPV4 address!

612 10/18/2005 12:04:02.810 SEV=9 IKEDBG/53 RPT=162
MODE_CFG: Received request for IPV4 net mask!

613 10/18/2005 12:04:02.810 SEV=9 IKEDBG/53 RPT=163
MODE_CFG: Received request for DNS server address!

614 10/18/2005 12:04:02.810 SEV=9 IKEDBG/53 RPT=164
MODE_CFG: Received request for WINS server address!
```

After pushing down the attributes, VPN 3000 concentrator displays a message indicating that the ISAKMP SA was successfully negotiated, as demonstrated in Example 6-5.

Example 6-5 *Log Output to Indicate Phase 1 Negotiations Are Completed*

```
670 10/18/2005 12:04:02.840 SEV=4 IKE/119 RPT=11 209.165.202.159
Group [NAC-Group] User [testuser]
PHASE 1 COMPLETED
```

After completing Phase 1 negotiations, the VPN peers try to negotiate Phase 2 SA by exchanging the proxy identities and the IPSec Phase 2 proposal. If they are acceptable, the Cisco VPN 3000 concentrator displays a message indicating that the IPSec SA proposal is acceptable, as shown in Example 6-6. It also shows the negotiated IPSec proposal—ESP-3DES-MD5, in this case.

Example 6-6   *Log Output to Show Phase 2 Proposal Is Accepted*

```
740 10/18/2005 12:04:02.850 SEV=7 IKEDBG/27 RPT=11 209.165.202.159
Group [NAC-Group] User [testuser]
IPSec SA Proposal # 11, Transform # 1 acceptable
Matches global IPSec SA entry # 2 Proposal (ESP-3DES-MD5)
```

After accepting the transform set values, both VPN devices complete IPSec SAs, also known as IKE Phase 2 SAs. Example 6-7 illustrates this. When the IPSec SAs have been created, both VPN devices should be capable of passing traffic bidirectionally across the tunnel.

Example 6-7   *Log Output to Indicate IPSec SA Negotiations Are Complete*

```
778 10/18/2005 12:04:02.860 SEV=4 IKE/120 RPT=11 209.165.202.159
Group [NAC-Group] User [testuser]
PHASE 2 COMPLETED (msgid=c1d569ac)
```

Because NAC is not configured on the concentrator, you will receive an informational message on the concentrator indicating that NAC is not enabled for this peer, as shown in Example 6-8.

Example 6-8   *Log Output to Indicate NAC Is Disabled for the Peer*

```
727 10/21/2005 00:42:17.770 SEV=4 NAC/27 RPT=3
NAC is disabled for peer - PUB_IP:209.165.202.159, PRV_IP:172.18.200.1
```

Remote-Access IPSec Tunnel from an Agentless Client

If the test VPN tunnel establishes successfully, the next step is to configure NAC on the VPN 3000 concentrator and then connect from the same test VPN client without installing the CTA agent. This emulates an agentless VPN client scenario. As shown in Example 6-9, as soon as IKE Phase 2 negotiations are complete, the VPN 3000 concentrator initiates the NAC process. It applies a default ACL called Default-Filter in this setup.

Example 6-9 *Log Output to Display NAC Process Initiation*

```
726 10/21/2005 00:45:31.460 SEV=4 IKE/120 RPT=23 209.165.202.159
Group [NAC-Group] User [testuser]
PHASE 2 COMPLETED (msgid=ac1f830a)

727 10/21/2005 00:45:31.460 SEV=4 NAC/2 RPT=11
NAC session initialized - PUB_IP:209.165.201.2 PRV_IP:172.18.0.2

728 10/21/2005 00:45:31.460 SEV=4 NAC/29 RPT=5
NAC Applying filter - PUB_IP: 209.165.201.2, PRV_IP: 172.18.0.2, Name:Default
-Filter, ID:7
```

The VPN 3000 concentrator sends EAPoUDP packets to the VPN client. Because CTA is not installed on the VPN client, the concentrator never receives a response from the client, and this fails the EAPoUDP communication, as shown in Example 6-10.

Example 6-10 *Log Output to Display EAPoUDP Failure*

```
749 10/21/2005 00:45:41.460 SEV=13 EAPOUDP/16 RPT=1577
EAPoUDP packet (TX)
0000: 00120008 D075A76D 00000000 80010004    .....u.m........
0010: D075A76D                               .u.m

752 10/21/2005 00:45:46.460 SEV=6 EAPOUDP/20 RPT=27
EAPoUDP response timer expiry - PRV_IP:172.18.200.1

753 10/21/2005 00:45:46.460 SEV=8 EAPOUDP/12 RPT=8
EAPoUDP failed to get a response from host - PRV_IP:172.18.200.1
```

After determining that the VPN client does not have CTA services active, the VPN 3000 concentrator sends the clientless user credentials to the RADIUS server. This process occurs only if clientless authentication is enabled under global NAC parameters. Example 6-11 shows this. The concentrator adds an event type of supplicant-failure to indicate that it is an agentless client that could not go through the posture-validation process.

Example 6-11 *Log Output to Show the VPN Client Failed EAPoUDP Communication*

```
753 10/21/2005 00:45:46.460 SEV=8 EAPOUDP/12 RPT=8
EAPoUDP failed to get a response from host - PRV_IP:172.18.200.1

754 10/21/2005 00:45:46.460 SEV=8 AUTHDBG/1 RPT=74
AUTH_Open() returns 73

757 10/21/2005 00:45:46.460 SEV=9 NAC/25 RPT=8
NAC NRH auth_attr #1: PUB_IP:209.165.202.159, PRV_IP:172.18.200.1
  un:clientless
  pw:cisco123cisco
  np:1017
  gs:209.165.202.159
```

Example 6-11 *Log Output to Show the VPN Client Failed EAPoUDP Communication (Continued)*

```
ds:172.18.0.2

759 10/21/2005 00:45:46.460 SEV=9 NAC/26 RPT=8
NAC NRH auth_attr #2: PUB_IP:209.165.202.159, PRV_IP:172.18.200.1
  as:aaa:service=ip-admission
  ae:aaa:event=supplicant-failure
  sv:1
  ig:NAC-Group
  ru:2
```

The RADIUS server authenticates the clientless user and, if the authentication is successful, sends policies that are applied on the users. In Example 6-12, the concentrator applies an ACL called Clientless-435513f6 on the VPN client after receiving it from the RADIUS server.

Example 6-12 *Log Output to Show an ACL Is Applied on the VPN Client*

```
865 10/21/2005 00:45:46.860 SEV=4 NAC/29 RPT=6
NAC Applying filter - PUB_IP:209.165.202.159, PRV_IP:172.18.200.1, Name:Clientless-
  435513f6, ID:8

867 10/21/2005 00:45:46.860 SEV=6 NAC/7 RPT=13
NAC Access Accept - PUB_IP:209.165.202.159, PRV_IP:172.18.200.1
```

Remote-Access IPSec Tunnel from a CTA Client

In the last test scenario, a CTA agent is installed on the VPN client machine. The idea is to have the VPN client to go through the entire posture-validation process. After establishing the IPSec SAs, the concentrator initiates the EAPoUDP process. If a response is received from the VPN client, the concentrator knows that the VPN client has an active CTA agent, as illustrated in Example 6-13.

Example 6-13 *Log Output to Indicate VPN Client Sends an EAPoUDP Response*

```
749 10/21/2005 02:07:39.630 SEV=13 EAPOUDP/18 RPT=1615
EAPoUDP packet (RX)
0000: 80120018 B501A90A B501A90A 8003000C      ...............
0010: B501A90A 935BC3FF 4603A87A 80010004      .....[..F..z....
0020: BE31E6FA                                 .1..

753 10/21/2005 02:07:39.630 SEV=8 EAPOUDP/3 RPT=13
EAPoUDP-Hello response received from host - PRV_IP:172.18.200.2

754 10/21/2005 02:07:39.630 SEV=7 EAPOUDP/4 RPT=13
NAC EAP association initiated - PRV_IP:172.18.200.2, EAP context:0x04096fd0
```

When the EAPoUDP session is successfully established between the VPN client and the concentrator, the concentrator contacts the RADIUS server to start a new posture-validation process, as shown in Example 6-14.

Example 6-14 *Log Output Displaying VPN 3000 Requesting a New PV*

```
778 10/21/2005 02:07:39.640 SEV=9 NAC/23 RPT=112
NAC EAP auth_attr #1: PUB_IP:209.165.202.160, PRV_IP:172.18.200.2
  un:64.102.44.254
  np:1022
  st:25
  gs:209.165.202.160
  ds:172.18.0.2

780 10/21/2005 02:07:39.640 SEV=9 NAC/24 RPT=112
NAC EAP auth_attr #2: PUB_IP: 209.165.202.160, PRV_IP:172.18.200.2
  em:0x02b00005
  as:aaa:service=ip-admission
  ae:aaa:event=new-session
  sv:1
  ig:NAC-Group
  ru:2
```

The RADIUS server analyzes the information received from the VPN client and returns an appropriate posture token to the concentrator. The VPN 3000 concentrator also receives the policies such as an ACL that is applied to the VPN clients. In Example 6-15, the RADIUS sends an ACL called Healthy-435513f6. The posture token is Healthy, indicating that the VPN client meets all the configured policies on the RADIUS server.

Example 6-15 *Log Output Displaying RADIUS Server Applying Policies*

```
865 10/21/2005 00:45:46.860 SEV=4 NAC/29 RPT=6
NAC Applying filter - PUB_IP: 209.165.202.160, PRV_IP:172.18.200.2, Name:Healthy-
 435513f6, ID:8

1513 10/21/2005 02:07:42.180 SEV=8 NAC/12 RPT=12
NAC Access Accept - PUB_IP: 209.165.202.160, PRV_IP:172.18.200.1,
user:AVCLIENTS:Administrator

1515 10/21/2005 02:07:42.180 SEV=8 NAC/14 RPT=12
NAC Access Accept - PUB_IP: 209.165.202.160, PRV_IP:172.18.200.2, Posture Token:
 Healthy

1517 10/21/2005 02:07:42.180 SEV=6 NAC/7 RPT=18
NAC Access Accept - PUB_IP: 209.165.202.160, PRV_IP:172.18.200.2
```

You can monitor the IPSec VPN sessions on the concentrator by browsing to **Monitoring > Sessions**. The L2TP over IPSec and Cisco remote-access VPN tunnels appear in the

Remote Access Sessions section. The concentrator shows the following important information about the VPN client:

- The public and assigned IP addresses of the VPN client
- The user-group membership
- The encryption protocol used
- The login time and the duration a connection is up for
- The operating system information and the version of VPN client
- The actual encrypted and decrypted data
- The status of NAC posture assessment

As shown in Figure 6-21, two VPN client connections are terminated on the VPN 3000 concentrator. The first connection is from an agentless host; consequently, the NAC result is Non-responsive. The second VPN connection is from a VPN client that has an active CTA client installed. The result of posture assessment is Accepted Healthy.

Figure 6-21 *Monitoring the VPN Connections*

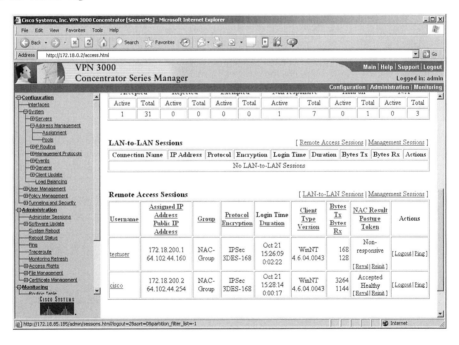

You can get detailed information about a VPN connection by clicking the username for the VPN tunnel you are interested in. You can get information such as IKE and IPSec sessions, NAC timers, and the ACL applied on the user. In Figure 6-22, an ACL is applied on a VPN user called testuser. The ACL name is Clientless-435955df, and it is applied under Dynamic Filters.

Figure 6-22 *Detailed Information on a VPN Connection*

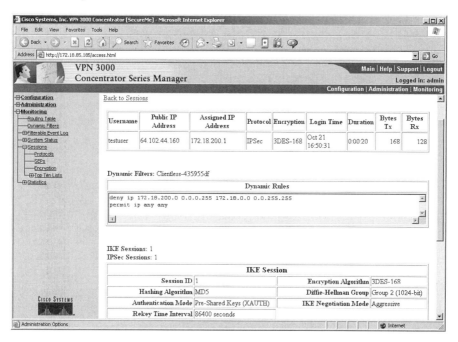

Summary

The NAC implementation on the VPN 3000 concentrator provides a complete solution to check the posture state of a VPN client. If the posture is not validated, the VPN 3000 concentrator applies appropriate ACLs to filter traffic. This chapter discussed the packet flow in a concentrator when NAC is enabled and then provided detailed configuration steps. This chapter provided guidance on how to monitor the remote-access VPN tunnels. For troubleshooting purposes, this chapter discussed various debug and log messages to help you isolate the issues related to remote-access tunnels and NAC.

Review Questions

You can find the answers to the review questions in Appendix A, "Answers to Review Questions."

1. The VPN 3000 concentrator uses UDP port _____ for EAPoUDP communication to the VPN client.

    a. 2182

    b. 3000

    c. 21862

    d. 3030

2. Cisco NAC solution is supported on which of the following VPN tunnels? (Multiple answers)

    a. PPTP

    b. L2TP

    c. IPSec

    d. L2TP over IPSec

3. True or false: A VPN client that has CTA installed will still be considered agentless if the CTA services are disabled on it.

4. True or false: During mode-config, the VPN 3000 concentrator validates the user against the configured authentication database.

5. True or false: The purpose of an exception ACL is to ensure that remote users do not send unnecessary traffic until their posture is fully validated.

6. When configuring a user-group, you need to specify these two mandatory parameters. (Multiple answers)

    a. Group name

    b. Group password

    c. Group mode-config attributes

    d. Group x-auth

7. True or false: The posture-validation process is initiated by the VPN 3000 concentrator.

8. True or false: The IPSec tunnel is torn down if the VPN client does not respond to the EAPoUDP request packet.

9. True or false: If a Healthy posture token is assigned to the VPN client, the VPN 3000 concentrator does not apply any ACL.

10. True or false: The assignment of an IP address to the VPN client is a mandatory parameter during tunnel negotiations.

This chapter covers the following topics:

- Architectural overview of NAC on Cisco security appliances
- Configuration steps of NAC on Cisco security appliances
- Testing, monitoring, and troubleshooting NAC on Cisco security appliances

## CHAPTER 7

Configuring NAC on Cisco ASA and PIX Security Appliances

Similar to the Cisco VPN 3000 series concentrators discussed in Chapter 6, "Configuring NAC on Cisco VPN 3000 Series Concentrators," the Cisco security appliances provide a complete solution for the site-to-site as well as remote-access VPN tunnels. Cisco security appliances consist of Cisco Adaptive Security Appliances (ASA) and the Cisco PIX Security Appliance. The NAC functionality on the Cisco security appliances enhances security of the IPSec tunnels. This chapter focuses on NAC implementation of the security appliances by providing a brief architectural overview of the solution and step-by-step configuration examples.

Architectural Overview of NAC on Cisco Security Appliances

The NAC implementation on the security appliances is identical to the implementation on Cisco VPN 3000 series concentrators. Refer to Chapter 6 for detailed information about the NAC architectural design on the security appliance. This section covers some of the significant changes from the VPN 3000 concentrator NAC implementation.

Stateless Failover for NAC

The security appliances support stateful failover for the traffic passing through the device. This includes Transmission Control Protocol (TCP), User Datagram Protocol (UDP), Internet Control Message Protocol (ICMP), and IPSec, to name a few protocols. However, the current implementation of NAC supports only stateless failover. This means that the NAC commands are replicated from the active appliance to the standby appliance; however, none of the active NAC connections will fail over to the standby appliance if the standby appliance becomes active. In a failover, all NAC postures that are validated by active appliance are disconnected, and the new NAC sessions are created on the newly active security appliance.

If you are using the stateful failover, the IPSec connections are switched over seamlessly after a failover. However, the remote-access VPN clients go through the posture-validation process. During this time, the security appliance applies a NAC default Access Control List (ACL), if defined, on the remote-access VPN clients.

Per-Group NAC Exception List

Unlike a VPN 3000 concentrator, a security appliance supports multiple NAC exception lists that are configured under user group-policy. Each NAC exception list can be set up with the reported operating system from the VPN client and an ACL. This list excludes the configured operating systems from going through the posture-validation process. The Cisco VPN client also provides the name of the operating system the host is using, and this string is compared with entries in the NAC Exception List.

NOTE   The security appliances support NAC for Cisco software clients and Microsoft L2TP over IPSec clients. Plans are underway to support NAC for the SSL-based VPN tunnels in future releases.

Configuration Steps of NAC on Cisco Security Appliances

Figure 7-1 illustrates a network topology in which a Cisco ASA 5500 appliance is terminating VPN client sessions from Cisco VPN clients. The public IP address of the appliance is 209.165.202.130; the private IP address is 10.10.0.2. The security appliance leverages a Cisco Secure ACS server for user authentication. The Cisco Secure ACS also participates in the client's posture validation and applies appropriate policies. The appliance is set up with a pool of addresses from the 10.10.200.0/24 subnet. During the mode-config phase of the VPN tunnel negotiations, the Cisco ASA 5500 appliance assigns an IP address from this pool to the VPN client.

NOTE   For more information about the mode-config phase, refer to Chapter 6.

Figure 7-1   *ASA 5500 Topology to Terminate IPSec Connections*

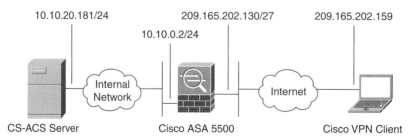

Pool: 10.10.200.0/24

NOTE	You need to run Version 7.2 or later on the security appliances to enable NAC.

The implementation of NAC on a security appliance can be divided into three stages:

1. VPN configuration on the security appliances

2. VPN configuration on the Cisco VPN client

3. NAC configuration on the security appliances

NOTE	This chapter focuses on the configuration of the security appliances and how they interact with the Cisco VPN clients.

NOTE	The operating system used by Cisco ASA and PIX is the same. Consequently, the configuration of NAC on the two security appliances is identical.

VPN Configuration on the Security Appliances

This section discusses the configuration of remote-access IPSec tunnels on the security appliances that can be used to accept connections from the Cisco VPN clients. The following 12 steps set up a basic remote-access IPSec tunnel.

Step 1 Enable ISAKMP.

Step 2 Create the ISAKMP policy.

Step 3 Configure remote-access attributes.

Step 4 Define the tunnel type.

Step 5 Configure preshared keys.

Step 6 Configure user authentication.

Step 7 Assign an IP address.

Step 8 Define the IPSec policy.

Step 9 Set up a dynamic crypto map.

Step 10 Configure the crypto map.

Step 11 Apply the crypto map on the interface.

Step 12 Configure traffic filtering.

NOTE   This chapter assumes that you have basic familiarity with the security appliance command-line interface (CLI) and that you have administrative rights to set up different functions and features. For more information about the security appliances, visit http://www.cisco.com/go/asa and http://www.cisco.com/go/pix.

Step 1: Enabling ISAKMP

By default, ISAKMP is disabled on all the interfaces. If the remote VPN device sends a tunnel-initialization message, the security appliance drops it until ISAKMP is enabled on the interface terminating the IPSec tunnels. Typically, it is enabled on the Internet-facing or the outside interface, as demonstrated in Example 7-1.

Example 7-1   *Enabling ISAKMP on the Outside Interface*

```
CiscoASA# configure terminal
CiscoASA(config)# isakmp enable outside
```

Step 2: Creating the ISAKMP Policy

The **isakmp policy** commands define ISAKMP Phase 1 attributes that are exchanged between the VPN peers. Example 7-2 shows an ISAKMP policy to negotiate preshared keys for authentication, Advanced Encryption Standard-256 (AES-256) for encryption, Secure Hash Algorithm (SHA) for hashing, group 2 for Diffie-Hellman (DH), and 86400 seconds for lifetime.

Example 7-2   *Configuration of ISAKMP Policy*

```
CiscoASA# configure terminal
CiscoASA(config)# isakmp policy 10 authentication pre-share
CiscoASA(config)# isakmp policy 10 encryption aes-256
CiscoASA(config)# isakmp policy 10 hash sha
CiscoASA(config)# isakmp policy 10 group 2
CiscoASA(config)# isakmp policy 10 lifetime 86400
```

Step 3: Configuring Remote-Access Attributes

The security appliance allows the configuration of the mode-config parameters in three different places:

- Under default group-policy
- Under user group-policy
- Under user policy

The security appliance implements an inheritance model in which a user inherits the mode-config attributes from the user policy, which inherits its attributes from the user group-policy, which, in turn, inherits its attributes from the default group-policy, as illustrated in Figure 7-2. A user, ciscouser, receives traffic filtering ACL and an assigned IP address from the user policy, the domain name from the user group-policy, and IP Compression, along with the number of simultaneous logins from the default group-policy.

Figure 7-2   *Mode-Config Inheritance Model*

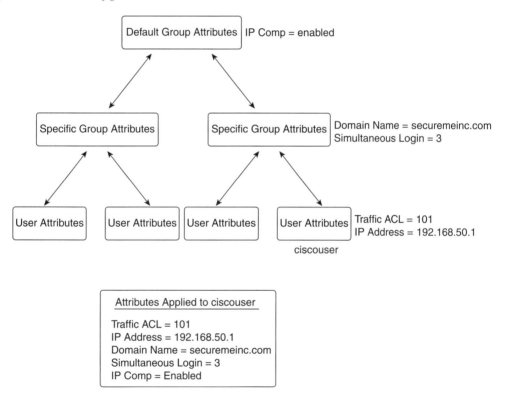

You can use the **group-policy attributes** command to specify the default and user group-policy mode-config attributes. Example 7-3 shows how to configure the default group attributes on the security appliances by setting DfltGrpPolicy as the group name in the group-policy. The administrator has limited the simultaneous logins to three and has enabled IP Compression for data payload.

Example 7-3   *Configuration of Default Group-Policy*

```
CiscoASA(config)# group-policy DfltGrpPolicy attributes
CiscoASA(config-group-policy)# vpn-simultaneous-logins 3
CiscoASA(config-group-policy)# ip-comp enable
```

NOTE	DfltGrpPolicy is a special group name, used solely for the default group-policy.

The user group-policy is set up similarly to a default group-policy, by configuring the attributes under the group-policy submenu. In Example 7-4, a group called SecureMeGrp is being set up to send the domain-name securemeinc.com attribute during mode-config exchange. One major difference between the default group-policy and the user group-policy is that you can define the latter as an internal or external group. In an internal group, all the policy attributes are defined locally on the security appliance. In an external group, all the attributes are stored on an external server such as RADIUS. In Example 7-4, SecureMeGrp is set up as an internal group, which is why the domain-name attribute is defined locally.

Example 7-4 *Configuration of Group-Specific Group Policy*

```
CiscoASA(config)# group-policy SecureMeGrp internal
CiscoASA(config)# group-policy SecureMeGrp attributes
CiscoASA(config-group-policy)# default-domain value securemeinc.com
```

Step 4: Defining the Tunnel Type

Cisco security appliances can be configured for two different tunnel types, as shown in Example 7-5.

Example 7-5 *Supported Tunnel Types*

```
CiscoASA(config)# tunnel-group NAC-Group type ?
  ipsec-l2l   IPSec Site to Site group
  ipsec-ra    IPSec Remote Access group
```

In this example, the tunnel-group tag is named NAC-Group, and the tunnel type is ipsec-ra. The **ipsec-ra** command stands for IPSec remote-access tunnels, and, when configured, the security appliance expects the Cisco VPN clients to initiate a tunnel and send vendor identity as a Cisco client during the ISAKMP negotiations. Example 7-6 shows the Cisco security appliance in CiscoASA configured for remote-access tunnels.

Example 7-6 *Configuration of Remote-Access Tunnels*

```
CiscoASA(config)# tunnel-group NAC-Group type ipsec-ra
```

NOTE   The tunnel-group name—NAC-Group in the preceding example—is the group name that needs to be configured on the Cisco VPN clients.

Step 5: Configuring ISAKMP Preshared Keys

If you want to use a preshared key as the authentication method, you must configure a shared secret that is used to validate the identity of both VPN devices. The preshared key is configured after the **ipsec-attributes** keyword of the **tunnel-group** command, as shown in Example 7-7.

Example 7-7   *Preshared Key Configuration*

```
CiscoASA(config)# tunnel-group NAC-Group ipsec-attributes
CiscoASA(config-ipsec)# pre-shared-key cisco123cisco
```

In Example 7-7, all Cisco VPN clients configured for the NAC-Group group must use cisco123cisco as the preshared key. If there is a mismatch on the key, the security appliance denies group authentication for the client.

NOTE   A preshared key is also known as a group password in the Cisco remote-access VPN client.

Step 6: Configuring User Authentication

The tunnel group must be configured with the corresponding authentication server, under general attributes. The **authentication-server-group** subcommand specifies the authentication server. Example 7-8 illustrates how to define a RADIUS server for user authentication. The RADIUS server is located on the inside interface and is set up for the 10.10.20.181 IP address. The RADIUS server is then mapped to the NAC-Group group for user authentication.

Example 7-8   *Authentication Using RADIUS Server*

```
CiscoASA(config)# aaa-server Radius (inside) host 10.10.20.181
CiscoASA(config-aaa-server-host)# key cisco123cisco
CiscoASA(config-aaa-server-host)# exit
CiscoASA(config)# tunnel-group NAC-Group general-attributes
CiscoASA((config-group-policy)# authentication-server-group Radius
```

Step 7: Assigning an IP Address

During the mode-configuration phase of the IPSec tunnel negotiations, the Cisco VPN client requests an IP address to be assigned to the VPN adapter of the workstation. The security appliance supports three different methods to assign an IP address back to the client:

- Local address pool
- DHCP server
- RADIUS server

Example 7-9 shows the available address-assignment methods in the **vpn-addr-assign** command.

Example 7-9 *Available Address-Assignment Methods*

```
CiscoASA(config)# vpn-addr-assign ?
  aaa    Allow AAA servers to specify an IP address
  dhcp   Allow DHCP servers to specify an IP address
  local  Allow local pools to specify an IP address
CiscoASA(config)# vpn-addr-assign local
```

These options are useful to meet any deployment methodology. Each address-assignment option is discussed here:

- **vpn-addr-assign aaa**—This option requires that an IP address be assigned from the RADIUS server. When a user is authenticated, the RADIUS server assigns an IP address in RADIUS attribute 8, Framed-IP-Address. This is a preferred method for large VPN deployments in which the pool of addresses is centrally managed on the authentication server.

- **vpn-addr-assign dhcp**—For ease of management, the security appliance can contact a DHCP server when allocating an IP address. After user authentication, the security appliance sends a request to the DHCP server and, after it is allocated, forwards it to the VPN client.

- **vpn-addr-assign local**—For small to midsize deployments, the preferred method for assigning an IP address is through the local database. When the client requests an IP address, the security appliance checks the local pool and assigns the next available IP address.

Example 7-10 shows the necessary commands to configure an address pool called vpnpool and map it for address assignment for a VPN group NAC-Group. The pool range starts at 10.10.200.1 and ends at 10.10.200.254.

Example 7-10 *Address Assignment from Local Pool*

```
CiscoASA(config)# ip local pool vpnpool 10.10.200.1-10.10.200.254
CiscoASA(config)# tunnel-group NAC-Group general-attributes
CiscoASA(config-general)# address-pool vpnpool
```

Many large enterprises prefer to authenticate users on the external RADIUS servers, which can assign IP addresses to the client after successfully authenticating the users. Example 7-11 shows the configuration of the security appliance if RADIUS, set up as an authenticating device, is assigning the IP address.

Example 7-11 *Address Assignment from an AAA Server*

```
CiscoASA(config)# aaa-server Radius protocol radius
CiscoASA(config-aaa-server-group)# exit
CiscoASA(config)# aaa-server Radius (inside) host 10.10.20.181
CiscoASA(config-aaa-server-host)# key cisco123cisco
CiscoASA(config-aaa-server-host)# exit
CiscoASA(config)# vpn-addr-assign aaa
```

NOTE   If all three methods are configured for address assignment, the security appliance prefers RADIUS over DHCP and an address pool. If the Cisco security appliance cannot get an address from the RADIUS server, it contacts the DHCP server for address allocation. If that method fails as well, the security appliance checks the local address pool as the last resort.

Step 8: Defining the IPSec Policy

An IPSec transform set specifies the encryption and hashing method to be used on the data packets when the tunnel is up. To configure the transform set, use the following command syntax:

```
crypto ipsec transform-set transform-set tag esp-3des | esp-aes | esp-aes-192
| esp-aes-256 | esp-des | esp-md5-hmac | esp-null | esp-none | esp-sha-hmac}
```

NOTE   If the security appliance does not have a license for the VPN-3DES-AES feature, the security appliance allows DES encryption only for ISAKMP and IPSec policies. Administrators can now obtain a 3DES-AES license free from the Cisco website. The software download page includes instructions for obtaining the license.

In Example 7-12, the security appliance in CiscoASA is set up for AES-256 encryption and SHA hashing. The transform set name is myset.

Example 7-12 *Transform Set Configuration*

```
CiscoASA(config)# crypto ipsec transform-set myset esp-aes-256 esp-sha-hmac
```

Step 9: Setting Up a Dynamic Crypto Map

VPN clients often get dynamic IP addresses from their ISPs. Therefore, it is impossible to statically map their IP addresses in the group settings. The Cisco security appliance solves this problem by allowing configuration of a dynamic crypto map. Example 7-13 demonstrates the configuration of the Cisco security appliance to use the defined transform set. The dynamic crypto map name is dynmap, and it is configured with a sequence number of 10. Setting up a transform set in a dynamic crypto map is a required attribute. The dynamic crypto map becomes incomplete if no transform set is applied to it.

Example 7-13 *Dynamic Crypto Map Configuration*

```
CiscoASA(config)# crypto dynamic-map dynmap 10 set transform-set myset
```

Step 10: Configuring the Crypto Map

The dynamic map is associated with a crypto map entry, which is eventually applied to the interface terminating the IPSec tunnels. Example 7-14 shows crypto map configuration on the CiscoASA security appliance. The crypto map name is IPSec_map, and the sequence number is 65535.

Example 7-14 *Crypto Map Configuration*

```
CiscoASA(config)# crypto map IPSec_map 65535 ipsec-isakmp dynamic dynmap
```

The Cisco security appliance limits you to one crypto map per interface. If there is a need to configure multiple VPN tunnels, use the same crypto map name with a different sequence number. However, the security appliance evaluates a VPN tunnel with the lowest sequence number first.

Step 11: Applying the Crypto Map to an Interface

The next step in setting up a remote-access tunnel is to bind the crypto map to an interface. In Example 7-15, the crypto map, IPSec_map, is applied to the outside interface of the security appliance.

Example 7-15 *Applying a Crypto Map to the Outside Interface*

```
CiscoASA# configure terminal
CiscoASA(config)# crypto map IPSec_map interface outside
```

Step 12: Configuring Traffic Filtering

If you trust all your private networks, including all your remote VPN clients, you can configure the security appliance to permit all decrypted IPSec packets to pass through it without inspecting them against the configured ACL. This is done with the use of the **sysopt connection permit-vpn** command, as shown in Example 7-16.

Example 7-16 *sysopt Configuration to Bypass Traffic Filtering*

```
CiscoASA(config)# sysopt connection permit-vpn
```

If NAT is configured on the security appliance but you do not want to change the source IP address of traffic going over the VPN tunnel, you need to configure the NAT exempt rules. You must create an access list to specify what traffic the NAT engine should bypass. Example 7-17 shows an access list that is permitting the VPN traffic from 10.10.0.0/16 to the pool of addresses in 10.10.200.0/24.

Example 7-17 *Access List to Bypass NAT*

```
CiscoASA(config)# access-list nonat extended permit ip 10.10.0.0 255.255.0.0
   10.10.200.0 255.255.255.0
```

After defining the access list, the next step is to configure the **nat 0** command. Example 7-18 demonstrates how to configure the **nat 0** statement if the private LAN that is being protected is toward the inside interface.

Example 7-18 *Configuration of NAT 0 Access List*

```
CiscoASA(config)# nat (inside) 0 access-list nonat
```

VPN Configuration on the Cisco VPN Client

The VPN client is set up identically to the process discussed in Chapter 6 in the section "VPN Configuration on the Cisco VPN client." Refer to Chapter 6 for configuration assistance with the VPN client.

NAC Configuration on the Cisco Security Appliances

This section discusses the configuration of NAC-related parameters on the security appliances. These parameters are applied after a VPN tunnel is established. The following four steps are required in configuring NAC on the security appliances:

Step 1   Set up the NAC global parameters.

Step 2   Configure NAC authentication.

Step 3   Enable NAC on user groups.

Step 4   Configure the NAC exception list.

This section discusses these configuration steps.

Step 1: Setting Up NAC Global Parameters

The first step in setting up NAC on the security appliances is to ensure that the global NAC parameters are properly configured. You can modify the default values of these parameters from the global configuration mode, as shown in Example 7-19, by using the **eou** commands.

Example 7-19   *Available EOU Parameters in Global Configuration Mode*

```
CiscoASA(config)# eou ?
configure mode commands/options:
  allow      Enable/Disable clientless authentication
  clientless Clientless host configuration
  max-retry  Set maximum number of times an EAP over UDP message is retransmitted
  port       Set EAP over UDP port number
  timeout    Set EAP over UDP timeout values
```

In Example 7-20, some of the NAC EAP over UDP (EOU) parameters are modified from their default values. The Retransmission Timer is modified from 3 seconds to 5 seconds. When the security appliance sends an EOU packet to the VPN client, it waits for 5 seconds before resending another request. This way, the VPN clients that use dialup connections to connect to the Internet can reply to the security appliance within a reasonable time. If a response is not received, the security appliance sends another request and starts the retransmission timer. The security appliance sends the EAPoUDP packets three times (**eou max-retry 3**) before failing the communication and initiating the hold timer. The hold time of 180 seconds ensures that no EAPoUDP requests are sent to the VPN client for 180 seconds (3 minutes). As soon as this timer expires, the security appliance initiates EAPoUDP communication with the VPN client and goes through the process discussed in Chapter 6 in the section "Architectural Overview of NAC on Cisco VPN 3000 Concentrators." EAPoUDP communication is done on UDP port 21862. It is recommended that you not change this port unless there is a port conflict in your network.

Example 7-20 *Modifying EOU Parameters*

```
CiscoASA(config)# eou max-retry 3
CiscoASA(config)# eou port 21862
CiscoASA(config)# eou timeout retransmit 5
CiscoASA(config)# eou timeout hold-period 180
```

For agentless hosts, you can enable the clientless authentication and specify a username and password. The user authentication credential is sent to the RADIUS server for proper action, such as applying appropriate ACLs or requesting an audit server to scan the host. In Example 7-21, a clientless user named clientless is set up with a password of cisco123cisco. It is recommended that clientless machines such as guest hosts and contractors' computers not be given access to the trusted network of the company. Therefore, the RADIUS server can send a downloadable ACL to be applied to the VPN clients that do not have a CTA agent installed.

Example 7-21 *EOU Clientless Authentication*

```
CiscoASA(config)# eou allow clientless
CiscoASA(config)# eou clientless username clientless
CiscoASA(config)# eou clientless password cisco123cisco
```

If clientless authentication is not enabled, the security appliance applies a default ACL, discussed in step 3. Traffic from the VPN client is subject to this ACL based on the permit and deny entries. The active VPN clients are periodically challenged to determine whether posture validation can be done on the client machine based on the configured value of the hold timer.

Additionally, you can use Adaptive Security Device Manager (ASDM) to manage a security appliance. ASDM provides an easy-to-navigate graphical interface to set up and monitor the different features that a Cisco security appliance provides. You can configure the NAC global parameters under **Configuration > VPN > NAC**, as shown in Figure 7-3.

Figure 7-3 *NAC Global Parameters in ASDM*

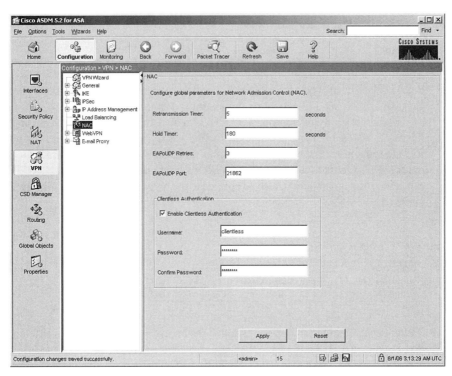

Step 2: Configuring NAC Authentication

For NAC posture validation, a RADIUS server must be defined under the tunnel group. The RADIUS server is available only for the remote-access tunnel groups: IPSec and L2TP over IPSec. If you don't define at least one RADIUS server for the NAC posture-validation process, the sessions will not get authenticated. A RADIUS server is mapped to the tunnel group by using the **nac-authentication-server-group** command followed by the server tag name. In Example 7-22, a RADIUS server is mapped to a NAC-Group tunnel group as Radius.

Example 7-22 *NAC Authentication Using RADIUS*

```
CiscoASA(config)# tunnel-group NAC-Group general-attributes
CiscoASA(config-tunnel-general)# nac-authentication-server-group Radius
```

In ASDM, the NAC authentication can be configured under the Authentication tab of the Edit Tunnel Group window by navigating to **Configuration > VPN > General > Tunnel Group**, as shown in Figure 7-4.

Figure 7-4 *NAC Authentication in ASDM*

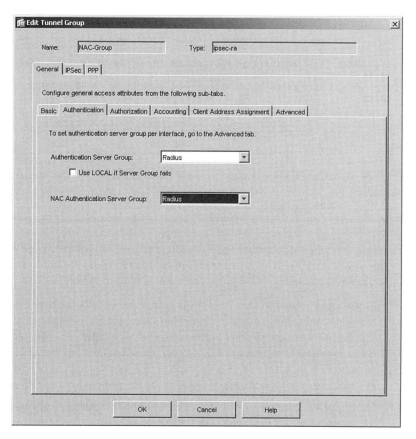

Step 3: Enabling NAC on a User Group-Policy

When a VPN tunnel is established, the security appliance initiates the posture-validation process. During this process, a default ACL is applied on the users to restrict traffic. The security appliance also applies this default ACL if the EAPoUDP communication fails between the client and the ACS server. The purpose of this default ACL is to ensure that remote users do not send unnecessary traffic until their posture is fully validated. You want this ACL to be as restrictive as possible. Therefore, it is recommended that you configure the appropriate inbound and outbound access-control entries (ACEs) to pass necessary packets and deny all other traffic passing through the security appliance. As shown in Example 7-23, an ACL is defined to allow the remote-access users to communicate with the ACS server and the DNS server, and vice versa. All other communication is dropped by the implicit deny of an ACL. This ACL is mapped to the NAC process under the user group-policy by using the **nac-default-acl** command. The user group-policy name is SecureMeGrp.

Example 7-23 *Default ACL for NAC*

```
CiscoASA(config)# access-list NAC-default permit ip host 10.10.20.181 10.10.200.0
 255.255.255.0
CiscoASA(config)# access-list NAC-default permit udp any eq 53 10.10.200.0
 255.255.255.0
CiscoASA(config)# access-list NAC-default permit ip 10.10.200.0 255.255.255.0 host
 10.10.20.181
CiscoASA(config)# access-list NAC-default permit udp 10.10.200.0 255.255.255.0 any
 eq 53
CiscoASA(config)# group-policy SecureMeGrp attributes
CiscoASA(config-group-policy)# nac-default-acl value NAC-default
```

NOTE   The NAC default ACL should allow traffic to pass from the VPN clients to the DNS server, and vice versa.

The security appliance supports two timers after successfully completing posture validation for the VPN clients. Both of these timers are configured under the user group-policy, as shown in Example 7-24:

- **Status query timer**—This timer ensures that the security appliance periodically checks the posture state of the VPN client, in case it has changed from the last time. The default status query timer is 300 seconds. In Example 7-24, the status query timer is changed to 600 seconds, which is recommended if the number of concurrent sessions is high. If this value is set too low, the security appliance will use a lot of system resources in sending status queries to the remote-access VPN clients.

- **Revalidation timer**—This timer initiates a complete posture-validation process on the remote-access VPN client. The default timer is set to 36,000 seconds (10 hours). You can lower this timer to 18,000 seconds (5 hours) if your organization requires you to revalidate the VPN clients more often. This is helpful when new antivirus patches are continuously updated on the servers and you want the VPN clients to update them as soon as they go through a new posture-validation process.

Example 7-24 *Status Query and Revalidation Timers*

```
CiscoASA(config)# group-policy SecureMeGrp attributes
CiscoASA(config-group-policy)# nac-sq-period 600
CiscoASA(config-group-policy)# nac-reval-period 18000
```

When all the parameters are set up, the last step is to enable NAC on the user group-policy. This is shown in Example 7-25 for a user group-policy called SecureMeGrp.

Example 7-25 *Enable NAC on a User Group-Policy*

```
CiscoASA(config)# group-policy SecureMeGrp attributes
CiscoASA(config-group-policy)# nac enable
```

NOTE   You can revalidate all the active NAC sessions by using the **eou revalidate all** command. To revalidate a specific host, you can use the **eou revalidate ip** command followed by the IP address of the host to be revalidated.

To configure these parameters in ASDM, navigate to **Configuration > VPN > General > Group Policy** and click the **NAC** tab, as shown in Figure 7-5.

Figure 7-5   *NAC Configuration of User Group-Policy Parameters in ASDM*

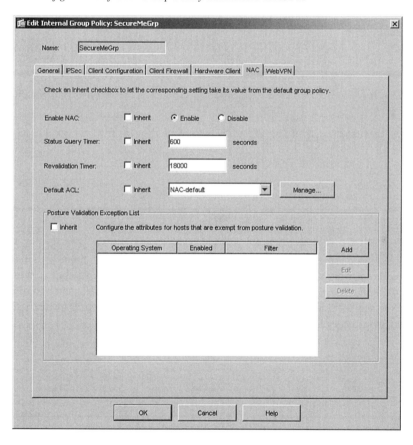

Step 4: Configuring the NAC Exception List

A number of operating systems support the Cisco VPN client, including Solaris, Mac OS X, Windows, and Linux. However, Cisco CTA is currently supported only on Windows, Linux, and Mac OS X. During the tunnel-negotiation process, the VPN client reports its version information, such as Windows 2000, Windows XP, or Mac OS X, to name a few. You can specify an exception list based on the reported version of the VPN client. This list excludes the configured operating systems to go through the posture-validation process. After the IPSec tunnel is negotiated, the VPN clients that are in the exception list can be subject to an ACL to restrict their activities on the network. For example, if you want only Solaris-based VPN clients to access an internal mainframe system, the exception list ACL should allow only traffic destined for the mainframe server in the ACL and should deny all other traffic.

In Example 7-26, an ACL called Solaris-ACL is being set up. This ACL will allow all bidirectional traffic to pass through if

- It is sourced from the mainframe server with an IP address of 10.10.50.100.
- It is destined to the Solaris VPN clients. Thus, the VPN client pool of 10.10.200.0 with a subnet mask of 255.255.255.0 is specified as the destination address.

Example 7-26 *ACL for NAC Exception List*

```
CiscoASA(config)# access-list Solaris-ACL extended permit ip host 10.10.50.100
  10.10.200.0 255.255.255.0
CiscoASA(config)# access-list Solaris-ACL extended permit ip 10.10.200.0
  255.255.255.0 host 10.10.50.100
```

When both the inbound and outbound entries are configured, the next step is to apply this ACL either globally or to a specific group. This is achieved by using the **vpn-nac-exempt** command followed by the operating system name and the ACL name to filter traffic. In Example 7-27, Solaris-ACL is mapped to the SecureMeGrp user group-policy for the Solaris operating system.

Example 7-27 *NAC Exception List*

```
CiscoASA(config-group-policy)# group-policy SecureMeGrp attributes
CiscoASA(config-group-policy)# vpn-nac-exempt os Solaris filter Solaris-ACL
```

If instead you want to define the NAC exception policies globally, specify the **vpn-nac-exempt** command under the default group policy, DfltGrpPolicy.

To define or manage an exception list in ASDM, navigate to **Configuration > VPN > General > Group Policy** and select the **NAC** tab, as shown in Figure 7-6. Under Posture Validation Exception List, click **Add** and specify the operating system and the NAC exception ACL.

Figure 7-6 *NAC Exception List in ASDM*

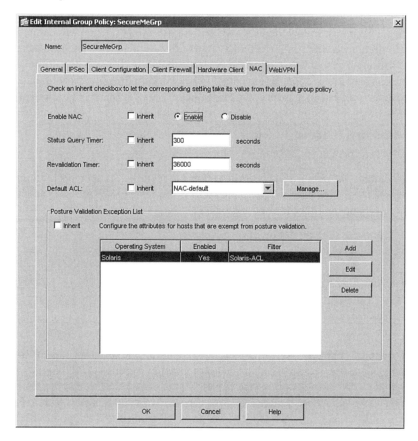

Testing, Monitoring, and Troubleshooting NAC on Cisco Security Appliances

This section discusses the different test scenarios that are useful in implementing the NAC solution on the security appliances. Each test scenario helps in gathering the statistical information about a connection. These scenarios also discuss the related debugs that are helpful in troubleshooting any IPSec or NAC deployments. The following test scenarios are discussed:

1. Remote-access IPSec tunnel without NAC

2. Remote-access IPSec tunnel from an agentless client

3. Remote-access IPSec tunnel from a CTA client

Remote-Access IPSec Tunnel Without NAC

If you are setting up a new group on the security appliance that will validate the posture on the VPN clients, follow the first two configuration stages, discussed earlier in the section "Configuration Steps of NAC on Cisco Security Appliances." The next step is to make a VPN tunnel from a test VPN client machine to ensure that you do not run into any misconfigurations. If the IPSec tunnel is not working for some reason, make sure that you have the proper debug turned on. The following are the two most important debugs to look at:

```
debug crypto isakmp [debug-level]

debug crypto ipsec [debug-level]
```

By default, the debug level is set to 1. You can increase the severity level up to 255 to get detailed logs. However, in most cases, setting this level to 127 provides enough information to determine the root cause of an issue.

In Example 7-28, the **debug crypto isakmp 127** and **debug crypto ipsec 127** commands have been enabled.

Example 7-28 *Enabling Crypto Debugs*

```
CiscoASA# debug crypto isakmp 127
CiscoASA# debug crypto ipsec 127
```

The tunnel negotiations begin by exchanging the ISAKMP proposals. If ISAKMP debugs are enabled, the security appliance shows the tunnel group—NAC-Group, in this case—that the VPN client is trying to connect to. If the proposal is acceptable, the debugs display a message indicating that the IKE SA proposal is acceptable, as shown in Example 7-29. Also displayed are the chosen IKE SA proposal number and the public IP address of the VPN client, which is 209.165.202.159.

Example 7-29 *debug Output to Show ISAKMP Proposal Is Acceptable*

```
Mar 22 19:31:50 [IKEv1]: IP = 209.165.202.159, Connection landed on tunnel_group
  NAC-Group
Mar 22 19:31:50 [IKEv1 DEBUG]: Group = NAC-Group, IP = 209.165.202.159, processing
  IKE SA payload
Mar 22 19:31:50 [IKEv1 DEBUG]: Group = NAC-Group, IP = 209.165.202.159, IKE SA
  Proposal # 1, Transform # 10 acceptable  Matches global IKE entry # 1
```

If the proposal is acceptable, the VPN devices try to discover whether they are NAT-T capable and whether an address-translation device lies between them. If NAT-Traversal (NAT-T) is not negotiated or a NAT/PAT device is not detected, the ISAKMP debugs display the "Remote end is NOT behind a NAT device. This end is NOT behind a NAT device" message, as shown in Example 7-30.

Example 7-30 *debug Output to Show NAT-T Discovery Process*

```
[IKEv1 DEBUG]: Group = NAC-Group, IP = 209.165.202.159, processing NAT-Discovery
 payload
[IKEv1 DEBUG]: Group = NAC-Group, IP = 209.165.202.159, computing NAT Discovery hash
[IKEv1 DEBUG]: Group = NAC-Group, IP = 209.165.202.159, processing NAT-Discovery
 payload
[IKEv1]: Group = NAC-Group, IP = 209.165.202.159, Automatic NAT Detection Status:
 Remote end is NOT behind a NAT device. This end is NOT behind a NAT device
```

After NAT-T negotiations, the Cisco security appliance prompts the user to specify user credentials. Upon successful user authentication, the ISAKMP debugs display a message indicating that the user (ciscouser, in this example) is authenticated, as shown in Example 7-31.

Example 7-31 *debug Output to Show User Is Authenticated*

```
[IKEv1]: Group = NAC-Group, Username = ciscouser, IP = 209.165.202.159, User
 (ciscouser) authenticated.,

[IKEv1 DEBUG]: Group = NAC-Group, Username = ciscouser, IP = 209.165.202.159,
 constructing blank hash
[IKEv1 DEBUG]: Group = NAC-Group, Username = ciscouser, IP = 209.165.202.159,
 constructing qm hash
```

The client requests mode-config attributes by sending a list of client-supported attributes, as shown in Example 7-32. The security appliance replies with all its supported attributes and the appropriate information.

Example 7-32 *debug Output to Show Mode-Config Requests*

```
[IKEv1 DEBUG]Processing cfg Request attributes,
[IKEv1 DEBUG]MODE_CFG: Received request for IPV4 address!,
[IKEv1 DEBUG]MODE_CFG: Received request for IPV4 net mask!,
[IKEv1 DEBUG]MODE_CFG: Received request for DNS server address!,
[IKEv1 DEBUG]MODE_CFG: Received request for WINS server address!,
```

After pushing down the attributes, the security appliance displays a message indicating that the ISAKMP SA was successfully negotiated, as demonstrated in Example 7-33.

Example 7-33 *debug Output to Show Phase 1 Negotiations Are Completed*

```
[IKEv1]: Group = NAC-Group, Username = ciscouser, IP = 209.165.202.159 PHASE 1
 COMPLETED
```

After completing Phase 1 negotiations, the VPN client and the security appliance try to negotiate Phase 2 SA by exchanging the proxy identities and the IPSec Phase 2 proposal. The remote host is the IP address that the security appliance assigned to the VPN client. If the proxy identities are acceptable, the ISAKMP debugs display a message indicating that the IPSec SA proposal is acceptable, as shown in Example 7-34.

Example 7-34 *debug Output to Show Proxy Identities and Phase 2 Proposal Are Accepted*

```
[IKEv1 DEBUG]: Group = NAC-Group, Username = ciscouser, IP = 209.165.202.159, IPSec
  SA Proposal # 12, Transform # 1 acceptable  Matches global IPSec SA entry # 10,
[IKEv1 DEBUG]: Group = NAC-Group, Username = ciscouser, IP = 209.165.202.159,
  Transmitting Proxy Id:
  Remote host: 10.10.200.1  Protocol 0  Port 0
  Local subnet:  0.0.0.0  mask 0.0.0.0 Protocol 0  Port 0
```

After accepting the transform set values, both VPN devices agree on the inbound and outbound IPSec SAs, as shown in Example 7-35. After the IPSec SAs have been created, both VPN devices should be capable of passing traffic bidirectionally across the tunnel.

Example 7-35 *debug Output to Show IPSec SAs Are Activated*

```
IKEv1 DEBUG]: Group = NAC-Group, Username = ciscouser, IP = 209.165.202.159, loading
  all IPSEC SAs
[IKEv1]: Group = NAC-Group, Username = ciscouser, IP = 209.165.202.159 Security
  negotiation complete for User (ciscouser)  Responder, Inbound SPI = 0x00c6bc19,
  Outbound SPI = 0xa472f8c1,
[IKEv1]: Group = NAC-Group, Username = ciscouser, IP = 209.165.202.159 Adding static
  route for client address: 10.10.200.1 ,
[IKEv1]: Group = NAC-Group, Username = ciscouser, IP = 209.165.202.159, PHASE 2
  COMPLETED (msgid=8732f056)
```

Remote-Access IPSec Tunnel from an Agentless Client

After successfully testing the VPN tunnel, the next step is to configure NAC on the security appliance and then connect from the same test VPN client without installing the CTA agent. This emulates an agentless VPN client scenario. The security appliance enables you to set up NAC logging and/or NAC debugging. NAC logging enables you to capture EAPoUDP, EAP, and NAC events such as EAP status query, posture-validation initializations and revalidations, exception list matches, ACS transactions, clientless authentications, and default ACL applications.

NAC debugging is useful if you want to gather detailed NAC-specific events such as the hexadecimal dump of EAP header and packet contents, EAPoUDP header and packet contents, EAPoUDP session-state changes, and timer events.

Example 7-36 illustrates how to enable NAC logging on a security appliance. An event list, called NAC, is defined to log the nac, eapoudp, and eap classes. The logging level is set as debugging. The NAC logs are sent to the internal buffer of the security appliance.

Example 7-36 *Enabling NAC Logging on a Security Appliance*

```
CiscoASA(config)# logging enable
CiscoASA(config)# logging list NAC level debugging class nac
CiscoASA(config)# logging list NAC level debugging class eapoudp
CiscoASA(config)# logging list NAC level debugging class eap
CiscoASA(config)# logging buffered NAC
```

NOTE   It is a best practice to send the log messages to an external syslog server for forensics and later analysis.

When NAC logging is turned on, establish an IPSec session from the VPN client that is clientless. As shown in Example 7-37, as soon as IKE Phase 2 negotiations are completed, the security appliance initiates the NAC process for 10.10.200.1. It applies a default ACL called Default-Filter on the VPN user session until the correct posture is determined.

This test scenario assumes that you are not running the CTA application on the VPN client. Consequently, the security appliance fails to receive a response from the host. The security appliance times out the request and sends an authentication request to the RADIUS server for the clientless user. If the RADIUS server authenticates this user, it sends a downloadable ACL, ACSACL#-IP-Clientless_ACL-4470a5d3, to the security appliance. Based on the access-control entries, the user gets limited access on the network.

Example 7-37 *NAC Logs for Clientless Agents*

```
CiscoASA(config)# show logging
<some output removed>
%ASA-6-335001: NAC session initialized - 10.10.200.1.
%ASA-5-335003: NAC Default ACL applied, ACL:NAC-default - 10.10.200.1.
%ASA-6-334001: EAPoUDP association initiated - 10.10.200.1.
%ASA-5-334006: EAPoUDP failed to get a response from host - 10.10.200.1.
%ASA-6-334004: Authentication request for NAC Clientless host - 10.10.200.1.
%ASA-6-335006: NAC Applying ACL:#ACSACL#-IP-Clientless_ACL-4470a5d3 - 10.10.200.1.
```

Alternatively, you can enable the appropriate debugs to troubleshoot issues related to NAC. Example 7-38 shows the recommended debugs on a security appliance for NAC troubleshooting.

Example 7-38 *Enabling NAC Logging on a Security Appliance*

```
CiscoASA# debug nac auth
CiscoASA# debug nac errors
CiscoASA# debug nac events
CiscoASA# debug eou eap
CiscoASA# debug eou errors
CiscoASA# debug eou events
```

As shown in Example 7-39, the security appliance applies NAC-Default ACL when it initiates a NAC session. It tries to determine whether CTA is active on the VPN client. The EAPoUDP queries time out and the security appliance initiates clientless authentication for the VPN client. The RADIUS server sends an Access-Accept message if clientless authentication is successful.

Example 7-39 *Enabling NAC Debugs for Clientless Hosts*

```
NAC default acl NAC-default applied - 10.10.200.1
EAPoUDP association initiated - 10.10.200.1
EAPoUDP response timer expiry - 10.10.200.1
EAPoUDP response timer expiry - 10.10.200.1
EAPoUDP response timer expiry - 10.10.200.1
EAPoUDP failed to get a response from the host - 10.10.200.1
NAC clientless Access Request successful - 10.10.200.1
EAPoUDP Authentication request for NAC Clientless host - 10.10.200.1
NAC Clientless Access Accept - 10.10.200.1
```

Remote-Access IPSec Tunnel from a CTA Client

If the "remote-access IPSec tunnel from an agentless client" test scenario is successful, the next test case is to install the CTA application on the VPN client and go through the posture-validation process on the security appliance. After establishing the IPSec SAs, the security appliance initiates the EAPoUDP process. If an EAPoUDP response is received from the VPN client, the security appliance knows that the VPN client is actively running the CTA service.

If you enable the debugs suggested in Example 7-37, the security appliance generates NAC-specific messages. As illustrated in Example 7-40, the security appliance initiates an EAPoUDP association. It receives a response from the VPN client and starts the posture-validation process. CTA forwards the host name and username of the client machine—SECUREME:Adminsitrator, in this example—through EAP. The security appliance receives the system posture token of Healthy from the RADIUS server and assigns it to the host machine.

Example 7-40 *NAC Debugs for CTA-Enabled VPN Client*

```
NAC default acl NAC-default applied - 10.10.200.1
EAPoUDP association initiated - 10.10.200.1
EAPoUDP-Hello response received from host - 10.10.200.1
NAC EAP association initiated - 10.10.200.1, EAP context:0x0463c490
NAC EAP Access Accept - 10.10.200.1
NAC EAP Access Accept - 10.10.200.1, user:SECUREME:Administrator
NAC EAP Access Accept - 10.10.200.1, Reval Period:36000 seconds
NAC Access Accept - 10.10.200.1, Posture Token:Healthy
NAC Access Accept - 10.10.200.1, Status Query Period:300 seconds
NAC PV complete - 10.10.200.1, posture:Healthy
EAPoUDP association successfully established - 10.10.200.1
```

After successfully testing the client posture, you are ready to start deploying NAC in your VPN environment. The CTA software can be distributed to the VPN client machines so that they can be assigned a correct posture based on their machine state.

Monitoring of NAC Sessions

You can use several **show** commands to monitor and report the state of NAC sessions. The **show vpn-sessiondb remote** command is one of the most commonly used because it displays IPSec as well as NAC statistics of all the VPN clients. As shown in Example 7-41, the session type is remote for remote-access tunnel, and the VPN username is ciscouser. The assigned IP address is 10.10.200.1 and the public IP address is 209.165.202.159. The security appliance has transmitted 15,790 bytes and has received 6,179 bytes. The NAC result was accepted by the RADIUS server, and a system posture token of Healthy is assigned to this user. The RADIUS server assigned a downloadable ACL called IP-NAC_HEALTHY_ACL-43c0876e.

Example 7-41 *Output of show vpn-sessiondb remote*

```
CiscoASA# show vpn-sessiondb remote
Session Type: Remote
Username     : ciscouser
Index        : 1
Assigned IP  : 10.10.200.1          Public IP    : 209.165.202.159
Protocol     : IPSec                Encryption   : 3DES
Hashing      : SHA1
Bytes Tx     : 15790                Bytes Rx     : 6179
Client Type  : WinNT                Client Ver   : 4.8.01.0300
Group Policy : SecureMeGrp
Tunnel Group : NAC-Group
Login Time   : 03:23:16 UTC Wed Aug 2 2006
Duration     : 0h:28m:13s
Filter Name  : #ACSACL#-IP-NAC_HEALTHY_ACL-43c0876e
NAC Result   : Accepted
Posture Token: Healthy
```

You can also use ASDM to monitor the IPSec and NAC session on the security appliance. Navigate to **Monitoring > VPN > VPN Statistics > Sessions** to check the NAC result and system posture token assigned to a user, as shown in Figure 7-7.

Figure 7-7 *IPSec and NAC Monitoring in ASDM*

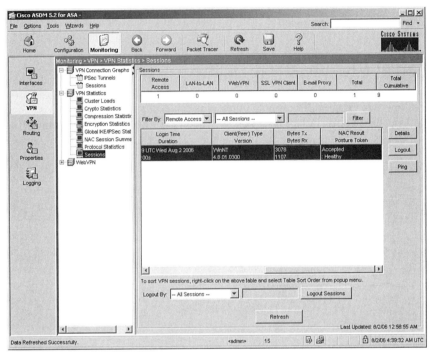

If you would rather get detailed information about a particular EAPoUDP session, you can use the **show vpn-sessiondb detail index** command followed by an index number to see a detailed connection of the host you are interested in. Example 7-42 shows the output of **show vpn-sessiondb detail index 1** to get detailed connection information about ciscouser. The index number is a local ID assigned to the user. Using this command, the security appliance can provide information about the EAPoUDP timers. The security appliance indicates that after 34,567 seconds, it will initiate EAPoUDP revalidation for this host. It also displays a Healthy system posture token associated for that host.

Example 7-42 *Displaying EOU Session Details for a Specific Host*

```
CiscoASA# show vpn-sessiondb detail index 1
Session Type: Remote Detailed
Username    : ciscouser
Index       : 1

<output removed>

NAC:
  Reval Int (T): 18000 Seconds     Reval Left(T): 17900 Seconds
  SQ Int (T)   : 600 Seconds       EoU Age(T)   : 100 Seconds
  Hold Left (T): 0 Seconds         Posture Token: Healthy
  Redirect URL :
```

Using ASDM, you can view the similar NAC session timers by navigating to **Monitoring > VPN > VPN Statistics > Sessions** and selecting the **Details** icon. Figure 7-8 illustrates this.

Figure 7-8 *NAC Session Timers in ASDM*

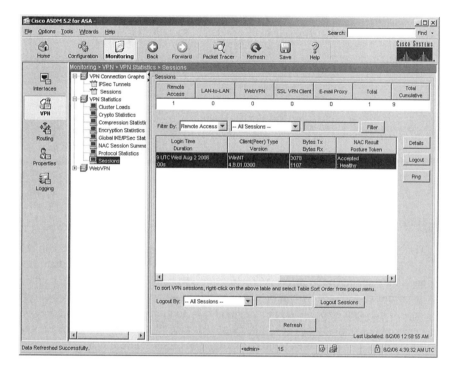

You can view a summary of all the VPN and NAC sessions on a security appliance by using the **show vpn-sessiondb summary** command. As shown in Example 7-43, it displays an active IPSec remote-access session. This session is an active accepted NAC session. Additionally, the security appliance displays cumulative NAC accepted and rejected sessions. This command is useful if you want to determine whether the RADIUS server is successfully assigning the appropriate posture token to the VPN client.

Example 7-43 *Displaying Active VPN and NAC Sessions*

```
CiscoASA# show vpn-sessiondb summary

Active Sessions:                          Session Information:
  IPSec LAN-to-LAN      : 0                 Peak Concurrent      : 1
  IPSec Remote Access   : 1                 IPSec Limit          : 750
  WebVPN                : 0                 WebVPN Limit         : 2
  SSL VPN Client (SVC)  : 0                 Cumulative Sessions  : 8
  Email Proxy           : 0
  Total Active Sessions : 1                 Percent Session Load : 0%
                                            VPN LB Mgmt Sessions : 0

Active NAC Sessions:                      Cumulative NAC Sessions:
  Accepted              : 1                 Accepted             : 14
  Rejected              : 0                 Rejected             : 1
  Exempted              : 0                 Exempted             : 0
  Non-responsive        : 0                 Non-responsive       : 14
  Hold-off              : 0                 Hold-off             : 1
  N/A                   : 0                 N/A                  : 0
```

Summary

The NAC implementation on the Cisco security appliances provides a complete solution to check the posture state of a VPN client. If the posture cannot be validated, the security appliance applies appropriate ACLs to filter traffic. This chapter discussed the packet flow in a security appliance when NAC is enabled and then provided detailed configuration steps. This chapter provided guidance on how to monitor the remote-access VPN tunnels. For troubleshooting purposes, this chapter discussed various debug and log messages to help you isolate the issues related to remote-access tunnels and NAC.

Review Questions

You can find the answers to the review questions in Appendix A, "Answers to Review Questions."

1. The default value for the revalidation timer on a security appliance is _____.

    a. 1,800 seconds

    b. 18,000 seconds

    c. 180,000 seconds

    d. None of the above

2. NAC exception polices can be set up under which of the following locations? (Multiple answers)

   a. Default group policies

   b. User group policies

   c. User policies

   d. Tunnel policies

3. True or false: A VPN tunnel is considered clientless if it does not report any software version information.

4. True or false: The NAC exception policies are configured under the tunnel group subconfiguration mode.

5. True or false: The NAC session's database cannot be statefully replicated to a standby appliance.

6. Mode-config attributes are configured under_____.

   a. User policy

   b. Default user-group

   c. User group-policy

   d. All of the above

7. True or false: Specifying a RADIUS server under tunnel-group is a mandatory step.

8. True or false: The IPSec tunnel is torn down if the VPN client does not respond to an EAPoUDP request packet.

9. True or false: The NAC exemption list must be applied on a per-group basis.

10. True or false: Clientless authentication is used for machines that do not have CTA installed.

This chapter covers the following topics:

- Installing Cisco Secure Access Control Server
- Performing initial ACS configuration
- Configuring posture validation
- Configuring posture enforcement
- Understanding and configuring network access profiles
- Understanding and configuring network access filtering
- Understanding and configuring nonresponsive policies
- Understanding user databases
- Importing vendors' attribute/value pairs
- Understanding and configuring ACS logging
- Understanding ACS replication
- Troubleshooting ACS

## CHAPTER 8

Cisco Secure Access Control Server

The Cisco Secure Access Control Server, hereafter referred to as ACS, is the central core component in the NAC Framework. Whereas switches, routers, concentrators, and access points are the brains of NAC (limiting access and enforcing policy), ACS is the brains. It is responsible for receiving the posture credentials from the end hosts and validating them against the policies defined by the administrator. It then sends the authorization policy to the enforcement device where it is applied. Additionally, in NAC-L2-802.1X deployments, ACS authenticates the user (or machine) to the network.

For clientless hosts (where CTA is not installed), ACS can trigger an external audit of the endpoint to determine its security posture. Alternatively, it can look up the MAC address of the endpoint in its database or on an external LDAP server.

On hosts that have CTA installed along with NAC partner applications, ACS can forward partner-specific posture information to the partner's management console. This allows for an additional posture assessment of the specific partner application. (A common example of this is validating antivirus definition files.) The partner application then returns an application posture token to ACS. ACS combines this posture token with all other application posture tokens associated with the host and derives the system posture token. Based on the overall system posture, ACS applies a policy to the host by way of the network enforcement device.

Besides the NAC capabilities that ACS has, it is a full-featured Authentication, Authorization, and Accounting (AAA) server. It is commonly used in networks to provide AAA services for remote-access (VPN, wireless, dialup) users and for management of network access devices (NADs). It supports both Remote Authentication Dial-In User Service (RADIUS) and Terminal Access Controller Access Control System (TACACS+) authentication protocols and provides support for several back-end databases, including Windows Active Directory (AD) and Security Accounts Manager (SAM), Lightweight Directory Access Protocol (LDAP), Novell NetWare, RSA ACE, any Open Database Connectivity (ODBC)–compliant relational database, and more. As an enterprise AAA server, ACS supports up to 300,000 users in its local database and 50,000 NADs.

Cisco sells two different flavors of the ACS server. One is the software itself, which can be installed on any medium-size Windows server that meets the minimum requirements. The other is the ACS Solution Engine, which is a 1-RU hardened hardware appliance with ACS preinstalled on it. Some functional differences exist between the two. The Cisco Secure

ACS Solution Engine uses a remote agent to receive logging information and to forward authentication requests to external databases. The Cisco Secure ACS software application performs these tasks natively. Therefore, you should evaluate both options before making a purchasing decision.

Installing ACS

This section covers the installation of ACS software on a Windows server.

Installation Prerequisites

Before installing the ACS software on a Windows server, make sure the server meets the minimum system requirements as indicated in Table 8-1.

Table 8-1   *ACS Windows Server Minimum System Requirements*

Component	Requirement
Operating System	Windows 2003 Server (Enterprise or Advanced) with SP1
	Windows 2000 Server with SP4
	Windows 2000 Advanced Server with SP4
Processor	Pentium IV, 1.8 GHz or faster
RAM	1 GB (minimum)
Virtual Memory	1 GB (minimum)
Free Hard Drive Space	1 GB (minimum)
File System	NTFS
Network Interface	Fast Ethernet or Gigabit Ethernet

Most midclass servers today easily meet the minimum requirements. However, be aware that NAC posture validation is the most computationally intensive service that ACS provides. Therefore, if your NAC deployment will consist of thousands of endpoints, I advise you to use a server with the fastest CPU available to you. Compared to the other networking components in your network (routers, switches, and so on), servers are by far the cheapest. Do not skimp on the hardware for the ACS server.

NOTE   Although ACS will run on a multiprocessor machine, the software was not designed with multiprocessors in mind. Therefore, you will notice little to no performance improvement on a multiprocessor machine over a single-processor one.

As for the hard drive, a bigger hard drive enables you to store the logs for a longer period of time. For most deployments, you should plan to retain the logs locally for 30 days. This usually amounts to less than 5GB of space.

For comparison purposes, the system specifications of the ACS Solution Engine (part number CSACSE-1113-K9) are listed in Table 8-2.

Table 8-2   *ACS Solution Engine System Specifications*

Component	Specification
Operating System	Windows 2000 Server
Processor	Pentium IV, 3.2 GHz
RAM	1 GB
Virtual Memory	1.5 GB
Hard Drive Size	80 GB

Now is a good time to point out that the ACS server hardware should be dedicated *only* to ACS. Do not host another enterprise application on the same server that ACS is installed on. This is unsupported and could substantially degrade the performance of ACS. Also note that, for Windows AD integration, ACS must be installed on a Domain Controller or on a member server.

Access to the ACS server and ACS Solution Engine are through a Java-enabled web browser. Table 8-3 lists the supported web browsers along with the supported Java plug-ins. You might find that other web browsers work just fine, but the ones listed here have been tested and are officially supported by Cisco.

Table 8-3   *Supported Web Browsers with Java Plug-In Versions*

Web Browser	Version
Microsoft Internet Explorer	6.0 with SP1, Sun Java plug-in Version 1.5
	5.5 with SP1, Sun Java plug-in Version 1.4.2_04
Netscape Communicator	8.0, 7.1 for Windows, with Sun Java plug-in Version 1.5
	7.0, 7.1, 7.2 for Windows, with Sun Java plug-in Version 1.4.2_04

Installing ACS on a Windows Server

Installing ACS on Windows is simple and straightforward. Like most Windows applications, ACS uses the Microsoft InstallShield installer. Therefore, you should be familiar with the process. To install ACS, complete these steps:

NOTE   Installing ACS over Terminal Services (or Remote Desktop) is not supported. However, you can use VNC (Virtual Network Computing's remote desktop utility) to install ACS remotely.

Step 1   Log in to the server using a local Administrator account.

Step 2   Insert the ACS CD into the CD-ROM drive. If autorun is enabled, the installation starts automatically. Otherwise, run setup.exe from the root directory on the CD. (If you downloaded the software from cisco.com, extract the archive file and then run setup.exe).

NOTE   If any of the minimum system requirements are not met, a dialog box appears indicating the missing components. It is recommended that you bring the system up to the minimum requirements before proceeding with the installation.

Step 3   The software license agreement appears. Read the software license agreement and, if you agree to it, select **Accept**.

Step 4   The welcome screen appears. Read the information on it, and then select **Next**.

Step 5   You are now presented with the Before You Begin dialog box. This step was originally designed to prevent common mistakes but is now out of date. Check off each of the items so that you can continue with the installation; then click **Next**.

Step 6   Choose a location where you want ACS installed; then click **Next**. The default directory is C:\Program Files\CiscoSecure ACS v4.x\.

Step 7   The Authentication Database Configuration box appears. If you plan to authenticate users against an external Windows database (SAM or AD), you can select the box here. Optionally, selecting **Grant Dial-In Permission to User** requires the Windows user to have dial-in rights before ACS can authenticate them. Note that all databases (including Windows databases) can be configured after the installation completes. Again, this is another legacy screen in the installation. Continue the installation by selecting **Next** to start copying the files.

Step 8   With the files copied, the Advanced Options dialog box appears. Selecting any of these options causes them to appear in the web interface. However, you can always enable them after the installation completes from the **Interface Configuration > Advanced Options** screen in ACS. Note that none of these options is required for NAC. If you do not know what to select, I recommend selecting all of them except the **Default Time of Day/Time of Week Specification**. Then click **Next**.

Step 9   The Active Service Monitoring dialog now appears. By default, ACS monitors its services and restarts them if it detects a failure. You can disable or modify this action by choosing a different script from the drop-down list. However, I recommend keeping the default **Restart All**. Optionally, select **Enable Mail Notifications** and fill in the SMTP server and e-mail address to be notified in case of an ACS service failure (highly recommended). Select **Next** to continue.

Step 10   Enter a password that will be used to encrypt the local ACS database. The password must be at least eight characters in length and should include both letters and numbers. The password you enter is kept encrypted in the Windows Registry. Record the password you used and keep in a secure place. If there is ever a critical problem with the database, the password might be needed to access the database manually. After you enter the password, click **Next** to continue.

Step 11   The installation is almost complete. A dialog box appears with three options checked: **Install ACS as a Windows Service**, **Launch ACS after the Installation**, and **Present the Readme File to the User**. Click **Next** to perform these actions and complete the installation.

Step 12   The Setup Complete dialog box appears. Select **Finish** to close ACS setup.

The ACS Admin icon should appear on your desktop. Double-click it to launch a web browser to the ACS GUI. By default, Internet Explorer is launched.

As with any application that runs on Windows, the question invariably arises, "Can I install the latest Windows hotfixes?" The short answer is, "Yes." Cisco documents the hotfixes they have tested with ACS in the Release Notes, but do not consider this list as a limit to the patches you can apply. Follow the security best practices and keep the operating system patched to protect against the latest security threats. In the rare case that a hotfix causes a problem with ACS, contact the Cisco TAC. The TAC will investigate and resolve the issue as quickly as possible.

Upgrading from Previous Versions of ACS Server

To upgrade from previous versions of ACS, follow the same steps as in the previous section. During the installation process, you are prompted to retain your existing data. If you choose **Yes**, to keep your existing configuration, it will be migrated to the new version.

A couple more notes on upgrading:

- Check the Release Notes for the supported upgrade paths. You can upgrade to ACS 4.1 directly from ACS 4.0. Upgrades to ACS 4.0 can be made from 3.3.3 and 3.3.2, but not directly from 3.3.1.

- *Always—I repeat, always—perform a backup* of your data from within ACS *before* you attempt your upgrade. Backing up your data ensures that you can return to your existing, working configuration if anything goes wrong with the upgrade.

- Most failed upgrades are caused by other applications placing locks on the ACS files or directories. Therefore, it is a good idea to reboot the server just before the upgrade attempt.

Post-Installation Tasks

Immediately after installing ACS, you can choose to perform one or more of the following tasks in this section. If you plan to administer ACS from a Windows 2003 server, you might need to add ACS as a trusted location. In addition, to administer ACS remotely, you must first create an administrator account. Finally, to improve the security of ACS from local physical access, you can disable automatic user logins. Each of these is covered shortly.

Launching the ACS GUI on Windows 2003

After installing ACS Server on a Windows 2003 default installation, you will not be able to access the ACS GUI from your web browser. This is because of the enhanced security features Microsoft has added to Internet Explorer. To resolve this, follow these steps:

Step 1   Double-click the ACS Admin icon on the desktop. This launches Internet Explorer to display the ACS GUI.

Step 2   If you do not see the ACS GUI interface, select the **Tools** menu and choose **Internet Options**.

Step 3   Select the **Security** tab and choose the **Local Intranet** icon. Next, select the **Sites** button.

Step 4   In the **Add This Web Site to the Zone** box, fill in **http://127.0.0.1** and choose **Add** followed by **Close**.

Step 5   Click the **OK** button to close the Internet Options window.

You should now be able to access the ACS GUI interface from Internet Explorer on the local machine. If you access the ACS server remotely from another Windows 2003 server, you might need to perform the same steps on that server, but replacing the 127.0.0.1 IP address with the IP address of the ACS server.

Creating an ACS Administrator Account

To access ACS from any machine other than the one it is installed on, an administrator account must be created. Follow these steps to create one or more administrator accounts.

Step 1 Double-click the ACS Admin icon on the desktop.

Step 2 From the navigation frame on the left, click the **Administration Control** button.

Step 3 The Administration Control configuration appears in the middle frame. Click the **Add Administrator** button.

Step 4 The Add Administrator frame appears. Fill in the new administrator name and passwords. In the Administrator Privileges section, select the **Grant All** button. Alternatively, you can select only the privileges you want to grant to this administrator, but we do not cover the individual privileges here.

Step 5 Click the **Submit** button at the bottom of the frame to finish adding the new administrator.

Repeat steps 3–5 to add ACS administrators. Make sure at least one of the new administrators has been granted all privileges.

Disabling Automatic Local Logins

With an administrator account created, it is time to secure access to ACS from the local machine by disabling automatic local logins. First, verify the new administrator account by logging in to ACS from a remote machine. Open a browser to http://*ACS_Server_IP*:2002/ and log in with the administrator account. (The :2002 after the ACS server's IP address tells the browser to connect to TCP port 2002, which is where the ACS web server is listening.) When you have successfully logged in, disable automatic local logins by selecting **Administration Control > Session Policy** and unchecking **Allow Automatic Local Login**; then click **Submit**.

Initial ACS Configuration

In this section, we walk through the steps necessary to configure ACS for NAC posture validation. First, we quickly review the main components of the ACS GUI. For reference, refer to Figure 8-1.

Figure 8-1 *ACS Main Page*

The ACS GUI screen is divided into three main frames. The frame on the left contains navigation buttons that, when selected, take you to that configuration component in the middle frame. The right frame contains localized help for the configuration component currently selected. It appears and disappears as you navigate around. (This frame is not shown in Figure 8-1.)

Most of the NAC configuration falls under the **Posture Validation** and **Network Access Profiles** buttons. However, before you can configure the NAC policies, you must configure ACS to support generic RADIUS authentications. The next few sections walk you through the configuration steps.

Configuring Network Device Groups (Optional)

Network Device Groups (NDGs) enable an administrator to group similar network devices in a group. Each group is assigned a name, and the administrator can refer to all devices in the group by the network device group name. This greatly simplifies the administration of large amounts of network devices.

Three key reasons exist for creating NDGs:

- They help simplify the administration of large amounts of network devices by dividing them into logical groups.
- All network devices in a NDG can share a common shared secret key.
- Users and groups of users can be permitted, denied, or given restricted access to an NDG, which automatically applies the same restriction to all the devices in the NDG.

Most network administrators create NDGs that align with their overall enterprise structure. For example, a large retail outlet might choose to create NDGs for each region in the country And then place the devices in that region into the corresponding NDG. Another company might have a couple large campuses and choose to create an NDG for each building. Alternatively, a multinational company might choose to create an NDG for each country it has offices in. Again, how you choose to segment the network devices is up to you, but generally, the best way is to segment along an existing business operational area.

To enable NDGs, follow these steps. If you choose not to enable NDGs now, you can always come back and do it at a later time, and then move your existing network devices into the corresponding NDG.

Step 1 From the navigation frame on the left, select **Interface Configuration > Advanced Options**.

Step 2 Select **Network Device Groups** from the list, and then click **Submit**.

With NDGs enabled, follow these steps to create NDGs:

Step 1 From the navigation frame on the left, select **Network Configuration**.

Step 2 Click the **Add** button to create a new NDG.

Step 3 Fill in the **Network Device Group Name** field. Do not use spaces in the NDG name. Instead, substitute an underscore where the space would be.

Step 4 (Optional) Fill in **Shared Secret** with the shared secret key that all devices in the NDG should use. If you prefer that each device have a unique key, leave this field blank, and the individual devices key will be used instead. When finished, click **Submit**.

NOTE   ACS 4.1 or later users will also notice the RADIUS Key Wrap section on the Network
Device Group configuration page. RADIUS Key Wrap is new to ACS 4.1 and currently
supports only Cisco 440*x* series WLAN controllers. It is used to securely encrypt session
keys during an EAP-TLS session. It is not used in the NAC Framework and can be ignored.

Repeat the previous steps to add NDGs. When all your NDGs have been created, proceed
to the next section.

Adding Network Access Devices

Before your switches, routers, concentrators, firewalls, and wireless access points can
communicate with ACS, you must add them in ACS as network access devices (NADs).
(NADs are also commonly referred to as AAA clients.) Adding the device in ACS tells ACS
what IP address the device has, what protocol it will be using to communicate, and what
key to use to decrypt the messages. Follow these steps to add your NAC enforcement points
to ACS:

Step 1   From the navigation frame on the left, select **Network Configuration**.

Step 2   (Optional) If you created Network Device Groups, select the NDG where
you want this client located.

Step 3   In the AAA Clients section, select **Add Entry**.

Step 4   In the **AAA Client Hostname** field, fill in a descriptive name for the
NAD. The name is not required to match the host name on the device; in
fact, the host name can represent multiple devices. Whatever name you
choose, it is advised that you standardize on a naming convention.

Step 5   In the **AAA Client IP Address** field, fill in the IP of the NAD. Optionally,
you can overload multiple NADs to this same entry by wildcarding any
part of the IP or by entering several IPs separated by pressing **Enter**. (See
the following tip.)

Step 6   If you are not using NDGs, fill in the key. The key is the shared secret key
you created on the NAD when defining the RADIUS server. When using
NDGs, the key is typically defined at the group level and applies to all
devices within that NDG.

Step 7   From the **Authenticate Using** drop-down box, select the appropriate
RADIUS dictionary. For switches and routers, choose **Cisco IOS/PIX
6.x**. For the VPN 3000 and ASA/PIX 7.x, choose **Cisco VPN 3000/ASA/
PIX7.x+**. For wireless access points, choose **Cisco Aironet**.

Step 8   Check the box next to **Log Update/Watchdog Packets from This AAA Client** and then click **Submit**.

This completes the steps necessary to add a NAD into ACS. Repeat these steps for each network device you plan to enable NAC on.

TIP   If you do not plan to restrict individual device access (to a user or groups of users), you might choose to wildcard your network devices. The most generic form of wildcarding involves matching all network devices to a single NAD. This is accomplished by defining a NAD with a host name of Any and an IP address of *.*.*.* The asterisks represent wildcarding that octet of the IP address. The key specified will be common to all your network devices. You can also wildcard classful networks, whereby all devices in the classful network are represented by the single NAD.

NOTE   If you want to wildcard all your network devices, the wildcard entry must be created before any other NADs are defined. Failure to do so results in an error message from ACS indicating overlapping IPs.

Configuring RADIUS Attributes and Advanced Options

After adding your RADIUS network devices, you need to globally add the RADIUS attributes that are used with NAC. Follow these steps to complete this task:

Step 1   From the navigation frame on the left, select **Interface Configuration**.

Step 2   Select the **RADIUS (IETF)** link and verify that the following attributes are selected:

☑ **[027] Session-Timeout**

☑ **[029] Termination-Action**

☑ **[064] Tunnel-Type**

☑ **[065] Tunnel-Medium-Type**

☑ **[081] Tunnel-Private-Group-ID**

NOTE   The RADIUS dictionaries appear in the Interface Configuration section only if ACS has at least one RADIUS NAD defined.

Step 3   Click **Submit**.

Step 4   Select the **RADIUS (Cisco IOS/PIX 6.0)** link and verify that the **[026/009/001] cisco-av-pair** attribute is selected. Scroll to the bottom of the page and select **Enable Authenticated Port cisco-av-pair** from the Advanced Configuration Options section.

Step 5   Click **Submit**.

Step 6   Select the **Advanced Options** link and select the following options:

☑ **Group-Level Shared Network Access Restrictions**

☑ **Group-Level Network Access Restrictions**

☑ **Group-Level Downloadable ACLs**

☑ **Network Access Filtering**

☑ **Distributed System Settings**

☑ **ACS Internal Database Replication**

Step 7   Click **Submit**.

Installing Certificates

NAC requires the use of digital certificates to form the secure tunnels (PEAP or EAP-FAST) between the clients and ACS. In Chapters 2, "Cisco Trust Agent," and 3, "Cisco Secure Services Client," we covered how to install the CA certificate (or ACS self-signed certificate) on the client. In this section, we cover how to install the certificates in ACS.

To review, ACS provides these two options for using digital certificates:

• Using an identity certificate signed by a CA

• Using a self-signed certificate

For NAC deployments, it is highly recommended that ACS use a certificate signed by a CA. This provides for the most scalable and secure deployment. A self-signed certificate can be used for very small deployments or in lab settings but should not really be considered for long-term production rollouts. One reason for this is that self-signed certificates are generally valid for only a year. When they expire, a new certificate must be installed in ACS and then distributed to all the endpoints.

If you are new to PKI and digital certificates, you have a couple options available. You can purchase a digital certificate from a public CA (such as VeriSign), or you can install your own CA. Purchasing a certificate from a public CA that Windows already trusts (the root CA is preinstalled in the trusted root store) eliminates the need to distribute the root CA certificate to the CTA clients.

<table>
<tr><td>**TIP**</td><td>Microsoft includes a free CA server with its Windows Server operating systems, and it is fairly easy to install and set up.</td></tr>
</table>

When you have decided between using a certificate from a CA and using a self-signed certificate, you must complete the steps in either the "Installing a Certificate from a CA" section or the "Using ACS to Generate a Self-Signed Certificate" section.

Installing a Certificate from a CA

ACS supports Base64-encoded X.509 certificates. Before receiving a certificate from a CA, you need to generate a certificate-signing request (CSR). The CSR is then supplied to the CA to generate ACS's identity (or server) certificate. Follow these steps to create the CSR:

Step 1 From the navigation frame on the left, select **System Configuration**.

Step 2 Select **ACS Certificate Setup** and then **Generate Certificate Signing Request**.

Step 3 Under the Generate New Request section, fill in the **Certificate Subject** box using the following format: *field=value, field=value,...* ACS requires only the commonName (**CN**) field, which is typically the server's name. The CA might require other fields. Check with the CA administrator if you are unsure what is required. The ACS help frame on the right lists the possible fields and their lengths. In Figure 8-2, the following fields and values were used to generate the CSR: CN=ACS01, O=Cisco, C=US, S=California, L=San Jose. However, only the CN and O fields are visible.

<table>
<tr><td>**TIP**</td><td>VeriSign requires Common Name, Organization, Country, State, and Locality (City). An Organizational Unit (OU) is optional.</td></tr>
</table>

Figure 8-2 *Generating a Certificate-Signing Request*

Step 4 In the **Private Key File** box, type the full directory path and filename where the private key will be saved (for example, C:\ACS01_privateKeyFile.pem).

Step 5 In the **Private Key Password** box, create a password used to protect the private key. This password should follow your business guidelines for strong passwords.

Step 6 In the **Retype Private Key Password** box, retype in the password you created in Step 5.

Step 7 From the **Key Length** list, select the length of key to use. The longer the key, the more secure, but the CA server must support the key length you select.

Step 8 From the **Digest to Sign With** list, select the hashing algorithm to use to encrypt the key. The default is SHA1; if you are uncertain what to select, leave the default.

Step 9 Next, click **Submit** to generate the CSR.

Step 10   The CSR appears in the right frame. Highlight the entire output, including the Begin and End Certificate Request lines, and copy the text into Notepad and save it to a file.

Use this CSR to request a certificate from the CA.

NOTE   You can install a Microsoft CA server by selecting **Add or Remove Programs** from the Control Panel. Next, select the **Add/Remove Windows Components** button. In the window that appears, select **Certificate Services** from the list and then click **Next.** For the CA type, select **Enterprise Root CA** and then click **Next.** Fill in the Common name for the CA and modify the Distinguished name suffix, if needed. When finished, click **Next.** Choose a location to save the certificate database and log file (the default is fine) and then click **Next.** The CA server now is installed.

NOTE   To request a certificate from a Microsoft CA server, open Internet Explorer and browse to http://*server-IP*/certsrv. Select **Request a Certificate** and then the **Advanced Certificate Request** option. Next, select **Submit a Certificate Request by Using a Base64-Encoded File**. Paste in the CSR, select the **Web Server** certificate template, and then submit the request. Finally, download the certificate as Base64 encoded.

When you receive a certificate for ACS from the CA, install it in ACS by following these steps:

Step 1   From the navigation frame on the left, select **System Configuration**.

Step 2   Select **ACS Certificate Setup** and then **Install ACS Certificate**.

Step 3   In the Install New Certificate section, select **Read Certificate from File** and fill in the full path to where you saved the certificate on the ACS machine. **Private Key File** should be filled in for you, but if not, go ahead and supply the full path to the private key file. Finally, fill in the password you used to secure the private key file and then click **Submit**. Figure 8-3 shows an example of this step.

Figure 8-3 *Installing ACS Certificate*

Install new certificate	?

⊙ Read certificate from file

Certificate file `C:\acs01.cer`

○ Use certificate from storage

Certificate CN

Private key file `C:\ACS01_privateKeyFi`

Private key password `••••••••••`

NOTE   If you are using an ACS appliance, you must place the ACS identity certificate on an FTP server where the appliance has access to it. In Step 3, select **Download Certificate File** to download the certificate to the appliance.

ACS installs the certificate and displays a summary of the certificate information. Finish the certificate configuration process by completing the steps in the section titled "Installing the CA Certificate in ACS."

Using ACS to Generate a Self-Signed Certificate

NOTE   Skip this section if you will be using a certificate for ACS that is signed by a CA.

If you do not want to purchase a certificate for ACS from a third-party CA and you also do not want to install your own CA, you can have ACS generate its own self-signed certificate. However, using self-signed certificates generally makes NAC deployments less scalable and is therefore discouraged for production use. However, using self-signed certificates in a lab environment is perfectly acceptable. Complete these steps to have ACS generate a self-signed certificate:

Step 1   From the navigation frame on the left, select **System Configuration**.

Step 2   Select **ACS Certificate Setup** and then **Generate Self-Signed Certificate**.

Step 3   In the Generate New Self-Signed Certificate section, fill in **Certificate Subject** using the following format: *field=value, field=value,....* ACS requires only the commonName (**CN**) field, which is typically the server's name. The ACS help frame on the right lists the possible fields and their lengths. One example for the certificate subject is: CN=ACS01, O=Cisco, C=US, S=California, L=San Jose.

Step 4 In the **Certificate File** box, fill in the full directory path and filename of the self-signed certificate ACS will create (for example, C:\ACS01-self-signed.cer).

Step 5 In the **Private Key File** box, type the full directory path and filename where the private key will be saved (for example, C:\ACS01_privateKeyFile.pem).

Step 6 In the **Private Key Password** box, create a password used to protect the private key. This password should follow your business guidelines for strong passwords.

Step 7 In the **Retype Private Key Password** box, retype the password you created in Step 6.

Step 8 From the **Key Length** list, select the length of key to use. The default length of 2048 bits is the most secure.

Step 9 From the **Digest to Sign With** list, select the hashing algorithm to use to encrypt the key. The default is SHA1; if you are uncertain what to select, leave the default.

Step 10 Next, check the box **Install Generated Certificate** and click **Submit**.

Step 11 Finally, restart the ACS services from **System Configuration > Services Control**.

This completes the installation steps to generate and install a self-signed certificate in ACS.

Installing the CA Certificate in ACS

Before you can use the ACS certificate, it must be trusted. Trust is established by installing the CA certificate in the root certificate store. Before completing the following steps, download the CA certificate to the machine ACS is installed on.

Step 1 From the navigation frame on the left, select **System Configuration**.

Step 2 Select **ACS Certificate Setup** and then **ACS Certification Authority Setup**.

Step 3 In the CA Operations section, fill in **CA Certificate File** with the full path to where you saved the CA certificate on the ACS machine; then click **Submit**.

To download the CA certificate from a Microsoft CA server, select the **Download a CA Certificate** option. Then select the correct CA certificate from the list and choose the Base64 encoding method. Finally, select **Download CA Certificate**.

On the right frame, you should see a message indicating that the CA certificate was successfully installed. Before proceeding, restart the ACS services from **System Configuration > Service Control > Restart**.

NOTE   If you are using an ACS appliance, you must place the CA certificate on an FTP server where the appliance has access to it. In Step 3, select **Download Certificate File** to download the certificate to the appliance.

The final step is to trust this CA by completing the steps in the next section, "Editing the Certificate Trust List."

Another component of digital certificates is Certificate Revocation Lists (CRLs). Sometimes you want to revoke an already issued certificate before it expires. (One example is when the device is stolen.) CRLs contain a list of such revoked certificates. You can configure ACS to retrieve a CRL to validate certificates against. For more information on this topic, see the ACS User Guide.

Editing the Certificate Trust List

The certificate trust list (CTL) is a further security step that ACS uses to decide whether to trust the CA certificate that is already installed. ACS implicitly trusts the CA that created the ACS identity certificate. Therefore, in many cases, this step is optional; however, for simplification, I recommend completing this step.

Follow these steps to add the CA server to the ACS certificate trust list:

Step 1   From the navigation frame on the left, select **System Configuration**.

Step 2   Select **ACS Certificate Setup** and then **Edit Certificate Trust List**.

Step 3   Scroll down the CTL until you find the CA that generated your certificates. (Private CAs are generally at the bottom of the list.) When you find the CA, select it and then click **Submit**.

Step 4   Finally, restart the ACS services to complete this process.

NOTE   If your end hosts use certificates to authenticate to ACS, the CA that signed their certificate must be installed in ACS and added to the CTL before ACS will authenticate the client with the certificate.

NOTE   If you use an external audit or posture-validation server, ACS typically communicates to that server using HTTPS. Before ACS can trust the server's certificate, you must add the CA to the computer's Trusted Root store and then select the CA in the CTL, as indicated earlier.

The single exception to the requirement that you must explicitly specify a CA as trustworthy occurs when the clients and ACS are getting their certificates from the same CA. You do not need to add this CA to the CTL because ACS automatically trusts the CA that issued its certificate.

Configuring Global Authentication Protocols

Out of the box, ACS will not authenticate NAC-enabled clients because the authentication protocols they use (PEAP or EAP-FAST) are not enabled by default. ACS provides the option of globally enabling or disabling authentication protocols from the **System Configuration > Global Authentication Setup** page. Later, in the "Protocols Policy" section, you will see that these protocols can also be selectively enabled or disabled on a per-profile basis. In this section, we walk you through the steps of enabling the NAC-specific protocols. However, if you are using other protocols in your network, you are free to enable them here as well. In fact, if you are unsure about what protocols to enable, there is no problem with enabling them all.

Follow these steps to configure the global authentication protocols:

Step 1   From the navigation frame on the left, select **System Configuration** and then **Global Authentication Setup**.

Step 2   The Global Authentication Setup page appears. In the PEAP section, select the following:

☑ **Allow EAP-MSCHAPv2**

☑ **Allow EAP-GTC**

☑ **Allow Posture Validation**

☑ **Cisco client initial message:** empty

☑ **PEAP session timeout (minutes): 120**

☑ **Enable Fast Reconnect**

Step 3   In the EAP-TLS section, select the following:

☑ **Allow EAP-TLS**

Select one or more of the following options:

☑ **Certificate SAN comparison**

☑ **Certificate CN comparison**

☑ **Certificate Binary comparison**

Step 4   Scroll down to the bottom of the page and verify that **Allow MS-CHAP Version 2 Authentication** is selected.

Step 5   Select the **Submit + Restart** button to save these changes.

Step 6   You should now be back at the System Configuration page. Select **Global Authentication Setup** again. Then click the **EAP-FAST Configuration** link.

Step 7   Configure the EAP-FAST section to match the options selected next. Leave the **Client Initial Message** blank, and supply the ACS server's name in the **Authority ID Info** field. Selecting **Allow Authenticated In-Band PAC Provisioning** along with **Accept Client on Authenticated Provisioning** allows the CTA clients to automatically receive a PAC during Phase 0 of the EAP-FAST negotiations, only after the client has authenticated. Refer to Figure 8-4 for a screen shot of properly configured EAP-FAST settings.

☑ **Allow EAP-FAST**

Active master key TTL: 1 month

Retired master key TTL: 3 months

Tunnel PAC TTL: 1 week

Client initial message: empty

Authority ID Info: *server-name*

☐ **Allow anonymous in-band PAC provisioning**

☑ **Allow authenticated in-band PAC provisioning**

☑ **Accept client on authenticated provisioning**

☐ **Require client certificate for provisioning**

Figure 8-4 *EAP-FAST Configuration Settings*

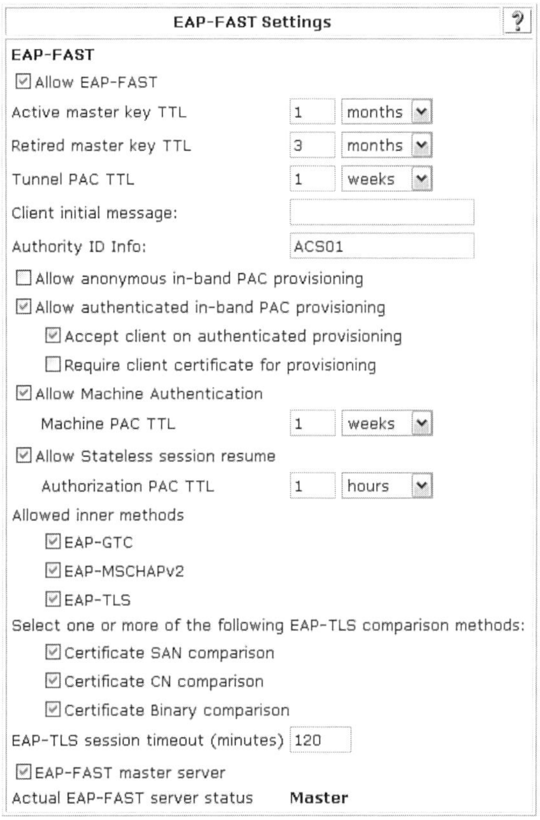

☑ **Allow Machine Authentication**

Machine PAC TTL: 1 week

☑ **Allow Stateless session resume**

Authorization PAC TTL: 1 hour

Allowed inner methods

☑ **EAP-GTC**

☑ **EAP-MSCHAPv2**

☑ **EAP-TLS**

Select one or more of the following EAP-TLS comparison methods:

☑ **Certificate SAN comparison**

☑ **Certificate CN comparison**

☑ **Certificate Binary comparison**

EAP-TLS session timeout (minutes): 120

☑ **EAP-FAST master server**

Step 8 Click **Submit + Restart** to save the changes.

You can change the timers in Step 7 to your liking, but the defaults shown represent a good balance between performance and security. Lowering the timers could increase security to the detriment of performance.

Creating Network Access Profiles Using NAC Templates

The NAC configuration on ACS really consists of the following four policies: Protocols, Authentication, Posture Validation, and Authorization. Each of these policies can also contain multiple components. The protocols policy separates the authentication requests based on protocol: EAP-FAST for NAC-L2-802.1X, and PEAP for NAC-L2-IP and NAC-L3-IP. The authentication policy defines what databases are used for authentication, and it also is used to set up the agentless host configuration. The posture-validation policy is really the core of NAC. End-host credentials are measured against this policy to determine the current security posture of the host. Finally, the authorization policy enforces the corporate security policy by restricting an end host's access to the network, based on the results of the posture validation. ACS glues these four policies together by way of a network access profile (NAP).

NOTE ACS 4.0 had only three policies: authentication, posture validation, and authorization. The protocols policy in ACS 4.1 was part of the authentication policy in ACS 4.0.

NOTE We cover NAPs in more detail later in this chapter in the section titled "Network Access Profiles."

Before ACS 4.0, the initial work required to configure NAC on ACS was quite daunting. However, ACS 4.0 introduced the concept of templates, through which you can easily create NAPs with prepopulated protocols (for ACS 4.1 only), authentication, posture-validation, and authorization policies.

These preconfigured NAPs enable you to quickly get started testing NAC in the lab because the templates also create sample RADIUS authorization components (RACs) with all the required NAC components in them. In addition, a sample CTA posture-validation policy is created. All these sample components can be quickly and easily modified to suit your lab or production environment. Because of the ease of use, we use templates to populate all our NAC policies. Currently, ACS has the following built-in templates available for NAC:

- NAC L3 IP
- NAC L2 IP
- NAC L2 802.1X
- Wireless (NAC L2 802.1X)
- Agentless Host for L2 (802.1X fallback)—or Authentication Bypass in ACS 4.0
- Agentless Host for L3

NOTE   Note that a template also exists for *Microsoft IEEE 802.1X*. However, this template is for straight 802.1X authentication (without NAC) using the Microsoft supplicant. The Microsoft supplicant currently does not support NAC over 802.1X. However, after 802.1X authentication, you could perform NAC-L2-IP or NAC-L3-IP posture validation.

Follow these steps to create NAC profiles using the ACS built-in templates. In later sections, we demonstrate how to edit these policies to match your corporate security policies.

Step 1   From the navigation frame on the left, select **Network Access Profiles**.

Step 2   The Network Access Profiles page appears. Click the **Add Template Profile** button.

Step 3   The Create Profile from Template page appears. From the **Template** drop-down list, select the NAC template that the new profile should be based on. If you are using more than one NAC validation method (L2-IP, L3-IP, or NAC 802.1X) in your network, select one now and repeat these steps for the remaining validation methods.

Step 4   Next, specify a name for the profile in the **Name** field. Note that spaces are not allowed; use underscores or hyphens instead.

TIP   I highly recommend that you name the profile after the template it was based on. Doing so will save a lot of confusion down the road.

Step 5   (Optional) Fill in the **Description** field with any comments you want to add to the profile.

Step 6   Finally, check the **Active** box and then click **Submit**.

A summary screen appears, as shown in Figure 8-5, indicating the objects created for the new profile.

Figure 8-5   *NAP Profile-Creation Summary Screen for L3-IP*

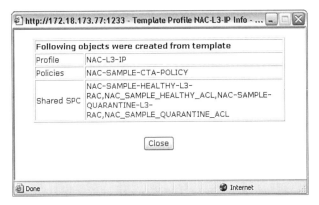

Repeat these steps to create additional NAPs using the built-in NAC templates. When finished, you should have a NAP for each NAC method you plan to use in your network. Figure 8-6 shows the network access profiles after creating several profiles from the NAC templates. Be sure to restart the ACS processes by clicking the **Apply and Restart** button from the bottom of the page for the changes to take affect.

Posture Validation

With the general configuration of ACS complete, it is time to define the posture-validation policies. However, before we begin that, let us review a key concept of posture validation: posture tokens.

Posture tokens are used to represent the result of the posture-validation process. Posture validation can be performed internally to ACS via user-defined policies, or it can be performed externally to ACS through third-party applications (such as antivirus or audit servers). When an end host's posture is evaluated against one of these policies (either internal or external), the result is returned by way of an application posture token (APT).

Figure 8-6   *Completed Network Access Profiles Screen Shot*

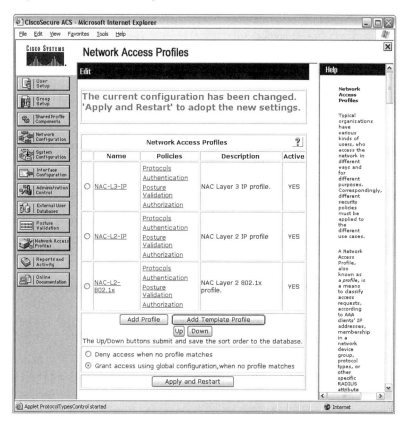

Six predefined, nonconfigurable posture tokens available. As an end host is postured, it is evaluated against all policies, and the resulting APTs from each policy are collected. ACS then assigns the host a system posture token (SPT) by taking the most severe APT returned. Thus, the SPT defines the end host's overall posture, and ACS sends the SPT to the NAD and the end host. Table 8-4 lists the possible posture tokens, from least to most severe, along with their descriptions.

Table 8-4 *NAC Posture Tokens*

Token	Description
Healthy	The endpoint complies with the current policies. Unrestricted access is generally granted.
Checkup	The endpoint is within the policy but does not have the latest security software; an update is recommended. Use this posture token to proactively remediate a host to the Healthy state.
Transition	The endpoint is in the process of having its posture checked and is given interim access pending a result from full posture validation. This is applicable during host boot, when all services might not be running or when audit results are not yet available.
Quarantine	The endpoint is out of policy and needs to be restricted to a remediation network. The device is not actively placing a threat on other hosts, but it is susceptible to attack or infection and should be updated as soon as possible.
Infected	The endpoint is an active threat to other hosts; network access should be severely restricted and placed into remediation or totally denied of all network access.
Unknown	The posture credentials of the endpoint cannot be determined. Quarantine the host and audit, or remediate until a definitive posture can be determined.

Even though the SPT indicates the overall posture of the end host, it by itself does not apply any restrictions to the host to grant, limit, or deny access to the network. Limiting the end host's access to the network is done with authorization rules, which are tied to the SPT. We cover the authorization rules in the section titled "Authorization Policy."

By using the built-in templates to create the network access profiles, ACS automatically creates and prepopulates policies for the Healthy and Quarantine SPTs. In this section, we walk through the creation of the posture-validation rules that will result in one of those SPTs. You optionally can create additional policies for the remaining four SPTs; however, there is something to be said for keeping things simple.

With the two posture tokens, Healthy and Quarantine, the end host is either Healthy or it is not. If it is Healthy, it is granted unrestricted access to the network. If it is not Healthy, access is restricted by either ACLs (NAC-L3-IP and NAC-L2-IP) or the VLAN (NAC-L2-802.1X). Optionally, the host can be redirected to a remediation server to download patches or updates and bring it back into compliance.

Internal Posture-Validation Policies

Creating posture-validation rules can be a little overwhelming in the beginning because many components link to create a policy. In this section, we walk you though those components and how they are linked.

A *posture-validation policy* contains one or more posture-validation rules and returns an application posture token (APT, which is combined with other application posture tokens in the network access profile to determine the system posture token, SPT). A *posture-*

validation rule contains one or more condition sets; if the condition sets evaluate to true, the posture token mapped to the rule is returned. A *condition set* contains one or more *condition elements,* which is a pairing of an attribute to a value.

Now you can see why this can be a bit overwhelming. However, do not worry—after we walk through an example, this will make more sense. Examine Figure 8-7 for a graphical representation of the components that make up the posture-validation policy.

Figure 8-7 *Components in the Posture-Validation Policy*

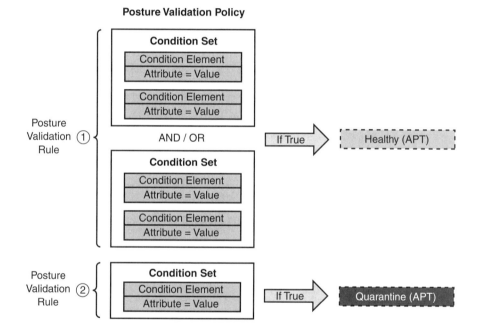

Now that you understand the components that make up a posture-validation policy, let us walk through a couple examples together.

Editing the NAC-SAMPLE-CTA-Policy

Previously, we used ACS's built-in NAC templates to create network access profiles for NAC. In doing so, ACS automatically created a posture-validation policy titled NAC-SAMPLE-CTA-POLICY. You can take a look at this policy by clicking the **Posture Validation** button on the left and then selecting **Internal Posture Validation Setup > NAC-SAMPLE-CTA-POLICY**.

Notice the two posture-validation rules. The first rule contains two condition elements within the condition set. The second is the default rule. (The *default rule* applies if the previous rules do not match.) The first rule has the following conditions:

Cisco:PA:PA-Name contains Cisco Trust Agent AND
Cisco:PA:PA-Version >= 1.0.0.0

This says, "If the posture agent name contains 'Cisco Trust Agent' and the posture agent version is greater than or equal to 1.0.0.0," the Healthy application posture token is assigned. If a client does not match the first posture-validation rule, the *default* rule is applied and assigns the Quarantine application posture token.

In this example, the first thing you will do is change the policy name to CTA-Policy. Next, you will modify the first rule so that an end-host is Healthy only if it has CTA installed and the version is greater than or equal to 2.0.0.30. This was the original FCS version of CTA that supports NAC Version 2. Then you will create a new policy-validation rule to check whether the host has CTA installed and is running a version less than 2.0.0.30. If so, you will assign the Quarantine posture token to let you know that CTA needs to be upgraded on this host. Complete this task by following these steps:

Step 1   From the navigation frame on the left, select **Posture Validation**.

Step 2   The Posture Validation Components Setup page appears. Select the **Internal Posture Validation Setup** button.

Step 3   Click the **NAC-SAMPLE-CTA-POLICY** link, and then click the **Rename** button.

Step 4   Change the name to **CTA-Policy**, add the description **Check for CTA Version 2.0**, and click **Submit**.

Step 5   Edit the first rule by clicking the link next to it. You will now see the condition set for that rule.

Step 6   Edit the condition set by selecting it again. The Add/Edit Condition window appears.

Step 7   From the Condition Elements table, select the **Cisco:PA:PA-Version >= 1.0.0.0** entry; then click **Remove**. The condition element is removed from the table and populated in the fields below.

Step 8   Change the **Value** field to 2.0.0.30 and select **Enter**. The condition element is added back to the table. Click **Submit**.

Step 9   Select **Submit** again to return to the posture-validation rules.

Step 10 Select **Add Rule**, and then **Add Condition Set** to create the new Quarantine rule.

Step 11   From the **Attribute** drop-down list, select **Cisco:PA:PA-Name**. From the **Operator** drop-down list, select **Contains**. In the **Value** field type in **Cisco Trust Agent**, then select **Enter**.

Step 12   From the **Attribute** drop-down, select **Cisco:PA:PA-Version**. From the **Operator** drop-down, select **<** (less than). In the **Value** field type in **2.0.0.30**, select **Enter**, followed by **Submit**.

Step 13   You are back on the posture-validation rule page. Change **Posture Token** from **Healthy** to **Quarantine**, and then click **Submit**. Leave the **Notification String** field empty.

Step 14   Verify that the posture-validation rules match what is shown in Figure 8-8; then click **Done**. Otherwise, go back and make the necessary corrections.

Figure 8-8   *Modified CTA-Policy*

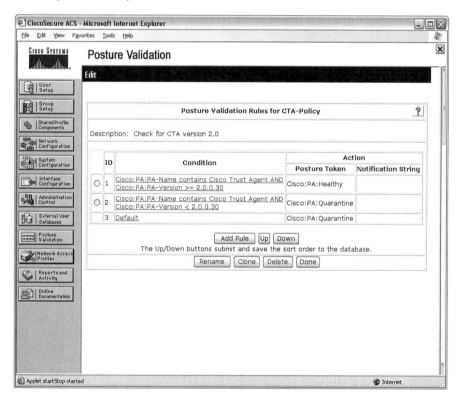

Creating a Policy to Validate the Windows Service Pack

Now that you have modified an existing policy, you go one step further by creating a new policy to check to make sure the hosts running Windows have the latest service packs installed. Complete this task by following these steps:

Step 1 From the navigation frame on the left, select **Posture Validation**.

Step 2 The Posture Validation Components Setup page appears. Click the **Internal Posture Validation Setup** button and then **Add Policy**.

Step 3 In the **Name** field, type **Windows-SP-Policy**. Optionally, enter the description **Check for the Latest Windows Service Packs**. Then click **Submit**.

Step 4 Click the **Add Rule** button, followed by **Add Condition Set**.

Step 5 Create a new condition element to check for Windows 2003 machines by selecting the following values and then choosing **Enter**:

Attribute: Cisco:PA:OS-Type

Operator: contains

Value: Windows 2003

Step 6 Create another condition element to check for the presence of Service Pack 1 by selecting the following values and then choosing **Enter:**

Attribute: Cisco:Host:ServicePacks

Operator: contains

Value: 1

Step 7 Now choose **Submit** to save the first condition set, followed by **Add Condition Set** to create the next one for Windows XP.

Step 8 Create a new condition element to check for Windows XP machines by selecting the following values, and then choosing **Enter**:

Attribute: Cisco:PA:OS-Type

Operator: contains

Value: Windows XP

Step 9 Create another condition element to check for the presence of Service Pack 2 by selecting the following values and then choosing **Enter**.

Attribute: Cisco:Host:ServicePacks

Operator: contains

Value: 2

Step 10 Now click **Submit** to save the second Condition Set, followed by **Add Condition Set** to create the next one for Windows 2000.

Step 11 Create a new condition element to check for Windows 2000 machines by selecting the following values and then choosing **Enter**:

Attribute: Cisco:PA:OS-Type

Operator: contains

Value: Windows 2000

Step 12 Create another condition element to check for the presence of Service Pack 4 by selecting the following values and then choosing **Enter**:

Attribute: Cisco:Host:ServicePacks

Operator: contains

Value: 4

Step 13 Click **Submit** to save the third condition set, followed by **Submit** again to return to the rules page.

Step 14 Select the Default rule and change **Posture Token** from **Unknown** to **Quarantine**. Then choose **Submit**.

Step 15 Verify that the posture-validation rules match what is shown in Figure 8-9; then click **Done**. Otherwise, go back and make the necessary corrections.

Figure 8-9 *Windows-SP-Policy*

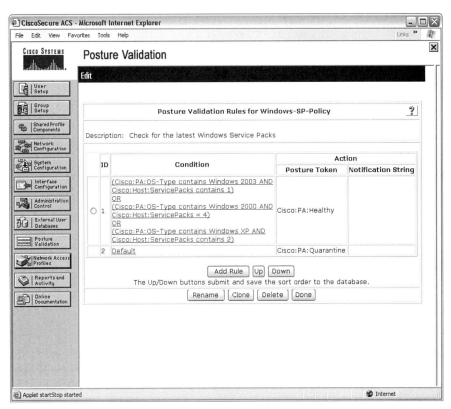

Creating a Policy to Check for a Specific Windows Hotfix

To reinforce what you have already learned, you will create one more policy to check for the presence of a specific Windows hotfix. Microsoft released hotfix KB912812 to protect against a critical remote code execution vulnerability in Internet Explorer. Your task is to create a Posture Validation policy to check for this specific hotfix. If the hotfix exists on the end host, return the Healthy posture token. Otherwise, return Quarantine.

I encourage you to attempt this one on your own. When finished, verify your results by checking them against the steps here. For the less inquisitive, follow the steps to complete this task.

NOTE   You can replace the actual hotfix ID with any one you are interested in; you can even check for multiple hotfixes at the same time.

Step 1   From the navigation frame on the left, select **Posture Validation**.

Step 2   The Posture Validation Components Setup page appears. Click the **Internal Posture Validation Setup** button and then **Add Policy**.

Step 3   In the **Name** field, type **Windows-Hotfix-Policy**. Optionally, enter the description **Check for Specific Windows Hotfixes**. Then click **Submit**.

Step 4   Select the **Add Rule** button, followed by **Add Condition Set**.

Step 5   Create a new condition element to check for Windows 2003 machines by selecting the following values and then choosing **Enter**:

Attribute: Cisco:PA:OS-Type

Operator: contains

Value: Windows 2003

Step 6   Create another condition element to check for the presence of hotfix KB912812 by selecting the following values and then choosing **Enter**.:

Attribute: Cisco:Host:HotFixes

Operator: contains

Value: KB912812

Step 7   Now click **Submit** to save the Condition Set, followed by **Add Condition Set** to create the next one.

Step 8   Repeat steps 5–7 for Windows XP and Windows 2000. When finished, select **Submit** to return to the rules page.

Step 9   Select the Default rule and change **Posture Token** from **Unknown** to **Quarantine**. Then choose **Submit**.

Step 10   Verify that the posture-validation rules match what is shown in Figure 8-10; then click **Done**. Otherwise, go back and make the necessary corrections.

Figure 8-10 *Windows-Hotfix-Policy*

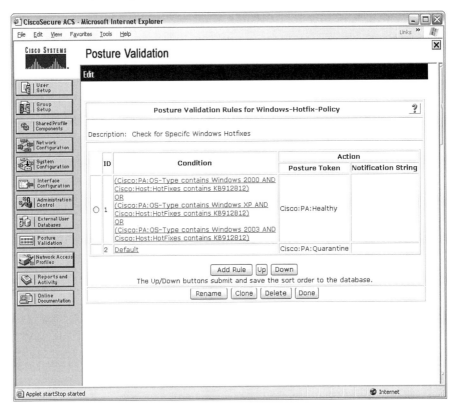

NOTE   For this specific task, you could have created a single condition set just to check for the hotfix, without validating the Windows OS. However, by first validating the Windows OS, this sets up a framework to enable you to check for additional hotfixes that are specific to a Windows OS.

Don't forget to restart the ACS processes by clicking the **Apply and Restart** button at the bottom of the Posture Validation Policies page.

External Posture Validation and Audit Servers

In the Posture Validation section, you can optionally configure both external posture-validation servers (antivirus servers) and external audit servers. When these servers are configured, ACS waits for the APT results from the external posture validation before combining it with the APTs from the internal posture validation to derive the SPT.

Chapters 10, "Antivirus Software Integration," and 11, "Audit Servers," cover the required steps to configure ACS for external posture validation.

Miscellaneous Posture-Validation Options

Before proceeding, it is important that we at least touch on a few miscellaneous items relating to the posture-validation process. One of these might even save you a lot of time during the posture-validation creation process, so pay attention!

Posture-Validation Rule Ordering

As seen earlier, an internal policy can contain one or more rules. When ACS receives posture credentials from an end host, they are evaluated against the rules in order from top to bottom. The first rule that matches the APT is returned, and processing stops for that policy. This allows lower rules to encompass upper rules. Said another way, the lower rules can be less specific than the upper rules. However, if each rule in a policy is independent from one another, for best performance, place the rule that will be hit most at the top of the list.

Rules can be reordered by selecting the radio button next to the rule and clicking the **Up** or **Down** buttons to reorder the rule.

In addition, multiple rules can return the same posture token. This gives you the flexibility of creating additional rules instead of creating multiple condition sets within the same rule. In the section titled "Creating a Policy to Check for a Specific Windows Hotfix," an alternative way of completing the task in that section is to create a unique rule for each Windows OS. In that case, each rule would contain one OS check and one hotfix check. Thus, you would have multiple rules that evaluate to a Healthy posture token.

Posture-Validation Rule Cloning

ACS also provides a way to clone posture-validation rules. You might wonder why this would be useful. Let me illustrate by continuing with the last example. We were just discussing the alternate way of checking multiple Windows OSes for a single hotfix—by creating a unique rule for each OS. Cloning would help here because after creating the first rule, you could just clone it and then edit the rule to change the OS. This saves a few steps in the policy-creation process.

To clone a rule, select **Internal Posture Validation Policy** and then select the link for the rule you want cloned. Click the **Clone** button at the bottom of the page to create a copy of the existing rule. Next, select the new cloned rule and edit it accordingly.

An entire policy can also be cloned by selecting the policy and then clicking the **Clone** button at the bottom of the page.

Deleting a Posture-Validation Rule

To delete a rule, select **Internal Posture Validation Policy** and then select the link for the rule you want deleted. Choose the **Delete** button at the bottom of the page. The rule is removed from the policy.

An entire policy can also be deleted by selecting the policy and then clicking the **Delete** button at the bottom of the page.

Notification String

You might have noticed that each posture-validation rule had its own notification string, which we left blank. The *notification string* sends a message back to the application that the Resultant Credential Type list indicates. The vendor determines the use of the text message. In most cases, this field is left blank. The third-party vendor will instruct you if this field needs to be filled in and what to place there.

Posture Enforcement

In the previous section, we went over how to create posture-validation policies. In this section, we cover the enforcement aspect of NAC: downloadable IP ACLs (NAC-L2-IP and NAC-L3-IP) and VLAN assignment (NAC-L2-802.1X).

Downloadable IP ACLs

Both NAC Layer 2 IP and Layer 3 IP use downloadable IP ACLs as the enforcement mechanism. After the posture-validation process, the resultant SPT is mapped to a downloadable IP ACL (in the Authorization policy of the network access profile), which is then pushed out to the NAD. The NAD then appends this ACL to the top of the interface ACL to further restrict (or permit) access to the network. If the SPT returned for the end-host is Healthy, the downloaded ACL is generally **permit ip any any**. However, if the SPT returned is Quarantine, you most likely want to restrict that host's access to a limited set of remediation servers or a quarantine network. Likewise, additional posture tokens can each have their own unique downloadable ACL.

NOTE   The Catalyst 6500 running CatOS (Hybrid mode) does not support downloadable IP ACLs for NAC-L2-IP. Instead, policy-based ACLs are used. See the section "Policy-Based ACLs," later in this chapter, for more information on this feature.

Before continuing on, decide what ACL you want to apply to Healthy end hosts and what ACL to apply to Quarantined end hosts. Examples 8-1 and 8-2 provide sample Healthy and Quarantine ACLs to assist you in this process.

Example 8-1   *Sample—Healthy Downloadable IP ACL*

```
remark If host is Healthy allow full network access
permit ip any any
```

Example 8-2   *Sample—Quarantine Downloadable IP ACL*

```
remark If host is Quarantine restrict access network
remark Allow DHCP and DNS
permit udp any any eq 67
permit udp any any eq 53
remark Allow EAPoUDP for CTA client
permit udp any any eq 21862
remark Allow access to Quarantine network
permit ip any 192.168.15.0 0.0.0.255
```

NOTE   In the examples in this section, you might have noticed that the source address used in the downloadable IP ACL definitions was always **any**. However, when ACS pushes the ACL to the NAD, the NAD changes the source IP address to the IP of the end host. Thus, the NAD personalizes the ACL for that host.

NOTE   If you make a mistake entering an ACL into ACS and that ACL is downloaded to the NAD, the authorization policy will most likely fail. Most switches will fail the authorization if the ACL is invalid.

When you have decided on the content of the ACLs, proceed with these steps to create them within ACS:

Step 1   From the navigation frame on the left, select **Shared Profile Components**.

Step 2   The Shared Profile Components page appears. Click the **Downloadable IP ACLs** link and then the **Add** button at the bottom of the page.

NOTE	If you do not see the link **Downloadable IP ACLs** off the Shared Profile Components page, you are skipping sections of this chapter. (Shame on you.) Go back and read the section titled "Configuring RADIUS Attributes and Advanced Options."

Step 3 In the **Name** field, fill in a name for the Healthy downloadable IP ACL (example: NAC_Healthy_ACL).

Step 4 Optionally, add a description to further explain the purpose of this downloadable IP ACL.

Step 5 Click the **Add** button to define elements in the ACL. The Downloadable IP ACL Content page appears.

Step 6 In the **Name** field, fill in the name of the ACL content (example: Healthy_ACL).

Step 7 In the **ACL Definitions** box, fill in the contents of the ACL. See Example 8-1 for a sample Healthy downloadable ACL.

Step 8 Click the **Submit** button to return to the Downloadable IP ACLs page. Then click **Submit** again to return to the Shared Profile Components— Downloadable IP ACLs page.

Step 9 Click the **Add** button to create the Quarantine downloadable ACL.

Step 10 In the **Name** field, fill in a name for the Quarantine downloadable IP ACL (example: NAC_Quarantine_ACL).

Step 11 Optionally, add a description to further explain the purpose of this downloadable IP ACL.

Step 12 Click the **Add** button to define elements in the ACL. The Downloadable IP ACL Content page appears.

Step 13 In the **Name** field, fill in the name of the ACL content (example: Quarantine_ACL).

Step 14 In the **ACL Definitions** box, fill in the contents of the ACL. See Example 8-2 for a sample Quarantine downloadable ACL.

Step 15 Click the **Submit** button to return to the Downloadable IP ACLs page. Then click **Submit** again to return to the Shared Profile Components— Downloadable IP ACLs page.

Because you previously created network access profiles from NAC templates, you should also see a few sample downloadable IP ACLs. These ACL names have the format NAC_SAMPLE_*Token*_ACL. If you created a network access profile from the Agentless Host for L3 template, you will notice that one of the ACLs has the name NAC_SAMPLE_TRANSITION_ACL. As you can guess, this ACL is tied to the Transition SPT. If you have not yet created a network access profile for agentless hosts, you can go back and do so now. Alternatively, you can skip the steps in this section and proceed to the next section.

The Transition SPT is typically used only if you are also using an external audit server (such as QualysGuard) to scan nonresponsive hosts (or hosts without CTA installed). ACS assigns the Transition token to the host (and, correspondingly, the Transition ACL) while the audit is performed. This provides the host with limited access to the network until the results of the full audit can be analyzed.

In the following steps, you rename the NAC_SAMPLE_TRANSITION_ACL and edit its contents to make them applicable to your network:

Step 1   From the Shared Profile Components—Downloadable IP ACLs page, click the **NAC_SAMPLE_TRANSITION_ACL** link.

Step 2   Modify the text in the **Name** field to read **NAC_Transition_ACL**.

Step 3   In the ACL Contents column, select the **L3_EXAMPLE** link to edit it. The Downloadable IP ACL Content page appears.

Step 4   In the **Name** field, replace **L3_EXAMPLE** with **Transition_ACL**.

Step 5   In the **ACL Definitions** box, fill in the contents of the Transition ACL. This can be as permissive as the Healthy ACL or as restrictive as the Quarantine ACL. It all depends on how much access you want an agentless host to have while it is being scanned. The default ACL is **permit ip any any**. Make your changes and then click **Submit**.

Step 6   Click the **Submit** button again to return to the Downloadable IP ACLs page.

Your screen should look similar to the one shown in Figure 8-11. You can delete the other sample ACLs by clicking their links, and then clicking the **Delete** button. You might receive a warning indicating that the ACL might be referenced by groups or users. This is because the sample RAC policy is referencing the ACL (which we have not covered yet). You can go ahead and click **OK** to remove the ACL. You will edit the RAC policy later.

Figure 8-11 *Downloadable IP ACLs Page*

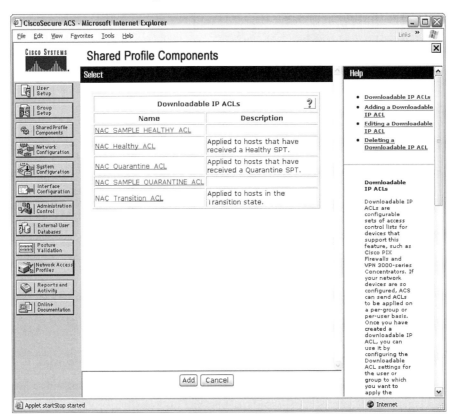

VLAN Assignment

VLAN assignment is the method of enforcement used when deploying NAC-L2-802.1X. (The one exception to this is for the Catalyst 6500 series switches; they also have the capability to use policy-based ACLs as an additional enforcement mechanism.) VLAN assignment is provided by sending the IETF RADIUS attributes 64 (Tunnel-Type), 65 (Tunnel-Medium-Type), and 81 (Tunnel-Private-Group-ID) to the switch in the RADIUS Access-Accept packet. Attribute 81 specifies either a VLAN name (as a case-sensitive string) or a VLAN ID (as an integer). Upon receiving these attributes, the switch places the port in the corresponding VLAN. However, before you can effectively use VLAN assignment as a way of quarantining non-Healthy hosts, some up-front planning must be done.

First, you must choose whether you will pass down a VLAN ID or a VLAN name to the switch. If a VLAN ID is used, the same VLAN must exist on every NAC-enabled L2-802.1X switch in your enterprise. In addition, that VLAN must be used for the same purpose—enterprise-wide. For example, if you decided you were going to use VLAN 300 as the Quarantine VLAN, VLAN 300 should not be assigned to any access port (enterprise-wide). The other option (which is more scalable and is, therefore, the preferred method) is to send down a VLAN name to the switch for the quarantined host. This enables you to use a different VLAN ID for the same VLAN name across multiple switches. For example, Switch-A might use VLAN 222 as the Quarantine VLAN, whereas Switch-B might use VLAN 333. The VLAN ID does not matter, as long as both VLANs are assigned the same name. This is useful when different geographic locations use different VLAN assignment policies.

Second, the Quarantine VLAN needs to be isolated from the Healthy devices in your network. If you have a small company, this can be accomplished by VLAN segmentation alone. Just place the remediation servers in the Quarantine VLAN, along with the quarantined hosts. However, for larger enterprises, this is best accomplished by applying Layer 3 ACLs to the routed interfaces in the Quarantine VLAN, restricting traffic only to the remediation servers (or network).

The upcoming "RADIUS Authorization Components" section covers the steps required to configure VLAN assignment on ACS.

Policy-Based ACLs

Policy-based ACLs are used exclusively on Catalyst 6500 switches running CatOS. They provide policy enforcement for NAC-L2-IP and provide additional enforcement (beyond VLAN assignment) for NAC-L2-802.1X. Unlike downloadable IP ACLs, policy-based ACLs are defined on the switch.

NOTE   Chapter 4, "Configuring Layer 2 NAC on Network Access Devices," covers the steps required to configure policy-based ACLs on the switch.

During the posture-validation process, ACS maps the resulting SPT to a RAC. The RAC then contains the name of the policy-based ACL that the switch is to apply to the end host's port. The switch receives the policy-based ACL name in the RADIUS Access-Accept packet by way of a Cisco-specific av-pair.

The following "RADIUS Authorization Components" section covers the steps required to configure policy-based ACLs on ACS.

RADIUS Authorization Components

RADIUS authorization components, or RACs, as they are more commonly referred to, are groupings of RADIUS attributes that map back to a NAC policy and are applied to a NAD during the posture-enforcement phase. These attributes apply NAC timers, assign ports to the specified VLAN, enforce policy-based ACLs, and apply URL redirect ACLs. Table 8-5 lists the NAC method along with the mandatory RADIUS attributes on the right.

Table 8-5   *RADIUS Attributes Used in NAC RADIUS Authorization Components*

NAC Method	RADIUS Attributes
L3-IP	[027]Session-Timeout
	[26/9/1]cisc-av-pair status-query-timeout
	[029] Termination-Action RADIUS-Request(1)
L2-IP	[027] Session-Timeout
	*[26/9/1] cisco-av-pair sec:pg
	[029] Termination-Action RADIUS-Request (1)
L2-802.1X	[027] Session-Timeout
	*[26/9/1] cisco-av-pair sec:pg
	[029] Termination-Action RADIUS-Request (1)
	[064] Tunnel-Type [T1] VLAN (13)
	[065] Tunnel-Medium-Type [T1] 802 (6)
	[081] Tunnel-Private-Group-ID (81)

* Required only for Catalyst 6500 switches running CatOS. Used to apply policy-based ACLs.

Because you previously created NAC profiles using ACS's built-in NAC templates, the required RACs have already been created and prepopulated for you. The only thing left to do is rename and edit them to meet your needs. Additionally, you will apply a URL redirect ACL for NAC-L2-IP and NAC-L3-IP quarantined hosts. Follow these steps to accomplish this task:

NOTE   For more information about using NAC templates, see the section "Create Network Access Profiles Using NAC Templates," earlier in this chapter.

Step 1   From the navigation frame on the left, select **Shared Profile Components**.

Step 2   The Shared Profile Components page appears. Select the **RADIUS Authorization Components** link to display the current RACs. Depending on the NAC profiles you created earlier, you might see L2 RACs or L3 RACs or both.

Step 3   If you see L3-RACs, continue with the next step. Otherwise, jump to step 17.

Step 4   Click the **NAC-SAMPLE-HEALTHY-L3-RAC** link.

Step 5   The RADIUS Authorization Components page appears. Edit the **Name** field to remove the word **SAMPLE**. Scroll down in the page to view the assigned attributes. The default for each attribute is fine; there is no need to edit them at this point.

Step 6   Select the **Submit** button to save the changes. You get a pop-up message indicating that the RAC might be referenced in a network access profile. Click **OK** to continue.

Step 7   Click the **NAC-SAMPLE-QUARANTINE-L3-RAC** link.

Step 8   The RADIUS Authorization Components page appears. Edit the **Name** field to remove the word **SAMPLE**.

Step 9   Scroll down to the bottom of the page. You will notice that for quarantined hosts, **Session-Timeout** was shortened from 10 hours (in the Healthy RAC) to just 1 hour (3600 seconds). Also, **status-query-timeout** (or how often CTA is polled to check for a status change) was shortened from 300 to 30 seconds.

Step 10   Specify the URL redirect ACL by adding a new Cisco av-pair. In the Add New Attribute section, select **cisco-av-pair (1)** from the **Cisco IOS/PIX 6.0** drop-down list. Then click the **Add** button.

Step 11   In the **Value** field, type **url-redirect-acl=**ACL_Name_defined_on_NAD (example: url-redirect-acl=quarantine_url_redir_acl). Then click **Submit**.

NOTE   The URL redirect ACL is defined on the router or switch and has a **deny** statement for your remediation server and **permit tcp any any eq 80** for everything else. See Chapter 5, "Configuring Layer 3 NAC on Network Access Devices," for more information on defining the redirect ACL.

Step 12 Click the **Submit** button again to save the changes. You might get a pop-up message indicating that the RAC might be referenced in a network access profile. If you do, click **OK** to continue.

Step 13 Click the **NAC-SAMPLE-TRANSITION-L3-RAC** link.

Step 14 The RADIUS Authorization Components page appears. Edit the **Name** field to remove the word **SAMPLE**.

Step 15 Scroll down to the bottom of the page. You will notice that, for transition hosts, **Session-Timeout** (the amount of time to wait before a full revalidation takes place) is only 60 seconds. Also note that **status-query-timeout** is missing. This is because the session timeout is so short that there is no need to query CTA between revalidations.

Step 16 Click the **Submit** button to save the changes. You might get a pop-up message indicating that the RAC might be referenced in a network access profile. If you do, click **OK** to continue. If you are doing only NAC-L3-IP, you can jump to the end of the steps. Otherwise, continue on.

Step 17 Click the **NAC-SAMPLE-HEALTHY-L2-RAC** link.

Step 18 The RADIUS Authorization Components page appears. Edit the **Name** field to remove the word **SAMPLE**.

Step 19 Scroll down in the page to view the assigned attributes. Notice that the **Tunnel-Private-Group-ID** has a value of **Healthy**. This is the VLAN name used in the VLAN assignment process of NAC-L2-802.1X. (If you are using only NAC-L2-IP, you can safely ignore this attribute.) For CatOS-based 6500 administrators, pay attention to the **cisco-av-pair** value. **sec:pg=healthy_hosts** is the name of the policy-based ACL that is sent to the switch. You can edit either of these values, although it is not recommended.

Step 20 Select the **Submit** button to save the changes. You might get a pop-up message indicating that the RAC might be referenced in a network access profile. If you do, click **OK** to continue.

Step 21 Click the **NAC-SAMPLE-QUARANTINE-L2-RAC** link.

Step 22 The RADIUS Authorization Components page appears. Edit the **Name** field to remove the word **SAMPLE**.

Step 23 Scroll down in the page to view the assigned attributes. Again, if you are deploying NAC-L2-802.1X, pay attention to the VLAN name used (**quarantine**); it is case sensitive. For CatOS-based 6500 administrators, the policy-based ACL name is **quarantine_hosts**; this is also case sensitive.

Step 24 To allow the quarantined host's web browsers to be automatically redirected to a server for guided remediation, a URL redirect ACL must be defined. Specify the URL redirect ACL by adding a new Cisco av-pair. In the Add New Attribute section, select **Cisco-av-pair (1)** from the **Cisco IOS/PIX 6.0** drop-down list. Then click the **Add** button.

Step 25 In the **Value** field, type **url-redirect-acl=**ACL_Name_defined_on_NAD (example: url-redirect-acl=quarantine_url_redir_acl). Then click **Submit**. The assigned attributes should look like the ones shown in Figure 8-12.

Figure 8-12 *RADIUS Authorization Components—Assigned Attributes*

Assigned Attributes		?
Vendor	**Attribute**	**Value**
IETF	Session-Timeout (27)	3600
Cisco IOS/PIX 6.0	cisco-av-pair (1)	secipq=quarantine_hosts
IETF	Termination-Action (29)	RADIUS-Request (1)
IETF	Tunnel-Type (64)	[T1] VLAN (13)
IETF	Tunnel-Medium-Type (65)	[T1] 802 (6)
IETF	Tunnel-Private-Group-ID (81)	[T1] quarantine
Cisco IOS/PIX 6.0	cisco-av-pair (1)	url-redirect-acl=quarantine_url_redirect

NOTE   If you plan to use automatic remediation through an external remediation server (such as Altiris or PatchLink), you do not need to add a URL redirect ACL in the Quarantine RAC.

For more information about remediation servers, see Chapter 12, "Remediation."

NOTE   The URL redirect ACL is defined on the switch and has a **deny** statement for your remediation server and **permit tcp any any eq 80** for everything else. See Chapter 4 for more information on defining the redirect ACL.

Step 26 Click the **Submit** button again to save the changes. You might get a pop-up message indicating that the RAC might be referenced in a network access profile. If you do, click **OK** to continue.

Step 27 Finally, with all the changes complete, you need to restart the ACS services from **System Configuration > Service Control > Restart**.

This completes the steps necessary to configure the RADIUS authorization components from within the shared profile components. Continue to the next section, "Network Access Profiles," to see how all these components fit together in the NAC solution.

Network Access Profiles

Before we look at network access profiles (NAPs) in more detail, let us review what we have done so far. Earlier, we created some NAP templates, which triggered the creation of a default posture-validation policy, along with default downloadable IP ACLs and RADIUS authorization components. Then we edited the CTA posture-validation policy and created some new ones for Windows. Likewise, we edited the downloadable IP ACL policies along with the RADIUS authorization components, which make up the enforcement policy. Now, with both the posture-validation and enforcement policies defined, we circle back to the NAPs to see how all this fits together. First, you need to understand what a NAP is.

Network access profiles classify incoming access requests and then apply a common policy to that type of request. This classification enables you to apply different policies to the same user, depending on how that user accesses the network. For example, you might want to apply a stricter policy when users access the network from home through a VPN connection than you would if those same users were sitting at their desks in the office. When accessing the VPN connection, you might want to authenticate those users to a one-time password server. However, when they are in the office, you might choose to authenticate them to the Windows Active Directory database. Similarly, you might want to place more restrictive access policies on wireless access points in public areas (lobbies, outside, and so on) than you would on the access points that are in secured areas. NAPs enable you to do all those things and more.

In relation to NAC, network access profiles are the glue that holds all the NAC components together. When ACS receives a RADIUS access request, it traverses the ordered list of active network access profiles, looking for a match. The request must match all the required conditions in the profile (such as the network device the request is coming from, the authentication protocol used, or even a specific RADIUS attribute value) before ACS can map the request to the profile. The first profile that the request matches is used. After mapping, the request is processed against the remaining policies that make up the profile. A NAC network access profile consists of the following policies: Protocols, Authentication, Posture Validation, and Authorization. As you will see, each one plays its part in the posture-validation process.

NOTE	The network access profiles feature was first added in ACS 4.0. It contained the Authentication, Posture Validation, and Authorization policies. In ACS 4.1 and later, the authentication protocols were removed from the Authentication policy and placed in a new Protocols policy. What remained in the Authentication policy were the credential validation database selection and the MAC auth-bypass configuration.

You should already have several existing NAPs, which you created earlier in this chapter in the section titled "Create Network Access Profiles Using NAC Templates." Look at your existing NAPs by clicking the **Network Access Profiles** button from the navigation frame on the left. You should see a screen similar to the one shown back in Figure 8-6. However, you might have more or fewer NAPs listed. In Figure 8-6, the following NAPs are displayed: NAC-L3-IP, NAC-L2-IP, and NAC-L2-802.1x. Notice the **Up** and **Down** buttons at the bottom of the page. This enables you to reorder the NAPs without deleting and re-creating them. Remember, ACS attempts to match the access request to a NAP in order (from top to bottom) until the first match.

Follow along as we walk though a NAP profile:

Step 1 Select one of the NAPs by clicking its name.

Step 2 The Profile Setup page appears. Notice the **Name** and **Description** fields, which we previously edited. The **Active** check box appears just below them. Deselecting the check box disables the profile without deleting it. This enables you to quickly test new profiles by deactivating the old ones and testing with the new ones.

Step 3 The Network Access Filter is the next section in the NAP. It enables you to filter the access requests on a per-NDG or even per-device basis. This enables you to apply a different policy, or even a different authentication method, to users based on the devices they are authenticating against. By default, the drop-down should say **(Any)**. We cover network access filters in more detail in the "Network Access Filtering" section, later in this chapter.

Step 4 The Protocol Types section enables you to filter the access request based on the RADIUS vendor that generated the request. This section is not currently used for NAC, and the default **Allow Any Protocol Type** should remain selected.

Step 5 The final section in the NAP, Advanced Filtering, enables you to filter the access request based on any combination of RADIUS attributes and their values. For NAC-L2-IP and NAC-L3-IP, ACS checks for the presence of the ip_admission service (NAC) and makes sure the service type is not call-check. The following rule elements accomplish this and are applied as filters:

[026/009/001]cisco-av-pair = aaa:service=ip_admission

[006]Service-Type != 10

For NAC-L2-802.1X, ACS checks that there is no AAA service request in the access request packet (because the NAC service is contained within the EAP-FAST packet) and that the service type is not call-check. The following rule elements accomplish this and are applied as filters:

[026/009/001]cisco-av-pair not-exist aaa:service

[006]Service-Type != 10

Step 6   Finally, at the bottom of the page, you will notice the **Clone** and **Delete** buttons. The **Clone** button comes in handy because it enables you to make a copy of an existing NAP, including all protocols, authentication, posture validation, and authorization policies (which we cover later), and then make modifications to the copied profile. This saves a lot of time over creating a new profile from scratch. The **Delete** button does exactly what you would think: It permanently deletes a profile.

This wraps up the overview and basic framework of the NAP. Although you can edit the NAP, typically the only modifications you might want to make are applying a network access filter or activating and deactivating the NAP to test the profile. Everything else has already been preconfigured because you used the built-in NAC templates when creating the NAP. In the following sections, we look at the policies applied to the profile.

Protocols Policy

The Protocols policy defines the authentication protocols allowed in the NAP. When ACS receives an inbound Access-Request from a NAD, it checks the list of NAPs (in order) to see if the protocol used in the request is allowed by the Authentication policy. If not, the next NAP in the list is checked. If the Protocols policy allows the protocol, processing continues. Because you created the NAC NAPs from ACS's built-in NAC templates, all the Protocol policies have already been configured. However, for completeness, I will cover the preconfigured options.

NOTE   The Protocols policy exists only in ACS 4.1 and higher versions. In ACS 4.0, the Protocols policy is contained within the Authentication policy.

For NAC-L2-IP and NAC-L3-IP NAPs, only the **Allow Posture Validation** option needs to be selected under the PEAP section of the EAP configuration.

For NAC-L2-802.1X NAPS, verify that these items selected with a check mark are also selected (enabled) in your configuration:

☑**Allow EAP-FAST**

☐**Allow anonymous in-band PAC provisioning**

☑**Allow authenticated in-band PAC provisioning**

   ☑**Accept client on authenticated provisioning**

   ☐**Require client certificate for provisioning**

☑**Allow Stateless session resume**

   Authorization PAC TTL: 1 hours

Allowed inner methods

☑**EAP-GTC**

☑**EAP-MSCHAPv2**

☐**EAP-TLS**

Posture Validation:

☐**None**

☑**Required**

☐**Optional—Client may not supply posture data. Use token Unknown**

☐**Posture only**

Now that you have covered the Protocols policies, continue on to the Authentication policy.

Authentication Policy

The Authentication policy contains the credential-validation databases (the databases you want to authenticate the users to), along with the MAC authentication bypass settings for NAC-L2-802.1X agentless hosts. The credential-authentication databases are used to authenticate NAC-L2-802.1X users. The ACS internal database is listed by default. Additional external databases can be configured by clicking the **External User Databases** button. When configured, the database appears in the Available Databases list and can be moved over to the Selected Databases list. Multiple databases can be selected, and ACS attempts to authenticate the user to the databases in the order they appear in the list.

The MAC authentication bypass section enables you to define a list of known MAC addresses for devices that do not have 802.1X supplicants and then authenticate those devices based on MAC addresses. The MAC addresses are mapped to user groups, where additional policies can be applied. Alternatively, you can authenticate the MAC addresses to an external LDAP server instead of defining them locally in ACS.

We cover both components of the Authentication policy in more detail in the sections titled "User Databases" and "Nonresponsive Hosts."

Posture Validation Policy

On the Posture Validation Policy page, contained within the NAP, you create posture-validation rules. Each rule comprises a condition and actions. If the condition is met, the actions are applied. Therefore, the condition can also be seen as a filter applied to the posture-validation policy.

The condition is defined as the set of required credential types. Said another way, the condition is met if the posture credentials received in the RADIUS request match all the selected credentials in the required credential types. If the RADIUS request maps to a NAP but does not contain the required credential types, the posture-validation request fails and is logged in the Failed Attempts log.

If the condition is met, the action is applied. The action is a list of internal posture-validation policies, external posture-validation policies, or both. ACS evaluates each posture-validation policy and returns an application posture token, which represents the endpoint's compliance with the policy. ACS then takes all the application posture tokens returned from the policies and selects the worst-case posture token to use as the system posture token. The system posture token then represents the overall posture of the endpoint. If this is still a bit fuzzy to you, do not worry: It will become clearer as we walk through an example.

Previously in this chapter, you created posture-validation policies to check for an endpoint's compliance with your business's security policy. You checked for things such as what Windows service pack or hotfixes are installed. You now apply those policies to the NAP to complete the overall posture-validation policy.

Follow along with these steps to modify the NAC-L2-IP profile to include the three posture-validation policies created earlier: CTA-Policy, Windows-SP-Policy, and Windows-Hotfix-Policy.

NOTE   If you are not using NAC-L2-IP in your enterprise, you can apply the same policies to your NAC-L3-IP or NAC-L2-802.1X network access profiles.

Step 1   From the navigation frame on the left, select **Network Access Profiles**.

Step 2   The Network Access Profiles page appears. Next, click the **Posture Validation** link next to the NAC-L2-IP profile.

Step 3   The Posture Validation page appears. Notice that the NAC Template already created a posture-validation rule for you named NAC-SAMPLE-POSTURE-RULE. Select the link for the rule name.

Step 4   The Posture Validation Rule page appears. Edit the **Name** field to, say, **NAC-L2-IP-POSTURE-RULE**.

Step 5   Under the Condition section, notice that **Cisco:PA** has been selected as a required credential type. There is no need to require any other credentials to be present.

NOTE   We recommend that you not add any more required credential types to your policies unless you understand the full consequences of that action. If a required credential type is specified and the client does not have that credential type, authentication will fail and no feedback will be provided to the user through CTA.

NOTE   Cisco: PA stands for the Cisco Posture Agent or, more specifically, the Cisco Trust Agent.

Step 6   Scroll down to the Action section. You will notice all your predefined internal and external posture-validation policies listed. Select the check boxes next to the policy names you want applied to this posture-validation rule. (In this example, select the check boxes next to **CTA-Policy**, **Windows-SP-Policy**, and **Windows-Hotfix-Policy**.) See Figure 8-13 for an example screenshot of this.

NOTE   Chapter 11, "Audit Servers," covers external posture-validation servers.

Figure 8-13 *Internal Posture-Validation Policies*

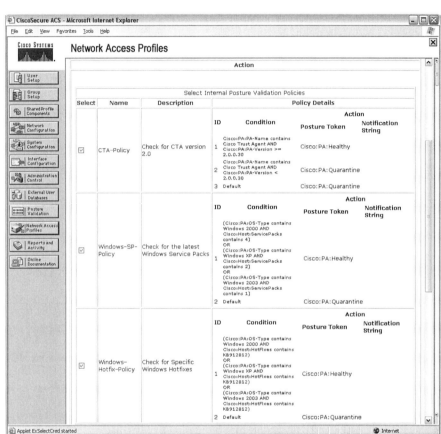

Step 7 Scroll down to the System Posture Token Configuration section. The six system-defined posture tokens are listed on the left. You can add a unique PA Message to each token, which pops up on the end user's screen at the end of the posture-validation process. This message should clearly and succinctly provide information or instructions to the user on what to do next. In this chapter, you have used only the Healthy and Quarantine system posture tokens. Therefore, you will apply the following PA messages to these tokens.

— **Healthy**—The security posture of this machine has been analyzed and found to comply with the company security policy. You have been granted access to the network.

        — **Quarantine**—The overall security posture of this host has been analyzed and does not meet the minimum security policy of this company. Please open a web browser and follow the instructions on the page. You will be asked to install security updates to bring the machine into compliance with the corporate security policy. Once complete, you will be granted access to the network.

Step 8 For the Quarantine system posture token, supply a link in the **URL Redirect** box to redirect the end user's browser to your remediation server. If you do not have a remediation server, you can redirect the user's browser to an internal web server. There you can supply the user with instructions on how to download and install the latest service packs and hotfixes, which will bring the user's machine back into compliance with your corporate security policy. See Figure 8-14 for an example screenshot of the system posture token configuration.

Figure 8-14 *System Posture Token Configuration*

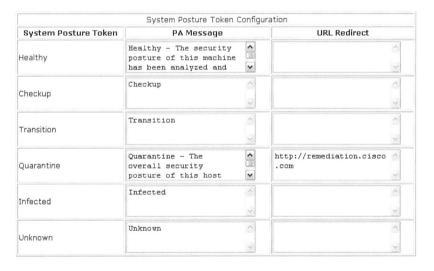

Step 9 Click **Submit** to return to the Posture Validation Rules page, followed by **Done** to return to the Network Access Profiles page.

Step 10 Finally, click **Apply and Restart** to apply the changes.

The posture-validation policy for NAC-L2-IP is now complete. Repeat these steps for the other NAPs to define the posture-validation rules, the PA message, and the redirect URL. In the next section, "Authorization Policy," you will apply the downloadable IP ACL and RADIUS authorization components to the NAD, based on the posture results of the end host.

Authorization Policy

The Authorization Policy in the NAP is where you apply authorization rules to limit an end host's access to the network, based on the system posture token returned from posture validation. Again, as with the posture validation rules you looked at in the last section, the authorization rules contain both a condition and an action.

The condition consists of a user group and a system posture token. If the condition is met, the action can be to deny access or apply the selected shared RAC and downloadable ACL. We defined both the shared RAC and the downloadable ACL earlier in this chapter.

NOTE   Downloadable ACLs are not used in NAC-L2-802.1X. Instead, the enforcement mechanism is VLAN assignment. For NAC-L2-802.1X, leave Downloadable ACLs blank.

Follow along with these steps to continue to configure your NAC-L2-IP NAP by editing its authorization policy and applying your RAC and downloadable IP ACL:

Step 1   From the navigation frame on the left, select **Network Access Profiles**.

Step 2   The Network Access Profiles page appears. Next, click the **Authorization** link next to the NAC-L2-IP profile. Two authorization rules have already been predefined from when the NAP was created from the NAC template. The first rule applies to all users whose system posture token (returned from the posture-validation policy) is Healthy; and the second applies to all users whose system posture token is Quarantine.

Step 3   For the Healthy authorization rule, select the drop-down box under **Shared RAC** and choose **NAC-HEALTHY-L2-RAC** from the list. Also choose **NAC_Healthy_ACL** from the **Downloadable ACL** drop-down list.

Step 4   For the Quarantine authorization rule, select the drop-down box under **Shared RAC** and choose **NAC-QUARANTINE-L2-RAC** from the list. Also choose **NAC_Quarantine_ACL** from the **Downloadable ACL** drop-down list.

Step 5   Finally, you can specify both a RAC and a downloadable ACL if the condition is not met for any of the authorization rules. In these cases, the recommended action is to apply the most restrictive policy. In this case, that is the Quarantine policy. Therefore, select **NAC-QUARANTINE-L2-RAC** for **Shared RAC** and **NAC_Quarantine_ACL** for **Downloadable ACL**.

Step 6 Leave both the **Include RADIUS Attributes from User's Group** and **Include RADIUS Attributes from User Record** check boxes unchecked. Your authorization rules should look like the ones shown in Figure 8-15.

Figure 8-15 *Authorization Rules for NAC L2-IP*

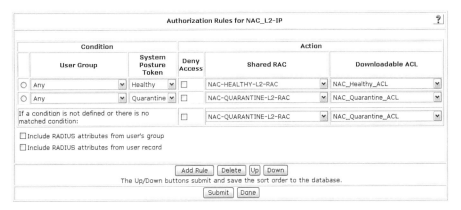

Step 7 Click the **Submit** button to save the changes and return to the Network Access Profiles page. Then choose **Apply and Restart** to apply the changes.

Repeat the same steps for the other NAC network access profiles you have configured. When you have finished configuring all your authorization policies, the required NAC configuration for ACS is complete. The only exception is NAC-L2-802.1X users, who must still populate their users in the user database and then select that database in the Authentication policy. See the "User Databases" section for more information on this step.

Network Access Filtering

Using network access filters (NAFs) is one method of filtering inbound RADIUS requests to the correct NAP. The other two methods are filtering on protocol type and filtering on specific RADIUS attributes. Both were covered previously in the "Network Access Profiles" section. Using NAFs, you can filter the inbound RADIUS request on the network access device's IP.

When configuring NAC, you can use NAFs to separate NAC-L3-IP devices from NAC-L2-IP devices, thus enabling you to apply a different network access profile to each. Without NAFs, the RADIUS request from a NAC-L3-IP device looks the same as one coming from a NAC-L2-IP device, and ACS cannot distinguish them. NAFs overcome this by filtering on a single IP or range of IPs, one or more network devices, and/or one or more network device groups. Thus, you can define all the NAC-L3-IP devices in a single NAF and then apply the NAF to a network access profile. When a RADIUS request comes in, the protocol type is checked, followed by the source IP. If the source IP does not match the NAF, the next profile is checked. Otherwise, processing of the request continues against that profile.

Another example is that you might be performing NAC-L3-IP on your concentrators for remote VPN access users, in addition to performing NAC-L3-IP at a remote branch site. By using NAFs, you can separate the requests from the two different devices and apply different posture-validation and authorization policies. You might want to perform fewer checks on the VPN users than the branch office users, but then further restrict their access to the network. On the other hand, for nonresponsive hosts, you might choose to audit them at the branch site and apply a very restrictive policy for VPN users (because the concentrators currently do not support auditing).

A final example is that you might choose to apply different policies to the same device type, but based on location. Switches or access points connecting public areas might have a different policy than the same devices located in more secured areas. As you can see, NAFs are flexible and, when applied to NAPs, enable you to filter the incoming request on the source IP address or any attribute in the packet. When filtered, you can apply any authentication, posture-validation, or authorization policy you want.

In the following steps, a NAF is created to group all VPN termination devices. Follow these steps to create a NAF, but you can select any device grouping you want:

Step 1 From the navigation frame on the left, select **Shared Profile Components**.

Step 2 The Shared Profile Components page appears. Next, click the **Network Access Filtering** link.

NOTE   If you do not see the Network Access Filtering link, you forgot to enable NAFs. Select **Interface Configuration** > **Advanced Options**, and then check **Network Access Filtering**.

Step 3 Click the **Add** button at the bottom of the page.

Step 4 The Network Access Filtering page appears. In the **Name** field, enter a name for this NAF (example: VPN_Devices).

| NOTE | The name of a NAF can contain up to 31 characters. Spaces are not allowed. Names cannot contain left or right brackets ([ ]), a comma (,), a slash (/), a hyphen (-), quotes ("), an apostrophe ('), or left or right angle brackets (< >). |

Step 5 (Optional) In the **Description** field, fill in a detailed description for this NAF.

Step 6 The final step is to select the devices you want in the NAF by selecting and moving items from the left to the **Selected Items** on the right. This is accomplished by either selecting a network device group from the list (choose (**Not Assigned**) if you are not using NDGs), selecting a network device from within the NDG, or specifying an IP (or wildcarded IP). After you make your selection, choose the right arrow (**->**) to move your selection to the **Selected Items** field. Repeat as many times as necessary until you have selected all NAC devices of the same type. For example, Figure 8-16 shows the VPN_Devices NAF with the following devices selected: TPA-ASA5550, ORD-VPN3000, Empire-VPN3000, and the device with IP address 10.70.9.87.

Step 7 When finished, click the **Submit+Restart** button to save and apply your changes.

With the NAF created, apply it to a network access profile to allow inbound RADIUS requests to be processed by the profile for only the devices you selected in the NAF. Create additional NAFs to group other like devices and apply the same policy to them. Remember, you can create a grouping of any devices that you want to apply the same policies to.

| NOTE | If you need to delete a NAF, first remove all references to the NAF from any network access profile. Then delete the NAF by clicking the **Delete** button from within the NAF. |

Figure 8-16 *L3-IP Network Access Filter*

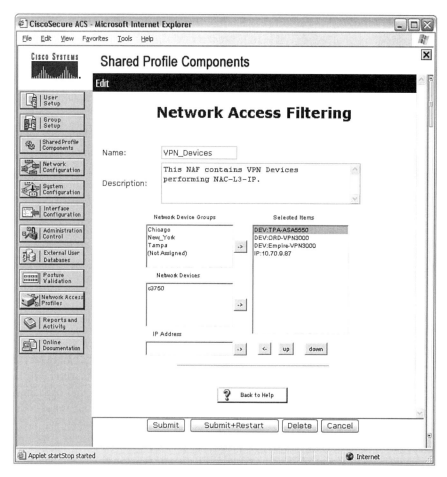

NAC Agentless Hosts

Agentless (or nonresponsive) hosts in NAC are hosts without CTA installed—or, more specifically, ones that cannot communicate with ACS through EAP over UDP, or EAP-FAST over 802.1X. In general, agentless hosts fall into one of the following categories: printers, IP Phones, hosts with operating systems not supported by CTA, and guests (external authorized visitors to your company). Additionally, you might have other devices plugged into your routers (or switchports) for which you want to exclude from NAC.

One question you might ask is why you cannot just disable NAC on the ports that have agentless hosts connected to them. The answer is, you can, but it might significantly weaken your network's overall security posture by providing unsecured ports sprinkled throughout your network. Any employee (or nonemployee, for that matter) can bypass your company's security policy just by disconnecting a printer and plugging in a laptop—or, worse, a wireless access point. So instead of disabling NAC on those ports, you can enable NAC but create an exception for the device out of the port.

Chapters 4 and 5 covered how to apply static NAC exceptions on the switches and routers. In this section, we cover how to configure exception policies on ACS that will apply globally to all devices. In addition to the static local exceptions on the switches/routers and the exception policies in ACS, you can use an audit server to scan the agentless hosts.

NOTE   Chapter 11 covers audit servers and the ACS configuration associated with them.

Centralized Agentless Host Policy for NAC-L3-IP and NAC-L2-IP

ACS provides a NAC template titled Agentless Host for L3, which covers all agentless hosts that the switch is attempting to posture through EAP over UDP. This includes both NAC-L3-IP and NAC-L2-IP.

The Agentless Host for L3 policy provides a way to authorize clientless hosts using a downloadable ACL and RAC, but without posturing them. Thus, these hosts will not be assigned a system posture token. Instead, the **show eou all** output on the switch/router will display the AuthType as CLIENTLESS with a blank posture token. However, the downloadable ACL will still be applied to the interface, and it can be as restrictive or permissive as you want. In general, it is best to limit agentless host access to your internal network because you cannot validate the security posture of those devices.

NOTE   In ACS 4.0, the Agentless Host for L3 NAC template was called just Agentless Host.

Centralized Agentless Host Policy for NAC-L2-802.1X (MAC Authentication Bypass)

Similar to the agentless host policy for NAC-L3-IP and NAC-L2-IP, ACS provides a NAC template to authenticate and authorize those agentless hosts in NAC-L2-802.1X–enabled networks. The NAC template used for this is titled Agentless Host for L2 (802.1X fallback).

The NAC-L2-802.1X Agentless Host Policy enables you to configure exceptions, based on MAC addresses, for hosts without the NAC-enabled 802.1X supplicant to connect to the network. The exceptions authenticate the hosts based on MAC address (which is sometimes referred to as MAC authentication bypass), and the authorization policy assigns them to a

VLAN based on the RAC applied. MAC addresses can be entered into ACS manually, or you can forward the MAC addresses to an external LDAP server to perform the authentication. If you are using LDAP-based authentication, first set up the external LDAP database under the **External User Databases** button. For more information, refer to the Cisco Secure ACS User Guide.

NOTE   In ACS 4.0, the Agentless Host for L2 (802.1X fallback) NAC template was called Authentication Bypass (802.1X fallback).

NOTE   Agentless Host Policy for NAC-L2-802.1X will be available for the 6500 series switches running Cisco IOS (native mode) in the middle of 2007.

Configuring the Agentless Host Policy on ACS

The steps required to configure the Agentless Host Policy for NAC-L3-IP, NAC-L2-IP, and NAC-L2-802.1X are almost identical. The only difference is the NAC template used to create the policy and the method of enforcement through the authorization policy.

Follow these steps to create a NAC Agentless Host Policy using ACS's built-in templates:

Step 1   From the navigation frame on the left, select **Network Access Profiles**.

Step 2   The Network Access Profiles page appears. Click the **Add Template Profile** button.

Step 3   The Create Profile from Template page appears. In the **Template** drop-down list, select **Agentless Host for L3** (for NAC-L3-IP and NAC-L2-IP) or **Agentless Host for L2 (802.1X Fallback)** for NAC-L2-802.1X.

Step 4   In the **Name** field, type in either **NAC-L3-Agentless-Host** (NAC-L3-IP or NAC-L2-IP) or **NAC-802.1X-Agentless-Host** (NAC-L2-802.1X).

Step 5   (Optional) Fill in the **Description** field with any comments you want to add to the profile.

Step 6   Next, check the **Active** box and then click **Submit**.

Step 7   A pop-up dialog box appears indicating what objects were created from the template. Click the **Close** button to return to the Network Access Profiles page.

Step 8 You should now see a profile for NAC-L3-Agentless-Host (or NAC-802.1X-Agentless-Host). Click the **Protocols** link next to the profile. (For ACS 4.0, is the Authentication link.)

Step 9 In the Authentication Protocols section, verify that the **Allow Agentless Request Processing** check box is selected; then click the **Submit** button. (For ACS 4.0, select **Allow MAC-Authentication-Bypass**.)

Step 10 Next, click the **Authentication** link next to the NAC-L3-Agentless-Host (or NAC-802.1X-Agentless-Host) profile.

Step 11 In the Authenticate MAC With section, select either **LDAP Server** (and choose a previously defined LDAP server from the drop-down list) or select **Internal ACS DB.** In this example, you should select **Internal ACS DB.**

Step 12 After selecting the **Internal ACS DB**, click the **Add** button to add a list of MAC addresses to exclude from your NAC policies.

Step 13 In the **MAC Address** field, fill in the MAC addresses of the devices you want to exclude from posture validation. Multiple entries can be entered but must be separated by commas. The following three MAC address formats are accepted: 00-13-c4-80-c5-19, 00:13:c4:80:c5:19, and 0013.c480.c519. Regardless of the format entered, ACS saves all MAC addresses internally in the same format.

NOTE ACS 4.0 saved the MAC addresses in the internal database as a string. This limited the implementation because it required the MAC addresses to be case sensitive and also required the user to enter the MAC address into the database in the same format that the router/switch used. This was sometimes problematic if a user moved between switches because Cisco IOS routers and switches use xxxx.xxxx.xxxx format and CatOS switches use xx-xx-xx-xx-xx-xx. Both Cisco IOS and CatOS use lowercase letters. Also, ACS 4.0 did not support the xx:xx:xx:xx:xx:xx format.

TIP MAC addresses can be wildcarded by specifying only the MAC prefix. For example, if you wanted to match all devices with MACs starting with 0013.c4, you could just enter that prefix without any wildcard characters. However, note that, when wildcarding, the prefixes must contain an even number of hex digits.

Step 14 When finished adding MAC addresses, select a user group from the drop-down list to map these agentless hosts to. This MAC address–to–group mapping represents an authentication rule. I recommend using a group that is above your normal user groups and renaming the group to indicate that it is used for agentless hosts.

NOTE   ACS supports up to 10,000 MAC addresses per authentication rule (MAC addresses–to–group mapping). Up to 100 authentication rules can be applied to a single network access profile. Each MAC authentication rule can be mapped to the same group or different groups.

Step 15 In the Default Action section, assign a group to Agentless Hosts whose MAC addresses are not found in either the internal or external databases. This should be a group that is not used for any other purpose. These hosts might be guests to the company or any other unmanaged device. See Figure 8-17 for an example screen shot of the last few steps.

Figure 8-17 *Agentless Hosts Definition*

Step 16 Click **Submit** to save the changes.

Step 17 Next, click the **Authorization** link next to the NAC-L3-Agentless-Host (or NAC-802.1X-Agentless-Host) profile.

Step 18 The Authorization Rules page appears. For the first authorization rule, select the same user group that you selected under the Authentication configuration.

Step 19 In the **System Posture Token** drop-down list, select **Any**. Because nonresponsive hosts do not undergo posture validation, no SPT is returned. Therefore, **Any** is the only valid option here.

Step 20 Select a RAC from the **Shared RAC** drop-down list. For NAC-L3-IP and NAC-L2-IP, the RAC is typically one of the Healthy RACs because only the timeout values will be used. However, for NAC-L2-802.1X, the RAC applies the VLAN assignment; therefore, you might want to apply the Quarantine RAC or create a new RAC just for agentless hosts. Again, this depends on your security policy and how you want to restrict agentless hosts.

Step 21 For NAC-L3-IP and NAC-L2-IP, select an ACL from the **Downloadable ACL** drop-down list. This is normally your Healthy ACL. However, you can create a unique ACL for agentless devices. For NAC-L2-802.1X, leave the **Downloadable ACL** drop-down list blank.

Step 22 You can delete or ignore the remaining Authorization rules because they will not be matched. However, a default rule is enabled that is matched by all agentless hosts whose MAC addresses are not defined. You can choose to apply a RAC and/or a downloadable ACL to these devices, or deny them access altogether by selecting the **Deny Access** check box. This default fallback rule allows another way to grant limited access to all undefined (or unauthorized) agentless hosts. However, you should map these unauthorized, agentless hosts to a dedicated group in the MAC authentication step. After making your default rule choices, select **Submit** to save the changes.

Step 23 Finally, restart the ACS services from **System Configuration > Service Control** for the changes to take effect.

NOTE   For the NAC-L3-IP and NAC-L2-IP Agentless Host Policy to be applied, the switch/router must be configured to allow clientless devices. For Cisco IOS switches, use the command **eou allow clientless**.

With agentless hosts, you have a few configuration options. In the previous steps, all agentless hosts were included in the same group, so the same policies were applied to all of them. However, you have the option of grouping agentless hosts into multiple groups.

For large enterprises, creating multiple groups gives you more flexibility. You can create a group for printers, a group for IP Phones, or a group for servers—or anything else you want. When you specify the MAC addresses under the authentication settings, just create additional MAC authentication mapping rules. Then apply a different user group to each rule. However, unique group mappings make sense only if you will apply a unique ACL (or VLAN) to each of these groups.

Continuing with the earlier NAC-L3-Agentless-Host example, create a unique downloadable ACL for your printers (probably to allow print jobs only from clients) and a different ACL for your phones or servers. (Remember, downloadable ACLs are created under **Shared Profile Components** > **Downloadable IP ACLs**.) Then in the authorization policy, create a new rule for each agentless user group and map the appropriate ACL to the rule. This way, you can apply unique policies to individual agentless devices based on their MAC addresses.

Figure 8-18 shows a sample MAC authentication mapping, with agentless hosts, printers, and IP Phones each mapped to a different user group.

Figure 8-18 *Agentless Hosts Authentication Policy—MAC Authentication Mapping Rules per Device Group*

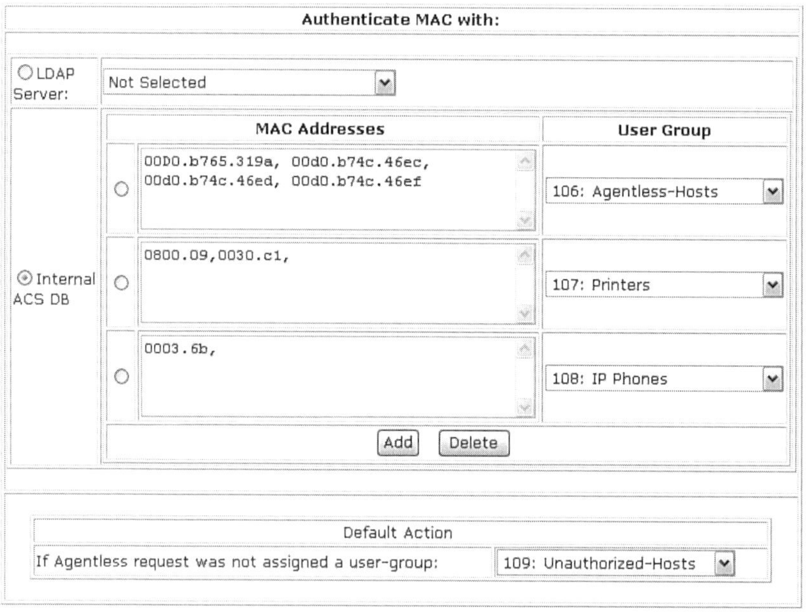

Figure 8-19 shows an example NAC-L3-Agentless-Host Authorization Policy with each agentless group of devices mapped to its own unique downloadable ACL, which allows only the traffic required for those devices.

Figure 8-19 *NAC-L3-Agentless-Host Authorization Policy—Unique Downloadable ACL Applied to*
Agentless Groups

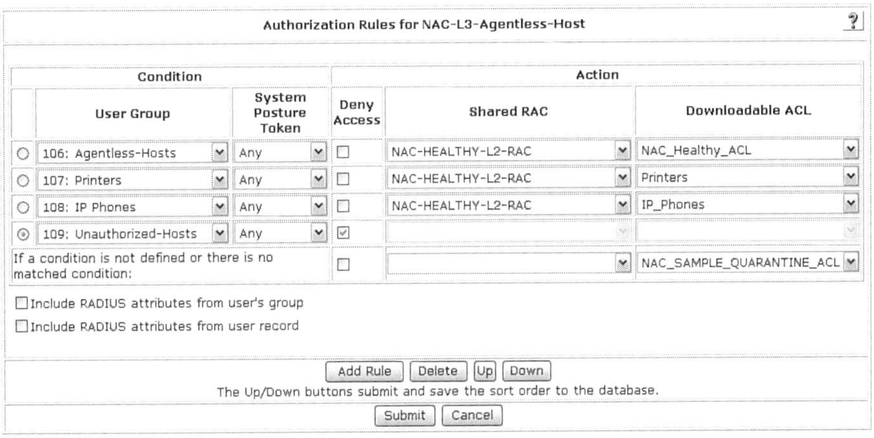

With the nonresponsive host policy configured, you need to only periodically edit the MAC
list to add agentless devices. You can also verify that the agentless devices are being
mapped to the correct group by checking your passed authentications log file. The group
name, network access profile name, shared RAC, and downloadable ACL are all listed,
along with the client's MAC address (in the Caller-ID field).

User Databases

ACS contains a robust internal user database where usernames and attributes applied to
those usernames are stored. ACS first checks this internal database for any user-
authentication request it receives. However, NAC-L2-IP and NAC-L3-IP perform no user
authentication, so no users need to be defined in ACS. NAC-L2-802.1X, on the other hand
requires user authentication. This is because the network admission control piece is
performed on top of the normal 802.1X authentication.

For small to medium-size businesses deploying NAC-L2-802.1X, ACS's internal database
will meet your needs fine. Just define new users under the **User Setup** button on the left
navigation frame and assign passwords to them. Large enterprises might want to leverage
one of their pre-existing user databases (Windows domain, Active Directory, LDAP, Token
Servers, and so on) to authenticate users against. Although it is outside the scope of this
chapter to cover the configuration of external user databases, it is prudent to mention the
following points regarding external databases when used with NAC-L2-802.1X:

- All token servers are not supported.
- External LDAP databases are supported.

- Both Windows Active Directory and Windows SAM databases fully support NAC-L2-802.1X.

- Machine authentication is supported only with the Windows Active Directory database when performing binary certificate matching.

NOTE   For more information about external database configuration, see the "User Databases" chapter of the ACS Users Guide.

Importing Vendor Attribute-Value Pairs

By default, ACS includes only Cisco-specific vendor attributes for NAC, which are used in the posture-validation process. If you have a partner application installed on the end hosts and you want to validate the state of that application (as in the current virus definition file), the vendor's Attribute Definition File (ADF) must be imported into ACS. The ADF contains multiple attribute/value pairs (AVPs) that define the attributes that ACS can query for posture compliance.

When this process is complete, you can include these attributes in the internal posture-validation rules to determine the overall security posture of the host. Complete these steps to add a NAC partner's ADF files to ACS.

Step 1   Obtain one or more ADFs from the NAC partner.

Step 2   Copy the ADFs to the following directory:

C:\Program Files\CiscoSecure ACS vX.X\bin

Step 3   From a DOS command prompt, change to the directory where you copied the ADFs and use the CSUtil.exe utility to import the ADFs. For example:

CSUtil.exe –addAVP *filename***.adf**

Step 4   After adding all the ADFs to ACS, restart the ACS processes from **System Configuration > Service Control**.

NOTE   For ACS appliances, AVPs are added through FTP from **System Configuration > NAC Attributes Management**.

Enabling Logging

ACS provides very robust logging options that are used both for monitoring the NAC deployment through external monitoring applications (like CS-MARS, which is covered in Chapter 17, "Monitoring the NAC Solution Using the Cisco Security Monitoring, Analysis, and Response System") and for troubleshooting NAC issues. By default, ACS stores the logs in comma-separated value (CSV) format on the local hard drive and provides a web interface to view the logs in a report format by selecting the **Reports and Activity** icon. Optionally, the log files can be downloaded and imported into any application that supports CSV files. ACS can also be configured to log to any Open Database Connectivity (ODBC) complaint relational database. And starting with ACS 4.1, logs can be sent out to an external syslog server. For more information on configuring syslog or ODBC logging, refer to the ACS User's Guide.

In this section, you will configure ACS to log both passed and failed authentication attempts, as well as RADIUS accounting information; this is all critical in your NAC deployment. In addition, you will customize the fields to include in the log files and enable directory management, to prevent the log files from filling up the hard disk.

Configuring Failed Attempts Logging

In this section, you will enable logging of failed attempts and add NAC-specific attributes to the Failed Attempts log. Doing so will aid in debugging NAC-related configuration errors. If an end host does not match any of the posture-validation rules, the result is logged in the Failed Attempts log file.

Complete these steps to accomplish these tasks:

Step 1 From the navigation frame on the left, select **System Configuration > Logging**.

Step 2 The Logging Configuration page appears. Click the **Configure** link in the CSV column for the Failed Attempts report.

Step 3 Verify that the **Log to CSV Failed Attempts Report** check box is selected.

Step 4 In the Select Columns to Log section, verify that the following attributes appear in the right column (Logged Attributes). If any item is not listed, select it from the left column (Attributes) and click the **->** button to move it to the right column. You can also select attributes other than those listed here. Attributes with asterisks are nondefault.

   — Message-Type

   — User-Name

   — Caller-ID

— Authen-Failure-Code

— NAS-Port

— NAS-IP-Address

— AAA Server*

— PEAP/EAP-FAST-Clear-Name

— EAP Type

— EAP Type Name

— Access Device

— Network Device Group

— Logged Remotely*

— Network Access Profile Name

— Shared RAC*

— Downloadable ACL*

— System-Posture-Token*

— Application-Posture-Token*

— Reason

— cisco-av-pair*

— Cisco:PA:PA-Name*

— Cisco:PA:PA-Version*

— Cisco:PA:OS-Type*

— Cisco:PA:OS-Version*

— Cisco:Host:ServicePacks*

— Cisco:Host:Hotfixes*

— Cisco:Host:Package*

TIP   I highly recommend that you log all the attributes that you are using in your posture-validation rules. Doing so enables you to quickly determine why end hosts did not receive the system posture token you thought they should have. The previous list represents the most common attributes.

Step 5   In the Log File Management section, specify how often you want a new log file to be created. The default of **Every Day** is the recommended option.

Step 6   (Optional) Specify where you want the log file to be created by modifying the path in the **Directory** field. The default location is C:\Program Files\CiscoSecure ACS v4.1\Logs\Failed Attempts\. Typically, this location is fine; modify it only if you have a specific reason to do so.

Step 7   Check the **Manage Directory** box and specify either how many files to keep or the number of days to keep them. A general rule of thumb is to keep a month's worth of files locally. You can also back up the files and save them in an alternate location if your security policy dictates it.

Step 8   Finally, click the **Submit** button at the bottom of the page to save the changes.

Configuring Passed Authentications Logging

In this section, you will enable logging of passed authentications and add NAC-specific attributes to the Passed Authentications log. ACS logs all posture-validation credentials to this log unless access is strictly denied. In that case, ACS logs the result in the Failed Attempts log. Adding the posture attributes to this log enables you to see what posture credentials the end host is sending to ACS. This will help you further define your posture-validation rules.

Complete these steps to accomplish these tasks:

Step 1   From the navigation frame on the left, select **System Configuration > Logging**.

Step 2   The Logging Configuration page appears. Click the **Configure** link in the CSV column for the Passed Authentication report.

Step 3   Check the **Log to CSV Passed Authentications Report** check box.

Step 4   In the Select Columns to Log section, verify that the following attributes appear in the right column (Logged Attributes). If any item is not listed, select it from the left column (Attributes) and click the **->** button to move it to the right column. You can also select attributes other than those listed below. Attributes with asterisks are nondefault.

   — Message-Type

   — User-Name

   — Caller-ID

— NAS-Port

— NAS-IP-Address

— AAA Server*

— Filter Information*

— PEAP/EAP-FAST-Clear-Name

— EAP Type

— EAP Type Name

— Access Device

— Network Device Group

— Logged Remotely*

— Outbound Class*

— Network Access Profile Name

— Shared RAC

— Downloadable ACL

— System-Posture-Token

— Application-Posture-Token

— Reason

— cisco-av-pair*

— Cisco:Host:HostFQDN*

— Cisco:PA:PA-Name*

— Cisco:PA:PA-Version*

— Cisco:PA:OS-Type*

— Cisco:PA:OS-Version*

— Cisco:Host:ServicePacks*

— Cisco:Host:Hotfixes*

— Cisco:Host:Package*

TIP   I highly recommend that you log all the attributes that you are using in your posture-validation rules. Doing so will enable you to quickly determine why end hosts did not receive the SPT you thought they should have. The previous list represents the most common attributes.

Step 5   In the Log File Management section, specify how often you want a new log file to be created. The default of **Every Day** is the recommended option.

Step 6   (Optional) Specify where you want the log file to be created by modifying the path in the **Directory** field. The default location is C:\Program Files\CiscoSecure ACS v4.1\Logs\Passed Authentications\. Typically, this location is fine; modify it only if you have a specific reason to do so.

Step 7   Check the **Manage Directory** box and specify either how many files to keep or the number of days to keep them. A general rule of thumb is to keep a month's worth of files locally. You can also back up the files and save them in an alternate location, if your security policy dictates it.

Step 8   Finally, click the **Submit** button at the bottom of the page to save the changes.

Configuring RADIUS Accounting Logging

Complete these steps to configure RADIUS accounting logging:

Step 1   From the navigation frame on the left, select **System Configuration > Logging**.

Step 2   The Logging Configuration page appears. Click the **Configure** link in the CSV column for the RADIUS Accounting report.

Step 3   Verify that the **Log to CSV RADIUS Accounting Report** check box is selected.

Step 4   In the Select Columns to Log section, verify that the following attributes appear in the right column (Logged Attributes). If any item is not listed, select it from the left column (Attributes) and click the **->** button to move it to the right column. You can also select attributes other than those listed below. Attributes with asterisks are nondefault.

— User-Name

— Group-Name

- — Calling-Station-Id
- — Acct-Status-Type
- — Acct-Session-Id
- — Acct-Session-Time
- — Acct-Input-Octets
- — Acct-Output-Octets
- — Acct-Input-Packets
- — Acct-Output-Packets
- — Framed-IP-Address
- — NAS-Port
- — NAS-IP-Address
- — Class*
- — Termination-Action*
- — Called-Station-Id*
- — AcctDelay-Time*
- — Acct-Authentic*
- — Acct-Terminate-Cause*
- — Event-Timestamp*
- — NAS-Port-Type*
- — Port-Limit*
- — NAS-Port-Id*
- — AAA-Server*
- — ExtDB Info*
- — Network Access Profile Name*
- — cisco-av-pair
- — Access Device*
- — Logged Remotely*

Step 5   In the Log File Management section, specify how often you want a new log file to be created. The default of **Every Day** is the recommended option.

Step 6   (Optional) Specify where you want the log file to be created by modifying the path in the **Directory** field. The default location is C:\Program Files\CiscoSecure ACS v4.1\Logs\RADIUS Accounting\. Typically, this location is fine; modify it only if you have a specific reason to do so.

Step 7   Check the **Manage Directory** box and specify either how many files to keep or the number of days to keep them. A general rule of thumb is to keep a month's worth of files locally. You can also back up the files and save them in an alternative location if your security policy dictates it.

Step 8   Finally, click the **Submit** button at the bottom of the page to save the changes.

Replication

Any time your organization relies on a single device, that device becomes a single point of failure. Using ACS to posture all the end hosts in your network is no exception. If the ACS server dies, you have a problem. Therefore, ACS provides a way to have multiple backup ACS servers that are all synced via replication. Each of the replication servers is a fully functioning ACS server and can actively process all types of authentication requests. Thus, you can use the replication partner servers in a load-balancing configuration (either locally or geographically dispersed).

The ACS replication feature has been around for a long time and has several options that an administrator can configure to meet the needs of the network. The configuration of ACS replication is outside the scope of this chapter, but more information on ACS replication options can be found in the "Advanced System Configuration" chapter of the ACS User Guide.

NOTE   Chapter 15, "Deploying and Troubleshooting NAC in Large Enterprises," covers the configuration required in ACS to replicate from a primary ACS server to one or more secondary ACS servers.

Troubleshooting ACS

In this section, we begin by covering how to troubleshoot problems that cannot be solved by looking in the Reports and Activity log files. In those cases, it might be necessary to examine the individual services' log files, which is where ACS stores verbose debugging information. Following that, we highlight a few common problems you might run into during your NAC deployment and discuss how to resolve the issues.

Enabling Service Debug Logging

Sometimes the information you need to troubleshoot a problem is not contained in the Failed Attempts, Passed Authentications, or RADIUS Accounting logs. In these cases, you can get additional debugging information by examining the AUTH.log or RDS.log files. These files contain detailed debugging information related to authentication attempts and RADIUS communications from the NAD to ACS. By default, these log files are set to record a low level of detail. At this level, most of the NAC-related information is not recorded.

During initial deployment and when troubleshooting problems, you might find it useful to increase the services logging level to Full. Be aware that this change affects only future log messages recorded in the file. Therefore, if you are troubleshooting an issue and then change the logging level, you will need to re-experience the issue to capture the additional logging information. For this reason, some customers configure logging to Full and leave it there. By enabling directory management, ACS purges old log files so they do not consume all your disk space.

Setting the Services Logging Level to Full

In the following steps, we walk through increasing the services logging level to Full and enabling directory management. You will configure ACS to generate a new log file every day and to purge files older than 31 days.

Step 1 From the navigation frame on the left, select **System Configuration > Service Control**. The Services Log File Configuration page appears.

Step 2 In the Level of Detail section, select **Full**.

Step 3 In the Generate New File section, select **Every Day**.

Step 4 Ensure that the **Manage Directory** box is checked and select **Delete Files Older Than 31 Days**.

Step 5 Click the **Restart** button to save and apply the changes.

NOTE When ACS has been deployed and running without any issues for a while, you might choose to lower the services logging level back to Low. This slightly improves performance while at the same time capturing any critical issue that might come up with ACS. If you need to debug a new NAC-related issue, you can always increase the logging level again.

Viewing the Logs

All the services log files are saved in the C:\Program Files\CiscoSecure ACS v4.*x**$SERVICE*\Logs\ directory, where *$SERVICE* is CSAuth, CSRadius, or similar. For example, the AUTH.log by default is saved in the following directory:

C:\Program Files\CiscoSecure ACS v4.1\CSAuth\Logs\

Likewise, the default location of the RDS.log is

C:\Program Files\CiscoSecure ACS v4.1\CSRadius\Logs\

The most recent logs are named AUTH.log and RDS.log, respectively. Older logs have a date-time stamp applied to their name, which indicates the time the log file was created. The AUTH.log file should be referenced when attempting to troubleshoot the host posture process. The RDS.log file is useful for troubleshooting the RADIUS communication between ACS and the NAD.

NOTE   The service logs are not directly accessible on the ACS appliance. Instead, the logs can be retrieved only by running the support utility and downloading the package.cab file. The support utility is accessible from **System Configuration > Support** and then selecting the **Run Support Now** button.

Example 8-3 shows the beginning of a NAC-L2-IP posture-validation request in the AUTH.log. The host being postured is identified on the first line by its MAC address: 00d0.b74c.46ec. The second line indicates that ACS is sending the posture query to CTA, and then CTA returns a few lines below the Incoming Posture Credentials.

Example 8-3 *L2-IP Posture-Validation Request in AUTH.log*

```
AUTH 05/11/2006 18:22:02 I 0897 0368 AuthenProcessResponse: process response for
'00d0.b74c.46ec'
AUTH 05/11/2006 18:22:02 I 0361 0368 EAP: TLV: Encoding specific PostureQuery, [32]
octets
AUTH 05/11/2006 18:22:02 I 5081 0368 Done RQ1027, client 50, status -2046
AUTH 05/11/2006 18:22:02 I 5094 0368     Worker 6 processing message 8.
AUTH 05/11/2006 18:22:02 I 5081 0368 Start RQ1027, client 50 (127.0.0.1)
AUTH 05/11/2006 18:22:02 I 0897 0368 AuthenProcessResponse: process response for
'SECURITY-TAC:Administrator'
AUTH 05/11/2006 18:22:02 I 0143 0368 [PDE]: [START] Incoming Posture credentials
(parsed)
AUTH 05/11/2006 18:22:02 I 0143 0368 [PDE]: PostureAttribute: [Cisco:PA:PA-Name]
value [Cisco Trust Agent]
```

continues

Example 8-3   *L2-IP Posture-Validation Request in AUTH.log (Continued)*

```
AUTH 05/11/2006 18:22:02 I 0143 0368 [PDE]: PostureAttribute: [Cisco:PA:PA-Version]
value [2.0.0.30]
AUTH 05/11/2006 18:22:02 I 0143 0368 [PDE]: PostureAttribute: [Cisco:Host:HotFixes]
value
[¦KB904706¦KB823980¦Q324720¦Q328310¦Q329048¦Q329170¦Q329390¦Q329441¦Q331953¦Q81057
7¦Q811493¦Q811630¦Q815021¦KB821557¦KB822603¦KB823182¦KB823559¦KB823980¦KB824105¦KB
824141¦KB824146¦KB824151¦KB825119¦KB828028¦KB828035¦KB828741¦KB835409¦KB835732¦KB8
37001¦KB839645¦KB840315¦KB840374¦KB841873¦KB842773¦KB887472¦KB892944¦KB905495¦KB91
4798¦Q323255¦Q327696¦Q328310¦Q329048¦Q329115¦Q329170¦Q329390¦Q329441¦Q329834¦Q3319
53¦Q810565¦Q810577¦Q810833¦Q811114¦Q811493¦Q811630¦Q814033¦Q814995¦Q815021¦Q817287
¦Q817606¦KB873339¦KB885835¦KB885836¦KB888113¦KB888302¦KB890046¦KB890859¦KB891781¦K
B893066¦KB893756¦KB893803v2¦KB896358¦KB896422¦KB896423¦KB896424¦KB896428¦KB898461¦
KB899587¦KB899589¦KB899591¦KB900725¦KB901017¦KB901214¦KB902400¦KB905414¦KB905749¦K
B908519¦KB908531¦KB910437¦KB911562¦KB911927¦KB912919¦KB913446¦KB913580¦]
AUTH 05/11/2006 18:22:02 I 0143 0368 [PDE]: [END] Incoming Posture credentials
(parsed)
```

As you can see, the AUTH.log will show you exactly what posture credentials CTA sent from the end host. This is useful in troubleshooting why a host might have been given a non-Healthy system posture token.

The RDS.log is useful for troubleshooting issues with the NAD. Example 8-4 shows a section of the RDS.log file. In this case, the user received a Healthy posture token but was unable to access the internal network after being postured. Checking the Passed Authentication log indicated that the downloadable ACL was not being applied. The next step was to check the RDS.log to see why.

As you can see from the first highlighted text, ACS cannot download the ACL because the NAD is defined as a RADIUS (IETF) device, not a Cisco device. The remaining highlighted sections show the NAD's IP address, the system posture token returned, the machine name and logged-in user, and finally the end-host's MAC address.

Example 8-4   *L2-IP Authorization Response in the RDS.log*

```
RDS 05/12/2006 20:36:48 I 0501 2312 AuthorExtensionPoint: Initiating scan of
configured extension points...
RDS 05/12/2006 20:36:48 I 0523 2312 AuthorExtensionPoint: Supplier [Cisco
Downloadable ACLs] not associated with vendor [RADIUS (IETF)], skipping...
RDS 05/12/2006 20:36:48 I 0537 2312 AuthorExtensionPoint: Calling
[AuthorisationExtension] for Supplier [Cisco Shared RACs]
RDS 05/12/2006 20:36:48 I 0805 2312 ExtensionPoint: [RadiusSPC] Starting RAC lookup
for user [SECURITY-TAC:Administrator] RAC [NAC-HEALTHY-L3-RAC]
RDS 05/12/2006 20:36:48 I 0805 2312 ExtensionPoint: [RadiusSPC] Found RAC [NAC-
HEALTHY-L3-RAC] for [SECURITY-TAC:Administrator]
RDS 05/12/2006 20:36:48 I 0805 2312 ExtensionPoint: [RadiusSPC] RAC lookup for
[SECURITY-TAC:Administrator] complete
RDS 05/12/2006 20:36:48 I 0542 2312 AuthorExtensionPoint: [RadiusSpc.dll-
>AuthorisationExtension] returned [20 - authorised]
RDS 05/12/2006 20:36:48 I 0537 2312 AuthorExtensionPoint: Calling
[AuthorisationExtension] for Supplier [Cisco Dynamic Session Dll]
RDS 05/12/2006 20:36:48 I 0542 2312 AuthorExtensionPoint: [DynaSession.dll-
>AuthorisationExtension] returned [20 - authorised]
```

Example 8-4 *L2-IP Authorization Response in the RDS.log (Continued)*

```
RDS 05/12/2006 20:36:48 I 0575 2312 AuthorExtensionPoint: Start of Attribute Set
 Returned From DynaSession.dll
RDS 05/12/2006 20:36:48 I 3047 2312    [026] Vendor-Specific           vsa id: 9
RDS 05/12/2006 20:36:48 I 3089 2312        [001] cisco-av-pair          value:
 posture-token=Healthy
RDS 05/12/2006 20:36:48 I 0577 2312 AuthorExtensionPoint: End of Attribute Set
RDS 05/12/2006 20:36:48 D 3934 2312 Sending response code 2, id 255 to 192.168.20.1
 on port 1645
RDS 05/12/2006 20:36:48 I 3017 2312    [027] Session-Timeout        value: 36000
RDS 05/12/2006 20:36:48 I 3017 2312    [029] Termination-Action        value: 1
RDS 05/12/2006 20:36:48 I 3047 2312    [026] Vendor-Specific           vsa id: 9
RDS 05/12/2006 20:36:48 I 3089 2312        [001] cisco-av-pair          value:
 status-query-timeout=300
RDS 05/12/2006 20:36:48 I 3047 2312    [026] Vendor-Specific           vsa id: 9
RDS 05/12/2006 20:36:48 I 3089 2312        [001] cisco-av-pair          value:
 posture-token=Healthy
RDS 05/12/2006 20:36:48 I 3042 2312    [008] Framed-IP-Address         value:
 255.255.255.255
RDS 05/12/2006 20:36:48 I 2999 2312    [079] EAP-Message              value:
 .V..
RDS 05/12/2006 20:36:48 I 3047 2312    [026] Vendor-Specific              vsa
 id: 311
RDS 05/12/2006 20:36:48 I 3089 2312        [016] MS-MPPE-Send-Key       value:
 ._.EW...!....yz...?V...J...*+8.I..>a.....8:.}J....
RDS 05/12/2006 20:36:48 I 3047 2312    [026] Vendor-Specific              vsa
 id: 311
RDS 05/12/2006 20:36:48 I 3089 2312        [017] MS-MPPE-Recv-Key       value:
 ...W...1.>.(U(...0 .....'.#L.0$....uR.8t.z?.%...Y.
RDS 05/12/2006 20:36:48 I 2999 2312    [001] User-Name               value:
 SECURITY-TAC:Administrator
RDS 05/12/2006 20:36:48 I 2999 2312    [025] Class                   value:
 CACS:d/a1a5/ac12ad63/00d0.b74c.46ec
RDS 05/12/2006 20:36:48 I 2999 2312    [080] Message-Authenticator   value:
 4E 4F 54 20 43 4F 4D 50 55 54 45 44 20 59 45 54
```

Invalid Protocol Data

If you have configured NAC-L2-802.1X and are unable to connect to the network, the first step is to check the Failed Attempts log. If the Authen-Failure-Code is "Invalid Protocol Data," this is likely because ACS cannot communicate with CTA on the client machine. If you are using the Cisco Secure Services Client, first make sure that you remembered to install CTA. Next, check that the CTA services are running, and execute **ctastat** to verify CTA's status. If still no luck, select the Network Access Profile and modify the Authentication policy under the profile you are using (the Failed Attempts log indicates which profile the client is falling under). Change the EAP-FAST Posture Validation section to **None**, restart the services, and see if you are able to connect. If so, the issue is with ACS being unable to communicate with CTA, and you must troubleshoot that part.

RADIUS Posture-Validation Requests Are Not Mapped to the Correct NAP

If you cannot connect to the network, check both the Passed Authentications and Failed Attempts log files to find the inbound authentication request. Then verify that the NAP the RADIUS requests are mapped to is the correct one. Remember that the NAPs are processed in order, and the first one that matches is applied. If your RADIUS request is being mapped to the wrong NAP, either reorder the NAPs or apply a network access filter to filter the requests by NAD or network device group. See the "Network Access Filtering" section earlier in this chapter for more information.

RADIUS Dictionaries Missing from the Interface Configuration Section

After clicking the **Interface Configuration** button from the left frame, if you do not see the RADIUS (IETF) or RADIUS (Cisco IOS/PIX 6.0) dictionaries listed, you have not defined a NAD using one of these dictionaries. See the section titled "Adding Network Access Devices (NADs)" for instructions on how to add NADs.

Certificate Issues—EAP-TLS or PEAP Authentication Failed During SSL Handshake in Failed Attempts Log

If you have a host that is not being postured properly, the first troubleshooting step is to check the Failed Attempts log. If you see the message "EAP-TLS or PEAP authentication failed during SSL handshake" in the Authen-Failure-Code column, this indicates a problem with the certificates. If other hosts have been postured fine, you know that ACS's certificate is fine. To resolve the problem, you need to check that the correct root CA certificate was installed in the trusted root store on the client. Both Chapters 2 and 3 cover the troubleshooting steps necessary on the client to resolve this issue.

Summary

In this chapter, we covered step by step the installation, configuration, and operation of NAC on the Cisco Secure Access Control Server. One unstated goal of this chapter is that a network administrator should be able to start reading the chapter with a server with only the OS installed on it, and by the end of the chapter, he should have a fully functioning ACS server configured for NAC. Along the way, we also covered troubleshooting NAC issues on ACS by examining the Reports and Activity log files, as well as the individual component log files. In summary, this chapter completely covers NAC on ACS.

Review Questions

You can find the answers to the review questions in Appendix A, "Answers to Review Questions."

1. True or false: You can access the ACS server remotely, by default, after installation.

2. True or false: The ACS server software that runs on the ACS Solution Engine (ACS appliance) is the same software that you can install on a standalone server.

3. Access to the ACS user interface is provided via what port?

   a. TCP/80

   b. TCP/8080

   c. TCP/2000

   d. TCP/2002

4. How can you further secure access to the ACS GUI interface?

5. Network device groups are:

   a. A way of grouping NAC policies to be applied to end hosts

   b. A way of grouping AAA clients so they can share a common shared secret key, and user access may be limited on a NDG basis

   c. A way of grouping users so common policies can be applied to all users in the group

   d. None of the above

6. Which of the following can you not add to a network access filter?

   a. Network device group

   b. Network access device

   c. Network access profile

   d. IP address

7. A network access profile contains which of the following policies? (Select two.)

   a. Authentication and Protocols

   b. Accounting and Posture Validation

   c. Posture Validation and Authorization

   d. Protocols and RADIUS Authorization Components

8. Which of the following is not contained in the Authorization policy for a network access profile?

   a. Deny access

   b. Shared RAC

   c. Downloadable ACL

   d. Network access filter

9. What type of external database can be used to authenticate Agentless Hosts by MAC address?

   a. Windows database

   b. LDAP database

   c. ODBC database

   d. Token server

10. If a client is being assigned the wrong system posture token, where is the first place you should look to troubleshoot the problem?

   a. Network access profiles configuration

   b. RADIUS authorization components configuration

   c. Failed Attempts log

   d. Passed Authentications log

This chapter covers the following topics:

- Cisco Security Agent architecture
- Installing Cisco Security Agent Management Center
- Configuring CSA NAC-related features

## CHAPTER 9

Cisco Security Agent

The Cisco Security Agent (CSA) is an optional component of the Cisco NAC Framework that provides endpoint security for servers and user desktop machines.

The CSA solution has two major components:

- **Cisco Security Agent Management Center (CSA MC)**—The management console where all groups, policies, and agent kits are configured
- **Cisco Security Agent**—The agent installed on end-user machines

CSA provides several more robust security features than a traditional antivirus or a personal firewall. CSA rich security features include the following:

- Host intrusion prevention
- Protection against spyware
- Protection against buffer-overflow attacks
- Distributed host firewall features
- Malicious mobile code protection
- Operating system integrity assurance
- Application inventory
- Extensive audit and logging capabilities
- Protection against file modification or deletion
- Windows Registry protection

The Cisco Security Agent Management Center (CSA MC)is the central management system that enables you to define and distribute policies, providing software updates and maintaining communications to the Cisco Security Agents (CSA) installed in end-user machines and servers. This chapter guides you on how to install and configure the CSA NAC–related features.

NOTE   You can refer to the Cisco Press book *Cisco Security Agent,* by Chad Sullivan (ISBN 1587052059), for a complete configuration and deployment guide of CSA. This chapter discusses CSA in the context of NAC.

Cisco Security Agent Architecture

In the CSA solution architecture, a central management center maintains a database of policies and information about the workstations and servers that have the Cisco Security Agent software installed. Agents register with CSA MC. Subsequently, CSA MC checks its configuration database and deploys a configured policy for that particular system.

NOTE   Starting with CSA Version 5.1, the CSA MC is a standalone system. Before Version 5.1, CSA MC was part of the CiscoWorks VPN and Security Management System (VMS).

The Cisco Security Agent software constantly monitors all activity on the end host and polls to the CSA MC at configurable intervals for policy updates, as illustrated in Figure 9-1.

Figure 9-1   *Cisco Security Agent Architecture*

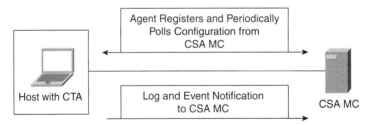

The agent sends events and alerts to the CSA MC's global event manager. The global event manager inspects the event logs and then alerts the administrator or triggers the agent to take action based on the specific alert.

NOTE   All the communication between the agents and the CSA MC is done through Secure Socket Layer (SSL). The administrator also connects to the CSA MC through SSL to manage and monitor the agents.

CSA MC has the following components:

- Database
- Web server
- Graphical user interface (GUI)
- Configuration manager
- Global event manager
- Report generator

Figure 9-2 illustrates the different components on CSA MC.

Figure 9-2   *CSA MC Architecture*

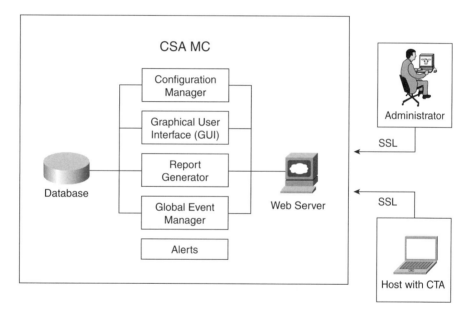

CSA MC installs Microsoft SQL Server Database Engine (MSDE) with Service Pack 4. You can alternatively install Microsoft SQL Server 2000 to host the agent-configuration database. This is recommended for any deployments with more than 500 agents. The Microsoft SQL Server 2000 should be patched to Service Pack 4. Later service packs for SQL Server are not qualified.

CSA MC Rule Definitions

CSA MC takes a structured, hierarchical approach to applying rules to the agents. Individual rules are created and applied to a rule module. One or more rule modules are then applied to a policy. Policies are then attached to a group, which contains one or more agents. Figure 9-3 illustrates the hierarchical nature of CSA MC.

Figure 9-3 *Relationship Between Rules and Agents*

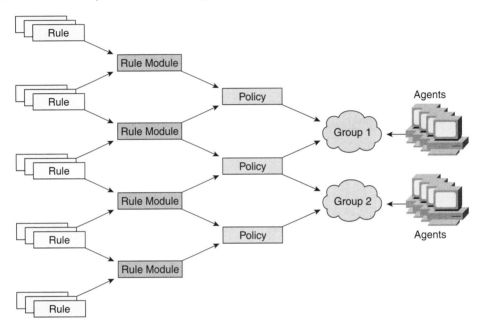

Any change to a rule is applied to any agent that is part of a group, to which a policy is attached, which contains the rule module with the modified rule in it. This sounds complicated but really is not. Figure 9-4 shows how the modification of a single rule can apply to all agents, even when the agents are members of different groups. The rule in the third group from the bottom is modified, and the dotted lines show how this rule is tied to a rule group, which is tied to two policies. One of these two policies is applied to both Group 1 and Group 2, which contains all the agents. Thus, modifying or adding any rule to that rule group affects all agents.

Figure 9-4 *A Single Rule Modification Can Affect All Agents*

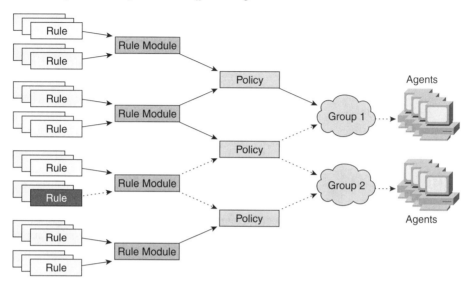

CSA MC comes with several predefined policies and rule sets to get you quickly up and running with minimal configuration. If changes to the rules are needed, a powerful exception wizard walks you through creating exceptions based on actual security events, which are then deployed to the agents.

Global Event Correlation

CSA MC also provides global event correlation of alerts from all agents and can dynamically push out new rules based on the alerts received. One example of this is a malicious executable attempting to be launched on several hosts within a short time period. Depending on the rule actions applied, an end user might be allowed to override the default action of deny. However, with global event correlation, CSA-MC can detect this potential threat and push out a new rule to quarantine this file on any host it is detected on. This prevents inexperienced users from overriding the default protection mechanism and possibly allowing them to become infected with a new, unknown virus or worm. The great thing about CSA is that it takes a "defense in-depth" approach to securing the host. A virus/worm has four stages:

- Installation
- Execution
- Exploitation
- Propagation

CSA prevents each of these threats independently from the others. This allows CSA to be installed on computers with viruses or worms already on them, and it prevents any further execution, exploitation, or propagation.

Another example of global event correlation is several hosts being scanned by the same source in a short period of time. The scan can be for one or more ports. CSA MC detects this and pushes out a rule to block all packets from the attacker's source IP on all agents. In this way, CSA MC acts as a distributed firewall, aggregating what would seem like a chance event (a single port scan on a host), along with all other similar occurrences of it to uncover the true threat.

Installing Cisco Security Agents Management Center

This section includes an overview of the installation of CSA MC. CSA MC Version 5.1 and later are supported only on Windows 2003 R2 Standard and Enterprise operating systems. Refer to the CSA MC release notes at www.cisco.com/go/csa for the minimum system requirements for your CSA MC version.

NOTE	Before you install CSA throughout your network, it is important that you create a detailed deployment plan. Chapter 16, "NAC Deployment and Management Best Practices," covers several best practices when deploying CSA.

CSA version 5.x and later can scale to up to 100,000 agents. Refer to the recommended multitiered CSA MC server system hardware, CPU, and memory requirements for deployment planning in the CSA Installation Guide at www.cisco.com/go/csa (select Install and Upgrade).

TIP	In large deployments (close to 100,000 agents), you want to ensure that no more than 20 agents are communicating with the CSA MC every second. To achieve this, you should not configure the polling interval to less than 1 hour. On average, the polling interval of 1 hour or higher is appropriate.

You must consider three installation configuration options before installing CSA MC:

- You can install CSA MC and the database on the same machine by selecting the **Local Database** radio button during the CSA MC installation. In this case, the CSA MC installation installs its own version of MSDE. You can alternatively install Microsoft SQL Server 2000 instead of MSDE on the same system. As previously mentioned, this is recommended if you are deploying more than 500 agents because MSDE has a 2GB database size limit.

- You can install CSA MC on one system and install the database on a remote system by selecting the **Remote Database** radio button during the CSA MC installation.

- You can install two CSA MCs on two separate systems and install the database on a remote machine. Both CSA MC systems use the same remote database. This is recommended for large deployments.

This section demonstrates how to install CSA MC and the database on the same system. Complete the following steps to install CSA MC:

Step 1   Log in to the system as Administrator.

Step 2   Click the CSA MC setup.exe file located at the CSA MC installation CD-ROM.

Step 3   The welcome screen appears. Click **Next**.

Step 4   Accept the license agreement by clicking **Yes**.

Step 5   Select the database location. In this example, the default selection of Local Database is selected, as shown in Figure 9-5. Click the **Next** button.

Figure 9-5   *Selecting Local Database*

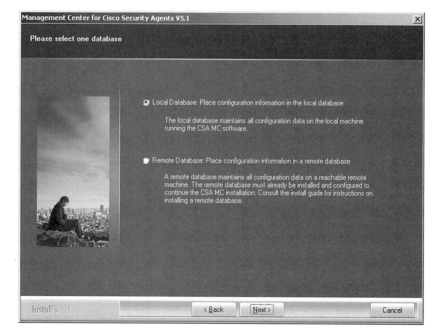

Step 6 The installation program checks the system to verify that MSDE is not installed. If it is not installed, you are prompted to install it, as shown in Figure 9-6.

Figure 9-6 *MSDE Prompt*

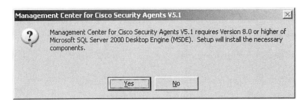

Step 7 Select the location you want to install MSDE. Click **Browse** to select a specific location or click **Next** to leave the default location. The default location is C:\Program Files\Microsoft SQL Server.

Step 8 After MSDE is installed, you are prompted to enter the location where you want to install CSA MC. Click **Browse** to select a specific location or click **Next** to leave the default location. The default location is C:\Program Files\Cisco Systems\CSAMC.

Step 9 Enter the administrator name and password information, as shown in Figure 9-7. This is the username and password you will use to log in to CSA MC.

Step 10 A dialog box appears asking if you want the system to automatically reboot when the installation is complete. You are required to reboot the system after the installation is complete. If you want the installation program to automatically reboot at the end of installation click **Yes**; otherwise, click **No**.

Step 11 All necessary files are copied to the system and CSA MC installs. If you selected Yes in the previous step, the system will reboot automatically after the installation is complete.

NOTE At the end of the installation process, an agent is installed to protect the system where you installed CSA MC.

Figure 9-7   *Entering the Administrator Credentials*

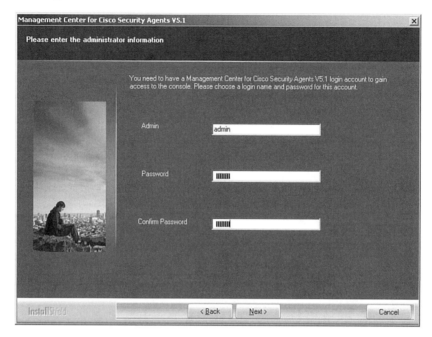

When installation is complete and the system has rebooted, you can access the CSA MC by launching a web browser and entering the CSA MC name or IP address in the address bar (for example, https://10.10.10.183).

Configuring CSA NAC-Related Features

CSA MC comes with numerous predefined agent kits, groups, policies, and configuration variables that are designed to offer high-level security measures for end-user systems and servers. You can use these default agent kits, groups, policies, rule modules, and configuration variables as a baseline and then monitor for possible tuning to your environment.

Cisco Trust Agent (CTA) can be bundled with CSA agent installations. This section guides you on how to configure an agent kit that will also install CTA for NAC deployments.

Creating Groups

CSA MC comes with a list of predefined groups that you can use to meet initial needs. A group is the only element required to build an agent kit. Using groups eases the management of a large number of agents. When using groups, you can consistently apply the same policy to a number of hosts.

Agent kits are the configuration and installation packages of the agent software to be deployed to end-user machines. Agent kits must be associated with configured groups. Agents installed on end-user hosts are automatically placed into their assigned group or groups when they register with CSA MC. The agents enforce the associated policies of each group. To modify or add a group, complete the following steps:

Step 1   Log on to the CSA MC console and choose **Systems > Groups**.

Step 2   Click the **New** button to create a new group. A dialog box appears and asks what operating system will be supported by this group (Windows, Linux, or Solaris), as illustrated in Figure 9-8. In this example, the Windows button is selected.

Figure 9-8   *Creating a Group in CSA MC*

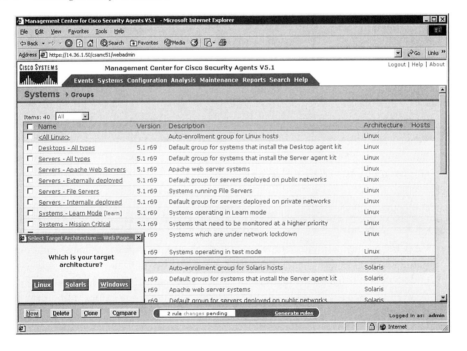

Step 3   Enter a unique name for this group of hosts.

NOTE   Group names are not case sensitive and must start with an alphabetic character. Group names can be up to 64 characters in length and can include alphanumeric characters, spaces, and underscores.

Step 4   (Optional) Enter a description for this group.

Step 5   You can also configure the polling interval for hosts within this group. The default is 10 minutes.

Creating Agent Kits

As previously mentioned, CSA MC comes with preconfigured agent kits that can be used to fulfill initial security needs. However, CSA MC enables you to create custom agent kits to fit your specific requirements. To create a new agent kit, complete the following steps:

Step 1   Choose **Systems** > **Agent Kits** from the CSA MC console.

Step 2   Click **New** at the bottom of the page displayed. A dialog box appears asking you which operating system this agent kit will be applied to, as shown in Figure 9-9.

Figure 9-9   *Creating an Agent Kit CSA MC*

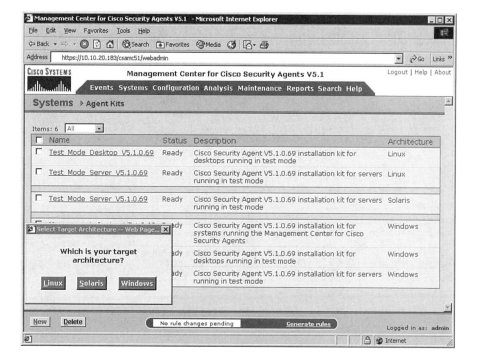

Step 3   Enter a name and description for the new agent kit, as illustrated in Figure 9-10. In this example, the agent kit is created for telecommuters and mobile workers. The name entered is Telecommuters.

Step 4   Select the groups that will be associated with this agent kit. In this example, **Desktops – Remote or Mobile** is selected.

Step 5   Optionally, you can select to reboot the system when the CSA installation is complete. You can also select a quiet install to avoid end-user interaction.

Step 6   Select **Install Cisco Trust Agent** to bundle CTA during the installation. You can select to install CTA Version 1, Version 2, or the version with the embedded 802.1.X supplicant, as illustrated in Figure 9-11. In this example, the ctasilent-supplicant-win-2.0.0.30.exe is selected. This installs CTA Version 2.0 with the embedded 802.1X supplicant.

Figure 9-10 *Agent Kit Attributes*

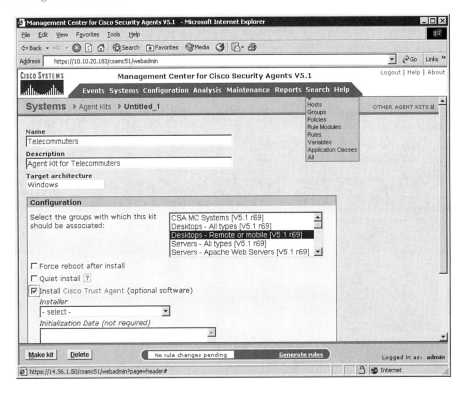

Figure 9-11 *Bundling CTA with CSA Installation*

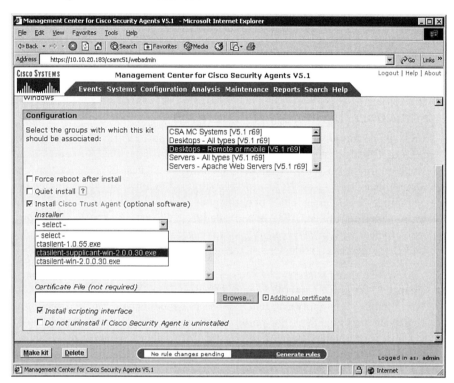

| NOTE | Refer to Chapter 2, "Cisco Trust Agent," for detailed information about CTA components and system requirements. |

Step 7 (Optional) You can enter instructions to create a custom ctad.ini file for CTA in the Initialization Data field.

Step 8 (Optional) You can install the Cisco Secure ACS server certificate along with CTA during CSA installation. To install the Cisco Secure ACS server certificate, click **Browse** next to the Certificate File field and locate the certificate file.

Step 9 In this example, the CTA scripting interface will be installed. This is an optional component of CTA. For more information about the scripting interface, refer to Chapter 2.

Step 10 Click **Make Kit** to create the new agent kit.

Step 11 Click **Generate Rules** to generate all pending rules. A new window appears with information about the rule generation. Click **Generate** after you have made the appropriate selections.

Step 12 All rules and configuration changes are applied at this point. A summary window is displayed when rule generation is successfully completed.

System State and NAC Posture Changes

CSA can perform dynamic policy updates on the end-user machine to change the NAC posture. Clients using CSA can be identified and trusted to have full network access. Nonconforming hosts can be quarantined until remediation is performed and they are brought into compliance. Rules can be configured to allow only quarantined devices to communicate with remediation or notification servers. In some cases, this is redundant with the Access Control List (ACL) downloaded from Cisco Secure ACS. On the other hand, in cases such as with NAC-L3-IP, it is useful because it prevents the quarantined host from infecting other adjacent devices on the network.

CSA system state parameters let you configure rules to be applied when certain conditions are met. These conditional rules can be based on the NAC posture of the end-host machine. For example, if you apply a system state to a rule module, you can dynamically activate and deactivate rules modules if the posture of the system has changed. For instance, if a machine is quarantined because of specific NAC policies, dynamic rules can be applied to allow the system to communicate with only specific remediation devices and/or services.

To configure system state parameters, follow these steps:

Step 1 Log on to CSA MC and select **Configuration > Rule Modules > System State Sets**.

Step 2 Click **New** to create a new system state. A new window appears, as shown in Figure 9-12.

Step 3 Enter a unique name for your system state. In this example, a system state rule is created for NAC quarantined hosts, and the name entered is Cisco Trust Agent Quarantine Posture.

Step 4 Enter a description.

Step 5 In the Network Admission Control section, you can select one or more Cisco Trust Agent posture state conditions.

NOTE   Hold down the Shift key while you click the mouse to choose multiple concurrent options. Hold down the Ctrl key to select nonconcurrent options.

Based on the NAC posture state that Cisco Secure ACS returns during posture validation, CSA can activate specific rules. For instance, if the system's antivirus software is not up-to-date or is disabled and the system posture is quarantined, CSA takes action based on that posture state and enforces a stricter policy to protect that system or alienate the quarantined system from the network.

Figure 9-12 *CSA System State Parameters*

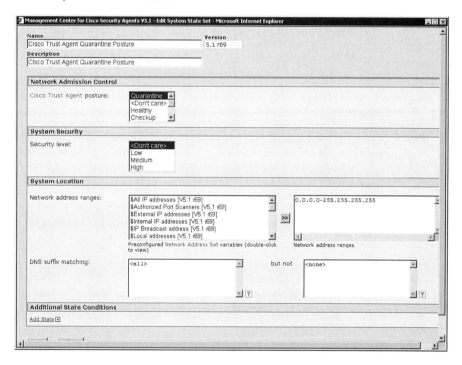

The following are the different available posture states:

— **<Don't care>**—This state is not provided by ACS. This state is currently the only valid posture state for UNIX-based machines.

— **Healthy**—The end-user machine is in Healthy state, and the risk to the network from this host is low.

— **Checkup**—Host credentials are not quite up-to-date, but the risk to the network is medium to low.

— **Quarantine**—The end-user machine does not comply with security policies configured in Cisco Secure ACS or any other policy server. The risk to the network from this host is high.

- **Transition**—The end-user machine is given temporary access to the network, pending a result from an audit server. For more information about audit servers, refer to Chapter 11, "Audit Servers."

- **Infected**—The end-user machine is infected with a virus or worm, or is severely vulnerable. The risk to the network from this host is very high. The host should be either removed from the network or remediated immediately.

- **Unknown**—The posture of the host cannot be determined.

- **Other**—This is shown if there is an incompatibility with posture state information received from ACS.

Step 6 In the System Security section, you can select one or more security-level conditions.

Step 7 In the System Location section, you can use the Network Address Ranges field to enter one or more addresses or address ranges to create a state condition based on system address. By default, no restrictions are configured.

Step 8 In the System Location section, you can use the DNS Suffix Matching Field to set a condition based on DNS server domain.

NOTE   Other system state parameters can be configured on CSA MC. This book concentrates only on the NAC-related system state parameters. For more information about all other system state parameters, refer to the Cisco Press Book titled *Cisco Security Agent,* by Chad Sullivan (ISBN 1587052059).

Step 9 Click the **Save** button to save the new system state configuration.

CSA gives you the flexibility to configure very customized and granular rules. It is important to carefully plan the rules to be applied when the system state changes because of different behavior, such as NAC posture. It is always a good idea to configure simple yet effective rules. An example of a simple, effective rule is, if a host is quarantined, CSA should allow this host to communicate with only a specific remediation server.

Summary

CSA is an optional component of the NAC solution that provides a robust framework to protect end-host machines. This chapter provided an overview of the CSA architecture and its components. It demonstrated how to install CSA MC on a Windows 2003 server. You also learned how to create new agent kits while bundling CTA during the agent installation. Finally, this chapter showed how CSA can be configured to react to NAC posture changes on a host as reported by CTA.

Review Questions

You can find the answers to the review questions in Appendix A, "Answers to Review Questions."

1. CSA Version 5.x and later can scale to up to

    a. 10,000

    b. 50,000

    c. 100,000

    d. 250,000

2. True or false: Agent kits are the configuration and installation packages of the agent software to be deployed to end-user machines. Agent kits must be associated with configured groups.

3. True or false: To connect to the CSA MC, you must first install an agent in your machine.

4. True or false: CSA version 3.x and above support NAC features and security posture–related policies.

5. True or false: Cisco Secure ACS can communicate with CSA MC through the GAME protocol for remediation purposes.

6. True or false: A group is the only element required to build an agent kit.

7. True or false: Groups can contain up to five policies.

8. The <Don't Care> posture state in CSA

    a. Is used when a client does not have CTA installed.

    b. Is not provided by ACS. This state is currently the only valid posture state for UNIX-based machines.

    c. Is used when antivirus software is not installed on the end-host machine.

    d. Does not exist.

9. You can install CSA MC and the database on the same machine by selecting the Local Database radio button during the CSA MC installation. In this case, the CSA MC installation installs the following:

    a. Its own version of MSDE

    b. Microsoft SQL Server 2000

    c. MSDE and Microsoft SQL Server 2000

    d. None of the above

10. True or False: if you are deploying more than 500 agents, the use of Microsoft SQL Server is recommended because MSDE has a 2GB database size limit.

This chapter covers the following topics:

- Supported antivirus software vendors
- Antivirus software posture plug-ins
- Antivirus policy servers and the Host Credential Authorization Protocol

## CHAPTER 10

Antivirus Software Integration

A core component of Cisco NAC is the capability to ensure that computers attempting to access your corporate network meet the requirements of your approved security policy for antivirus software. As a result, many antivirus software vendors are working with Cisco to integrate their software with Cisco NAC. This chapter covers how to integrate third-party antivirus software with the Cisco NAC Framework solution.

Supported Antivirus Software Vendors

The number of the antivirus program participants is growing every day. Some major participants include these:

- Computer Associates
- McAfee
- Symantec
- Trend Micro

Table 10-1 lists the antivirus software versions that are compatible with Cisco NAC.

Table 10-1   *Antivirus Software Versions Compatible with Cisco NAC*

Vendor	Version Compatible with Cisco NAC
Computer Associates eTrust AntiVirus	Versions 6, 7, and 7.1 or later
Computer Associates eTrust Patrol	Version 5 or later
McAfee VirusScan	Version 8.0i or later
Symantec Antivirus	Version 9.0 or later (Version 10 recommended)
Trend Micro OfficeScan Corporate Edition	Version 6.5 or later

Not all antivirus vendors have a policy server that is compatible with NAC. An example of a vendor that is compatible with the NAC solution is the Trend Micro Policy Server.

NOTE   Details on the Trend Micro Policy Server are discussed later in this chapter.

Antivirus Software Posture Plug-Ins

Posture plug-ins enable Cisco Trust Agent (CTA) to retrieve posture credentials from third-party applications (such as antivirus software) installed on a client machine.

NOTE   Chapter 2, "Cisco Trust Agent," covers the installation and configuration of CTA in detail.

In most cases, two files make up a posture plug-in. For Windows-based systems, a posture plug-in consists minimally of the following:

- A Dynamic Link Library (.dll) file
- An Information File (.inf) file

On Linux-based systems, posture plug-ins consist of the following:

- A Shared Object (.so) file
- An Information File (.inf) file

Posture credentials can be different for each NAC-compliant application. The antivirus application is responsible for installing its own posture plug-in in the correct location at the client machine. Plug-ins for Windows environments are installed in the \Program Files\Common Files\PostureAgent\Plugins\Install directory:

NOTE   This directory is different in CTA Version 1. When upgrading, CTA Version 2 moves the plug-ins to the \Program Files\Common Files\PostureAgent\Plugins\Install directory.

On Linux-based machines, plug-ins are installed in the /opt/PostureAgent/Plugins/install directory.

During posture validation, CTA checks the install/ folder for new or updated posture plug-ins. If the posture plug-in does not exist in the PostureAgent/Plug-Ins folder, CTA moves the plug-in files from the install/ folder to the PostureAgent/Plug-Ins folder. If the posture plug-in does exist in the PostureAgent/Plug-Ins folder, CTA checks to see if the plug-in under the install/ folder is newer than the one in the Plug-Ins folder and moves the newer plug-in to PostureAgent/Plug-Ins, overwriting the older one. If the plug-in in the install/ folder is older, CTA deletes it and continues to use the original plug-in.

TIP	Because all plug-ins are stored in a common directory, you do not need to install CTA before any antivirus software for CTA to make use of their plug-ins.

CTA gathers all posture plug-in data/attributes and sends it to the network-access device (NAD), which subsequently sends it to Cisco Secure ACS.

All NAC attributes are sent using a namespace based on the vendor and application type. Each vendor and application type is represented by numbers within the EAP exchange; they are commonly referred to in the following format:

Vendor-ID : Application-Type : Attribute

The Vendor-ID is a 32-bit field containing a globally unique vendor identifier. The Vendor-ID for Cisco is 9. The Application-Type is a 16-bit field indicating a globally unique posture application type. The Application-Type for antivirus software is 3. Table 10-2 lists and describes the antivirus software attributes.

Table 10-2   *Antivirus Software Attributes*

Attribute Name	Type	Description
Software-Name	String	Name of the antivirus software product.
Software-ID	Unsigned32	Numeral identifier of the antivirus software product.
Version	Version	Version of the antivirus software.
Scan-Engine-Version	Version	Version of the antivirus scan engine.
DAT-Version	Version	Version of the antivirus signature file.
DAT-Date	Time	Release time of the antivirus signature file.
Protection-Enabled	Unsigned32	0 = Disabled. 1 = Enabled.
Action	String	Format and content are vendor specific. Maximum length to be supported is 255 chars.

Antivirus Policy Servers and the Host Credential Authorization Protocol (HCAP)

Cisco Systems developed the Host Credential Authorization Protocol (HCAP) to provide the communication channel between Cisco Secure Access Control Server (ACS) and third-party posture-validation servers, such as antivirus software. HCAP uses Secure Socket Layer (SSL) as the communication medium to exchange EAP-based credentials between Cisco Secure ACS and the posture-validation servers. ACS forwards client credentials to one or more antivirus vendor servers and receives posture token response and optional notification messages, as illustrated in Figure 10-1.

Figure 10-1 *External Posture Validation with Antivirus Policy Server*

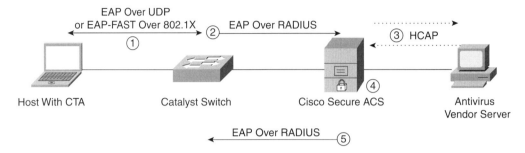

The following explains the numbered process illustrated in Figure 10-1 during posture validation to an external antivirus policy server:

1. The Cisco Trust Agent collects security state information from antivirus software on the client machine and communicates this to the NAD using EAPoUDP or 802.1X (EAP-FAST).

2. The NAD relays this information to the Cisco Secure ACS server for an admission decision.

3. Cisco Secure ACS forwards the antivirus software information to the external policy server over the HCAP protocol. The antivirus policy server sends posture token response and optional notification messages to Cisco Secure ACS. On Cisco Secure ACS, you can specify a text message that is sent to the third-party antivirus application. The vendor determines use of this text message. Some NAC-compliant applications do not implement the use of this notification string.

4. Cisco Secure ACS applies the respective policies based on the token received from the antivirus policy server.

5. After Cisco Secure ACS determines the appropriate access policy to be applied (permit, deny, quarantine, or restrict), it sends this information to the NAD for policy enforcement.

Adding External Antivirus Policy Servers in Cisco Secure ACS

Before you add any external antivirus policy server to Cisco Secure ACS, you must import a NAC attribute definition file (ADF) provided by the antivirus vendor. To import the ADF to ACS, complete the following steps:

Step 1 Copy the ADF file to a directory accessible by the Cisco Secure ACS utility CSUtil.exe.

Step 2   On the server running Cisco Secure ACS, open a command prompt and change directories to the directory containing CSUtil.exe.

Step 3   Import the ADF to ACS using the command **CSUtil.exe -addAVP** *filename*.**adf**. (*filename*.**adf** is the ADF provided by the antivirus vendor.) In Example 10-1, the Trend Micro ADF is imported to Cisco Secure ACS.

Example 10-1 *Importing the Trend Micro ADF*

```
C:\Program Files\CiscoSecure ACS v4.0\bin> CSUtil.exe -addAVP Trend-AV.adf
CSUtil v4.0(1.27), Copyright 1997-2005, Cisco Systems Inc
Attribute 6101:3:1 (Application-Posture-Token) automatically added to dictionary
 (DB).
Attribute 6101:3:2 (System-Posture-Token) automatically added to dictionary (DB)
[attr#2]: Attribute 6101:3:3 (Software-Name) added to the dictionary (DB).
[attr#3]: Attribute 6101:3:4 (Software-ID) added to the dictionary (DB).
[attr#4]: Attribute 6101:3:5 (Software-Version) added to the dictionary (DB).
[attr#5]: Attribute 6101:3:6 (Scan-Engine-Version) added to the dictionary (DB)
[attr#6]: Attribute 6101:3:7 (Dat-Version) added to the dictionary (DB).
[attr#7]: Attribute 6101:3:8 (Dat-Date) added to the dictionary (DB).
[attr#8]: Attribute 6101:3:9 (Protection-Enabled) added to the dictionary (DB).
[attr#9]: Attribute 6101:3:10 (Action) added to the dictionary (DB).
=== AVP Summary ===
8 AVPs have been added to the dictionary (DB).
=== IMPORTANT NOTICE ===
Please restart the following services:
(If more attributes are to be deleted, the services can be restarted once all delete
 operations are done)
- CSAdmin
- CSAuth
- CSLog
```

Step 4   Be sure to restart the CSAdmin, CSAuth, and CSLog services after successfully importing the ADF. To restart the Cisco Secure ACS services, go to **System Configuration > Service Control** and click **Restart**.

After you have successfully imported the ADF, complete the following steps to add the external antivirus policy server in Cisco Secure ACS:

Step 1   Access the Cisco Secure ACS administration window and click **Posture Validation**.

Step 2   Click **External Posture Validation Setup**, as illustrated in Figure 10-2.

Figure 10-2 *Configuring External Posture Validation*

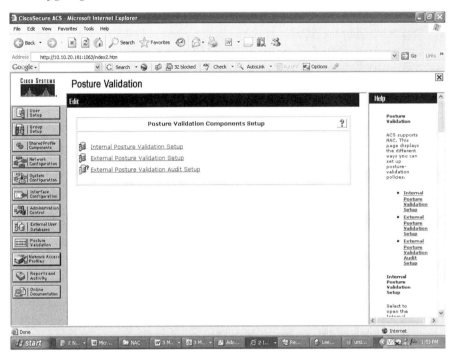

Step 3 Click **Add Server** to add a new antivirus policy server, as shown in Figure 10-3.

Figure 10-3 *Adding a New External Posture Validation Server*

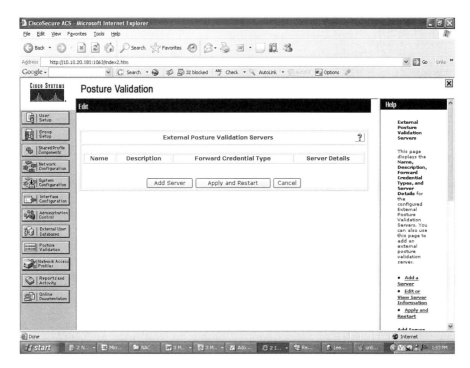

Step 4   Type a name in the Name field and a description in the Description field. The name and description are arbitrary attributes. Select the Primary Server Configuration check box. Specify the HTTP or HTTPS URL for the external antivirus policy server, as illustrated in Figure 10-4. In this example, the antivirus policy server is a Trend Micro server, and the port used is 4343.

Figure 10-4 *External Posture Validation Server Configuration*

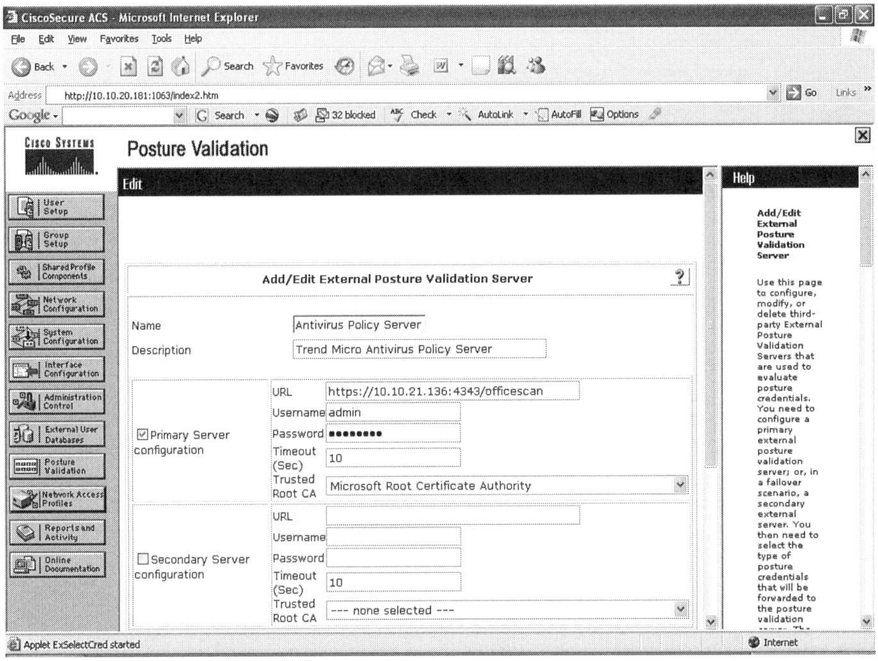

NOTE Refer to your antivirus server documentation for the correct URL. If you do not have a secondary policy server, be sure to unselect the Secondary Server Configuration box.

Step 5 Enter the user credentials that Cisco Secure ACS will use to access the external antivirus policy server.

Step 6 Set the Timeout (Sec) value to the number of seconds that Cisco Secure ACS waits for a result from the external server. This also includes the time that is taken for domain name resolution. The default is 10 seconds.

Step 7 Select the Trusted Root CA to be used.

Step 8 Select the credentials to be sent to the antivirus policy server, as shown in Figure 10-5. In this example, Trend:Av is selected.

Step 9 Click **Add** to add the antivirus policy server.

Figure 10-5 *Selecting Credential Type*

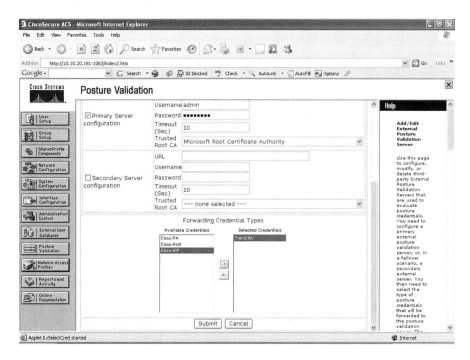

NOTE	Refer to your antivirus vendor documentation to configure the external policy server and its respective rules and policies.

On Cisco Secure ACS, you can specify a secondary external posture-validation server, in case the primary server fails. For each posture-validation request, Cisco Secure ACS attempts to use the first server configured in the policy that is enabled. If Cisco Secure ACS cannot reach the primary server or the primary server fails to respond to the request, Cisco Secure ACS uses the secondary server, if it is configured and enabled. Cisco Secure ACS checks the first server in the list in every posture validation. Subsequently, you will experience an estimated 10-second delay on each posture validation if the primary server is down.

Cisco recommends using the Cisco IOS Server Load Balancing (SLB) feature to load-balance requests to multiple posture-validation servers. The SLB feature is a Cisco IOS–based solution that provides server load balancing. This feature enables you to define a virtual server that represents a cluster of real servers. In this case, when Cisco Secure ACS initiates a connection to the virtual server, SLB load-balances the connection to a chosen external policy server, depending on the configured load-balance algorithm or predictor. In this case, you do not have to wait 10 seconds if one server is down.

Summary

One of the major features of the Cisco NAC solution is the capability to evaluate the status of antivirus software before a machine can access the organization's network. This chapter provided an overview of the different antivirus software that the Cisco NAC solution supports. It included detailed information about CTA posture plug-ins and the different attributes sent from the client machine to the policy servers. This chapter also provided an overview of the HCAP protocol and how to add antivirus vendor attribute definition files and external antivirus policy servers into Cisco Secure ACS.

Review Questions

You can find the answers to the review questions in Appendix A, "Answers to Review Questions."

1. True or false: The HPAC protocol is used as the communication mechanism when using external posture validation to a third-party antivirus server.

2. Why does Cisco recommend the use of SLB when using external antivirus policy servers?

   a. Because NAC is dependent on the SLB Cisco IOS feature to perform posture validation.

   b. Because SLB creates a secure channel between Cisco Secure ACS and the antivirus server.

   c. Because Cisco Secure ACS checks the first external policy server in the list in every posture validation. Subsequently, you will experience an estimated 10-second delay on each posture validation if the primary server is down. Cisco recommends using SLB as a load-balancing and failover mechanism to avoid this unnecessary delay.

   d. SLB is faster.

3. What port does the HCAP protocol use for its communication?

   a. TCP port 8080

   b. TCP port 80

   c. TCP port 4343

   d. TCP port 443

4. What utility can you use to import the antivirus ADF files on Cisco Secure ACS?

   a. ADFUtil.exe

   b. CSUtil.exe

   c. CSADF.exe

   d. ADFinstall.exe

5. True or false: Cisco Secure ACS can send a notification message to the third-party antivirus software installed at the end host.

6. True or false: Cisco Secure ACS can download the latest antivirus updates from each vendor's website automatically.

This chapter covers the following topics:

- Options for handling agentless hosts
- Architectural overview of NAC for agentless hosts
- Configuring audit servers
- Monitoring of agentless hosts

## CHAPTER 11

Audit Servers

Using the Network Admission Control (NAC) functionality, the Cisco network access devices (NADs) validate endpoint device posture by comparing them with the security policies on the access control server (ACS). However, this requires that you load the Cisco Trust Agent (CTA) on the end hosts. In a typical network topology, some hosts will use non-Windows, non-Linux, or non-MAC-based operating systems. Such devices might include network printers and Solaris-based workstations that cannot run CTA. These devices are referred to as agentless, clientless, or nonresponsive hosts.

Cisco NAC Framework can leverage an audit server to scan agentless hosts and determine the device type (printer, phone, PC, and so on), the operating system (Solaris, Windows XP, and so on), and any potential vulnerabilities not patched on the host. Based on the results of the scan, an application posture token is applied to the host and returned to Cisco Secure ACS.

Options for Handling Agentless Hosts

As discussed in the earlier chapters, three options exist for handling the agentless hosts:

- Exception lists in the NADs
- MAC authentication bypass
- Audit servers

Exception Lists in the NADs

In this option, when an agentless host tries to go through a network access device (NAD), it is checked against the local exception list on the NAD. If it is defined in the exception list, the posture-validation process is bypassed and the host is granted access based on the access policies. The exception list can exclude hosts for the posture-validation process, depending on their MAC address, IP address, operating system, or CDP device identity. However, not all NADs support configuration of all these attributes. Refer to Chapters 4–7 for a complete list of all the supported attributes related to a specific NAD.

NOTE	Exception lists are supported for the NAC deployments based on L2-IP and L3-IP.

Additionally, some NADs, such as the VPN 3000 Concentrator and Cisco security appliances, can be configured with a clientless username and password. These credentials are validated on a Cisco Secure Access Control Server (CS-ACS). If authentication is successful, the CS-ACS server can optionally send an access-control list (ACL) for the user session to limit its access.

In Cisco IOS–based NADs, such as Cisco IOS routers and Catalyst switches, you do not have to specify the clientless user account.

NOTE	If you use an audit server to determine the posture state of an agentless machine, you cannot use the exception lists on the NADs. You must define exception policies on the Cisco Secure ACS server.

MAC Authentication Bypass

If a NAD is not set up to use an exception list or a host does not exist in the exception list, the NAD can forward the request to the ACS server for posture validation if configured to do so. This request contains the MAC address of the end host. When the CS-ACS receives an authentication request, it checks the MAC Authorization bypass list to determine whether the received MAC address is present in the list. If a MAC address is found in its list, it associates the host with a particular user group on CS-ACS to apply appropriate attributes.

NOTE	The MAC authentication bypass feature is supported only on Cisco Catalyst switches that support 802.1X authentication. It is also called Agentless Host Configuration in the Cisco Secure ACS 4.1 version of code.

MAC authentication bypass is used in conjunction with 802.1X authentication. Centralized Agentless Host L2 (802.1X fallback) is supported on Cisco Secure ACS without configuring it on a per-port basis.

NOTE	You cannot use the MAC authentication bypass feature on the Layer 3 devices and on the Layer 2 switches implementing Layer 2 IP.

Audit Servers

The third option, to support the agentless hosts in the NAC Framework environment, is to use an external audit server. An audit server collects information from the agentless machines and determines their compliance based on the security policies of an organization. The audit servers usually use well-known assessment methods, such as remote login, fingerprinting, scanning, and active probes. In some other implementations, user web sessions are redirected to an audit server for assessment. During this process, an applet is downloaded on the client machine that initiates the audit.

NOTE   Audit server support is available only for NAC deployments based on L2-IP and L3-IP.

When an agentless machine tries to pass traffic through a NAD, the ACS server contacts an external audit server to initiate the vulnerability scan on the agentless machines. When an assessment is finished, the Cisco Secure ACS server retrieves the vulnerability report from the audit server and assigns a proper posture token to the host. Figure 11-1 illustrates how an ACS server communicates with an audit server. The Cisco NAD uses RADIUS to talk to the CS-ACS server; CS-ACS uses the Generic Authorization Message Exchange (GAME) protocol to communicate with the audit server. Using GAME, the Cisco Secure ACS retrieves authorization decisions and attributes from the audit server.

Figure 11-1 *Communication Between Audit Server and CS-ACS*

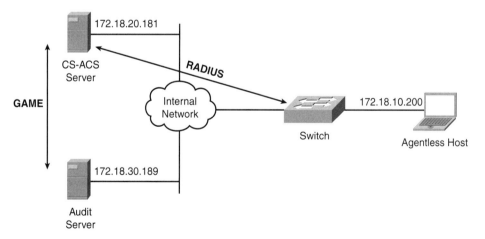

The use of an audit server is recommended for midsize to large enterprises, where there could be hundreds and thousands of hosts that are not running the Cisco Trust Agent (CTA) software.

NOTE   The audit server feature exits for NADs implementing Layer 2 IP (NAC-L2-IP). If you want to enable audit server support for L3-IP on Cisco routers, you need to run 12.4(6)T or higher version of code.

Architectural Overview of NAC for Agentless Hosts

The posture-validation process is crucial in determining the correct status of a network device. When CTA is not present on a device, the NAD can leverage an audit server when an end machine requests access to the network. Figure 11-2 provides a complete flow of the posture-validation process on a Cisco NAD. A Cisco switch is set up for NAC-L2-IP to validate an end host's posture before allowing access to the corporate network.

Figure 11-2 *Posture-Validation Process for a Host*

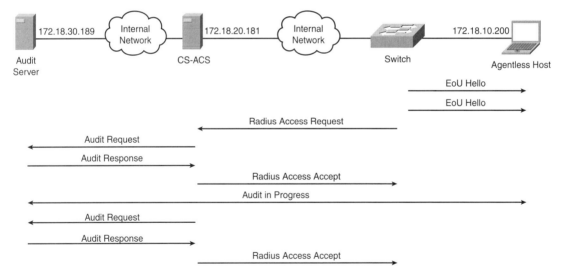

When an agentless host connects to a NAC-L2-IP-enabled network, the following steps take place:

1. A network host tries to access the network by sending traffic. The NAD identifies a new host when it intercepts traffic. It sends out an EAPoUDP hello packet to determine whether the host is actively running the CTA service.

2. If the NAD does not get an acknowledgment from the host, it declares the host as an agentless host. The ACS server checks to see whether an exception has been configured for the agentless host. If not, ACS initiates a request to the audit server to scan and then determine the overall posture of the host.

3. Based on the information sent by the NAD, the CS-ACS server sends the following attributes to the audit server:

    — Service-Type [6] = Call Check [10]

    — Calling-Station-Id [30] = IP address of agentless host

    — Framed-IP-Address [8] = IP address of agentless host

    — Cisco VSA "aaa:service" = "ip_admission"

    — Cisco VSA "audit-session-id" = Unique session identifier

NOTE	Use the **eou allow ip-station-id** command to use the agentless host's IP address as the calling station ID. Otherwise, it uses the MAC address of the host machine.

The Service-Type attribute is set as *Call Check* to indicate that the NAD received a request for authentication and that the RADIUS server should send either an access-accept to answer the NAC request or an access-reject to decline it. The Calling-Station-Id and the Framed-IP-Address attributes indicate the IP address of the agentless machines. Additionally, Cisco Secure ACS sends two vendor-specific attributes of aaa:service and audit-session-id. For NAC implementations, the aaa:service attribute is always *ip_admission,* and the audit-session-id is a unique session ID that the NAD and the RADIUS server use for a specific agentless host. The aaa:service and Service-Type attributes are automatically populated if you use one of the agentless host templates in ACS when creating the network access profile.

4. The Cisco Secure ACS server is typically set up to assign a Transition token during an audit server's posture assessment. The audit server posture assessment could take a while in determining the current posture of the agentless host. Therefore, after it contacts the audit server, the Cisco Secure ACS server sends an access-accept packet to the NAD with the following attributes:

    — Termination-Action [29] = 0 or 1

    — State [24] = State attribute value

— Session-Timeout [6] = Session timeout in seconds

— Cisco VSA "posture-token" = "Transition"

— Cisco VSA "ACS:CiscoSecure-Defined-ACL" = ACL name

— Optional attributes, such as url-redirect and url-redirect-acl

The Termination-Action attribute defines what action a NAD should perform when a session times out. If the Termination-Action value is 1, the NAD sends another access-request packet to authenticate the agentless host. If the Termination-Action value is set to the default value of 0, the RADIUS server specifies the current posture state of the agentless host after the session timeout. The Session-Timeout value specifies how long a NAD should wait before timing out the agentless host session. The vendor-specific posture-token attribute indicates a posture token that is applied to the agentless host while the audit server is determining the current posture. The "ACS:CiscoSecure-Defined-ACL" is the attribute that is forwarded to the NAD so that a temporary filtering ACL is applied to the agentless host session. Optionally, url-redirect and url-redirect-acl are vendor-specific attributes that can be applied to the agentless host session so that their web traffic can be redirected to a server, if necessary.

5. The Cisco Secure ACS server contacts the audit server using the GAME protocol and specifies the following parameters:

   — An indication that this is a request for a new scan for the agentless machine

   — The name of the policy that the audit server will use for this agentless machine

   — The IP address of the agentless machine

6. The audit server starts the scan by contacting the agentless host directly.

7. The NAD declares the end station as agentless after receiving the access-accept message from the RADIUS server. It assigns the received session-timeout value and the configured revalidation timer on the agentless host session. The host is seen as clientless if the EOU status is checked from the command-line interface (CLI) on the NADs.

8. When the session timeout expires, the NAD sends another request to the RADIUS server for agentless host authentication if the Termination-Action attribute in the access-accept message was 1. If the value of the Termination-Action attribute was 0, the session is deleted from the NAD table.

9. When the NAD sends a revalidation request, the RADIUS server contacts the audit server to determine whether the assessment result is available. If it is available, the RADIUS server pushes a new set of policies to the NAD for the agentless host. This

policy includes a new session-timeout attribute, the current posture token, and an updated ACL. If the RADIUS server does not have an assessment from the audit server, it sends out a short session-timeout attribute. This process continues until an assessment result is available from the audit server.

10. If the RADIUS server does not receive an assessment result from the audit server within the configured amount of time, the audit server is expected to send an error to the RADIUS server. The RADIUS server sends an access-reject to the NAD along with the Termination-Action to delete the agentless session.

NOTE   In the current implementation, the audit server cannot initiate communication with the Cisco Secure ACS server when an assessment result is available. The Cisco Secure ACS server needs to query the audit server periodically.

---

11. If during the entire assessment process the NAD receives an EAPoUDP Hello response packet from the host, it goes through the regular posture-validation process and ignores the audit server assessment.

NOTE   The GAME protocol can use both http and https connections between the RADIUS server and the audit server.

Configuring Audit Servers

The NAC Framework solution supports a number of audit servers:

- QualysGuard Scanner Appliance
- Altiris SecurityExpressions
- Symantec WholeSecurity

This chapter focuses on the configuration of QualysGuard Scanner Appliance because it is the most commonly used audit server in the NAC Framework environments. The integration of QualysGuard Scanner Appliance into CS-ACS server can be divided into three stages:

Step 1   Installation of QualysGuard Scanner Appliance

Step 2   Configuration of QualysGuard Scanner Appliance

Step 3   Configuration of CS-ACS Server

Installation of QualysGuard Scanner Appliance

The QualysGuard Scanner Appliance is a hardware-based appliance that provides an out-of-the-box integration for the NAC Framework. When you are ready to install the Scanner Appliance into your network, consider the following things first:

- IP address to be assigned to the LAN interface
- IP address to be assigned to the WAN interface

Even though you can assign a DHCP address on the LAN and WAN interfaces, it is highly recommended that you configure static IP addresses on the interfaces. The QualysGuard Scanner Appliance uses the WAN interface to establish a connection to QualysGuard platform over SSL. The Scanner Appliance uses this connection to get software updates, vulnerability signatures, and security scan results. Consequently, it is important for a WAN interface to have Internet connectivity to reach the QualysGuard platform. On the other hand, the LAN interface is used to scan hosts on the internal network. When the QualysGuard Scanner Appliance is integrated with NAC, the LAN interface scans the agentless hosts and provides results to the ACS server.

| NOTE | You must contact Qualys, Inc. directly to order a QualysGuard Scanner Appliance. |

The QualysGuard Scanner Appliance is 1 rack unit (RU) in height. When it is rack-mounted and using the split configuration, ensure that the LAN interface is connected to your inside network and that the WAN interface is connected to the network providing Internet access.

| NOTE | The QualysGuard Scanner Appliance supports two network traffic configurations:

 • **Standard traffic configuration**—Uses one interface for both network scans and management traffic

 • **Split**—Uses the WAN interface for management traffic and the LAN interface for network scans |

Connect the power cable to the Scanner Appliance to turn it on. The power LED is lit amber, indicating that the Scanner Appliance is powering up. It takes a few minutes for the appliance to boot up. During the boot-up process, the Scanner appliance displays the following message:

```
Welcome to QualysGuard
Qualys Scanner is starting up
Filesystem check in progress
Qualys Scanner is coming up
```

NOTE   If you deploy the QualysGuard Scanner Appliance in the Standard traffic-configuration mode, connect the LAN interface to the network because the WAN interface is not used.

By default, the QualysGuard Scanner Appliance is set up as a DHCP client. As the Scanner Appliance boots up, it sends a request for a DHCP address. If it receives an IP address, it should display the SA LOGIN prompt for you to log in. If it fails to receive an IP address, it displays a "NETWORK ERROR" message.

If the "NETWORK ERROR" message appears, press the **Enter** button (the circular button) to start the network-setup process. Press the **up** arrow to navigate through the menu. Select the **Enable Static IP on LAN** option and press the **Enter** button. When you see "CFG LAN STATIC NETWORK PARAMS?", press the **Enter** button again. The appliance prompts for LAN IP ADDR. Use the **up** and **down** arrow buttons to configure a single digit. Use the **left** and **right** arrow buttons to move to the next digit. Press the **Enter** button to accept the IP address. Similarly, configure the LAN NETMASK, LAN GATEWAY, LAN DNS1, LAN DNS2, LAN WINS1, and LAN WINS2 addresses, and the DOMAIN NAME. When these parameters are configured, the "REALLY SET LAN STATIC NETWORK" message appears. Press **Enter** if you want to accept the current parameters. If you do not have a WINS server, you can skip defining those addresses. However, you must define at least one DNS server.

Similarly, configure an IP address on the WAN interface of the Scanner Appliance if you deploy the appliance in the Split network configuration. When both the interfaces are set up and the Scanner Appliance has access to the QualysGuard platform, you are ready to move on to configure NAC-specific policies after logging into the appliance.

Configuration of QualysGuard Scanner Appliance

After setting up the Scanner Appliance, you can access it through the Qualys website, at http://qualysguard.qualys.com. The web page prompts you to specify a username and a password. When your authentication credentials are successful, the Qualys website shows all the options to manage your Scanner Appliance. Browse to **Preferences > Account** and click the **Edit** icon for your Scanner Appliance. A new browser window pops up showing the Scanner Appliance Information. Make sure that Enable NAC is checked under NAC/NAM Access Protocol. You can close the browser window after verifying the current settings. This is shown in Figure 11-3.

NOTE   You must make sure that the QualysGuard Scanner Appliance is set up for NAC. If it is not, you must contact Qualys, Inc., for a NAC subscription. You cannot create NAC-specific policies if your Scanner Appliance does not have NAC subscription from Qualys.

When you have verified that the Enable NAC option is turned on, the next step is to configure the NAC-specific policies on the Scanner Appliance. You must log into the Scanner Appliance by opening an HTTP or HTTPS session to its LAN interface's IP address. The scanner prompts for the user credentials again. After the user credentials are authenticated, you can create a new policy or use the existing default policy. If you want to create a new NAC policy, click the **New Policy** icon. Under Policy Title, enter the name of the NAC policy. As shown in Figure 11-4, the name of this NAC policy is NAC-Policy and is made the default NAC policy. Therefore, this policy will be analyzed when the ACS server contacts the Scanner Appliance for an audit and does not specify a policy name.

Figure 11-3 *Verification of Scanner Appliance Information*

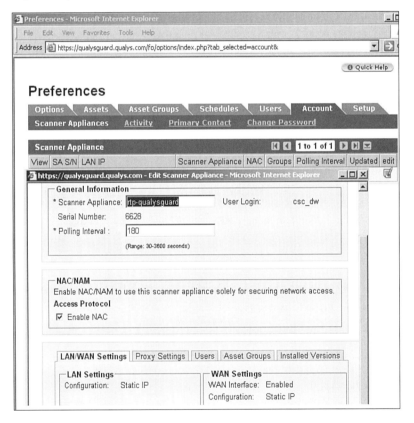

The QualysGuard Scanner Appliance supports two polling intervals. The preliminary polling interval instructs the CS-ACS server to check back with the Scanner Appliance after the configured interval when an initial request for an audit is submitted. The preliminary polling interval is set to 60 seconds to allow the scanner appliance to complete the scan. When the preliminary polling interval expires, the ACS server contacts the Scanner

Appliance to determine the current posture of the agentless machine. If the Scanner Appliance is not finished with the scanning process, it sends back a 30-second polling interval, which tells ACS to check back in 30 seconds to see if the posture assessment is ready. The following polling interval is set to 30 seconds so that the ACS server can have plenty of time to check back with the scanner appliance about the NAC posture-assessment result.

Figure 11-4 *NAC Policy Setup on QualysGuard*

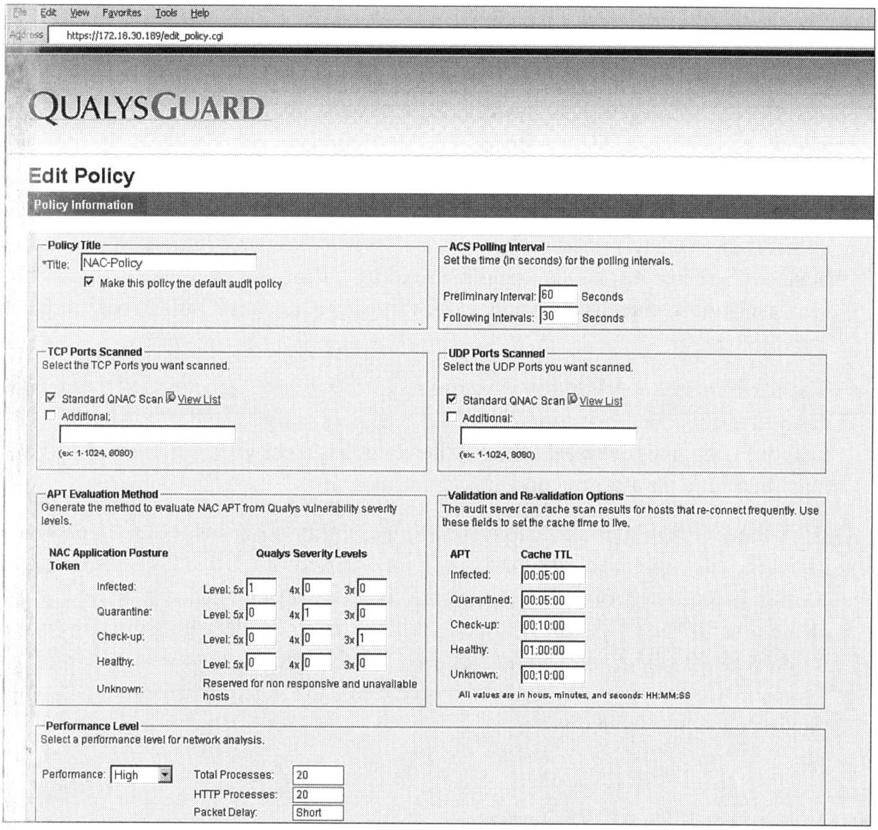

NOTE	The QualysGuard Scanner Appliance usually takes between 15 and 30 seconds to complete an audit. However, scanning time can vary, depending on your implementation and configured NAC policies.

In Figure 11-4, the TCP and UDP ports are selected with the default NAC scanlist. You can view the list of all the ports by clicking the View List option. If you want to add more ports, you can specify them in the Additional option.

The QualysGuard Scanner Appliance uses the application posture token (APT) evaluation method to determine the correct posture token for the agentless machine. It maps the severity levels of different threats with the posture tokens. In Figure 11-4, if there is at least one Severity 5–level vulnerability on the agentless host, the QualysGuard Scanner Appliance assigns an Infected posture token to the host. Similarly, if there is at least one Severity 4–level vulnerability on the host, the Scanner Appliance assigns a Quarantine posture token. A Checkup posture token is assigned if at least one Severity 3–level vulnerability is determined. If there are no Severity 3, 4, or 5 vulnerabilities on the agentless host, the Scanner Appliance assigns a Healthy posture token to the agentless host. The QualysGuard scanner assigns an Unknown posture token if it fails to communicate with the agentless host.

The performance-level option is useful to specify what type of agentless hosts will be analyzed. If the network connection between the Qualys scanner and the agentless hosts is fast, use High under Performance. If the connection between the scanner and the agentless machines is slow, use Low under Performance.

After the Scanner Appliance has done a vulnerability assessment of an agentless host, it can cache the assessment results for a configured period of time. It is recommended that all posture tokens except for the Healthy token have a shorter cache time. In Figure 11-4, the cache time to live (TTL) is 5 minutes for Infected and Quarantine posture tokens and 10 minutes for Checkup and Unknown hosts. For the Healthy posture token, the cache TTL is 1 hour so that the hosts do not have to go through the posture-validation process every time they reconnect to the network.

Configuration of CS-ACS Server

Follow these steps to configure the CS-ACS server:

Step 1   Load the ADF.

Step 2   Define the QualysGuard Scanner Appliance.

Step 3   Set up network access profiles for the audit server.

Step 4   Configure shared profiles.

Step 5   Set up authorization policy for network access profiles.

Step 6   (Optional) Install QualysGuard Root CA into CS-ACS.

The following sections cover these steps.

Step 1: Loading the ADF

Before you configure the audit server on CS-ACS, you need to import the attribute definition file (ADF) for the QualysGuard Scanner Appliance into CS-ACS. As discussed in Chapter 8, "Cisco Secure Access Control Server," the ADF defines the attributes that the CS-ACS requires to communicate with the configured server. Example 11-1 shows the template ADF for the QualysGuard Scanner Appliance.

Example 11-1 *Template ADF to Be Imported into CS-ACS*

```
[attr#0]
vendor-id=22282
vendor-name=Qualys
application-id=6
application-name=Audit
attribute-id=00003
attribute-name=Dummy-attr
attribute-profile=out
attribute-type=unsigned integer
```

NOTE   You must obtain the ADF from Qualys directly. Consult Chapter 8 for how to load the ADF file into Cisco Secure ACS.

Save the attributes in a text file and import it using the following methods:

Step 1   **CS-ACS software server**—Import the saved ADF using the CSUtil.exe utility, found under the *root* \ Program Files\CiscoSecure ACS v4.0\bin\ directory. Use the **CSUtil.exe –addAVP** *filename*.**adf** syntax when adding the ADF into CS-ACS.

Step 2   **CS-ACS appliance**—Save the ADF to an FTP server and load it in the appliance by browsing to **System Configuration > NAC Attribute Management** and specifying the FTP server IP address, user credentials, and the remote directory and ADF name.

NOTE   Ensure that you restart the CSAdmin, CSLog, and CSAuth services after loading the ADF.

Step 2: Defining the QualysGuard Scanner Appliance

To add an audit server, log into the CS-ACS server and navigate to **Posture Validation > External Posture Validation Audit Setup**. Click **Add Server** to add a new QualysGuard Scanner Appliance. You must specify a name for this server. In Figure 11-5, we have given Qualys as the name to this server configuration. A description of Qualys Audit Server is added.

Figure 11-5 *Defining QualysGuard Server on CS-ACS*

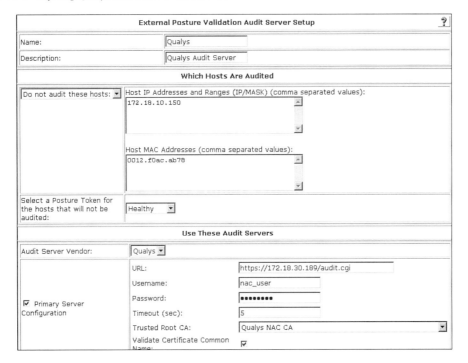

Under Which Hosts Are Audited, you can specify whether you want to exclude selected agentless hosts to be audited by this server. You can exclude hosts based on their IP addresses or their MAC addresses or both. As shown in Figure 11-5, a host with an IP address of 172.18.10.150 and a host with a MAC address of 0012.f0ac.ab78 are excluded from the audit process. The CS-ACS server grants these hosts a Healthy token. The audit server scans all the other agentless hosts.

Select Qualys as the Audit Server Vendor under Use These Audit Servers. Specify the location of the audit server where the CS-ACS server can submit the audit request for an agentless host under the Primary Server Configuration. In Figure 11-5, the URL to submit the request is https://172.18.30.189/audit.cgi. The username is nac_user and the password is cisco123 (shown as asterisks). These user credentials must match the account information on the QualysGuard Scanner Appliance. The server timeout specifies how long the CS-ACS server should wait to get a response from the audit server when a communication attempt is made. If the audit server does not respond within the configured timeout value (5 seconds, in this case), the CS-ACS tries to contact the secondary server, if defined.

The CS-ACS can contact the audit server using the HTTP or HTTPS protocols specified in the URL. The recommended option is to use the HTTPS protocol because the sessions from the CS-ACS to the Qualys scanner will be encrypted. If you are using the HTTPS protocol, you must select the Certificate Authority (CA) from the drop-down list of available servers. For additional security, you can enable the Validate Certificate Common Name option to ensure that the CS-ACS validates the common name (CN) in the received certificate before establishing a secured session.

After defining the QualysGuard Scanner Appliance, you must specify what posture token the CS-ACS should assign when the audit server is determining the current posture of the agentless hosts. This posture token is assigned to the agentless host by the time it is discovered and by the time an audit server has the assessment ready. In Figure 11-6, the CS-ACS server is set up to assign a posture token of Transition. This parameter is configured in the drop-down list under Audit Flow Settings.

NOTE   When you assign a Transition posture token to the agentless host, make sure that you allow the traffic to pass to the audit server in your downloadable ACL.

It is recommended that you set Polling Intervals and Session-Timeout to be Use Timeouts Sent by Audit Server for Polling Intervals and Session-Timeout. This way, the QualysGuard Scanner Appliance specifies a timeout value to CS-ACS when it starts the scanning process. When this timeout value expires, CS-ACS contacts the audit server to determine whether the scanning process is complete. If the audit server is still determining the posture state of the agentless machine, it sends back an updated timeout value to CS-ACS. In Figure 11-6, CS-ACS is set up to query the audit server three times. If the QualysGuard appliance is configured to scan the agentless hosts on ports other than the standard Qualys NAC (QNAC) ports, it can take a while to complete the scan; you need to increase the number of times CS-ACS contacts the Qualys appliance. The last thing you need to configure under Audit Flow Settings is the policy name that CS-ACS sends to the QualysGuard appliance. This policy name should match the NAC policy that you configure on the Qualys appliance, as discussed in the section "Configuration of QualysGuard Scanner Appliance."

Figure 11-6 *Defining Posture Token for Audit Process*

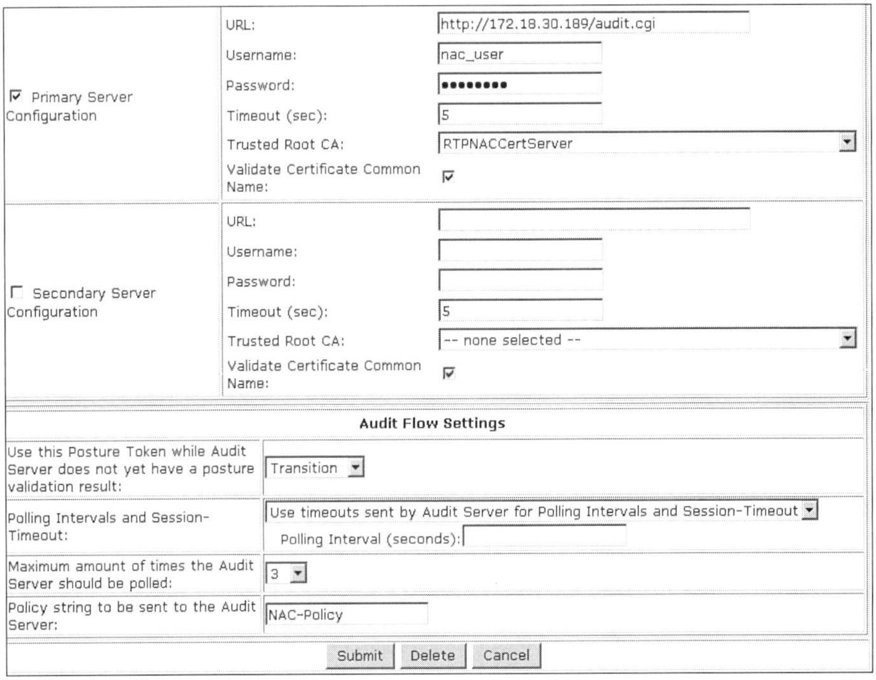

Step 3: Setting Up Network Access Profiles for Audit Server

The CS-ACS server needs to know which network access profile (NAP) needs to use the audit server for agentless hosts. For example, you do not want to use the QualysGuard scanner to assess the 802.1X-based agentless machines. Therefore, the audit server is typically assigned to the Layer 2 IP and Layer 3–based NAPs. To assign the configured audit server to a NAP, browse to Network Access Profiles and select Posture Validation of a NAC-L2-IP or NAC-L3-IP-based NAP. Under Determine Posture Validation for NAH, click the Select Audit option. You should see the audit server that you defined earlier, listed under Select Audit Server. Select the Qualys Audit Server, as shown in Figure 11-7.

If the QualysGuard Scanner is not reachable from the CS-ACS server, we can optionally set up the fail-open method. In Figure 11-7, the fail-open policy involves assigning a Checkup posture token if the scanner appliance does not respond within 30 seconds of the request. If you want the CS-ACS server to reject the posture-validation request from the agentless machine if the audit server is not available, do not enable the fail-open option. After defining the mapping to a NAP, click **Submit** and **Done** to complete this step.

NOTE   Make sure that you apply appropriate access-control lists and RADIUS authorization components to the Checkup token in the authorization section under Network Access Profiles.

Figure 11-7   *Mapping of Qualys Scanner to a NAP*

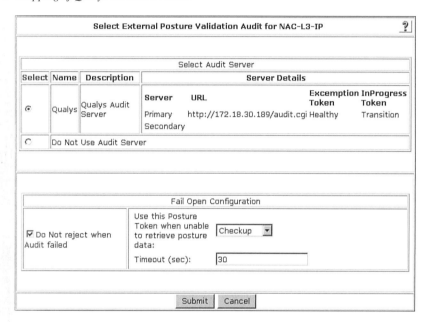

Step 4: Configuring Shared Profiles

When CS-ACS assigns a Transition posture token to an agentless host, it also pushes down two additional RADIUS attributes:

- Downloadable IP ACL
- RADIUS Authorization Components (RACs)

The purpose of these attributes is to restrict the capability of agentless hosts to communicate on the network unless they are fully scanned. While they are being scanned, the agentless hosts should have access to the QualysGuard appliance so that their current states can be determined. Table 11-1 lists the contents of the downloadable IP ACL and the RAC.

Table 11-1 *Shared Profiles for Agentless Hosts*

Shared Profile	Name of Shared Profile	Attribute Type	Content of Shared Profile
Download able IP ACL	Transition_ACL	—	**Permit ip any host** *Qualys-IP-Addr*
RAC	Transition_RAC (for Layer 2 and Layer 3 NAC)	cisco-av-pair (string)	**url-redirect=http://***Qualys-IP-Addr***/viewreport.cgi?nac_session_id=$host_session_id**
RAC	L2_IP_Transition_RAC (for Layer 2 NAC)	cisco-av-pair (string)	**url-redirect-acl=***name-of-ACL*

NOTE   The **url-redirect=http://***Qualys-IP-Addr***/viewreport.cgi?nac_session_id=$host_session_id** attribute redirects the web session to the URL that has the NAC assessment report unique for the host that was audited.

To learn more about shared profile components, consult Chapter 8.

TIP   The url-redirect-acl RAC needs to match the ACL name defined locally on the Layer 2 Cisco IOS switch. The ACL should have the following entries:

```
ip access-list extended transition_redir_acl
 deny ip any host 172.18.30.189
 permit tcp any any eq www
```

Here, 172.18.30.189 is the IP address of the Qualys scanner.

Step 5: Setting Up Authorization Policy for Network Access Profiles

The last mandatory step in setting up the audit server configuration on CS-ACS is to map the shared profiles (downloadable ACL and RACs) to a NAP. When a NAP is in use and the CS-ACS server assigns a Transition posture token to an agentless host, you want to apply the appropriate policies to it. You can configure this mapping by browsing to **Network Access Profiles** and selecting **Authorization of a NAC-L2-IP or NAC-L3-IP-Based NAP**. Click **Add Rule** and add a condition for the Transition posture token, as shown in Figure 11-8.

Figure 11-8 *Authorization Rules for Transition Token*

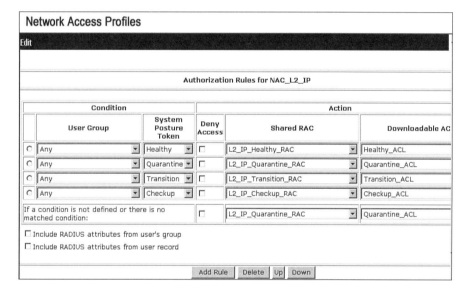

Under the new rule, select the user group as **Any** and select **Transition** from the **System Posture Token** drop-down list. The shared profiles defined in Step 3 are applied under Action. L2_IP_Transition_RAC is selected from the drop-down menu of Shared RAC, and Transition_ACL is selected from the Downloadable ACL drop-down list. After defining the mappings, click **Submit** and restart the CS-ACS services.

Step 6: Installing QualysGuard Root CA into CS-ACS (Optional)

If you are using an SSL connection for the GAME protocol between the audit server and CS-ACS, you must install the QualysGuard root certificate into Cisco Secure ACS. Consequently, this root certificate, once installed, must be added to the trusted root certificate store on Cisco Secure ACS. To install the root certificate from the QualysGuard scanner into Cisco Secure ACS, follow these instructions:

Step 1   Log in to your CS-ACS server and open a browser such as Microsoft Internet Explorer.

Step 2   Point your URL to the scanner's LAN interfaces. For example, if the IP address of your QualysGuard's LAN interface is 172.18.30.189, use https://172.18.30.189/ca.crt as your URL.

Step 3   The QualysGuard scanner presents you the root certificate as a file to download. Click **Open** to open the certificate file. Click **Install Certificate** to install this certificate on CS-ACS.

NOTE   If you are using an ACS appliance, you can save the root certificate from QualysGuard as a file on an FTP server; then you can load it into the CS-ACS appliance by browsing to **System Configuration > ACS Certificate Setup > Install ACS Certificate > Download Certificate**. You can specify your FTP user credentials and the certificate file that is stored on the FTP server.

Step 4   Internet Explorer brings up the Certificate Import Wizard. Click **Next** to proceed further.

Step 5   Under **Certificate Store**, select **Place All Certificates in the Following Store** and click **Browse**.

Step 6   Enable the **Show Physical Stores** option and browse to **Trusted Root Certification Authorities > Local Computer**. Click **OK,** then **Next,** and finally **Finish** to import the certificate into CS-ACS. You should receive the message "The import was successful," indicating that the certificate has been added successfully.

After loading the QualysGuard scanner root certificate into CS-ACS, the next process is to add this certificate into the ACS Certificate Trust List. Navigate to **System Configuration > ACS Certificate Setup > Edit Certificate Trust List** and select **Qualys NAC CA** from the list. Click **Submit** and restart the ACS services. This certificate can be used in Step 2 of the "Configuration of CS-ACS Server" section.

Monitoring of Agentless Hosts

To monitor the status of the agentless machines, you can either check the audit report on the Qualys scanner or look at the logs on the CS-ACS server.

Monitoring Agentless Hosts on QualysGuard Scanner

When the Qualys server scans an agentless machine, it generates the audit report. This audit report can be viewed from any machine on the network, as long as it specifies either the NAC session ID or the IP address of the agentless machine in the URL string. To view an audit report by the IP address of a host, the URL is

https://*X.X.X.X*/viewreport.cgi?ip=*Y.Y.Y.Y*

Here, *X.X.X.X* is the IP address of the Qualys scanner and *Y.Y.Y.Y* is the IP address of the agentless host.

To view an audit report based on the NAC session ID, the URL is

https://*X.X.X.X*/viewreport.cgi?nac_session_id=*session_id*

Here, *X.X.X.X* is the IP address of the Qualys scanner and *session_id* is the ID of the NAC session for that particular scan.

Figure 11-9 shows an audit report for 172.18.10.200. The IP address of the QualysGuard scanner is 172.18.30.189. The Qualys scanner assigned a posture token of Checkup to this host because it discovered three Severity 3 vulnerabilities on the host. Based on OS fingerprinting, the scanner determined that it was a Windows XP machine running Service Pack 2, and it took about 28 seconds to complete the scan.

Figure 11-9 *Audit Report for 172.18.10.200*

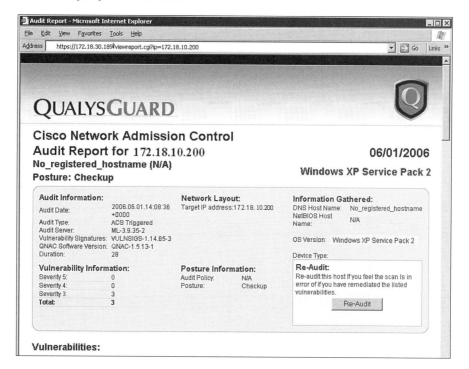

The audit report also provides detailed information about each vulnerability and the recommendation for how to mitigate it. As discussed in the configuration section, you can send the URL-redirect attribute along with the audit server report link. In this case, the user browser session will be redirected to this audit report, and the user can follow the recommendation to fix the vulnerability on the agentless machine.

If the user feels that he or she has fixed all the vulnerabilities or this result is not accurate, the user can restart a new scan from the QualysGuard scanner by clicking the Re-Audit button, shown in Figure 11-9.

Monitoring CS-ACS Logs

To determine whether your Cisco Secure ACS is assigning the correct RAC and the downloadable ACL when the audit initiates, you can navigate to **Reports and Activities > Passed Authentications > Passed Authentication active.csv** and check the Shared RAC, Downloadable ACL, and System-Posture-Token columns. As shown in Figure 11-10, the CS-ACS server assigns a Transition token when the audit server initiates a scan. It applies L2_IP_Transition_RAC as the shared RAC and Transition_ACL as the downloadable A CL. After the audit server assigns the Checkup system-posture token, CS-ACS server applies L2_IP_Quarantine_RAC as the shared RAC and Quarantine_ACL as the downloadable ACL.

Figure 11-10   *Passed Authentication Report on CS-ACS Server*

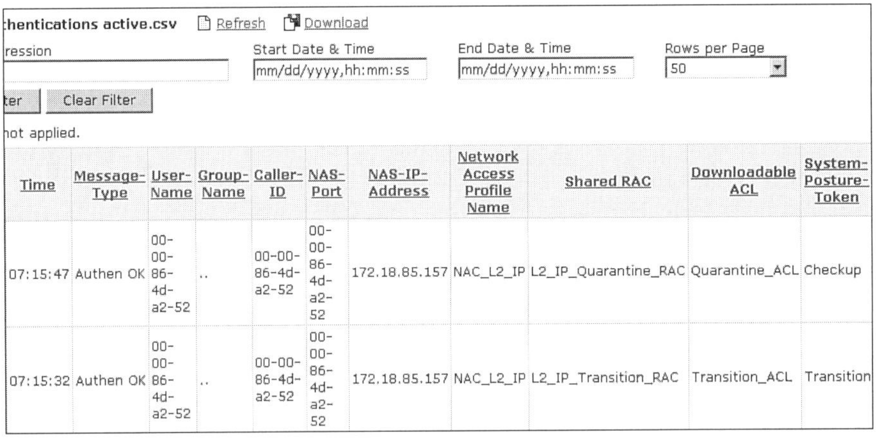

Time	Message-Type	User-Name	Group-Name	Caller-ID	NAS-Port	NAS-IP-Address	Network Access Profile Name	Shared RAC	Downloadable ACL	System-Posture-Token
07:15:47	Authen OK	00-00-86-4d-a2-52	..	00-00-86-4d-a2-52	00-00-86-4d-a2-52	172.18.85.157	NAC_L2_IP	L2_IP_Quarantine_RAC	Quarantine_ACL	Checkup
07:15:32	Authen OK	00-00-86-4d-a2-52	..	00-00-86-4d-a2-52	00-00-86-4d-a2-52	172.18.85.157	NAC_L2_IP	L2_IP_Transition_RAC	Transition_ACL	Transition

Monitoring Agentless Hosts on a Cisco NAD

The NAC Framework solution enables you to check the state of an agentless machine on the NADs. When a new host is detected on the network, the NAD sends out the EAPoUDP hello packet, as shown in Example 11-2. This output was taken from a Cisco 6500 switch running CatOS. The agentless host IP address is 172.18.10.200, and the current state is hello. The host is connected to port 1/48 on the switch.

Example 11-2   *Output of the **show eou all** Command for EAPoUDP Hello Packet*

```
Console> (enable) show eou all
Eou Summary
-----------
Eou Global State = enabled

Currently Validating EOU Sessions = 0
mNo/pNo   Host Ip           Nac_Token   Host_Fsm_State   Username
-------   ---------------   ---------   --------------   --------
 1/48     172.18.10.200         -          hello            -
```

After determining that the host machine is agentless, the NAD contacts the CS-ACS server, which, in turn, contacts the audit server. When the audit initiates a scan on the host, the CS-ACS server assigns a Transition token to the agentless machine, as shown in Example 11-3.

Example 11-3   *Output of the **show eou all** Command for Transition Token*

```
Console> (enable) show eou all
Eou Summary
-----------
Eou Global State = enabled

Currently Validating EOU Sessions = 0
mNo/pNo   Host Ip           Nac_Token    Host_Fsm_State   Username
-------   ---------------   ---------    --------------   --------
 1/48     172.18.10.200     Transition   clientless           -
```

When the audit server completes its scanning process, it assigns the Checkup token. The CS-ACS server assigns that token to the host along with the appropriate ACLs and other attributes. As shown in Example 11-4, the NAC token is Checkup for the agentless host with an IP address of 172.18.10.200.

Example 11-4 *Output of the show eou all Command for Checkup Token*

```
Console> (enable) show eou all
Eou Summary
- - - - - - - - - - -
Eou Global State = enabled

Currently Validating EOU Sessions = 0
mNo/pNo   Host Ip            Nac_Token   Host_Fsm_State   Username
- - - - - - -   - - - - - - - - - - - - - - - -   - - - - - - - - -   - - - - - - - - - - - - - -   - - - - - - - -
  1/48      172.18.10.200      Checkup     clientless        -
```

Summary

The NAC Framework solution integrates Cisco partners in providing an end-to-end solution for determining the current posture state of a network device. The QualysGuard appliance not only can determine the posture state of a host, but it also can provide recommendations on how to fix the open vulnerabilities on the host. By providing the posture state of a machine, the QualysGuard appliance can update the CS-ACS server about an agentless machine. Using this information, the CS-ACS server can apply appropriate policies that are specific to those agentless machines.

Review Questions

You can find the answers to the review questions in Appendix A, "Answers to Review Questions."

1. The CS-ACS server supports which of the following audit servers? (Multiple answers)

   a. QualysGuard Scanner Appliance

   b. Microsoft IAS server

   c. Altiris SecurityExpressions

   d. Symantec WholeSecurity

2. Audit server support is available on which of the following Cisco NADs? (Multiple answers)

   a. Cisco IOS routers

   b. Cisco switches in 802.1X mode

   c. Cisco switches in NAC-L2-IP mode

   d. Cisco VPN 3000 concentrators

3. True or false: The audit servers use only SSL communication for the GAME protocol.

4. True or false: The Cisco Secure ACS server pulls the audit report from the QualysGuard server.

5. True or false: You must use both interfaces on the QualysGuard scanner when assessing the internal network.

6. What is the commend to load a QualysGuard ADF file into CS-ACS?

   a. **CSUtil.exe** *filename***.adf –addAVP**

   b. **CSUtil.exe –addAVP** *filename***.adf**

   c. **addAVP CSUtil** *filename***.adf**

   d. **addAVP –CSUtil** *filename***.adf**

7. True or false: The CS-ACS server cannot apply the shared RAC and downloadable ACL on the agentless machine because they are assigned by the audit server.

8. True or false: You can assign a Checkup posture token only if the QualysGuard scanner is not reachable from the Cisco Secure ACS server.

9. True or false: The CS-ACS usually assigns a Transition posture token to the agentless hosts while an audit is in progress.

10. True or false: You cannot use the MAC authentication bypass feature on the Layer 3 devices and on the Layer 2 devices implementing Layer 2 IP.

This chapter covers the following topics:

- Altiris remediation solution
- PatchLink remediation solution

## CHAPTER 12

Remediation

Cisco has partnered with several vendors to integrate different software-distribution solutions to enable you to reduce the time and expense of manually patching and fixing noncompliant systems trying to connect to the corporate network. Their integration with Cisco NAC enables you to leverage your existing investment by extending functionality to include network access-control policies. The number of NAC partners is growing every day. The following are some of the vendors that have remediation solutions:

- Altiris
- PatchLink
- Citadel
- LANDesk
- BigFix

This chapter includes an overview of the integration of the Altiris and PatchLink remediation solutions with Cisco NAC.

Altiris

Altiris has a very robust software-distribution and remediation solution called the Altiris Quarantine Solution. The Altiris Notification Server plays a crucial role in this solution, as illustrated on Figure 12-1.

Figure 12-1 *Altiris Quarantine Solution*

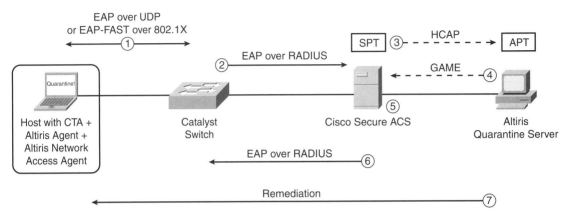

The following remediation steps are illustrated in Figure 12-1:

1. A host attempts to access the network, and posture validation is started via EAPoUDP or EAP over 802.1X.

2. The network access device (a switch, in this example) forwards the host credentials to Cisco Secure ACS for validation.

3. When the Cisco Trust Agent (CTA), the Altiris Agent, the Altiris Network Access Agent, and the Posture Plug-in are installed on the end-user machine, Cisco Secure ACS uses the Host Credential Authorization Protocol (HCAP) to send information to the Altiris Quarantine Server about the software, and the relevant information, installed on the client machine.

4. When the Altiris Network Access Agent or the Posture Plug-in are not installed on the end host, Cisco Secure ACS uses the GAME protocol to communicate with the Altiris Quarantine Server. Cisco Secure ACS still receives posture information from CTA; however, you cannot have full network enforcement unless you install the Altiris Agent, the Altiris Network Access Agent, and the Posture Plug-in.

5. In this example, the end-user machine is not compliant with Cisco Secure ACS policies. Cisco Secure ACS also evaluates the response from the Altiris Notification and enforces the quarantine policy.

NOTE   The Altiris Notification Server and the add-on Quarantine Solution grant the Application Posture Token (APT). Subsequently, Cisco Secure ACS compiles all application posture tokens within the System Posture Token (SPT).

---

6. The response is sent back to the network access device (switch).

7. The end host is remediated automatically. The Altiris Quarantine Server sends instructions to the Altiris Agent installed on the end-user machine to automatically start the remediation process. The agent downloads and installs the necessary patches or software to the machine from the remediation server.

Four different pieces of software must be installed on the end host before you can begin granting or denying access to the network and perform remediation on the machine with the Altiris Quarantine Solution:

- Altiris Agent
- Cisco Trust Agent
- Altiris Network Access Agent
- Altiris Posture Plug-in

Figure 12-2 shows how each agent communicates with each other.

Figure 12-2 *Altiris Agents*

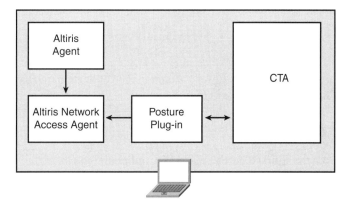

The Notification Server installs the Altiris Agent to systems connected to the network by using policies that point to a collection of end-user machines. The Altiris Network Access Agent communicates with the Altiris Agent and the Posture Plug-in. The Posture Plug-in is the interface between the Altiris Network Access Agent and CTA. When posture validation occurs, users receive a pop-up balloon notification that their machine posture has changed through the Altiris Network Access Agent and CTA.

NOTE Cisco and Altiris recommend that you install all the agents in the following order:

1. Altiris Agent

2. Cisco Trust Agent

3. Altiris Network Access Agent

4. Posture Plug-in

Altiris Network Discovery

The Altiris Network Discovery is a free plug-in component to the Notification Server that is used to discover all end-user machines connected to the network.

NOTE   For the Altiris Notification Server installation guidelines and minimum system requirements, refer to Altiris documentation at www.altiris.com.

The Altiris Quarantine Solution does not require the use of Network Discovery to function; however, it is recommended that you use Network Discovery to have an accurate database of end-user machines that you will use to apply NAC policies and for remediation capabilities.

NOTE   The Network Discovery information is stored in the notification database and can be used by other Altiris network software components.

Complete the following steps to run Network Discovery:

Step 1   From the Altiris Console, click the **Configuration** tab.

Step 2   Select **Solutions Settings > Network Discovery > Scan Groups**. You can create different scan policies to discover end-user machines by entering either an IP address range or the IP address of a seed device. A Seed Device is a machine that has a list or inventory of all your end-user systems (this can be another Altiris server).

Step 3   Right-click on the **Default Scan Group** policy and select **Clone**. Then enter a name for the new policy.

Step 4   Click the **Schedule** tab.

Step 5   Select a time to run the policy from the pull-down list.

Step 6   Click **Apply**.

Step 7   Click **Discovered Devices** in the left pane. A table with the list of discovered devices appears on the screen.

Importing Attribute Files to Cisco Secure ACS

For Cisco Secure ACS to communicate with the external Notification Server, you must import the Altiris attributes file. Complete the following steps to import the attributes file on Cisco Secure ACS:

Step 1 On the Notification Server, locate the Altiris_ACS_Attrs.txt file under Program Files\Altiris\Notification Server\NSCap\Quarantine.

Step 2 Copy the Altiris_ACS_Attrs.txt file to the Cisco Secure ACS Server.

Step 3 From a command prompt, run the CSUtil.exe utility using the following attributes:

```
CSUtil.exe -addAVP Altiris_ACS_Attrs.txt
```

The CSUtil.exe file is located on a folder called bin under the directory where you installed Cisco Secure ACS.

C:\Program Files\CiscoSecure ACS v4.0\bin>**CSUtil.exe -addAVP Altiris_ACS_Attrs.txt**

CSUtil v4.0(1.27), Copyright 1997-2005, Cisco Systems Inc

[attr#0]: Error: attribute [12999:1:1] is reserved for (Application-Posture-Token) and is generated automatically.

This attribute cannot be added manually or redefined. Skipping.

[attr#1]: Error: attribute [12999:1:2] is reserved for (System-Posture-Token) and is generated automatically.

This attribute cannot be added manually or redefined. Skipping.

Attribute 12999:1:1 (Application-Posture-Token) automatically added to dictionary (DB).

Attribute 12999:1:2 (System-Posture-Token) automatically added to dictionary (DB).

[attr#2]: Attribute 12999:1:7 (PA-User-Notification) added to the dictionary (DB).

[attr#3]: Attribute 12999:1:32768 (AppName) added to the dictionary (DB).

[attr#4]: Attribute 12999:1:32769 (Version) added to the dictionary (DB).

[attr#5]: Attribute 12999:1:32770 (ClientGUID) added to the dictionary (DB).

[attr#6]: Attribute 12999:1:32771 (HostName) added to the dictionary (DB).

[attr#7]: Attribute 12999:1:32772 (IPAddress) added to the dictionary (DB).

[attr#8]: Attribute 12999:1:32773 (MACAddress) added to the dictionary (DB).

=== AVP Summary ===

7 AVPs have been added to the dictionary (DB).

=== IMPORTANT NOTICE ===

Please restart the following services:

(If more attributes are to be deleted, the services can be restarted once all delete operations are done)

- CSAdmin

- CSAuth

- CSLog

Step 4 After the Altiris attribute file is imported to Cisco Secure ACS, the option to select the Altiris Notification Server as an external audit server becomes available.

Setting External Posture Validation Audit Server on Cisco Secure ACS

Now that you have added the ADF file to Cisco Secure ACS, you need to add the Altiris Notification Server to Cisco Secure ACS. To add the Altiris server information to Cisco Secure ACS, complete the following steps:

Step 1   Log in to the Cisco Secure ACS web console.

Step 2   Select **Posture Validation**.

Step 3   Click the **External Posture Validation Audit Setup** page.

Step 4   Click **Add Server**.

Step 5   Type a name for the new server entry in the **Name** box and a description in the **Description** box.

Step 6   In the Which Hosts Are Audited section, select **Audit All Hosts** to audit all hosts that do not contain a posture agent.

Step 7   Select **Healthy** on the pull-down menu under **Select a Token for the Hosts That Will Not Be Audited**.

Step 8   Select **Altiris** under the **Audit Server Vendor** drop-down list.

Step 9   Select the **Primary Server Configuration** check box and enter the applicable information in the boxes to the right of the check box (such as the server URL, username, password, timeout, and trusted root certificate).

Step 10 Configure the Audit Flow settings. Under **Use This Token While the Audit Server Does Not Yet Have a Posture Validation Result**, select the **Transition** token from the drop-down list.

Step 11 Click **Submit**.

Installing the Altiris Network Access Agent and Posture Plug-In

The Altiris Network Access Agent and Posture Plug-in must be installed to establish communications among the Notification Server, the Cisco Secure ACS Server, and end-user machines with the Altiris Agent. Complete the following steps to install the Network Access Agent and Posture Plug-in to the end-user machines:

Step 1   Access the Altiris Console and click the **Configuration** tab.

Step 2   Select **Solutions Settings > Network Access > Agent Configuration**.

Step 3   Select **Network Access Agent/NAC Posture Plug-in Package**.

Step 4 Click the **Package**, **Programs**, **Package Servers**, and **Advanced** tabs to change values as necessary, and click **Apply**. Refer to Altiris Notification Server documentation for more information.

Step 5 Click the **Network Access Agent/NAC Posture Plug-in Installation** policy in the left pane of the Altiris Console, and select the **Enable** check box to install the package.

Step 6 Select the **Scheduling Options** for rolling out the agents and click **Apply**.

Exception Policies

Exception policies specify what devices should be exempt of posture validation. When you configure exception policies in the Altiris Notification Server, the status of the device running the policy is set to Healthy, granting it access to the network. You can alternatively create exception lists on the network access devices or Cisco Secure ACS. Complete the following steps to configure   exception policies in the Altiris Notification Server:

Step 1 Access the Altiris Notification Server Console and click the **Configuration** tab.

Step 2 Select Solutions **Settings** > **Network Access** > **Policies**.

Step 3 Right-click the **Exception** folder.

Step 4 Select **New** > **Exception Policy**.

Step 5 Right-click **New Exception Policy** and select **Rename** to change the policy name to a name that is more intuitive for you.

Step 6 Select the **Enable** check box to run the policy.

Step 7 Enter a description for the exception policy.

Step 8 Click the **Collection** link and use the Collection Selector to select the collections to which you want to apply the exemption policy; then click **Apply**.

Step 9 Click the **Impact Analysis** tab. This shows a list of devices that will be impacted when the policy runs.

Creating Posture Policies on the Altiris Notification Server

This section shows you how to create a posture policy on the Altiris Notification Server to determine whether end-user machines are running a specific version of software before being granted access to the network. If the end-user machine does not meet minimum requirements, a client message can direct users to a URL for more instructions or can start the automatic installation of software on such machines. Complete the following steps to configure posture policies on the Altiris Notification Server:

Step 1   Access the Altiris Notification Server Console and click the **Configuration** tab.

Step 2   Navigate to **Solutions Settings** > **Network Access** > **Policies**.

Step 3   Right-click the **Posture** folder.

Step 4   Select **New** > **Posture Policy**.

Step 5   Right-click **New Posture Policy** and select **Rename** to enter a more descriptive name.

Step 6   Select the **Enable** check box to run the policy.

Step 7   Enter a description for the posture policy.

Step 8   Select a posture from the drop-down list.

Step 9   Click the **Collection** link and, using the Collection Selector, select the collections to be applied.

Step 10 Enter a message to display on end-user devices when the criteria of the policy is met.

Step 11 Enter a URL that users can be redirected to for more information about their device and posture.

Step 12 Enter command-line utilities or programs that will automatically run on client devices when the policy criteria is met, and click **Apply**.

Step 13 To verify the configuration, click the **Impact Analysis** tab to view a list of devices that will be impacted when the policy runs.

TIP   It is important that you test the impact of quarantine and remediation policies in a lab or pilot environment before you configure the Altiris Quarantine Solution, Cisco Secure ACS server, network access devices, and rolled-out agents to client machines in a production environment.

PatchLink

PatchLink is another Cisco partner that provides remediation features to the NAC solution. PatchLink Quarantine for NAC is an add-on feature to the PatchLink Update server, and it works very similarly to the Altiris solution. An agent is installed on the client machine that talks to CTA through a posture plug-in. The PatchLink Update server can then discover end-user machines connected to the network. You can also use the Agent Management Utility of the PatchLink Update server to install and remove PatchLink agents on end-user machines.

The installation and configuration documentation of PatchLink Update server and agents are publicly available on PatchLink's website at www.patchlink.com/support/documentation.html.

Figure 12-3 illustrates how the PatchLink Agent and Posture Plug-in communicate with CTA and the Windows Registry.

Figure 12-3 *PatchLink Agent*

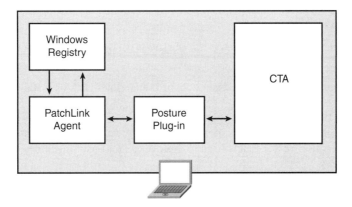

The PatchLink Agent communicates with CTA via the Posture Plug-in. It also reads and updates Windows Registry entries.

Similar to Altiris, the PatchLink Quarantine attributes need to be installed on Cisco Secure ACS server before you configure the PatchLink Update server as an external remediation server. In this case, PatchLink provides an installation package called PatchLink Quarantine ACS.msi. When executing this file on the Cisco Secure ACS server, all necessary PatchLink attributes are installed, and the csauth, cslog, and csadmin services are restarted.

NOTE   The Cisco Secure ACS configuration steps are exactly the same as the steps mentioned in the previous section.

Summary

Remediation is one of the key elements of the Cisco NAC solution. If machines do not comply with security policies and are therefore being quarantined, the capability to easily or automatically install security patches and updates on these machines is crucial. This chapter covered some of the different remediation techniques that the Cisco NAC solution supports. It provided information about CTA posture plug-ins for remediation software solutions and the different attributes sent from the client machine to the notification and patching servers. This chapter also provided an overview of how to add remediation vendor attribute-definition files and external notification servers into Cisco Secure ACS.

Review Questions

You can find the answers to the review questions in Appendix A, "Answers to Review Questions."

1. True or false: The Altiris Agent can be bundled with CTA's installation.

2. True or false: Cisco recommends installing the Altiris Agent after installing CTA.

3. True or false: The Altiris Network Discovery is a free plug-in component to the Notification Server that is used to discover all end-user machines connected to the network.

4. Which one of the following is not a Cisco NAC program remediation partner:

   a. Altiris

   b. BigFix

   c. RemediaCorp

   d. Citadel

5. What command you can use to install the attributes file for remediation servers on Cisco Secure ACS?

   a. CSUtility.exe

   b. CSUtil.exe

   c. CSACSUtil.exe

   d. CSImport.exe

Deployment Scenarios

This chapter covers the following topics:

- Defining the business requirements for deploying NAC in small businesses
- Reviewing the small businesses network topology
- Configuring NAC in a small business
- Troubleshooting the small businesses NAC deployment

## CHAPTER 13

Deploying and Troubleshooting NAC in Small Businesses

This is the first of three chapters devoted to helping you deploy NAC in your business. In the previous chapters, we covered all the individual pieces that make up the NAC Framework. Now we bring together all those components to demonstrate how to deploy NAC in a small business.

In this chapter, we examine the typical small business with fewer then 100 employees, all located in the same building. If your business resembles the one presented here, use this chapter as your deployment template. Larger businesses might want to use one of the following two chapters as a template. However, the principals presented in this chapter apply to all businesses. As the network size grows, the policies, redundancy, third-party support, and complexity also grow—but the fundamentals are still the same.

For the small-business network administrator, the goal is to help secure the network by requiring the machines that connect to the network to adhere to minimum-security requirements. To meet the requirements, the administrator has chosen to deploy NAC in the network. Users who meet the security requirements should be granted full access to the network. Those who fail to meet the minimum requirements should be granted limited access to the network.

In this chapter, we explain the requirements, go over the network topology, and walk through the steps needed to configure and enforce the requirements using NAC. We close with a troubleshooting section.

NAC Requirements for a Small Business

The purpose of NAC is to enforce a minimum-security policy across all the end hosts in your network. The network administrator enforces this policy using NAC. However, the requirements for the policy must come from the business leaders, working jointly with the network administrators, to define not only the minimum-security policy, but also the restrictions imposed on the end hosts that fail to meet the policy.

| NOTE | After the initial deployment, you might receive complaints from end users who fail to comply with the minimum-security policy and are quarantined with restricted access. These complaints usually make it up to the business leaders. Therefore, it is imperative that the business leaders participate and sign off on the policies that will be enforced. Without their buy-in, you could run into some problems. |

In the small business example presented here, network administrators and business leaders held joint meetings in which they agreed on the following policies and actions:

Policies:

- All access ports on the switches must have NAC enabled on them.
- All Windows machines must be running the latest service pack available. (Windows 2003, Windows XP, and Windows 2000 are the only supported OSes.)
- All Windows machines must install all critical hotfixes. (The network administrator determines which hotfixes are critical to the company, based on the severity of the hotfix and its applicability to the end hosts.)
- All Windows machines must be running the Trend antivirus software; it must be installed and enabled.
- All Windows machines must have the latest version of the antivirus signatures installed.
- Printers must have network access to print, but nothing else.
- Guest access must be allowed to provide vendors and other guests access to the Internet but not to the internal network.

Enforcement actions based on state:

- **Healthy**—End hosts that meet the minimum-security policy are granted unrestricted access to the network.
- **Quarantine**—End hosts that fail to meet the minimum-security policy are quarantined and redirected to an internal web server. The web server provides information on the company's minimum-security requirements and instructions on how to bring the host in compliance with the policy.
- **Clientless**—End hosts without CTA are assumed to be guests. Guests are allowed to access the Internet and the internal web server. If the guest's machine needs to access the corporate network for a business reason, the guest can download CTA from the internal web server and bring the machine up to the company's minimum-security policy.

TIP   Preparing your end users for NAC is the best way to avoid problems after deployment. Besides the typical messaging (e-mails, announcements, and so on), you can deploy NAC with a grace period, such as 30 days. In other words, you can deploy NAC, but the enforcement action for all states will continue to be **permit ip any any** for the grace period. For non-Healthy hosts, you can use the Posture Assessment (PA) message to give end users information on the upcoming enforcement policy change and tell them how to get their machines updated with the minimum-security policy. This allows for a soft transition period instead of a hard one and should prevent many help-desk calls when the real enforcement policy goes live.

TIP   During the grace period, you should periodically review the Cisco Secure ACS logs, or MARS reports, to verify that the number of agentless host devices is trending downward and that the majority of devices are in a Healthy state. Toward the end of the grace period, you should update the PA message to end users, especially those who are not in a Healthy state, warning them of the imminent policy-enforcement change. Additionally, you should attempt to investigate the non-Healthy hosts to determine why they have not made the changes necessary to meet the minimum-security policy. It is advisable to check that your boss's and senior executive staff's devices are reporting a Healthy state before you enforce more restrictive policies for non-Healthy hosts.

Small Business Network Topology

The typical topology in a small business consists of one or more switches connected to a router, which, in turn, connects to the Internet. A dedicated firewall also might function between the Internet-facing router and the switches, or the router might have firewalling capabilities (one example is Cisco IOS Firewall running on a Cisco router).

In this chapter, we use the topology shown in Figure 13-1 to represent the topology of a standard small business. The business is connected to the Internet through the GW_Router. The GW_Router is connected to a Layer 3 Catalyst 3750 switch on port GigabitEthernet 1/0/1. Following best practices, the business separates user traffic from server traffic by using VLANs. Each VLAN is defined as a Layer 3 switched virtual interface (SVI) on the 3750 and is assigned the .1 address in the Class C network. The devices connected to the 3750 (with the exception of the GW_Router) use the 3750 as the default gateway.

Figure 13-1 *Small Business Topology*

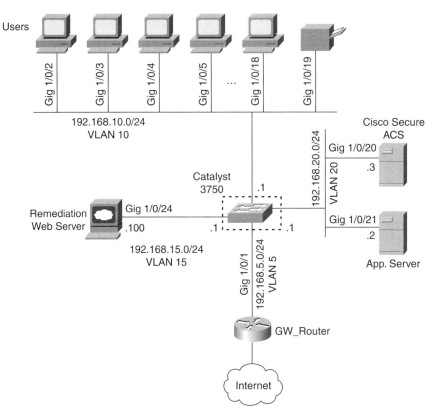

NOTE   For simplicity, Figure 13-1 shows only one switch in the topology, even though the typical small business might have several switches. However, the additional switches provide additional port capacity for servers and end hosts. Therefore, you can replicate the configuration to scale across all the switches in your network.

As shown in Figure 13-1 and detailed in Table 13-1, the 3750 is divided into four VLANs. VLAN 5 is the Internet segment, VLAN 10 is dedicated for end users, VLAN 15 is the quarantine network, and VLAN 20 is for servers. The quarantine network (VLAN 15) contains only a web server, which we use as a notification server and rudimentary remediation server.

Table 13-1   *3750 Switch Port Configuration*

Network Segment	VLAN	Port(s)
Internet	5	GigabitEthernet1/0/1
End user	10	GigabitEthernet1/0/2 to GigabitEthernet1/0/19
Quarantine	15	GigabitEthernet1/0/24
Server	20	GigabitEthernet1/0/20 to GigabitEthernet1/0/23

Configuring NAC in a Small Business

In this section, we cover the configuration needed to meet the requirements listed in the section "NAC Requirements for a Small Business." However, before you can start configuring the individual components, you must decide on the type of NAC to deploy: NAC-L3-IP, NAC-L2-IP, or NAC-L2-802.1X.

Because you do not have a requirement to authenticate the end users before granting them network access, you can rule out NAC-L2-801.X. Now the choice remains between NAC-L3-IP and NAC-L2-IP. This is actually an easy decision to make. Remember that NAC-L3-IP provides posture enforcement at the Layer 3 interface, whereas NAC-L2-IP provides posture enforcement at the Layer 2 switchport. With NAC-L3-IP, hosts can still communicate with one another on the same segment (Layer 2) without being postured. With NAC-L2-IP, all hosts must be postured before they can communicate with one another. This is important because network security best practices indicate that the security enforcement point should be pushed as close to the end device as possible. This leaves you with only NAC-L2-IP. Finally, if that were not enough, the first requirement mentioned earlier is that all access ports on the switches must have NAC enabled on them. This can be accomplished only using NAC-L2-IP.

With the requirements laid out and the type of NAC to deploy settled on, you can proceed with the configuration.

Cisco Secure ACS

Install and configure Cisco Secure ACS following the procedure described in Chapter 8, "Cisco Secure Access Control Server (ACS)." Then follow the steps in this section to create both a NAC-L2-IP profile and an Agentless Host profile (for guests). For the NAC-L2-IP profile, you create policies to validate the requirements listed earlier and then create authorization rules to enforce them. For the Agentless Host profile, you use a default authorization rule, tied to a downloadable ACL to restrict guest access to the internal network.

NOTE	If you already created the internal posture-validation policies as described in the Cisco Secure ACS chapter, you do not need to re-create them here. Just edit them where needed.

Complete the following steps to configure Cisco Secure ACS:

Step 1 Create an L2-IP Network Access Profile using the NAC L2 IP template and name it NAC-L2-IP. Do not forget to mark it Active.

Step 2 Create an Agentless Host profile using the Agentless Host template, and name it NAC_Agentless-Hosts.

Step 3 Import Trend's ADF file into Cisco Secure ACS using the command **CSUtil.exe –addAVP Trend-AV.adf.** Do not forget to restart CSAdmin, CSAuth, and CSLog from the services control panel.

Step 4 Edit the existing posture-validation policy, NAC-SAMPLE-CTA-POLICY, to check whether the version of CTA is greater than or equal to 2.0.0.30. Also, rename the policy to just CTA-Policy.

Step 5 Create a new internal posture-validation policy named Windows-SP-Policy that will check that the latest service pack is installed for that OS. Add the conditions shown in Table 13-2 to accomplish this.

Table 13-2 *Windows Service Pack Posture-Validation Rule*

No.	Condition	Posture Token
1	(Cisco:PA:OS-Type contains Windows 2003 AND Cisco:Host:ServicePacks contains 1) OR (Cisco:PA:OS-Type contains Windows XP AND Cisco:Host:ServicePacks contains 2) OR (Cisco:PA:OS-Type contains Windows 2000 AND Cisco:Host:ServicePacks contains 4)	Cisco:PA:Healthy
2	Default	Cisco:PA:Quarantine

Step 6 Create a new internal posture-validation policy named Windows-Hotfix-Policy that will check that the critical hotfixes are installed for the respective OSes. Add the conditions shown in Table 13-3 to accomplish this.

Table 13-3 *Windows Hotfix Posture-Validation Rule*

No.	Condition	Posture Token
1	Cisco:PA:OS-Type contains Windows 2003 AND Cisco:Host:HotFixes contains KB912812 AND Cisco:Host:HotFixes contains KB899585 AND Cisco:Host:HotFixes contains KB908531 AND Cisco:Host:HotFixes contains KB911562 AND Cisco:Host:HotFixes contains KB911565 AND Cisco:Host:HotFixes contains KB918222	Cisco:PA:Healthy
2	Cisco:PA:OS-Type contains Windows XP AND Cisco:Host:HotFixes contains KB912812 AND Cisco:Host:HotFixes contains KB899585 AND Cisco:Host:HotFixes contains KB918222	Cisco:PA:Healthy
3	Cisco:PA:OS-Type contains Windows 2000 AND Cisco:Host:HotFixes contains KB912812 AND Cisco:Host:HotFixes contains KB899585 AND Cisco:Host:HotFixes contains KB918222	Cisco:PA:Healthy
4	Default	Cisco:PA:Quarantine

NOTE   For simplicity, Table 13-3 does not list all the critical hotfixes. Instead, you can use this table as a framework to check for as many hotfixes as you want. Just add or remove condition elements to the condition set for the appropriate OS.

Step 7   Create a new internal posture-validation policy named Trend-AV-Policy that will check that Trend's antivirus software is enabled and that the latest virus-definition file is loaded. Add the conditions shown in Table 13-4 to accomplish this.

Table 13-4   *Trend Antivirus Posture-Validation Rule*

No	Condition	Posture Token
1	Cisco:PA:OS-Type contains Windows AND Trend:AV:Protection-Enabled = 1 AND Trend:AV:Dat-Version >= 3.456.0.0	Cisco:PA:Healthy
2	Default	Cisco:PA:Quarantine

Step 8   Create the downloadable IP ACLs shown in Table 13-5. Remember that downloadable IP ACLs are under the Shared Profile Components.

Table 13-5   *Downloadable IP ACLs*

Name	ACL Contents	ACL Definitions
NAC_Healthy_ACL	Healthy_ACL	`permit ip any any`

NAC_Quarantine_ACL	Quarantine_ACL	`remark If host is Quarantine restrict`
		`network access`
		`remark Allow DHCP and DNS`
		`permit udp any any eq 67`
		`permit udp any any eq 53`
		`remark Allow EAPoUDP for CTA client`
		`permit udp any any eq 21862`
		`remark Allow access to Quarantine`
		`network`
		`permit ip any 192.168.15.0 0.0.0.255`
		`remark Allow Updates from`
		`Microsoft.com`
		`permit tcp any host 207.46.253.157`
		`permit tcp any host 207.46.20.93`
		`permit tcp any host 207.46.157.61`
		`permit tcp any host 207.46.225.221`
		`permit tcp any host 207.46.156.254`
		`remark Allow Updates from`
		`TrendMicro.com`
		`permit tcp any host 64.62.243.182`
		`permit tcp any host 64.62.243.191`

Table 13-5 *Downloadable IP ACLs (Continued)*

Name	ACL Contents	ACL Definitions
| NAC_Clientless_ACL | Clientless_ACL | ```
remark Allow DHCP and DNS
permit udp any any eq 67
permit udp any any eq 53
remark Deny access to Internal networks
deny ip any 192.168.10.0 0.0.0.255
deny ip any 192.168.20.0 0.0.0.255
remark Permit web and IPSec access to
the Internet
permit tcp any any eq 80
permit tcp any any eq 443
permit udp any any eq 500
permit esp any any
permit udp any any eq 4500
``` |

Step 9 Create the RADIUS Authorization Components (RACs) shown in Table 13-6. Remember that RACs are also under the Shared Profile Components.

Table 13-6 *RADIUS Authorization Components*

Name	Assigned Attributes		
	Vendor	Attribute	Value
NAC-HEALTHY-L2-RAC	IETF	Session-Timeout(27)	36000
	Cisco IOS/ PIX 6.0	cisco-av-pair(1)	sec:pg=healthy_hosts
	IETF	Termination-Action (29)	RADIUS-Request(1)
NAC-QUARANTINE-L2-RAC	IETF	Session-Timeout(27)	36000
	Cisco IOS/ PIX 6.0	cisco-av-pair(1)	sec:pg=healthy_hosts
	IETF	Termination-Action (29)	RADIUS-Request(1)
	Cisco IOS/ PIX 6.0	cisco-av-pair(1)	url-redirect-acl=quarantine_url_redir_acl

NOTE Although the sec:pg=healthy_hosts attributes are included in the table, they are applicable only to the Catalyst 6500 series of switches. The other switches just ignore this attribute. For the Catalyst 6500s, this attribute is used to download a policy-based ACL.
```

Step 10 Configure the posture-validation rules for the NAC-L2-IP profile by selecting the appropriate link under Network Access Profiles.

Step 11 No modifications to the Required Credential Types are needed. In the Action section, select the following Internal Posture Validation Policies: CTA-Policy, Windows-SP-Policy, Windows-Hotfix-Policy, and Trend-AV-Policy.

Step 12 In the System Posture Token Configuration section, fill in a PA Message for both the Healthy and Quarantine System Posture Tokens. Example messages are shown here:

— **Healthy**—The security posture of this machine has been analyzed and found to comply with the company security policy. You have been granted access to the network.

— **Quarantine**—The overall security posture of this host has been analyzed and does not meet the minimum-security policy of this company. Please open a web browser and follow the instructions on the page. You will be asked to install security updates to bring the machine into compliance with the corporate security policy. Once complete, you will be granted access to the network.

Step 13 For the Quarantine System Posture Token, fill in the **URL Redirect** field with the URL of the web/remediation server on the quarantine network (Example: http://192.168.15.100).

Step 14 Configure the authorization rules for the NAC-L2-IP profile by selecting the **Authorization** link next to the profile and configuring the rules according to Table 13-7.

Table 13-7 *L2-IP Authorization Rules*

Condition		Action		
User Group	**System Posture Token**	**Deny Access**	**Shared RAC**	**Downloadable ACL**
Any	Healthy		NAC-HEALTHY-L2-RAC	NAC_Healthy_ACL
Any	Quarantine		NAC-QUARANTINE-L2-RAC	NAC_Quarantine_ACL
If a condition is not defined or there is no matched condition			NAC-QUARANTINE-L2-RAC	NAC_Quarantine_ACL

Step 15 Rename group 106 to Clientless by selecting the **Rename Group** option under the **Group Setup** button.

Step 16 Configure the authentication rules for the NAC_Agentless-Hosts profile by selecting the **Authentication** link under Network Access Profiles. Under the **Default Action** section, select **106: Clientless** from the drop-down list.

Step 17 Configure the authorization rules for the NAC_Agentless-Hosts profile by selecting the **Authorization** link next to the profile and configuring the rules according to Table 13-8.

Table 13-8 *Agentless-Host Authorization Rules*

Condition		Action		
User Group	System Posture Token	Deny Access	Shared RAC	Downloadable ACL
106: Clientless	Any	☐	NAC-HEALTHY-L2-RAC	NAC_Clientless_ACL
If a condition is not defined or there is no matched condition		☑		

Step 18 Restart the ACS processes from **System Configuration > Services Control**.

This completes the configuration steps for Cisco Secure ACS.

End-User Clients

The configuration of the end-user clients consists of creating a silent distribution package of CTA and deploying it to your end users. Follow these steps to accomplish this task:

Step 1 Extract the CTA silent installation package from the CtaAdminEx executable file.

Step 2 Customize both the ctad.ini and ctalogd.ini files as appropriate for your business.

Step 3 Package, deploy, and install CTA on all company-owned hosts. Make sure you include the root CA certificate (or Cisco Secure ACS self-signed certificate) in the deployment package. For more information, refer to the section "Deploying CTA in a Production Network" in Chapter 2, "Cisco Trust Agent."

Step 4 It is assumed that the Trend antivirus software application is already installed on the hosts. Verify that Trend's posture plug-in for CTA is installed by checking for the existence of Trend's .dll and .inf files in the \Program Files\Common Files\PostureAgent\Plugins\Install directory. If the plug-in files do not exist, obtain them from Trend and install them in that directory.

This completes the configuration steps for the end-user clients.

Switches

Configure the switch(es) for NAC-L2-IP by following these steps:

Step 1 Configure Authentication, Authorization, and Accounting by adding the following commands:

```
aaa new-model
aaa authentication eou default group radius
aaa authorization network default group radius
aaa accounting network default start-stop group radius
```

Step 2 Configure RADIUS on the switch by adding the following commands:

```
radius-server host Cisco-Secure-ACS-IP
radius-server key shared-secret-key
radius-server attribute 8 include-in-access-req
radius-server vsa send authentication
ip radius source-interface interface-name
```

Step 3 Enable device tracking to trigger the NAC-L2-IP posture validation by adding the following command:

```
ip device tracking
```

Step 4 Create an interface ACL that is applied to the switchport before posture validation. An example ACL is shown here:

```
ip access-list extended interface_acl
  permit udp any any eq 21862
  permit udp any any eq 67
  permit udp any any eq 53
  permit tcp any quarantine-network mask
```

Step 5 Create an IP admission rule to enable NAC:

```
ip admission name L2-IP eapoudp
```

Step 6 Allow clientless devices to connect and use the Agentless host policy:

```
eou allow clientless
```

Step 7 Enable EAP over UDP logging:

```
eou logging
```

Step 8 Configure a local NAC policy to authorize printer and server access to the network:

```
identity profile eapoudp
  device authorize ip-address Printer-IP policy Printers
  device authorize ip-address Server-IP policy Servers
identity policy Printers
  access-group printers
identity policy Servers
  access-group servers
ip access-list extended printers
  permit tcp any eq 9100 any
ip access-list extended servers
  permit ip any any
```

Step 9   Enable the HTTP server and configure the URL redirect ACL for
quarantined hosts to be redirected to the web/remediation server. You
might also want to exclude the windowsupdate.microsoft.com and Trend
update servers from being redirected back to the remediation server:

```
ip http server
ip access-list extended quarantine_url_redir_acl
  deny tcp any host web/remediation server IP eq www
  deny tcp any host http://windowsupdate.microsoft.com eq www
  deny tcp any host http://www.trendmicro.com eq www
  permit tcp any any eq www
```

Step 10   Finally, apply the interface ACL and IP admission rule to each
switchport. The only exception to this is the switchport out which Cisco
Secure ACS connects and the switchport that connects to your upstream
gateway router:

```
interface GigabitEthernet1/0/x
  ip access-group interface_acl in
  ip admission L2-IP
```

This completes the configuration of the Catalyst 3750 switch for NAC-L2-IP. Example 13-1
shows output of the full configuration of the switch after adding these commands.

Example 13-1 *Catalyst 3750 Switch Configuration for NAC-L2-IP*

```
Current configuration : 6236 bytes
!
version 12.2
no service pad
service timestamps debug uptime
service timestamps log uptime
service password-encryption
!
hostname c3750
!
enable password <removed>
!
aaa new-model
aaa authentication login no-login none
aaa authentication eou default group radius
aaa authorization network default group radius
aaa accounting network default start-stop group radius
!
```

continues

Example 13-1 *Catalyst 3750 Switch Configuration for NAC-L2-IP (Continued)*

```
aaa session-id common
switch 1 provision ws-c3750g-24ps
ip subnet-zero
ip routing
ip cef accounting non-recursive
ip admission name L2-IP eapoudp
ip device tracking
!
eou allow clientless
eou logging
identity profile eapoudp
 description Exemption policy for Servers and Printers
 device authorize ip-address 192.168.10.19 policy Printers
 device authorize ip-address 192.168.20.2 policy Servers
identity policy Servers
 access-group servers
identity policy Printers
 access-group printers
!
no file verify auto
spanning-tree mode pvst
spanning-tree extend system-id
!
vlan internal allocation policy ascending
!
interface GigabitEthernet1/0/1
 description Connection to GW_Router
 switchport access vlan 5
 switchport mode access
!
interface GigabitEthernet1/0/2
switchport access vlan 10
 switchport mode access
 ip access-group interface_acl in
 spanning-tree portfast
 ip admission L2-IP
!
interface GigabitEthernet1/0/3
switchport access vlan 10
 switchport mode access
 ip access-group interface_acl in
 spanning-tree portfast
 ip admission L2-IP
!
! The configuration for Ports 1/0/4 through 1/0/18
!  has been removed to simply the output. The
!   configuration of those ports are identical to
!   port 1/0/3 shown above.
!
interface GigabitEthernet1/0/19
description Connection to HP Printer
 switchport access vlan 10
```

Example 13-1 *Catalyst 3750 Switch Configuration for NAC-L2-IP (Continued)*

```
 switchport mode access
 ip access-group interface_acl in
 spanning-tree portfast
 ip admission L2-IP
 !
interface GigabitEthernet1/0/20
 description Connection to ACS Server
 switchport access vlan 20
 switchport mode access
 spanning-tree portfast
 !
interface GigabitEthernet1/0/21
 description Connection to Application Server
 switchport access vlan 20
 switchport mode access
 ip access-group interface_acl in
 spanning-tree portfast
 ip admission L2-IP
 !
interface GigabitEthernet1/0/22
 !
interface GigabitEthernet1/0/23
 !
interface GigabitEthernet1/0/24
 description Web / Remediation Server
 switchport access vlan 15
 switchport mode access
 spanning-tree portfast
 !
interface GigabitEthernet1/0/25
 !
interface GigabitEthernet1/0/26
 !
interface GigabitEthernet1/0/27
 !
interface GigabitEthernet1/0/28
 !
interface Vlan1
 ip address dhcp
 shutdown
 !
interface Vlan5
 description Connection to GW_Router
 ip address 192.168.5.1 255.255.255.0
 !
interface Vlan10
 description End-User VLAN
 ip address 192.168.10.1 255.255.255.0
 !
interface Vlan15
 description Quarantine VLAN
 ip address 192.168.15.1 255.255.255.0
```

continues

Example 13-1 *Catalyst 3750 Switch Configuration for NAC-L2-IP (Continued)*

```
!
interface Vlan20
 description Server VLAN
 ip address 192.168.20.1 255.255.255.0
!
ip classless
ip route 0.0.0.0 0.0.0.0 192.168.5.2
ip http server
ip http authentication aaa
!
ip radius source-interface Vlan20
!
ip access-list extended interface_acl
 permit udp any any eq 21862
 permit udp any any eq bootps
 permit udp any any eq domain
 permit tcp any 192.168.15.0 0.0.0.255
ip access-list extended printers
 permit tcp any eq 9100 any
ip access-list extended quarantine_url_redir_acl
 deny   tcp any host 192.168.15.100 eq www
remark Allow Updates from Microsoft.com
deny   tcp any host 207.46.253.157
deny   tcp any host 207.46.20.93
deny   tcp any host 207.46.157.61
deny   tcp any host 207.46.225.221
deny   tcp any host 207.46.156.254
remark Allow Updates from Trend.com
deny   tcp any host 64.62.243.182
deny   tcp any host 64.62.243.191
 permit tcp any any eq www
ip access-list extended servers
 permit ip any any
!
radius-server attribute 8 include-in-access-req
radius-server host 192.168.20.3 auth-port 1812 acct-port 1813
radius-server key <removed>
radius-server vsa send authentication
!
control-plane
!
line con 0
line vty 0 4
 exec-timeout 60 0
 password <removed>
 login authentication no-login
line vty 5 15
!
end
```

Web Server

The web server shown in Figure 13-1 doubles as a very basic form of a remediation server. Its primary purpose is to supply information to quarantined users that are redirected to the server. It must contain information on why they were redirected there, as well as information on how to bring their computer up to the company standard.

In the case of this small business example, configure the web server's main index.html page to explain that the network has quarantined the user because the computer fails to meet minimum security. Next, provide instructions on how the users can install the latest patches, hotfixes, virus-definition files, and so on to bring the computer up-to-date and thus remove them from being quarantined.

This can be as simple as providing links to http://windowsupdate.microsoft.com that users can click to follow the steps to install the latest patches. Or you can provide steps on running Windows update from **Start** > **Programs**. The same holds true for obtaining the latest antivirus file definitions. Alternatively, you can even download the files locally to the web/ remediation server and just have the user click them to download and install them. The simple rule of thumb is to gauge the knowledge base of your general users and then design the web page to be a self-help guide that walks users through the process to update their computers.

Finally, yet importantly, always include the help-desk phone number that users can call if they get stuck. The last thing you want is an employee who is locked out of the network and is no longer being productive.

Troubleshooting NAC Deployment in a Small Business

This section covers some common troubleshooting methods you can use when diagnosing NAC-related problems. The first two methods pertain to the switch, and the last two pertain to Cisco Secure ACS and the client running CTA. All four methods combined provide you with a complete end-to-end picture of how, when, where, and why an end host was posture-validated by NAC.

show Commands

show commands are useful in determining the current state and posture of an end host. However, they do not provide a historical reference of how (or why) the host ended up there. The two most useful **show** commands are **show eou all** and **show eou ip** *ip-address*.

NOTE   Cisco IOS uses **eou** commands to represent EAP over UDP, or what we generally refer to as EAPoUDP. All three—EAP over UDP, EAPoUDP, and EOU—are equivalent terms and can be used interchangeably.

The **show eou all** command displays a table of all clients connected to NAC-enabled ports on the switch. The output contains the IP address of the client, the port it is connected to, the authentication method it used to authenticate itself, the system posture token assigned to it, and the time since the last posture validation. Example 13-2 shows sample output from this command.

Example 13-2 *show eou all Command Output*

```
c3750#show eou all
-------------------------------------------------------------------
Address           Interface              AuthType   Posture-Token Age(min)
-------------------------------------------------------------------
192.168.10.67     GigabitEthernet1/0/2   EAP        HEALTHY          23
192.168.10.69     GigabitEthernet1/0/4   CLIENTLESS -------         148
```

The **show eou ip** *ip-address* command displays the NAC policy applied to the host, including the assigned system posture token, the downloadable IP ACL, and the URL redirect link and ACL; all are important in determining what authorization components are applied to the end host after the posture-validation process completes. Example 13-3 shows sample output from this command for a quarantined host.

Example 13-3 *show eou ip ip-address Command Output*

```
c3750#show eou ip 192.168.10.73
Address             : 192.168.10.73
MAC Address         : 00d0.b73c.76ac
Interface           : GigabitEthernet1/0/5
AuthType            : EAP
Audit Session ID    : 000000007D8518FC00000085AC12AD45
PostureToken        : Quarantine
Age(min)            : 0
URL Redirect        : http://192.168.15.100
URL Redirect ACL    : quarantine_url_redir_acl
ACL Name            : #ACSACL#-IP-NAC_Quarantine_ACL-44665573
User Name           : SECURITY-TAC:wbeach
Revalidation Period : 3600 Seconds
Status Query Period : 300 Seconds
Current State       : AUTHENTICATED
```

EAP over UDP Logging

You enabled EAP over UDP (or EOU, for short) logging on the switch during its configuration. Therefore, when a host is postured, the switch generates the EOU logs, which can be viewed by enabling logging on the switch at Level 6 or higher. The logs are standard syslogs and can be viewed in the local buffer, on the console/monitor session, or on the syslog server. Example 13-4 illustrates an example from an agentless (clientless) host connecting to the switch.

Example 13-4 *Clientless Host EOU Logs*

```
3w3d: %EOU-6-SESSION: IP=192.168.10.69¦ HOST=DETECTED¦ Interface=GigabitEthernet1/
  0/4
3w3d: %EOU-6-POLICY: IP=192.168.10.69¦ ACLNAME=#ACSACL#-IP-NAC_Clientless_ACL-
  44665562
3w3d: %EOU-6-POLICY: IP=192.168.10.69¦ HOSTNAME=Unknown User
3w3d: %EOU-6-POSTURE: IP=192.168.10.69¦ HOST=AUTHORIZED¦
  Interface=GigabitEthernet1/0/4
3w3d: %EOU-6-AUTHTYPE: IP=192.168.10.69¦ AuthType=CLIENTLESS
3w3d: %EOU-6-CTA: IP=192.168.10.69¦ CiscoTrustAgent=NOT DETECTED
```

The EOU logs provide you with critical troubleshooting information, including the IP address of the end host, the port it is connecting to, the posture token (or, in this case, the CLIENTLESS AuthType is shown), the downloadable ACL applied, and, if CTA was enabled on the host, the username logged into the device. This information goes a long way in troubleshooting any client-connectivity issue.

Cisco Secure ACS Logging

As discussed in Chapter 8, Cisco Secure ACS provides robust NAC logging capabilities with the Passed Authentications and Failed Attempts log files. Enable and configure Cisco Secure ACS logging from **System Configuration > Logging**.

NOTE   For detailed steps on configuring logging in Cisco Secure ACS, refer to the "Enabling Logging" section in Chapter 8.

The Cisco Secure ACS log files contain critical information about not only the end host, but also the NAD that the end host is connecting to and the policies, profiles, and rules that the end host is mapped to in Cisco Secure ACS. These are some of the items contained in the logs:

- IP address and name of the device the end host is connecting to
- MAC and IP address of the end host

- Domain/username of the person logged in to the end host
- The Network Access Profile the end host is mapped to
- The RADIUS Authorization Component applied
- The downloadable ACL applied
- The system posture token assigned
- All the application posture tokens
- The posture-validation policies
- All the values returned from the posture plug-ins

Don't forget that the logs are also configurable, so you can add even more information to them.

As you can see, Cisco Secure ACS logging is very robust and enables you to easily diagnose configuration errors on Cisco Secure ACS. In addition, you can use the Cisco Secure ACS logs to determine why an end host failed to receive a Healthy system posture token. Typically, the Cisco Secure ACS logs is the first place you look to diagnose any NAC-related issues.

Certificate Issues: EAP-TLS or PEAP Authentication Failed During SSL Handshake

If you have a host that is not being postured properly, the first troubleshooting step is to check the Cisco Secure ACS logs. Specifically, check the Failed Attempts log. If you see the message "EAP-TLS or PEAP authentication failed during SSL handshake" in the Authen-Failure-Code column, this indicates a problem with the certificates.

Missing or Incorrect Root CA Certificate

The most common cause of this error is forgetting to install the root CA certificate (that signed Cisco Secure ACS certificate) into the client's trusted root certificate store. Without the root CA certificate, the client cannot validate the certificate presented from Cisco Secure ACS, and authentication fails during the Secure Socket Layer (SSL) handshake.

NOTE   If you are using a self-signed certificate on Cisco Secure ACS, this same self-signed certificate needs to be imported into the client's trusted root certificate store.

The easiest way to check whether the correct root certificate is installed is to select **System Configuration > ACS Certificate Setup > Install ACS Certificate in ACS**. This presents you with the currently installed ACS certificate. Record the name in the Issued By field. This is the name of the root CA that signed the ACS certificate.

Now follow these steps to verify that the root CA's certificate is installed on the client:

Step 1   Go to the client that is generating the "EAP-TLS or PEAP authentication failed during SSL handshake" messages and open Internet Explorer.

Step 2   Select **Tools > Internet Options.**

Step 3   Select the **Content** tab, followed by the **Certificates** button.

Step 4   A new Certificates window opens up. Select the **Trusted Root Certification Authorities** tab.

Step 5   Scroll through the list of trusted root CAs, and verify that the CA name you wrote down earlier appears in the list.

If you do not see the root CA that issued the Cisco Secure ACS certificate in the list, you need to import that certificate into the trusted root CA store. From the same screen that appears in step 5, select the **Import** button to import the certificate.

Incorrect Time or Date

After you have verified that the root CA that signed the Cisco Secure ACS certificate is in the client's trusted root CA store, and authentication is still failing, the next step is to verify the time and date. Certificates are valid for only a given period of time. If either the Cisco Secure ACS clock or the client's clock is off, the certificate might not be valid and authentication will fail.

Verify that the clock on Cisco Secure ACS and the client are accurate. (Do not forget to check for the correct year!) Also, if they are in different time zones, verify that the time zone is properly selected on both.

TIP   It is highly suggested that you run a Network Time Protocol (NTP) application on the Cisco Secure ACS server to keep the Cisco Secure ACS clock accurate. Windows 2003 has an NTP client automatically built in. If you double-click the time in the taskbar, the Date and Time Properties window appears. If you select the **Internet Time** tab, you have the option **Automatically Synchronize with an Internet Time Server**. Selecting the check box enables the Windows NTP client.

Summary

In this chapter, we walked through the steps required for a typical small business to deploy NAC-L2-IP in the network. We started by creating a list of requirements developed jointly by the network administrators and business leaders. Next, we reviewed the network topology used throughout this chapter. With solid requirements and a good idea of the network topology, we walked through the steps required to configure Cisco Secure ACS, the clients, the switches, and the web/remediation server. Finally, we closed with a troubleshooting section that covered common problems encountered in the deployment.

Review Questions

You can find the answers to the review questions in Appendix A, "Answers to Review Questions."

1. What two business groups must be involved in developing the NAC requirements?

   a. Network administrators and users

   b. Users and human resources

   c. Human resources and business leaders

   d. Business leaders and network administrators

2. Why was NAC-L2-IP chosen over NAC-L3-IP or NAC-L2-802.1X?

   a. L2-802.1X was too complicated.

   b. User authentication was not a requirement, and NAC-L2-IP pushed the enforcement point as close as possible to the end host.

   c. User authentication was a requirement that could be performed only with NAC-L2-IP.

   d. NAC-L3-IP is older and was replaced by NAC-L2-IP.

3. Why were only two system posture tokens used?

   a. Cisco Secure ACS has only two predefined system posture tokens.

   b. The other system posture tokens apply only when using NAC partner applications.

   c. Three posture tokens were used.

   d. The requirements called for only two different types of enforcement, for users with CTA installed.

4. What two system posture tokens were used?

   a. Healthy and Quarantine

   b. Healthy and Transition

   c. Healthy and Unknown

   d. Quarantine and Infected

5. True or false: End hosts without CTA installed cannot get access to the network.

6. True or false: Guests visiting the business must connect to a non-NAC-enabled switch to get access to the Internet.

7. True or false: Printers and servers can be authorized by a local policy on the switch or a central policy on Cisco Secure ACS.

8. What two things must be applied to each switchport interface to enable NAC?

   a. Admission and authorization policy

   b. Authentication and authorization policy

   c. Admission policy and interface ACL

   d. Interface ACL and authorization policy

9. What is the identity policy used for?

   a. To tie an access list to an authorized device

   b. To tell Cisco Secure ACS the identity of the device connected to the switchport

   c. To tell the switch the identity of the device connected to the switchport

   d. To spy on users

10. What can be configured to send a message to users after they have been postured?

   a. The configured MOTD on the switch is sent to users.

   b. CTA displays the message associated with the posture token in the cta_message.ini file.

   c. CTA can display the PA message to end users.

   d. It is not possible to send a user a message.

This chapter covers the following topics:

- Deployment overview of NAC in a medium-size enterprise
- Business requirements for NAC in a medium-size enterprise
- NAC solution highlights in a medium-size enterprise
- Steps for configuring NAC in a medium-size enterprise
- Monitoring and troubleshooting NAC in a medium-size enterprise

CHAPTER **14**

Deploying and Troubleshooting NAC in Medium-Size Enterprises

All companies, whether small, medium, or large, focus on securing their network infrastructure. This not only includes updating their security devices, but it also requires updating security policies to deal with new and emerging security threats. This chapter provides a detailed deployment scenario of the Cisco NAC solution for a medium-size enterprise.

This chapter presents real-life examples of how the Cisco NAC solution can be deployed at a medium-size organization. It discusses the typical requirements of an organization and the solution to achieve those requirements. These solutions are based on the industry best practices and are commonly used by enterprises.

NOTE   This chapter builds on the content in Chapter 13, "Deploying and Troubleshooting NAC in Small Businesses." Review Chapter 13 even if you plan to deploy NAC Framework in a medium-size enterprise.

Deployment Overview of NAC in a Medium-Size Enterprise

In this chapter, we discuss the deployment scenario of NAC in a fictitious company called SecureMe, Inc. This company, based in Chicago, has around a thousand employees and is looking to provide admissions control for the users logging in to the network. Figure 14-1 shows the network topology of SecureMe, Inc.

NOTE   Preparing your end users for NAC is the best way to avoid problems after deployment. Besides the typical messaging (e-mails, announcements, and so on), you can deploy NAC with a grace period—say, 30 days. In other words, deploy NAC, but the enforcement action for all states will continue to be **permit ip any any** for the grace period. For non-Healthy hosts, you can use the Posture Assessment (PA) message to provide the end users with information on the upcoming enforcement policy change and how to get their machines updated with the minimum-security policy. This allows for a soft transition period instead of a hard one and should prevent many help-desk calls when the real enforcement policy goes live.

Figure 14-1 *Network Topology of a Medium-Size Enterprise*

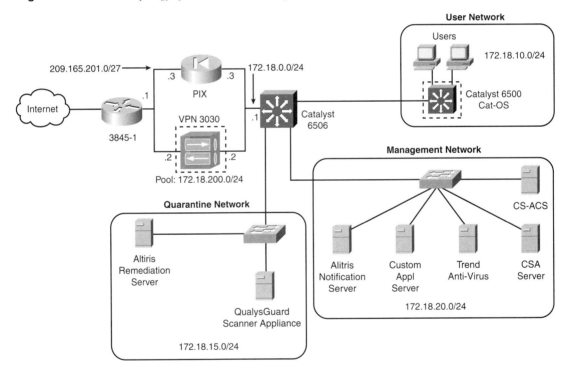

NOTE   The design scenarios discussed in this section should be used solely to reinforce learning. They should be used for reference purposes only.

In Figure 14-1, a 3845 Cisco IOS router is used to provide Internet connectivity. On the LAN segment of the router, SecureMe, Inc., has implemented a security appliance (a PIX firewall) to filter inbound and outbound traffic. SecureMe, Inc., provides VPN services to its employees who require full network access from their home offices. The VPN 3000 concentrator also provides access to a number of contractors who access only one application server on the internal network. All these devices are connected to a core 6506 switch that links devices on the internal network.

The 6506 switch connects to three distinct networks:

- User network
- Management network
- Quarantine network

The User Network

The User network consists of SecureMe employees who plug in their laptops and other devices to gain network access. Each user is connected to a unique port on the Cisco Layer 2 switches. SecureMe uses a number of Cisco switches, including Catalyst 6500 and 2924XL. A trunk connection exists between the Catalyst 6500 switch and the 2900XL switches. Most of the users are connected directly to the Catalyst 6500 switch. However, some users still connect to the Cisco 2924XL switches, as shown in Figure 14-2. The Catalyst 6500 switch is using the CatOS system image, while the 2924XLs are using the Cisco IOS code. The User network also hosts a number of network devices such as printers and IP phones.

In this topology, the User network uses a 172.18.10.0 Class C subnet. Therefore, it can accommodate more than 250 network devices on that subnet. For a medium-size enterprise, multiple user networks are trunked to the Catalyst 6506 switch. Currently, SecureMe has five user networks, ranging from 172.18.10.0 to 172.18.14.0. The red dotted box around the 6500 Catalyst switch indicates that it is configured with the NAC Framework to check posture from the machines in the User network.

NOTE   After the initial deployment, you might receive complaints from end users who fail to comply with the minimum-security policy and are quarantined with restricted access. These complaints usually make it up to the business leaders. Therefore, it is imperative that the business leaders participate and sign off on the policies that will be enforced. Without their buy-in, you could run into some problems.

Figure 14-2 *User Network in a Medium-Size Enterprise*

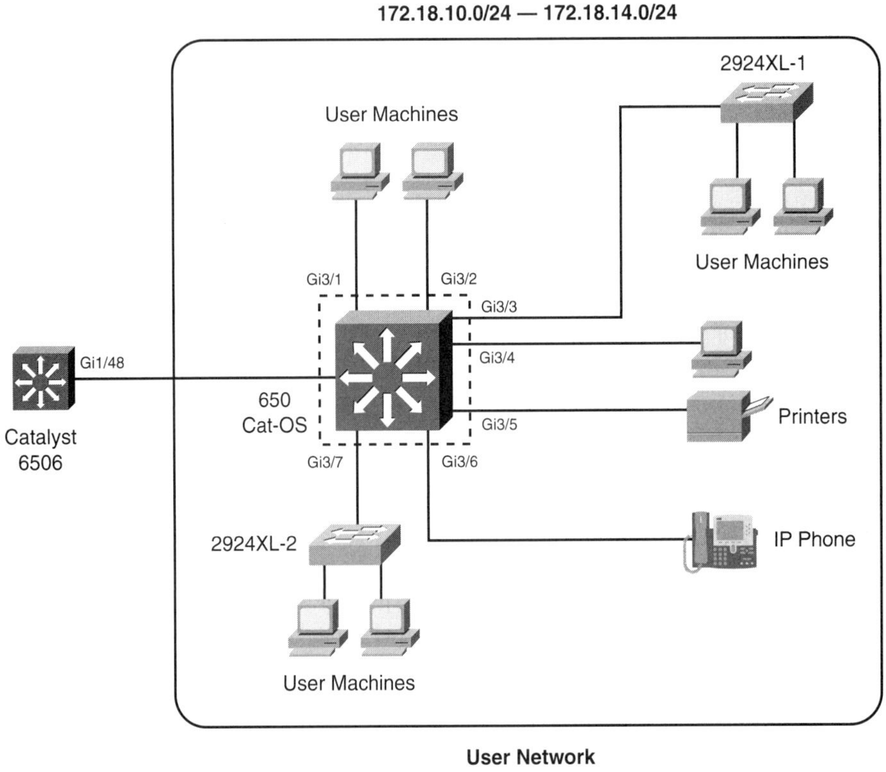

172.18.10.0/24 — 172.18.14.0/24

User Network

The Management Network

The Management network hosts most of the network-management and user-authentication servers. Additionally, all the Cisco network access devices (NADs), including routers and switches, have their IP addresses in the Management network. Figure 14-3 shows five servers on the Management network:

- **CS-ACS**—Cisco Secure Access Control Server is the authentication server that is currently used for validating user credentials on the network. All the Cisco NADs check with Cisco Secure ACS when users try to gain access to the devices.

- **CSA Server**—Cisco Security Agent management console server. All end-user machines are expected to run the CSA agent to protect them against unforeseeable events.

- **Trend Micro Policy Server**—Trend Micro Policy Server downloads latest antivirus signatures from the Trend labs and then pushes them onto the machines running the Trend antivirus client software. This server is also acting as the OfficeScan server.

- **Altiris Notification Server**—Altiris Notification Server contacts the remediation Server to update software and other patches on a quarantined or noncompliant host.

- **Application Server**—The application server is used by the contractors who log in to SecureMe's network over the VPN tunnel. The application uses TCP port 2005.

Figure 14-3 *Management Network in a Medium-Size Enterprise*

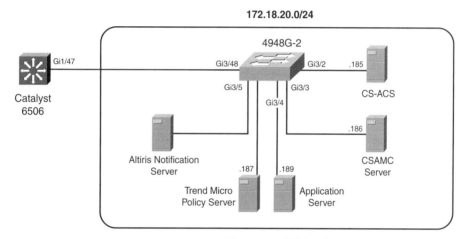

Management Network

The Quarantine Network

The Quarantine network consists of a number of servers that are solely used to identify and patch noncompliant hosts. In Figure 14-4, SecureMe has three servers on this network:

- **Remediation server**—The remediation server updates software and patches on the end-host machines.

- **QualysGuard Audit Scanner Appliance**—The QualysGuard Scanner Appliance scans hosts that do not identify themselves on the network. This way, it can check machine-specific credentials or policies to determine whether they are running updated patches.

Figure 14-4 *Quarantine Network in a Medium-Size Enterprise*

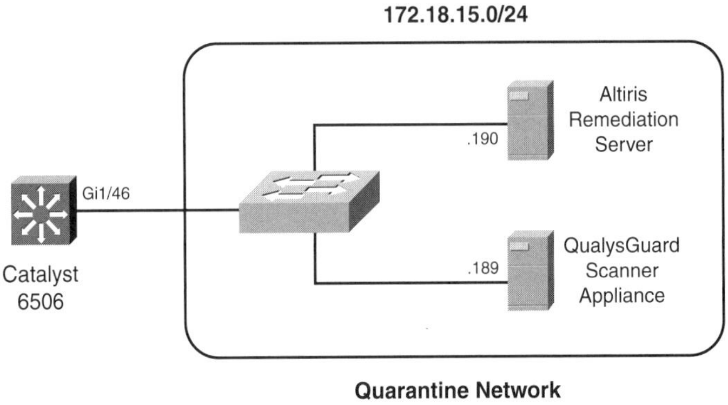

Business Requirements for NAC in a Medium-Size Enterprise

SecureMe is concerned about outbreaks of new network worms. A few months ago, the network infrastructure was severely degraded by a number of laptops. During the post-analysis phase of the incident, it was determined that those machines were not using the latest antivirus signature files and did not even have the Cisco Security Agent (CSA) application installed.

The chief security officer (CSO) of SecureMe, Inc., is concerned about the findings of the port-analysis report and wants to look into a solution that can achieve the following requirements:

- The solution should check for policy compliance for the host machines trying to get network access.

- The solution should check for policy compliance for all types of users, whether those are VPN- or LAN-based users.

- The solution, based on the compliance policies, should assign an appropriate level of access to the users.

- If the solution determines that the hosts are not in compliance based on the policies, it should initiate the remediation process.

- The solution should be capable of detecting the following:

  — Version of antivirus software, including the signature file

  — Operating system information, including any service packs and hotfixes

  — Status of certain security applications, such as CSA, running on the machines

- The solution should seamlessly integrate with the network infrastructure without the need to install new devices.

- The solution should be capable of differentiating among the VPN users. SecureMe employees and the contractor should have appropriate policies applied to them based on their user credentials.

- The solution should quarantine the host machines if they are not in compliance with the corporate policies.

Based on these requirements, SecureMe has decided to implement Cisco's NAC Framework solution.

Medium-Size Enterprise NAC Solution Highlights

Before a solution is deployed in the production environment, SecureMe wants to document all the major highlights of the solution. This is necessary in case new network or security requirements come up later and they need to expand this solution to meet those requirements. The major highlights of the solution include the following:

- The NAC Framework solution will install the CTA agent on all the host machines owned by SecureMe. SecureMe already has the Altiris Quarantine solution deployed for software management.

- For the machines that SecureMe does not own or the machines that do not have the CTA agent installed, the NAC Framework solution will use a QualysGuard Scanner Appliance to scan for well-known vulnerabilities.

- The NAC Framework solution will be implemented on the following devices:

  — **VPN 3000 concentrator**—SecureMe already has a VPN 3000 concentrator deployed to provide remote-access connectivity to its employees and other contractors. The concentrator will be enabled for NAC to ensure that users are given appropriate access based on their compliance with the corporate policies.

  — **Cisco Catalyst 6500 Switch**—SecureMe is using an access 6500 switch in its network infrastructure. Most of the user networks are directly connected to this switch. However, many legacy switches, such as Cisco 2924XL switches, are also connected to this 6500 switch. The Catalyst 6500 switch will be enabled for NAC in Layer 2 IP (NAC-L2-IP) mode. This way, it can accommodate host machines that are connected behind the 2924XL switches. The 2924XL switches do not support the NAC Framework solution.

- All the policies for compliance will be checked on the Cisco Secure ACS. Any host that is not in compliance with the policies will be given restrictive access to the network so that their machines can be updated. All Windows machines must be running the latest service pack available. (Windows 2003, Windows XP, and Windows 2000 are the only supported OSes.)

- SecureMe already uses Altiris Quarantine solution. This solution will be integrated with the NAC Framework to ensure that hosts that do not meet corporate compliance policies are treated accordingly. The Network Discovery option is not enabled, but the CSO would like to use this functionality to get a list of all the devices that exist in SecureMe's network.

- The quarantined hosts should be given access only to the remediation server so that software updates and proper patches can be applied to those hosts.

- SecureMe uses Trend Micro Policy Server for antivirus management. The solution will incorporate the antivirus server to ensure compliance with security policies. All Windows machines must be running the Trend antivirus software; it must be installed and enabled.

- During the audit process, the hosts are given access to only the audit servers so that their posture can be determined.

- The Cisco Security Agent (CSA) can generate an agent kit with the CTA software preinstalled.

Enforcement Actions

The following enforcement actions are outlined by SecureMe's leadership staff:

- **Healthy**—End hosts that meet the minimum-security policy will be granted unrestricted access to the network.

- **Quarantine**—End hosts that fail to meet the minimum-security policy will be quarantined and redirected to an internal web server. The web server will provide information on the company's minimum-security requirements, and Altiris remediation servers will be used to update end-user machines.

- **Transition**—This state is applicable either during host boot, when all NAC-enabled applications might not be running, or during an audit when posture information has not yet been obtained from the host.

- **Checkup**—This state is applicable if the hosts' antivirus definitions are at least five versions old. If the Cisco Secure ACS server cannot communicate with the audit server, the user is assigned a Checkup posture token. Additionally, if the audit server detects at least one Severity 4 vulnerability on the end-user machine, a Checkup posture token is assigned.

- **Infected**—This state is applicable if either the Antivirus real-time engine is not active or the audit server detects at least one Severity 5 vulnerability on the host.

The Internet, end-user, quarantine, and management VLANs continue to be configured as described in Chapter 13. Table 14-1 lists the different network segments in SecureMe.

Table 14-1   *VLAN Assignment*

Network Segment	VLAN
Internet	5
End-user	10–14
Quarantine/Remediation	15
Management	20

Steps for Configuring NAC in a Medium-Size Enterprise

In this section, we cover the configuration needed to meet the requirements listed in the "Network Requirements" section. The major configuration stages are listed as follows:

- Catalyst 6500 CatOS configuration
- VPN 3000 concentrator configuration
- QualysGuard Audit Server configuration
- Altiris Server configuration
- Trend Micro Policy Server configuration
- Cisco Secure ACS configuration
- CSA-MC Server configuration
- End-user clients

Catalyst 6500 CatOS Configuration

To meet the requirements that SecureMe has listed for the NAC Framework solution, the following are the major configuration steps on the Catalyst 6500 switch running CatOS. The solution requires you to configure NAC-L2-IP because you do not have a requirement to authenticate the end users before granting them network access. This way you can rule out NAC-L2-801.X and configure the switch for NAC-L2-IP.

Step 1   Configure the RADIUS server information on the switch. The RADIUS server in this example is 172.18.20.185 and is declared as the primary RADIUS server. The RADIUS shared secret key is cisco123cisco.

```
set radius server 172.18.20.185 primary
set radius key cisco123cisco
```

Step 2 Enable EAP over UDP (EOU) on the switch.

```
set eou enable
```

Step 3 Enable EOU on the switch ports that require posture validation. Port 3/
48 is exempt from posture validation because it is a trunk port connected
to Catalyst 6506 core switch. Therefore, EOU is enabled on the switch
ports 3/1 through 3/47.

```
set port eou 3/1-47 auto
```

Step 4 Optionally, if you have any previously configured Access Control Lists
on the switch, you can remove them by using the **clear security acl all**
command, as shown here:

```
clear security acl all
```

Step 5 Configure a policy-based ACL to allow the necessary services for NAC-
L2-IP and to restrict access based on the posture of the end-host
machines.

Permit ARP:

```
set security acl ip nac permit arp
set security acl ip nac permit arp-inspection any any
```

Permit DHCP snooping:

```
set security acl ip nac permit dhcp-snooping
```

Allow EAPoUDP communication:

```
set security acl ip nac permit eapoudp
```

Allow DHCP communication:

```
set security acl ip nac permit udp any eq 67 any
set security acl ip nac permit udp any eq 68 any
```

Optionally, permit DNS services to resolve any internal hosts for
remediation or used by URL redirect.

```
set security acl ip nac permit udp any any eq 53
```

Create an Access Control List entry (ACE) that defines the level of access
Healthy hosts will have after security posture validation. In the SecureMe
network, Healthy hosts get full access to the network. The name of the
Healthy policy group is Healthy_hosts. This name must match the
Healthy policy group name defined in the Cisco Secure ACS server,
shown in the section "Cisco Secure ACS Configuration."

```
set security acl ip nac permit ip group Healthy_hosts any
```

For the hosts that are not in compliance with security policies, allow them limited access as quarantined hosts. In this example, the Quarantine policy group name is Quarantine_hosts. The Quarantine hosts should access only the Quarantine network (172.18.15.0). This way, the Altiris Quarantine solution can update the necessary software on the end hosts. The Quarantine hosts are also given access to the Trend Micro Policy Server so that they can update their latest antivirus signature files.

```
set security acl ip nac permit ip group Quarantine_hosts 172.18.15.0
  0.0.0.255
set security acl ip nac permit ip 172.18.15.0 0.0.0.255 group
  Quarantine_hosts
set security acl ip nac permit ip group Quarantine_hosts host
  172.18.20.187
set security acl ip nac permit ip host 172.18.20.187 group
  Quarantine_hosts
```

For hosts that are declared infected or are assigned a Checkup posture token, you can allow them limited access in the network so that they are patched accordingly. In this example, two policy group names are defined: Infected_hosts and Checkup_hosts. Both Infected hosts and Checkup hosts should access only the remediation server in the Quarantine network (172.18.15.190) and the Trend Micro Policy Server in the Management network (172.18.20.187).

```
set security acl ip nac permit ip group Infected_hosts host
  172.18.15.190
set security acl ip nac permit ip host 172.18.15.190 group
  Infected_hosts
set security acl ip nac permit ip group Infected_hosts host
  172.18.20.187
set security acl ip nac permit ip host 172.18.20.187 group
  Infected_hosts
set security acl ip nac permit ip group Checkup_hosts host 172.18.15.190
set security acl ip nac permit ip host 172.18.15.190 group Checkup_hosts
set security acl ip nac permit ip group Checkup_hosts host 172.18.20.187
set security acl ip nac permit ip host 172.18.20.187 group Checkup_hosts
```

If an end-user machine is declared agentless, the Cisco Secure ACS server can assign a Transition posture token. The hosts in that state should be allowed to access the audit server. In this example, the policy group name Transition_hosts is defined. Transition hosts should access only the audit server in the Quarantine network (172.18.15.189).

```
set security acl ip nac permit ip group Transition_hosts host
  172.18.15.189
set security acl ip nac permit ip host 172.18.15.189 group
  Transition_hosts
```

Step 6 Commit the configured ACL.

```
commit security acl all
```

Step 7 Map the ACL to the VLAN that will be used for NAC Layer 2 IP. In this case, VLAN 10 is used for the user network. Apply the **set security acl map nac** command to all user VLANs.

```
set security acl map nac 10
```

This completes the configuration of the Catalyst 6500 switch for NAC-L2-IP.

VPN 3000 Concentrator Configuration

Based on the requirements put forward by SecureMe, the VPN 3000 concentrator is set up for two user groups:

- **SecureMe**—This group is used by SecureMe employees when they need access to the corporate network over the remote-access VPN tunnel. All employee machines are required to run CTA. If their machines are Healthy, they get full access to the network. If their machines are not compliant, they are quarantined until they update their software and apply appropriate patches to become compliant.

- **Contractors**—This group is used by contractors who log in to the corporate network to access a certain application (using TCP port 2005). The application resides on the management network and has an IP address of 172.18.20.100. The access to this application is controlled by using filters on this group. The contractors are not expected to have CTA installed on their machines.

The user groups are set up on the concentrator under **Configuration > User Management > Groups > Add Group**. Table 14-2 lists the two groups with their passwords and group type.

Table 14-2 *Adding User Groups in VPN 3000 Concentrator*

Group Name	Password	Type
SecureMe	S3cur3M3	Internal
Contractor	C0ntract0r	Internal

You need to configure two filters on the concentrators to achieve the listed requirements. The first filter (default filter for NAC) is configured to restrict SecureMe employees from gaining full network access until their posture is fully verified. The other filter is used to limit contractors to the application that they need access to. Before you configure a filter, you need to define the inbound and outbound rules. Table 14-3 shows the configuration of four rules: NAC-Def-In, NAC-Def-Out, Consult-In, and Consult-Out.

Table 14-3   *Inbound and Outbound Rules in the Filters*

Parameters	NAC-Def-In	NAC-Def-Out	Consult_In	Consult_Out
Direction	Inbound	Outbound	Inbound	Outbound
Action	Forward	Forward	Forward	Forward
Protocol	UDP	UDP	TCP	TCP
Source address	172.18.200.0	172.18.0.2	172.18.200.0	172.18.20.189
Source wildcard mask	0.0.0.255	0.0.0.0	0.0.0.255	0.0.0.0
Source port	Range 21862–21862	Range 0–65535	Range 0–65535	Range 2005–2005
Destination address	172.18.0.2	172.18.200.0	172.18.20.189	172.18.200.0
Destination wildcard Mask	0.0.0.0	0.0.0.255	0.0.0.0	0.0.0.255
Destination port	Range 0–65535	Range 21862–21862	Range 2005–2005	Range 0–65535

After the rules have been added into the system, the next step is to define two filters that were described earlier. The filters are defined at **Configuration > Policy Management > Traffic Management > Filters > Add Filter**. Table 14-4 lists the two filters, the default action of each filter, and the rules that each filter contains. The NAC-Default filter contains NAC-Def-In and NAC-Def-Out; the Contract-fltr contains Consult-In and Consult-Out.

Table 14-4   *Filters to Restrict Traffic on Groups*

Filter Name	Default Action	Rules in Filter
NAC-Default	Drop	NAC-Def-In, NAC-Def-Out
Contract-fltr	Drop	Consult-In, Consult-Out

After the filters are defined, you can apply Contract-fltr to the Contractor user group by navigating to **Configuration > User Management > Groups > Modify Contractor > General** and by selecting **Contract-fltr** from the **Filter** drop-down menu. Click **Apply** when finished.

Apply the NAC-Default filter to the SecureMe group, defined earlier under **Configuration > User Management > Groups > Modify SecureMe > NAC**. Select **NAC-Default** from the **Default ACL** drop-down menu. As the last step, select the **Enable NAC** option and click **Apply**.

Audit Server Configuration

The audit server (QualysGuard Scanner Appliance) needs to be installed on the network before it can be configured for NAC. After installing the appliance, log into it by browsing to the LAN interfaces IP address. Create a new NAC policy by clicking the **New Policy** icon. Under **Policy Title**, enter the name of the NAC policy as **NAC-Policy** and make it the default NAC policy.

Configure the polling intervals, APT evaluation method, and validation and revalidation options, as shown in Figure 14-5.

Figure 14-5 *QualysGuard NAC Configuration*

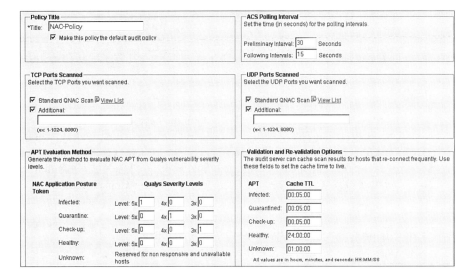

The preliminary polling interval is set to 30 seconds to instruct the Cisco Secure ACS server to check back with the Scanner Appliance. This provides enough time for the Scanner Appliance to complete the host scan. If the Scanner Appliance is still busy auditing a host, the Cisco Secure ACS server contacts it when the preliminary polling interval expires. The Qualys scanner sends back a new polling interval (following interval), configured as 15 seconds. After this interval, Cisco Secure ACS server attempts to contact the Qualys scanner again to see if it has finished the scan. Table 14-5 shows a mapping of different posture tokens with respect to the number of vulnerabilities detected on the end-user machine.

Table 14-5 *Number of Vulnerabilities to Posture Token Mapping*

Number of Vulnerabilities	Posture Token
At least one Severity 5	Infected
At least one Severity 4	Quarantine
At least one Severity 3	Checkup

For a machine that does not have any level 3, 4, or 5 severities, the Scanner Appliance assigns a Healthy posture token.

The cache TTL for Infected, Quarantined, and Checkup is set to 5 minutes. This way, a host in either Infected, Quarantine, or Checkup state will be reaudited if the machine is patched using the Altiris patch-management software. Click **Save** to store the settings.

Altiris Quarantine Solution Configuration

SecureMe wants to ensure that it has a database of all the end-host machines that exist in its network. Even though the Altiris Quarantine solution is already deployed, SecureMe wants to take advantage of its Network Discovery feature. To enable this feature, consult Chapter 12, "Remediation," and follow the steps described in the "Altiris Network Discovery" section.

The Altiris Notification Server determines whether end-user machines are running a specific version of software before being granted access to the network. If the end-user machine does not meet minimum requirements, a client message can direct users to the URL of the remediation server in the Quarantine network. Complete the following steps to configure posture policies on the Altiris Notification Server:

Step 1 Access the Altiris Notification Server Console and click the **Configuration** tab.

Step 2 **Select Solutions Settings > Network Access > Policies.**

Step 3 Right-click the **Posture** folder.

Step 4 Select **New > Posture Policy**.

Step 5 Right-click the **New Posture Policy** and select **Rename**; enter **Quarantine Policy** as the policy name.

Step 6 Select the **Enable** check box to run the policy.

Step 7 Enter a description of **This Policy Is for Quarantined Hosts**.

Step 8 Select the **Quarantine** posture from the drop-down list.

Step 9 Click the **Collection** link and select **All Computers**.

Step 10 Enter a message such as **Your Connection Is Limited to the Quarantine Network As Your Machine Is Not Compliant with the Security Policies**. This message will be displayed on end-user devices when the criteria of the policy are met.

Step 11 Enter a URL of **http://172.18.15.190**. This way, the Quarantine hosts will be redirected to the Altiris remediation server.

Trend Micro Policy Server Configuration

SecureMe already has a Trend Micro Policy Server deployed for its antivirus solution. The NAC Framework solution can leverage the server and define rules to meet the security posture criteria. Based on the information from the end-host machine, the policy server can assign the appropriate application posture token to the end-host machine.

Table 14-6 shows the configuration of security posture criteria that the policy server uses to assign the appropriate posture token. The Client Real-Time Scan status checks whether the end-host machine has the real-time scan enabled. The Client Scan Engine Version Currency is used to check whether the end host machine's scan engine is up-to-date. Finally, the Client Virus Pattern File Status determines how up-to-date the signature file is. Based on the application posture token, the policy server can take the configured action, such as to update the signature file on the end-host machine.

By default, the policy server has the security criteria defined in Table 14-6. You can tweak this as necessary to meet any future needs.

Table 14-6   *Application Posture Token and Security Posture Criteria*

Posture Token	Client Real-Time Scan Status	Client Scan Engine Version	Client Virus Pattern File Status	Action
Healthy	Enabled	Up-to-date	Up-to-date	None
Checkup	Enabled	Up-to-date	At least one version older	1) Update components 2) Perform automatic cleanup
Quarantine	Enabled	Up-to-date	At least five versions older	1) Update components 2) Perform automatic cleanup and scan
Infected	Disabled	Unknown	Unknown	1) Enable real-time scan 2) Send a message to client

Cisco Secure ACS Configuration

Install and configure ACS following the procedure described in Chapter 8, "Cisco Secure Access Control Server." Then follow the next steps to create both a NAC-L2-IP profile and a NAC-L3-IP-VPN profile (for VPN users). For the NAC-L2-IP profile, you will create policies to validate the previously listed requirements and then create authorization rules to enforce them. You will map the audit server to scan the hosts that are not currently running CTA. For the NAC-L3-IP-VPN, you will create policies to check the posture state for the VPN user who are SecureMe employees and connect to SecureMe user group. However, those machines will not be audited if they are declared agentless. Configuration of the Cisco Secure ACS server can be completed by following these tasks.

NOTE   If you have already defined the internal posture-validation policies as described in Chapter 8, you do not need to re-create them here. Just edit them where needed.

Import ADF Files

Complete the following steps to import ADF files:

Step 1   Import Trend's ADF file into ACS using this command:

```
CSUtil.exe -addAVP Trend-AV.adf
```

Step 2   Import QualysGuard's ADF file into ACS using this command:

```
CSUtil.exe -addAVP Qualys-AV.adf
```

Step 3   Import Altiris's ADF file into ACS using this command:

```
CSUtil.exe -addAVP Altiris-AV.adf
```

Do not forget to restart CSAdmin, CSAuth, and CSLog from the services control panel.

NOTE   The .adf files must be obtained from the respective companies providing the NAC partner software.

Configure Network Access Filters

NAFs are used to separate NAC-L3-IP devices from NAC-L2-IP devices, thus enabling you to apply a different network access profile to each. Create a NAF named NAF-L2 that will include the Catalyst 6500 switch and a NAF named NAF-L3 to include the VPN 3000 concentrator. These NAFs will be mapped to the network access profiles (NAPs) so that inbound RADIUS requests are processed by the profile for only the devices you selected in the NAF. Follow these steps to create NAPs:

Step 1   Create an L2-IP network access profile using the NAC L2 IP template and name it **NAC-L2-IP**. Do not forget to mark it **Active**.

Step 2   Create an L3-IP network access profile using the NAC L3 IP template and name it **NAC-L3-IP-VPN**. Mark it **Active**.

Step 3   Select **NAC-L2-IP** and apply **NAF-L2** to it.

Step 4   Select **NAC-L3-IP-VPN** and apply **NAF-L3** to it.

Create Posture-Validation Policies

Complete the following steps to create posture-validation policies:

Step 1   Navigate to **Posture Validation > Internal Posture Validation Setup**.

Step 2   Edit the existing posture-validation policy, NAC-SAMPLE-CTA-POLICY, to check whether the version of CTA is greater than or equal to 2.0.0.30. Also rename the policy to just **CTA-Policy**.

Step 3   Create a new internal posture-validation policy named **Windows-SP-Policy** that will checked if the latest service pack is installed for that OS. Add the conditions shown in Table 14-7 to accomplish this.

Table 14-7   *Windows Service Pack Posture-Validation Rule*

#	Condition	Posture Token
1	(Cisco:PA:OS-Type contains Windows 2003 AND Cisco:Host:ServicePacks contains 1) OR (Cisco:PA:OS-Type contains Windows XP AND Cisco:Host:ServicePacks contains 2) OR (Cisco:PA:OS-Type contains Windows 2000 AND Cisco:Host:ServicePacks contains 4)	Cisco:PA:Healthy
2	Default	Cisco:PA:Quarantine

Step 4   Create a new internal posture-validation policy named **Windows-Hotfix-Policy** that checks whether the critical hotfixes are installed for the respective OSes. Add the conditions shown in Table 14-8 to accomplish this.

Table 14-8   *Windows Hotfix Posture-Validation Rule*

#	Condition	Posture Token
1	Cisco:PA:OS-Type contains Windows 2003 AND	Cisco:PA:Healthy
	Cisco:Host:HotFixes contains KB912812 AND	
	Cisco:Host:HotFixes contains KB899585 AND	
	Cisco:Host:HotFixes contains KB908531 AND	
	Cisco:Host:HotFixes contains KB911562 AND	
	Cisco:Host:HotFixes contains KB911565 AND	
	Cisco:Host:HotFixes contains KB918222	
2	Cisco:PA:OS-Type contains Windows XP AND	Cisco:PA:Healthy
	Cisco:Host:HotFixes contains KB912812 AND	
	Cisco:Host:HotFixes contains KB899585 AND	
	Cisco:Host:HotFixes contains KB918222	
3	Cisco:PA:OS-Type contains Windows 2000 AND	Cisco:PA:Healthy
	Cisco:Host:HotFixes contains KB912812 AND	
	Cisco:Host:HotFixes contains KB899585 AND	
	Cisco:Host:HotFixes contains KB918222	
4	Default	Cisco:PA:Quarantine

Set Up Trend Micro Policy Server

After you have successfully imported the ADF, complete the following steps to add the external antivirus policy server in Cisco Secure ACS:

Step 1   Access the Cisco Secure ACS administration window, click **Posture Validation**, and click **External Posture Validation.**

Step 2   Click **Add Server** to add a new antivirus policy server and specify a name of **Trend-Policy** in the **Name** field. In the **Description** field, add a description of **This Is Trend Micro Antivirus Server Definition**. Select the **Primary Server Configuration** check box. Specify the URL of **http://172.18.20.187:4343/officescan** for the external antivirus policy server.

Step 3   Enter the user credentials (username = **admin,** password = **cisco123**, in this case) that Cisco Secure ACS will use to access the external antivirus policy server.

Step 4   A Timeout value of 10 seconds is configured so that Cisco Secure ACS waits for a result from the external server and domain name resolution.

Step 5 Select **Trend:AV** as the credentials to be sent to the antivirus policy server, and then click **Add** to add the antivirus policy server.

When the Trend Micro Policy Server is defined, the Cisco Secure ACS server can forward AV information from the end-host machines to the policy server.

Set Up Altiris Server

Complete the following steps to add the Altiris server in Cisco Secure ACS:

Step 1 Access the Cisco Secure ACS administration window, click **Posture Validation**, and click **External Posture Validation.**

Step 2 Click **Add Server** to add the Altiris server, and specify a name of **Altiris-Policy** in the **Name** field. In the **Description** field, add a description of **This Is Altiris Notification Server Definition**. Select the **Primary Server Configuration** check box. Specify the URL of **http://172.18.20.188/altiris/QuarantineSolution/NACPostureValidationServer.aspx**.

Step 3 Select **Altiris:PA** as the credentials to be sent to the Altiris server and then click **Add** to add the server.

Set Up QualysGuard Scanner

To add an audit server, navigate to **Posture Validation > External Posture Validation Audit Setup**. Click **Add Server** to add a new QualysGuard Scanner Appliance. Specify **Qualys** as the name and select **Do Not Audit These Hosts**. Specify the IP addresses of the printers and IP Phones that will not be audited.

Select **Qualys** as the **Audit Server Vendor** under **Use These Audit Servers** and enable **Primary Server Configuration**. Specify the URL for the audit server to submit the audit request to. In our example, the URL to submit the request is **http://172.18.15.189/audit.cgi**. The username is *nac_user* and the password is *cisco123* (shown as asterisks).

Table 14-9 lists the **Audit Flow Settings** for the audit server.

Table 14-9 *Audit Flow Settings for Audit Server*

#	Attribute	Value
1	Use This Posture Token While Audit Server Does Not Yet Have a Posture-Validation result	Transition
2	Polling Intervals and Session Timeout	Use timeouts Sent by Audit Server for Polling Intervals and Session-Timeout
3	Maximum Amount of Times the Audit Server Should Be Polled	3
2	Policy String to Be Sent to the Audit Server	NAC-Policy

The QualysGuard is mapped to Network Access Profile (NAP) to provide the audit server services for agentless hosts. Browse to **Network Access Profiles** and select the **Posture Validation** link next to the L2-IP NAP. Under **Determine Posture Validation for NAH**, click the **Select Audit** button and select the Qualys Audit Server. Define a fail-open policy so that a posture token of Checkup is assigned to the user if the ACS cannot communicate with the Scanner Appliance within 30 seconds of the request. After defining the mapping to a NAP, click **Submit** and **Done** to complete this step.

Configure Shared Components Profile

Complete the following steps to configure shared components on the Cisco Secure ACS server:

Step 1 Create the downloadable IP ACLs shown in Table 14-10. Remember that downloadable IP ACLs are under Shared Profile Components. These downloadable ACLs are mapped to the VPN sessions on the VPN 3000 concentrator.

Table 14-10 *Downloadable IP ACLs*

Name	Name	ACL Definitions
NAC_Healthy_ACL	Healthy_ACL	permit ip any any
NAC_Quarantine_ACL	Quarantine_ACL	remark If host is Quarantine restrict network access
		remark Allow DHCP and DNS
		permit udp any any eq 67
		permit udp any any eq 53
		remark Allow EAPoUDP for CTA client
		permit udp any any eq 21862
		remark Allow access to Quarantine network
		permit ip any 172.18.15.0 0.0.0.255
NAC_Checkup_ACL	Checkup_ACL	remark If host is in Checkup State
		remark Allow DHCP and DNS
		permit udp any any eq 67
		permit udp any any eq 53
		remark Allow EAPoUDP for CTA client
		permit udp any any eq 21862
		remark Allow access to Quarantine network
		permit ip any 172.18.15.0 0.0.0.255

continues

Table 14-10 *Downloadable IP ACLs (Continued)*

Name	Name	ACL Definitions
NAC_Infected_ACL	Infected_ACL	remark If host is Infected
		remark Allow DHCP and DNS
		permit udp any any eq 67
		permit udp any any eq 53
		remark Allow EAPoUDP for CTA client
		permit udp any any eq 21862
		remark Allow access to Remediation Server
		permit ip any host 172.18.15.190
NAC_Transition_ACL	Transition_ACL	remark If host is in Transition
		remark Allow DHCP and DNS
		permit udp any any eq 67
		permit udp any any eq 53
		remark Allow EAPoUDP for CTA client
		permit udp any any eq 21862
		remark Allow access to QualysGuard Scanner
		permit ip any host 172.18.15.189

Step 2 Create the RADIUS Authorization Components shown in Table 14-11.
Remember that RACs are also defined under Shared Profile Components.

Table 14-11 *RADIUS Authorization Components*

Name	Assigned Attributes		
	Vendor	Attribute	Value
NAC-HEALTHY-L2-RAC	IETF	Session-Timeout(27)	36000
	Cisco IOS/PIX 6.0	cisco-av-pair(1)	sec:pg=Healthy_hosts
	IETF	Termination-Action (29)	RADIUS-Request(1)
NAC-QUARANTINE-L2-RAC	IETF	Session-Timeout(27)	3600
	Cisco IOS/PIX 6.0	cisco-av-pair(1)	sec:pg=Quarantine_hosts
	IETF	Termination-Action (29)	RADIUS-Request(1)
	Cisco IOS/PIX 6.0	cisco-av-pair(1)	url-redirect=http// 172.18.15.190
NAC-TRANSITION-L2-RAC	IETF	Session-Timeout(27)	3600
	Cisco IOS/PIX 6.0	cisco-av-pair(1)	sec:pg=Transition_hosts
	IETF	Termination-Action (29)	RADIUS-Request(1)

Table 14-11 *RADIUS Authorization Components (Continued)*

| Name | Assigned Attributes | | |
	Vendor	Attribute	Value
	IETF	Session-Timeout(27)	3600
	Cisco IOS/PIX 6.0	cisco-av-pair(1)	sec:pg=Infected_hosts
	IETF	Termination-Action (29)	RADIUS-Request(1)
	Cisco IOS/PIX 6.0	cisco-av-pair(1)	url-redirect=http// 172.18.15.190
NAC-CHECKUP-L2-RAC	IETF	Session-Timeout(27)	3600
	Cisco IOS/PIX 6.0	cisco-av-pair(1)	sec:pg=Checkup_hosts
	IETF	Termination-Action (29)	RADIUS-Request(1)
	Cisco IOS/PIX 6.0	cisco-av-pair(1)	url-redirect=http// 172.18.15.190

Configure Posture-Validation Rules for NAPs

Complete the following steps to configure posture-validation rules for NAPs:

Step 1   Configure the posture-validation rules for the NAC-L2-IP profile by selecting the appropriate link under Network Access Profiles.

Step 2   No modifications are needed for the required credential types. In the Action section, select the following internal posture-validation policies: **CTA-Policy**, **Windows-SP-Policy**, and **Windows-Hotfix-Policy**.

Step 3   Under Select External Posture Validation Server, select **Altiris**. As a failure action policy, select **Cisco:PA** with a posture token of **Checkup**. Disable **Reject User** if it has a check mark.

Step 4   Under Select External Posture Validation Server, select **Trend-Policy**. As a failure action policy, select **Cisco:PA** with a posture token of **Checkup**. Disable **Reject User** if it has a check mark.

Step 5   Under the System Posture Token Configuration section, fill in a PA message for the Healthy, Checkup, Infected, Transition, and Quarantine System Posture Tokens. Examples are as follows:

— **Healthy**—The security posture of this machine has been analyzed and found to comply with the company security policy. You have been granted access to the network.

— **Infected**—The overall security posture of this host has been analyzed, and you are identified as an infected host. Please open a web browser and follow the instructions on the page. The installation of updated software will start automatically once the Altiris server pushes those updates to bring the machine into compliance with the corporate security policy. Once complete, you will be granted access to the network.

— **Checkup**—The security posture of this host has not been confirmed, or this host has been identified as a host that does not meet the minimum security policies. Please open a web browser and follow the instructions on the page. The installation of updated software will start automatically once the Altiris server pushes those updates to bring the machine into compliance with the corporate security policy. Once complete, you will be granted access to the network.

— **Transition**—The security posture of this machine is being determined. You have limited access to the network until the posture-assessment process is completed.

— **Quarantine**—The overall security posture of this host has been analyzed and does not meet the minimum security policy of this company. Please open a web browser and follow the instructions on the page. The installation of updated software will start automatically once the Altiris server pushes those updates to bring the machine into compliance with the corporate security policy. Once complete, you will be granted access to the network.

For the Quarantine system posture token, fill in the **URL Redirect** field with the URL of the web server on the quarantine network (example: http://172.18.15.190).

Configure Authorization Rules for NAPs

Complete the following steps to configure authorization rules for NAPs:

Step 1 Configure the authorization rules for the NAC-L2-IP profile by selecting the **Authorization** link next to the profile and configuring the rules according to Table 14-12.

Table 14-12 *L2-IP Authorization Rules*

Condition		Action		
User Group	**System Posture Token**	**Deny Access**	**Shared RAC**	**Downloadable ACL**
Any	Healthy	❏	NAC-HEALTHY-L2-RAC	NAC_Healthy_ACL
Any	Infected	❏	NAC-INFECTED-L2-RAC	NAC_Infected_ACL
Any	Checkup	❏	NAC-CHECKUP-L2-RAC	NAC_Checkup_ACL

Table 14-12 *L2-IP Authorization Rules (Continued)*

Condition		Action		
User Group	**System Posture Token**	**Deny Access**	**Shared RAC**	**Downloadable ACL**
Any	Transition	❏	NAC-TRANSITION-L2-RAC	NAC_Transition_ACL
Any	Quarantine	❏	NAC-QUARANTINE-L2-RAC	NAC_Quarantine_ACL
If a condition is not defined or there is no matched condition		❏	NAC-QUARANTINE-L2-RAC	NAC_Quarantine_ACL

> **Step 2**   Configure the authentication rules for the NAC-L3-IP-VPN profile by selecting the **Authentication** link under the Network Access Profiles and configuring the rules according to Table 14-13.

Table 14-13 *L3-IP-VPN Authorization Rules*

Condition		Action		
User Group	**System Posture Token**	**Deny Access**	**Shared RAC**	**Downloadable ACL**
Any	Healthy	❏	NAC-HEALTHY-L2-RAC	NAC_Healthy_ACL
Any	Infected	❏	NAC-INFECTED-L2-RAC	NAC_Infected_ACL
Any	Checkup	❏	NAC-CHECKUP-L2-RAC	NAC_Checkup_ACL
Any	Quarantine	❏	NAC-QUARANTINE-L2-RAC	NAC_Quarantine_ACL
If a condition is not defined or there is no matched condition		❏	NAC-QUARANTINE-L2-RAC	NAC_Quarantine_ACL

> **Step 3**   Restart the ACS processes from **System Configuration > Services Control**.

This completes the configuration steps for ACS.

CSA-MC Server Configuration

You can leverage the CSA-MC server, already installed in the SecureMe network, to create a CSA agent kit that has the CTA software preconfigured.

Select **Install Cisco Trust Agent** to bundle CTA during the installation and then select **ctasilent-win-2.x.x.x.exe** under the installer drop-down menu. The CTA version depends on the version of the CSAMC server that you are using in your network.

End-User Clients

The configuration of the end-user clients simply consists of deploying the CSA agent kit to your end users. You can push the updated CSA agent kit by using the Altiris server.

This completes the configuration steps for the end-user clients.

Monitoring and Troubleshooting NAC in a Medium-Size Enterprise

This section covers some common troubleshooting methods you can use when diagnosing NAC-related problems. The first two methods pertain to the NADs, and the last pertains to Cisco Secure ACS. All three methods combined provide you with a complete end-to-end picture of how, when, where, and why NCA posture-validated an end host.

Diagnosing NAC on Catalyst 6500 Switch

show commands are very useful in determining the current state and posture of an end host. However, they do not provide a historical reference of how (or why) the host ended up there. In the Catalyst 6500 switch running CAT OS, you can verify the NAC Layer 2 IP functionality and posture using the **show policy group all** command. It shows you the configured NAC group name and the hosts that are bound to each group. In Example 14-1, a Healthy group name is displayed; the associated IP address is 172.18.10.100, and this host is connected to switch port 3/10.

Example 14-1 *Verifying NAC Layer 2 IP Posture in CatOS*

```
6500 (enable) show policy group all
-------------------------------------------------
Group Name            = Healthy
Group Id              = 1
No.of IP Addresses    = 1
Is Changed flag       = 0
Src Type              = ACL CLI
      List of Hosts in group.
      -----------------------
      Interface    = GigabitEthernet3/10
      IpAddress    = 172.18.10.100
      Src type     = NAC
```

In the Catalyst 6500 switch, you can also use **show eou all** to display a table of all clients connected to NAC-enabled ports on the switch. The output contains the IP address of the client, the port it is connected to, the authentication method it used to authenticate itself, the system posture token assigned to it, and the time since the last posture validation. Example 14-2 shows sample output from this command.

Example 14-2 *show eou all* Command Output

```
6500# show eou all


Eou Summary
-----------
Eou Global State = enabled
```

Example 14-2   *show eou all Command Output (Continued)*

```
Currently Validating EOU Sessions = 0
mNo/pNo   Host Ip              Nac_Token   Host_Fsm_State   Username
-------   ---------------      ---------   -------------    --------
3/10      172.18.10.100        Healthy     authenticated    SECURITY:JaneFranklin
3/16      172.18.10.73         Quarantine  authenticated    SECURITY:JackFranklin
```

The **show eou ip** *ip-address* command displays the NAC policy applied to the host, including the assigned system posture token, the downloadable IP ACL, and the URL Redirect link and ACL—all are important in determining what authorization components are applied to the end host after the posture-validation process completes. Example 14-3 shows sample output from this command for a Quarantined host.

Example 14-3   *show eou ip ip-address Command Output*

```
6500 (enable) show eou ip-address 172.18.10.73
Port      EOU-State IP Address       MAC Address          Critical-Status
--------  --------- ---------------  ----------------- ---------------
 3/16     auto      172.18.10.73     00-00-86-4d-a2-52 No

Port      FSM State     Auth Type    SQ-Timeout Session Timeout
--------  ------------- -----------  ---------- ---------------
 3/16     authenticated eap          300        60

Port      Posture       URL Redirect
--------  ------------- -------------------
 3/16     Quarantine    http://172.18.15.190


Port      Termination action Session id
--------  ------------------ --------------------------------
 3/16     initialize         00000db9000013a2000017f60000122f

Port      PolicyGroups
--------  ------------------------------------------------------
 3/16     Quarantine-hosts
```

Additionally, you can use the **show eou config** command to display the current EoU configuration on the 6500 switch.

The EOU logs provide you with critical troubleshooting information, including the IP address of the end host, the port it is connecting to, the posture token, the downloadable ACL applied, and information on whether CTA was enabled on the host. This is helpful in troubleshooting any client connectivity issue. Example 14-4 shows an example from a Quarantined host connecting to the Catalyst 6500 switch. When a new end-user machine (172.18.10.73) tries to pass traffic through the switch, the switch identifies it as a new host and starts the posture-validation process. It detects that the host is running CTA and contacts the Cisco Secure ACS server and successfully authenticates the host machine. The

Cisco Secure ACS server assigns a Quarantine system posture token and sends a Quarantine_hosts policy group.

Example 14-4 *Quarantine Host EOU Logs*

```
%EOU-6-EOU_NEW_IP_LEARNT:EOU: New IP (172.18.10.73) and MAC (00-00-86-4d-a2-52)
  seen on port (3/16)
%EOU-6-EOU_CTA_DETECT:EOU: CTA detected on host with IP 172.18.10.73 and MAC 00-00-
  86-4d-a2-52 on port 3/16
%EOU-6-EOU_AUTH_STATUS_SUCCESS:EOU: Host with IP 172.18.10.73 and MAC 00-00-86-4d-
  a2-52 successful authenticated on port 3/16
%EOU-6-EOU_HOST_POLICY:EOU: IP 172.18.10.73 received policy group Quarantine_hosts
  on port 3/16
%EOU-6-EOU_POSTURE_TOKEN:EOU: Recvd token (Quarantine) for host IP 172.18.10.73 and
  MAC 00-00-86-4d-a2-52 on port 3/16
%EOU-6-EOU_HOSTNAME:EOU: Host Security:JackFranklin with IP 172.18.10.73 and MAC 00-
  00-86-4d-a2-52 authenticated on port 3/16
%EOU-6-EOU_AUTHTYPE:EOU: Host with IP 172.18.10.73 and MAC 00-00-86-4d-a2-52 on port
  3/16 authenticated using eap
```

Diagnosing NAC on a VPN 3000 Concentrator

As described earlier in the chapter, SecureMe provides VPN services to its employees and wants the VPN client machines to go through the posture-validation process after the IPsec tunnels are established. After establishing the IPsec SAs, the concentrator initiates the EAPoUDP process. If a response is received from the VPN client, the concentrator knows that the VPN client has an active CTA agent, as illustrated in Example 14-5. You can view the output of these logs under **Monitoring > Filterable Event Log**.

Example 14-5 *Log Output to Indicate VPN Client Sends an EAPoUDP Response*

```
749 10/21/2005 02:07:39.630 SEV=13 EAPOUDP/18 RPT=1615
EAPoUDP packet (RX)
0000: 80120018 B501A90A B501A90A 8003000C    ...............
0010: B501A90A 935BC3FF 4603A87A 80010004    .....[..F..z....
0020: BE31E6FA                               .1..

753 10/21/2005 02:07:39.630 SEV=8 EAPOUDP/3 RPT=13
EAPoUDP-Hello response received from host - PRV_IP:172.18.200.2

754 10/21/2005 02:07:39.630 SEV=7 EAPOUDP/4 RPT=13
NAC EAP association initiated - PRV_IP:172.18.200.2, EAP context:0x04096fd0
```

When the EAPoUDP session is successfully established between the VPN client and the concentrator, the concentrator contacts the RADIUS server to start a new posture-validation process by sending aaa:service=ip-admission and aaa:event=new-session RADIUS attributes. This is shown in Example 14-6.

Example 14-6 *Log Output Displaying VPN 3000 Requesting a New PV*

```
778 10/21/2005 02:07:39.640 SEV=9 NAC/23 RPT=112
NAC EAP auth_attr #1: PUB_IP:209.165.202.160, PRV_IP:172.18.200.2
  un:64.102.44.254
```

Example 14-6 *Log Output Displaying VPN 3000 Requesting a New PV (Continued)*

```
np:1022
st:25
gs:209.165.202.160
ds:172.18.0.2

780 10/21/2005 02:07:39.640 SEV=9 NAC/24 RPT=112
NAC EAP auth_attr #2: PUB_IP: 209.165.202.160, PRV_IP:172.18.200.2
  em:0x02b00005
  as:aaa:service=ip-admission
  ae:aaa:event=new-session
  sv:1
  ig:SecureMe
  ru:2
```

The RADIUS server analyzes the information received from the VPN client and returns an appropriate posture token to the concentrator. The VPN 3000 concentrator also receives the policies, such as an ACL that is applied to the VPN clients. In Example 14-7, the RADIUS sends an ACL called Healthy-435513f6. The posture token is Healthy, indicating that the VPN client meets all the configured policies on the RADIUS server.

Example 14-7 *Log Output Displaying RADIUS Server Applying Policies*

```
865 10/21/2005 00:45:46.860 SEV=4 NAC/29 RPT=6
NAC Applying filter - PUB_IP: 209.165.202.160, PRV_IP:172.18.200.2, Name:Healthy-
  435513f6, ID:8

1513 10/21/2005 02:07:42.180 SEV=8 NAC/12 RPT=12
NAC Access Accept - PUB_IP: 209.165.202.160, PRV_IP:172.18.200.1,
 user:AVCLIENTS:Administrator

1515 10/21/2005 02:07:42.180 SEV=8 NAC/14 RPT=12
NAC Access Accept - PUB_IP: 209.165.202.160, PRV_IP:172.18.200.2, Posture Token:
Healthy

1517 10/21/2005 02:07:42.180 SEV=6 NAC/7 RPT=18
NAC Access Accept - PUB_IP: 209.165.202.160, PRV_IP:172.18.200.2
```

You can monitor the IPsec VPN sessions on the concentrator by browsing to **Monitoring > Sessions**. The concentrator shows the following important information about the VPN client:

- The public and assigned IP addresses of the VPN client
- The user-group membership
- The encryption protocol used
- The login time and the duration a connection is up for
- The operating system information and the version of VPN client

- The actual encrypted and decrypted data
- The status of NAC posture assessment

Cisco Secure ACS Logging

Cisco Secure ACS provides robust NAC logging capabilities through the Passed Authentications and Failed Attempts log files. Enable and configure Cisco Secure ACS logging from **System Configuration > Logging**. The Cisco Secure ACS log files contain critical information about not only the end host, but also the NAD the end host is connecting to and the policies, profiles, and rules the end host is mapped to in Cisco Secure ACS. Consult Chapter 13, which discusses most of the common issues that occur on the Cisco Secure ACS server and how to troubleshoot them.

Summary

This chapter focused on the requirements of a medium-size enterprise to protect its network from both internal and external unknown threats. Based on the requirements, a solution was presented to the company. This chapter showed step-by-step configurations of all the devices involved. We discussed NAC-L2-IP on a Catalyst switch, NAC-L3-IP on a VPN 3000 concentrator, and the configurations of an Altiris server for remediation and QualysGuard server for agentless hosts auditing. We walked through the steps required to configure ACS and defined all the policies. Finally, we closed with a troubleshooting section that covered common problems encountered in the deployment.

Review Questions

You can find the answers to the review questions in Appendix A, "Answers to Review Questions."

1. Why was NAC-L2-IP chosen over L2-802.1X on Catalyst 6500?

    a. L2-802.1X was too complicated.

    b. Legacy switches that do not support NAC were connected to 6500.

    c. User authentication was a requirement that could be performed only with NAC-L2-IP.

    d. L3-IP is older and was replaced by NAC-L2-IP.

2. What is the purpose of the Transition system posture token?

    a. It is used for transitioning a machine from Healthy to Quarantine.

    b. It is used for transitioning a machine from Quarantine to Healthy.

    c. It is used for transitioning a machine from Agentless to Quarantine.

    d. It is used for transitioning a machine from Agentless to a system posture token determined by the audit server.

3. What are the system posture tokens used? (Multiple answers)

    a. Healthy

    b. Transition

    c. Unknown

    d. Quarantine

4. True or false: End hosts without CTA installed cannot get access to the network if they are connected to the switches.

5. True or false: Printers are authorized by defining MAC addresses in the exception list on the audit server.

This chapter covers the following topics:

- The business requirements for deploying NAC in a large enterprise
- Design and network topology for NAC in a large enterprise
- Configuring NAC in a large enterprise
- Troubleshooting NAC deployment in a large enterprise

Deploying and Troubleshooting NAC in Large Enterprises

In the previous two chapters, you learned the typical deployment scenarios in small and medium-size enterprises. This chapter demonstrates how to deploy NAC in a large enterprise, where most of the previous concepts still apply in a larger scheme.

The typical large enterprise is an organization with more than 5,000 users, all located in different geographical locations. If your business resembles the one presented here, use this chapter, along with the previous two chapters, as your deployment template.

SecureMe has grown dramatically and now has a new headquarters office in New York. It has also acquired the small company described in Chapter 13, "Deploying and Troubleshooting NAC in Small Businesses." That acquisition has become a small branch office in the Tampa, Florida, area. The SecureMe Chicago office described in Chapter 14, "Deploying and Troubleshooting NAC in Medium-Size Enterprises," has become a regional office. Figure 15-1 illustrates a high-level overview of the new infrastructure.

This chapter explains the new business and technical requirements for Network Admission Control (NAC) now that it's being deployed in a large enterprise. It details the steps necessary to integrate the small and medium sites with the new headquarters office. Network administrators, security engineers, and the management team need to develop new global security policies for admission control and authentication.

This chapter serves as a guide to network designers considering the security requirements of a large enterprise network. It takes a defense-in-depth approach to NAC and security design. This type of design focuses on the expected threats and their methods of mitigation and is based on typical scenarios for large enterprises. This strategy results in a layered approach to security, where the failure of one security system is not likely to lead to the compromise of network resources. By taking the defense-in-depth approach, this chapter provides network security engineers with information for making sound network security choices when deploying the NAC Framework.

Figure 15-1 *SecureMe's New Infrastructure*

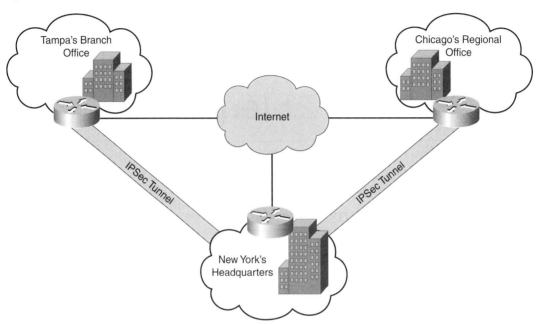

Business Requirements for Deploying NAC in a Large Enterprise

The business drivers and technical requirements outlined in Chapters 13 and 14 are still valid. However, SecureMe's business leaders are working jointly with the network administrators to define global policies and integrate existing and new NAC features within the enterprise network.

Security Policies

The following are the pre-existing and new security policies:

1. All access ports on the switches must have NAC enabled on them.

2. All Windows machines must be running the latest Service Pack available. (Windows 2003, Windows XP, and Windows 2000 are the only supported OSes.)

3. All Windows machines must install all critical hotfixes. (The network administrator determines which hotfixes are critical to the company, based on the severity of the hotfix and its applicability to the end hosts.)

4. All Windows machines must be running the Trend Micro antivirus software.

5. All Windows machines must have the latest version of the Trend antivirus signatures installed. Trend Micro policy servers communicating with Cisco Secure ACS server through the HCAP protocol control this.

6. Printers must have network access to print, but nothing else.

7. Guest access must be allowed to grant vendors and other guests' access to the Internet but not the internal network. Agentless machines, including guests, must be scanned by Qualys audit servers.

8. Admission control logs must be monitored by using CS-MARS and archived every week.

9. Remediation should be automatic through the Altiris Quarantine Solution.

Enforcement Actions

The following enforcement actions are outlined by SecureMe's leadership staff:

- **Healthy**—End hosts meeting the minimum-security policy will be granted unrestricted access to the network.

- **Quarantine**—End hosts failing to meet the minimum-security policy will be quarantined and redirected to an internal web server. The web server will provide information on the company's minimum-security requirements, and Altiris remediation servers are used to update end-user machines.

- **Transition**—This state is applicable either during host boot when all NAC-enabled applications might not be running or during an audit when posture information has not yet been obtained from the host.

- **Clientless**—End hosts without CTA will be assumed to be guests. Guests will be allowed to access the Internet but not corporate internal resources. If a business need arises for the guest's machine to access the corporate network, the guest can download CTA from the internal web server and bring the machine up to the company's minimum-security policy.

Design and Network Topology for NAC in a Large Enterprise

This section details SecureMe's new network topology:

- Branch office
- Regional office
- Corporate headquarters

Branch Office

The branch office topology is the same described in Chapter 13 for the small business. It consists of one or more switches connected to a router, which, in turn, connects to the New York corporate headquarters through a site-to-site IPsec VPN tunnel. Figure 15-2 shows the topology.

Figure 15-2 *Tampa's Branch Office*

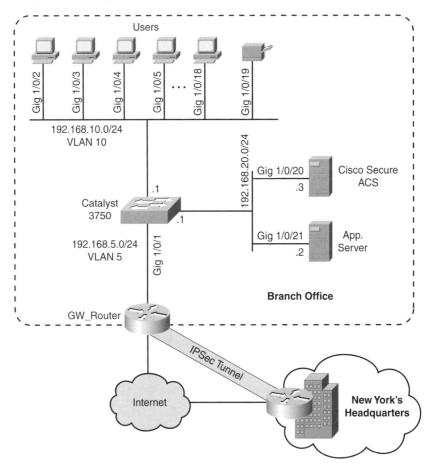

The branch office is connected to the Internet through the GW_Router and to SecureMe's New York headquarters through the site-to-site IPsec VPN tunnel. This is done to avoid the use of expensive leased lines and to encrypt data over the Internet.

NOTE Notice that the quarantine/remediation segment is removed from the topology previously illustrated in Chapter 13. This is because now the quarantined hosts are redirected to a web server in the quarantine zone at the corporate headquarters. Quarantined hosts at the branch office are also updated by an Altiris remediation server at New York's headquarters. This is discussed later in this chapter.

As mentioned in previous chapters, you should initially run NAC policies in monitor mode only. This enables you to quantify the impact of the NAC policies within your organization.

Table 15-1 lists the different network segments at the branch office in Tampa, Florida.

Table 15-1   *Branch Office 3750 Switch Port Configuration*

Network Segment	VLAN	Port(s)
Internet	5	GigabitEthernet1/0/1
End user	10	GigabitEthernet1/0/2 to GigabitEthernet1/0/19
Management	20	GigabitEthernet1/0/20 to GigabitEthernet1/0/23

As part of the integration and standardization efforts, all end-user machines at the branch office are now running the Altiris Agent, Altiris Network Access Agent, and Posture Plug-in. SecureMe's staff faced a challenge when integrating their remediation techniques at the branch office. If the Internet connection goes down, their remediation and external policy capabilities will fail because the Altiris remediation and notification servers are located at the corporate headquarters, along with the external Trend policy server. Consequently, security posture for all users attempting to connect to the network will fail and will be prevented to communicate with corporate resources. Deploying notification, remediation, and antivirus policy servers at each branch office is not a cost-effective solution. The management staff decided to put a low-cost backup DSL connection at the branch office. If their main Internet connection goes down, now they have an alternative method to connect to the corporate site.

This is something that many organizations face when deploying NAC at branch offices. In some cases, NAC is deployed at a Layer 3 router at the headquarters site. However, by doing so, none of the end-user machines at the branch office are validated unless they attempt to communicate with the resources at the corporate headquarters.

The Cisco Security Agent (CSA) is also installed in all end hosts at the branch office. CSA communicates with the CSA Management Console (CSA MC) at the corporate headquarters.

Regional Office

SecureMe's Chicago office has become a regional (medium-size) office, and the new office in New York is now the corporate headquarters. The topology at the Chicago office remains the same; however, it is now connected through a site-to-site IPsec VPN tunnel to the New York office. Figure 15-3 illustrates this.

Figure 15-3 *Chicago's Regional Office*

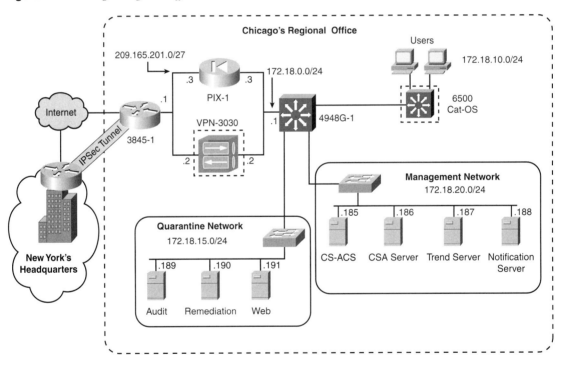

NAC Layer 3 is enabled at the VPN 3000 concentrator, and NAC-L2-IP is enabled at the Catalyst 6500 access switches. The Internet, end-user, quarantine, and management VLANs continue to be configured as described in Chapter 14. Table 15-2 lists the different network segments at the regional office in Chicago.

Table 15-2   *Chicago's Regional Office VLAN Assignment*

Network Segment	VLAN
Internet	5
End user	10
Quarantine/remediation	15
Management	20

Headquarters

The new headquarters in New York serves around 2,000 users in a 15-floor building. Each floor hosts several access Layer 2 switches. Each floor is connected to distribution switches with Layer 2 links, as illustrated in Figure 15-4.

Figure 15-4   *New York Headquarters*

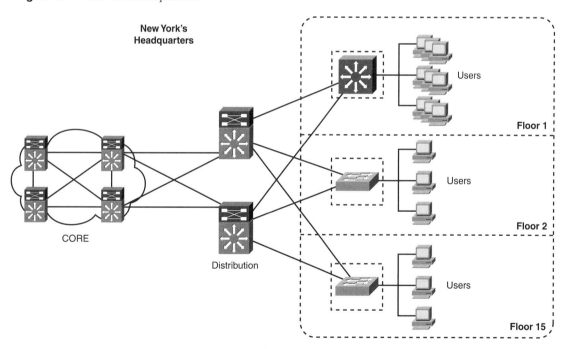

The distribution switches have redundant connections to core switches for high availability. Access switches range from Catalyst 3750s and Catalyst 4948s, to Catalyst 6500 switches in floors that have a large population of devices.

NAC-L2-802.1X is configured in most of the access switches at the New York office. The headquarters building has the following different departments:

- Call center
- Human Resources Department
- Finance Department
- Sales Department
- Engineering
- Conference center
- Data center

The following sections show how NAC is deployed on each of the different network segments at SecureMe's New York headquarters.

Call Center

The call center is one of the most populated sections of SecureMe's network. More than 800 contractors handle customer and third-party calls at SecureMe's call center. Each user's desk is equipped with a workstation connected behind a Cisco IP Phone.

TIP   Cisco IP phones are supported in NAC-L2-IP and NAC-L2-802.1X when Cisco Discovery Protocol (CDP) is enabled to provide a seamless NAC bypass function. SecureMe's network staff enables CDP to allow this functionality.

Contractors should have access only to limited corporate resources. Role-based authentication is necessary to only allow these contractors to access a customer database and an electronic ticketing system. SecureMe's network administrator configures NAC-L2-802.1X to authenticate each contractor and allow them access to limited resources based on his or her identity.

In one incident, one of these contractors brought an unauthorized wireless access point to the call center and connected several other machines to the network. SecureMe's network engineering staff was informed of the incident. To keep this from happening again, NAC-L2-802.1X machine authentication was configured on the access switches.

Human Resources, Finance, and Sales Departments

Most of SecureMe's sales representatives are now at branch offices. However, several sales representatives reside at the fourth floor in the New York office. The human resources and finance departments are also on the same floor. Role-based authentication is important for these areas because each group should not have access to the others' data. NAC-L2-802.1X is configured to authenticate all users at these segments. SecureMe uses Microsoft Windows Active Directory for the user database. Cisco Secure ACS is configured to authenticate all NAC-L2-802.1X users against the Microsoft Active Directory user database.

The human resources, finance, and sales personnel use different specialized printers and scanners to handle large printouts and high-resolution imaging. MAC Auth Bypass is configured on the Cisco Secure ACS to allow these printers and scanners to communicate to other devices within the corporate network.

Engineering

The engineering group includes SecureMe's network engineering staff, desktop support, and security teams. Most of them have two separate workstations: one for normal applications, such as email and web, and another that resides in a management VLAN to access all network resources, including routers, switches, firewalls, VPN concentrators, Cisco Secure ACS, and others. NAC-L2-IP is enabled on the management VLAN because some of their workstations are Linux systems that do not have an 802.1X supplicant. NAC-L2-802.1X is enabled on the other segment.

Conference Center

The first floor has the conference center, where SecureMe's customers and visitors can attend meetings and presentations. NAC-L2-802.1X is enabled at each port of the conference center. Guest machines are assigned to VLAN 60. Guests assigned to VLAN 60 have access to the Internet only via HTTP and HTTPS. SecureMe's partners and guests are required to have access to the Internet because they are allowed to connect to their corporate VPN devices using IPsec. The following ports and protocols are allowed for IPsec VPN and for guests to access the Internet:

- UDP port 500: Internet Key Exchange (IKE)
- Protocol 50: Encapsulation Security Protocol (ESP)
- Protocol 51: Authentication header (AH)
- UDP port 4500: Network Address Translation (NAT) traversal
- TCP port 80: HTTP
- TCP port 443: HTTPS

Data Center

NAC is not enabled at SecureMe's data center because the servers are tightly controlled with both physical security and good patch management. On the other hand, CSA is installed and running in all servers in the data center.

Remote Access VPN

SecureMe's New York headquarters have a cluster of Cisco Adaptive Security Appliance (ASA) 5550s to terminate their remote access VPN connections. Four Cisco ASA 5550s have been configured for load balancing. They run WebVPN and IPsec VPN for remote users and telecommuters. However, NAC is applied only for IPsec VPN users. Figure 15-5 illustrates how the Cisco ASA appliances are configured within New York's headquarter offices.

All Cisco ASA appliances outside/public interfaces are directly connected to the Internet routers (VLAN 5). The inside/private interfaces of each Cisco ASA are connected to a DMZ in the Catalyst 6500 Firewall Services Modules (FWSM) in VLAN 50. The pool of IP addresses to be assigned to the remote access VPN users are in the range of 10.10.200.0/24.

NOTE	Different pools of IP addresses are assigned to the remote access VPN users. However, for simplicity, in this example, 10.10.200.0/24 is used.

Each Internet-edge Catalyst 6500 is connected to other Catalyst 6500s that are connected to the rest of the corporate network.

Figure 15-5 *New York's Cisco ASAs*

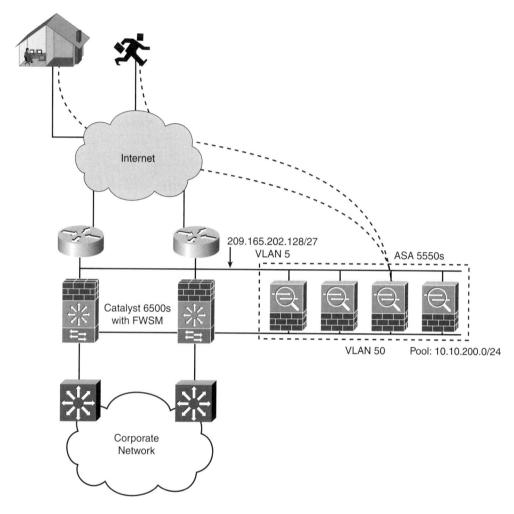

VLAN Assignments at the Headquarters with NAC-L2-802.1X

This section describes SecureMe's New York headquarters infrastructure. Figure 15-6 shows how the user, management, VPN, and quarantine segments are configured in the offices in New York.

Figure 15-6 *Scanning PDAs*

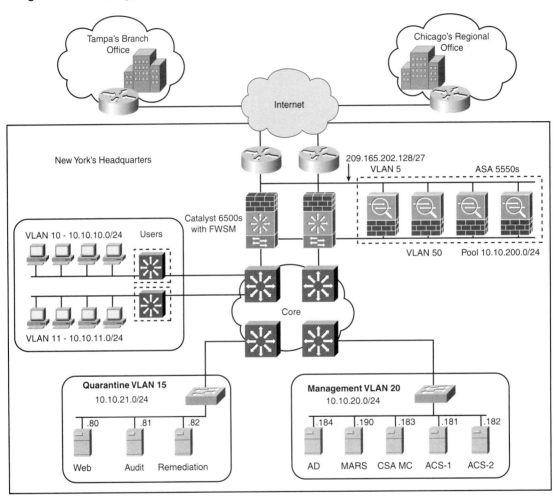

NOTE Figure 15-6 illustrates two user VLANs (VLAN 10 and 11). The office in New York has several other user VLANs; however, only two are illustrated for simplicity.

Table 15-3 lists the different network segments at the headquarters office in New York.

Table 15-3   *New York's Headquarters VLAN Assignment*

Network Segment	VLAN
Internet	5
End-user segments	10, 11, 12, 13, 14
Quarantine/remediation	15
Management	20
Remote access VPN	50
Guests	60
Contractors	70

Configuring NAC in a Large Enterprise

In this section, we cover the configuration needed to meet the requirements listed in the section "Business Requirements for Deploying NAC in a Large Enterprise" section.

NOTE   The switch, routers, and VPN concentrator configurations at the branch and regional offices are identical to the ones described in Chapters 13 and 14. The only changes are in the configuration of the Cisco Secure ACS for database replication. Additionally, the Cisco Secure ACS server at the branch office connects to external policy and audit servers at the New York headquarters office.

ACS

NAC-L2-802.1X is deployed throughout the headquarters offices in New York. This section guides you on how to configure Cisco Secure ACS for NAC-L2-802.1X.

The configuration of Cisco Secure ACS at the branch and regional offices is almost the same as demonstrated in Chapters 13 and 14. The only differences are that the Cisco Secure ACS now replicates to the ACS server(s) at the headquarters offices in New York, and the branch ACS server uses the remediation and external antivirus policy servers in New York.

Configuring NAC-L2-802.1X

NOTE Refer to Chapter 8, "Cisco Secure Access Control Server," for the installation and initial configuration of Cisco Secure ACS. The steps listed next assume that you already know how to navigate the Cisco Secure ACS web admin console.

Complete the following steps to configure NAC-L2-802.1X in Cisco Secure ACS:

Step 1 Create a NAC-L2-802.1X Network access profile using the NAC L2 IP template and name it **NAC_L2-802.1X**. Make sure that the policy is Active.

Step 2 Import Trend Micro, Qualys, and Altiris ADF files into ACS using the **CSUtil.exe** command, as you learned in previous chapters. Do not forget to restart CSAdmin, CSAuth, and CSLog from the services control panel. This file is obtained from Trend Micro when purchasing the Trend Office Scan product(s).

Step 3 Create a new policy to check whether the version of CTA is greater than or equal to 2.0.0.30. Name this policy **CTA-Policy**.

Step 4 In Chapter 13, you created an internal posture-validation policy named Windows-SP-Policy, which will check that the latest Service Pack is installed. Similarly, create one at the New York Cisco Secure ACS server. Add the conditions shown in Table 15-4 to accomplish this.

Table 15-4 *Windows Service Pack Posture-Validation Rule*

#	Condition	Posture Token
1	(Cisco:PA:OS-Type contains Windows 2003 AND Cisco:Host:ServicePacks contains 1) OR (Cisco:PA:OS-Type contains Windows XP AND Cisco:Host:ServicePacks contains 2) OR (Cisco:PA:OS-Type contains Windows 2000 AND Cisco:Host:ServicePacks contains 4)	Cisco:PA:Healthy
2	Default	Cisco:PA:Quarantine

Step 5 Create a new internal posture-validation policy named Windows-Hotfix-Policy that checks that the critical hotfixes are installed for the respective OSes, as shown in Table 15-5.

Table 15-5 *Windows Hotfix Posture-Validation Rule*

#	Condition	Posture Token
1	Cisco:PA:OS-Type contains Windows 2003 AND Cisco:Host:HotFixes contains KB912812 AND Cisco:Host:HotFixes contains KB899585 AND Cisco:Host:HotFixes contains KB908531 AND Cisco:Host:HotFixes contains KB911562 AND Cisco:Host:HotFixes contains KB911565 AND Cisco:Host:HotFixes contains KB918222	Cisco:PA:Healthy
2	Cisco:PA:OS-Type contains Windows XP AND Cisco:Host:HotFixes contains KB912812 AND Cisco:Host:HotFixes contains KB899585 AND Cisco:Host:HotFixes contains KB918222	Cisco:PA:Healthy
3	Cisco:PA:OS-Type contains Windows 2000 AND Cisco:Host:HotFixes contains KB912812 AND Cisco:Host:HotFixes contains KB899585 AND Cisco:Host:HotFixes contains KB918222	Cisco:PA:Healthy
4	Default	Cisco:PA:Quarantine

NOTE The steps to create new policies for Service Packs, hotfixes, and antivirus versions are detailed in this section. However, they can be replicated from existing Cisco Secure ACS servers. Later in this chapter, you learn how to configure database replication in Cisco Secure ACS.

Step 6 In Chapter 13, an internal posture-validation policy named Trend-AV-Policy was created. This policy checks that Trend's antivirus software is enabled and that the latest virus-definition file is loaded. On the other hand, SecureMe has integrated the antivirus posture checks with the

Trend antivirus server. Configure Cisco Secure ACS to query the Trend server for antivirus posture validation, as shown in the configuration section in Chapter 10, "Antivirus Software Integration."

Step 7 In NAC-L2-IP, downloadable IP ACLs are used as the policy-enforcement method. In NAC-L2-802.1X, VLAN assignment is used for policy enforcement. Configure Cisco Secure ACS to assign the VLANs in Table 15-6, depending on the different posture tokens and health of the machine.

Table 15-6 *Posture Tokens and VLAN Assignment*

Posture Token Name	VLAN
Healthy	VLAN 10
Quarantine	VLAN 15
Guest	VLAN 60
Contractors	VLAN 70

Step 8 Use the 10.10.21.80 web server in the **URL Redirect** field under the Radius Authorization Components (RAC). (Example: http://10.10.21.80.) Refer to Chapter 8 for complete RAC configuration in Cisco Secure ACS.

Cisco Secure ACS Database Replication

This section covers how to configure database replication on Cisco Secure ACS. Database replication enables an administrator to duplicate parts of the primary Cisco Secure ACS configuration to one or more secondary Cisco Secure ACS servers. In this case, you can configure the NAC network access devices (NADs) to use these secondary Cisco Secure ACS servers if the primary server is not reachable. When you configure database replication, you can select the specific functionality of the primary Cisco Secure ACS configuration to be replicated. You can also create automatic replication schedules.

NOTE   You have the capability of selecting the time and date for replication. These timers depend on how often you change your Cisco Secure ACS policies and configuration. Cisco Secure ACS stops authentication services during replication. The replication process does not take a long time to complete. However, because authentication services are stopped during replication, typically replication is scheduled after hours.

Cisco Secure ACS cannot be replicated with these items:

- IP address pools
- Digital certificate and private key files
- Unknown user group mappings
- Dynamically mapped users
- Service management services (under the System Configuration section)
- RDBMS synchronization parameters

NOTE   Cisco Secure ACS database replication will fail in a NAT environment. If a primary or secondary address is NATed, the database replication file will indicate a shared secret mismatch. NAT is bypassed in the branch, regional, and headquarters offices for their site-to-site VPN tunnels. Cisco Secure ACS database replication is done over TCP port 2000.

Complete the following steps to configure database replication on Cisco Secure ACS server:

Step 1   Before you start configuring replication parameters, you need to make sure that internal database replication and distributed system settings are enabled on the primary Cisco Secure ACS server and each of the secondary servers. To enable replication capabilities in Cisco Secure ACS server, go to **Interface Configuration > Advanced Options**. Make sure that the **ACS Internal Database Replication** and the **Distributed System Settings** check boxes are selected, as illustrated in Figure 15-7. Click **Submit**.

Step 2   Navigate to **System Configuration** and click **ACS Internal Database Replication**, as illustrated in Figure 15-8.

Figure 15-7 *Enabling Database-Replication Capabilities*

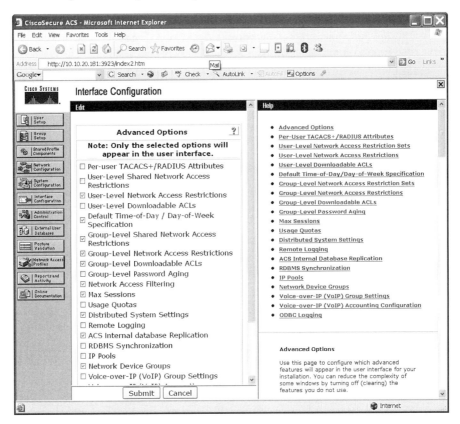

Figure 15-8 *Configuring Internal Database Replication*

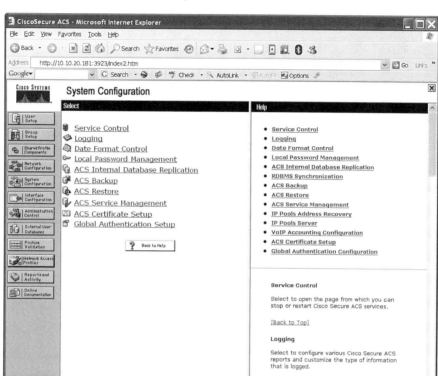

Step 3 Under Replication Components in the primary server (only), make sure that the following options are selected under the **Send** column, as illustrated in Figure 15-9.

— User and Group Database

— Distribution Table

— Interface Configuration

— Interface Security Settings

— Password Validation Settings

— EAP-FAST Master Keys and Policies

— Network Access Profiles

Figure 15-9 *Selecting Replication Components*

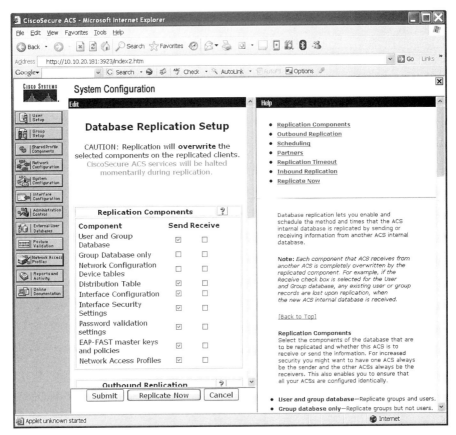

Step 4 Under each secondary server, make sure that the same replication components are selected under the **Receive** column.

Step 5 Configure the scheduling parameters as illustrated in Figure 15-10. In this example, automatic replication is scheduled for 12:00 a.m. (midnight) every day of the week. Select the times that best suit your deployment strategies and your security policies and procedures.

Figure 15-10   *Scheduling Replication and Adding Replication Partners*

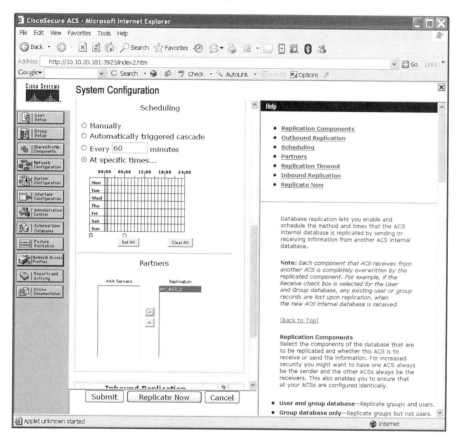

Step 6   Move the secondary server(s) to the replication partners column, as illustrated in Figure 15-10. In this example, the server called NY_ACS_2 is added. If you do not see any of the secondary servers listed in the AAA Servers column, add your AAA servers under **Network Configuration > AAA Servers**.

Step 7   On the secondary Cisco Secure ACS servers (where replication is done inbound), select the primary ACS server under **Accept Replication** from pull-down menu.

Step 8   Select the replication timeout. The default value is 5 minutes and is appropriate in most environments.

Step 9   Click **Submit**. If you want to start replication immediately, click **Replicate Now**.

End-User Clients

As described in Chapter 13, the configuration of the end-user clients consists of creating a silent distribution package of CTA and deploying it to your end users. In this case, the CTA distribution must include the 802.1X supplicant for users in the New York Office.

TIP   You can also bundle the CTA with wired-supplicant in the CSA Agent Kit. Instructions and detailed steps on how to do this are covered in Chapter 9, "Cisco Security Agent."

Switches

Configure the switch(es) for NAC-L2-802.1X by following these steps:

Step 1   Configure Authentication, Authorization, and Accounting:

```
Switch# configure terminal
Switch(config)# aaa new-model
Switch(config)# aaa authentication dot1x default group radius
Switch(config)# aaa authorization network default group radius
Switch(config)# aaa accounting network default start-stop group radius
```

Step 2   Configure the RADIUS server on the switch (the RADIUS server with IP address 10.10.20.181 is used in this example):

```
Switch(config)# radius-server host 10.10.20.181
Switch(config)# radius-server host 10.10.20.182
Switch(config)# radius-server key cisco123cisco
Switch(config)# radius-server attribute 8 include-in-access-req
Switch(config)# radius-server vsa send authentication
```

Step 3   Enable 802.1X globally in the switch:

```
Switch(config)# dot1x system-auth-control
```

Step 4   Under each interface where you want to enable NAC-L2-802.1X on the switch, configure the following commands:

```
Switch(config)# interface interface-name
Switch(config-if)#dot1x port-control auto
Switch(config-if)#dot1x timeout reauth-period server
Switch(config-if)#dot1x reauthentication
```

Troubleshooting NAC Deployment in a Large Enterprise

In this section, you learn some of the common techniques to use when troubleshooting NAC-related problems in a large organization. The first two methods pertain to the switch, and the last pertains to ACS. All three methods combined provide you with a complete end-to-end picture of how, when, where, and why an end host was posture validated by NAC.

show Commands

The **show** commands you learned about in Chapters 13 and 14 still apply when troubleshooting NAC problems in a large enterprise. They are very useful in determining the state and posture of an end host. In the previous chapters, you learned that the two most useful **show** commands are **show eou all** and **show eou ip** *ip-address* in NAC-L3-IP and NAC-L2-IP scenarios.

Several **show** commands are also useful in NAC-L2-802.1X environments. You can use the **show dot1x all** command to display 802.1X capabilities and information related to 802.1X users, groups, VLANs, and VLAN groups. Example 15-1 shows the output of the **show dot1x all** command.

Example 15-1 *show dot1x all Command Output*

```
Switch#show dot1x all
Dot1x Info for interface GigabitEthernet 3/8
-------------------------------------------------
Supplicant MAC 000d.32ac.1234
    AuthSM State    = AUTHENTICATED
    BendSM State    = IDLE
    Posture         = Healthy
    ReAuthPeriod    = 3600 Seconds (From Authentication Server)
    ReAuthAction    = Terminate
    TimeToNextReauth = 3570 Seconds
PortStatus         = AUTHORIZED
MaxReq             = 2
MaxAuthReq         = 2
HostMode           = Single
PortControl        = Auto
ControlDirection   = Both
QuietPeriod        = 60 Seconds
Re-authentication  = Enabled
ReAuthPeriod       = From Authentication Server
ServerTimeout      = 30 Seconds
SuppTimeout        = 30 Seconds
TxPeriod           = 30 Seconds
Guest-Vlan         = 0
```

In Example 15-1, an end user with a machine residing on switch port GigabitEthernet 3/8 was successfully authenticated. The highlighted lines show that the security posture is Healthy and that the machine was authorized on that port.

After an authentication and posture attempt, you can also use the **show vlan** command to verify that the client switch port has been placed in the correct VLAN.

debug Commands

In previous chapters, you learned about the EoU logging capabilities on the Cisco IOS routers running NAC-L3-IP and Cisco Catalyst switches running NAC-L2-IP. EoU logging still applies when troubleshooting NAC-L3-IP and NAC-L2-IP in large organizations. However, in case of NAC-L2-802.1X, the **debug dot1x events** is a very useful command when troubleshooting 802.1X-related problems. Example 15-2 shows the output of the **debug dot1x events** for a quarantined host.

Example 15-2 *debug dot1x events Output*

```
00:55:00: dot1x-ev:auth_initialize_enter:000d.32ac.1234: Current ID=0
00:55:00: dot1x-ev:dot1x_update_port_direction: Updating oper direction for Ge3/8
  (admin=Both, current oper=Both)
00:55:00: dot1x-ev:dot1x_update_port_direction: New oper direction for Ge3/8 is Both
00:55:00: dot1x-ev:dot1x_port_cleanup_author: cleanup author on interface
  GigabitEthernet3/8
00:55:00: dot1x-ev:dot1x_update_port_status: Called with host_mode=0 state
  UNAUTHORIZED
00:55:00: dot1x-ev:dot1x_update_port_status: using mac 000d.32ac.1234 to send port
  to unauthorized on vlan 15
00:55:00: dot1x-ev:Found a supplicant block for mac 000d.32ac.1234 1E113F0
00:55:00: dot1x-ev:dot1x_port_unauthorized: Host-mode=0 radius/guest vlan=15 on
  GigabitEthernet3/8
```

In the shaded lines in Example 15-2, you can see that the client machine has been placed in the UNAUTHORIZED state and is placed in the quarantined VLAN (VLAN 15).

NOTE Use caution when enabling debugs in busy switches because they can impact performance.

Other debug commands mentioned in Chapter 4, "Configuring Layer 2 NAC on Network Access Devices," such as **debug aaa authentication** and **debug radius**, are also good for authentication problems in large organizations. However, they need to be enabled with caution.

ACS Logs and CS-MARS

Cisco Secure ACS provides robust NAC logging capabilities through the Passed Authentications and Failed Attempts log files. You can enable and configure ACS logging from **System Configuration > Logging**.

NOTE   For detailed steps on configuring logging in Cisco Secure ACS, refer to the "Enabling Logging" section in Chapter 8.

ACS log files contain a long list of attributes and other information about the end host and the network access device. This information can be very overwhelming in large environments. Consequently, it is recommended that you use a monitoring tool, such as CS-MARS, to correlate these events. Chapter 17, "Monitoring the NAC Solution Using the Cisco Security Monitoring, Analysis, and Response System," details how to integrate CS-MARS with ACS and each different network access device.

Summary

Many aspects must be considered when deploying NAC in a large organization. The breakdown of the business drivers and technical requirements should be carefully analyzed. NAC has different approaches and features that can be deployed to satisfy those business and technical needs. This chapter detailed several key items to consider and analyze while deploying NAC in a large organization. It presented a real-life scenario on where SecureMe integrated existing NAC approaches discussed in Chapters 13 and 14.

This chapter covered the deployment of NAC policies for user and machine authentication using NAC-L2-802.1X features at a large headquarters site. It also covered how, in other sites and areas of the network, NAC-L2-IP and NAC Layer 3 IP were better choices to fulfill the previously mentioned business and technical requirements. In this chapter, you also learned how to take high availability and scalability into consideration while designing and deploying NAC. The chapter elaborated on the different third-party application integration methods that were discussed earlier on this book.

Review Questions

You can find the answers to the review questions in Appendix A, "Answers to Review Questions."

  1. True or false: Cisco Secure ACS can replicate only internal users and groups; it cannot replicate other configurations.

   2. True or false: NAC Layer 2 IP and NAC-L2-802.1X require a third-party supplicant to do security posture validation.

   3. What underlying protocol does Cisco Secure ACS use to communicate with third-party antivirus servers?

   a. HCAP

   b. HAAP

   c. GAME

   d. FTP

   4. What is the system posture token used during an audit for NAC agentless hosts?

   a. Quarantine

   b. Checkup

   c. Transition

   d. Audit

   5. Where in the network are remediation servers typically located?

   a. Internet edge

   b. Quarantine segment

   c. Datacenter

   d. All of the above

Managing and Monitoring NAC

This chapter covers the following topics:

- A phased approach to deploying NAC
- Provisioning of user/client software
- CSA management
- NAC policy maintenance
- Technical support
- Education and awareness

CHAPTER 16

NAC Deployment and Management Best Practices

NAC is an architecture-based framework solution intended to use a collection of both Cisco networking and security technologies, as well as existing deployments of security and management solutions from other vendors. To achieve a successful enterprise-wide deployment of the Cisco NAC Framework solution, it is first necessary to have a solid background in the operational, management, and support functions required by such a deployment.

The previous chapters explained how to configure and deploy all the major NAC components and features. This chapter provides guidelines on best practices to successfully plan, manage, and maintain the NAC solution within your organization.

A Phased Approach to Deploying NAC Framework

Every organization faces its own challenges and pitfalls when deploying new technologies, products, and tools. The NAC Framework introduces new technologies that leverage existing network infrastructure. It is important that you create a clear and detailed test and implementation plan to overcome these challenges. Network and security best-practice procedures strongly recommend that any new technology or product be tested first in a lab environment. Subsequently, a pilot within a limited production environment should be completed and carefully evaluated. If at all possible, this environment should include a sample of the systems available within the rest of the production network. This enables your network and security staff to quantify the effects of the new NAC solution on the organization without actually affecting the production network. This might not be easy to do in many smaller environments; however, it is still recommended. Your security and network staff will gain valuable training and experience with the new technologies being deployed and will understand their interaction with the existing infrastructure.

The up-front planning, time, and willingness to work through several iterations before a final deployment will save your organization a great deal in time and effort. The steps required to successfully evaluate, test, and deploy the NAC Framework components throughout your organization include the following:

Step 1 **Readiness assessment**—Complete a readiness assessment of your current infrastructure. Assuming that the organization has a corporate security policy, complete a gap analysis determining what NAC policies need to be developed.

Step 2 **Stakeholders**—Identify who will be the stakeholders during the initial tests and the rest of the deployment.

Step 3 **Lab**—Build an initial lab environment.

Step 4 **Test plans**—Create a detailed test plan for lab and limited-production pilot.

Step 5 **Initial tuning**—Complete any initial tuning of policies, configurations, and procedures on the test network.

Step 6 **Final deployment strategy**—Start the deployment in the production environment in accordance with the deployment model devised from the pilot environment. Monitor the deployment stages and tune accordingly.

Readiness Assessment

The first step in completing a readiness assessment is to create a list of requirements and determine what NAC features will help fulfill those requirements. For example, if one of the organization's requirements is to be able to perform user and machine authentication while performing security posture, 802.1X is a required feature. Subsequently, you need to understand the technical requirements to successfully deploy Layer 2 NAC with 802.1X within your environment. In this case, you need to consider what supplicants to use, how they will be deployed, how the switches will be configured, and any other related tasks.

After the list of requirements (technical and nontechnical) is completed, a complete inventory of existing network devices and systems must be evaluated to determine what software and equipment needs to be upgraded. An upgrade plan allows an organization to properly plan its budget and allocate resources. Without this upgrade plan and its definitions, an organization typically experiences an increase in compatibility issues because of software and hardware requirements.

TIP	Release notes should be reviewed during the readiness-assessment phase to ensure that all required hardware and software support exists and to understand any migration issues, including different default behavior or upgrade requirements. The NAC release notes are posted on Cisco's website at www.cisco.com/go/nac.

TIP	Products from NAC program partners, such as Great Bay's Beacon Endpoint Profiler, help in the discovery phase of NAC readiness assessments.

The readiness assessment also evaluates how capable your engineering, help-desk, and network-management staff is to support the new implementation. User education and back-end support are critical for a successful deployment. This is discussed later in this chapter.

NOTE	Cisco Advanced Services for Network Security provides numerous services that can help your organization successfully complete a readiness assessment and implementation plans. More information about these services can be obtained from Cisco's website at http://www.cisco.com/go/securityconsulting.

Stakeholders

Another critical administrative step is to identify individuals from architecture, desktop support, InfoSec, engineering, the help desk, and any other groups within your organization that will be needed during the planning, test/pilot, and deployment phases. The group should first consider business goals and resource capabilities to ensure that the deployment will have continued success. Next, assign individuals or groups overall responsibility for key steps in the planning and deployment process, including track management, life-cycle upgrade definitions, testing, validation, and pilots. Each of these areas should be defined, approved, and formally communicated within the organization.

Initial Lab Environment

Testing and validation is a critical best practice. Proper lab testing can significantly reduce production downtime, help your network and security support staff become familiar with the NAC solution, and assist in streamlining the implementation processes. To be effective, however, the organization must allocate the necessary resources to build and maintain the appropriate lab environment, apply necessary resources to perform the correct tests, and use a recommended testing methodology that includes measurement collection. Without giving each of these areas detailed attention, the testing and validation process might not meet an organization's expectations.

Many organizations do not take the time to build the recommended test lab environment. Consequently, they have deployed solutions incorrectly and have experienced network failures that could have been isolated in a lab environment. In some environments, this is acceptable because the cost of downtime does not offset the cost of a sophisticated lab environment. In many organizations, however, downtime cannot be tolerated. These organizations are strongly urged to develop the recommended test labs, test types, and test methodologies to improve production network quality.

Lab Isolation

The lab should be an isolated area that is equipped to mimic the production environment.

TIP   Physical security is recommended to help maintain a test environment while tests are in progress. This helps prevent a lab test from being disrupted.

TIP   Logical security is also recommended to prevent test traffic from entering the production network. This can be done with routing filters, with extended access lists on a lab gateway router/firewall, or by simply not connecting the equipment to the production environment.

As previously mentioned, the lab topology should be capable of mimicking some of the production environment for specific test plans. Reproducing hardware, network topology, and feature configurations is recommended. However, reproducing the actual topology is nearly impossible. Because of this, after the initial lab tests, a pilot within the production network is recommended. This is important for feature interaction between new and existing devices that cannot be reproduced in a pure lab environment.

Lab Management

In large organizations, the lab also requires some management. Lab-management responsibilities include these:

- Ordering lab equipment
- Performing asset tracking

- Handling cabling
- Managing physical space
- Performing lab scheduling
- Performing lab documentation
- Setting up lab topologies

Test Plans

When you have determined what NAC features will be tested, a test methodology and validation process should be developed. The purpose of a best-practice testing methodology is to help ensure that all features and capabilities are well documented, easily reproducible, and valuable in terms of finding potential risks. Try to document everything.

Common steps of a testing methodology are as follows (some can be performed concurrently):

Step 1 Create a test topology that simulates the production environment under test. For example, a remote-access VPN test might include only one type of network-access device (NAD) and few components, whereas a LAN Layer 2 approach might include more devices that can best represent the environment.

Step 2 The configuration of lab devices must closely match the expected production device hardware and software configurations. For example, take into consideration Voice over IP (VoIP) interoperability, NAC agentless hosts, audit services, and all other details that closely match the production environment.

Step 3 Document the test plan, defining goals and functionality based on requirements tests. Tests should include basic protocol and feature validation, outage testing, and redundancy when applicable.

Step 4 Baseline expected results and define the metrics that will be used to measure success.

Step 5 Simulate load, which would be expected in the production environment. This will probably be more feasible to achieve in the limited-production environment. Validate expected network device utilization variables, such as CPU and memory utilization of NADs.

Step 6 Documented test results and device-measurement tests should be repeatable.

Limited-Production Pilot Site

It is important to identify a section of the network in which you can successfully test the new NAC features and devices you might be implementing. This helps minimize potential exposure and more safely identifies any production issues. For example, in the previous chapters, you learned how to successfully deploy Layer 2, Layer 3, wireless, and remote-access VPN NAC features on different sites within an organization. During the pilot-selection phase, you might identify an area or branch office where you can test the specific features to be deployed. Pilot selection identifies where and how the pilot will be completed. The limited-production pilot might start with one device in a low-impact area and extend to multiple devices in a higher-impact area. You should perform a risk analysis to identify what areas and users can deal with some possible production impacts. You can also use the "monitor-mode" approach. In other words, you can configure the Cisco Secure ACS policies for Healthy, Quarantine, and Transition, yet still allow users to access the network. This way, you can quantify the impact of enforcing the configured policies and determine what machines are getting quarantined or placed into any other state—and why.

The duration of this pilot should be based on the time it takes to sufficiently test and evaluate all the software, hardware, and third-party features and their dependencies. During the pilot phase, it is critical to monitor and document results in a similar manner as initial lab testing. This can include user surveys, pilot data collection, problem identification, and success/failure criteria.

Initial Tuning

It is important to start the policy and configuration tuning process during the pilot phase. This will minimize numerous administrative hindrances. The tuning process includes these actions:

- **Tuning of ACS policies**—Cisco ACS is the main policy decision point. It is the only component that provides details on the state of the credential checking, what those credentials are, and the authorization policy that is used.

- **Tuning of CSA policies**—During the initial CSA tuning phase, you determine which rules would have a negative impact on the production systems. The tuning wizard helps modify the policy or policies applied by creating "allow rules" for the appropriate actions. This is discussed later in this chapter.

- **Creation of exception lists, white-lists, and audit server policies (when applicable)**—As covered in previous chapters, you can create exception lists on the NADs, create white-lists on ACS, or configure audit servers for NAC unresponsive hosts. Products from Cisco partners such as Altiris, Great Bay Software, and others can help you create exception lists for NAC unresponsive hosts.

Final Deployment Strategy

When the pilot phase has been completed within the limited-production network, begin the full NAC implementation phase. The implementation phase includes several steps to ensure software/hardware upgrade and configuration success, including these:

Step 1   Slow-start implementation

Step 2   Final software certification

Step 3   Upgrade preparation

Step 4   Upgrade and client software automation

Step 5   Final validation

The slow-start NAC implementation process ensures that the new technologies have full exposure to the production environment before final validation and full-scale conversion. It is recommended to start configuring only some devices (NADs) within the production network and allow at least one day of exposure within the NAC environment before moving on to the rest of the network. In some cases, continuing in monitor mode during the initial deployment is recommended. This way, you can continue to do more reconnaissance and measure the impact more effectively. Upon final validation, the organization can more rapidly deploy the NAC solution with a much higher confidence level. Some organizations do this right after the limited-production pilot; however, in large environments, it is recommended to carefully use the slow-start strategy.

When starting the full-scale deployment, all devices identified for upgrade should be reviewed and validated using the device inventory that was collected during the readiness assessment, along with a matrix of the minimum Cisco IOS, CATOS, and other software standards, to ensure that the minimum requirements are met.

TIP   If a large number of similar devices (such as Cisco IOS routers or switches) need to be upgraded, it is strongly recommended that you use an automated method or tool. Automation has been shown to improve upgrade efficiency and to improve the percentage of device upgrade successes on large deployments. You can use the Cisco's SoftWare Image Manager (SWIM) tool of CiscoWorks Interface Configuration Manager (ICM), Resource Manager Essentials (RME), or any other partner tools, such as Great Bay Software.

During the deployment phase, it is recommended to create standards with configuration templates and maintain a configuration version-control system. A configuration version-control system upholds the running configurations of all the network-access devices. This information is useful for troubleshooting and change audits. When troubleshooting, you can compare the current running configuration to previous working versions to help understand if a configuration is linked to the problem in any way.

Provisioning of User Client Software

NAC uses the Cisco Trust Agent (CTA) on hosts whose host policy state requires validation before permitting network access. An optional component is the Cisco Security Agent (CSA), antivirus software, or other required third-party security or management software. This section provides some tips on how to provision this type of software to the client machines.

CTA is bundled with other client software, such as the following:

- CSA version 4.0.2 and later
- InfoExpress CyberGatekeeper Server 3.1
- CyberGatekeeper Policy Manager 3.1
- Trend Micro OfficeScan Corporate Edition 6.5

NOTE   The number of vendors that bundle CTA within their software grows continuously. The most current list of vendors can be obtained from Cisco's website at www.cisco.com/go/nac.

In this section, we focus on the provisioning of CTA bundled within CSA.

You should determine the impact of the user client software in the lab tests or in the limited-production pilot. After the impact is quantified, the next step is the deployment of the software across the entire production environment. In large organizations, it is recommended that you do a staged distribution within your production environment. In smaller deployments, you can do a single distribution.

The suggested method for deploying the CSA/CTA across the client machines is based on the group or their network roles. This enables you to deploy the agent kits on similar client machines and helps you when troubleshooting unexpected problems.

TIP   It is recommended that you start the deployment of CSA with the appropriate policies set to the test mode. After each group of client machines runs CSA for a short period of time, you can enforce the applicable policies.

Large-scale enterprise deployments might require the use of sophisticated software-installation tools such as Microsoft's System Management Server (SMS) and Altiris. These types of deployment projects have become more complex because of the difficulty and cost associated with the installation and upgrades of software in numerous client systems. Software-provisioning tools deliver end-to-end capabilities to help enable the seamless deployment of CSA/CTA, while reducing the burden on the networking staff and also reducing costs.

NOTE   To obtain information about Microsoft SMS, visit Microsoft's website at www.microsoft.com/sms. To obtain information about Altiris software, go to www.altiris.com.

When installing CTA by itself (without CSA), you should consider creating a custom installation package. Creating a custom installation package enables you to set CTA configuration parameters, provision certificates, and install any third-party plug-ins.

NOTE   Chapter 2 covers the packaging and custom installation of CTA.

CSA Management

Chapter 9, "Cisco Security Agent," discusses the installation and configuration of the Cisco Security Agent Management Center (CSA MC). This section provides a series of tips on how to plan, deploy, and maintain CSA MC and the agent software.

CSA MC provides a central policy-management and distribution point for the CSA agent kits. It is recommended that you place the CSA MC server on your management network (management VLAN). When doing this, you need to understand how the agents communicate with CSA MC, and vice versa. The agents communicate with CSA MC over TCP port 5401 with a fallback to TCP port 443 (if TCP port 5401 communication is not possible). The CSA Profiler uses TCP port 5402 to communicate with CSA MC. Make sure that any firewalls or filtering devices allow this communication. All systems running the agent should reach CSA MC.

Another important factor is that the system (hardware) running CSA MC must be sized appropriately.

NOTE   For a list of hardware requirements, refer to the release notes on Cisco's website at www.cisco.com/go/csa.

The current version of CSA MC is capable of managing up to 100,000 agents. However, it is recommended that you install and strategically deploy additional CSA MC servers, depending on your network topology and geographical needs.

During the lab test and pilot phases, it is recommended that you start by using the default CSA policies (depending on the type of system where the agent is installed).

NOTE   The default CSA policies provide a good level of protection to the end hosts. Tuning of these is recommended; however, these default policies are known for stopping new and unknown threats.

When you start your CSA deployment, the initial hosts where CSA will be installed should be selected based on the following guidelines:

- Select at least one host per each distinct application environment.
- During the pilot, the test hosts should be a mirror sample of the production systems.
- When installing CSA on servers, use a test machine per each server type to avoid negative impact from CSA agent software installation.

It is also recommended that you create a group for each type of application environment that needs to be protected.

NOTE   Chapter 9 covers CSA MC group configuration.

The following are some examples of different application environments:

- Engineering desktop machines
- Remote sales staff laptops
- Web servers
- Database servers

Building and tuning CSA policies is a continuous task. It is important to have the proper staff and procedures to minimize the administrative burden. The security staff is responsible not only for maintaining the CSA MC policies, but also for creating and organizing exception rules appropriately and for monitoring user activity. You can organize the exception rules as follows:

- Create a global exception policy to allow legitimate traffic and application behavior that is required on all the systems within the organization. Subsequently, add these global exception rules to this exception policy.

- Create one exception policy for each group.

- Apply these policies to their respective groups and collect all necessary data to complete any additional tuning.

The following summarizes the steps that your security staff should take when deploying the agent kits throughout the organization:

Step 1 Deploy the CSA agents in test mode throughout your organization.

Step 2 Collect and analyze results. Subsequently, start policy tuning (as needed).

Step 3 Enable protection mode.

Step 4 Make sure that your security, operations, and engineering staff are comfortable with the support of your deployment.

Maintaining NAC Policies

Cisco Secure ACS is one of the major components of the NAC solution. It determines the appropriate action based on the device compliancy and the policies that you configure. It is important to recognize the administrative tasks that are involved in maintaining all the NAC policies in ACS and third-party vendor software. For example, some of the most common administrative tasks include the following:

- Keeping the operating system (OS) policies up-to-date

- Keeping your antivirus policies up-to-date

- Maintaining remediation servers and third-party software

Keeping Operating System Policies Up-to-Date

The network-access devices forward to Cisco Secure ACS all host credentials that CTA gathers. This information can include the device OS version, patch level (hotfixes), and antivirus software levels. Subsequently, it is important that you update your ACS NAC policies every time that a new OS critical patch is made available. If not, the host is allowed to access the network without having this update installed.

This can be an administrative headache. That is why it is important that you have clear procedures in place and the correct staff to be able to support these important tasks.

Keeping Your Antivirus Policies Up-to-Date

Similar to the OS policies, you must also keep your antivirus software policies up-to-date in ACS. Cisco Secure ACS works in concert with antivirus vendor software (such as Trend Micro OfficeScan policy server) to validate endpoint antivirus credentials. In this case, you also have to keep up with the latest signatures in the antivirus server. Commonly, this is done by automatic mechanisms helping with the administrative overhead of such tasks.

Maintenance of Remediation Servers and Third-Party Software

The number of remediation servers (partners) is growing daily. Some examples are PatchLink Update with PatchLink Quarantine for NAC and the Altiris server. It is crucial that these servers also be up-to-date so you can successfully remediate machines that are put into quarantine for not having the latest version of the required software dictated in the configured NAC policies.

TIP   You can obtain the most current list of third-party remediation partners from www.cisco.com/go/nac.

It is important that your security staff is aware of all the previously mentioned administrative tasks. In addition, it is important that your organization's management team allocate the necessary resources to be able to fully support the NAC solution.

Technical Support

It is important that you use a well-structured call-routing process to give end users the correct resources as quickly as possible. To ensure that all service requests are reported in a standard format, it is recommended that your organization establish service request severity definitions. The following are some examples:

- Severity 1 (S1): Network down situation.
- Severity 2 (S2): Network access degraded.
- Severity 3 (S3): Operational performance of the network/device is impaired, but most business operations remain functional.

Most of the NAC-related calls will involve users who cannot access the network (or are granted limited access) because their machines do not meet the standards that the security policy is enforcing. Consequently, these calls will most likely be Severity 1 or Severity 2 calls. If the production network is down or severely degraded, or if users do not have network access, they most likely will contact your help desk or technical support group by telephone. Engineers must be assigned immediately to S1 and S2 service requests to help keep business operations running smoothly. This is an important consideration when you are planning the deployment of the NAC solution and evaluating the impact on your support staff.

Educating users on setting the severity of the service request accurately, based on the effect on the organization, enables you to allocate the appropriate resources to resolve problems more efficiently. Additionally, using online resources and education material will help alleviate the support process.

The "life expectancy" of these calls depends on the nature of why the user can't access the network. For instance, a user might open a service request because her or his machine has been placed into quarantine and has failed to install an OS patch or antivirus signature update. However, alternatively, a user might be infected and more detailed work needs to be done to his or her workstation.

It is also important to have clearly defined escalation procedures. Having solid escalation procedures avoids service requests being escalated prematurely. During the troubleshooting process, the engineer assigned to assist the user might determine that an onsite engineer is required to resolve the issue. A clear process should be in place for the engineer to contact a resource onsite.

Education and Awareness

The deployment of a NAC solution involves varying levels of education and training for the support, implementation, and engineering staff, as well as the end users within the organization. Education of these different groups varies based on the impact and involvement of the NAC implementation.

End-User Education and Awareness

Some organizations already have extensive security-awareness programs that can be leveraged to provide much of the end-user education. Other organizations do not have these types of activities. It is highly recommended that you at least make your end users aware of what the impact might be when you start the deployment of NAC within your organization. This avoids confusion and might reduce the number of calls to your help-desk groups.

Some of the awareness activities that can be leveraged include the training of employees on rethinking the importance of security and understanding that it is everyone's job, not just the security staff. You should explain to the end users how important it is to keep workstations updated with the latest security patches and antivirus software.

Your organization can create an awareness campaign that notifies end users that access to the network will be denied to devices that do not comply with the minimum security standards.

Help-Desk Staff Training

The help desk is the organization that will receive the first phone call when a user cannot connect or has limited access to the network. Part of the training that needs to be supplied to the help-desk staff is how to determine whether the issue is related to NAC. This training includes guidance on how to get the posture status of the end host, what the policy applied is, and what the remediation steps are. The help desk should also understand where the remediation systems are located and how to help the user remediate the device or get an exception granted.

Engineering and Networking Staff Training

Your organization might have several groups responsible for the configuration of NAC components. Subsequently, they must be trained appropriately on all the new features, configuration, management, and maintenance of the NAC solution. Training should include troubleshooting the underlying protocols and technologies to determine whether the communication and interaction of all systems is functional.

Some organizations have sophisticated training programs and dedicated staff; others don't. One of the most common methodologies that enable information to be delivered in a more customized, learner-centric format is the implementation of e-learning technologies. This can help reduce training costs, provide easier access to educational materials, increase collaboration, and improve accountability.

Summary

In this chapter, you learned several best practices for managing a successful NAC deployment. The chapter described how to follow a phased approach when deploying NAC within your organization. This chapter also covered the provisioning and management of user client software such as CTA and CSA. It also provided guidance on how to prepare and educate your staff and improve processes for a successful deployment.

References

Cisco NAC website, http://www.cisco.com/go/nac

NAC technical documentation, http://www.cisco.com/en/US/netsol/ns617/ networking_solutions_sub_solution_home.html

Cisco's collateral material on third-party vendors, http://www.cisco.com/en/US/partners/ pr46/nac/partners.html

Review Questions

You can find the answers to the review questions in Appendix A, "Answers to Review Questions."

1. True or false: Documenting detailed test plans during the initial pilot phase is not important because it adds unnecessary administrative overhead.

2. A slow-start NAC implementation is

   a. Not recommended because it delays the implementation process.

   b. Recommended because it ensures that the new technologies have full exposure to the production environment before final validation and full-scale conversion.

   c. None of the above.

3. Automation tools have been shown to improve upgrade efficiency on large NAC deployments when numerous network devices need to be upgraded. An example of an automation tool you can use is

   a. Cisco Secure ACS

   b. CiscoWorks SWIM

   c. PatchLink Update

   d. All of the above

4. True or false: To avoid confusion, you should not notify end users before NAC is fully deployed within your organization.

5. True or false: The default CSA policies do not provide a good level of protection to the end hosts.

6. True or false: NAC deployment and support commonly do not affect your help-desk staff because the solution should be transparent to the end users.

This chapter covers the following topics:

- CS-MARS overview
- Setting up Cisco IOS routers to report to CS-MARS
- Setting up Cisco switches to report to CS-MARS
- Configuring ACS to send events to CS-MARS
- Configuring CSA to send events to CS-MARS
- Configuring VPN 3000 concentrators to send events to CS-MARS
- Configuring the ASA and PIX security appliances to send events to CS-MARS
- Configuring QualysGuard to send events to CS-MARS
- Generating reports in CS-MARS
- Troubleshooting CS-MARS

Monitoring the NAC Solution Using the Cisco Security Monitoring, Analysis, and Response System

Implementing the NAC Framework into your organization's network takes a well-thought-out plan from the beginning for things to flow smoothly. One thing you should not leave out of that plan is a way to monitor the devices connecting to your NAC-enabled network.

In this last chapter, we cover how to monitor the NAC solution using the Cisco Security Monitoring, Analysis, and Response System (CS-MARS).

NOTE	This chapter includes several references to *Protego Networks* (or *pn*, for short)—an example is the pnlog agent. All such references refer to CS-MARS. CS-MARS was originally designed and created by Protego Networks before it was acquired by Cisco Systems, Inc., in January 2005.

CS-MARS Overview

CS-MARS is a hardware appliance solution that you plug into your network and then forward network events to it from your network devices. It acts as an information sink, absorbing all the events thrown at it. CS-MARS correlates and then sessionizes these events across all devices. Thus, it can recognize malicious activity taking place anywhere in the network. It can then alert you to not only the attack, but also the attacker, the victim, and the path the attack is taking through the network. In addition, it can provide the best mitigation point to stop the attack, while also suggesting the commands needed to enter on the mitigation device to stop the attack. CS-MARS also interrogates the endpoints to determine the host OS and whether they are actually vulnerable to the attack. It uses this information to prioritize the attack and rule out false positives.

All configuration information and reporting that CS-MARS provides works through a web browser interface. You must use Internet Explorer 6.0 SP1 or later to access the appliance. In addition, CS-MARS uses Adobe's SVG viewer plug-in to display graphs and charts. If you do not have the plug-in installed, when you access CS-MARS for the first time, it directs you to the Adobe SVG download page to install the plug-in. After installation, you are redirected back to the CS-MARS summary page.

NOTE   When navigating through the CS-MARS user interface, do not use your browser's Forward and Back buttons. Doing so might lead to unpredictable behavior.

NOTE   For non-Windows clients, browsers other than Internet Explorer have been shown to work, but they are not officially supported. I have used Netscape 7.0 on MAC OS without any problems, although there are some cosmetic display issues.

The back end consists of an embedded Oracle database where the raw messages, sessions, incidents, reports, and configuration reside. The back end is self-maintaining and needs no periodic user intervention. This means your organization does not need to know anything about databases or Oracle to effectively use, operate, and maintain CS-MARS.

CS-MARS is a turnkey appliance solution. A stand-alone software version is not available. Cisco sells various models of CS-MARS appliances. The main differences among them include how many events they can process per second and how long they can store the received events locally on the file system. Table 17-1 lists the current CS-MARS appliances.

Table 17-1   *CS-MARS Appliances*

Product	Events/Sec	NetFlows/Sec	Storage
CS-MARS-20R-K9	50	1,500	120 GB (no RAID)
CS-MARS-20-K9	500	15,000	120 GB (no RAID)
CS-MARS-50-K9	1000	30,000	240 GB, RAID 0
CS-MARS-100e-K9	3000	75,000	750 GB, RAID 10
CS-MARS-100-K9	5000	150,000	750 GB, RAID 10
CS-MARS-200-K9	10,000	300,000	1 TB, RAID 10

In addition to the appliances in Table 17-1, Cisco offers a CS-MARS Global Controller (GC), which can manage and aggregate the incidents from several CS-MARS appliances spread out in a large enterprise. This allows for a total centralized configuration and management solution.

CS-MARS can receive events in the form of NetFlow export data, syslogs, SNMP traps, SDEE, and other security vendors' protocols. In the support of NAC, CS-MARS receives events from the following NAC components:

- Cisco IOS routers
- Cisco switches
- Cisco Secure Access Control Servers (ACS)
- Cisco Security Agent Management Centers (CSA-MC)
- Cisco VPN 3000 series concentrators
- Cisco Adaptive Security Appliances and PIX security appliances
- QualysGuard network appliances

In the next several sections, we walk through the steps needed to set up the devices to send events to CS-MARS and for CS-MARS to become aware of the network devices. We focus mainly on the setup necessary to receive NAC events, but we also cover general setup of these devices. Be aware that CS-MARS is a feature-packed product that offers high levels of customization and extensive reporting capabilities. Covering the NAC-related reporting available in CS-MARS barely even skims the surface of what CS-MARS is capable of. The assumption is that this chapter is for those who already have the CS-MARS product installed or plan to acquire it to monitor NAC and want to know more information on how to use it related to a NAC deployment. To fully understand the value that CS-MARS provides to your overall network and to get a complete list of the current devices CS-MARS supports, refer to the online datasheets and documentation found at http://www.cisco.com/go/mars/.

Setting Up Cisco IOS Routers to Report to CS-MARS

In a standard CS-MARS deployment, Cisco IOS routers are configured to forward syslogs and NetFlow events to CS-MARS. The syslogs allow CS-MARS to be aware of incidents occurring on the router; the NetFlow events allow CS-MARS to be aware of all the sessions that are flowing through the router. This allows CS-MARS to perform anomaly detection for Day Zero viruses and worms.

When deploying NAC Framework in your network, if the NAC router is already set up to send syslogs and NetFlow events to CS-MARS, all you have left to do is configure the router to send NAC specific syslogs.

To accomplish this, add the following commands to the router:

```
eou allow ip-station-id
eou logging
```

NOTE   Enabling the **eou allow ip-station-id** command causes the router to send the client's IP address in the Calling-Station-Id field in the RADIUS Access-Request packet (instead of the client's MAC address). This allows CS-MARS to run reports displaying the client's IP. However, in doing so, because the client's MAC is no longer sent, you will not be able to use centralized MAC-based exceptions (for agentless devices) on ACS.

However, if the Cisco IOS router has not been previously defined in CS-MARS or been configured to forward events to CS-MARS, you must complete the following tasks:

- Define the Cisco IOS router as a reporting device within CS-MARS.
- Configure the Cisco IOS router to forward events to CS-MARS.

In the next two sections, we walk through completing these tasks.

Defining the Cisco IOS Router as a Reporting Device within CS-MARS

Before you can begin to add the Cisco IOS router into CS-MARS, you need to bootstrap the router so that CS-MARS can discover and import it. CS-MARS discovers Cisco IOS routers through SNMP, SSH, Telnet, or a saved configuration on an FTP server. If the router has ACLs defined or NAT configured, it is recommended that you discover the router through either SSH or Telnet. In addition, you need to supply the SNMP Read-Only (RO) community string. The SNMP community string allows CS-MARS to query the routing table, interface MIBs, and resource utilization.

To bootstrap a Cisco IOS router for CS-MARS to access it through SSH, the router must be running a crypto image (–k8 or –k9) and must have the SSH Server feature in the version you are running. Issue the command **ip ssh ?** from config mode. If you see a list of options, the version you are running has support for SSH. Additionally, SSH requires that the user authenticate with a username/password pair. This means that AAA must be enabled on the router to query either the local database or a remote TACACS+ or RADIUS server. Example 17-1 shows an example of how to bootstrap a Cisco IOS router to allow SSH access while authenticating the user to an external TACACS+ server at 172.18.124.101.

Example 17-1 *Bootstrapping a Cisco IOS Router for SSH Access*

```
7206-D(config)# tacacs-server host 172.18.124.101 key c1scs3cr3tA
7206-D(config)# aaa new-model
7206-D(config)# aaa authentication login default group tacacs+
7206-D(config)# aaa authentication enable default group tacacs+
7206-D(config)# ip domain-name securemeinc.com
7206-D(config)# crypto key generate rsa
The name for the keys will be: 7206-D.securemeinc.com
Choose the size of the key modulus in the range of 360 to 2048 for your
```

Example 17-1 *Bootstrapping a Cisco IOS Router for SSH Access (Continued)*

```
General Purpose Keys. Choosing a key modulus greater than 512 may take
  a few minutes.

How many bits in the modulus [512]: 2048
% Generating 2048 bit RSA keys ...[OK]
7206-D(config)#
```

Alternatively, instead of SSH access, you can have CS-MARS access the device via Telnet. However, this method is less secure because the contents of the session are not encrypted. The only requirements for the router are that you have not disabled Telnet access under the vty lines and that a password has been set.

Next, add the following command to bootstrap the Cisco IOS router for CS-MARS to access it through SNMP:

> **snmp-server community** *community-string* **ro** *optional-acl*

With the router bootstrapped, follow these steps to add it as a monitored device within CS-MARS:

Step 1   Log in to the CS-MARS GUI interface and select the **Admin** tab.

Step 2   In the Device Configuration and Discovery Information section, click the **Security and Monitor Devices** link.

Step 3   Click the **Add** box on the far right of the screen.

Step 4   In the **Device Type** drop-down list, select **Cisco IOS 12.2**.

NOTE   In CS-MARS, all Cisco IOS routers are represented as **Device Type: Cisco IOS 12.2**, regardless of the actual Cisco IOS version they are running.

Step 5   Fill in the **Device Name** with the host name of the router.

Step 6   Fill in the **Access IP** and **Reporting IP**. These should be the same. The Access IP is the address CS-MARS uses to discover the router. The Reporting IP is the address CS-MARS uses to match events received for the correct monitored device.

Step 7   For **Access Type**, choose **SSH** from the drop-down list and select either **3DES** or **DES** as the encryption strength.

Step 8   Add the username in the **Login** field, and add the password in the **Password** field. Also fill in the **Enable Password** field.

Step 9   Fill in the **SNMP RO Community** field with the read-only community string that you set when bootstrapping the router earlier.

Step 10   Under **Monitor Resource Usage**, I recommend that you select **Yes** from the drop-down list. This allows CS-MARS to monitor the memory and CPU for abnormal activity. Figure 17-1 shows an example of this screen.

Figure 17-1   *Example: Adding a Cisco IOS Router to CS-MARS as a Reporting Device*

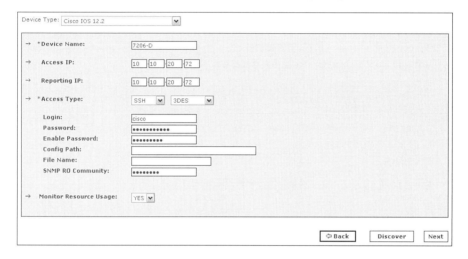

Step 11   Select the **Discover** button. In a few seconds, you should see a pop-up message indicating that the discovery is complete. Choose **OK**.

Step 12   Select **Submit**.

Step 13   Select **Activate** in the upper-right corner.

Repeat these steps to add other Cisco IOS NADs into CS-MARS.

Configuring the Cisco IOS Router to Forward Events to CS-MARS

Now that the Cisco IOS router has been added into the CS-MARS GUI interface, it needs to be configured to forward events to CS-MARS.

First, configure the router to send syslogs to CS-MARS by adding the following commands:

```
logging source-interface interface
logging trap level
logging CS-MARS-IP
logging on
```

NOTE	To be most effective, CS-MARS needs to receive a high level of logging. This corresponds to a logging level of 6 (Informational) on the router.

Although sending NetFlow events to CS-MARS is not required to monitor the NAC solution, it is a highly recommended best practice and allows CS-MARS to detect attacks and other anomalous events in the network. For completeness, I have added the configuration needed on the router to send NetFlow events to CS-MARS:

```
ip flow-export version 5
ip flow-export destination CS-MARS-IP 2055
ip flow-export source source-interface
```

In addition, you need to enable **ip route-cache flow** under each interface so the router can track the flows going through the interface:

```
interface interface
   ip route-cache flow
```

NOTE	Specifying the source-interface in both the logging and flow-export commands is not required. However, on multi-interface routers, where packets could arrive to CS-MARS out more than one interface (and with a different source IP), it should be used. Remember that CS-MARS classifies received events from devices based on the *reporting IP*. If the IP address changes, CS-MARS considers the event to be coming from an unknown reporting device. Finally, as a security best practice, you should always specify the source interface and tie it to a loopback interface.

The last step is to enable the generation of NAC-specific events. They are sent through the existing syslog facility to CS-MARS:

```
eou allow ip-station-id
eou logging
```

NOTE	Enabling the **eou allow ip-station-id** command causes the router to send the client's IP address in the Calling-Station-Id field in the RADIUS Access-Request packet (instead of the client's MAC address). This allows CS-MARS to run reports displaying the client's IP. However, in doing so, because the client's MAC is no longer sent, you will not be able to use centralized MAC-based exceptions (for agentless devices) on ACS.

When you complete these steps, the Cisco IOS router is properly configured to send events to CS-MARS. Repeat these steps for the remaining NADs in your network.

NOTE For large numbers of routers, importing each one individually into CS-MARS is not very practical. Therefore, CS-MARS provides a mechanism to import large numbers of devices using a comma-delimited seed file. See the CS-MARS User Guide for more information about this process.

Setting Up Cisco Switches to Report to CS-MARS

If you have already defined your switches in CS-MARS and they are forwarding syslog messages to CS-MARS, very little is left for you to do. The only NAC-specific configuration that needs to be applied depends on whether the switch is being used for L2-IP or L3-IP. In that case, you need to configure the switch to send EAP over UDP logs to CS-MARS.

Add the following commands to the switch to accomplish this.

Cisco IOS switch:

```
eou allow ip-station-id
eou logging
```

CatOS switch:

```
set eou allow ip-station-id enable
set eou logging enable
```

NOTE Enabling the **eou allow ip-station-id** command causes the switch to send the client's IP address in the Calling-Station-Id field in the RADIUS Access-Request packet (instead of the client's MAC address). This allows CS-MARS to run reports displaying the client's IP. However, in doing so, because the client's MAC is no longer sent, you cannot use centralized MAC-based exceptions (for agentless devices) on ACS.

However, if the switch has not been previously defined in CS-MARS or configured to forward events to CS-MARS, you must complete the following tasks:

1. Define the Cisco Switch as a reporting device within CS-MARS.

2. Configure the Cisco Switch to forward events to CS-MARS.

In the next two sections, we walk through completing these tasks.

Defining the Cisco Switch as a Reporting Device within CS-MARS

CS-MARS supports both Cisco IOS–based switches and CatOS-based Cisco switches. The procedure to add them into the CS-MARS GUI is exactly the same. The only difference is that for Cisco IOS–based switches, the **Device Type** is **Cisco Switch-IOS 12.2**; for CatOS-based switches, the **Device Type** is **Cisco Switch-CatOS ANY**.

Before you can begin adding the switch into CS-MARS, you first need to bootstrap it so that CS-MARS can discover and import it. CS-MARS discovers switches through SNMP, SSH, Telnet, or a saved configuration on an FTP server. If the switch has ACLs defined or NAT configured, it is recommended that you discover the switch through either SSH or Telnet. In addition, you need to supply the SNMP read-only community string. The SNMP community string allows CS-MARS to query the content addressable memory (CAM) table, the spanning-tree table, interface MIBs, and resource utilization.

NOTE   If you want CS-MARS to push out L2 mitigation policies to your switches, you must define a read-write SNMP community string on the switch and supply it to CS-MARS during the L2 mitigation push.

To bootstrap a switch for CS-MARS to access it through SSH, the switch must be running a crypto image (–k8 or –k9), and it must have the SSH Server feature in the version you are running. For Cisco IOS switches, issue the command **ip ssh ?** from config mode. For CatOS switches, issue the command **set ssh mode ?** from enable mode. If you see a list of options, the version you are running has support for SSH. Additionally, SSH requires that the user authenticate with a username/password pair. This means that AAA must be enabled on the switch to query either the local database or a remote TACACS+ or RADIUS server. Example 17-2 shows an example of how to bootstrap a Cisco IOS switch to authenticate against an external TACACS+ server at 172.18.124.101 and allow SSH access.

Example 17-2   *Bootstrapping a Cisco IOS Switch for SSH Access*

```
6503-A(config)# tacacs-server host 172.18.124.101 key c1scs3cr3tA
6503-A(config)# aaa new-model
6503-A(config)# aaa authentication login default group tacacs+
6503-A(config)# aaa authentication enable default group tacacs+
6503-A(config)# ip domain-name securemeinc.com
6503-A(config)# crypto key generate rsa
The name for the keys will be: 6503-A.securemeinc.com
Choose the size of the key modulus in the range of 360 to 2048 for your
  General Purpose Keys. Choosing a key modulus greater than 512 may take
  a few minutes.

  How many bits in the modulus [512]: 2048
  % Generating 2048 bit RSA keys ...[OK]
6503-A(config)#
```

Example 17-3 shows how to bootstrap a CatOS switch to allow SSH access, authenticating to an external TACACS+ server at 172.18.124.101 and from management IPs on the 10.10.20.0/24 network.

Example 17-3 *Bootstrapping a CatOS Switch for SSH Access*

```
6503-B (enable) set tacacs server 172.18.124.101 primary
6503-B (enable) set tacacs key c1sc0s3cr3t
6503-B (enable) set authentication login tacacs enable primary
6503-B (enable) set authentication enable tacacs enable primary
6503-B (enable) set ip permit 10.10.20.0 255.255.255.0
6503-B (enable) set crypto key rsa 2048
Generating RSA keys.......................... [OK]
```

Alternatively, instead of SSH access, you can have CS-MARS access the device via Telnet. However, this method is less secure because the contents of the session are not encrypted.

Next, add the following command to bootstrap the switch for CS-MARS to access it via SNMP:

Cisco IOS switch:

```
snmp-server community community-string {ro | rw} optional-acl
```

CatOS switch:

```
set snmp community {read-only | read-write} community-string
```

Now that the switch is bootstrapped, follow these steps to add the switch as a monitored device within CS-MARS:

Step 1 Log in to the CS-MARS GUI interface and select the **Admin** tab.

Step 2 Under the Device Configuration and Discovery Information section, click the **Security and Monitor Devices** link.

Step 3 Click the **Add** box on the far right of the screen.

Step 4 In the **Device Type** drop-down list, select **Cisco Switch-IOS 12.2** for a Cisco IOS-based switch or **Cisco Switch-CatOS ANY** for a switch running CAT-OS.

Step 5 Fill in the **Device Name** with the host name of the switch.

Step 6 Fill in the **Access IP** and **Reporting IP**. These should be the same. The Access IP is the address CS-MARS uses to discover the switch. The Reporting IP is the address CS-MARS uses to match events received to the correct monitored device.

Step 7 For **Access Type**, choose **SSH** from the drop-down list and select either **3DES** or **DES** as the encryption strength.

Step 8   Add the username in the **Login** field and the password in the **Password** field. Also fill in the **Enable Password** field.

Step 9   Fill in the **SNMP RO Community** field with the read-only community string that you set when bootstrapping the switch earlier.

Step 10 Under **Monitor Resource Usage**, I recommend that you select **Yes** from the drop-down list. This allows CS-MARS to monitor the memory and CPU for abnormal activity. Figure 17-2 shows an example of this screen for a CatOS-based switch.

Figure 17-2   *Example: Adding a CatOS Switch to CS-MARS as a Reporting Device*

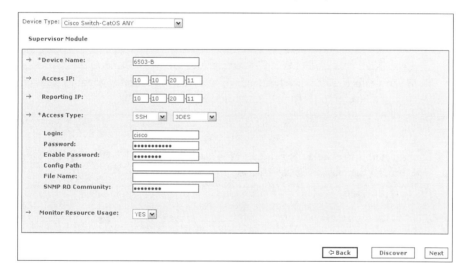

Step 11 Click the **Discover** button. In a few seconds, you should see a pop-up message indicating that the discovery is complete. Choose **OK**.

Step 12 Select **Submit**.

Step 13 Select **Activate** in the upper-right corner.

Repeat these steps to add other Cisco Switches into CS-MARS.

Configuring the Cisco Switch to Forward Events to CS-MARS

With the switch added to CS-MARS, the next step is to configure the switch to forward events to CS-MARS. First, configure the switch to send syslogs to CS-MARS by adding the following commands:

Cisco IOS switch:

```
logging source-interface interface
logging trap level
logging CS-MARS-IP
logging on
```

CatOS switch:

```
set logging server severity level
set logging server CS-MARS-IP
set logging server enable
set snmp rmon enable
```

NOTE   To be most effective, CS-MARS needs to receive a high level of logging. This corresponds to a logging level of 6 (Informational) on the switch.

The last step is to enable the generation of NAC L2-IP and L3-IP specific events. They are sent through the existing syslog facility to CS-MARS:

Cisco IOS switch:

```
eou allow ip-station-id
eou logging
```

CatOS switch:

```
set eou allow ip-station-id enable
set eou logging enable
! Also add the following if doing L2-802.1x
set dot1x radius-accounting enable
```

NOTE   Enabling the **eou allow ip-station-id** command causes the switch to send the client's IP address in the Calling-Station-Id field in the RADIUS Access-Request packet (instead of the client's MAC address). This allows CS-MARS to run reports displaying the client's IP. However, in doing so, because the client's MAC is no longer sent, you cannot use centralized MAC-based exceptions (for agentless devices) on ACS.

After you complete these steps, the switch is properly configured to send events to CS-MARS. Repeat these steps for the remaining NADs in your network.

NOTE	For large numbers of switches, importing each one individually into CS-MARS is not very practical. Therefore, CS-MARS provide a mechanism to import large numbers of devices using a comma-delimited seed file. See the CS-MARS User Guide for more information about this process.

Configuring ACS to Send Events to CS-MARS

Complete the following tasks to send events from ACS to the CS-MARS appliance:

1. Define ACS as a reporting device within CS-MARS.

2. Configure logging on ACS.

3. Configure 802.1X NADs in ACS to report to CS-MARS.

4. Install the pnlog agent on ACS.

In the next few sections, we walk through all these tasks.

Defining ACS as a Reporting Device within CS-MARS

Before CS-MARS will analyze the events received from ACS, you must define ACS as a monitored device within CS-MARS. Follow these steps to accomplish this task:

Step 1   Log in to the CS-MARS GUI interface and select the **Admin** tab.

Step 2   In the Device Configuration and Discovery Information section, click the **Security and Monitor Devices** link.

Step 3   Click the **Add** box on the far right of the screen.

Step 4   In the **Device Type** drop-down list, select **Add SW Security Apps on New Host**.

Step 5   Under the General Information section, fill in **Device Name**, **Access IP**, and **Reporting IP**. Under the interface information section, fill in the IP address and netmask of the ACS machine. Figure 17-3 shows an example of this screen.

NOTE	The access IP, reporting IP, and interface IP should all be the IP address of the machine running the pnlog agent, which is generating the syslogs and sending them to CS-MARS. For ACS Software users, this is the IP of the ACS machine itself. For ACS appliance users, this is the IP of the machine where the Remote Agent is installed. If you have more than one ACS machine, each one must be added independently.

Figure 17-3 *Example: Adding ACS to CS-MARS as a Reporting Device*

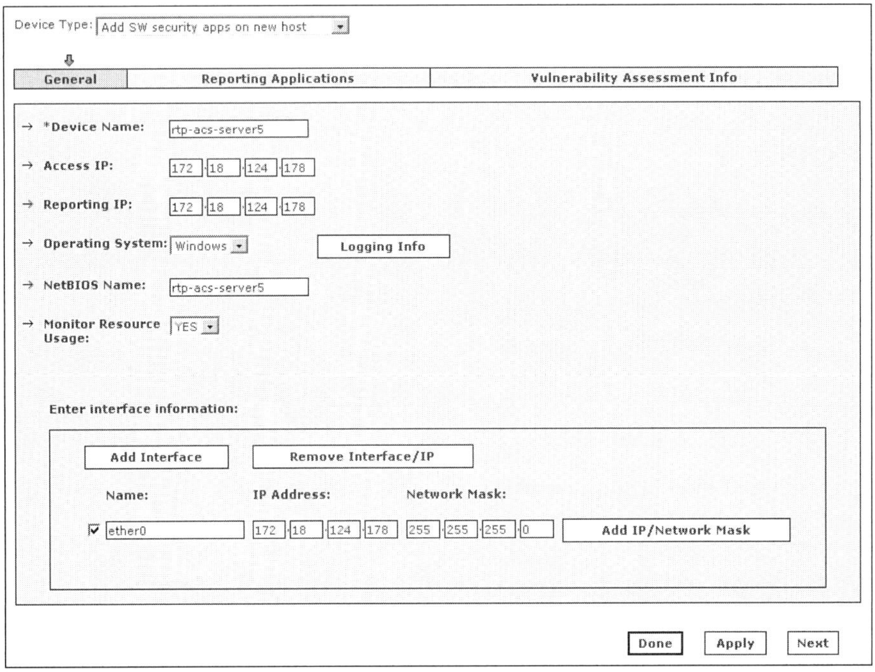

Step 6 Click the **Apply** button.

Step 7 Click the **Next** button to advance to the **Reporting Applications** tab.

Step 8 From the **Select Application** drop-down list, choose **Cisco ACS 3.x** and then click the **Add** button. Figure 17-4 shows an example of this screen.

NOTE   In CS-MARS, all ACS versions are represented as **Device Type: Cisco ACS 3.x**, regardless of the actual version of ACS.

Step 9 The Cisco ACS 3.x Windows Requirements window appears, indicating that you need to install the pnlog agent on the ACS machine. Click the **Submit** button.

Step 10 Cisco ACS 3.x appears as a device type. Click **Done** to save the changes.

Step 11 The last step (which people often forget) is to select the **Activate** button in the upper-right corner of the page.

Figure 17-4 *Example: Adding ACS to CS-MARS as a Reporting Application*

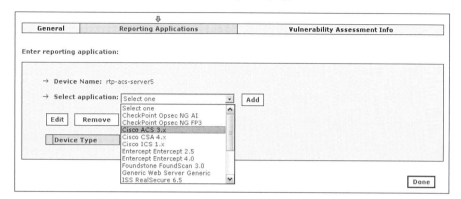

These steps are all you need to do to set up CS-MARS to receive events from ACS. In the next section, you will configure ACS to generate the correct events in its log files.

Configuring Logging on ACS

In this section, we walk through the steps needed to configure the logging attributes on ACS that CS-MARS needs to monitor the NAC implementation. Keep in mind that you will most likely want to log additional attributes (other than those mentioned here) to the log files to assist in troubleshooting client connectivity issues. CS-MARS can receive these additional attributes without any issues.

NOTE   If you are using an ACS appliance, the following steps apply to the *Remote Agent logging configuration*, not to the *local logging configuration* on the appliance. Because appliance users do not have direct access to the file system, the pnlog agent cannot be installed on the appliance. Instead, the ACS Remote Agent utility is used to forward the logs to another Windows machine where the pnlog agent is also installed.

Step 1   Log in to the ACS GUI interface; select the **System Configuration** button on the left and then the **Logging** link.

Step 2   Select the **Configure** link in the CSV column for the **Passed Authentications** report. (For ACS Appliance users, the **Passed Authentications** report is configured under the Remote Agent Logging Configuration section.)

Step 3   Verify that the **Log to CSV Passed Authentications Report** box is checked.

Step 4   In the Select Columns to Log section, ensure that, at a minimum, the following attributes appear under the **Logged Attributes** list:

- User-Name

- Group-Name

- Caller-ID

- NAS-Port

- NAS-IP-Address

- System-Posture-Token

- Message-Type

- EAP Type

- EAP Type Name

- AAA Server

Step 5   Select **Submit**.

Step 6   Select the **Configure** link in the CSV column for the **Failed Attempts** report. (For ACS Appliance users, the **Failed Attempts** report is configured under the Remote Agent Logging Configuration section.)

Step 7   Verify that the **Log to CSV Failed Attempts Report** box is checked.

Step 8   In the Select Columns to Log section, ensure that, at a minimum, the following attributes appear under the **Logged Attributes** list:

- User-Name

- Group-Name

- Caller-ID

- NAS-Port

- NAS-IP-Address

- Message-Type

- Authen-Failure-Code

- AAA Server

- Cisco-av-pair

Step 9   Select **Submit**.

Step 10 Select the **Configure** link in the CSV column for the **RADIUS Accounting** report. (For ACS Appliance users, the **RADIUS Accounting** report is configured under the Remote Agent Logging Configuration section.)

Step 11 Verify that the **Log to CSV RADIUS Accounting Report** box is checked.

Step 12 Under the Select Columns to Log section, ensure that, at a minimum, the following attributes appear under the **Logged Attributes** list:

— User-Name

— Calling-Station-Id

— Acct-Status-Type

— NAS-Port

— NAS-IP-Address

— Framed-IP-address

— AAA Server

— cisco-av-pair

Step 13 Select **Submit**.

ACS is now set up to log NAC-related events to the local logging files. In a later section, you will install the pnlog agent to forward events from the log files to CS-MARS.

TIP   If left at their default settings, the ACS log files will eventually grow out of control and consume all the disk space on the machine. ACS has built-in log-file management, but it is disabled by default. To enable it, select **System Configuration > Logging**, and then select each log file independently. At the bottom of the log-file configuration is a section entitled Log File Management. Select the **Manage Directory** box to allow ACS to delete log files older than a specified time. A good practice is to generate a new log file every day and to keep files for 30 days.

Configuring 802.1X NADs in ACS to Report to CS-MARS

Chapter 8, "Cisco Secure Access Control Server," covered how to add the NADs as AAA clients in ACS. For NADs that are performing 802.1X authentication, CS-MARS needs to receive the incremental 802.1X update messages. Enable this within ACS under **Network Configuration > AAA Clients**. Select the specific AAA client and configure it to authenticate using the **RADIUS (Cisco IOS/PIX 6.0)** or **RADIUS (IETF)** dictionary. In addition, make sure **Log Update/Watchdog Packets from This AAA Client** is checked. Refer to Figure 17-5 for an example screen shot of a properly configured 802.1X NAD.

Figure 17-5 *Properly Configured 802.1X NAD in ACS*

Installing the pnlog Agent on ACS

ACS currently does not have a mechanism to forward events to CS-MARS. Instead, CS-MARS receives events from ACS through the pnlog agent. The pnlog agent is an application that you install on the ACS machine—or, if using an ACS Appliance, install the pnlog agent on the same machine as the Remote Agent. The pnlog agent monitors the log files ACS (or the Remote Agent) writes to disk, and then forwards events in the log files as syslog messages to CS-MARS. CS-MARS receives these syslog messages and parses them to retrieve the original event. All events are analyzed against other events that have come in; where applicable, events are sessionized and incidents are created.

Begin by downloading the pnlog agent from cisco.com at http://www.cisco.com/cgi-bin/tablebuild.pl/cs-mars-misc.

NOTE   Two versions of the pnlog agent are available. Version 1.1 is the latest and should be used with CS-MARS Versions 4.1.3 and later. It includes enhancements to the earlier 1.0 version. One important enhancement is the capability to send events to CS-MARS that are larger than 1024 bytes.

| NOTE | To upgrade from the earlier pnlog agent to Version 1.1, install the new agent in the same directory as the old one. Note, however, that the CS-MARS IP address information is lost in the upgrade process and must be re-entered. |

Step 1 Download the pnLogAgent.zip file to a temporary directory and unzip it. The pnLogAgentInstall.exe file is extracted.

Step 2 Double-click the pnLogAgentInstall.exe file to begin the installation.

Step 3 Accept the license agreement and click **Next** to advance the install. By default, the pnlog agent is installed in the following directory:

C:\Program Files\Protego Networks\PNLogAgent\

Step 4 Upon completion of the install, the agent automatically starts, and the Protego Networks Log Agent window appears.

| NOTE | The pnlog agent is installed as a Windows Service with the name pnLogAgentService. It is set to start automatically on boot and uses the Local System Account. |

Step 5 From the menu at the top, select **Edit > PN-MARS Config...**

Step 6 The PNLog Agent Configuration box appears. Fill in the IP address of the CS-MARS appliance, as shown in Figure 17-6.

Figure 17-6 *pnlog Agent Configuration Box*

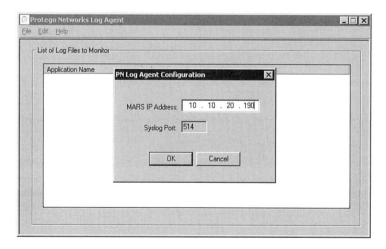

Step 7   Select **Edit > Log File Config > Add**.

Step 8   The Add/Edit File Details dialog box appears. Under **Application Name**, select **Cisco ACS—Failed Attempts** from the drop-down list. For the **Log File**, select the box with the three dots to browse to the file on disk. Browse to the **Failed Attempts active.csv** file, select it, and choose **Open**. See Figure 17-7 for an example of this step.

NOTE   The failed attempts active log file is located in the following default directory:

ACS 4.0 software:

C:\Program Files\CiscoSecure ACS v4.0\Logs\Failed Attempts\

ACS appliance - Remote Agent:

C:\Program Files\Cisco\CiscoSecure ACS Agent\Logs\Failed Attempts\

Figure 17-7   *Mapping the Failed Attempts Log File*

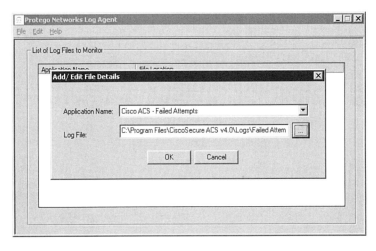

Step 9   Repeat steps 7 and 8 for both the Passed Authentications and RADIUS Accounting log files.

Step 10   The pnlog agent should now be configured with all three log files mapped to their respective locations on disk, as shown in Figure 17-8.

Step 11   The final step is to select **File > Activate** to tell the agent to start monitoring the log files. After you select **Activate**, it is grayed out.

Figure 17-8 *Completed Log File Mapping*

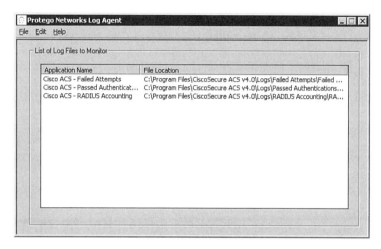

At this point, the pnlog agent will forward all new log events to CS-MARS for analysis using the syslog protocol on UDP port 514. If you encounter any trouble receiving events from the pnlog agent, verify that you do not have a firewall in place blocking traffic on UDP/514 from the pnlog agent to CS-MARS.

NOTE   The pnlog agent writes errors to the Windows Application Log in the Event Viewer. If CS-MARS is not receiving events from ACS through the pnlog agent, take a look in the Windows event log to see if the pnlog agent is having any problems starting or sending messages to CS-MARS. The pnlog agent messages have a source of ProtegoNetworks, as displayed in the Event Viewer.

NOTE   CS-MARS currently cannot parse out the Server field in the messages sent to it through the pnlog agent. This means if you have multiple ACS appliances reporting to the same Remote Agent with the pnlog agent installed, CS-MARS will not be capable of distinguishing between events coming from the individual ACS appliances. In addition, CS-MARS will see all events coming from the pnlog agent's IP address instead of from the ACS appliances IP. This should be resolved in later releases of CS-MARS.

Configuring CSA to Send Events to CS-MARS

Individual CSA agents send events to the CSA-MC that they are registered with. The CSA-MC can, in turn, forward the events to CS-MARS through SNMP traps. As CS-MARS receives the traps, it recognizes the individual CSA agent and associates it with the corresponding CSA-MC.

Complete the following tasks for CS-MARS to receive and understand events sent from CSA-MC:

1. Define CSA-MC as a reporting device within CS-MARS.

2. Configure CSA-MC to forward events to CS-MARS.

In the next two sections, we walk through completing these tasks.

Defining CSA-MC as a Reporting Device within CS-MARS

Before CS-MARS will analyze the events received from CSA-MC, you must define CSA-MC as a monitored device within CS-MARS. Follow these steps to accomplish this task:

Step 1   Log in to the CS-MARS GUI interface and select the **Admin** tab.

Step 2   In the Device Configuration and Discovery Information section, click the **Security and Monitor Devices** link.

Step 3   Click the **Add** box on the far right of the screen.

Step 4   In the **Device Type** drop-down list, select **Add SW Security Apps on New Host**.

Step 5   In the General Information section, fill in **Device Name**, **Access IP**, and **Reporting IP**. In the interface information section, fill in the IP address and netmask of the CSA-MC machine. Figure 17-9 shows an example of this screen.

NOTE   The access IP, reporting IP, and interface IP should all be the IP address of the CSA-MC. If you have more than one CSA-MC machine, each one must be defined independently.

Step 6   Click the **Apply** button.

Step 7   Click the **Next** button to advance to the **Reporting Applications** tab.

Step 8   From the **Select Application** drop-down list, choose **Cisco CSA 4.x**; then click the **Add** button. Figure 17-10 shows an example of this screen.

Figure 17-9 *Example: Adding CSA-MC to CS-MARS as a Reporting Device*

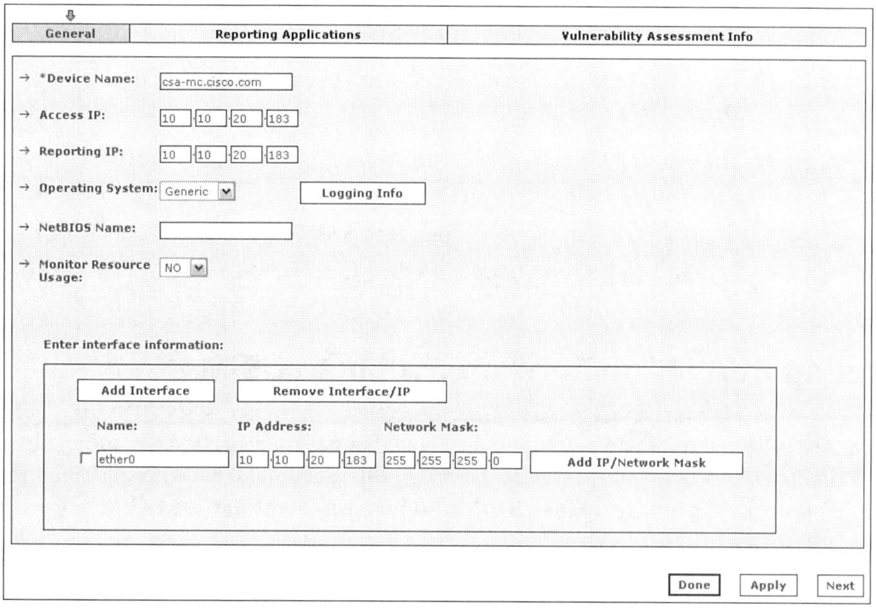

NOTE   In CS-MARS, all CSA versions are represented as **Device Type: Cisco CSA 4.x**, regardless of the actual version of CSA.

Figure 17-10 *Example: Adding CSA-MC as a Reporting Application*

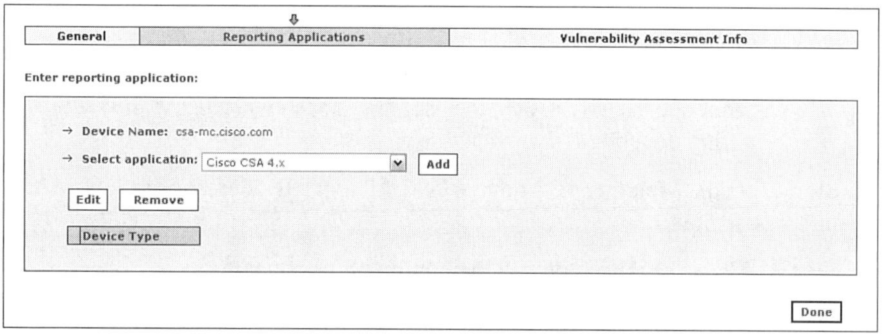

Step 9 The Management Console window appears, where you can manually add CSA agents. Instead, click the **Submit** button. (Starting with Version 4.1, CS-MARS can automatically discover the agents.)

Step 10 Cisco CSA Management Center now appears as a device type. Click **Done** to save the changes.

Step 11 The last step (which people often forget) is to select the **Activate** button in the upper-right corner of the page.

These steps are all you need to do to set up CS-MARS to receive events from CSA-MC. In the next section, you will configure CSA-MC to forward agent events to CS-MARS.

Configuring CSA-MC to Forward Events to CS-MARS

CSA-MC is capable of forwarding all received agent events as SNMP traps. CS-MARS can receive these traps and determine the agent that generated the event, automatically add the agent as a reporting device under the CSA-MC, and analyze the event. Complete the following steps to configure CSA-MC to forward events to CS-MARS:

Step 1 Log in to the Cisco Works Desktop and launch CSA-MC.

Step 2 Select the **Events** link at the top and then **Alerts**.

Step 3 Create a new alert by clicking the **New** button at the bottom of the page.

Step 4 Fill in the **Name** and **Description** fields. I highly recommend that you make these entries descriptive. For **Name**, you could use "Forward events to <Mars_appliance_name>". An example of the **Description** field could be, "Send events as SNMP traps to the CS-MARS appliance."

Step 5 In the Send Alerts section, select **Event Set—All Events**.

Step 6 Scroll down the page to select the **SNMP** check box under the **Alert Method**.

Step 7 Fill in the SNMP **Community name** field with the community name of your choice. CS-MARS does not use this, so you can use the standard string of public if you want.

Step 8 In the **Manager IP Address** field, fill in the IP address of the CS-MARS appliance.

Step 9 Click the **Save** button at the bottom of the page.

This completes the required configuration needed in CSA-MC.

TIP   When you install CS-MARS in a network that is being protected by CSA, you will receive a lot of events from the CSA agents when CS-MARS performs its vulnerability scans against the endpoints. You can prevent these alerts by adding CS-MARS to the $Authorized_Port_Scanners variable, which is included in the default rule module, IP Stack Hardening Module—Internal Systems. To add a CS-MARS IP address to the $Authorized_Port_Scanners variable in CSA-MC, click **Configuration** > **Variables** > **Network Address Sets** > **Authorized Port Scanners**. Then click **Save** and **Generate Rules**.

Configuring VPN 3000 Concentrators to Send Events to CS-MARS

The VPN 3000 concentrator can forward events to CS-MARS relating to client access. This includes the username and IP address of the client who is connecting to the concentrator, along with the host OS and the duration of the connection. This information assists with the end-to-end attack path for attacks destined to or from VPN users. This enables you to single out a specific user's machine instead of just an IP address from a DHCP pool.

Complete the following tasks for CS-MARS to receive and understand events sent from a VPN 3000 concentrator:

1. Define the VPN 3000 concentrator as a reporting device within CS-MARS.

2. Configure the VPN 3000 concentrator to forward events to CS-MARS.

In the next two sections, we walk through completing these tasks.

Defining the VPN 3000 Concentrator as a Reporting Device within CS-MARS

Before the VPN 3000 concentrator can be imported as a reporting device within CS-MARS, you must bootstrap it. This is done by enabling SNMP and setting a read-only community string. Follow these below to accomplish this task:

Step 1   Enable SNMP by navigating to **Configuration** > **System** > **Management Protocols** > **SNMP**. Check the **Enable** box and click **Apply**.

Step 2   Next, set the SNMP community string by navigating to **Configuration** > **System** > **Management Protocols** > **SNMP Communities**. Click the **Add** button. Fill in the **Community String** field and click **Add**.

Step 3   Finally, click the **Save Needed** button.

With the concentrator properly bootstrapped, follow these steps to add it as a monitored device within CS-MARS:

Step 1   Log in to the CS-MARS GUI interface and select the **Admin** tab.

Step 2   In the Device Configuration and Discovery Information section, click the **Security and Monitor Devices** link.

Step 3   Click the **Add** box on the far right of the screen.

Step 4   In the Device Type drop-down list, select **Cisco VPN Concentrator 4.7**.

Step 5   Fill in **Access IP** and **Reporting IP**. These should be the same. The access IP is the address CS-MARS uses to discover the concentrator. The reporting IP is the address CS-MARS uses to match events received to the correct monitored device.

Step 6   For **Access Type**, choose **SNMP** from the drop-down list and fill in the **SNMP RO Community** string.

Step 7   Under **Monitor Resource Usage**, choose **Yes**. Figure 17-11 shows an example of this screen.

Figure 17-11   *Example: Adding a VPN 3000 Concentrator to CS-MARS as a Reporting Device*

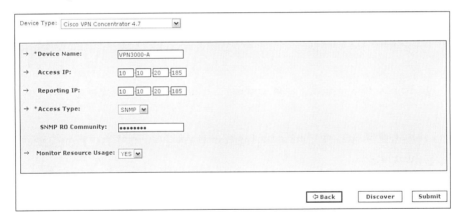

Step 8   Select the **Discover** button. In a few seconds, you should see a pop-up message indicating that the discovery is complete. Choose **OK**.

Step 9   Select **Submit**.

Step 10 Select **Activate** in the upper-right corner.

Repeat the above steps to add other VPN 3000 concentrators into CS-MARS.

Configuring the VPN 3000 Concentrator to Forward Events to CS-MARS

With the VPN 3000 concentrator added in CS-MARS, the next task is to configure it to send syslog events to CS-MARS. Follow these steps to accomplish this:

Step 1   Log in to the VPN 3000 GUI interface and navigate to **Configuration > System > Events > General**.

Step 2   Set the **Save Log Format** to **Multiline**.

Step 3   Set **Syslog Format** to **Original**.

Step 4   Under **Events to Log**, select **Severities 1–5**.

Step 5   Under **Events to Syslog**, select **Severities 1–5**.

Step 6   Under **Events to Trap**, select **Severities 1–3**.

Figure 17-12 shows an example of configuring syslog levels on the VPN 3000 concentrator.

Figure 17-12   *Example: Configuring Syslog Levels on the VPN 3000 Concentrator*

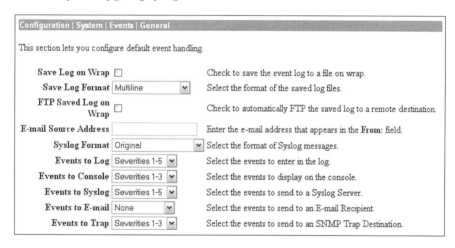

Step 7   Click **Apply**.

Step 8   Navigate to **Configuration > System > Events > Syslog Servers**.

Step 9   Click **Add** to add CS-MARS as a syslog server.

Step 10   In the **Syslog Server** field, fill in the IP address of CS-MARS, and then click **Add**.

Step 11   Click the **Save Needed** icon in the upper-right corner.

This completes the configuration needed on the VPN 3000 concentrator to forward events to CS-MARS.

Configuring the Adaptive Security Appliance and PIX Security Appliance to Send Events to CS-MARS

The ASA and PIX security appliances support NAC-L3-IP NAC for remote access VPN clients starting with Version 7.2. This includes the username and IP address of the client who is connecting to the appliance, along with the host OS and the duration of the connection. This information assists with the end-to-end attack path for attacks destined to or from VPN users. This enables you to single out a specific user's machine instead of just an IP address from a DHCP pool.

Besides the NAC-specific features CS-MARS can monitor, the firewall appliance is a critical network security device. It is typically the device that is performing Network Address Translation (NAT) in your network. Because of this, CS-MARS must know about the firewall's configuration to retrieve the NAT rules. In addition, it needs to receive the built and teardown connection-related messages to properly sessionize events received from other devices in your network.

Complete the following tasks for CS-MARS to receive and understand events sent from the ASA or PIX appliance:

1. Define the ASA/PIX appliance as a reporting device within CS-MARS.

2. Configure the ASA/PIX appliance to forward events to CS-MARS.

In the next two sections, we walk through completing these tasks.

Defining the ASA/PIX Appliance as a Reporting Device within CS-MARS

Before the ASA or PIX appliance can be imported as a reporting device within CS-MARS, you must bootstrap it. This is done by enabling SSH or Telnet access to the appliance for the IP address assigned to CS-MARS and defining an SNMP read-only community string. CS-MARS uses the SSH or Telnet access to import the appliance's configuration. The SNMP read-only community string is optional, but it allows CS-MARS to monitor the CPU, memory, and interface utilization of the appliance. Apply the following commands to bootstrap the appliance:

```
crypto key generate rsa modulus modulus-size
ssh CS-MARS-IP 255.255.255.255 interface
snmp-server host interface CS-MARS-IP poll community community-string
```

The first command generates an RSA key that is used to encrypt the SSH session. The second command tells the appliance to accept incoming SSH sessions from CS-MARS IP addresses on the specified interface. The interface listed is the one packets would leave out of to reach the CS-MARS appliance. The third command allows CS-MARS to poll the appliance via SNMP.

Now that the appliance is bootstrapped, follow these steps to add it to CS-MARS as a monitored device:

Step 1   Log in to the CS-MARS GUI interface and select the **Admin** tab.

Step 2   In the Device Configuration and Discovery Information section, click the **Security and Monitor Devices** link.

Step 3   Click the **Add** box on the far right of the screen.

Step 4   In the **Device Type** drop-down list, select **Cisco ASA 7.0** for an ASA, or **Cisco PIX 7.0** for a PIX appliance.

NOTE   In CS-MARS, all ASA versions greater than 7.0 are represented as **Device Type: Cisco ASA 7.x**, regardless of the actual version of ASA. The same is true of the PIX. Versions greater than 7.0 are represented as **Device Type: Cisco PIX 7.0**.

Step 5   Fill in **Device Name** with the host name of the appliance.

Step 6   Fill in **Access IP** and **Reporting IP**. These should be the same. The access IP is the address CS-MARS uses to discover the appliance. The reporting IP is the address CS-MARS uses to match events received to the correct monitored device.

Step 7   For **Access Type**, choose **SSH** from the drop-down list and select either **3DES** or **DES** as the encryption strength.

Step 8   Add the username in the **Login** field and the password in the **Password** field. Also fill in the **Enable Password** field.

NOTE   If you do not have authentication setup on the ASA/PIX for SSH access, use the default username of pix. The password for this user is the exec password.

Step 9   Fill in the **SNMP RO Community** field with the read-only community string that you set when bootstrapping the appliance earlier.

Step 10 Under **Monitor Resource Usage**, I recommend that you select **Yes** from the drop-down list. This allows CS-MARS to monitor the memory and CPU for abnormal activity. Figure 17-13 shows an example of this screen for an ASA appliance.

Figure 17-13 *Example: Adding an ASA Appliance to CS-MARS as a Reporting Device*

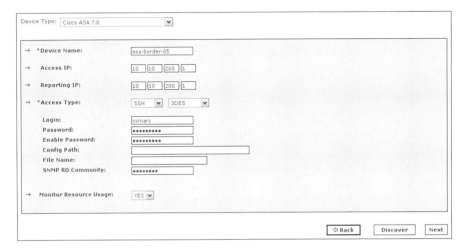

Step 11 Click the **Discover** button. In a few seconds, you should see a pop-up message indicating that the discovery is complete. Choose **OK**.

Step 12 Select **Submit**.

Step 13 Select **Activate** in the upper-right corner.

Repeat these steps to add other ASA or PIX appliances to CS-MARS.

Configuring the ASA/PIX Appliance to Forward Events to CS-MARS

Now that the ASA or PIX appliance has been added into CS-MARS as a monitored device, it needs to be configured to forward events to CS-MARS. The ASA or PIX uses syslogs as the mechanism to generate and forward events. CS-MARS prefers to see a high level of syslogs (levels 6 or 7) to properly sessionize events in the network.

Configure the ASA or PIX to send syslogs to CS-MARS by adding the following commands:

```
logging host interface> CS-MARS-IP
logging trap level
logging enable
```

NOTE   On highly utilized firewall appliances, setting the logging level above level 4 (Warning) might cause higher than normal CPU usage because of the number of syslogs generated. If the CPU usage is above 50 percent before enabling the previous logging, use caution when choosing a logging level. You can monitor the CPU usage by using the command **show cpu usage**. If the CPU usage is at 99 percent, the appliance will start dropping packets.

NOTE   Starting with Version 4.2.1, CS-MARS can correctly parse syslogs that have customized logging levels. This enables you to move the syslogs that CS-MARS needs to see down to a lower level and then log at that level. Use the command **logging message** *message-id* **level** *level* on the ASA, or PIX, to move a syslog to a new level.

Configuring QualysGuard to Send Events to CS-MARS

Qualys provides network security audits and vulnerability assessments of your network using the QualysGuard solution. When used with the NAC Framework, QualysGuard can receive messages from ACS to scan nonresponsive hosts to assist in determining their system posture token.

If you have a subscription with QualysGuard, you can configure CS-MARS to connect to the QualysGuard API server and retrieve the vulnerability analysis reports. These reports are then parsed and inserted into the CS-MARS back-end database. This per-host vulnerability assessment data augments the built-in capabilities of CS-MARS and results in high-fidelity attack analysis. If hosts that are under attack are not vulnerable to that exploit, CS-MARS can lower the incident severity. Likewise, if a host is vulnerable, the severity can be increased.

Because CS-MARS queries the QualysGuard API server, no configuration changes or bootstrap settings need to be configured on QualysGuard. For the CS-MARS side, you just need to add QualysGuard as a monitored device.

Follow these steps to add QualysGuard as a monitored device within CS-MARS:

Step 1   Log in to the CS-MARS GUI interface and select the **Admin** tab.

Step 2   Under the Device Configuration and Discovery Information section, click the **Security and Monitor Devices** link.

Step 3   Click the **Add** box on the far right of the screen.

Step 4   In the **Device Type** drop-down list, select **QualysGuard 3.x**.

Step 5   Fill in the **Device Name** field. This name is used in reports and query results to identify the QualysGuard. I suggest using the name QualysGuard.

Step 6   The **Access IP** is filled in for you: 165.193.18.12. This is the address assigned to the QualysGuard API server on the Internet. In addition, the URL to retrieve the audit reports is prepopulated in the **URL** field. Fill in the **Login** and **Password** fields with your credentials to the QualysGuard subscription service. Figure 17-14 shows an example of this screen.

Figure 17-14   *Example: Adding QualysGuard to CS-MARS as a Reporting Device*

Step 7   Click the **Test Connectivity** button to verify your login credentials and network connectivity. In a few seconds, you should see a pop-up message indicating that the connectivity was successful. Choose **OK**.

Step 8   Select **Submit**.

Step 9   Select **Activate** in the upper-right corner.

This completes the steps needed to add QualysGuard to CS-MARS.

Generating Reports in CS-MARS

Up until now in this chapter, we have talked about how to configure CS-MARS to receive events from your NADs. However, what you really want to know about is how CS-MARS can help you monitor your network for NAC-specific events and map those to your company's overall security policies. This is where CS-MARS really shines. It takes in all the events generated by the various devices in your network and correlates, consolidates, rules out false positives, and alerts you to what is important to you.

Out of the box, CS-MARS has a number of built-in reports to assist you with monitoring your NAC solution:

- Activity: AAA Failed Auth—All Events (Total View)
- Activity: AAA Failed Auth—Top NADs (Total View)

- Activity: AAA Failed Auth—Top Users (Total View)
- Activity: Security Posture: Healthy—Top Users (Total View)
- Activity: Security Posture: NAC—Top NADs (Total View)
- Activity: Security Posture: NAC—Top NADs and Tokens (Total View)
- Activity: Security Posture: NAC—Top Tokens (Total View)
- Activity: Security Posture: NAC Agentless—Top Hosts (Total View)
- Activity: Security Posture: NAC Agentless—Top NADs (Total View)
- Activity: Security Posture: NAC Agentless—Top Tokens (Total View)
- Activity: Security Posture: NAC Audit Server Issues—All Events (Total View)
- Activity: Security Posture: NAC End Host Details—All Events (Total View)
- Activity: Security Posture: NAC Infected/Quarantine—All Events (Total View)
- Activity: Security Posture: NAC Infected/Quarantine—Top Hosts (Total View)
- Activity: Security Posture: NAC L2 802.1X—Top Tokens (Total View)
- Activity: Security Posture: NAC L2IP—Top Tokens (Total View)
- Activity: Security Posture: NAC Static Auth—Top Hosts (Total View)
- Activity: Security Posture: NAC Static Auth—Top NADs (Total View)
- Activity: Security Posture: NAC Status Query Failure—Top Hosts (Total View)
- Activity: Security Posture: Not Healthy—All Events (Total View)
- Activity: Vulnerable Host Found (Total View)
- Activity: Vulnerable Host Found via VA Scanner (Total View)

One question on your mind might be, "How easy is it to access and use these reports?" The answer to that is, it is very simple. After logging in to the GUI, you select the **Query/Reports** tab from the top. Then in the first drop-down list, choose **System: Security Posture Compliance (Cisco NAC)**. A second drop-down lists all the NAC-related reports. Figure 17-15 shows a screenshot of this.

These reports can be run on demand, anytime you want. Alternatively, you can schedule any or all of them to be run at a predetermined time, and the report can be sent to you by e-mail.

Figure 17-15   *Screenshot Showing Built-In NAC Reports*

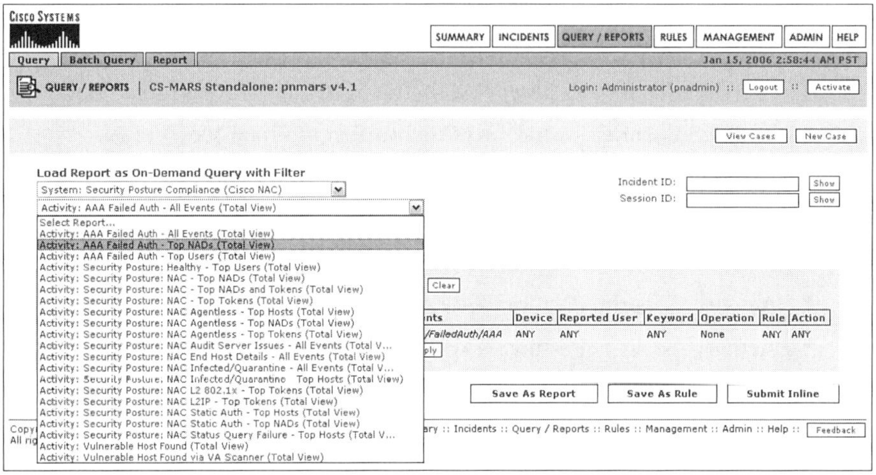

NAC Report—Top Tokens

One of the most important reports to run is the Activity: Security Posture: NAC—Top Tokens (Total View), which shows you the overall security posture of your network. This report gives you a summary of the number of hosts at the various NAC posture states.

Let us walk through an example to see how easy it is to generate this report.

Step 1   Log in to the CS-MARS GUI and click the **Query/Reports** tab at the top of the page.

Step 2   In the Load Report as On-Demand Query with Filter section, choose **System: Security Posture Compliance (Cisco NAC)** from the first drop-down list, and then choose **Activity: Security Posture: NAC—Top Tokens (Total View)** from the second drop-down list.

Step 3   Choose the **Submit Inline** button to generate the report.

By default, the report is generated from the events over the last hour, but you can easily edit this to be the last 24 hours, or any period you desire. Figure 17-16 shows an example of this report.

Figure 17-16 *Report: NAC—Top Tokens*

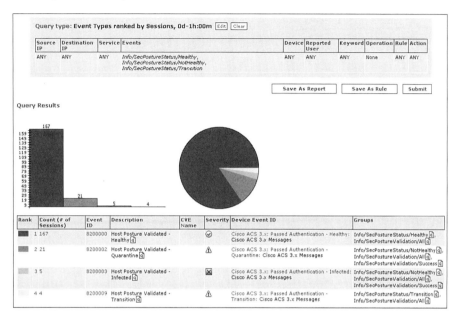

NAC Report—Infected/Quarantine—Top Hosts

Another report you might to run is the Activity: Security Posture: NAC Infected/
Quarantine—Top Hosts (Total View). This report shows you the number of hosts that are in
an Infected or Quarantine state, along with the user logged into the host. The steps to
generate this report are similar to the previous steps:

Step 1   Log in to the CS-MARS GUI and click the **Query/Reports** tab at the top
of the page.

Step 2   In the Load Report as On-Demand Query with Filter section, choose
System: Security Posture Compliance (Cisco NAC) from the first
drop-down list, and then choose **Activity: Security Posture: NAC—
Infected/Quarantine—Top Hosts (Total View)** from the second drop-
down list.

Step 3   Click the **Submit Inline** button to generate the report.

Figure 17-17 shows an example of this report.

Figure 17-17 *Report: NAC—Infected/Quarantine—Top Hosts*

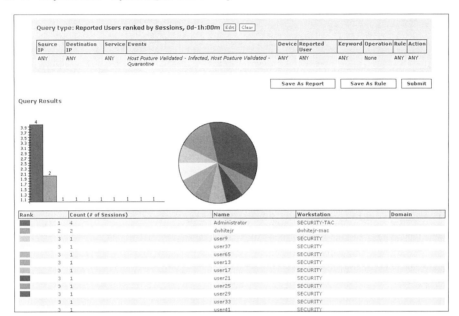

NAC Report—Agentless (Clientless) Hosts

Another very useful piece of information to know during the rollout of NAC is the number of agentless (clientless) hosts in your network. These hosts represent users who have not installed the CTA agent. Before implementing any restrictive policy, you will want the number of agentless hosts to less than 10 percent. You can keep a close eye on this number by running the agentless hosts report with a small customization, as follows:

Step 1 Log in to the CS-MARS GUI and click the **Query/Reports** tab at the top of the page.

Step 2 In the Load Report as On-Demand Query with Filter section, choose **System: Security Posture Compliance (Cisco NAC)** from the first drop-down list, and then choose **Activity: Security Posture: NAC Agentless—Top Hosts (Total View)** from the second drop-down list.

Step 3 Select the link under the Events column to edit the events to query on.

Step 4 Under the Filter by Event Type section, change the filter drop-down list from Event Type Groups to **All Event Types**; then type **Passed AAA** in the free text search box and then click **Search**.

Step 5   The result list is provided in the box below. Select **Passed AAA Authentication** and move it to the left box. Then click the **Apply** button.

Step 6   Click the **Submit Inline** button to generate the report.

Figure 17-18 shows an example of this customized agentless report.

Figure 17-18   *Report: NAC Agentless—Top Hosts*

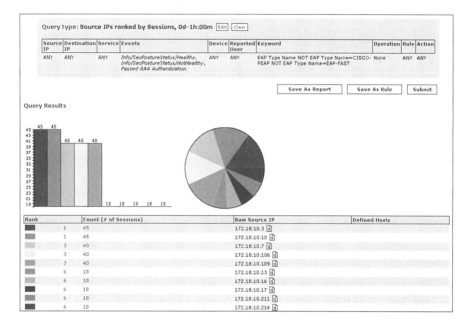

Running the Agentless Hosts report without modification returns only the agentless hosts that have been scanned by an audit server and been assigned a posture token. However, including the Passed AAA Authentication events to the report, as shown in the previous steps, ensures that all agentless hosts are reported.

Creating Scheduled NAC Reports

Running these on-demand style reports is neat, but the real beauty is configuring CS-MARS to e-mail you the reports at the schedule you specify. For example, you might find it useful to receive a report every morning of the hosts that are Infected or in a Quarantine state. To create a scheduled report, follow these steps:

Step 1   Log in to the CS-MARS GUI and click the **Query/Reports** tab at the top of the page.

Step 2 In the Load Report as On-Demand Query with Filter section, choose **System: Security Posture Compliance (Cisco NAC)** from the first drop-down list, and then choose **Activity: Security Posture: NAC Infected/Quarantine—Top Hosts (Total View)** from the second drop-down list.

Step 3 Next, click the **Edit** button to change the time interval from 1 hour to 1 day, and then click **Apply**.

Step 4 Click the **Save As Report** button to save this customized report.

Step 5 On the next page, you need to specify the report name. What you type here will be the Subject line in the e-mail report CS-MARS generates. I chose Daily Report: NAC Infected/Quarantined Hosts for mine. You also need to fill in the **Report Description** field. When finished, click **Next**.

Step 6 For the schedule, choose **Daily** and specify a time to start the report. I suggest running the report an hour before you normally arrive in the office. The report then will be in your e-mail inbox when you arrive.

Step 7 Under **View Type**, leave the default of **Total View** and click **Next**.

Step 8 You now need to list which users should receive this report. You can specify a group of users or, from the drop-down list, select **All Users** to choose individual users who should receive the report. When the users are selected, click **Next**.

Step 9 You now see a summary of the report criteria. Click **Next**.

Step 10 The final page in the wizard appears. Click the **Submit** button to save the custom report. The Reports screen appears, and the new custom report is listed at the top of the table. Figure 17-19 shows this step.

Repeat this process to deliver as many reports as you want—whenever you want—to your inbox every day. This will help you stay on top of your NAC deployment and as other events occurring in your network.

In this section, we examined the built-in reports that CS-MARS provides for NAC-related events. We also walked through customizing one of these reports to be generated daily and e-mailed to users. However, this is only a very small sampling of what CS-MARS can do with respect to reporting. Besides generating all the built-in reports, you can configure CS-MARS to generate your own fully customized reports—matching on whatever criteria you deem is important. You could generate different reports for different branches or different departments. Then you could e-mail the reports to the local administrators of those networks. Whatever you can dream up, CS-MARS can probably handle.

Figure 17-19   *Custom Daily Report: NAC Non-Healthy Hosts*

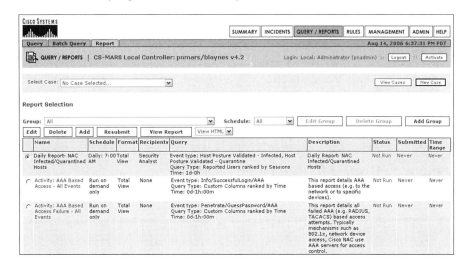

Troubleshooting CS-MARS

In this section, we cover some common problems users experience with CS-MARS. Troubleshooting steps are provided to assist in resolving the issue.

Events from a Specific Device Are Not Showing Up

You can determine whether CS-MARS is receiving events from a given device in two ways:

- Submit an inline query for all raw messages
- Use tcpdump to display packets from that device

Submitting an Inline Query for All Raw Messages

The easiest way to determine whether events are arriving to CS-MARS from a specified device is to submit an inline query for all raw messages that CS-MARS is receiving. To do this, click the **Query/Reports** tab. In the middle of the page, the query type Event Types ranked by sessions is shown. Click the **Edit** box and, under **Result Format**, select **All Matching Event Raw Messages** from the drop-down list. Under the Filter by Time section, select **Real Time.** Next, choose **Apply.** Select the link for the **Source IP.** Remove Any from the selected addresses (the box on the left) and, below, fill in the IP address of the device you are troubleshooting and select the double up arrow icon to add it to the source IP box. Then click **Apply.** Finally, click **Submit Inline** to start the query.

Any new events from the device automatically appear on the page. If you do not see any events, the device either is not sending them or is sending them with the incorrect IP, or they are being filtered along the path.

NOTE   In addition, when troubleshooting why a host has been quarantined (or assigned any non-Healthy token), you can choose to view the raw messages from ACS because this enables you to see the attributes sent from the client and the various application posture tokens.

Using tcpdump to Display Packets from a Device

The second option to determine whether events are arriving to CS-MARS from a specified device is to SSH into the CS-MARS appliance. From there, execute the **tcpdump host** *device-ip* command to verify the events are making it from the device to the CS-MARS interface. In Example 17-4, tcpdump is executed, filtering packets from the ACS server at 10.10.20.181. From the output, you can see that CS-MARS is receiving syslogs from ACS.

Example 17-4   *Executing tcpdump to Verify That Events Are Arriving at CS-MARS*

```
[pnadmin]$ tcpdump host 10.10.20.181
tcpdump: listening on eth0
00:55:34.450306 10.10.20.181.1523 > 10.10.20.190.syslog:  udp 665
00:55:34.489659 10.10.20.181.1499 > 10.10.20.190.syslog:  udp 230
```

tcpdump is terminated by issuing **Ctrl+C**. If tcpdump does not display the packets from the network device, the next step is to verify that the device is actually generating the traffic. Next, verify that the packets are being generated with the source IP you expect. (Remember, you can always use the source-interface option.) Finally, verify that the packets are not being dropped by an access list or some other filtering mechanism between the originator and CS-MARS.

Events Are Showing Up from an Unknown Reporting Device

If you run a Raw Event Query and see events arriving from an Unknown Reporting Device, but the IP matches one that you have defined on a monitored device, pat yourself on the back. You have just made the number one mistake that every CS-MARS owner hits about ten times in the first week. You forgot to click the **Activate** button in the upper-right corner of the page. The GUI front end is aware of the monitored device you configured. However, the database back end has not been made aware of it. Clicking the **Activate** button synchronizes the GUI configuration to the back-end database. So click the **Activate** button and let us move on.

NOTE	In a future version of CS-MARS, we hope to change the **Activate** button into a flashing strobe light when you make changes to the front-end GUI. Until then, history has shown us that we humans will still forget to click the button.

Trouble Discovering a Monitored Device

When adding a Reporting/Monitoring device into CS-MARS, you click the **Discover** button for CS-MARS to attempt to access the device and pull in its configuration. If discovery fails, click the **View Error** button at the bottom of the page. A pop-up window appears indicating why discovery failed. Note the protocol that CS-MARS used to try to discover the device. Ensure that this is the protocol CS-MARS should be using. Also verify that you correctly bootstrapped the device to allow CS-MARS to access it through the protocol. This often means allowing the IP address of CS-MARS in the vty access-list, or in the SSH/Telnet/SNMP filter list. Also verify that all usernames/passwords are correct.

If you still have problems, SSH into CS-MARS itself and from there attempt to SSH/Telnet to the device using the same credentials that you specified in the GUI. If this is not successful, check the logs on the device to ensure that your access attempt is reaching the device. If not, a device in between is either filtering the packets or possibly NATing them.

Summary

In this chapter, we covered a brief overview of the CS-MARS appliance family. Then we showed, step by step, how to bootstrap and import the following devices in CS-MARS:

- Cisco IOS routers
- Cisco switches
- Cisco Secure Access Control Servers (ACS)
- Cisco Security Agent Management Centers (CSA-MC)
- Cisco VPN 3000 series concentrators
- Cisco ASA and PIX security appliances
- QualysGuard network appliances

Next, we covered the reporting capabilities CS-MARS provides that are specific to the NAC Framework. Finally, we finished with our usual troubleshooting section.

Reference

CS-MARS User Guide

Review Questions

You can find the answers to the review questions in Appendix A, "Answers to Review Questions."

1. After adding any new monitored device into CS-MARS, what must be done before CS-MARS analyzes events sent from that device?

   a. CS-MARS must be rebooted.

   b. The **Activate** button must be clicked to synchronize the GUI to the back-end database.

   c. You must select the **Analyze Events** button next to the device on the Report tab.

   d. Nothing needs to be done after adding the new device through the GUI.

2. What protocol/port do Cisco IOS routers (by default) use to send NetFlow data to CS-MARS?

   a. UDP/5520

   b. TCP/5520

   c. UDP/2055

   d. TCP/2055

3. What version(s) of NetFlow does CS-MARS support?

   a. 5

   b. 7

   c. 9

   d. 5 and 7

   e. 7 and 9

4. When discovering a monitored device, which of the following protocols is not supported by CS-MARS?

   a. FTP

   b. SSH

   c. Syslog

   d. Telnet

5. What utility is used to send ACS events as syslogs to CS-MARS?

   a. pnlog agent

   b. mars-syslog.exe

   c. syslog.exe

   d. csagent

6. Events from which log file are not forwarded to CS-MARS from the ACS server?

   a. Failed Attempts

   b. Passed Authentications

   c. RADIUS Accounting

   d. TACACS+ Accounting

7. When adding a new monitored device into CS-MARS, which protocol used during discovery requires the access IP and reporting IP to be different?

   a. FTP

   b. SNMP

   c. SSH

   d. Telnet

8. When sending syslogs from monitored devices to CS-MARS, if the traffic flow passes through a firewall, what protocol and port must be allowed through for the syslogs to reach CS-MARS?

   a. TCP/21

   b. TCP/513

   c. TCP/514

   d. UDP/513

   e. UDP/514

9. CSA agents send events to CS-MARS . . .

   a. Directly, via syslog

   b. Indirectly; the CSA-MC sends the events via Syslog

   c. Directly, via SNMP traps

   d. Indirectly; the CSA-MC sends the events via SNMP traps

   e. CS-MARS cannot receive individual agent events.

10. True or false: CS-MARS can automatically discover CSA agents and add them to the database.

PART V

Appendix

Answers to Review Questions

Chapter 1

1. Which of the following is a required component of NAC?

   a. Remediation server

   b. Antivirus server

   c. Cisco Security Agent

   d. Cisco Secure Access Control Server

   Answer: D

2. What is the posture-enforcement method for NAC-L3-IP?

   Answer: NAC-L3-IP uses a downloadable ACL to permit, restrict, or deny access to the network, based on the overall posture of the endpoint along with the policy defined on Cisco Secure ACS.

3. What is the posture-enforcement method for NAC-L2-802.1X?

   Answer: NAC-L2-802.1X uses VLAN assignment as the posture enforcement. However, on the Catalyst 6500 series switches, policy-based ACL might optionally be applied to the switch port as well. On Layer 3 switches, the network administrator might additionally apply an ACL to the Layer 3 VLAN interface (or switch virtual interface) to further restrict network access.

4. NAC-L3-IP and NAC-L2-IP use which of the following protocols to secure the communication between the endpoint and Cisco Secure ACS?

   a. EAP over UDP

   b. EAP-FAST

   c. RADIUS

   d. PEAP

   Answer: D

5. The network-access device uses what protocol to send NAC-related messages to Cisco Secure ACS?

   a. EAP over UDP

   b. EAP-FAST

   c. RADIUS

   d. PEAP

   Answer: C

6. The VPN 3000 concentrator and the ASA and PIX security appliances support NAC on which of the following:

   a. Remote-access IPSec and L2TP over IPSec connections

   b. Remote-access and LAN-to-LAN IPSec connections

   c. Remote-access PPTP and L2TP over IPSec connections

   d. Remote-access IPSec connections only

   Answer: A

Chapter 2

1. What port does CTA use to communicate with the NAD?

   a. 12628

   b. 1812

   c. 1813

   d. 21862

   Answer: D

2. What type of certificate is required to be installed on the CTA client?

   a. Identity certificate

   b. Root or self-signed certificate

   c. Authoritative certificate

   Answer: B

3. The 802.1X supplicant bundled with CTA supports what interface types?

   a. Wired interfaces only

   b. Wireless interfaces only

   c. Both wired and wireless interfaces

   Answer: A

4. On default CTA installs, logging is

   a. Enabled at level High

   b. Enabled at level Medium

   c. Enabled at level Low

   d. Disabled

   Answer: D

5. To temporarily enable CTA logging:

   a. Manually start the ctalogd service

   b. Execute the **clogcli** command

   c. Create a log.ini file

   Answer: B

6. What command will allow you to view the current status of CTA?

   a. **show status**

   b. **ctad -status**

   c. **ctastat**

   Answer: C

7. What file must be edited to disable user notifications?

   a. ctalogd.ini

   b. ctad.ini

   c. ctaconfig.ini

   Answer: B

8. True or false: The CTA Scripting Interface is installed by default.

   Answer: False—with one notable exception. The CTA Linux installation always installs the Scripting Interface.

9. When using the Scripting Interface, which of the following is not true:

   a. The AppType value in the .inf file must match the application-id used in the posture data file.

   b. The application-id can be any positive integer.

   c. The ctasi executable is used to load the output of your custom script into the posture database on the client.

   Answer: B

10. How do you add custom attributes to the ACS database?

    a. Use CSUtil.exe

    b. Import a csv file, attributes.def, into ACS

    c. Enter each one into the GUI under the Posture Validation section

    Answer: A

Chapter 3

1. What is the difference between the Administrator version and the End-User version of the Cisco Secure Services Client?

   a. The End-User Client version has a different .msi executable file than the Administrator version.

   b. The Administrator version is licensed separately.

   c. The clients are the same; the only difference is the configuration files.

   Answer: C

2. The Cisco Secure Services End-Client configuration is defined by what three files?

   a. *-networks.xml, *-config.xml, *-profile.xml

   b. *-config.xml, *-profile.xml, *-policy.xml

   c. *-config.xml, *-networks.xml, *-policy.xml

   d. *-networks.xml, *-policy.xml, *-credentials.xml

   Answer: D

3. True or false: The Cisco Secure Services Client must always validate ACS's identity certificate.

   Answer: False

4. True or false: Cisco Secure Services Preset Clients cannot add new networks to their profile.

   Answer: True

5. The Cisco Secure Services Client must be configured for which Authentication method to support NAC-L2-802.1X?

   a. EAP-MD5

   b. EAP-TLS

   c. FAST

   d. PEAP

   Answer: C

6. What utility is included with the Cisco Secure Services Client to assist you in troubleshooting client issues?

   a. Debugger

   b. System Report

   c. Cisco Secure Services Troubleshooter

   d. None of the Above

   Answer: B

Chapter 4

1. What command do you use to enable 802.1X globally on a switch running CatOS?

   a. **dot1x system-auth-control**

   b. **set dot1x system-auth-control**

   c. **dot1x enable**

   d. **set dot1x enable**

   Answer: B

2. True or false: EAP-FAST Phase 0 is used very frequently to enable the client to be dynamically provisioned with a PAC. Phases 1 and 2 cannot complete without Phase 0.

   Answer: False

3. True or false: VLAN assignment is the method used in NAC-L2-802.1X for policy enforcement.

   Answer: True

4. True or false: The output of the **debug dot1x packets** command can be very lengthy and might impact performance on busy switches.

   Answer: True

5. NAC nonresponsive hosts are often referred to as NAC agentless hosts (NAH). These are devices that do not or cannot run CTA. What command can you use to statically authorize a NAH though its IP address in a Catalyst switch running IOS?

   a.   **set device authorize ip** *ip-address*

   b.   **device authorize ip-address** *ip-address*

   c.   **ip device authorize** *ip-address*

   d.   **device ip authorize** *ip-address*

   Answer: B

6. What command is used to enable EoU logging on a Catalyst switch running Cisco IOS?

   a.   **eou logging enable**

   b.   **set eou logging**

   c.   **ip logging eou**

   d.   **eou logging**

   Answer: D

7. True or false: In NAC-L2-IP, the security posture process is triggered by a EAP-START.

   Answer: False

8. True or false: You can configure only one RADIUS server on a Catalyst switch running CatOS.

   Answer: False

9. True or false: The connection between CTA and a Catalyst switch running EoU is encrypted using IPSec.

   Answer: False

10. True or false: By default, a Catalyst switch configured for NAC-L2-IP and running Cisco IOS will reauthenticate every 275 seconds.

    Answer: False

Chapter 5

1. You can exempt devices from the posture-validation process by using the following attributes: (Multiple answers)

   a. IP address

   b. MAC address

   c. Operating system

   d. Type

   Answer: A, B, D

2. True or false: The Cisco IOS NAD does not allow you to use an audit server for determining the current state of clientless machines.

   Answer: False

3. True or false: The **radius-server key cisco123** command encrypts the shared secret defined on Cisco IOS NAD.

   Answer: False

4. The Cisco IOS NAD supports the following EAPoUDP timeouts when a machine goes through the posture-validation process: (Multiple answers)

   a. AAA timeout

   b. NAD timeout

   c. Retransmission timeout

   d. Max-retry timeout

   Answer: A, C

   5. True or false: In the hold-off state, the NAD ceases the EAPoUDP and other NAC-
   related activities until the hold-off timer expires.

   Answer: True

   6. The purpose of a NAC Intercept Access Control List is to

   a. Define the interesting hosts and networks that are bypassed from the posture-
   validation process.

   b. Define the interesting hosts and networks that are subject to the posture-
   validation process.

   c. Define the interesting hosts and networks that are considered clientless hosts and
   networks.

   d. Define the interesting hosts and networks that are allowed to pass traffic even if
   they are infected.

   Answer: B

Chapter 6

   1. The VPN 3000 concentrator uses UDP port _____ for EAPoUDP communication
   to the VPN client.

   a. 2182

   b. 3000

   c. 21862

   d. 3030

   Answer: C

   2. Cisco NAC solution is supported on which of the following VPN tunnels? (Multiple
   answers)

   a. PPTP

   b. L2TP

   c. IPSec

   d. L2TP over IPSec

   Answer: C, D

3. True or false: A VPN client that has CTA installed will still be considered agentless if the CTA services are disabled on it.

Answer: True

4. True or false: During mode-config, the VPN 3000 concentrator validates the user against the configured authentication database.

Answer: False

5. True or false: The purpose of an exception ACL is to ensure that remote users do not send unnecessary traffic until their posture is fully validated.

Answer: False

6. When configuring a user-group, you need to specify these two mandatory parameters. (Multiple answers)

   a. Group name

   b. Group password

   c. Group mode-config attributes

   d. Group x-auth

Answer: A, B

7. True or false: The posture-validation process is initiated by the VPN 3000 concentrator.

Answer: True

8. True or false: The IPSec tunnel is torn down if the VPN client does not respond to the EAPoUDP request packet.

Answer: False

9. True or false: If a Healthy posture token is assigned to the VPN client, the VPN 3000 concentrator does not apply any ACL.

Answer: False

10. True or false: The assignment of an IP address to the VPN client is a mandatory parameter during tunnel negotiations.

Answer: True

Chapter 7

1. The default value for the revalidation timer on a security appliance is _____.

   a. 1,800 seconds

   b. 18,000 seconds

   c. 180,000 seconds

   d. None of the above

   Answer: D

2. NAC exception polices can be set up under which of the following locations? (Multiple answers)

   a. Default group policies

   b. User group policies

   c. User policies

   d. Tunnel policies

   Answer: A, B

3. True or false: A VPN tunnel is considered clientless if it does not report any software version information.

   Answer: False

4. True or false: The NAC exception policies are configured under the tunnel group subconfiguration mode.

   Answer: False

5. True or false: The NAC session's database cannot be statefully replicated to a standby appliance.

   Answer: True

6. Mode-config attributes are configured under_____.

   a. User policy

   b. Default user-group

   c. User group-policy

   d. All of the above

   Answer: D

7. True or false: Specifying a RADIUS server under tunnel-group is a mandatory step.

   Answer: True

8. True or false: The IPSec tunnel is torn down if the VPN client does not respond to an EAPoUDP request packet.

   Answer: False

9. True or false: The NAC exemption list must be applied on a per-group basis.

   Answer: False

10. True or false: Clientless authentication is used for machines that do not have CTA installed.

    Answer: True

Chapter 8

1. True or false: You can access the ACS server remotely, by default, after installation.

   Answer: False. All remote users must authenticate before accessing the ACS GUI interface. After installation, no administrative users are defined; therefore, you cannot be authenticated to access the GUI.

2. True or false: The ACS server software that runs on the ACS Solution Engine (ACS appliance) is the same software that you can install on a standalone server.

   Answer: False. Because an administrator cannot access the Windows GUI interface on the ACS Solution Engine, some features needed to be moved off the Solution Engine and are handled by the Remote Agent. This includes authenticating to remote databases, along with some logging capabilities.

3. Access to the ACS user interface is provided via what port?

   a. TCP/80

   b. TCP/8080

   c. TCP/2000

   d. TCP/2002

   Answer: D

4. How can you further secure access to the ACS GUI interface?

   Answer: You can enable SSL encryption to the ACS GUI interface to protect the contents of the HTTP session. In addition, you can restrict access to the GUI by allowing only specified IP addresses to connect. Finally, authenticated users can be limited based on what configuration rights they have.

5. Network device groups are

   a. A way of grouping NAC policies, to be applied to end hosts

   b. A way of grouping AAA clients so they can share a common shared secret key, and user access may be limited on a NDG basis

   c. A way of grouping users so common policies can be applied to all users in the group

   d. None of the above

   Answer: B

6. Which of the following can you not add to a network access filter?

   a. Network device group

   b. Network access device

   c. Network access profile

   d. IP address

   Answer: C

7. A network access profile contains which of the following policies? (Select two.)

   a. Authentication and Protocols

   b. Accounting and Posture Validation

   c. Posture Validation and Authorization

   d. Protocols and RADIUS Authorization Components

   Answer: A and C

8. Which of the following is not contained in the Authorization policy for a network access profile?

   a. Deny access

   b. Shared RAC

   c. Downloadable ACL

   d. Network access filter

   Answer: D

9. What type of external database can be used to authenticate Agentless Hosts by MAC address?

   a. Windows database

   b. LDAP database

   c. ODBC database

   d. Token server

   Answer: B

10. If a client is being assigned the wrong system posture token, where is the first place you should look to troubleshoot the problem?

    a. Network access profiles configuration

    b. RADIUS authorization components configuration

    c. Failed Attempts log

    d. Passed Authentications log

    Answer: D

Chapter 9

1. CSA Version 5.*x* and later can scale to up to

   a. 10,000

   b. 50,000

   c. 100,000

   d. 250,000

   Answer: C

2. True or false: Agent kits are the configuration and installation packages of the agent software to be deployed to end-user machines. Agent kits must be associated with configured groups.

   Answer: True

3. True or false: To connect to the CSA MC, you must first install an agent in your machine.

   Answer: False

4. True or false: CSA version 3.*x* and above support NAC features and security posture–related policies.

   Answer: False

5. True or false: Cisco Secure ACS can communicate with CSA MC through the GAME protocol for remediation purposes.

   Answer: False

6. True or false: A group is the only element required to build an agent kit.

   Answer: True

7. True or false: Groups can contain up to five policies.

   Answer: False

8. The <Don't Care> posture state in CSA

   a. Is used when a client does not have CTA installed.

   b. Is Not provided by ACS. This state is currently the only valid posture state for UNIX-based machines.

   c. Is used when antivirus software is not installed on the end-host machine.

   d. Does not exist.

   Answer: B

9. You can install CSA MC and the database on the same machine by selecting the Local Database radio button during the CSA MC installation. In this case, the CSA MC installation installs the following:

    a. Its own version of MSDE

    b. Microsoft SQL Server 2000

    c. MSDE and Microsoft SQL Server 2000

    d. None of the above

    Answer: A

10. True or False: if you are deploying more than 500 agents, the use of Microsoft SQL Server is recommended because MSDE has a 2GB database size limit.

    Answer: True

Chapter 10

1. True or false: The HPAC protocol is used as the communication mechanism when using external posture validation to a third-party antivirus server.

    Answer: False. The Host Credential Authorization Protocol (HCAP) is used as the communication mechanism when using external posture validation to a third-party antivirus server.

2. Why does Cisco recommend the use of SLB when using external antivirus policy servers?

    a. Because NAC is dependent on the SLB Cisco IOS feature to perform posture validation.

    b. Because SLB creates a secure channel between Cisco Secure ACS and the antivirus server.

    c. Because Cisco Secure ACS checks the first external policy server in the list in every posture validation. Subsequently, you will experience an estimated 10-second delay on each posture validation if the primary server is down. Cisco recommends using SLB as a load-balancing and failover mechanism to avoid this unnecessary delay.

    d. SLB is faster.

Answer: C. Cisco Secure ACS checks the first external policy server in the list in every posture validation. Subsequently, you will experience an estimated 10-second delay on each posture validation if the primary server is down. Cisco recommends using SLB as a load-balancing and failover mechanism to avoid this unnecessary delay.

3. What port does the HCAP protocol use for its communication?

   a. TCP port 8080

   b. TCP port 80

   c. TCP port 4343

   d. TCP port 443

   Answer: D. HCAP uses SSL/TLS as the underlying communication protocol. SSL/TLS uses TCP port 443.

4. What utility can you use to import the antivirus ADF files on Cisco Secure ACS?

   a. ADFUtil.exe

   b. CSUtil.exe

   c. CSADF.exe

   d. ADFinstall.exe

   Answer: B. To import an antivirus vendor ADF file to ACS, use the command **CSUtil.exe -addAVP** *filename*.**adf** (*filename*.**adf** is the ADF provided by the antivirus vendor).

5. True or false: Cisco Secure ACS can send a notification message to the third-party antivirus software installed at the end host.

   Answer: True. An optional notification message can be sent to the third-party antivirus software installed at the end host.

6. True or false: Cisco Secure ACS can download the latest antivirus updates from each vendor's website automatically.

   Answer: False. This feature does not exist. Cisco Secure ACS can query an external antivirus posture-validation server; however, it does not download the latest antivirus updates from any antivirus vendor website.

Chapter 11

1. The CS-ACS server supports which of the following audit servers? (Multiple answers)

   a. QualysGuard Scanner Appliance

   b. Microsoft IAS server

   c. Altiris SecurityExpressions

   d. Symantec WholeSecurity

   Answer: A, C, D

2. Audit server support is available on which of the following Cisco NADs? (Multiple answers)

   a. Cisco IOS routers

   b. Cisco switches in 802.1X mode

   c. Cisco switches in NAC-L2-IP mode

   d. Cisco VPN 3000 concentrators

   Answer: A, C

3. True or false: The audit servers use only SSL communication for the GAME protocol.

   Answer: False

4. True or false: The Cisco Secure ACS server pulls the audit report from the QualysGuard server.

   Answer: True

5. True or false: You must use both interfaces on the QualysGuard scanner when assessing the internal network.

   Answer: False

6. What is the commend to load a QualysGuard ADF file into CS-ACS?

   a. **CSUtil.exe** *filename*.**adf –addAVP**

   b. **CSUtil.exe –addAVP** *filename*.**adf**

   c. **addAVP CSUtil** *filename*.**adf**

   d. **addAVP –CSUtil** *filename*.**adf**

   Answer: B

7. True or false: The CS-ACS server cannot apply the shared RAC and downloadable ACL on the agentless machine because they are assigned by the audit server.

   Answer: False

8. True or false: You can assign a Checkup posture token only if the QualysGuard Scanner is not reachable from the Cisco Secure ACS server.

   Answer: False

9. True or false: The CS-ACS usually assigns a Transition posture token to the agentless hosts while an audit is in progress.

   Answer: True

10. True or false: You cannot use the MAC authentication bypass feature on the Layer 3 devices and on the Layer 2 devices implementing Layer 2 IP.

   Answer: False

Chapter 12

1. True or false: The Altiris Agent can be bundled with CTA's installation.
   Answer: False

2. True or false: Cisco recommends installing the Altiris Agent after installing CTA.

   Answer: False

3. True or false: The Altiris Network Discovery is a free plug-in component to the Notification Server that is used to discover all end-user machines connected to the network.

   Answer: True

4. Which one of the following is not a Cisco NAC program remediation partner:

   a. Altiris

   b. BigFix

   c. RemediaCorp

   d. Citadel

   Answer: C

5. What command you can use to install the attributes file for remediation servers on Cisco Secure ACS?

   a. CSUtility.exe

   b. CSUtil.exe

   c. CSACSUtil.exe

   d. CSImport.exe

   Answer: B

Chapter 13

1. What two business groups must be involved in developing the NAC requirements?

   a. Network administrators and users

   b. Users and human resources

   c. Human resources and business leaders

   d. Business leaders and network administrators

   Answer: D

2. Why was NAC-L2-IP chosen over NAC-L3-IP or NAC-L2-802.1X?

   a. L2-802.1X was too complicated.

   b. User authentication was not a requirement, and NAC-L2-IP pushed the enforcement point as close as possible to the end host.

   c. User authentication was a requirement that could be performed only with NAC-L2-IP.

   d. NAC-L3-IP is older and was replaced by NAC-L2-IP.

   Answer: B

3. Why were only two system posture tokens used?

    a. Cisco Secure ACS has only two predefined system posture tokens.

    b. The other system posture tokens apply only when using NAC partner applications.

    c. Three posture tokens were used.

    d. The requirements called for only two different types of enforcement for users with CTA installed.

Answer: D

5. What two system posture tokens were used?

    a. Healthy and Quarantine

    b. Healthy and Transition

    c. Healthy and Unknown

    d. Quarantine and Infected

Answer: A

5. True or false: End hosts without CTA installed cannot get access to the network.

Answer: False

6. True or false: Guests visiting the business must connect to a non-NAC-enabled switch to get access to the Internet.

Answer: False

7. True or false: Printers and servers can be authorized by a local policy on the switch or a central policy on Cisco Secure ACS.

Answer: True

8. What two things must be applied to each switchport interface to enable NAC?

    a. Admission and authorization policy

    b. Authentication and authorization policy

    c. Admission policy and interface ACL

    d. Interface ACL and authorization policy

Answer: C

9. What is the identity policy used for?

   a. To tie an access list to an authorized device

   b. To tell Cisco Secure ACS the identity of the device connected to the switchport

   c. To tell the switch the identity of the device connected to the switchport

   d. To spy on users

   Answer: A

10. What can be configured to send a message to users after they have been postured?

    a. The configured MOTD on the switch is sent to users.

    b. CTA displays the message associated with the posture token in the cta_message.ini file.

    c. CTA can display the PA message to end users.

    d. It is not possible to send a user a message.

    Answer: C

Chapter 14

1. Why was NAC-L2-IP chosen over L2-802.1X on Catalyst 6500?

   a. L2-802.1X was too complicated.

   b. Legacy switches that do not support NAC were connected to 6500.

   c. User authentication was a requirement that could be performed only with NAC-L2-IP.

   d. L3-IP is older and was replaced by NAC-L2-IP.

   Answer: B

2. What is the purpose of the Transition system posture token?

    a. It is used for transitioning a machine from Healthy to Quarantine.

    b. It is used for transitioning a machine from Quarantine to Healthy.

    c. It is used for transitioning a machine from Agentless to Quarantine.

    d. It is used for transitioning a machine from Agentless to a system posture token determined by the audit server.

    Answer: D

3. What are the system posture tokens used? (Multiple answers)

    a. Healthy

    b. Transition

    c. Unknown

    d. Quarantine

    Answer: A, B, D

5. True or false: End hosts without CTA installed cannot get access to the network if they are connected to the switches.

    Answer: False

6. True or false: Printers are authorized by defining MAC addresses in the exception list on the audit server.

    Answer: False

Chapter 15

1. True or false: Cisco Secure ACS can replicate only internal users and groups; it cannot replicate other configurations.

    Answer: False

2. True or false: NAC Layer 2 IP and NAC-L2-802.1X require a third-party supplicant to do security posture validation.

    Answer: False

3. What underlying protocol does Cisco Secure ACS use to communicate with third-party antivirus servers?

   a. HCAP

   b. HAAP

   c. GAME

   d. FTP

   Answer: A

4. What is the system posture token used during an audit for NAC agentless hosts?

   a. Quarantine

   b. Checkup

   c. Transition

   d. Audit

   Answer: C

5. Where in the network are remediation servers typically located?

   a. Internet edge

   b. Quarantine segment

   c. Datacenter

   d. All of the above

   Answer: B

Chapter 16

1. True or false: Documenting detailed test plans during the initial pilot phase is not important because it adds unnecessary administrative overhead.
   Answer: False

2. A slow-start NAC implementation is

   a. Not recommended because it delays the implementation process.

   b. Recommended because it ensures that the new technologies have full exposure to the production environment before final validation and full-scale conversion.

   c. None of the above.

   Answer: B

3. Automation tools have been shown to improve upgrade efficiency on large NAC deployments when numerous network devices need to be upgraded. An example of an automation tool you can use is

   a. Cisco Secure ACS

   b. CiscoWorks SWIM

   c. PatchLink Update

   d. All of the above

   Answer: C

4. True or false: To avoid confusion, you should not notify end users before NAC is fully deployed within your organization.

   Answer: False

5. True or false: The default CSA policies do not provide a good level of protection to the end hosts.

   Answer: False

6. True or false: NAC deployment and support commonly do not affect your help-desk staff because the solution should be transparent to the end users.

   Answer: False

Chapter 17

1. After adding any new monitored device into CS-MARS, what must be done before CS-MARS analyzes events sent from that device?

   a. CS-MARS must be rebooted.

   b. The **Activate** button must be clicked to synchronize the GUI to the back-end database.

c. You must select the **Analyze Events** button, next to the device on the Report tab.

d. Nothing needs to be done after adding the new device through the GUI.

Answer: B

2. What protocol/port do Cisco IOS routers (by default) use to send NetFlow data to CS-MARS?

   a. UDP/5520

   b. TCP/5520

   c. UDP/2055

   d. TCP/2055

Answer: C

3. What version(s) of NetFlow does CS-MARS support?

   a. 5

   b. 7

   c. 9

   d. 5 and 7

   e. 7 and 9

Answer: D

4. When discovering a monitored device, which of the following protocols is not supported by CS-MARS?

   a. FTP

   b. SSH

   c. Syslog

   d. Telnet

Answer: C

5. What utility is used to send ACS events as syslogs to CS-MARS?

   a. pnlog agent

   b. mars-syslog.exe

   c. syslog.exe

   d. csagent

   Answer: A

6. Events from which log file are not forwarded to CS-MARS from the ACS server?

   a. Failed Attempts

   b. Passed Authentications

   c. RADIUS Accounting

   d. TACACS+ Accounting

   Answer: D

7. When adding a new monitored device into CS-MARS, which protocol used during discovery requires the access IP and reporting IP to be different?

   a. FTP

   b. SNMP

   c. SSH

   d. Telnet

   Answer: A

8. When sending syslogs from monitored devices to CS-MARS, if the traffic flow passes through a firewall, what protocol and port must be allowed through for the syslogs to reach CS-MARS?

    a. TCP/21

    b. TCP/513

    c. TCP/514

    d. UDP/513

    e. UDP/514

    Answer: E

9. CSA agents send events to CS-MARS . . .

    a. Directly, via syslog

    b. Indirectly; the CSA-MC sends the events via Syslog

    c. Directly, via SNMP traps

    d. Indirectly; the CSA-MC sends the events via SNMP traps

    e. CS-MARS cannot receive individual agent events

    Answer: D

10. True or false: CS-MARS can automatically discover CSA agents and add them to the database.

    Answer: True

INDEX

Numbers

A

Linux, CTA (Cisco Trust Agent)
  CA certificate, 47
  installation packages, 33
  lab environment installation, 45
  operating system support, 31
  production environment deployment, 76–77
logging, ACS, 307
  failed attempts configuration, 307–309
  passed authentication configuration, 309–311
  RADIUS accounting logging, 311–313
logging services, CTA (Cisco Trust Agent), 63–64
  clogcli utility, 68–69
  ctalogd.ini file creation, 64–68
  troubleshooting, 80–81

M

MAC
  agentless hosts handling, authentication bypass, 356
  CTA (Cisco Trust Agent)
    CA certificate, 47
    installation packages, 33
    lab environment installation, 42–44
    operating system support, 31
  NAC-L2-802.1X authentication bypass, 144–145
  production environment deployment, 75–76
management networks, medium enterprise NAC deployment, 422–423
McAfee, supported antivirus vendors, 343
medium enterprises
  business requirements, 424–425
  configuration steps, 427
    Altiris Quarantine solution configuration, 433–434
    audit server configuration, 432–433
    CatOS configuration, 427–430
    Cisco Secure ACS configuration, 435–443
    CSA-MC server configuration, 443
    end-user clients, 443
    Trend Micro Policy Server configuration, 434
    VPN 300 concentrator configuration, 430–431

  major NAC solution highlights, 425–427
  NAC deployment overview, 419, 421
    management network, 422–423
    quarantine network, 423
    user network, 421
  troubleshooting
    NAC on Catalyst 6500 switch, 444–446
    NAC on VPN 3000 concentrator, 446–448
    secure ACS logging, 448
Meetinghouse AEGIS SecureConnect client. *See* Cisco Secure Services Client
mode-config assignment, IPSec remote-access tunnels, 189
monitoring
  agentless hosts, 375–376
    CS-ACS logs, 376
    NADs, 377–378
  Layer 3 NAC, 168–169
  medium enterprises
    NAC on Catalyst 6500 switch, 444–446
    NAC on VPN 3000 concentrator, 446–448
    secure ACS logging, 448
  NAC components, 23–24
  security appliances, 229
    NAC sessions, 235–238
    remote-access IPSec tunnel from agentless client, 232–234
    remote-access IPSec tunnel from CTA client, 234–235
    remote-access IPSec tunnel without NAC, 230–232
  VPN 3000 series concentrators, 200
    remote-access IPSec tunnel from agentless client, 203–205
    remote-access IPSec tunnel from CTA client, 205–207
    remote-access IPSec tunnel without NAC, 200–203

N

NAC (Network Admission Control), 5
  basics, 5–7
    Phase I, 7–8
    Phase II, 9–11
    program participation, 12

Learn more about
Cisco Network Admission Control

Volume 1 is now available from Cisco Press

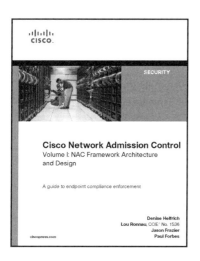

Cisco Network Admission Control,
Volume I: NAC Architecture and Design

Authors: Denise Helfrich, Jason Frazier,
Paul Bigbee, Lou Ronnau

ISBN: 1587052415

Published December 2006

Secure the network edge with the premier book on NAC

Cisco Network Admission Control, Volume I describes the Cisco NAC solution.
It also describes how to plan and design each component as well as an overall
NAC-enabled architecture. This first book on the Cisco NAC solution focuses on
the system architecture and design and it also addresses the security risks of
remote and mobile computer users connecting to corporate networks.

Visit **www.ciscopress.com** to find out more about this
and other Cisco Press titles.

Cisco Press

3 STEPS TO LEARNING

STEP 1

First-Step

STEP 2

STEP 3

Fundamentals

**Networking
Technology Guides**

STEP 1 **First-Step**—Benefit from easy-to-grasp explanations.
No experience required!

STEP 2 **Fundamentals**—Understand the purpose, application,
and management of technology.

STEP 3 **Networking Technology Guides**—Gain the knowledge
to master the challenge of the network.

NETWORK BUSINESS SERIES

The Network Business series helps professionals tackle the
business issues surrounding the network. Whether you are a
seasoned IT professional or a business manager with minimal
technical expertise, this series will help you understand the
business case for technologies.

Justify Your Network Investment.

Look for Cisco Press titles at your favorite bookseller today.

Visit **www.ciscopress.com/series** for details on each of these book series.

CISCO SYSTEMS

Cisco Press

Your **first-step** to networking starts here

Are you new to the world of networking? Whether you are beginning your networking career or simply need a better understanding of a specific technology to have more meaningful discussions with networking experts, Cisco Press First-Step books are right for you.

➤ **No experience required**

➤ **Includes clear and easily understood explanations**

➤ **Makes learning easy**

Check out each of these First-Step books that cover key networking topics

Computer Networking First-Step
ISBN: 1-58720-101-1

LAN Switching First-Step
ISBN: 1-58720-100-3

Network Security First-Step
ISBN: 1-58720-099-6

TCP/IP First-Step
ISBN: 1-58720-108-9

Voice over IP First-Step
ISBN: 1-58720-156-9

Routing First-Step
ISBN: 1-58720-122-4

Wireless Networks First-Step
ISBN: 1-58720-111-9

Visit **www.ciscopress.com/firststep** to learn more.

What's your next step?

Eager to dig deeper into networking technology? Cisco Press has the books that will help you move to the next level. Learn more at **www.ciscopress.com/series**.

ciscopress.com   **Learning begins with a first step.**

CISCO SYSTEMS

Cisco Press

FUNDAMENTALS SERIES
ESSENTIAL EXPLANATIONS AND SOLUTIONS

Voice over IP Fundamentals

A systematic approach to understanding the basics of Voice over IP

Jonathan Davidson, CCIE® No. 2560
James Peters

1-57870-168-6

When you need an authoritative introduction to a key networking topic, **reach for a Cisco Press Fundamentals book**. Learn about network topologies, deployment concepts, protocols, and management techniques and **master essential networking concepts and solutions**.

Look for Fundamentals titles at your favorite bookseller

802.11 Wireless LAN Fundamentals
ISBN: 1-58705-077-3

**Cisco CallManager Fundamentals:
A Cisco AVVID Solution**
ISBN: 1-58705-008-0

Cisco LAN Switching Fundamentals
ISBN: 1-58705-089-7

Cisco Unity Fundamentals
ISBN: 1-58705-098-6

Data Center Fundamentals
ISBN: 1-58705-023-4

IP Addressing Fundamentals
ISBN: 1-58705-067-6

IP Routing Fundamentals
ISBN: 1-57870-071-X

Network Security Fundamentals
ISBN: 1-58705-167-2

Storage Networking Fundamentals
ISBN: 1-58705-162-1

Voice over IP Fundamentals
ISBN: 1-57870-168-6

Coming in Fall 2005
**Cisco CallManager Fundamentals:
A Cisco AVVID Solution**, Second Edition
ISBN: 1-58705-192-3

Visit **www.ciscopress.com/series** for details about the Fundamentals series and a complete list of titles.

CISCO SYSTEMS

Cisco Press

NETWORKING TECHNOLOGY GUIDES
MASTER THE NETWORK

Turn to Networking Technology Guides whenever you need **in-depth knowledge of complex networking technologies**. Written by leading networking authorities, these guides offer theoretical and practical knowledge for **real-world networking applications and solutions**.

Look for Networking Technology Guides at your favorite bookseller

Cisco CallManager Best Practices: A Cisco AVVID Solution
ISBN: 1-58705-139-7

Cisco IP Telephony: Planning, Design, Implementation, Operation, and Optimization
ISBN: 1-58705-157-5

Cisco PIX Firewall and ASA Handbook
ISBN: 1-58705-158-3

Cisco Wireless LAN Security
ISBN: 1-58705-154-0

End-to-End QoS Network Design: Quality of Service in LANs, WANs, and VPNs
ISBN: 1-58705-176-1

Network Security Architectures
ISBN: 1-58705-115-X

Optimal Routing Design
ISBN: 1-58705-187-7

Top-Down Network Design, Second Edition
ISBN: 1-58705-152-4

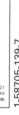

Visit **www.ciscopress.com/series** for details about Networking Technology Guides and a complete list of titles.

Learning is serious business.
Invest wisely.

SEARCH THOUSANDS OF BOOKS FROM LEADING PUBLISHERS

Safari® Bookshelf is a searchable electronic reference library for IT professionals that features more than 2,000 titles from technical publishers, including Cisco Press.

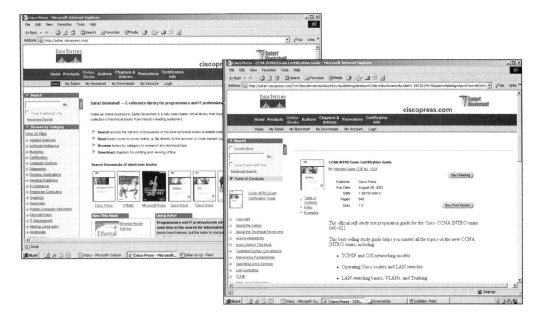

With Safari Bookshelf you can

- **Search** the full text of thousands of technical books, including more than 70 Cisco Press titles from authors such as Wendell Odom, Jeff Doyle, Bill Parkhurst, Sam Halabi, and Karl Solie.

- **Read** the books on My Bookshelf from cover to cover, or just flip to the information you need.

- **Browse** books by category to research any technical topic.

- **Download** chapters for printing and viewing offline.

With a customized library, you'll have access to your books when and where you need them—and all you need is a user name and password.

TRY SAFARI BOOKSHELF FREE FOR 14 DAYS!

You can sign up to get a 10-slot Bookshelf free for the first 14 days. Visit **http://safari.ciscopress.com** to register.

Cisco Press

CISCO CERTIFICATION SELF-STUDY
#1 BEST-SELLING TITLES FROM CCNA® TO CCIE®

Look for Cisco Press Certification Self-Study resources at your favorite bookseller

Learn the test topics with **Self-Study Guides**

1-58705-142-7

Gain hands-on experience with **Practical Studies** books

1-58720-046-5

Prepare for the exam with **Exam Certification Guides**

1-58720-083-X

Practice testing skills and build confidence with **Flash Cards and Exam Practice Packs**

1-58720-079-1

Visit **www.ciscopress.com/series** to learn more about the Certification Self-Study product family and associated series.

Learning is serious business.
Invest wisely.

Cisco Systems

Cisco Press

CCIE PROFESSIONAL DEVELOPMENT
RESOURCES FROM EXPERTS IN THE FIELD

CCIE Professional Development books are the **ultimate resource for advanced networking professionals**, providing practical insights for effective network design, deployment, and management. **Expert perspectives, in-depth technology discussions, and real-world implementation advice** also make these titles essential for anyone preparing for a CCIE® exam.

CCIE® Professional Development
Routing TCP/IP
Volume I

A detailed examination of interior routing protocols

Jeff Doyle, CCIE No. 1919

1-57870-041-8

Look for CCIE Professional Development titles at your favorite bookseller

Cisco BGP-4 Command and Configuration Handbook
ISBN: 1-58705-017-X

Cisco OSPF Command and Configuration Handbook
ISBN: 1-58705-071-4

Inside Cisco IOS® Software Architecture
ISBN: 1-57870-181-3

Network Security Principles and Practices
ISBN: 1-58705-025-0

Routing TCP/IP, Volume I
ISBN: 1-57870-041-8

Troubleshooting IP Routing Protocols
ISBN: 1-58705-019-6

Troubleshooting Remote Access Networks
ISBN: 1-58705-076-5

Coming in Fall 2005

Cisco LAN Switching, Volume I, Second Edition
ISBN: 1-58705-216-4

Routing TCP/IP, Volume I, Second Edition
ISBN: 1-58705-202-4

Visit **www.ciscopress.com/series** for details about the CCIE Professional Development series and a complete list of titles.

Learning is serious business.
Invest wisely.

CISCO SYSTEMS

Cisco Press

NETWORK BUSINESS SERIES

JUSTIFY YOUR NETWORK INVESTMENT

Understand the business case for technologies with Network Business books from Cisco Press. Designed to support anyone **searching for optimal network systems,** Network Business titles help you justify your network investments.

Look for Network Business titles at your favorite bookseller

The Business Case for E-Learning
Kelly / Nanjiani • ISBN: 1-58720-086-4

The Business Case for Network Security
Paquet / Saxe • ISBN: 1-58720-121-6

The Business Case for Storage Networks
Williams • ISBN: 1-58720-118-6

The Case for Virtual Business Processes
Young / Jude • ISBN: 1-58720-087-2

IP Telephony Unveiled
Brown • ISBN: 1-58720-075-9

Power Up Your Small-Medium Business
Aber • ISBN: 1-58705-135-4

The Road to IP Telephony
Carhee • ISBN: 1-58720-088-0

Taking Charge of Your VoIP Project
Walker / Hicks • ISBN: 1-58720-092-9

Coming in Fall 2005

The Business Case for Enterprise-Class Wireless LANs
Castaneda / Alasdair / Vinckier • ISBN: 1-58720-125-9

MPLS for Decision Makers
Sayeed / Morrow • ISBN: 1-58720-120-8

Network Business Series.   **Justify Your Network Investment.**

Visit **www.ciscopress.com/netbus** for details about the Network Business series and a complete list of titles.

Cisco Press

SAVE UP TO 30%

Become a member and save at ciscopress.com!

Complete a **user profile** at ciscopress.com today to become a member and benefit from **discounts up to 30% on every purchase** at ciscopress.com, as well as a more customized user experience. Your membership will also allow you access to the entire Informit network of sites.

Don't forget to subscribe to the monthly Cisco Press newsletter to be the first to learn about new releases and special promotions. You can also sign up to get your first **30 days FREE on Safari Bookshelf** and preview Cisco Press content. Safari Bookshelf lets you access Cisco Press books online and build your own customized, searchable electronic reference library.

Visit **www.ciscopress.com/register** to sign up and start saving today!

The profile information we collect is used in aggregate to provide us with better insight into your technology interests and to create a better user experience for you. You must be logged into ciscopress.com to receive your discount. Discount is on Cisco Press products only; shipping and handling are not included.

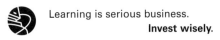

Learning is serious business.
Invest wisely.

THIS BOOK IS SAFARI ENABLED

INCLUDES FREE 45-DAY ACCESS TO THE ONLINE EDITION

The Safari® Enabled icon on the cover of your favorite technology book means the book is available through Safari Bookshelf. When you buy this book, you get free access to the online edition for 45 days.

Safari Bookshelf is an electronic reference library that lets you easily search thousands of technical books, find code samples, download chapters, and access technical information whenever and wherever you need it.

TO GAIN 45-DAY SAFARI ENABLED ACCESS TO THIS BOOK:

- Go to **http://www.ciscopress.com/safarienabled**

- Complete the brief registration form

- Enter the coupon code found in the front of this book before the "Contents at a Glance" page

If you have difficulty registering on Safari Bookshelf or accessing the online edition, please e-mail customer-service@safaribooksonline.com.